# Personality Development Across the Lifespan

# Personality Development Across the Lifespan

*Edited by*

## Jule Specht

ELSEVIER

ACADEMIC PRESS

An imprint of Elsevier

Academic Press is an imprint of Elsevier
125 London Wall, London EC2Y 5AS, United Kingdom
525 B Street, Suite 1800, San Diego, CA 92101-4495, United States
50 Hampshire Street, 5th Floor, Cambridge, MA 02139, United States
The Boulevard, Langford Lane, Kidlington, Oxford OX5 1GB, United Kingdom

**Notices**
Knowledge and best practice in this field are constantly changing. As new research and experience broaden our
understanding, changes in research methods, professional practices, or medical treatment may become
necessary.

Practitioners and researchers must always rely on their own experience and knowledge in evaluating and using
any information, methods, compounds, or experiments described herein. In using such information or methods
they should be mindful of their own safety and the safety of others, including parties for whom they have a
professional responsibility.

To the fullest extent of the law, neither the Publisher nor the authors, contributors, or editors, assume any
liability for any injury and/or damage to persons or property as a matter of products liability, negligence or
otherwise, or from any use or operation of any methods, products, instructions, or ideas contained in the
material herein.

**British Library Cataloguing-in-Publication Data**
A catalogue record for this book is available from the British Library

**Library of Congress Cataloging-in-Publication Data**
A catalog record for this book is available from the Library of Congress

ISBN: 978-0-12-804674-6

For Information on all Academic Press publications
visit our website at https://www.elsevier.com/books-and-journals

Working together
to grow libraries in
developing countries

www.elsevier.com • www.bookaid.org

*Publisher:* Nikki Levy
*Acquisition Editor:* Emily Ekle
*Editorial Project Manager:* Timothy J. Bennett
*Production Project Manager:* Punithavathy Govindaradjane
*Designer:* Alan Studholme

Typeset by MPS Limited, Chennai, India

Transferred to Digital Printing in 2017

Being a personality psychologist means loving diversity.

# Contents

# List of Contributors

**Mathias Allemand** University of Zurich, Zurich, Switzerland

**Mitja D. Back** University of Münster, Münster, Germany

**Wiebke Bleidorn** University of California, Davis, CA, United States

**Elien De Caluwé** Ghent University, Ghent, Belgium

**Barbara De Clercq** Ghent University, Ghent, Belgium

**Filip De Fruyt** Ghent University, Ghent, Belgium

**Grant W. Edmonds** Oregon Research Institute, Eugene, OR, United States

**Christine Finn** Friedrich Schiller University Jena, Jena, Germany

**R. Chris Fraley** University of Illinois at Urbana-Champaign, Champaign, IL, United States

**Alexandra M. Freund** University of Zurich, Zurich, Switzerland

**Denis Gerstorf** Humboldt-Universität zu Berlin, Berlin, Germany; German Institute for Economic Research (DIW Berlin), Berlin, Germany

**Katharina Geukes** University of Münster, Münster, Germany

**Marie Hennecke** University of Zurich, Zurich, Switzerland

**Kathrin Herzhoff** Northwestern University, Evanston, IL, United States

**Patrick L. Hill** Washington University in St. Louis, St. Louis, MO, United States

**Nathan W. Hudson** Michigan State University, East Lansing, MI, United States

**Gizem Hülür** University of Zurich, Zurich, Switzerland

**Charles J. Infurna** Children's Institute, Rochester, NY, United States; St. John Fisher College, Rochester, NY, United States

**Frank J. Infurna** Arizona State University, Tempe, AZ, United States

**Joshua J. Jackson** Washington University in St. Louis, St. Louis, MO, United States

**Bertus F. Jeronimus** University Medical Center Groningen, University of Groningen, Groningen, The Netherlands

**Christian Kandler** Bielefeld University, Bielefeld, Germany; Medical School Berlin, Berlin, Germany

**Hyunji Kim** York University, Toronto, ON, Canada

**Theo A. Klimstra** Tilburg University, Tilburg, The Netherlands

**Shauna C. Kushner** University of Toronto, Toronto, ON, Canada

**Maike Luhmann** Ruhr University Bochum, Bochum, Germany

**Kate C. McLean** Western Washington University, Bellingham, WA, United States

**Matthias R. Mehl** University of Arizona, Tucson, AZ, United States

**René Mõttus** University of Edinburgh, Edinburgh, United Kingdom

**Swantje Mueller** Humboldt-Universität zu Berlin, Berlin, Germany

**Franz J. Neyer** Friedrich Schiller University Jena, Jena, Germany

**Lauren B. Nickel** University of Illinois, Urbana-Champaign, IL, United States

**Johan Ormel** University Medical Center Groningen, University of Groningen, Groningen, The Netherlands

**Ulrich Orth** University of Bern, Bern, Switzerland

**Michael Papendick** Bielefeld University, Bielefeld, Germany

**John F. Rauthmann** Wake Forest University, Winston-Salem, NC, United States

**Anne K. Reitz** Columbia University, New York, NY, United States; New York University, New York, NY, United States

**Harriëtte Riese** University Medical Center Groningen, University of Groningen, Groningen, The Netherlands

**Brent W. Roberts** University of Illinois, Urbana-Champaign, IL, United States

**Joni Y. Sasaki** York University, Toronto, ON, Canada

**Florian Schmiedek** German Institute for International Educational Research (DIPF), Frankfurt am Main, Germany

**Leah H. Schultz** Washington University in St. Louis, St. Louis, MO, United States

**Ted Schwaba** University of California, Davis, CA, United States

**Conor G. Smith** The University of Edinburgh, Edinburgh, United Kingdom

**Jule Specht** Humboldt-Universität zu Berlin, Berlin, Germany; German Institute for Economic Research (DIW Berlin), Berlin, Germany

**Ursula M. Staudinger** Columbia University, New York, NY, United States

**Gundula Stoll** University of Tübingen, Tübingen, Germany

**Jennifer L. Tackett** Northwestern University, Evanston, IL, United States

**Ulrich Trautwein** University of Tübingen, Tübingen, Germany

**Lotte van Doeselaar** Tilburg University, Tilburg, The Netherlands

**Maarten H.W. van Zalk** University of Münster, Münster, Germany

**Lize Verbeke** Ghent University, Ghent, Belgium

**Manuel C. Voelkle** Humboldt-Universität zu Berlin, Berlin, Germany; Max Planck Institute for Human Development, Berlin, Germany

**Michael VonKorff** Group Health Research Institute, Group Health Cooperative, Seattle, WA, United States

**Jenny Wagner** Humboldt-Universität zu Berlin, Berlin, Germany; Leibniz Institute for Science and Mathematics Education (IPN), Kiel, Germany

**Alexander Weiss** The University of Edinburgh, Edinburgh, United Kingdom

**Sara J. Weston** Washington University in St. Louis, St. Louis, MO, United States

**Alexandra Zapko-Willmes** Bielefeld University, Bielefeld, Germany; Medical School Berlin, Berlin, Germany

**Julia Zimmermann** FernUniversität Hagen, Hagen, Germany

# Part One

# Introduction

# Personality development research: State-of-the-art and future directions

*Jule Specht*[1,2,]*
[1]Humboldt-Universität zu Berlin, Berlin, Germany, [2]German Institute for Economic Research (DIW Berlin), Berlin, Germany

What can we predict for the future of an individual who happens to be a sociable, talkative, and lively young boy? Or for an open-minded, unconventional, and curious woman who enters young adulthood? From personality psychology research, we know that individuals are characterized by stable individual differences like, e.g., extraversion and openness to experience. But from developmental psychology research, we know that individuals change systematically across time depending, among other things, on their biological maturation and the developmental tasks they are faced with.

Personality development research combines these two research traditions assuming that there are relatively stable individual differences that may change in the long run. Based on the findings of these two psychological disciplines, we now have good reason to predict that the extraverted boy from the introductory example is likely to become an energetic, happy, and self-confident man. And that he is more likely to become popular, to have a lot of friends, and that he will later likely be at ease attracting romantic partners compared to a more introverted person. We can also be quite confident that these experiences will retroact on his personality, strengthening his extraversion and stimulating changes in other personality traits of his own or his social network.

We can furthermore expect on good grounds that the woman of the second introductory example, who has particularly high levels in the personality trait openness to experience, will likely remain among the most open-minded individuals of her age during the course of her life. It is likely that she will think, feel, and behave more extraordinarily even in old age compared to others of her age group. However, empirical research also suggests that she will likely be less open to new experience at age 80 compared to the time of her college years because openness to experience tends to decline during adulthood.

Taken together, recent findings from personality development research highlight the fact that personality trait levels are surprisingly stable even across several decades and even when faced with major changes in life circumstances. At the

*While writing this chapter, Jule Specht was also affiliated at Freie Universität Berlin, Berlin, Universität zu Lübeck, Lübeck, and the German Institute for Economic Research (DIW Berlin), Berlin.

**Personality Development Across the Lifespan.** DOI: http://dx.doi.org/10.1016/B978-0-12-804674-6.00001-6

same time, it is very unlikely that a person remains at the same personality trait level across all of childhood, adolescence, adulthood, and old age or that a person remains at the exact same position on a personality trait relative to others of the same age group across time. Personality development researchers are eager to understand why personality is highly stable even under instable life conditions, why personality changes in some people more than in others, and how life shapes who we are and who we become.

## A new focus: from stability to changeability of personality traits

Personality psychologists and social psychologists have long struggled about the question of whether enduring individual characteristics or momentary situational characteristics are most relevant for predicting how a person will act in a given context. Most colleagues now agree that both—the personality and the (social) situation—have an important influence on behavior. Personality is assumed to have a particularly high impact in situations with low social pressure to behave in a specific way. For example, personality is more likely to result in individual differences at a Sunday afternoon with no obligations to go to work, and the freedom to choose between relaxing at home, doing sports, going to a museum, or meeting with friends. In contrast, personality is less likely to result in strong individual differences at a busy working day that comes along with specific demands about how to behave to comply to the situation. Thus even though individual differences can occur in every situation, they are more likely in situations that are free of specific social expectations about how to behave.

The need to argue for the important impact of enduring individual differences—compared to situational characteristics—is likely a reason for the strong focus on the stability of individual differences in personality traits in early personality psychology research. Now we can be sure that individuals show different behaviors in the same situation as a result of differences in their personality traits. Also, we now know that individuals will show similar behavior across different situations as a result of relatively stable personality traits. Thus the scientific debate between personality psychologists and social psychologists about whether personality actually exists is now largely overcome, and the idea of stable individual differences is widely acknowledged across disciplines within psychology.

The initial focus on the high stability of personality traits has lost sight of the fact that personality is far from being perfectly stable. Instead, personality changes systematically across time, with age, and in reaction to the environment. Modern personality psychology therefore shifted its focus from stability to changeability of personality traits, which resulted in a new area of research, namely personality development research.

Research on personality development has flourished during the last decade. Nowadays, it is continuously represented with scientific talks and posters at each of the major conferences of our field (e.g., International Convention of Psychological Science, Society for Personality and Social Psychology Convention, Association for Research in Personality Conference, European Conference on Personality). It gets published in the major journals of our field (e.g., *Psychological Science, Journal of Personality and Social Psychology, Developmental Psychology*) and was topic of two special issues in the *European Journal of Personality* in 2006 (Neyer, 2006) and in 2014 (Denissen, 2014). At the moment, *Web of Science* (https://apps. webofknowledge.com) lists more than 8000 published papers on personality development since 2006, which is more than twice the number of papers on that topic compared to the decade before and the number is still increasing every year.

# Central topics within the personality development literature

The number of researchers interested in the question of how and why personality changes across the lifespan is obviously increasing considerably, resulting in an overwhelming number of new research findings on that topic. At the same time, there is still no up-to-date book summarizing the most important findings in the most central areas of research on personality development and this is exactly what this book aims at changing.

The first part of this book deals with the question of how personality changes in different life phases by summarizing empirical findings on personality development. This includes childhood (Herzhoff, Kushner, & Tackett, Chapter 2), adolescence (Hill & Edmonds, Chapter 3), emerging adulthood (Bleidorn & Schwaba, Chapter 4), adulthood (Specht, Chapter 5), and the end of life (Mueller, Wagner, & Gerstorf, Chapter 6).

The second part of this book then introduces theoretical perspectives on personality development including Five-Factor Theory of Personality (Mõttus, Chapter 7), theoretical perspectives on the interplay of nature and nurture (Kandler & Zapko-Willmes, Chapter 8), Set-Point Theory (Ormel, VonKorff, Jeronimus, & Riese, Chapter 9), evolutionary perspectives (Smith & Weiss, Chapter 10), and the Neo-Socioanalytic Model (Roberts & Nickel, Chapter 11).

Most research within personality psychology is based on the well-known Big Five model but of course there are other important individual differences beyond emotional stability, extraversion, openness to experience, agreeableness, and conscientiousness that require special attention. These personality characteristics and their lifespan development are summarized in the third part of this book, including self-esteem (Orth, Chapter 12), subjective well-being (Luhmann, Chapter 13), positive personality development (Reitz & Staudinger, Chapter 14), perceived control (F. J. Infurna & C. J. Infurna, Chapter 15), goals and motivation (Hennecke & Freund, Chapter 16), attachment style (Fraley & Hudson, Chapter 17), identity formation (Klimstra & van Doeselaar, Chapter 18), cognition and intelligence (Schmiedek, Chapter 19), and personal narratives (McLean, Chapter 20).

Personality development does not occur in isolation. How the context individuals are in impacts their personality is the topic of the fourth part of this book. It includes reviews on the impact of major life events (Specht, Chapter 21), close relationships (Finn, Zimmermann, & Neyer, Chapter 22), health (Jackson, Weston, & Schultz, Chapter 23), psychopathology (De Fruyt, De Clercq, De Caluwé, & Verbeke, Chapter 24), educational and organizational environments (Stoll & Trautwein, Chapter 25), and culture (Kim & Sasaki, Chapter 26) on personality development and shows that a considerable amount of systematic changes in personality can be traced back to these contexts.

The fifth part of this book offers insight into methods used to come to meaningful conclusions about how personality changes across time. It includes information about how this area of research can benefit from personality assessment in daily life (Allemand & Mehl, Chapter 27), how microprocesses of personality development likely take place (Geukes, van Zalk, & Back, Chapter 28), about the impact of genetic effects (Kandler & Papendick, Chapter 29), and statistical approaches aiming at analyzing personality change (Voelkle & Wagner, Chapter 30).

In the sixth and last part of this book, three promising new areas of research are introduced that have not received much attention in the last 10 years and therefore remain, at this point, rather speculative. However, they are also visionary because these areas of research will likely advance our understanding of personality development in the upcoming years. The first topic under consideration deals with generational changes in personality (Hülür, Chapter 31) that have been controversially discussed in the context of self-esteem and that received less attention with regard to other personality characteristics. A second topic deals with the question of how implicit aspects of personality develop with age (Rauthmann, Chapter 32), a topic that might fruitfully complement the findings that mainly—even though not exclusively—focused on explicit self-reports nowadays. The third chapter deals with the question of whether personality can be changed intentionally (Hudson & Fraley, Chapter 33), which could allow individuals to adapt to their life circumstances in a goal-directed way.

Taken together, these chapters aim at providing a comprehensive picture of the state-of-the-art of personality development by bringing together a multifaceted set of theoretical perspectives, empirical evidence, methodological tools, and trends for future research. Due to the diverse perspectives included here, this book will hopefully result in a differentiated understanding of the diversity of personality traits and developments that makes each personality in its unique way valuable.

# References

Denissen, J. J. A. (2014). Editorial: A roadmap for further progress in research on personality development. *European Journal of Personality*, 28, 213—215.

Neyer, F. J. (2006). Editorial: EJP special edition on personality change. *European Journal of Personality*, 20, 419—420.

# Part Two

# Personality Development in Different Life Phases

# Personality development in childhood

**2**

*Kathrin Herzhoff[1], Shauna C. Kushner[2], and Jennifer L. Tackett[1]*
[1]Northwestern University, Evanston, IL, United States, [2]University of Toronto, Toronto, ON, Canada

The need for a thorough understanding of personality development in childhood becomes clear when reviewing the effect of early personality on later life outcomes. Early personality—commonly organized into the Big Five personality traits Neuroticism, Extraversion, Openness-to-Experience, Agreeableness, and Conscientiousness—is highly relevant and important for later outcomes. For example, multiple studies support the importance of early personality in predicting adult outcomes such as mental and physical health, interpersonal relationships, and educational and occupational success (Caspi, Roberts, & Shiner, 2005; Hampson, 2008; Shiner, 2000; Shiner, Masten, & Roberts, 2003). As a prime example, mortality is predicted by childhood personality. Specifically, more conscientious children live longer and are healthier (Friedman et al., 1995; Hampson, 2008). Proposed mechanisms by which early Conscientiousness predicts these adult outcomes include better stress management, greater self-regulation, and increased health behaviors (Hampson, 2008). Childhood Conscientiousness also predicted adult academic success and good conduct (Shiner, 2000; Shiner et al., 2003). Childhood Agreeableness also predicted adult academic success, good conduct, in addition to good outcomes in adult friendships (Shiner, 2000; Shiner et al., 2003). Disagreeable children, however, were more likely to be unemployed in adulthood (Caspi, Wright, Moffitt, & Silva, 1998; Kokko, Bergman, & Pulkkinen, 2003; Kokko & Pulkkinen, 2000) and aggressive children were more likely to engage in abuse in adult romantic relationships (Ehrensaft, Moffitt, & Caspi, 2004). Like Agreeableness, childhood Surgency/Extraversion predicted positive outcomes in adult friendships in addition to romantic relationships (Shiner, 2000; Shiner et al., 2003). Many of these predictions were evident even after controlling for IQ (Shiner, 2000; Shiner et al., 2003), underlining the robustness with which early personality affects individuals' lives.

The associations between early personality and outcomes in adulthood may be driven by mediation and/or moderation processes (Hampson, 2008), i.e., personality may cause later outcomes through another variable (mediation) or it may interact with another variable to predict different levels of an outcome. In addition, it may be necessary to examine the effects of personality traits during critical periods when they may have stronger effects on later outcomes (Hampson, 2008). At present, the exact mechanisms underlying the associations among early personality and

Personality Development Across the Lifespan. DOI: http://dx.doi.org/10.1016/B978-0-12-804674-6.00002-8

important life outcomes are not fully understood. Given the relevance and importance of early personality for later life outcomes (Caspi et al., 2005; Hampson, 2008; Shiner, 2000; Shiner et al., 2003), in this chapter, we will describe the development of the Big Five personality traits in childhood and review evidence for their associations with temperament.

# Big Five personality traits in childhood

## Big Five personality traits versus temperament

Before describing Big Five personality traits in childhood, it is pertinent to differentiate personality from temperament, which in the past was used almost exclusively to describe individual differences in childhood. Personality and temperament were historically conceptualized as distinct constructs and were studied in parallel, non-overlapping bodies of research. Whereas personality has traditionally been used to describe individual differences in adulthood (John, Naumann, & Soto, 2008), temperament has been used to describe individual differences in infants, toddlers, and preschool-aged children (Buss & Plomin, 1984; Rothbart, 1981; Rothbart & Ahadi, 1994; Thomas, Chess, Birch, Hertzig, & Korn, 1963). Specifically, temperament has been used to describe biologically based, innate, and relatively stable patterns of emotional reactivity, behavioral activity, and self-regulation (Goldsmith et al., 1987; Mervielde, De Clercq, De Fruyt, & Van Leeuwen, 2005; Rothbart, 2004). Despite their distinction, temperament is believed to represent the core emotional, cognitive, and behavioral characteristics around which later personality traits develop (Buss & Plomin, 1984; De Pauw, 2016; Rothbart & Bates, 2006).

Contemporary perspectives maintain that personality and temperament are more alike than different (Caspi & Shiner, 2007, 2008; Caspi et al., 2005; De Pauw & Mervielde, 2010; Mervielde et al., 2005; Shiner, 1998; Shiner & Caspi, 2003; Shiner & DeYoung, 2013). For example, most personality and temperament models include overlapping content and common traits (e.g., tendencies toward experiencing negative and positive emotions; Rothbart & Bates, 2006; Shiner, 1998). Analogous traits in temperament and personality models (e.g., Neuroticism and Negative Affect; Extraversion and Positive Emotions/Surgency; Conscientiousness and Effortful Control/Constraint) are robustly correlated in both children (De Pauw & Mervielde, 2011; De Pauw, Mervielde, & Van Leeuwen, 2009; De Pauw, Mervielde, Van Leeuwen, & De Clercq, 2011; Deal, Halverson, Martin, Victor, & Baker, 2007; Grist, Socha, & McCord, 2012; Halverson et al., 2003; Tackett, Kushner, De Fruyt, & Mervielde, 2013) and adults (Angleitner & Ostendorf, 1994; Evans & Rothbart, 2007; McCrae & Costa, 1985). Both personality and temperament traits share biological underpinnings (e.g., both are strongly determined by genetics; Eysenck, 1990; Loehlin, McCrae, Costa, & John, 1998; Saudino, 2005). Likewise, both personality and temperament traits are influenced by early social and environmental factors (e.g., parenting, stress). For example, early environmental adversity appears to impede temperament development (Laceulle, Nederhof,

Karreman, Ormel, & Aken, 2012) and is associated with vulnerable personality traits (i.e., higher neuroticism; Rogosch & Cicchetti, 2004). Finally, both show substantial stability over time (Neppl et al., 2010; Roberts & DelVecchio, 2000; Rothbart & Bates, 2006).

Despite these similarities, there are important distinctions between personality and temperament. Convergence between personality and temperament traits, even for aforementioned analogs, is imperfect (De Pauw, 2016); rather, personality and temperament measures capture both common and unique variance in important outcomes (De Pauw et al., 2009, 2011; Tackett, Kushner et al., 2013). For example, there was greater convergence between two child personality measures than there was between either child personality measure and a temperament measure (Tackett, Kushner et al., 2013). Additionally, in a joint factor analysis of personality and temperament scales, Big Five factors were differentially made up of personality and temperament scales (e.g., Conscientiousness and Disagreeableness showed predominant loadings from personality scales whereas Activity, Emotionality, and Sensitivity showed predominant loadings from temperament scales; De Pauw et al., 2009). Finally, this joint personality/temperament model predicted greater variance in problem behaviors than the personality or temperament models on their own (De Pauw et al., 2009). Further, personality traits are generally described more broadly than temperamental traits (De Pauw, 2016; Rothbart & Bates, 2006; Shiner & DeYoung, 2013). As such, personality traits may have added utility for understanding individual differences across the life span and will be described next.

## Content of child personality traits

Like adult personality, child personality has predominantly been described using the Big Five traits: Neuroticism, Extraversion, Openness-to-Experience, Agreeableness, and Conscientiousness. However, it is important to acknowledge differences in the content of adult and child personality traits, which may shed light on personality development across the life span. We will first define the traits, followed by a general discussion of the manner in which they differ from adult traits. Whenever relevant, we will also discuss content differences between child temperament and adult personality traits (see Fig. 2.1 for a depiction of temperamental−personality analogs and correlations).

In adults, Neuroticism describes an individual's tendency to experience negative emotions, such as anger, fear, and sadness, which compose two lower order dimensions: fearfulness/inhibition and anger/irritability (Caspi et al., 2005). Extraversion describes an individual's tendency to experience positive emotions, and be active and assertive. Openness-to-Experience describes an individual's tendency to be intellectually curious and value new experiences. Agreeableness describes an individual's tendency to be altruistic, trusting, and tender-minded. Conscientiousness describes an individual's tendency to be self-disciplined, achievement oriented, and orderly.

Of all Big Five traits, Openness-to-Experience is the most controversial in child personality models (and not represented in child temperament models).

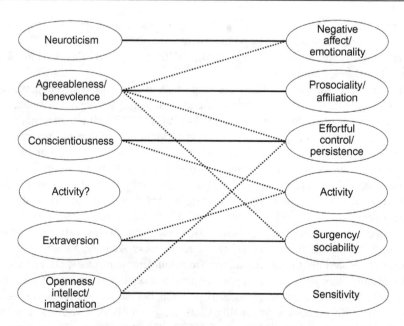

**Figure 2.1** The left side reflects personality in terms of the Big Five model as well as Activity as a potential "Little Six" addition (Soto & John, 2014; Soto & Tackett, 2015; Shiner & DeYoung, 2013). The right side reflects common dimensions of temperament (based on De Pauw & Mervielde, 2010; De Pauw et al., 2009) in addition to Affiliation and Sensitivity from Rothbart's temperament model. Solid lines denote clear temperamental−personality analogs, whereas broken lines denote correlations observed in the existing literature.

Specifically, some researchers have not included it in child personality models (Eder, 1990). In adults, Openness-to-Experience is composed of two dimensions: Openness and intellect (DeYoung, Peterson, & Higgins, 2005; DeYoung, Shamosh, Green, Braver, & Gray, 2009). In contrast, child Openness-to-Experience is largely composed of intellect (De Fruyt, Mervielde, & Van Leeuwen, 2002; Halverson et al., 2003). Thus child personality instruments do not fully capture the full range of openness, such as content regarding appreciation of esthetics and culture. However, adding item-coverage from a temperament measure provided evidence that perceptual sensitivity, which covered content regarding being sensitive to changes in the environment, showed evidence for convergence with intellect aspects of openness from a child personality measure (Herzhoff & Tackett, 2012).

Another main distinction between child and adult personality is greater overlap between Neuroticism and Disagreeableness in children compared to adults. In children, Agreeableness was composed of antagonistic aspects of Neuroticism whereas in young adolescents, the facets composing Agreeableness appeared more adult-like (i.e., empathy and compassion; Tackett et al., 2012). Like Openness-to-Experience, Agreeableness is not well represented in temperament models. Self-regulatory aspects of child Agreeableness and Conscientiousness are correlated with the temperament trait Effortful Control (Tackett et al., 2012); however, Effortful Control shows a greater degree of overlap with Conscientiousness than Agreeableness (Tackett, Kushner et al., 2013). In fact, the overlap between Effortful Control and Conscientiousness was greater than for any other temperament and personality traits. In addition, a mixed "agreeableness compliance" factor differentiates into separate Agreeableness and Conscientiousness factors across development (Tackett et al., 2012). That means although Tackett et al. found more content from Conscientiousness in their Agreeableness factor at younger ages (3–8 years), the factors split off more cleanly in older children.

Finally, another example of a developmentally specific difference in traits involves the trait of Activity Level. This trait is often not measured in adults—when it is, it typically defines a facet of Extraversion—but is highly salient and relevant in measures of temperament and child personality (De Pauw & Mervielde, 2010; Soto & John, 2014). Activity Level may represent a primary trait in childhood that actually decreases in importance across development, when it assumes a more secondary role in adulthood (Soto & Tackett, 2015). Overall, it is clear that although similar in many respects, child personality is also distinct from adult personality. Given that the measurement of personality also changes across developmental periods, it is challenging to tease apart developmental and measurement causes of these differences in content. The unique challenges for measurement of child personality will be presented next.

## Personality measurement in childhood

One of the relatively distinctive aspects of child personality research, relative to analogous work with adults, includes a host of additional measurement considerations. Although use of questionnaires—typically completed by parents or teachers—is likely the most common approach, they are accompanied by limitations including informant bias and constraints of role specificity (regarding the informant's relation to the child; Rothbart & Bates, 2006). Popular instruments include measures of temperament traits (Rothbart, Ahadi, Hershey, & Fisher, 2001; Simonds & Rothbart, 2004), measures of child personality (Halverson et al., 2003; Mervielde & De Fruyt, 1999), and any number of measures initially developed for adults that have been adapted (or administered without adaptation) to children.

A second fairly common approach to measuring temperament and child personality involves the use of standardized laboratory paradigms, which has certain advantages over questionnaires but brings with it different limitations. Some notable limitations include the resource-intensive nature of collecting and coding these data, as well as potential bias and constraint based on situational selection (Rothbart & Bates, 2006). Nonetheless, these methods are used frequently, often in complement to more typical questionnaire data (Kochanska, Barry, Jimenez, Hollatz, & Woodard, 2009; Kochanska, Murray, & Harlan, 2000). More recent extensions of lab-based observations include harnessing the thin-slice approach, which relies on the valid information contained in snap judgments of person characteristics, including personality (Borkenau, Brecke, Möttig, & Paelecke, 2009; Rule & Ambady, 2008;

Rule, Garrett, & Ambady, 2010). Specifically, snap judgments of children's personalities contain valid and predictive variance (Tackett, Herzhoff, Kushner, & Rule, 2016), which have applicability and relevance for clinical and other applied settings (Tackett et al., under review), and may even outperform more resource-intensive microcoding efforts (Prime, Perlman, Tackett, & Jenkins, 2014).

Self-report methods, while used, are used much less often than these alternative methods, particularly given concerns around validity of children as informants, the constraints of cognitive development, and lack of psychometrically validated measures for self-report at younger ages (Tackett et al., 2016). Some successful methods, although resource-intensive, include self-report gathered in an interview format (Brown, Mangelsdorf, Agathen, & Ho, 2008; Eder, 1990; Markey, Markey, Tinsley, & Ericksen, 2002; Measelle, John, Ablow, Cowan, & Cowan, 2005). Current considerations include expanding our toolboxes beyond traditional measures and particularly avoiding reliance on a single measure. Other exciting future directions can be identified when we look outside of personality psychology, as well—for example, incorporating some of the interesting and important work being done on combining multiple informant reports for child behavior and other characteristics (De Los Reyes et al., 2015; Tackett, 2011).

## Hierarchical structure of personality in childhood

As in adulthood, childhood personality traits are hierarchically structured (Markon, 2009; Soto & Tackett, 2015; see Fig. 2.2). Specifically, major childhood personality traits are hierarchically organized, such that predominant five-factor models of personality are composed of broader traits at higher levels of the hierarchy

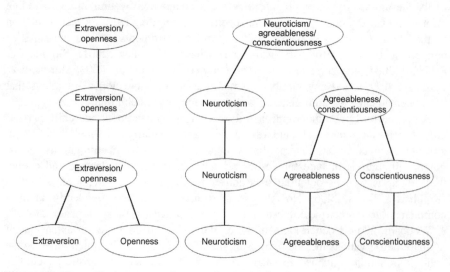

**Figure 2.2** Hierarchical structure of personality in childhood.

(Soto & John, 2014; Tackett et al., 2012, 2008). As with virtually any major measure or model of broad individual differences, two-factor models can be identified that correspond in some way to traits reflecting approach and avoidance. In Big Five terms, these two broad traits are typically made up of Extraversion/Openness and Neuroticism/Agreeableness/Conscientiousness, respectively. At the third level of the hierarchy, the broader avoidance trait typically bifurcates into Neuroticism and Agreeableness/Conscientiousness, with some developmental exceptions (discussed in the following text). At the fourth level of the hierarchy, Agreeableness and Conscientiousness break down into distinct aspects of interpersonal and intrapersonal self-regulation, respectively. Finally, moving further to a fifth level typically sees a distinct Openness trait differentiating from Extraversion. In addition to generalization across adult and youth populations, this hierarchical structure is largely robust across different measures of child personality (Soto & John, 2014; Tackett et al., 2008, 2012), across different age groups in childhood and adolescence (Soto & John, 2014; Tackett et al., 2012), and across children from a variety of countries around the world (Tackett et al., 2012).

Despite robust similarities in this hierarchical organization of personality traits when comparing children to adults, some important differences emerge as well. One notable difference reflects the relative difficulty in measuring "pure" Neuroticism (e.g., internal sadness and distress) and "pure" Agreeableness (e.g., compassion and altruistic tendencies) in children. Given the reliance on adult informants, it is somewhat reasonable to expect that access to such information would be more difficult to obtain from outside observers, particularly those in a position of power and authority over the target (Tackett et al., 2012). Perhaps as a result, those aspects of Neuroticism (e.g., anger and frustration) and Agreeableness (e.g., antagonism and stubbornness) that are more observable, and likely more salient to parents and teachers, tend to dominate trait measure ratings in children (Soto & Tackett, 2015). This results in some differences in hierarchical structure, including a tighter covariation between Neuroticism and Agreeableness across multiple levels of the hierarchy. A similar issue of covariation arises with Conscientiousness and Openness, which do not tend to covary highly in adults, but do in children, and result in a differentiated profile relative to that of adults (Soto & Tackett, 2015). These examples illustrate the importance of establishing robust effects across developmental populations while still seeking to understand the nature of specific differences across age, and the function of these differences on behavior and measurement.

## Developmental trajectory of personality traits in childhood

In addition to changes in the hierarchical structure, personality traits also have a unique developmental trajectory in childhood. Specifically, their developmental trajectory seems to support two conclusions: the cumulative-continuity principle and the disruption hypothesis (Soto & Tackett, 2015). In support of the cumulative-continuity principle, the rank-order stability of personality increases with age, i.e., an individual's relative standing on a trait becomes more stable with age (Roberts & DelVecchio, 2000). Although rank-order stability increases from childhood to adulthood, even in early childhood it is surprisingly high. Of the Big Five traits, Neuroticism tends to show the lowest rank-order stability across both adulthood and childhood (De Fruyt et al., 2006; Hampson & Goldberg, 2006; Roberts & DelVecchio, 2000; Tackett et al., 2008).

In support of the disruption hypothesis, mean-level changes of personality indicate dips in maturity during the transition from childhood to adolescence, i.e., an individual's absolute standing on traits changes toward less maturity during this transitional period (Soto & Tackett, 2015). Specifically, most robust across studies is the finding that Conscientiousness and at least some facets of Openness decrease from childhood to adolescence (Denissen, Van Aken, Penke, & Wood, 2013; Soto, 2015; Soto, John, Gosling, & Potter, 2011). Findings for the other Big Five traits differed slightly across studies. For instance, a meta-analysis that focused on the age between 10 and 20 years found that Neuroticism, Extraversion, and Agreeableness did not significantly change during this developmental period, at least not when effect sizes were aggregated within samples (Denissen et al., 2013). In contrast, two large, cross-sectional studies and a five-wave longitudinal study on mean-level changes in self-reported as well as in parent-reported personality traits found that Extraversion (and Activity) and Agreeableness decreased from childhood to adolescence (Soto, 2015; Soto et al., 2011; Van den Akker, Deković, Asscher, & Prinzie, 2014). Gender differences in mean levels of personality were also first evident during this transitional period (Soto, 2015; Soto et al., 2011; Van den Akker et al., 2014). Specifically, Neuroticism increased from childhood into adolescence for females whereas it did not for males (Soto, 2015; Soto et al., 2011; Van den Akker et al., 2014). Despite these general trends, at least one study also found evidence for informant differences with respect to changes in Conscientiousness, Extraversion, and Neuroticism (Göllner et al., 2016). This finding underlines the importance of taking into account the source of personality ratings when drawing conclusions regarding developmental trajectories of personality traits.

Despite the importance of even early personality for later outcomes, few longitudinal studies have focused on personality traits before late childhood. Two notable exceptions to this are studies by Van den Akker et al. (2014) and De Fruyt et al. (2006). In Van den Akker et al. five-wave study, mean levels of Neuroticism, Agreeableness, and Conscientiousness increased from middle to late childhood. De Fruyt et al. study examined multiple types of developmental trajectories and deserves more elaborate review. In brief, De Fruyt et al. found that parent-reported personality remained relatively stable across a 3-year period in their sample of 6- to 13-year-old children. Due to the inclusion of a twin sample, the authors were also able to conclude that personality stability was mostly due to genetic and nonshared environmental factors. Specifically, in their study, the authors examined five types of personality continuity in childhood (and adolescence) and, at the Big Five level, found evidence for (1) structural continuity (i.e., invariance of the five-factor structure); (2) rank-order consistency (i.e., coefficients were generally greater than 0.70, except for Neuroticism, which was greater than 0.60); (3) lack of mean-level changes in the 6–7 and 8–9 year age groups (and otherwise generally only small mean-level changes); and (4) stable trait profiles (i.e., less than 10% of the sample showed changes in their profile shape). Given the relative dearth of studies that focus on the earlier childhood years, one important future direction for research in this area is the longitudinal study of early childhood personality, which may help to uncover all the predictive value of early individual differences.

In sum, childhood and especially the transition from childhood to adolescence are key periods for the developmental trajectories of personality traits for multiple reasons: (1) mean-level changes in traits are especially salient, (2) these changes are often opposite to changes in adults, and (3) there are gender-related differences in these changes (Soto et al., 2011). These findings underline the importance of examining personality changes not only early in life but also over short periods of time (because changes often happen quickly and in a curvilinear fashion; Soto & Tackett, 2015).

## Conclusion and future directions

In summary, while describing the Big Five traits in childhood, it becomes clear that child personality is more than temperament and not quite adult personality. This might suggest developmental progression/maturational processes at play, but more work is needed before we can be confident how much of the perceived differences are due to differences in measurement versus developmental changes. For example, although personality and temperament literatures have historically been studied in separation, current research generally agrees that personality and temperament are more alike than different. Nevertheless, there are important distinctions between personality and temperament and both capture common and unique variance in important outcomes. Similarly, there are also important distinctions between child and adult personality content that are crucial to take into account when studying personality development across the life span. Some examples include the greater content overlap among traits (e.g., Neuroticism and Agreeableness) and the greater salience of certain characteristics (e.g., Activity Level in child Extraversion; Intellect in child Openness-to-Experience). Some of these distinctions among child and adult personality traits may be due to differences in approaches to measurement. Greater reliance on informant reports is a unique issue in child research that offers great opportunities to develop strategies for combining multiple informants on a construct of interest. A hierarchical structure of personality in childhood could help organize the historically separate literatures on child temperament and personality across the life span.

A significant challenge for longitudinal research concerns the potential for personality assessment instruments to change across subsequent study waves. For example, different scales have been developed and validated for measuring dispositional traits during limited developmental windows (e.g., the Children's Behavior

Questionnaire for 3- to 7-year-old children versus the Temperament in Middle Children Questionnaire for 7- to 10-year-old children; Rothbart et al., 2001; Simonds & Rothbart, 2004). Likewise, researchers may have greater reliance on parent informants at earlier waves, and greater reliance on self-report at later waves of the study. As such, it becomes challenging to conclude whether an observed change is due to true changes in personality, changes in the measure, or changes in the informant (see Göllner et al., 2016, for an example of how informants affect observed changes in mean levels of personality traits). A "thin-slice" approach to measurement of personality in early life may at least partially address these challenges. As noted previously, this approach involves observers' snap judgments about children's personality based on thin slices of their behavior and has recently been shown to be an efficient, reliable, and valid indicator of children's personalities (Tackett et al., 2016). Given their reliance on random observers, a thin-slice approach would be in the unique position to hold the informant on the individual's personality consistent across waves of a longitudinal study even into adulthood, when parents may have less insight into their children's functioning compared to when their children were young. Other future directions include establishing optimal approaches to combining multiple informant reports for child behavior broadly and child personality specifically (De Los Reyes et al., 2015; Tackett, 2011). Such research would likewise benefit from thin-slice measures of personality, which would provide a consistent backdrop against which to compare different informant reports. Such a comparison would illustrate common as well as unique variance in different informants' reports, thereby contributing to efforts toward uncovering optimal strategies for combining multi-informant data.

In conclusion, the development of the Big Five personality traits not only begins early in childhood but already shows its predictive validity for later adulthood at an early age. Longitudinal studies beginning in early life are needed to understand the full extent of the impact of early personality on life outcomes. This work may benefit from thin-slice measures of child personality, which may ultimately help to overcome challenges inherent in multi-informant data.

# References

Angleitner, A., & Ostendorf, F. (1994). Temperament and the Big Five factors of personality. In C. F. Halverson, G. A. Kohnstamm, & R. P. Martin (Eds.), *The developing structure of temperament and personality from infancy to adulthood* (pp. 69−90). Hillsdale, NJ: Lawrence Erlbaum Associates.

Borkenau, P., Brecke, S., Möttig, C., & Paelecke, M. (2009). Extraversion is accurately perceived after a 50-ms exposure to a face. *Journal of Research in Personality, 43*, 703−706.

Brown, G. L., Mangelsdorf, S. C., Agathen, J. M., & Ho, M.-H. (2008). Young children's psychological selves: Convergence with maternal reports of child personality. *Social Development, 17*, 161−182.

Buss, A. H., & Plomin, R. (1984). *Temperament: Early developing personality traits.* Hillsdale: Erlbaum.

Caspi, A., Roberts, B. W., & Shiner, R. L. (2005). Personality development: Stability and change. *Annual Review of Psychology, 56,* 453–484.

Caspi, A., & Shiner, R. L. (2007). Personality development. In W. Damon, & R. M. Lerner (Eds.), *Handbook of child psychology.* Hoboken, NJ: John Wiley & Sons, Inc. Retrieved from http://doi.wiley.com/10.1002/9780470147658.chpsy0306.

Caspi, A., & Shiner, R. (2008). Temperament and personality. In M. Rutter, D. V. M. Bishop, D. S. Pine, S. Scott, J. Stevenson, E. Taylor, & A. Thapar (Eds.), *Rutter's child and adolescent psychiatry* (pp. 182–198). Oxford, UK: Blackwell Publishing Ltd.

Caspi, A., Wright, B. R. E., Moffitt, T. E., & Silva, P. A. (1998). Early failure in the labor market: Childhood and adolescent predictors of unemployment in the transition to adulthood. *American Sociological Review, 63,* 424–451.

Deal, J. E., Halverson, C. F., Martin, R. P., Victor, J., & Baker, S. (2007). The inventory of children's individual differences: Development and validation of a short version. *Journal of Personality Assessment, 89,* 162–166.

De Fruyt, F., Bartels, M., Van Leeuwen, K. G., De Clercq, B., Decuyper, M., & Mervielde, I. (2006). Five types of personality continuity in childhood and adolescence. *Journal of Personality and Social Psychology, 91,* 538–552.

De Fruyt, F., Mervielde, I., & Van Leeuwen, K. (2002). The consistency of personality type classification across samples and five-factor measures. *European Journal of Personality, 16,* S57–S72.

De Los Reyes, A., Augenstein, T. M., Wang, M., Thomas, S. A., Drabick, D. A. G., Burgers, D. E., & Rabinowitz, J. (2015). The validity of the multi-informant approach to assessing child and adolescent mental health. *Psychological Bulletin, 141,* 858–900.

De Pauw, S. S. W. (2016). Childhood personality and temperament. In T. A. Widiger (Ed.), *Oxford handbook of the five factor model.* New York: Oxford Press.

De Pauw, S. S. W., & Mervielde, I. (2010). Temperament, personality and developmental psychopathology: A review based on the conceptual dimensions underlying childhood traits. *Child Psychiatry & Human Development, 41,* 313–329.

De Pauw, S. S. W., & Mervielde, I. (2011). The role of temperament and personality in problem behaviors of children with ADHD. *Journal of Abnormal Child Psychology, 39,* 277–291.

De Pauw, S. S. W., Mervielde, I., & Van Leeuwen, K. G. (2009). How are traits related to problem behavior in preschoolers? Similarities and contrasts between temperament and personality. *Journal of Abnormal Child Psychology, 37,* 309–325.

De Pauw, S. S. W., Mervielde, I., Van Leeuwen, K. G., & De Clercq, B. (2011). How temperament and personality contribute to the maladjustment of children with autism. *Journal of Autism and Developmental Disorders, 41,* 196–212.

Denissen, J. J. A., van Aken, M. A., Penke, L., & Wood, D. (2013). Self-regulation underlies temperament and personality: An integrative developmental framework. *Child Development Perspectives, 7,* 255–260.

DeYoung, C. G., Peterson, J. B., & Higgins, D. M. (2005). Sources of Openness/Intellect: Cognitive and neuropsychological correlates of the fifth factor of personality. *Journal of Personality, 73,* 825–858.

DeYoung, C. G., Shamosh, N. A., Green, A. E., Braver, T. S., & Gray, J. R. (2009). Intellect as distinct from openness: Differences revealed by fMRI of working memory. *Journal of Personality and Social Psychology, 97,* 883–892.

Eder, R. A. (1990). Uncovering young children's psychological selves: Individual and developmental differences. *Child Development*, *61*, 849−863.

Ehrensaft, M. K., Moffitt, T. E., & Caspi, A. (2004). Clinically abusive relationships in an unselected birth cohort: Men's and women's participation and developmental antecedents. *Journal of Abnormal Psychology*, *113*, 258−270.

Evans, D. E., & Rothbart, M. K. (2007). Developing a model for adult temperament. *Journal of Research in Personality*, *41*, 868−888.

Eysenck, H. J. (1990). *Biological dimensions of personality. Handbook of personality: Theory and research* (pp. 244−276). New York, NY: Guilford Press.

Friedman, H. S., Tucker, J. S., Schwartz, J. E., Tomlinson-Keasey, C., Martin, L. R., Wingard, D. L., & Criqui, M. H. (1995). Psychosocial and behavioral predictors of longevity: The aging and death of the "Termites". *American Psychologist*, *50*, 69−78.

Goldsmith, H. H., Buss, A. H., Plomin, R., Rothbart, M. K., Thomas, A., Chess, S., ... McCull, R. B. (1987). Roundtable: What is temperament? Four approaches. *Child Development*, *58*, 505−529.

Göllner, R., Roberts, B. W., Damian, R. I., Lüdtke, O., Jonkmann, K., & Trautwein, U. (2016). Whose "storm and stress" is it? Parent and child reports of personality development in the transition to early adolescence. *Journal of Personality*, Advance online publication.

Grist, C. L., Socha, A., & McCord, D. M. (2012). The M5−PS−35: A Five-Factor personality questionnaire for preschool children. *Journal of Personality Assessment*, *94*, 287−295.

Halverson, C. F., Havill, V. L., Deal, J., Baker, S. R., Victor, J. B., Pavlopoulos, V., ... Wen, L. (2003). Personality structure as derived from parental ratings of free descriptions of children: The inventory of child individual differences. *Journal of Personality*, *71*, 995−1026.

Hampson, S. E. (2008). Mechanisms by which childhood personality traits influence adult well-being. *Current Directions in Psychological Science*, *17*, 264−268.

Hampson, S. E., & Goldberg, L. R. (2006). A first large cohort study of personality trait stability over the 40 years between elementary school and midlife. *Journal of Personality and Social Psychology*, *91*, 763−779.

Herzhoff, K., & Tackett, J. L. (2012). Establishing construct validity for openness-to-experience in middle childhood: Contributions from personality and temperament. *Journal of Research in Personality*, *46*, 286−294.

John, O. P., Naumann, L. P., & Soto, C. J. (2008). Paradigm shift to the integrative Big Five trait taxonomy. Retrieved from http://www.colby.edu/psychology/labs/personality/publications/John_et_al_2008.pdf.

Kochanska, G., Barry, R. A., Jimenez, N. B., Hollatz, A. L., & Woodard, J. (2009). Guilt and effortful control: Two mechanisms that prevent disruptive developmental trajectories. *Journal of Personality and Social Psychology*, *97*, 322−333.

Kochanska, G., Murray, K. T., & Harlan, E. T. (2000). Effortful control in early childhood: Continuity and change, antecedents, and implications for social development. *Developmental Psychology*, *36*, 220−232.

Kokko, K., Bergman, L., & Pulkkinen, L. (2003). Child personality characteristics and selection into long-term unemployment in Finnish and Swedish longitudinal samples. *International Journal of Behavioral Development*, *27*, 134−144.

Kokko, K., & Pulkkinen, L. (2000). Aggression in childhood and long-term unemployment in adulthood: A cycle of maladaptation and some protective factors. *Developmental Psychology*, *36*, 463−472.

Laceulle, O. M., Nederhof, E., Karreman, A., Ormel, J., & Aken, M. A. G. (2012). Stressful events and temperament change during early and middle adolescence: The TRAILS study. *European Journal of Personality, 26,* 276–284.

Loehlin, J. C., McCrae, R. R., Costa, P. T., & John, O. P. (1998). Heritabilities of common and measure-specific components of the Big Five personality factors. *Journal of Research in Personality, 32,* 431–453.

Markey, P. M., Markey, C. N., Tinsley, B. J., & Ericksen, A. J. (2002). A preliminary validation of preadolescents' self-reports using the Five-Factor Model of personality. *Journal of Research in Personality, 36,* 173–181.

Markon, K. E. (2009). Hierarchies in the structure of personality traits. *Social and Personality Psychology Compass, 3,* 812–826.

McCrae, R. R., & Costa, P. T. (1985). Updating Norman's "adequacy taxonomy": Intelligence and personality dimensions in natural language and in questionnaires. *Journal of Personality and Social Psychology, 49,* 710–721.

Measelle, J. R., John, O. P., Ablow, J. C., Cowan, P. A., & Cowan, C. P. (2005). Can children provide coherent, stable, and valid self-reports on the Big Five dimensions? A longitudinal study from ages 5 to 7. *Journal of Personality and Social Psychology, 89,* 90–106.

Mervielde, I., De Clercq, B. J., De Fruyt, F., & Van Leeuwen, K. (2005). Temperament, personality, and developmental psychopathology as childhood antecedents of personality disorders. *Journal of Personality Disorders, 19,* 171–201.

Mervielde, I., & De Fruyt, F. (1999). Construction of the Hierarchical Personality Inventory for Children (HiPIC). In I. Mervielde, I. Deary, F. De Fruyt, & F. Ostendorf (Eds.), *Personality psychology in Europe. Proceedings of the eight European conference on personality psychology* (1999, pp. 107–127). Tilburg: Tilburg University Press.

Neppl, T. K., Donnellan, M. B., Scaramella, L. V., Widaman, K. F., Spilman, S. K., Ontai, L. L., & Conger, R. D. (2010). Differential stability of temperament and personality from toddlerhood to middle childhood. *Journal of Research in Personality, 44,* 386–396.

Prime, H., Perlman, M., Tackett, J. L., & Jenkins, J. M. (2014). Cognitive sensitivity in sibling interactions: Development of the construct and comparison of two coding methodologies. *Early Education and Development, 25,* 240–258.

Roberts, B. W., & DelVecchio, W. F. (2000). The rank-order consistency of personality traits from childhood to old age: A quantitative review of longitudinal studies. *Psychological Bulletin, 126,* 3–25.

Rogosch, F. A., & Cicchetti, D. (2004). Child maltreatment and emergent personality organization: Perspectives from the Five-Factor Model. *Journal of Abnormal Child Psychology, 32,* 123–145.

Rothbart, M. K. (1981). Measurement of temperament in infancy. *Child Development, 52,* 569–578.

Rothbart, M. K. (2004). Temperament and the pursuit of an integrated developmental psychology. *Merrill-Palmer Quarterly, 50,* 492–505.

Rothbart, M. K., & Ahadi, S. A. (1994). Temperament and the development of personality. *Journal of Abnormal Psychology, 103,* 55–66.

Rothbart, M. K., Ahadi, S. A., Hershey, K. L., & Fisher, P. (2001). Investigations of temperament at three to seven years: The Children's Behavior Questionnaire. *Child Development, 72,* 1394–1408.

Rothbart, M. K., & Bates, J. E. (2006). Temperament. In W. Damon, & R. M. Lerner (Eds.), *Handbook of child psychology* (Vol. 3, 3rd ed.)., Hoboken, NJ: Wiley. Retrieved from http://www.bowdoin.edu/~sputnam/rothbart-temperament-questionnaires/cv/publications/pdf/2006_Chp%203_Temperament_Rothbart-Bates.pdf.

Rule, N. O., & Ambady, N. (2008). Brief exposures: Male sexual orientation is accurately perceived at 50 ms. *Journal of Experimental Social Psychology, 44*, 1100−1105.

Rule, N. O., Garrett, J. V., & Ambady, N. (2010). Places and faces: Geographic environment influences the ingroup memory advantage. *Journal of Personality and Social Psychology, 98*, 343−355.

Saudino, K. J. (2005). Behavioral genetics and child temperament. *Journal of Developmental and Behavioral Pediatrics: JDBP, 26*, 214−223.

Shiner, R. L. (1998). How shall we speak of children's personalities in middle childhood? A preliminary taxonomy. *Annual Progress in Child Psychiatry and Child Development,* 77−126.

Shiner, R. L. (2000). Linking childhood personality with adaptation: Evidence for continuity and change across time into late adolescence. *Journal of Personality and Social Psychology, 78*, 310−325.

Shiner, R. L., & Caspi, A. (2003). Personality differences in childhood and adolescence: Measurement, development, and consequences. *Journal of Child Psychology and Psychiatry, 44*, 2−32.

Shiner, R. L., & DeYoung, C. G. (2013). The structure of temperament and personality traits: A developmental perspective. In *The Oxford handbook of developmental psychology,* (pp. 113−141). New York: Oxford University Press.

Shiner, R. L., Masten, A. S., & Roberts, J. M. (2003). Childhood personality foreshadows adult personality and life outcomes two decades later. *Journal of Personality, 71*, 1145−1170.

Simonds, J., & Rothbart, M. K. (2004). The Temperament in Middle Childhood Questionnaire (TMCQ): A computerized self-report instrument for ages 7 − 10. Presented at the Occasional Temperament Conference, Athens, GA.

Soto, C. J. (2015). The Little Six personality dimensions from early childhood to early adulthood: Mean-level age and gender differences in parents' reports. *Journal of Personality,* Advance online publication.

Soto, C. J., & John, O. P. (2014). Traits in transition: The structure of parent-reported personality traits from early childhood to early adulthood. *Journal of Personality, 82*, 182−199.

Soto, C. J., John, O. P., Gosling, S. D., & Potter, J. (2011). Age differences in personality traits from 10 to 65: Big Five domains and facets in a large cross-sectional sample. *Journal of Personality and Social Psychology, 100*, 330−348.

Soto, C. J., & Tackett, J. L. (2015). Personality traits in childhood and adolescence: Structure, development, and outcomes. *Current Directions in Psychological Science, 24*, 358−362.

Tackett, J. L. (2011). Parent informants for child personality: Agreement, discrepancies, and clinical utility. *Journal of Personality Assessment, 93*, 539−544.

Tackett, J. L., Herzhoff, K., Kushner, S. C., & Rule, N. (2016). Thin slices of child personality: Perceptual, situational, and behavioral contributions. *Journal of Personality and Social Psychology, 110*, 150−166.

Tackett, J. L., Krueger, R. F., Iacono, W. G., & McGue, M. (2008). Personality in middle childhood: A hierarchical structure and longitudinal connections with personality in late adolescence. *Journal of Research in Personality, 42*, 1456−1462.

Tackett, J. L., Kushner, S. C., De Fruyt, F., & Mervielde, I. (2013). Delineating personality traits in childhood and adolescence: Associations across measures, temperament, and behavioral problems. *Assessment*, *20*, 738−751.

Tackett, J. L., Slobodskaya, H. R., Mar, R. A., Deal, J., Halverson, C. F., Baker, S. R., ... Besevegis, E. (2012). The hierarchical structure of childhood personality in five countries: Continuity from early childhood to early adolescence. *Journal of Personality*, *80*, 847−879.

Tackett, J. L., Smack, A. J., Herzhoff, K., Reardon, K. W., Daoud, S. L. S. B., & Granic, I. (under review). Measuring child personality when child personality was not measured: Application of a thin-slice approach.

Thomas, A., Chess, S., Birch, H. G., Hertzig, M. E., & Korn, S. (1963). *Behavioral individuality in early childhood*. New York: New York University.

Van den Akker, A. L., Deković, M., Asscher, J., & Prinzie, P. (2014). Mean-level personality development across childhood and adolescence: A temporary defiance of the maturity principle and bidirectional associations with parenting. *Journal of Personality and Social Psychology*, *107*, 736−750.

# Personality development in adolescence

3

*Patrick L. Hill[1] and Grant W. Edmonds[2]*
[1]Washington University in St. Louis, St. Louis, MO, United States, [2]Oregon Research Institute, Eugene, OR, United States

Adolescence as a developmental period often is viewed as one typified more by instability than stability. This viewpoint is in part justified by the tendency for adolescence to serve as a period of self and identity development, with marked fluctuations in how one perceives oneself (Erikson, 1959; Marcia, 1980; Waterman, 1982). With respect to personality psychology, during this period, research has demonstrated the capacity for change in goal commitments (Crone & Dahl, 2012) as well as self-concepts (Cole et al., 2001; Savin-Williams & Demo, 1984). Moreover, meta-analytic work suggests that personality traits exhibit lower levels of stability during adolescence than at any point thereafter (Roberts & DelVecchio, 2000). As such, it may appear problematic to describe adolescents' dispositional characteristics, thus leaving researchers to wonder about whether and how best to employ personality trait taxonomies for understanding adolescents.

This chapter will discuss personality trait development in adolescence, through exposition on three primary topics of interest. First, we will discuss common trait typologies and taxonomies employed for research with adolescents. Second, we consider the current state of evidence for personality trait stability and change during adolescence, focusing on taxonomies that bridge adolescent and adult literatures. Third, we discuss personality traits outside of the Big Five, focusing on subtypes of narcissistic tendencies given the prominence of research on this topic in recent years. Afterward, we conclude by providing future directions for longitudinal work on trait fluctuations during this developmental period.

## Personality trait taxonomies and classification schemes

When considering personality trait classification schemes, two varieties tend to arise in adolescent research. The first is an effort to classify adolescents into specific personality types, defined by their relative scores on given personality dimensions. The second set includes taxonomies such as the Big Five. Our primary focus in this chapter will be on research focused on the second front, though we begin by with a brief discussion of how the typological approach has been applied to understanding adolescent personality development.

Personality Development Across the Lifespan. DOI: http://dx.doi.org/10.1016/B978-0-12-804674-6.00003-X

## Considering typologies

The ARC (Asendorpf-Robins-Caspi) types (Asendorpf, Borkenau, Ostendorf, & Van Aken, 2001; Caspi & Silva, 1995; Costa, Herbst, McCrae, Samuels, & Ozer, 2002; Robins, John, Caspi, Moffitt, & Stouthamer-Loeber, 1996) represent one of the most commonly used personality typologies. Originally conceptualized by Block (1971) and Block and Block (1980), the theoretical background focuses on individual differences in ego resiliency, or the ability to functionally fluctuate one's control of impulses and desires in respond to the given situational demands (Block & Block, 1980). Individuals able to flexibly tailor their inhibitory control are referred to as resilient, while those on either end of the continuum have been labeled under-controlled and over-controlled. These three personality types have been replicated in child (Asendorpf & van Aken, 1999) and adolescent samples (Robins et al., 1996), as well as older samples (Specht, Luhmann, & Geiser, 2014). ARC-type structures have been identified using diverse methods, often employing Q-sort techniques and reverse factor analysis, as Block and coworkers initially suggested, or cluster analysis (Chapman & Goldberg, 2011). Moreover, these three personality types have proven valuable for understanding trajectories of adolescent development (Klimstra, Hale, Raaijmakers, Branje, & Meeus, 2010). Multiple studies have demonstrated that individuals within the resilient group tend to fare better than their peers on outcomes such as psychological well-being (van Aken & Dubas, 2004) and rates of delinquent activity (Klimstra et al., 2010; Robins et al., 1996). In addition, resilient children appear more likely to participate in volunteer activities during adolescence (Atkins, Hart, & Donnelly, 2005).

An important question then is whether these personality types hold across adolescence, or if normative developmental changes lead one to greater resilience in route to adulthood. Longitudinal research on personality types suggests moderate stability in class membership over time (Akse, Hale, Engels, Raaijmakers, & Meeus, 2007; van Aken & Dubas, 2004). Indeed, one five-wave study of adolescents from ages 12 to 20 found that 74% of participants retained their personality type membership across the five waves (Meeus, van de Schoot, Klimstra, & Branje, 2011). That said, the two most common transitions evidenced were both in the form of individuals becoming more resilient, from either an initial under-controlled or over-controlled status. When these changes occur, they too appear valuable for predicting adolescent well-being, insofar that transitions toward resilience coincide with reductions in anxiety, though the opposite is true for adolescents who become more over-controlled.

Given the apparent utility of this typology, researchers have sought to examine its connection to trait taxonomies more common in adulthood, with mixed results. Some research does suggest that class membership classifications will differ based on the personality trait assessment (De Fruyt, Mervielde, & Van Leeuwen, 2002). However, researchers have demonstrated that personality types can be characterized by taxonomies such as the Big Five (Klimstra, Luyckx, Teppers, Goossens, & De Fruyt, 2011), which may hold true for adolescents and adults alike (Asendorpf et al., 2001). While resilient youth appear to hold largely adaptive Big Five profiles (higher than average levels of emotional stability, extraversion, openness, agreeableness, and conscientiousness), under-controlled youth are characterized by lower than average levels on those domains (outside of extraversion) and over-controlled youth tend to exhibit the lowest scores on extraversion and emotional stability (Klimstra et al., 2011; Robins et al., 1996). This work was built upon a now substantial foundation of studies providing evidence that the Big Five taxonomy has the ability to characterize individual differences in personality during adolescence.

## Big Five taxonomy in adolescence

Certainly the most common trait taxonomy in personality psychology today is the Big Five, or Five-Factor, framework (John & Srivastava, 1999; McCrae & Costa, 1999). These five traits (extraversion, agreeableness, conscientiousness, emotional stability or neuroticism, and openness to experience) have been widely replicated across multiple cultures worldwide (John, Soto, & Naumann, 2008). Initial work establishing the Big Five depended heavily on teacher ratings of child personality (Digman, 1990; Goldberg, 1993). That said, the construction of modern Big Five measures had largely focused on adult samples. One notable exception being the HiPIC (Mervielde & De Fruyt, 1999), an instrument designed to assess Big Five personality in children and adolescents using parent ratings. There is robust evidence that a Big Five structure can be replicated in child samples using parents or teachers as raters (see also Herzhoff, Kushner, & Tackett, Chapter 2). However, one area that received less attention is adolescents' self-reported personality.

Concerns related to the validity of adolescent self-reports include both rater characteristics, and potential structural changes in personality constructs across development. Adolescence represents a time where cognitive faculties, linguistic abilities, and metacognitive perspectives including identity development and self-concept may all affect the validity of self-ratings. Shifts in the construct coherence and age appropriate expression of traits further complicate trait assessment (Caspi & Shiner, 2006). Adolescence then represents a unique measurement scenario, as it straddles the space between self-ratings in adulthood and observer rating methods in childhood. Developmental models and attempts to characterize personality change within and across adolescence faced multiple methodological challenges. Differences in trait content and development across time are confounded with differences due to changing rater perspectives and characteristics. These measurement concerns have been investigated using the Big Five Inventory (BFI; John & Srivastava, 1999), among participants ranging in age from 10 to 20 (Soto, John, Gosling, & Potter, 2008). In contrast to other measures, the BFI uses easily readable and short phrases more appropriate for youth. All five domains gained in coherence (assessed by inter-item correlations within a domain) when comparing across participants' ages from 10 to 20. In other words, adolescence appears as an important period for the crystallization and coherence of the Big Five domains with respect to self-reports, and it may be especially important to consider acquiescence bias in younger samples. However, the broader issue of construct coherence and its relationship to developmental trait change, and biases resulting from different rater characteristics during the transition from childhood and across adolescence have yet to be fully integrated into a comprehensive measurement or theoretical model.

In line with the research on personality types, longitudinal work on the Big Five during adolescence provides a nuanced portrayal of stability over time. The gestalt of this work suggests that adolescence is an important development period with respect to building continuity and stability on trait dimensions over time. One meta-analysis found that the rank-order consistency, or the extent to which people rank similarly on a trait over longitudinal assessments, tends to be higher in adolescence than childhood but still remains at levels much lower than seen in adult research (Roberts & DelVecchio, 2000). These rank-order stability estimates are slightly lower than evidenced for vocational interests (Low, Yoon, Roberts, & Rounds, 2005), suggesting that traits may be more malleable during adolescence than alternative personality characteristics.

Another approach to considering change on the Big Five traits during adolescence is to understand what occurs at the mean level, or how the sample as a whole changes on a given trait over time. Meta-analytic work on this front suggests that adolescence is not a time of large mean-level trends, with moderate increases on emotional stability and social dominance (a facet of extraversion), and marginal increases on openness to experience (Roberts, Walton, & Viechtbauer, 2006). Since that meta-analysis, only a few additional longitudinal studies have examined Big Five personality changes across adolescence, once again showing mixed results. A five-wave longitudinal study of Dutch adolescents found evidence for increases on agreeableness and emotional stability (Klimstra, Hale, Raaijmakers, Branje, & Meeus, 2009). Other work with Dutch youth has suggested sex differences, in that boys decrease on openness and extraversion, with girls showing increases on agreeableness, emotional stability, conscientiousness, and openness (Branje, van Lieshout, & Gerris, 2007). In contrast, research in Swiss adolescents, surveyed twice 1 year apart, found no significant mean-level trends for any of the Big Five traits (Hill et al., 2013). Low levels of rank-order stability compared to later age periods, coupled with inconsistent and modest evidence of mean-level changes in adolescence suggest adolescence is a time where changes do occur, although not in consistent ways for all samples or individuals. This uncertainty has lead researchers to focus on understanding the predictors of interindividual fluctuations on personality traits during adolescence.

## Predictors and correlates of Big Five trait change during adolescence

Theorists have posited a number of developmental challenges that confront individuals during adolescence, two of which may prove particularly influential with respect to personality development. First, adolescence is viewed as a primary period of identity development (Erikson, 1959; Marcia, 1980; Waterman, 1982), and as such, individual differences in the capacity to navigate this identity crisis likely will influence adolescents' personality dimensions. Second, the preadult years are commonly viewed with the expectation of maturation, and it has been suggested that age-graded role expectations may generate a press encouraging individuals to develop higher levels of certain personality traits (Hogan & Roberts, 2004). More specifically, maturity might entail developing those dispositional characteristics that assist individuals with taking on their socially expected roles; for instance, postindustrial cultures have increasingly encouraged adolescents to continue their education after high school (Arnett, 2000), and thus the transition to university, as well as the preparation for this transition may influence personality trait development. Though the challenges of maturation and identity formation are unique in their own right, they are similar with respect to how they define "successful" development. Indeed, successes with respect to identity development, maturation, and at school all seem to entail leading one toward being a more responsible and reliable individual, as well as being more stable and able to work with others. We take up each of these potential influences on personality development below, starting with understanding the relations between identity and personality change, given that this literature has received relatively more attention in longitudinal work.

## Identity development as a catalyst for personality change

Classically, adolescence was defined as a period during which individuals achieve identity formation and consolidation, or are mired in a state of identity confusion and profuse exploration (Erikson, 1959; Marcia, 1980). Additional work in this handbook describes identity development in greater detail (Klimstra & van Doeselar, Chapter 18), and thus we focus our attention here to its role specific to the Big Five. First, researchers have considered identity aspects, or subcomponents of feeling a consolidated sense of identity, in line with definitions of Erikson (1959) and others. For instance, Hill et al. (2013) examined whether adolescents perceived a sense of personal authenticity, control over their environments, as well as whether they were facing similar or inconsistent expectations across social roles. Each of the Big Five traits was initially related to at least one identity aspect, suggesting a relationship between personality and identity during adolescence. Moreover, over the span of a year, all traits with the exception of openness evidenced correlated changes with the identity aspects. For instance, adolescents who reported higher levels of conscientiousness over the year tended also to report higher authenticity and environmental control. Increases on emotional stability coincided with reports of greater environmental control and more consistency in expectations across social roles. Accordingly, it appears that the process of navigating identity formation may coincide with developments with respect to the Big Five personality traits.

Second, research has demonstrated the importance of considering how individuals process information relevant for self-knowledge. Specifically, Berzonsky (1990, 1992) has suggested that individuals tend to adopt one of three methods for processing identity-relevant information: (1) an informational approach, marked by deliberation and more active knowledge-seeking, (2) a normative approach, defined by a tendency to follow norms and the information provided by close associates, and (3) a diffuse style, in which the individual is uninterested in thinking about one's identity. Work with late adolescents suggests that openness to experience appears highly related to informational processing, while conscientiousness is associated with a more normative style (Duriez & Soenens, 2006; Duriez, Soenens, & Beyers, 2004). In addition, this work demonstrates that a more diffuse approach appears to coincide with a maladaptive personality profile, insofar that diffusion scores correlated with lower levels on agreeableness, conscientiousness, and openness to experience. As such, at least in cross-sectional data, research exists to suggest that the linkages between personality and identity development are even found with respect to the social-cognitive mechanisms underlying identity formation.

Third, research has targeted two processes central to identity development: (1) commitment to an identity and (2) exploration of identity options. Work with adolescents suggests that openness is linked to greater exploration, while neuroticism is negatively associated with commitment but positively with exploration (Klimstra, Luyckx, Goossens, Teppers, & De Fruyt, 2013). Though longitudinal work is needed with adolescents, work with emerging adults suggests that identity exploration and commitment do appear to change in tandem with the Big Five traits (Luyckx, Soenens, & Goossens, 2006). Support for personality and identity co-development has also been found with respect to the domain of *educational* identity development (Klimstra, Luyckx, Germeijs, Meeus, & Goossens, 2012). Across the three years of assessment, college students who increased their commitment to an educational identity (a sense that one is certain and confident in the educational path chosen) tended also to increase on extraversion, agreeableness, and conscientiousness. This work also points to the potential for commitments to societally prescribed roles, such as identifying as a student, to play a role in personality development, a central tenet of maturation theories.

## *Maturation, societal role adoption, and personality development*

Although disagreements may exist regarding the defining characteristics of the mature individual, most would agree that the preadult years are a period during which society expects some maturation to occur. Interestingly, biological maturation (as assessed by self-reported pubertal timing) has been found to hold little influence on personality trait trajectories during adolescence (Branje et al., 2007), suggesting the need to take a broader approach to defining maturity. Personality psychologists have described maturity with respect to developing higher levels on conscientiousness, agreeableness, and emotional stability, in line with the belief that these traits tend to be socially valued across the primary life domains (Hogan & Roberts, 2004). Evidence that maturation occurs during adolescence comes in part from cross-sectional and meta-analytic studies of personality trait change. As mentioned earlier, previous meta-analytic work suggests that adolescence is a period during which individuals tend to become more emotionally stable (Roberts et al., 2006). These trends have been confirmed in a recent online study of over a million participants between ages 10 and 65 (Soto, John, Gosling, & Potter, 2011). Moreover, that work suggests higher levels of conscientiousness in emerging adulthood when contrasted with early adolescence. If maturation is driven by societal role commitment, the trends in conscientiousness may be expected in part due to the educational experiences individuals experience during the preadult years.

Conscientiousness is associated with greater academic effort and motivation to achieve in school (Corker, Oswald, & Donnellan, 2012; Noftle & Robins, 2007; Trautwein, Lüdtke, Roberts, Schnyder, & Niggli, 2009) and ultimately higher grade point averages (Noftle & Robins, 2007; O'Connor & Paunonen, 2007). Accordingly, education itself can be viewed as an "intervention" of sorts to promote conscientious activity. Teachers encourage students from an early age toward being behaviors aligned with being reliable, punctual, and industrious, which are all facets of conscientiousness (Jackson et al., 2010). Indeed, research suggests that teachers' reports of their adolescent students' conscientiousness tend to coincide with their ratings of their students' school adjustment (Graziano & Ward, 1992). Recent work has advanced the notion that individuals develop conscientiousness in part due to their realization of the benefits associated with investing in the future (Hill & Jackson, in press). Schools should provide excellent environments for such realizations, and thus one would anticipate that educational contexts could play an important role in developing conscientiousness.

Research also demonstrates that academic experiences may influence development with respect to the other Big Five traits. For instance, one longitudinal study followed high school students through their transition to university, and examined the role of educational (and other) life events on personality development (Lüdtke, Roberts, Trautwein, & Nagy, 2011). In that study, students who studied abroad tended to be more likely to increase on extraversion, neuroticism, and agreeableness. As another example, students who changed their university studies over the four years tended to decrease on extraversion and openness to experience, but show increases on agreeableness and neuroticism. Research is needed to further understand the pathways involved, but this work suggests that even single academic events may hold the potential to influence personality development during the late adolescent and emerging adult years.

## Narcissistic ideation in adolescent development

Though several studies have focused on personality types or the Big Five traits, additional specific traits are worth mentioning when discussing personality research with adolescent samples. Among these specific traits, perhaps none has received more attention than those associated with narcissistic self-perceptions. Similar to the discussion earlier, the development of adolescent narcissism also appears tied to the ongoing identity crisis during adolescence. Theoretical literatures in fact suggest that inflated self-perceptions, to an extent, could prove valuable and even normative during the adolescent years (Blos, 1962; Hill & Lapsley, 2011; Lapsley, 1993). This argument builds from the notion that the adolescent years are particularly important for self- and identity formation, as well as for beginning to make important life decisions absent parental safeguards. Accordingly, individuals will necessarily make mistakes during these initial attempts at autonomous decision-making. If true, then adolescents have an increased susceptibility for self-doubt and self-esteem issues.

Theoretical traditions point to the potential for adolescents then to form "personal fables" about their personal uniqueness, importance, or invulnerability (Elkind, 1967; Lapsley, 1993), which may be viewed as adolescence-specific forms of narcissistic ideation (Hill & Lapsley, 2011). These inflated self-perceptions may serve to support adolescents' self-worth during their initial trial-and-error stage, and during the difficult travails of identity formation. Consistent with this idea, adolescents who report higher levels of either subjective omnipotence or invulnerability against psychological concerns tend also to report greater well-being (Aalsma, Lapsley, & Flannery, 2006; Hill, Duggan, & Lapsley, 2012; Lapsley & Hill, 2010). However, not all of these self-perceptions appear valuable, as evidenced by the negative psychological consequences that appear to present for those who perceive a profound sense of uniqueness and peculiarity from others (Hill & Lapsley, 2011). In other words, adolescents who believe others cannot understand them may be at greatest risk for psychological concerns. Similarly, research has delineated between more adaptive and maladaptive forms of narcissistic traits in adolescent samples (Barry & Kauten, 2014; Barry & Malkin, 2010; Barry, Frick, Adler, & Grafeman, 2007), based on the distinction that adaptive narcissism reflects perceived authority and self-sufficiency, while maladaptive facets include entitlement, exploitativeness, and exhibitionism (Barry, Frick, & Killian, 2003). This work suggests that the link between adolescents who report higher levels of pathological narcissism is more likely to experience self-esteem and internalizing issues, while nonpathological (adaptive) forms may negatively associate with these concerns.

Narcissism has received extensive research attention over the past decade mostly as a result of examinations into whether cultural changes through the years have encouraged adolescents and emerging adults into greater narcissistic tendencies, leading some to claim an "epidemic" of narcissism (Twenge, 2013; Twenge & Campbell, 2009; Twenge & Foster, 2010). Empirical research into cohort differences has suggested a fairly modest increase on narcissism levels over time (Donnellan, Trzesniewski, & Robins, 2009), with studies finding little to no cohort difference (Roberts, Edmonds, & Grijalva, 2010). Moreover, longitudinal work also has failed to show significant increases in narcissism among adolescents over time (Barry & Lee-Rowland, 2015). The inconsistent evidence for cohort or longitudinal differences in narcissism has led some to suggest research should focus on whether adolescence is a developmental period associated with normative increases on narcissism paired with later declines, possibly due to maturation (Roberts et al., 2010). Longitudinal research is needed to investigate these self-perceptions into adulthood, but if holding specific varieties of narcissistic self-perceptions can serve to benefit individuals during the identity travails of adolescence, one would predict these characteristics are only normative during this period (Blos, 1962; Lapsley, 1993).

# Conclusion and future directions

Research on personality trait development during adolescence has increased significantly over the past two decades. This growth has been due in part to the consistent demonstration that trait taxonomies well known to personality researchers (e.g., the Big Five) appear applicable even during the adolescent years. The most prominent need for research in the years ahead though is continued efforts to chart personality trait development during adolescence, using multiwave assessments that, ideally, follow participants across developmental periods, from childhood to the early teenage years, through their transition to adulthood. Most longitudinal work discussed earlier has focused solely on the preadult years, with limited information on how the transition to adulthood influences individual trajectories. Such efforts would substantially advance our understanding of whether (1) normative mean-level trends exist for the Big Five during adolescence, (2) significant variability exists with respect to individual-level patterns of change, and (3) identity formation and maturation serve as valuable theoretical frameworks from which to predict trajectories in trait change during adolescence. While there is strong evidence for measurement validity at the basic structural level has been established for each of these developmental periods, questions remain regarding the content and structural coherence of traits across these periods, and confounds between these and rater characteristics. More work is needed to create theoretical and measurement models to address these measurement concerns.

Additional avenues for future research include the need for longitudinal studies of the developmental role aspects of narcissism from childhood into adulthood. Based on the past literature (Hill & Lapsley, 2011; Roberts et al., 2010), one would anticipate that individuals would naturally increase their narcissistic tendencies as they progress toward the transition into adulthood, with concomitant decreases once faced with societal pressures to decline. Some components though may remain at elevated levels, if they prove adaptive for entering the work force. Research has shown that individuals' shifting work experiences coincide with personality trait changes, in the form of positive work experiences being associated with developing those traits that promote workplace success (Hudson, Lodi-Smith, & Roberts, 2012; Hudson & Roberts, 2016). As such, perceptions of oneself as an authority or leader, two components of more "adaptive" forms of narcissism (Ackerman, Donnellan, Roberts, & Fraley, 2015; Ackerman et al., 2011), might actually increase when building commitments to adult work roles.

Finally, further research is needed to understand how adolescents perceive trait changes and their potential utility. Similar work has been conducted with emerging adult samples, asking individuals about their goals for personality change (see Hudson & Fraley, Chapter 33); however, it is unknown whether adolescents will desire personality trait changes seen as adaptive to society as a whole. Such work will be valuable to test a central tenet of theories of personality trait change in adulthood (Hill, & Jackson, in press; Roberts, Wood, & Caspi, 2008), namely that individuals may alter their personality profiles after observing the utility of doing so (e.g., seeing the value of being conscientious). If adolescents hold differing goals for personality change, either with respect to adults or their own peer groups, these motivations may help explain the inconsistent evidence for mean-level trait trends in this period. In sum, though the theoretical frameworks appear in place to help understand adolescent personality development (i.e., maturation, identity formation studies, and social role investment), future research is needed to support their potential as explanatory frameworks. Understanding these processes will open new avenues to understanding positive development in an important and often tumultuous time in the lifespan.

# References

Aalsma, M. C., Lapsley, D. K., & Flannery, D. J. (2006). Personal fables, narcissism, and adolescent adjustment. *Psychology in the Schools, 43*, 481–491.

Ackerman, R. A., Donnellan, M. B., Roberts, B. W., & Fraley, R. C. (2015). The effect of response format on the psychometric properties of the Narcissistic Personality Inventory: Consequences for item meaning and factor structure. *Assessment.*

Ackerman, R. A., Witt, E. A., Donnellan, M. B., Trzesniewski, K. H., Robins, R. W., & Kashy, D. A. (2011). What does the narcissistic personality inventory really measure? *Assessment, 18*, 67–87.

Akse, J., Hale, W. W., Engels, R. C., Raaijmakers, Q. A., & Meeus, W. H. (2007). Stability and change in personality type membership and anxiety in adolescence. *Journal of Adolescence, 30*, 813–834.

Arnett, J. J. (2000). Emerging adulthood: A theory of development from the late teens through the twenties. *American Psychologist, 55*, 469–480.

Asendorpf, J. B., & van Aken, M. A. (1999). Resilient, overcontrolled, and undercontroleed personality prototypes in childhood: Replicability, predictive power, and the trait-type issue. *Journal of Personality and Social Psychology, 77*, 815–832.

Asendorpf, J. B., Borkenau, P., Ostendorf, F., & Van Aken, M. A. (2001). Carving personality description at its joints: Confirmation of three replicable personality prototypes for both children and adults. *European Journal of Personality, 15*, 169–198.

Atkins, R., Hart, D., & Donnelly, T. M. (2005). The association of childhood personality type with volunteering during adolescence. *Merrill-Palmer Quarterly, 51*, 145–163.

Barry, C. T., & Kauten, R. L. (2014). Nonpathological and pathological narcissism: Which self-reported characteristics are most problematic in adolescents? *Journal of Personality Assessment, 96*, 212–219.

Barry, C. T., & Lee-Rowland, L. M. (2015). Has there been a recent increase in adolescent narcissism? Evidence from a sample of at-risk adolescents (2005–2014). *Personality and Individual Differences, 87*, 153–157.

Barry, C. T., & Malkin, M. L. (2010). The relation between adolescent narcissism and internalizing problems depends on the conceptualization of narcissism. *Journal of Research in Personality, 44*, 684–690.

Barry, C. T., Frick, P. J., & Killian, A. L. (2003). The relation of narcissism and self-esteem to conduct problems in children: A preliminary investigation. *Journal of Clinical Child and Adolescent Psychology, 32*, 139–152.

Barry, C. T., Frick, P. J., Adler, K. K., & Grafeman, S. J. (2007). The predictive utility of narcissism among children and adolescents: Evidence for a distinction between adaptive and maladaptive narcissism. *Journal of Child and Family Studies, 16*, 508–521.

Berzonsky, M. D. (1990). Self-construction over the life-span: A process perspective on identity formation. In G. J. Neimeyer, & R. A. Neimeyer (Eds.), *Advances in personal construct psychology* (pp. 155–186). Greenwich, CT: JAI Press.

Berzonsky, M. D. (1992). A process perspective on identity and stress management. In G. R. Adams, T. P. Gullotta, & R. Montemayor (Eds.), *Adolescent identity formation (Advances in adolescent development)* (Vol. 4, pp. 193–215). Newbury Park, CA: Sage.

Block, J. (1971). *Lives through time*. Berkeley, CA: Bancroft.

Block, J. H., & Block, J. (1980). The role of ego-control and ego-resiliency in the organization of behavior. In W. A. Collins (Ed.), *Minnesota symposia on child psychology* (pp. 39–101). Hillsdale, NJ: Erlbaum.

Blos, P. (1962). *On adolescence*. New York, NY: Free Press of Glencoe.

Branje, S. J., Van Lieshout, C. F., & Gerris, J. R. (2007). Big Five personality development in adolescence and adulthood. *European Journal of Personality, 21*, 45–62.

Caspi, A., & Silva, P. A. (1995). Temperamental qualities at age three predict personality traits in young adulthood: Longitudinal evidence from a birth cohort. *Child Development, 66*(2), 486–498.

Chapman, B. P., & Goldberg, L. R. (2011). Replicability and 40-year predictive power of childhood ARC types. *Journal of Personality and Social Psychology, 101*, 593–606.

Cole, D. A., Maxwell, S. E., Martin, J. M., Peeke, L. G., Seroczynski, A. D., Tram, J. M., . . . Maschman, T. (2001). The development of multiple domains of child and adolescent self-concept: A cohort sequential longitudinal design. *Child Development, 72*, 1723–1746.

Corker, K. S., Oswald, F. L., & Donnellan, M. B. (2012). Conscientiousness in the classroom: A process explanation. *Journal of Personality, 80*, 995–1028.

Costa, P. T., Herbst, J. H., McCrae, R. R., Samuels, J., & Ozer, D. J. (2002). The replicability and utility of three personality types. *European Journal of Personality, 16*, S73–S87.

Crone, E. A., & Dahl, R. E. (2012). Understanding adolescence as a period of social-affective engagement and goal flexibility. *Nature Reviews Neuroscience, 13*, 636–650.

De Fruyt, F., Mervielde, I., & Van Leeuwen, K. (2002). The consistency of personality type classification across samples and five-factor measures. *European Journal of Personality, 16*, S57–S72.

Digman, J. M. (1990). Personality structure: Emergence of the five-factor model. *Annual Review of Psychology, 41*, 417–440.

Donnellan, M. B., Trzesniewski, K. H., & Robins, R. W. (2009). An emerging epidemic of narcissism or much ado about nothing? *Journal of Research in Personality, 43*, 498–501.

Duriez, B., & Soenens, B. (2006). Personality, identity styles, and religiosity: An integrative study among late and middle adolescents. *Journal of Adolescence, 29*, 119–135.

Duriez, B., Soenens, B., & Beyers, W. (2004). Personality, identity styles, and religiosity: An integrative study among late adolescents in Flanders (Belgium). *Journal of Personality, 72*, 877–910.

Elkind, D. (1967). Egocentrism in adolescence. *Child Development, 38*, 1025–1034.

Erikson, E. H. (1959). *Identity and the life cycle*. New York, NY: International University Press.

Goldberg, L. R. (1993). The structure of phenotypic personality traits. *American Psychologist, 48*, 26–34.

Graziano, W. G., & Ward, D. (1992). Probing the Big Five in adolescence: Personality and adjustment during a developmental transition. *Journal of Personality, 60*, 425–439.

Hill, P. L., & Jackson, J. J. (in press). The invest-and-accrue model of conscientiousness. *Review of General Psychology*.

Hill, P. L., & Lapsley, D. K. (2011). Adaptive and maladaptive narcissism in adolescent development. In C. T. Barry, P. Kerig, K. Stellwagen, & T. D. Barry (Eds.), *Implications of narcissism and Machiavellianism for the development of prosocial and antisocial behavior in youth* (pp. 89−105). Washington, DC: APA Books.

Hill, P. L., Allemand, M., Grob, S. Z., Peng, A., Morgenthaler, C., & Käppler, C. (2013). Longitudinal relations between personality traits and aspects of identity formation during adolescence. *Journal of Adolescence, 36*, 413−421.

Hill, P. L., Duggan, P. M., & Lapsley, D. K. (2012). Subjective invulnerability, risk behavior, and adjustment in early adolescence. *The Journal of Early Adolescence, 32*, 489−501.

Hogan, R., & Roberts, B. W. (2004). A socioanalytic model of maturity. *Journal of Career Assessment, 12*, 207−217.

Hudson, N. W., & Roberts, B. W. (2016). Social investment in work reliably predicts change in conscientiousness and agreeableness: A direct replication and extension of Hudson, Roberts, and Lodi-Smith (2012). *Journal of Research in Personality, 60*, 12−23.

Hudson, N. W., Roberts, B. W., & Lodi-Smith, J. (2012). Personality trait development and social investment in work. *Journal of Research in Personality, 46*, 334−344.

Jackson, J. J., Wood, D., Bogg, T., Walton, K. E., Harms, P. D., & Roberts, B. W. (2010). What do conscientious people do? Development and validation of the Behavioral Indicators of Conscientiousness (BIC). *Journal of Research in Personality, 44*, 501−511.

John, O. P., & Srivastava, S. (1999). The Big Five trait taxonomy: History, measurement, and theoretical perspectives. In L. A. Pervin, & O. P. John (Eds.), *Handbook of personality: Theory and research,* (2nd ed., pp. 102−138). New York, NY: Guilford.

John, O. P., Naumann, L. P., & Soto, C. J. (2008). Paradigm shift to the integrative big five trait taxonomy. In O. P. John, R. W. Robins, & L. A. Pervin (Eds.), *Handbook of personality: Theory and research,* (3rd ed., pp. 114−158). New York, NY: Guilford.

Klimstra, T. A., Hale, W. W., III, Raaijmakers, Q. A., Branje, S. J., & Meeus, W. H. (2009). Maturation of personality in adolescence. *Journal of Personality and Social Psychology, 96*, 898−912.

Klimstra, T. A., Hale, W. W., Raaijmakers, Q. A., Branje, S. J., & Meeus, W. H. (2010). A developmental typology of adolescent personality. *European Journal of Personality, 24*, 309−323.

Klimstra, T. A., Luyckx, K., Germeijs, V., Meeus, W. H., & Goossens, L. (2012). Personality traits and educational identity formation in late adolescents: Longitudinal associations and academic progress. *Journal of Youth and Adolescence, 41*, 346−361.

Klimstra, T. A., Luyckx, K., Goossens, L., Teppers, E., & De Fruyt, F. (2013). Associations of identity dimensions with Big Five personality domains and facets. *European Journal of Personality, 27*, 213−221.

Klimstra, T. A., Luyckx, K., Teppers, E., Goossens, L., & De Fruyt, F. (2011). Congruence between adolescent personality types based on the Big Five domains and the 30 NEO-PI-3 personality facets. *Journal of Research in Personality, 45*, 513−517.

Lapsley, D. K. (1993). Toward an integrated theory of adolescent ego development: The "new look" at adolescent egocentrism. *American Journal of Orthopsychiatry, 63*, 562−571.

Lapsley, D. K., & Hill, P. L. (2010). Subjective invulnerability, optimism bias and adjustment in emerging adulthood. *Journal of Youth and Adolescence, 39*, 847−857.

Low, K. D., Yoon, M., Roberts, B. W., & Rounds, J. (2005). The stability of vocational interests from early adolescence to middle adulthood: A quantitative review of longitudinal studies. *Psychological Bulletin, 131*, 713−737.

Lüdtke, O., Roberts, B. W., Trautwein, U., & Nagy, G. (2011). A random walk down university avenue: Life paths, life events, and personality trait change at the transition to university life. *Journal of Personality and Social Psychology, 101*, 620–637.

Luyckx, K., Soenens, B., & Goossens, L. (2006). The personality–identity interplay in emerging adult women: Convergent findings from complementary analyses. *European Journal of Personality, 20*, 195–215.

Marcia, J. E. (1980). Identity in adolescence. In J. Adelson (Ed.), *Handbook of adolescent psychology* (pp. 159–187). New York, NY: Wiley & Sons.

McCrae, R. R., & Costa, P. T., Jr. (1999). A five-factor theory of personality. In L. A. Pervin, & O. P. John (Eds.), *Handbook of personality: Theory and research,* (2nd ed., pp. 139–153). New York, NY: Guilford.

Mervielde, I., & De Fruyt, F. (1999). Construction of the Hierarchical Personality Inventory for Children (HiPIC). In I. Mervielde, I. Deary, F. De Fruyt, & F. Ostendorf (Eds.), *Personality psychology in Europe. Proceedings of the eight European conference on personality psychology* (pp. 107–127). Tilburg: Tilburg University Press.

Meeus, W., Van de Schoot, R., Klimstra, T., & Branje, S. (2011). Personality types in adolescence: change and stability and links with adjustment and relationships: A five-wave longitudinal study. *Developmental Psychology, 47*, 1181–1195.

Noftle, E. E., & Robins, R. W. (2007). Personality predictors of academic outcomes: Big Five correlates of GPA and SAT scores. *Journal of Personality and Social Psychology, 93*, 116–130.

O'Connor, M. C., & Paunonen, S. V. (2007). Big Five personality predictors of post-secondary academic performance. *Personality and Individual Differences, 43*, 971–990.

Roberts, B. W., & DelVecchio, W. F. (2000). The rank-order consistency of personality traits from childhood to old age: A quantitative review of longitudinal studies. *Psychological Bulletin, 126*, 3–25.

Roberts, B. W., Edmonds, G., & Grijalva, E. (2010). It is developmental me, not generation me developmental changes are more important than generational changes in narcissism—Commentary on Trzesniewski & Donnellan (2010). *Perspectives on Psychological Science, 5*, 97–102.

Roberts, B. W., Walton, K. E., & Viechtbauer, W. (2006). Patterns of mean-level change in personality traits across the life course: A meta-analysis of longitudinal studies. *Psychological Bulletin, 132*, 1–25.

Roberts, B. W., Wood, D., & Caspi, A. (2008). The development of personality traits in adulthood. In O. P. John, R. W. Robins, & L. A. Pervin (Eds.), *Handbook of personality: Theory and research,* (3rd ed., pp. 375–398). New York, NY: Guilford.

Robins, R. W., John, O. P., Caspi, A., Moffitt, T. E., & Stouthamer-Loeber, M. (1996). Resilient, overcontrolled, and undercontrolled boys: Three replicable personality types. *Journal of Personality and Social Psychology, 70*, 157–171.

Savin-Williams, R. C., & Demo, D. H. (1984). Developmental change and stability in adolescent self-concept. *Developmental Psychology, 20*, 1100–1110.

Soto, C. J., John, O. P., Gosling, S. D., & Potter, J. (2008). The developmental psychometrics of big five self-reports: Acquiescence, factor structure, coherence, and differentiation from ages 10 to 20. *Journal of Personality and Social Psychology, 94*, 718–737.

Soto, C. J., John, O. P., Gosling, S. D., & Potter, J. (2011). Age differences in personality traits from 10 to 65: Big Five domains and facets in a large cross-sectional sample. *Journal of Personality and Social Psychology, 100*, 330–348.

Specht, J., Luhmann, M., & Geiser, C. (2014). On the consistency of personality types across adulthood: Latent profile analyses in two large-scale panel studies. *Journal of Personality and Social Psychology, 107*, 540–556.

Trautwein, U., Lüdtke, O., Roberts, B. W., Schnyder, I., & Niggli, A. (2009). Different forces, same consequence: Conscientiousness and competence beliefs are independent predictors of academic effort and achievement. *Journal of Personality and Social Psychology, 97,* 1115−1128.

Twenge, J. M. (2013). The evidence for generation me and against generation we. *Emerging Adulthood, 1,* 11−16.

Twenge, J. M., & Campbell, W. K. (2009). *The narcissism epidemic: Living in the age of entitlement.* New York, NY: Simon and Schuster.

Twenge, J. M., & Foster, J. D. (2010). Birth cohort increases in narcissistic personality traits among American college students, 1982−2009. *Social Psychological and Personality Science, 1,* 99−106.

van Aken, M. A., & Semon Dubas, J. (2004). Personality type, social relationships, and problem behaviour in adolescence. *European Journal of Developmental Psychology, 1,* 331−348.

Waterman, A. S. (1982). Identity development from adolescence to adulthood: An extension of theory and a review of research. *Developmental Psychology, 18,* 341−358.

# Personality development in emerging adulthood

4

*Wiebke Bleidorn and Ted Schwaba*
University of California, Davis, CA, United States

What is the common thread between a 20-year-old college junior beginning a new relationship, a 19-year-old part-time sandwich shop manager going through a breakup, and a 23-year old working a full-time job but living single at her parent's house? One answer—all three of these people will probably be in completely different living situations next year.

Compared to other ages, a day in the life of an 18- to 25-year old living in a developed country is particularly hard to generalize. All three of the hypothetical people described above are uncommitted to their present role identities, whether by choice or by economic necessity. According to Jeffrey Arnett (2000, 2007), this time—the period between the late teens and the mid- to late 20s—can be best described as *emerging adulthood*, a demographically and subjectively distinct period within the adult life course in modern Western industrialized countries.

This chapter examines if and how emerging adulthood is related to personality trait change. Specifically, in the following we lay out Arnett's conception of emerging adulthood, present a brief overview of previous research on personality trait development in young adulthood, and then review the empirical evidence for two specific hypotheses about personality trait change in emerging adulthood. Finally, we discuss the implications of emerging adulthood on future directions for theory and research on personality trait development.

## What is emerging adulthood?

Emerging adulthood is a stage of the lifespan between adolescence and full-fledged adulthood encompassing the late teens and mid- to late 20s that has been proposed by Jeffrey Arnett (2000, 2004, 2007). The term describes young adults who do not have children, do not live in their own home, or do not have sufficient income to become fully independent. According to Arnett (2000), emerging adulthood can be best described as a "roleless role" (Arnett, 2000, p. 471).

The idea of a transitory period between adolescence and adulthood has existed in the sociological literature for some time (Keniston, 1971), but has recently attracted more attention. One of the most important features of emerging adulthood is that this period allows for identity exploration more than any other age period in

Personality Development Across the Lifespan. DOI: http://dx.doi.org/10.1016/B978-0-12-804674-6.00004-1

the adult life course. This is because emerging adults have not yet made strong commitments to roles or a particular identity (Arnett, 2000).

Much of this exploration takes place in the domains of worldviews and work, as the transition from an industrial to an information-based economy has led to an increase in postsecondary education and a delaying of career entrance (Tanner & Arnett, 2009). Emerging adults also explore the domain of love; as women are afforded more opportunities in education and occupation, and as mores on premarital sex dissipate, there is less pressure to start a family or get married when one is young (Tanner & Arnett, 2009).

Emerging adulthood has also been described as the "age of being in-between" (Arnett, 2007, p. 69). Overwhelmingly, 18- to 25-year olds do not feel like adolescents or adults, but like they are not much of either (Arnett, 2000). Contrasted with past generations, in which entrance into adult roles, such as spouse, parent, or jobholder, typically came immediately after finishing education, today's twentysomethings seem to take their time, entering into adult roles more gradually. In a way, emerging adulthood may be thus seen as a prolonged version of the moratorium stage of Erikson's (1959) theory of lifespan development. To the extent that these demographic shifts are permanent, or may grow more pronounced in the future, emerging adulthood can be expected to continue to be a normative life stage.

The proposition of a new and distinct life stage between adolescence and young adulthood raises important questions about its relevance to emerging adults for their socio-emotional development in general and their personality development in particular. Assuming that emerging adulthood is indeed a subjectively and demographically distinct period in the adult life course, how does this affect theory and research on personality development? Do emerging adults experience personality trait changes that are specific to this life stage, and are these changes different from normative personality trait changes observed in young adulthood?

## Personality trait development in young adulthood

During the past two decades, a large number of studies have examined when and how broad personality characteristics, such as the Big Five or self-esteem, change throughout adulthood (for reviews, see Orth & Robins, 2014; Roberts, Walton, & Viechtbauer, 2006; Roberts, Wood, & Caspi, 2008; Specht et al., 2014). The vast majority of these studies have focused generally on the years between age 18 and 40 (Bleidorn, 2015). That is, most previous research on personality trait development has focused on the all-embracing period of young adulthood rather than treating emerging adulthood and young adulthood as discrete developmental periods with distinct developmental tasks and themes.

One robust finding to emerge from this literature is that young adults tend to show remarkable increases in traits that indicate greater social maturity (Roberts & Mroczek, 2008). Specifically, between ages 18 and 40, the average individual shows increases in emotional stability, conscientiousness, agreeableness, and self-esteem (Bleidorn, 2015; Bleidorn et al., 2016a; Orth & Robins, 2014; Roberts et al., 2006). This pattern has been often referred to as the maturity principle of personality development, because increases in these traits have been theorized to be functional for mastering adult role transitions such as entering the labor force or becoming a parent (Bleidorn et al., 2013; Hudson, Roberts, & Lodi-Smith, 2012; Hutteman et al., 2014; Roberts & Mroczek, 2008; van Scheppingen et al., 2016).

Research on changes in openness to experience and extraversion has led to results that are less clear: Some studies reported increases (Bleidorn, 2012; Roberts et al., 2006), some reported decreases (Wortman, Lucas, & Donnellan, 2012), and others reported no significant changes in openness and extraversion (Soto, John, Gosling, & Potter, 2011). Overall, the evidence seems to suggest that most people likely experience no more than modest changes in extraversion and openness across young adulthood.

How well do these findings describe normative personality trait change when narrowing in on emerging adulthood? Is it reasonable to generalize from 18- to 40-year olds to 18- to 25-year olds in particular?

Arnett's conception of emerging adulthood outlined above (2000, 2007) suggests that this life phase is marked by specific themes and developmental challenges that are different from those that characterize young adulthood. So, while developmental trajectories in young adulthood may be shaped by commitment to and investment in adult social roles, developmental trajectories in emerging adults who have not yet committed to these roles and responsibilities may instead be a product of identity exploration and delayed maturity. As a result, these trajectories may take a different shape. In other words, the widely observed pattern of personality maturation might apply to young adults who are invested in adult roles; it might, however, not apply to emerging adults who are relatively independent from these social roles and the normative expectations that come with them.

Based on theory and research on emerging adulthood as a distinct life stage, we derived two broad hypotheses about the nature and shape of personality trait change in emerging adults. First, based on the claim that emerging adulthood is marked by freedom from adult role responsibilities, it can be predicted that personality maturation due to role investment is attenuated during this period. Second, consistent with the proposition that emerging adulthood is best described as a time of exploration, it can be predicted that emerging adulthood is characterized by normative increases in openness to experience. In the following, we detail the theoretical background for these two hypotheses, review the existing empirical evidence, and discuss the implications for theory and future research on adult personality development.

## Is personality maturation attenuated during emerging adulthood?

As outlined above, during young adulthood, individuals tend to increase in personality traits that mark greater social maturity (for reviews, see Bleidorn,

2015; Roberts & Mroczek, 2008; Specht et al., 2014). A leading explanatory account of these positive personality trait changes in young adulthood has been offered within the framework of social investment principle (SIP; Roberts, Wood, & Smith, 2005). SIP proposes that age-graded life transitions into adult roles, such as entering the labor force, marrying, or becoming a parent, are triggers of the widely observed increases in emotional stability, agreeableness, and conscientiousness during young adulthood. According to SIP, increases in these traits derive from the new behavioral demands and responsibilities that are associated with mastering adult social roles.

Thus, from the perspective of SIP, the normative pattern of personality maturation should be attenuated as long as emerging adults are delaying firm commitments to adult role responsibilities. This is not to say that there is no personality maturation at all in emerging adulthood. Theory and research suggest that personality trait changes in young adulthood are at least partly influenced by genetically influenced biological maturation processes (Bleidorn, Kandler, & Caspi, 2014; Bleidorn, Kandler, Riemann, Angleitner, & Spinath, 2009; McCrae & Costa, 2008), and that comparable patterns of personality maturation can even be observed in nonhuman animals (Weiss & King, 2015). However, if SIP is correct in proposing that investments into adult social roles catalyze normative increases in emotional stability, agreeableness, and conscientiousness, then there is reason to predict that these increases are substantially attenuated during the period of emerging adulthood.

## Cross-sectional studies

Does the empirical evidence on personality trait change support this prediction? When looking at large-scale cross-sectional research on age difference in personality traits, the evidence suggests that emerging adulthood is marked by relatively strong age-related increases in conscientiousness, emotional stability, and agreeableness (Soto et al., 2011). Consistent with our prediction, however, a cross-cultural examination of these age trends suggested that age-graded increases in maturity-related traits are delayed in developed nations with prolonged periods of emerging adulthood (Bleidorn et al., 2013, 2014). Specifically, cultures with a later normative timing of job-role transitions, such as the United States or the Netherlands, were marked by a later onset of age-graded increases in conscientiousness, emotional stability, and to a lesser degree also agreeableness. This finding provides some support for the position that prolonged periods of emerging adulthood and a delayed commitment to adult roles may influence the personality trajectories of emerging and young adults.

## Longitudinal studies

The findings of longitudinal studies provide mixed evidence for the hypothesis that emerging adulthood is a time of attenuated personality maturation. A meta-analysis of longitudinal studies found that, during the college years, the average person does experience increases in emotional stability and to a lesser degree also in agreeableness (Roberts et al., 2006). Yet, more consistent with the conception of emerging adulthood, this study also found that mean-level increases in conscientiousness do not appear until after the college years.

Notably, the majority of studies included in the meta-analysis by Roberts and colleagues tracked personality trait change across only two assessment waves with often relatively lengthy time intervals between assessments (the average time interval between assessments was 9 years). These kinds of studies do not allow modeling the shape of change, nor do they allow for a more fine-grained investigation of changes in the magnitude of mean-level trait changes from emerging to young adulthood (Luhmann, Orth, Specht, Kandler, & Lucas, 2014).

Also, the cohorts analyzed in the meta-analysis by Roberts and colleagues ranged in birth year from 1889 to 1982 (Mean = 1942). This aggregates together recent cohorts that experienced emerging adulthood with older cohorts that did not, making it difficult to draw conclusions about the specific effects that emerging adulthood might have had on developmental trajectories.

More recent longitudinal studies have begun to track personality trait change in cohorts of emerging adults over shorter time periods, across multiple measurement waves, and in relation to life events that are more likely to occur during emerging adulthood, allowing us to better investigate the hypothesis that personality maturation is attenuated during this life stage. For example, Jackson, Thoemmes, Jonkmann, Lüdtke, and Trautwein (2012) followed a sample of German high schoolers who, upon graduation, participated either in military service or civilian community service. This study found that both military recruits and people who chose civilian community service reported increases in maturity-related personality traits. However, after completing their training, military recruits were significantly lower in agreeableness than people who chose civilian community service. Another study using the same sample found that conscientiousness increased more slowly in those who attended college than in those who went into vocational training or work after high school (Lüdtke, Roberts, Trautwein, & Nagy, 2011). These findings suggest that, even though emerging adults do not necessarily adopt traditional adult or stable social roles, they do experience positive personality trait changes that can be related to role transitions that are salient during this life stage.

Further support for different avenues through emerging adulthood leading to personality maturation comes from research on the dynamic transactions between personality trait change and relationship experiences in emerging adults. For example, Neyer and Lehnart (2007) found that entering into a romantic relationship for the first time is related to increases in emotional stability and conscientiousness. Notably, the changes in these traits seemed to sustain even if people are separated from or changed their partner. Emerging adults may enter into more relationships before committing to partnership than past generations, but this difference alone does not seem to affect personality maturation.

## Summary and future directions for the study of personality trait development

In summary, previous cross-sectional and longitudinal studies on personality trait development provide an ambiguous answer to the question as to whether personality maturation is attenuated during emerging adulthood. To the best of our knowledge, not a single study reported a complete absence of positive personality trait change in emerging adults. The vast majority of studies found at least some symptoms of personality maturation as indicated by increases in one or more maturity-related personality traits. At the same time, however, there is some evidence to suggest that personality maturation is somewhat attenuated during emerging adulthood.

There are at least three possible explanations for why research on personality maturation during emerging adulthood remains inconclusive. First, personality trait change in emerging adulthood might be largely controlled by genetically determined biological influences, with only a negligible role played by life transitions and socio-environmental influences. This interpretation is consistent with the propositions of Five-Factor Theory (FFT, McCrae & Costa, 2008). According to FFT, personality traits can be defined as "endogenous dispositions that follow intrinsic paths of development essentially independent of environmental influences" (McCrae et al., 2000, p. 173). In other words, the observed changes in some (but not all) traits may reflect an intrinsic maturation program that is largely independent of external influences, implying that it does not matter whether adulthood "emerges" or not.

A second possible explanation, in stark contrast to the aforementioned FFT account, is that personality trait changes in emerging adulthood occur in response to life transitions and developmental tasks that are salient during this particular life stage, even if these transitions and tasks don't necessarily lead directly into traditional, committed adult roles. For example, graduating from school or college, dating, moving out of one's parental home, or making new friends are developmental tasks that may have an influence on emerging adults standing on emotional stability, agreeableness, or conscientiousness (Hutteman, Hennecke, Orth, Reitz, & Specht, 2014). This explanation is consistent with recent studies on personality trait change and major life events (Bleidorn, 2012; Bleidorn, Hopwood, & Lucas, 2016; Jackson et al., 2012; Zimmermann & Neyer, 2013) and would suggest that emerging adulthood is not such a roleless role after all.

A third possible explanation is that previous studies were not suited to discriminate between changes in emerging adulthood and changes in young adulthood, and that stronger research designs are needed to more definitively examine when, why, and how personality trait change occurs in emerging adulthood. Specifically, more longitudinal studies with frequent and well-timed measurement occasions throughout adolescence, emerging adulthood, and young adulthood are needed to detect similarities and differences in personality trait change in and outside the context of social role transitions (Bleidorn, 2015; Luhmann et al., 2014). Ideally, these studies would employ multiple methods, including self- and other reports, and measure a broad range of personality characteristics and social role experiences. Moreover, to disentangle intrinsic, biologically based changes from extrinsic, event-related changes, future studies need to include control groups of participants who did not experience a particular event or role transition (Bleidorn et al., 2016b; Jackson et al., 2012; van Scheppingen et al., 2016).

# Does openness to experience increase during emerging adulthood?

Perhaps even more than the apparent freedom from adult role responsibilities, the most central feature of emerging adulthood is that it is a period of identity exploration (Arnett, 2000). Emerging adults explore the domains of love, work, and worldviews before eventually committing to role-based identities. They have romantic relationships without necessarily committing to a partner; they intern without signing long-term contracts; they are exposed to worldviews that are often distinctively different from how they were raised.

This theme of identity exploration may have implications for the development of openness. More specifically, because emerging adults presumably engage in exploratory behavior, thoughts, and feelings, they should be frequently in highly open states (cf. Bleidorn, 2009; Fleeson, 2001, 2007). The frequent manifestation of increased state openness may then—if it becomes habitual and generalized—translate into increases in the broader trait domain of openness (Hennecke, Bleidorn, Denissen, & Wood, 2014; Roberts & Jackson, 2008). In other words, emerging adults who engage in identity exploration should experience an increase in openness, and, since identity exploration is the key theme of emerging adulthood, the majority of people should report openness increases between ages 18 and 25.

## Cross-sectional studies

Although studies have found conflicting results when examining openness development throughout young adulthood, one area where cross-sectional studies converge is in finding substantial mean-level increases from age 18 to 22 (Soto et al., 2011). These years correspond with the college years, a time that seems particularly important for identity exploration in multiple domains (Arnett, 2007).

Attending college may trigger increases in openness in multiple ways, some of which may be related to formal aspects of postsecondary education, such as intellectually demanding coursework or the exploration of possible identities through deciding on a major. Other aspects of the college experience that potentially influence emerging adults' openness to experience may be more informal, such as exploring different worldviews while socializing with new friends and student groups. Indirect support for an enriching effect of college experiences on openness through intellectual activity comes from more fine-grained facet-level analyses, which showed an increase in openness to ideas but a relatively flat trajectory of openness to esthetics from age 18 to 22 (Soto et al., 2011).

Cross-cultural research provided further evidence for the proposition that the period of emerging adulthood is related to age-graded increases in openness. Specifically, Bleidorn et al. (2013) found more pronounced age-graded increases in openness in countries in which people tend to delay the transition to adult social roles, such as marriage, parenthood, or their first job. In other words, cultures in which young people tend to experience extended periods of exploration (vs role commitment) were marked by more pronounced mean-level increases in openness.

## Longitudinal studies

Longitudinal studies examining change in openness in emerging adults allow us to chart the course of development within individuals, extending cross-sectional points into developmental trajectories. The results of the aforementioned meta-analysis by Roberts et al. (2006) support the hypothesis that openness increases in emerging adulthood. Specifically, this study found that people show statistically significant increases in openness only during the college years, whereas in adolescence and in the decades following emerging adulthood, openness either did not change or declined.

More specific hypotheses about the links between openness and exploration during emerging adulthood were tested in a longitudinal study by Lüdtke et al. (2011). In this research, approximately 2000 students were tracked from high school to university or to vocational training or work, with 3 assessments over 4 years. The findings indicated that high-school graduates with higher initial levels in openness were more likely to enter college. Yet, independent of their particular career path, all participants reported significant mean-level changes in openness to experience, with the most pronounced changes occurring between approximately ages 19 and 22. The latter finding suggests that identity exploration and potentially related increases in openness are not an idiosyncrasy of college students. Rather, the findings of this study indicate that emerging adults who enter the labor market early may also increase in openness to experience—potentially from identity exploration outside the domain of work.

More evidence for the effect of identity exploration on change in openness has been provided by Zimmermann and Neyer (2013), who analyzed personality trait change in college students who spent time studying abroad. Compared to a control group who did not travel during the research period, students who spent time abroad were found to increase on openness. These changes were partly mediated by changes in the exchange students' everyday social behavior and the exploration of new relationships. The latter finding supports the notion that, during emerging adulthood, changes in openness to experience are likely preceded by changes in everyday (exploratory) behavior.

Just as identity exploration in emerging adulthood may lead to increases in openness, committing to adult roles may end this exploration and lead to decreases. Thus there is a potential *washing out* of trait increases that occurs during this stage by the time that emerging adults have entered into full-fledged adulthood. Some support for this hypothesis has been provided by Specht, Egloff, and Schmuckle (2011). Examining the influence of several life events on personality trait change in a representative German sample, these authors found a negative effect of marriage on openness to experience. Specifically, participants who got married showed decreases in openness to experience, whereas men who divorced from their partner reported increases in openness. Interestingly, no other single life event examined by Specht et al. (2011) was related to mean-level changes in openness, suggesting that the commitment to marriage has a particularly strong effect on this trait. Whether this effect is mediated by a decrease in (romantic) exploratory behavior remains an open question that needs to be addressed by future studies.

## Summary and future directions for the study of personality trait development

In summary, there is evidence to support the hypothesis that mean-level change in openness to experience is normative during the period of emerging adulthood. Both cross-sectional and longitudinal studies on personality trait change suggest that emerging adults experience significant increases in openness.

Although most studies examined samples of college students, there is evidence to suggest that increases in openness may also generalize to emerging adults who choose to follow a vocational career path (Lüdtke et al., 2011). An open question remains whether the observed changes in openness are indeed related to increases in emerging adults' identity exploration. Future research is needed to examine whether increased exploratory behavior in the domains of love, work, and world-views has the potential to trigger increases in emerging adults' openness.

Moreover, it is important to note that Arnett's conception of emerging adulthood stresses the heterogeneity of this life stage. Even in developed societies, not all young people experience their 20s as years of exploration; some lack the opportunities and others may be more inclined to limit their explorations (Arnett, 2007). Generally, emerging adulthood is often considered the most heterogeneous and least structured period of the life course. In view of this presumed variability in the degree to which individuals explore their identity in emerging adulthood, it can be predicted that this period is marked by substantial individual differences in emerging adults' openness trajectories. To the best of our knowledge, no research to date has examined whether the period of emerging adulthood is marked by greater variability in openness trajectories than the periods of adolescence or young adulthood. Future studies on the development of variance in individual personality trait trajectories are needed to test this hypothesis.

# Concluding remarks

Emerging adulthood has been proposed to be a distinct period of the life course for young people in developed, industrialized societies. It has been characterized as a period of exploration for most people as they examine possible life paths and gradually arrive at more stable roles in the process of making commitments in the domains of love, work, and worldviews (Arnett, 2000).

From a personality trait development perspective, previous research has provided some support for the idea that emerging adulthood is a distinct life stage with unique developmental tasks and trajectories. Specifically, the findings of cross-sectional, cross-cultural, and longitudinal studies suggest that the time between the late teens and the early 20s is marked by distinctive patterns of personality trait change that are (partly) different from the patterns observed during the broader period of young adulthood. First, there is some evidence to suggest that personality maturation—as indicated by normative increases in emotional stability, agreeableness, and conscientiousness during young adulthood—is somewhat less pronounced during emerging adulthood. It remains to be tested whether the attenuated patterns of personality maturation in emerging adulthood are indeed related to delayed transitions into adult role responsibilities. Second, mean-level increases in openness to experience seem to be a unique characteristic of the period of emerging adulthood. Whether and how these changes in openness are related to increases in emerging adults' exploratory behavior remains a topic for future research.

# References

Arnett, J. J. (2000). Emerging adulthood: A theory of development from the late teens through the twenties. *American Psychologist*, *55*, 469—480. Available from http://dx. doi.org/10.1037//0003-066X.55.5.469.

Arnett, J. J. (2004). *Emerging adulthood: The winding road from the late teens through the twenties*. New York: Oxford University Press.

Arnett, J. J. (2007). Emerging adulthood: What is it, and what is it good for? *Child Development Perspectives*, *1*, 68—73. Available from http://dx.doi.org/10.1111/j.1750-8606.2007.00016.x.

Bleidorn, W. (2009). Linking personality states, current social roles and major life goals. *European Journal of Personality*, *23*, 509—530. Available from http://dx.doi.org/10.1002/per.731.

Bleidorn, W. (2012). Hitting the road to adulthood: Short-term personality development during a major life transition. *Personality and Social Psychology Bulletin*, *38*, 1594—1608.

Bleidorn, W. (2015). What accounts for personality maturation in early adulthood? *Current Directions in Psychological Science*, *24*, 245—252. Available from http://dx.doi.org/10.1177/0963721414568662.

Bleidorn, W., Arslan, R., Denissen, J. J. A., Rentfrow, P. E., Gebauer, J. E., Potter, J., et al. (2016a). Age and gender differences in self-esteem — A cross-cultural window. *Journal of Personality and Social Psychology*, *111*, 396—410. Available from http://dx.doi.org/10.1037/pspp0000078.

Bleidorn, W., Buyukcan-Tetik, A., Schwaba, T., van Scheppingen, M. A., Denissen, J. J. A., & Finkenauer, C. (2016b). Stability and change in self-esteem during the transition to parenthood. *Social Psychological and Personality Science*, *7*, 560—569. Available from http://dx.doi.org/10.1177/1948550616646428.

Bleidorn, W., Hopwood, C. J., & Lucas, R. E. (2016). Life events and personality trait change. *Journal of Personality. Advance online publication*, . Available from http://dx. doi.org/10.1111/jopy.12286.

Bleidorn, W., Kandler, C., & Caspi, A. (2014). The behavioral genetics of personality development in adulthood—Classic, contemporary, and future trends. *European Journal of Personality*, 28, 244−255. Available from http://dx.doi.org/10.1002/per.1957.

Bleidorn, W., Kandler, C., Riemann, R., Angleitner, A., & Spinath, F. M. (2009). Patterns and sources of adult personality development: Growth curve analyses of the NEO-PI-R scales in a longitudinal twin study. *Journal of Personality and Social Psychology*, 97, 142−155. Available from http://dx.doi.org/10.1037/a0015434.

Bleidorn, W., Klimstra, T. A., Denissen, J. J. A., Rentfrow, P. J., Potter, J., & Gosling, S. D. (2013). Personality maturation around the world—A cross-cultural examination of Social Investment Theory. *Psychological Science*, 24(12), 2530−2540. Available from http://dx.doi.org/10.1177/0956797613498396.

Bleidorn, W., Klimstra, T. A., Denissen, J. J. A., Rentfrow, P. J., Potter, J., & Gosling, S. D. (2014). Let the data speak. A response to Terracciano (2014). *Psychological Science*, 25, 1051−1053.

Erikson, E. H. (1959). Identity and the life cycle: Selected papers. *Psychological Issues*, 1, 1−171.

Fleeson, W. (2001). Toward a structure- and process-integrated view of personality: Traits as density distributions of states. *Journal of Personality and Social Psychology*, 80, 1011−1027. Available from http://dx.doi.org/10.1037/0022-3514.80.6.1011.

Fleeson, W. (2007). Situation-based contingencies underlying trait-content manifestation in behavior. *Journal of Personality*, 75, 825−862. Available from http://dx.doi.org/ 10.1111/j.1467-6494.2007.00458.x.

Hennecke, M., Bleidorn, W., Denissen, J. J., & Wood, D. (2014). A three-part framework for self-regulated personality development across adulthood. *European Journal of Personality*, 28, 289−299. Available from http://dx.doi.org/10.1002/per.1945.

Hudson, N. W., Roberts, B. W., & Lodi-Smith, J. (2012). Personality trait development and social investment in work. *Journal of Research in Personality*, 46(3), 334−344. Available from http://dx.doi.org/10.1016/j.jrp.2012.03.002.

Hutteman, R., Bleidorn, W., Kereteš, G., Brković, I., Butković, A., & Denissen, J. J. (2014). Reciprocal associations between parenting challenges and parents' personality development in young and middle adulthood. *European Journal of Personality*, 28(2), 168−179. Available from http://dx.doi.org/10.1002/per.1932.

Hutteman, R., Hennecke, M., Orth, U., Reitz, A. K., & Specht, J. (2014). Developmental tasks as a framework to study personality development in adulthood and old age. *European Journal of Personality*, 28, 267−278.

Jackson, J. J., Thoemmes, F., Jonkmann, K., Lüdtke, O., & Trautwein, U. (2012). Military training and personality trait development: Does the military make the man, or does the man make the military? *Psychological Science*, 23, 270−277. Available from http://dx. doi.org/10.1177/0956797611423545.

Keniston, K. (1971). *Youth and dissent: The rise of a new opposition*. New York: Harcourt Brace Jovanovich.

Lüdtke, O., Roberts, B. W., Trautwein, U., & Nagy, G. (2011). A random walk down university avenue: Life paths, life events, and personality trait change at the transition to university life. *Journal of Personality and Social Psychology*, 101, 620−637. Available from http://dx.doi.org/10.1037/a0023743.

Luhmann, M., Orth, U., Specht, J., Kandler, C., & Lucas, R. E. (2014). Studying changes in life circumstances and personality: It's about time. *European Journal of Personality*, *28*, 256−266. Available from http://dx.doi.org/10.1002/per.1951.

McCrae, R. R., & Costa, P. (2008). The Five-Factor Theory of personality. In O. P. John, R. W. Robins, & L. A. Pervin (Eds.), *Handbook of personality: Theory and research* (3rd ed., pp. 1−58). New York, NY: Guilford Press.

McCrae, R. R., Costa Jr, P. T., Ostendorf, F., Angleitner, A., Hřebíčková, M., Avia, M. D., & Saunders, P. R. (2000). Nature over nurture: Temperament, personality, and life span development. *Journal of Personality and Social Psychology*, *78*, 173. Available from http://dx.doi.org/10.1037/0022-3514.78.1.173.

Neyer, F. J., & Lehnart, J. (2007). Relationships matter in personality development: Evidence from an 8-year longitudinal study across young adulthood. *Journal of Personality*, *75*, 535−568. Available from http://dx.doi.org/10.1111/j.1467-6494.2007.00448.x.

Orth, U., & Robins, R. W. (2014). The development of self-esteem. *Current Directions in Psychological Science*, *23*, 381−387. Available from http://dx.doi.org/10.1177/0963721414547414.

Roberts, B. W., & Jackson, J. J. (2008). Sociogenomic personality psychology. *Journal of Personality*, *76*, 1523−1544. Available from http://dx.doi.org/10.1111/j.1467-6494.2008.00530.x.

Roberts, B. W., & Mroczek, D. (2008). Personality trait change in adulthood. *Current Directions in Psychological Science*, *17*, 31−35. Available from http://dx.doi.org/10.1111/j.1467-8721.2008.00543.x.

Roberts, B. W., Walton, K. E., & Viechtbauer, W. (2006). Patterns of mean-level change in personality traits across the life course: A meta-analysis of longitudinal studies. *Psychological Bulletin*, *132*, 1−25. Available from http://dx.doi.org/10.1037/0033-2909.132.1.1.

Roberts, B. W., Wood, D., & Caspi, A. (2008). The development of personality traits in adulthood. In O. P. John (Ed.), *Handbook of personality: Theory and research* (3rd ed., pp. 375−398). New York: Guilford Press.

Roberts, B. W., Wood, D., & Smith, J. L. (2005). Evaluating Five Factor Theory and social investment perspectives on personality trait development. *Journal of Research in Personality*, *39*, 166−184. Available from http://dx.doi.org/10.1016/j.jrp.2004.08.002.

Soto, C. J., John, O. P., Gosling, S. D., & Potter, J. (2011). Age differences in personality traits from 10 to 65: Big Five domains and facets in a large cross-sectional sample. *Journal of Personality and Social Psychology*, *100*, 330−348. Available from http://dx.doi.org/10.1037/a0021717.

Specht, J., Bleidorn, W., Denissen, J. J., Hennecke, M., Hutteman, R., Kandler, C., ... Zimmermann, J. (2014). What drives adult personality development? A comparison of theoretical perspectives and empirical evidence. *European Journal of Personality*, *28*, 216−230. Available from http://dx.doi.org/10.1002/per.1966.

Specht, J., Egloff, B., & Schmukle, S. C. (2011). Stability and change of personality across the life course: The impact of age and major life events on mean-level and rank-order stability of the Big Five. *Journal of Personality and Social Psychology*, *101*, 862. Available from http://dx.doi.org/10.1037/a0024950.

Tanner, J. L., & Arnett, J. J. (2009). The emergence of "emerging adulthood": The new life stage between adolescence and young adulthood. In A. Furlong (Ed.), *Handbook of youth and young adulthood: New perspectives and agendas* (pp. 39−45). London, England: Routledge.

van Scheppingen, M. A., Jackson, J. J., Specht, J., Hutteman, R., Denissen, J. J. A., & Bleidorn, W. (2016). Personality development during the transition to parenthood: A test of social investment theory. *Social Psychological and Personality Science, 7,* 452−462.

Weiss, A., & King, J. E. (2015). Great ape origins of personality maturation and sex differences: A study of orangutans and chimpanzees. *Journal of Personality and Social Psychology, 108,* 648−664. Available from http://dx.doi.org/10.1037/pspp0000022.

Wortman, J., Lucas, R. E., & Donnellan, M. B. (2012). Stability and change in the Big Five personality domains: Evidence from a longitudinal study of Australians. *Psychology and aging, 27*(4), 867. Available from http://dx.doi.org/10.1037/a0029322.

Zimmermann, J., & Neyer, F. J. (2013). Do we become a different person when hitting the road? Personality development of sojourners. *Journal of Personality and Social Psychology, 105,* 515−530.

# Personality development in adulthood and old age

**5**

*Jule Specht*[1,2,*]

[1]Humboldt-Universität zu Berlin, Berlin, Germany, [2]German Institute for Economic Research (DIW Berlin), Berlin, Germany

Ten years before writing this chapter, Brent Roberts and colleagues published their extensive and highly influential meta-analysis on mean-level changes in personality traits across the life course (Roberts, Walton, & Viechtbauer, 2006). Since then, hundreds of studies have built on that knowledge and several new studies on the development of the Big Five personality traits—the most prevalent personality model to date—have emerged (for overviews, see Caspi, Roberts, & Shiner, 2005; Roberts & Mroczek, 2008; Roberts, Wood, & Caspi, 2008). These studies were oftentimes based on the rich data from large and representative panel studies like the Socio-Economic Panel Study (SOEP; Wagner, Frick, & Schupp, 2007), the Household, Income and Labour Dynamics in Australia Survey (HILDA; Summerfield et al., 2011), and the British Household Panel Study (BHPS; Taylor, Brice, Buck, & Prentice-Lane, 2010). Combined, these results offer deep insight into the question of how personality changes across adulthood.

This chapter aims at summarizing the main findings on the development of the Big Five personality traits in young adulthood, middle adulthood, and old age. Personality development is considered in terms of mean-level changes and rank-order consistencies. Furthermore, a brief insight is given into other types of personality change that have been examined, even though less frequently so far. In a conclusion, avenues for future research are pointed out.

## Measuring personality change

Personality change comprises different forms of change in different aspects of personality. Most studies within personality psychology are based on the Big Five model (John, Naumann, & Soto, 2008) and therefore this chapter will focus on this model as well. It is based on the idea that every meaningful personality trait is represented in language and therefore part of a (comprehensive) dictionary. Thus all traits that can be identified in dictionaries were collected in large samples of individuals and condensed using factor analytical techniques. The Big Five model summarizes the large number of personality traits into a hierarchy with

*While writing this chapter, Jule Specht was also affiliated at Freie Universität Berlin, Berlin, Universität zu Lübeck, Lübeck, and the German Institute for Economic Research (DIW Berlin), Berlin.

**Personality Development Across the Lifespan.** DOI: http://dx.doi.org/10.1016/B978-0-12-804674-6.00005-3

five personality factors at the highest level of abstraction (i.e., emotional stability, extraversion, openness to experience, agreeableness, and conscientiousness). The Big Five have been replicated by a large number of scientists across a large number of age groups, languages, and cultures.

Personality change has often been examined using two population indices, namely mean-level changes and rank-order consistencies. Mean-level changes describe how the average levels of single personality traits in groups of same-aged individuals change across time. Mean-level increases reflect that a personality trait—on average—increases in an age group whereas mean-level decreases reflect that the respective personality trait—on average—decreases in an age group. Mean-level changes do not inform about how single individuals change across time or about how similar individuals change within an age group across time.

Rank-order consistencies describe how stable the ordering of individuals in groups of same-aged individuals is on single personality traits across time. High rank-order consistencies reflect that individuals remain their relative ordering on a personality trait. That is, individuals who were among those with the highest, medium, and lowest trait values tend to have the highest, medium, and lowest trait values, respectively, across time. Low rank-order consistencies, in contrast, reflect that individuals change their relative ordering. For example, individuals who were among those with the highest trait values might have lower trait values than others of that age group at later time points. Similarly, those with low trait values might, for example, have higher trait values than others of their age group at later time points. Rank-order consistencies do not inform about how single individuals change across time or whether the average level of a personality trait increases or decreases with time. Further details on how rank-order consistency informs about developmental processes are provided by Fraley and Roberts (2005).

Another, somewhat less frequently used, approach for examining personality change focuses on changes in personality profiles or personality types instead of single traits. It aims at describing personality in a more holistic way by considering several traits at once. Most often, at least three personality types with distinct personality profiles are distinguished: resilients, overcontrollers, and undercontrollers (Asendorpf, 2015). Resilient individuals are characterized by profiles with comparatively high values in emotional stability and all of the other four Big Five traits. In contrast, undercontrollers are characterized by profiles with comparatively low values in agreeableness and conscientiousness whereas overcontrollers are characterized by profiles with comparatively low values in extraversion and openness to experience (Specht, Luhmann, & Geiser, 2014). Changes in type membership generally require changes of either several personality traits simultaneously or change in one personality trait that is comparatively strong. Thus personality type membership tends to be relatively stable across time.

There are lots of other forms of conceptualizing and measuring personality change that have been largely neglected so far. Ozer (1986) provides a comprehensive overview on a large number of these. It includes, among others, information on stability (and change) in the structure of personality across time and/or age groups and similarities in developmental trends either across individuals or across personality traits. Whereas a high number of studies confirm that the structure of personality remains largely stable across time (which is a precondition for a straightforward test of the stability in mean levels and rank ordering), there is a lack of knowledge about how personality changes using other than the above-mentioned approaches. A deeper understanding in this regard would enable to gain insight into individual differences and processes of personality development.

# Age effects on personality across adulthood and old age

Adulthood can be subdivided into (at least) three age periods that typically come along with different developmental tasks and trends (Hutteman, Hennecke, Orth, Reitz, & Specht, 2014). Young adulthood lasts until about age 30 even though some researchers assume that this period of adulthood might be prolonged nowadays due to later career entry and older age at the birth of the first child. Middle adulthood describes the period between about ages 30 and 60 that is when individuals have typically started a family and their career and focus on maintaining and extending the social roles they have in these contexts. Old age then starts at about age 60 when individuals typically start to enter retirement sooner or later. In the following, changes in personality in each of these three age periods are summarized.

## Young adulthood

Young adulthood starts with a (sub-)period labeled emerging adulthood (Arnett, 2000) that marks the transition from teenage years to adulthood (for an overview on personality development in this age group, see Bleidorn & Schwaba, Chapter 4). In this period of life, most individuals have not yet committed to adult social roles but most of them do so later on during young adulthood.

There is strong consensus that emotional stability tends to increase during young adulthood. That means individuals tend—on average—to become more even-tempered and calm in the face of stress and suffer less from anxiety or rumination (in a subclinical sense). Findings from Roberts and colleagues (2006) suggest that this is true for individuals during all of early adulthood. Additional support comes from more recent findings from large-scale panel studies (Donnellan & Lucas, 2008; Lucas & Donnellan, 2011; Specht, Egloff, & Schmukle, 2011; Wortman, Lucas, & Donnellan, 2012) that are national representative for the Australian, British, and German population. Also, an intercultural study comprising cross-sectional data from altogether more than 800,000 individuals from more than 60 countries replicates this finding as well (Bleidorn et al., 2013). In fact, no study on the development of the Big Five personality traits from the last years seemed to find something contrary (Lehmann, Denissen, Allemand, & Penke, 2013; Lüdtke, Trautwein, & Husemann, 2009; Mund & Neyer, 2014; Soto & John, 2012; Vaidya, Gray, Haig, Mroczek, & Watson, 2008; Wille, Beyers, & De Fruyt, 2012).

There is similar consensus that conscientiousness increases strongly during young adulthood. That means individuals tend—on average—to be better able to control their impulses, become more reliable, purposeful, and responsible. This was found for twens in the meta-analysis by Roberts and colleagues (2006) as well as in national representative panel data (Donnellan & Lucas, 2008; Lucas & Donnellan, 2011; Specht et al., 2011; Wortman et al., 2012) and other studies on that topic (Bleidorn et al., 2013).

Openness to experience seems to follow a curvilinear pattern in young adulthood. Specifically, most findings suggest that it first increases and that it then either remains stable or decreases in the later course of young adulthood. For example, Roberts et al. (2006) found in their meta-analysis that the average level of openness to experience first increases for the age group 18–22 years but remains stable for older age groups. The studies that used data from national representative panels found openness to experience to decrease in young adulthood (Donnellan & Lucas, 2008; Lucas & Donnellan, 2011; Specht et al., 2011; Wortman et al., 2012). Inconsistent with that, a very large intercultural study (Bleidorn et al., 2013) found small increases in this trait during young adulthood, which might be due to the fact that the data came from an Internet sample whose sample composition might be biased with regard to this trait. However, other studies found increases across all of young adulthood as well (Lehmann et al., 2013) whereas other studies found openness to be stable across young adulthood (Mund & Neyer, 2014). Thus trajectories of openness to experience might be more sensitive to biases in sample composition, especially with regard to the collection mode (i.e., online collection might attract more individuals who are open to experience) and educational background (i.e., more educated individuals might be higher in openness to experience). Taken together, individuals seem—on average—to increase in their curiosity and open-mindedness during the first years of adulthood but do not seem to continue to do so during the later course of young adulthood.

Extraversion can be subdivided into two facets that follow different developmental trajectories. Roberts and colleagues (2006) found that social dominance increases during all of young adulthood but that social vitality only increased in the age group of 18–22 years but decreased later on. Thus individuals tend—on average—to become more dominant, independent, and self-confident during adulthood. Similarly, they become more sociable and energetic but only at the beginning of young adulthood and become less so during the later course of young adulthood. Findings from large-scale panel studies either captured more of the social vitality than of the social dominance facet or did not differentiate between both and generally found decreases in extraversion during young adulthood (Donnellan & Lucas, 2008; Lucas & Donnellan, 2011; Specht et al., 2011; Wortman et al., 2012). However, there are divergences in some other recent studies that found extraversion to be slightly increasing (Bleidorn et al., 2013; Lüdtke et al., 2009), decreasing

(Lehmann et al., 2013; Mund & Neyer, 2014) or to be rather stable across young adulthood (Soto & John, 2012; Wille et al., 2012). Results by Lehmann et al. (2013) suggest that such divergences are likely due to the use of different questionnaires that focus on different facets of extraversion that, as mentioned above, each follow different developmental trajectories.

There seems to be least consensus with regard to the development of agreeableness in young adulthood, which has oftentimes been found to remain stable but has also repeatedly been found to increase during that time. In their meta-analysis, Roberts and colleagues (2006) indeed found slight increases in the average levels of agreeableness, however, these were not significant. Nevertheless, these nonsignificant increases have led to the proposition of the maturity principle (Roberts & Wood, 2006; for a revision, see Roberts & Nickel, Chapter 11). Similarly, analyses using national representative panel data find no meaningful increases in agreeableness during young adulthood (Donnellan & Lucas, 2008; Lucas & Donnellan, 2011; Specht et al., 2011; Wortman et al., 2012). On the contrary, other studies did find increases in agreeableness at this age (Bleidorn et al. 2013; Lehmann et al., 2013; Lüdtke et al., 2009; Mund & Neyer, 2014; Soto & John, 2012; Vaidya et al., 2008; Wille et al., 2012). To date, it is hard to say what the reason for these diverging results is. Both, differences across subpopulations (as it is the case for openness to experience) as well as differences across facets (as it is the case for extraversion) are plausible in this regard. For example, Jackson et al. (2012) found that agreeableness remains stable in male military recruits but increases in men who participate in civilian community service and that these different developmental trends continue even years after finishing service. Thus findings on developmental trends differ greatly between subpopulations that might—at least in part—explain different findings across samples especially if these do not come from national representative samples. In sum, results suggest that individuals tend—on average—to remain rather stable in their prosocial orientation and do not seem to become (much) more benevolent and cooperative during young adulthood.

All of the above-mentioned results inform about the average change in mean levels of the Big Five personality traits. In contrast, findings on the rank-order consistency of individuals are much more similar across these traits. In two independent meta-analyses of rank-order stability in personality by Ardelt (2000) and Roberts and DelVecchio (2000), it was found that young adulthood is a period of life with slightly more stability compared to adolescence but less stability compared to middle adulthood. Furthermore, both meta-analyses found that individuals are less stable in their relative ordering at the beginning of young adulthood compared to individuals at the end of young adulthood. Similarly, recent studies using longitudinal data from national representative samples from Australia and Germany found that rank-order stability increases during young adulthood for all of the Big Five personality traits (Lucas & Donnellan, 2011; Specht et al., 2011; Wortman et al., 2012). In sum, these findings suggest that individuals differ considerably in their developmental trajectories during young adulthood but that the relative ordering of individuals becomes increasingly stable during this period of life.

Studies on the stability of personality type membership are less common than those on mean-level changes and rank-order stability. Findings from a large and national representative sample from Germany by Specht and colleagues (2014) suggest that the number of individuals with a resilient personality type slightly increases during young adulthood. Stronger age effects were found for the other two personality types: whereas the proportion of individuals with an under-controlled personality type strongly decreased during young adulthood, the number of individuals with an overcontrolled personality type strongly increased during the same time. Most longitudinal changes in type membership could be found for individuals who were initially classified as undercontrollers and who were most likely to change to a resilient type across time. There were slightly different results for individuals from a sample that was national representative for Australia. However, again, the number of individuals with a resilient personality type increased with age (see Specht et al., 2014, for details as well as for a review of findings from other studies on that topic).

## Middle adulthood

Emotional stability continues to increase during middle adulthood. In their meta-analysis, Roberts et al. (2006) found it to be increasing particularly strongly for individuals aged 30–40 years and less so afterward. Similar results were obtained by more recent studies using large-scale panel data. However, there seemed to be stronger increases in emotional stability in Australian and British people (Donnellan, 2008; Wortman et al., 2012) compared to German people (Lucas & Donnellan, 2011; Specht et al., 2011). Also, other studies using different question-naires and sample compositions equally found that emotional stability continues to increase in middle adulthood (Allemand, Gomez, & Jackson, 2010; Hill, Turiano, Mroczek, & Roberts, 2012; Lehmann et al., 2013), but there are also other more mixed findings (Branje, van Lieshout, & Gerris, 2007). Taken together, results suggest that emotional stability tends—on average—to continue its positive development from young adulthood into middle age but that the strength of this effect decreases with increasing age.

Similarly, conscientiousness continues to increase during middle adulthood. Again, Roberts et al. (2006) found it to be increasing particularly strongly in the first part of middle adulthood and less so at the end of this age period. Data from national representative panel studies also suggest that conscientiousness keeps increasing in Australians (Wortman et al., 2012) but that it remains quite stable after age 40 in British and German samples (Donnellan & Lucas, 2008; Lucas & Donnellan, 2011; Specht et al., 2011). Stability in conscientiousness was also found in US samples (Allemand et al., 2010) even though other studies found some increases in middle adulthood (Hill et al., 2012; Lehmann et al., 2013) and another study found stability in men but increases in women (Branje et al., 2007). In sum, conscientiousness seems to increase—on average—during middle adulthood, but mostly until age 40 and less so afterward.

As with the other traits mentioned so far, openness to experience tends to be comparatively stable in middle adulthood. Meta-analytical findings suggest that it remains stable across all of middle adulthood (Roberts et al., 2006) whereas findings from national representative data suggest that openness either remains relatively stable or decreases during middle adulthood (Donnellan & Lucas, 2008; Lucas & Donnellan, 2011; Specht et al., 2011; Wortman et al., 2012). Estimated trajectories are also somewhat mixed in other studies that either found decreases in openness to experience during middle adulthood (Allemand et al., 2010; Hill et al., 2012) or stability (Branje et al., 2007; Lehmann et al., 2013). Combined, these findings suggest that openness to experience reaches its peak level during young adulthood and that it either remains stable or decreases between ages 30 and 60.

Facets of extraversion continue to follow different developmental trajectories in middle adulthood. Roberts et al. (2006) found that whereas social dominance still increases at the beginning of middle adulthood and remains stable afterward, social vitality remains at a stable level throughout all of middle adulthood. In contrast, national representative panel data suggests that extraversion tends to be lower with increasing age (Donnellan & Lucas, 2008; Lucas & Donnellan, 2011; Specht et al., 2011; Wortman et al., 2012). Other studies just as well found decreases in this trait during middle adulthood (Allemand et al., 2010; Branje et al., 2007; Hill et al., 2012) but again there was also studies that found stable or even increasing levels in extraversion during middle adulthood (Lehmann et al., 2013). Taken together, findings on the development of extraversion are mixed. Whereas some studies found increases or decreases, most studies speak in favor of the idea that the average level of extraversion is stable during most parts of middle adulthood.

Agreeableness seems to finally increase at the end of middle adulthood after it has been surprisingly stable in young adulthood and the beginning of middle adulthood. In their meta-analysis, Roberts et al. (2006) found increases in agreeableness in individuals aged 50−60 years. However, the sample only included a handful of studies with altogether less than 300 individuals. Results from national representative panel studies suggest that agreeableness is still rather stable across all of middle adulthood (Donnellan & Lucas, 2008; Lucas & Donnellan, 2011; Specht et al., 2011; Wortman et al., 2012). Findings from other studies were again mixed with some finding increases (Lehmann et al., 2013), some finding stability (Allemand et al., 2010), or even decreases (Branje et al., 2007; Hill et al., 2012). In sum, agreeableness seems to be still relatively stable during middle adulthood.

Similarly to findings on comparatively stable mean levels of personality in middle adulthood, there is also high rank-order consistency in middle adulthood compared to younger and older age groups. Both meta-analyses on that topic (Ardelt, 2000; Roberts & DelVecchio, 2000) found that the rank order of individuals is highest in middle adulthood for all of the Big Five personality traits. The same was found using national representative panel data (Lucas & Donnellan, 2011; Specht et al., 2011; Wortman et al., 2012). Thus middle adulthood seems to be a period of life in which personality trait levels are maintained at a relatively stable level with comparatively few individual differences in change trajectories. However, this is not to say that there are no personality changes at all but that these are less common than in other periods of life.

With regard to type membership, there is more stability than change as well in a German sample but there were some age effects on type membership in an Australian sample (Specht et al., 2014). In the Australian population, the percentage of individuals with a resilient personality type keeps increasing. However, longitudinally, there is also very high stability of type membership throughout middle adulthood in Australians.

The findings of these three measures of change all suggest that middle adulthood is a period of life with comparatively high stability that might be due to the fact that social roles that have been established in young adulthood remain stable in this period of life which might mean that social pressures to change personality are not as strong as in other periods of life.

## Old age

Personality development in old age has received increasingly more attention in recent years after it seemed to be less of interest before. This is likely due to, first, the increasing number of older individuals that has reached a historical maximum in western societies resulting in an increased necessity to come to a better understanding of psychological processes in this age group (Specht, 2015). And, second, to the finding that there are surprisingly strong personality changes in old aged individuals (Specht, Bleidorn et al., 2014).

Emotional stability tends—on average—to remain rather stable in old age, at least in young old individuals. In their meta-analysis, Roberts et al. (2006) found no mean-level changes in a group of 60- to 70-year olds as well as in individuals older than 70 years. Results from national representative panel studies show that emotional stability might further increase in old age (Donnellan & Lucas, 2008; Lucas & Donnellan, 2011; Specht et al., 2011; Wortman et al., 2012). Contrary, other studies found either no significant mean-level change in emotional stability (Mõttus, Johnson, & Deary, 2012) or decreases until the ninth decade of life (Kandler, Kornadt, Hagemeyer, & Neyer, 2015; Wagner, Ram, Smith, & Gerstorf, in press). Taken together, results suggest that increases in emotional stability that have been observed in young and, in part, in middle adulthood, seem to be less prevalent in older age groups. However, old age is not necessarily a period of life with strong decreases in this trait. Mixed findings on trajectories of emotional stability can probably be explained by the fact that individuals remain at a stable level during young old age but become less emotionally stable in old old age when approaching death (Wagner et al., in press; see also Mueller, Wagner, & Gerstorf, Chapter 6).

For conscientiousness, studies have also yielded mixed results for older age. In their meta-analysis, Roberts et al. (2006) found increases for individuals aged 60–70 years and stability afterward. However, the number of studies and sample sizes that could be considered were not very large in this age group. Similar age trends were found in a national representative Australian sample, however, cross-sectional and longitudinal results indicated different age trends (Wortman et al., 2012). National representative panel studies using British and German data both found decreases in conscientiousness (Donnellan & Lucas, 2008; Lucas & Donnellan, 2011; Specht et al., 2011). Other studies found stability in mean levels at about age 70 but considerable decreases in the ninth decade of life (Mõttus et al., 2012) or decreases across all of older age (Kandler et al., 2015). When combining these findings, it seems that individuals tend—on average—to have relatively stable levels in conscientiousness in young old age but decreasing levels in old old age. This might probably be the case because mental and physical resources are not sufficient enough anymore to maintain a high level in this trait.

Compared to the other two traits mentioned above, stronger changes have been observed for openness to experience that tends to decrease in old age. Meta-analytical findings indicate decreases for individuals aged 60–70 years and also later on, even though this trend was then not significant anymore. Again, the number of studies and sample sizes considered were much smaller compared to younger age groups. Also, data from national representative panel studies show consistently that openness decreases considerable in old age (Donnellan & Lucas, 2008; Lucas & Donnellan, 2011; Specht et al., 2011; Wortman et al., 2012). Other studies found that there is stability for individuals aged about 70 years but that openness to experience decreases in the ninth decade of life (Mõttus et al., 2012; for similar results see also Kandler et al., 2015; Wagner et al., in press). Thus there is strong consensus across studies that people decrease on average in openness to experience during old age.

Extraversion tends to decrease in old age. Social vitality, one of its facets, has been shown to decrease at least at the beginning of old age and to remain stable after age 70 (Roberts et al., 2006). Due to the lack of studies, no information was available on the development of social dominance, the second facet of extraversion, in the meta-analysis by Roberts and colleagues. National representative panel studies found extraversion to be decreasing across all of old age (Donnellan & Lucas, 2008; Lucas & Donnellan, 2011; Specht et al., 2011; Wortman et al., 2012). Other studies equally found decreases in old age (Kandler et al., 2015; Mõttus et al., 2012; Wagner et al., in press) even though Mõttus and colleagues also found a small increase in extraversion at the beginning of old age. In sum, information on the development of social dominance is missing for old age but at least social vitality has repeatedly been found to decrease in older age groups.

Agreeableness tends to finally increase in old age after it has been relatively stable in young and middle adulthood even though the scarce information to date remains mixed. In their meta-analysis, Roberts et al. (2006) found slight increases in agreeableness. However, these were not significant, which might be due to the lack of studies that could be considered. Results from British and German samples indicate that older individuals are more agreeable than younger individuals (Donnellan & Lucas, 2008; Lucas & Donnellan, 2011; Specht et al., 2011), however, there were some inconsistencies between cross-sectional and longitudinal results as well as findings from Australia that rather indicate decreases in agreeableness in old age (Wortman et al., 2012). Kandler et al. (2015) and Mõttus and colleagues (2012) found stable levels of agreeableness. However, Mõttus and colleagues also found some decreases for old old age. Taken together, results are scarce and mixed. Some results indicate that levels of agreeableness increase in old age whereas other found stable or even decreasing levels.

With regard to rank-order stability, there seems to be equally much change in the rank ordering of individuals in old age compared to young adulthood. In the meta-analysis on that topic by Roberts and DelVecchio (2000), there were more rank-order changes between age 60 and 73 compared to the years before but information for individuals older than that was missing. Ardelt (2000) found in her meta-analysis that rank-order stability follows an inverted U-shaped trajectory with higher stability in middle adulthood and lower stability in young adulthood and old age. Likewise, more recent data from national representative panels also found inverted U-shaped stabilities that also indicate that old aged individuals differ in their personality development considerably (Lucas & Donnellan, 2011; Specht et al., 2011; Wortman et al., 2012). However, there are also studies that found comparatively high rank-order stability until old age (Ferguson, 2010; Terracciano, Costa, & McCrae, 2006).

Individual differences in developmental trajectories are also apparent when examining changes of personality type membership in old age (Specht et al., 2014). Individuals were almost equally likely to change from a resilient to an under- or overcontrolled personality type or to change from being an undercontrolled personality type to a resilient type or from an over- to an undercontrolled type. Thus there doesn't seem to be one normative trajectory that applies to most individuals of old age but rather high individual differences in development.

## Summary and outlook

Personality changes during all of adulthood with most changes occurring in young adulthood and old age (for a summarizing overview, see Table 5.1). A majority of changes in personality trait levels are in a direction of greater maturity (Roberts & Wood, 2006). This includes that individuals tend to become more emotionally stable, more socially dominant, and more conscientious during young and middle adulthood and, later on in old age, also more agreeable. These traits have all been found to be adaptive with regard to developmental tasks individuals are faced with during their life (Hutteman et al., 2014). However, other personality changes seem to be less adaptive. For example, openness to experience tends to decrease as people age even though high levels on that trait have been associated with educational attainments and cognitive flexibility until old age (Ziegler, Cengia, Mussel, & Gerstorf, 2015). Developmental trends in old age that partly deviate from what is called "personality maturation" have been vividly labeled "la dolce vita" effect (Marsh, Nagengast, & Morin, 2013). This term underlines that individuals might

**Table 5.1  Age effects on the Big Five personality traits**

| Big Five personality traits | Young adulthood | Middle adulthood | Old age |
|---|---|---|---|
| Emotional Stability | Increase | Increase | Stability |
| Social Dominance (Extraversion) | Increase | First increase, then stability | *(lack of data)* |
| Social Vitality (Extraversion) | First increase, then decrease | Stability/decrease | Decrease |
| Openness to Experience | First increase, then stability/decrease | Stability/decrease | Decrease |
| Agreeableness | Stability | Stability | Increase |
| Conscientiousness | Increase | Increase | First stability, then decrease |

*Note*: See text for more differentiated information.

then tend to become more self-content, more laid back, and less preoccupied with productivity, which could also be considered as being—in a sense—"mature."

Despite changes at the trait levels that have been summarized above, some developmental differences across personality facets have also been found (Terracciano, McCrae, Brant, & Costa, 2005; see also Lucas & Donnellan, 2009; Soto, John, Gosling, & Potter, 2011). In most cases, all facets follow the same overall developmental trajectory but to a stronger or weaker degree. For example, even though all facets of emotional stability tend to increase during adulthood, stronger age effects have been found for moodiness and less age effects have been found for calmness. Similarly, openness to values decreases much more than openness to esthetics. The same can be found with regard to agreeableness: All facets follow a positive age trend but effects are stronger for compliance compared to modesty. And with regard to conscientiousness, deliberation increased more clearly than self-discipline. However, as mentioned above, developmental trends for facets of extraversion are more diverse. Thus, with the exception of extraversion, developmental trends seem to be more similar than different within personality traits.

Besides these average developmental trajectories, individuals follow very different life paths and this is also reflected in high diversity in personality development. Most individual differences occur in young adulthood and old age, presumably because both periods of life are marked with strong changes in social roles that either need to be established (i.e., in young adulthood) or need to be adapted to losses (i.e., in old age). Individuals do not only differ to which social roles they commit but also when they commit to these which both likely impacts the timing of personality changes (Specht et al., 2011).

Importantly, this chapter is confined to a detailed description of age trends that is typically observed in research on personality development in adulthood. However, these age trends do not automatically prove (or disapprove) a theoretical prediction on causes and mechanisms of personality development. Instead, systematic changes in personality may be due to intrinsic maturation (cf. Mõttus, Chapter 7), biological changes (cf. Smith & Weiss, Chapter 10), genetic effects (cf. Kandler & Zapko-Willmes, Chapter 8), environmental changes (cf. Ormel, VonKorff, Jeronimus, & Riese, Chapter 9), or changes in social roles (cf. Roberts & Nickel, Chapter 11). Most likely, these personality changes are due to a combination of these potential causes. However, what this chapter does imply is that personality is not "set like plaster" but can and does change in all periods of life.

Future studies will hopefully continue to have a closer look at personality changes in old age. This period of life has long awakened less interest but is highly susceptible to changes in personality that are not yet well understood. Also, research on personality development has mainly—with notable exceptions—focused on differences across biological age groups but less so on other indicators of age, namely distance to death (Mueller, Wagner, & Gerstorf, Chapter 6) and the future time perspective (Carstensen, 2006), how old a person feels like (i.e., subjective age; Settersten & Mayer, 1997) or is perceived to be by others (i.e., perceived age; Christensen et al., 2009), and with regard to different indicators of biological age (Belsky et al., 2015). Hopefully, an update of this chapter in 10 years will be able to include many more indicators of age despite chronological age to enable a comprehensive understanding of developmental trends of the Big Five personality traits in adulthood.

## Acknowledgment

I thank Ulrich Orth for valuable comments on an earlier version of this chapter.

## References

Allemand, M., Gomez, V., & Jackson, J. J. (2010). Personality trait development in midlife: Exploring the impact of psychological turning points. *European Journal of Ageing, 7,* 147—155.

Ardelt, M. (2000). Still stable after all these years? Personality stability theory revisited. *Social Psychology Quarterly, 63,* 392—405.

Arnett, J. J. (2000). Emerging adulthood: A theory of development from the late teens through the twenties. *American Psychologist, 55,* 469—480.

Asendorpf, J. B. (2015). Person-centered approaches to personality. In M. L. Cooper, & R. J. Larsen (Eds.), *Handbook of personality and social psychology. Vol. 4: Personality processes and individual differences* (pp. 403—424). Washington, DC: American Psychological Association.

Belsky, D. W., Caspi, A., Houts, R., Cohen, H. J., Corcoran, D. L., Danese, A., ... Moffitt, T. E. (2015). Quantification of biological aging in young adults. *Proceedings of the National Academy of Sciences.*

Bleidorn, W., Klimstra, T. A., Denissen, J. J. A., Rentfrow, P. J., Potter, J., & Gosling, S. D. (2013). Personality maturation around the world—A cross-cultural examination of Social Investment Theory. *Psychological Science, 24*, 2530—2540.

Branje, S. J. T., van Lieshout, C. F. M., & Gerris, J. R. M. (2007). Big Five personality development in adolescence and adulthood. *European Journal of Personality, 21*, 45—62.

Carstensen, L. L. (2006). The influence of a sense of time on human development. *Science, 312*, 1913—1915.

Caspi, A., Roberts, B. W., & Shiner, R. L. (2005). Personality development: Stability and change. *Annual Review of Psychology, 56*, 453—484.

Christensen, K., Thinggaard, M., McGue, M., Rexbye, H., Hjelmborg, J. V. B., Aviv, A., ... Vaupel, J. W. (2009). Perceived age as clinically useful biomarker of ageing: Cohort study. *BMJ, 339*, b5262.

Donnellan, M. B., & Lucas, R. E. (2008). Age differences in the Big Five across the life span: Evidence from two national samples. *Psychology and Aging, 23*, 558—566.

Ferguson, C. J. (2010). A meta-analysis of normal and disordered personality across the life span. *Journal of Personality and Social Psychology, 98*, 659—667.

Fraley, R. C., & Roberts, B. W. (2005). Patterns of continuity: A dynamic model for conceptualizing the stability of individual differences in psychological constructs across the life course. *Psychological Review, 112*, 60—74.

Hill, P. L., Turiano, N. A., Mroczek, D. K., & Roberts, R. W. (2012). Examining concurrent and longitudinal relations between personality traits and social well-being in adulthood. *Social Psychological and Personality Science, 3*, 698—705.

Hutteman, R., Hennecke, M., Orth, U., Reitz, A. K., & Specht, J. (2014). Developmental tasks as a framework to study personality development in adulthood and old age. *European Journal of Personality, 28*, 267—278.

Jackson, J. J., Thoemmes, F., Jonkmann, K., Lüdtke, O., & Trautwein, U. (2012). Military training and personality trait development: Does the military make the man, or does the man make the military? *Psychological Science, 23*, 270—277.

John, O. P., Naumann, L. P., & Soto, C. J. (2008). Paradigm shift to the integrative Big Five trait taxonomy: History, measurement, and conceptual issues. In O. P. John, R. W. Robins, & L. A. Pervin (Eds.), *Handbook of personality: Theory and research* (3rd ed., pp. 114—158). New York, NY: The Guilford Press.

Kandler, C., Kornadt, A. E., Hagemeyer, B., & Neyer, F. J. (2015). Patterns and sources of personality development in old age. *Journal of Personality and Social Psychology, 109*, 175—191.

Lehmann, R., Denissen, J. J. A., Allemann, M., & Penke, L. (2013). Age and gender differences in motivational manifestations of the Big Five from age 16 to 60. *Developmental Psychology, 49*, 365—383.

Lucas, R. E., & Donnellan, M. B. (2009). Age differences in personality: Evidence from a nationally representative Australian sample. *Developmental Psychology, 45*, 1353—1363.

Lucas, R. E., & Donnellan, M. B. (2011). Personality development across the life span: Longitudinal analyses with a national sample from Germany. *Journal of Personality and Social Psychology, 101*, 847—861.

Lüdtke, O., Trautwein, U., & Husemann, N. (2009). Goal and personality trait development in a transitional period: Assessing change and stability in personality development. *Personality and Social Psychology Bulletin, 35*, 428—441.

Marsh, H. W., Nagengast, B., & Morin, A. J. S. (2013). Measurement invariance of Big-Five factors over the life span: ESEM tests of gender, age, plasticity, maturity, and la dolce vita effects. *Developmental Psychology*, *49*, 1194−1218.

Mõttus, R., Johnson, W., & Deary, I. J. (2012). Personality traits in old age: Measurement and rank-order stability and some mean-level change. *Psychology and Aging*, *27*, 243−249.

Mund, M., & Neyer, F. J. (2014). Treating personality-relationship transactions with respect: Narrow facets, advanced models, and extended time frames. *Journal of Personality and Social Psychology*, *107*, 352−368.

Ozer, D. J. (1986). *Consistency in personality: A methodological framework*. Heidelberg: Springer-Verlag.

Roberts, B. W., & DelVecchio, W. F. (2000). The rank-order consistency of personality traits from childhood to old age: A quantitative review of longitudinal studies. *Psychological Bulletin*, *126*, 3−25.

Roberts, B. W., & Mroczek, D. (2008). Personality trait change in adulthood. *Current Directions in Psychological Science*, *17*, 31−35.

Roberts, B. W., Walton, K. E., & Viechtbauer, W. (2006). Patterns of mean-level change in personality traits across the life course: A meta-analysis of longitudinal studies. *Psychological Bulletin*, *132*, 1−25.

Roberts, B. W., & Wood, D. (2006). Personality development in the context of the neo-socioanalytic model of personality. In D. K. Mroczek, T. D. Little, D. K. Mroczek, & T. D. Little (Eds.), *Handbook of personality development* (pp. 11−39). Mahwah, NJ: Lawrence Erlbaum Associates Publishers.

Roberts, B. W., Wood, D., & Caspi, A. (2008). The development of personality traits in adulthood. In O. P. John, R. W. Robins, & L. A. Pervin (Eds.), *Handbook of personality: Theory and research* (pp. 375−398). New York, NY: Guilford.

Settersten, R. A., & Mayer, K. U. (1997). The measurement of age, age structuring, and the life course. *Annual Review of Sociology*, *23*, 233−261.

Soto, C. J., & John, O. P. (2012). Development of Big Five domains and facets in adulthood: Mean-level age trends and broadly versus narrowly acting mechanisms. *Journal of Personality*, *80*, 881−914.

Soto, C. J., John, O. P., Gosling, S. D., & Potter, J. (2011). Age differences in personality traits from 10 to 65: Big Five domains and facets in a large cross-sectional sample. *Journal of Personality and Social Psychology*, *100*, 330−348.

Specht, J. (2015). Psychologie des hohen Lebensalters [Psychology of old age]. *Aus Politik und Zeitgeschichte*, *65*, 3−10.

Specht, J., Bleidorn, W., Denissen, J. J. A., Hennecke, M., Hutteman, R., Kandler, C., ... Zimmermann, J. (2014). What drives adult personality development? A comparison of theoretical perspectives and empirical evidence. *European Journal of Personality*, *28*, 216−230.

Specht, J., Egloff, B., & Schmukle, S. C. (2011). Stability and change of personality across the life course: The impact of age and major life events on mean-level and rank-order stability of the Big Five. *Journal of Personality and Social Psychology*, *101*, 862−882.

Specht, J., Luhmann, M., & Geiser, C. (2014). On the consistency of personality types across adulthood: Latent profile analyses in two large-scale panel studies. *Journal of Personality and Social Psychology*, *107*, 540−556.

Summerfield, M., Dunn, R., Freidin, S., Hahn, M., Ittak, P., Kecmanovic, M., ... Wooden, M. (2011). *HILDA user manual—Release 10*. Melbourne, Australia: Melbourne Institute of Applied Economic and Social Research, University of Melbourne.

Taylor, M. F., Brice, J., Buck, N., & Prentice-Lane, E. (Eds.), (2010). *British Household Panel Survey User Manual Volume A: Introduction, technical report and appendices* Colchester: University of Essex.

Terracciano, A., Costa, P. T., & McCrae, R. R. (2006). Personality plasticity after age 30. *Personality and Social Psychology Bulletin, 32,* 999–1009.

Terracciano, A., McCrae, R. R., Brant, L. J., & Costa, P. T. (2005). Hierarchical linear modeling analyses of the NEO-PI-R scales in the Baltimore Longitudinal Study of Aging. *Psychology and Aging, 20,* 493–506.

Vaidya, J. G., Gray, E. K., Haig, J. R., Mroczek, D. K., & Watson, D. (2008). Differential stability and individual growth trajectories of Big Five and affective traits during young adulthood. *Journal of Personality, 76,* 267–304.

Wagner, G. G., Frick, J. R., & Schupp, J. (2007). The German Socio-Economic Panel Study (SOEP): Scope, evolution and enhancements. *Journal of Applied Social Science Studies, 127,* 139–169.

Wagner, J., Ram, N., Smith, J., & Gerstorf, D. (in press). Personality trait development at the end of life: Antecedents and correlates of mean-level trajectories. *Journal of Personality and Social Psychology.*

Wille, B., Beyers, W., & De Fruyt, F. (2012). A transactional approach to person-environment fit: Reciprocal relations between personality development and career role growth across young to middle adulthood. *Journal of Vocational Behavior, 81,* 307–321.

Wortman, J., Lucas, R. E., & Donnellan, M. B. (2012). Stability and change in the Big Five personality domains: Evidence from a longitudinal study of Australians. *Psychology and Aging, 27,* 867–874.

Ziegler, M., Cengia, A., Mussel, P., & Gerstorf, D. (2015). Openness as a buffer against cognitive decline: The openness-fluid-crystallized-intelligence (OFCI) model applied to late adulthood. *Psychology and Aging, 30,* 573–588.

# On the role of personality in late life

# 6

*Swantje Mueller[1], Jenny Wagner[1,2], and Denis Gerstorf[1,3]*
[1]Humboldt-Universität zu Berlin, Berlin, Germany, [2]Leibniz Institute for Science and Mathematics Education (IPN), Kiel, Germany, [3]German Institute for Economic Research (DIW Berlin), Berlin, Germany

## Introduction

Who are we and who do we become before we die? The first years of life are shaped by rapid rates of developmental growth in cognitive, physical, sensory, and psychosocial domains. In contrast, the last years of life are typically marked by pronounced decrements in multiple domains of individual functioning—a phenomenon referred to as terminal decline (Hülür, Ram, & Gerstorf, in press). Drawing from seminal work conducted in the 1960s and 1970s (Kleemeier, 1962; Siegler, 1975), research has accumulated to suggest that mortality-related processes leading toward death bring about steep declines in cognitive performance (Bäckman & MacDonald, 2006), physical and sensory functioning (Gerstorf, Ram, Lindenberger, & Smith, 2013; Wilson et al., 2012), as well as subjective accounts of functional health and well-being (Diehr, Williamson, Burke, & Psaty, 2002; Gerstorf & Ram, 2013; Luhmann, Chapter 13). In the context of these seemingly inevitable declines, huge individual differences exist. Some people experience dramatic and profound declines, whereas others enjoy their last years in reasonably good health. Despite this abundant body of research, we know surprisingly little about how personality traits—defined as basic building blocks of human thinking, feeling, and behavior—might shape and be shaped by the often multifaceted loss experiences in late life. To guide and encourage research toward that end, we review and discuss in this chapter theoretical notions and empirical evidence revolving around three major questions: How do personality traits operate as antecedents of and buffers against late-life decline? How do personality traits themselves change in response to and as a consequence of late-life decline in central areas of life? What would be defining features of adaptive personality development in late life?

## Personality as an antecedent and buffer of late-life decline

Across many central areas of life, vast individual differences exist in levels of late-life functioning, and in the onset and rate of decline (Gerstorf & Ram, 2013). We argue in the following that between-person differences in personality traits

Personality Development Across the Lifespan. DOI: http://dx.doi.org/10.1016/B978-0-12-804674-6.00006-5

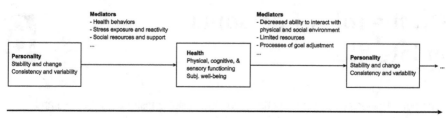

**Figure 6.1** Conceptual model of the mediators and moderators of the personality—health interplay. We note that research on processes of personality development in late life is still in its infancy. Thus this model is only a tentative suggestion and might be modified as research progresses.

operate as both antecedent conditions for and buffer against late-life declines, thereby contributing to the heterogeneity observed. The conceptual model guiding our argumentation is illustrated in Fig. 6.1. Focusing first on the left-hand part of the figure, we consider theoretical notions and empirical evidence suggesting that personality traits impact multiple behavioral, physiological, and social pathways that accumulatively shape health across life. We acknowledge that changes in living conditions and the growing importance of biological factors might reduce the room for personality traits to buffer health declines late in life. Nonetheless, we propose that within this limited space, personality remains an important psychological resource that helps people adjust to (and alleviate) functional declines in the health domain.

## Mechanisms linking personality and health

Lifespan scholars have long noted that personality operates as an adaptive capacity that helps people adjust to age-related challenges and thereby contributes to health and longevity (Staudinger & Fleeson, 1996). We distinguish two theoretically plausible pathways through which personality traits might affect late-life trajectories of health and well-being: First, from an action theoretical perspective, personality traits might influence the degree to which individuals are motivated to engage in and pursue health-relevant goals and behaviors (Friedman, 2000; Smith, 2006). For example, the tendency of conscientious individuals to be responsible and self-disciplined might lead them to be both more concerned about their health as well as more successful in starting and keeping up healthy behaviors, such as regular exercise. In contrast, neurotic individuals who tend to be nervous and easily stressed might have more self-regulatory difficulties, thus being less likely to successfully commit to a workout plan and more likely to engage in detrimental health behaviors. Supporting this notion, lower levels of conscientiousness and higher levels of neuroticism have frequently been linked to poor exercise behavior, smoking, and unhealthy eating habits (Bogg & Roberts, 2004; Malouff, Thorsteinsson, & Schutte, 2006; Rhodes & Smith, 2006).

   Second, according to the transactional stress-moderation model, personality dispositions might impact health through stress-related physiological processes by influencing how individuals shape and interact with their environment (Segerstrom, 2000; Smith, 2006). To illustrate, personality traits might influence how individuals actively form their (social) environment, whether they enter or avoid certain situations, and which reactions they evoke from others. This in turn affects the frequency, severity, and persistence of everyday stressors (e.g., interpersonal conflict) as well as the amount and quality of stress-reducing coping resources (e.g., social support). In line with that view, an increasing number of studies indicates that individuals who are more emotionally stable, extraverted, agreeable, and conscientious tend to experience less (interpersonal) stress (Bolger & Schilling, 1991; Day, Therrien, & Carroll, 2005; Smith & Zautra, 2002), receive more social support (Cukrowicz, Franzese, Thorp, Cheavens, & Lynch, 2008; Hoth, Christensen, Ehlers, Raichle, & Lawton, 2007; Russell & Booth, 1997), and have more favorable constellations on neuroendocrine, inflammatory, or cardiovascular risk factors (Chapman et al., 2009; Nater, Hoppmann, & Klumb, 2010; Sutin et al., 2010).

However, both theoretical models and empirical investigations have rarely explicitly considered how personality might shape health and well-being late in life. To what extent do these associations generalize to the last years of life? Borrowing from research on healthy aging, there are two different perspectives on how age— or vulnerability more generally—modulates the relevance of psychosocial resources. First, higher vulnerability could amplify the effect of personality on health because psychosocial resources gain in importance (Duberstein et al., 2003). For example, the tendency of conscientious individuals to be diligent and well-organized might be particularly important in very old age when people need to follow strict dietary regimen or adhere to complex medication schedules. Second, personality might become less relevant for health late in life because the growing importance of physiological constraints overshadows the health benefits conveyed by psychosocial resources (Baltes & Smith, 2003; Scheier & Bridges, 1995). Although these assumptions seem contradictory at first, we find support for both, suggesting a curvilinear association between personality and health. The health risks or benefits conveyed by personality traits might indeed be magnified in old age, but their relevance likely decreases again when a critical point of physiological vulnerability and compromised psychosocial reserve capacity is reached, the so-called "fourth age" (at around 80−85 years of age; Baltes & Smith, 2003; Löckenhoff, Sutin, Ferrucci, & Costa, 2008).

## Health behaviors

It appears intuitively plausible that links between personality and health behaviors are age- and context dependent. To begin with, approximately 15% of people aged 85+ live in long-term care facilities and two-thirds of those who still live in the community require assistance with multiple activities of daily life (Federal Interagency Forum on Aging-Related Statistics, 2012). As a consequence, effects of personality on health behaviors might wane late in life. Instead of the individual being responsible for planning his or her activities, a close relative or professional caregiver might take on much of this responsibility. Rather than being determined by one's level of conscientiousness, whether or not one engages in physical activity might then be more dependent on the availability of assistance and on one's overall physical condition. Likewise, as individuals become particularly frail, medication might be administered by a nurse or close relative, diminishing the importance of conscientiousness for adherence to medication (in fact, it is rather the nurse's or relative's level of conscientiousness that might be relevant here). Supporting this view, a meta-analysis of conscientiousness and health behaviors found that conscientiousness was a stronger predictor of activity level, smoking, and unhealthy eating habits in younger than in older adults (Bogg & Roberts, 2004). Moreover, Hill and Roberts (2011) reported initial evidence suggesting that age moderates associations between conscientiousness and medication adherence, such that the relationship weakens with advancing age.

## Stress exposure and reactivity

In a similar vein, the effects of personality traits on processes of stress exposure and reactivity might change late in life. As individuals suffer from severe age-related and morbidity-related losses, their ability to prevent or alleviate stressful experiences through active situation selection might be limited due to their decreased mobility and increased dependence on others. In addition, the sources of stress are likely very different at the end of life as compared to midlife and old age (Aldwin, Sutton, Chiara, & Spiro, 1996). In earlier phases of life, work-related issues (e.g., disagreements with one's superior) are a major source of stress. In very old age, stress might be more often triggered by factors the individual has little control over, including adverse life events (e.g., death of a close friend) or physical disabilities. As a consequence, personality might have less influence on the *occurrence* of potential stressors. However, personality traits might still affect the *appraisal* of (and coping with) stressful events. For instance, it has been suggested that individuals low in neuroticism are better able to focus on positive aspects of a situation and are thus more successful in using effective emotion-focused coping strategies such as positive reappraisal (Suls & Martin, 2005; Watson & Hubbard, 1996). This might be particularly beneficial in very old age when opportunities for problem-focused coping often are limited.

## Social resources and support

In addition, social environmental characteristics often change considerably at the end of life. It is well established that as individuals age, their social networks get smaller (Carstensen, 1991; Smith & Ryan, 2016; Wrzus, Hänel, Wagner, & Neyer, 2013). Older individuals tend to maintain increasingly fewer peripheral contacts and focus more on their closest friends and family members (Lang & Carstensen, 1994). In the very last years of life, even this close circle of confidants is often reduced because same-aged friends and partners pass away, further increasing the importance of (younger) family members (Broese van Groenou, Hoogendijk, & Van Tilburg, 2013). As a consequence, personality may be less relevant for the maintenance of social relationships late in life because such network losses are often caused by factors beyond the reach of personality—relationship transactions. Nonetheless, some individuals appear to be able to (partially) compensate network losses through establishing new social relationships (Broese van Groenou et al., 2013). It is thus possible that personality traits related to the development of new relationships (e.g., extraversion and openness; Wagner, Lüdtke, Roberts, & Trautwein, 2014) continue to be relevant for social integration and support late in life.

## Mortality- and pathology-related processes

It is long established that trajectories of psychological change late in life reflect a combination of age-related, but also of mortality-related, and pathology-related processes (Ram, Gerstorf, Fauth, Zarit, & Malmberg, 2010). These factors may also operate as moderators for pathways linking personality to health. To illustrate, many studies on personality and health focus on the effect of personality on the onset of disease. In very old age, however, individuals most likely already suffer from a myriad of comorbidities (Baltes & Smith, 2003). Rather than finding ways to prevent getting sick, it becomes more important to adjust to the pervasive health constraints very old individuals are commonly faced with. This may have important implications for personality—health associations late in life because the impact of personality-related health behaviors and social resources might vary depending on the stage in the disease process (Scheier & Bridges, 1995; Smith & Spiro, 2002). For example, clinical studies suggest that although psychosocial factors affect disease outcomes at early stages, the relevance of personality might wane as diseases progress. In very frail individuals (close to death), health outcomes appear to be increasingly determined by biological factors, limiting the health benefits conveyed by psychosocial resources. However, the nature and strength of personality—health associations may vary depending upon the kind and severity of health constraints, such as acute versus chronic disease. For example, first evidence suggests that personality profiles related to higher activity and social engagement continue to benefit health outcomes throughout the course of HIV (Ironson, O'Cleirigh, Schneiderman, Weiss, & Costa, 2008).

In sum, there is reason to believe that associations of personality with objective health outcomes might be attenuated very late in life. However, given that the discrepancy between objective and subjective health assessments substantially increases in old age (Steinhagen-Thiessen & Borchelt, 1999), personality might continue to be highly relevant for subjective perceptions of health.

## Empirical evidence for personality—health associations in late life

Only very few empirical studies have systematically investigated the potential effects of age or closeness to death on associations between personality and facets of health. One of the reasons is that studies rarely include sufficiently large sample sizes for very old people or those close to death. The few exceptions support theoretical notions summarized above, suggesting that the influence of personality on objective health does indeed wane with advancing age (Scheier & Bridges, 1995; Schulz, Bookwala, Knapp, Scheier, & Williamson, 1996). In contrast, studies using subjective rather than objective or performance-based measures of health and well-being indicate that personality might still play an important role in shaping subjective perceptions late in life (Berg, Hassing, Thorvaldsson, & Johansson, 2011; Duberstein et al., 2003; Quinn, Johnson, Poon, & Martin, 1999). Importantly, we note that the evidence is primarily cross-sectional and should therefore be interpreted with caution.

We also note that there is (mixed) evidence regarding the predictive effects of personality on mortality hazards. For example, Weiss and Costa (2005) reported that lower levels of neuroticism, agreeableness, and conscientiousness each predicted higher 5-year mortality hazards in a sample of Medicare recipients (aged 65−100) suffering from multiple functional limitations (see also Korten et al., 1999). Conversely, Mroczek and Spiro (2007) found that higher levels of and increases in neuroticism were positively related to all-cause mortality in men aged 43−91 (see also Read, Vogler, Pedersen, & Johansson, 2006; Wilson et al., 2005). All these reports refer to all-cause mortality, which may be related to, but not necessarily caused by health issues. In fact, an individual's health status might moderate associations between personality and mortality hazards, with different traits being adaptive in healthy versus health-impaired individuals. To illustrate, neuroticism is generally seen as a risk factor for physical health (Friedman, 2000). However, (moderate) increases in neuroticism might actually be very adaptive for chronically ill and frail individuals because heightened awareness of health issues and resource constraints might prevent people from engaging in risky behaviors, such as trying to cross a busy street alone despite suffering from severe vision loss (see Roberts, Smith, Jackson, & Edmonds, 2009). Such a moderating effect of health might be one potential explanation for previous controversial findings.

In sum, theoretical notions and empirical evidence indicate that personality operates both as antecedent condition for and buffer against late-life declines of function. Because of the growing importance of physiological constraints, health risks or benefits conveyed by personality traits might be more pronounced for subjective than for objective indicators of health and well-being late in life. Empirical tests of such an assertion have not revealed conclusive evidence though because a myriad of alternative explanations are yet to be ruled out (e.g., lack of personality assessments tailored to people's life stage and no within-person change study designs).

## Stability and change in personality as a consequence of late-life decline

Over and above personality operating as a resource and risk factor for late-life decline, lifespan developmental theory has long noted that an increasingly negative ratio of gains to losses late in life might also bring about changes in personality itself (Baltes, Lindenberger, & Staudinger, 2006; Staudinger & Fleeson, 1996). In the following, we focus on the right-hand portion of our conceptual model depicted in Fig. 6.1, discussing how stability and change in personality is shaped by what happens in key facets of health.

## *Physical health*

Debilitating and chronic diseases can be expected to threaten older individuals' capacity to maintain an acquired lifestyle and to meet the environmental demands they are confronted with, thereby prompting long-term change in people's personality (Baltes et al., 2006; Roberts & Wood, 2006). For example, sudden or severe health issues could cause feelings of vulnerability and anxiety (Hayman et al., 2007), which may eventually result in long-term increases in neuroticism. Moreover, health constraints often force older adults to be more selective in the activities and social relationships they engage in (Wrzus et al., 2013), potentially leading to decreases in extraversion and agreeableness (Hill, Turiano, Mroczek, & Roberts, 2012; Stephan, Sutin, & Terracciano, 2014). Similarly, compromised physical health may limit older individuals' capacity to engage in cultural and intellectual endeavors or to maintain their previous levels of orderliness, manifesting in reduced openness and conscientiousness.

In line with predictions from lifespan theory, initial evidence suggests that personality traits do indeed continue to change up until the very end of life. For example, Mroczek and Spiro (2003) found that extraversion mean levels continue to decline in very old age, whereas levels of neuroticism substantially decrease until age 80 and then increase again. Similar trends have been reported by Mõttus, Johnson, and Deary (2012) who additionally observed significant declines in openness, agreeableness, and conscientiousness in a cohort of octogenarians. To our knowledge, only one study has tested how mortality-related processes—as indexed by time-to-death— shape personality development at the end of life. Studying trajectories of neuroticism, extraversion, and openness over 13 years in by now deceased participants aged 70−103 initially, Wagner, Ram, Smith, and Gerstorf (2016) found that average levels of neuroticism increased with approaching death. Conversely, levels of extraversion and openness increased over time in study, but rates of change were unaffected by time-to-death. Interestingly, in this sample age did not moderate rates of change in any of the three traits, indicating that factors other than age per se (or for extraversion and openness, time-to-death) may be operating to shape personality development late in life. Consistent with this interpretation, the authors showed that suffering from disabilities was associated with steeper late-life declines in extraversion and openness. Similarly, a recent meta-analysis (mean age = 56) suggests that individuals become less extraverted, open, and conscientious, but more neurotic after the (self-reported) onset of a chronic disease (Jokela, Hakulinen, Singh-Manoux, & Kivimäki, 2014; see also Sutin, Zonderman, Ferrucci, & Terracciano, 2013).

Conversely, little evidence for health-related personality change was found in studies using more objective indicators of health (Berg & Johansson, 2014; Mõttus, Johnson, Starr, & Deary, 2012; Wagner et al., 2016). Examining personality trajectories between ages 81 and 87, Mõttus and colleagues reported that decreases in physical fitness were associated with steeper declines in conscientiousness, but unrelated to other Big Five traits. Similarly, neither physician-diagnosed comorbidities nor self-reported functional limitations predicted patterns of personality stability and change in a sample aged 80 to 98 (Berg & Johansson, 2014). However, relying on moderate sample sizes, both studies might have been underpowered to detect potentially small effects.

## Cognitive functioning

In addition to physical constraints, age-related declines in cognitive performance are likely to contribute to late-life personality change. Specifically, reduced cognitive functioning might prevent very old adults from seeking out new experiences and (social) contexts (Köhncke et al., 2016), leading to decreases in extraversion and openness. Compromised cognitive functioning might further challenge people's ability to make and carry out plans, thereby contributing to decreases in conscientiousness and increased feelings of vulnerability, and thus higher neuroticism.

Supporting this view, poor cognitive performance has been associated with higher levels of or increases in neuroticism and with lower and decreasing levels of openness to experience (Graham & Lachman, 2012; Ziegler, Cengia, Mussel, & Gerstorf, 2015), as well as with accelerated declines in conscientiousness (Mõttus, Johnson, Starr et al., 2012). Personality changes have also been observed in relation to neurodegenerative conditions such as Alzheimer's disease (AD). A review of informant-rated personality changes in AD patients revealed substantial mean-level increases in neuroticism and significant declines in extraversion, openness, agreeableness, and conscientiousness after the onset of AD (Robins Wahlin & Byrne, 2011). Changes were largest for conscientiousness, amounting up to three standard deviations relative to premorbid levels of personality. It remains an open question whether, in these severe cases, changes in personality are direct outcomes of brain pathology or rather indicative of psychological adjustments in reaction to chronic conditions.

## Sensory functioning

Finally, declines in sensory functioning may play a considerable role in shaping patterns of personality stability and change late in life. Losses in hearing and vision are highly prevalent in very old age and often have severe psychological consequences (Wahl et al., 2013). Apart from reduced mobility and everyday competence, sensory declines limit older adults' ability to successfully interact with their social environment and might thus take a particularly dramatic toll on social integration and functioning (Hawthorne, 2008). As a consequence, increases in neuroticism and decreases in extraversion might be especially pronounced. Initial evidence suggests that worse hearing is indeed associated with steeper decreases in extraversion and stronger increases in neuroticism, whereas vision loss was only related to accelerated increases in neuroticism (Berg & Johansson, 2014; Lißmann, 2003).

Taken together, theoretical notions and empirical evidence suggest that age-, pathology-, and mortality-related vulnerabilities as well as specific physical, cognitive, and sensory losses drive patterns of personality stability and change late in life. Specifically, very late life seems to be characterized by increases in neuroticism and decreases in all of the other Big Five traits.

# What is adaptive personality development in late life?

After having discussed multifaceted ways in which personality traits do shape and are shaped by late-life functioning and development in physical health, cognitive functioning, and sensory functioning, the next section will integrate these insights and discuss probable defining features of adaptive personality development in late life.

An intuitive way to evaluate the adaptive utility of a personality trait or trait change is to consider whether or not it might contribute to the mastery of age-specific developmental tasks (Havighurst, 1972). Following this line of thought, normative increases in emotional stability (i.e., decreases in neuroticism), agreeableness, and conscientiousness from adolescence up until old age may reflect processes of personality maturation that enable people to better master the challenges associated with these life periods, such as starting a family or establishing a career (Hogan & Roberts, 2004; Hutteman, Hennecke, Orth, Reitz, & Specht, 2014). Consequently, developing and maintaining lower levels of neuroticism and higher levels of agreeableness and conscientiousness has often been labeled positive personality development (Staudinger & Kunzmann, 2005). Such a pattern of personality stability and change certainly proves to be beneficial in most contexts throughout most of the lifespan.

At the same time, lifespan theoretical notions suggest that the situation might change late in life, when an increasingly negative ratio of developmental gains to losses necessitates a shift from processes of growth to the management of losses (Baltes & Baltes, 1990; Heckhausen, Wrosch, & Schulz, 2010). Late in life, severe health complaints often compromise older individuals' everyday competence and resources, thereby threatening their ability to maintain a previously acquired lifestyle and to meet the environmental demands they are confronted with. Thus, rather than trying to achieve or maintain higher levels of functioning, very old people might increasingly benefit from so-called compensatory secondary control strategies (Heckhausen et al., 2010), which involve replacing no longer achievable goals and refocusing one's remaining resources on goals and activities that are still manageable.

Against this backdrop, a reversal of maturation trends as reflected in increasing levels of neuroticism and declining agreeableness and conscientiousness might in fact be adaptive in very old age and with increasing functional limitations. To illustrate, (moderate) increases in neuroticism and therefore heightened awareness of health and resource constraints might help very old individuals to disengage from unattainable goals and prevent people from engaging in activities that might cause too much exhaustion and frustration (e.g., going shopping alone despite being barely able to walk without assistance). Similarly, age- and health-related decreases in agreeableness and extraversion may mirror processes of adaptation, in which no longer attainable social goals (e.g., attending crowded parties in public spaces) are replaced with still attainable ones (e.g., having a small dinner party at home). With increasing functional limitations, it might also be beneficial to relax one's standards of orderliness and diligence and focus more selectively on the most important aspects of everyday life (e.g., adherence to medication), which could be reflected in decreasing levels of conscientiousness. Finally, declines in openness to experience might also represent a process of adaptive age-specific goal adjustment in which goals related to seeking out new experiences and contexts are replaced with goals that can be attained within a more familiar environment. For example, instead of going on adventurous hikes, older individuals might rather enjoy a walk in the park around the corner.

Importantly, however, it might not be beneficial to disengage too early from goals that are difficult, but not impossible to attain (Wrosch, Scheier, Carver, & Schulz, 2003). For example, if individuals refrain from physically or cognitively challenging activities even before the first signs of fatigue, functional declines might be accelerated, not prevented. Thus, when asking what constitutes adaptive personality development late in life, the most correct answer might in fact be: it depends. Rather than labeling a particular pattern of trait change as adaptive, we suggest that successful adaptation at the end of life is highly dependent on individual resources and burdens. For those suffering from severe and debilitating chronic diseases, increases in neuroticism and declines in the other Big Five traits might reflect adaptive processes of goal adjustment. In contrast, individuals who are still in relatively good cognitive and physical shape and blessed with a good (social) infrastructure might rather benefit from personality stability. Moreover, in addition to the direction and amount of trait change, across-situation consistency of personality traits (or states) might be an important defining feature of adaptive personality development (Fleeson & Jayawickreme, 2014). Borrowing from extant research on functional implications of intraindividual variability in other domains of functioning (Ram & Gerstorf, 2009; Röcke, Li, & Smith, 2009), we would expect that very low across-situation consistency might reflect an increased lability of the personality system. In contrast, extremely high consistency may indicate that a person has become too rigid in his or her personality, losing the ability to flexibly adapt to changing situational demands and opportunities (see Human et al., 2015, for initial evidence on the adaptive utility of moderate affect variability).

To thoroughly describe, understand, and potentially encourage adaptive personality development late in life, future research needs to move from examining personality—health associations to investigating more complex interactions between personality traits, environmental characteristics, as well as age-related, mortality-related, and pathology-related resources and burdens. Specifically, we suggest to carefully consider the following aspects: What kind of personality trait change (how much, in which direction, in which trait or constellation of traits) might be adaptive in which context (acute or chronic disease), under which circumstances (individual living alone vs in a nursing home), and with respect to what kind of outcome (well-being, subjective or objective health, mortality).

## Conclusion

There is a dearth of research investigating how personality traits might shape and be shaped by the often multifaceted loss experiences in late life. In this chapter, we discussed theoretical notions and initial empirical evidence suggesting that trajectories of personality and health are closely intertwined late in life. Research suggests that personality operates as antecedent condition for and buffer against late-life declines in the health domain via its influence on health behaviors, stress-related processes, and social resources. At the same time, pervasive health declines in late-life challenge an individual's ability to maintain an acquired lifestyle and to successfully interact with the social and physical environment, often resulting in substantial changes in personality. Based on lifespan theory, we argue that such health-related personality changes reflect processes of adaptation involving the adjustment to changing developmental opportunities and constraints through the selection of age-appropriate goals and activities.

# References

Aldwin, C. M., Sutton, K. J., Chiara, G., & Spiro, A. (1996). Age differences in stress, coping, and appraisal: Findings from the Normative Aging Study. *The Journals of Gerontology: Series B: Psychological Sciences and Social Sciences, 51,* 179—188. Available from http://dx.doi.org/10.1093/geronb/51B.4.P179.

Bäckman, L., & MacDonald, S. W. S. (2006). Death and cognition. *European Psychologist, 11,* 224—235. Available from http://dx.doi.org/10.1027/1016-9040.11.3.224.

Baltes, P. B., & Baltes, M. M. (1990). Psychological perspectives on successful aging: The model of selective optimization with compensation. In P. B. Baltes, & M. M. Baltes (Eds.), *Successful aging: Perspectives from the behavioral sciences* (pp. 1—34). New York, NY: Cambridge University Press.

Baltes, P. B., Lindenberger, U., & Staudinger, U. M. (2006). Life span theory in developmental psychology. In R. M. Lerner (Ed.), *Handbook of child psychology: Theoretical models of human development* (6th ed. (Vol. 1). New York, NY: Wiley.

Baltes, P. B., & Smith, J. (2003). New frontiers in the future of aging: From successful aging of the young old to the dilemmas of the fourth age. *Gerontology, 49,* 123—135. Available from http://dx.doi.org/10.1159/000067946.

Berg, A. I., Hassing, L. B., Thorvaldsson, V., & Johansson, B. (2011). Personality and personal control make a difference for life satisfaction in the oldest-old: Findings in a longitudinal population-based study of individuals 80 and older. *European Journal of Ageing, 8,* 13—20. Available from http://dx.doi.org/10.1007/s10433-011-0181-9.

Berg, A. I., & Johansson, B. (2014). Personality change in the oldest-old: Is it a matter of compromised health and functioning? *Journal of Personality, 82,* 25—31. Available from http://dx.doi.org/10.1111/jopy.12030.

Bogg, T., & Roberts, B. W. (2004). Conscientiousness and health-related behaviors: A meta-analysis of the leading behavioral contributors to mortality. *Psychological Bulletin, 130,* 887—919. Available from http://dx.doi.org/10.1037/0033-2909.130.6.887.

Bolger, N., & Schilling, E. A. (1991). Personality and the problems of everyday life: The role of neuroticism in exposure and reactivity to daily stressors. *Journal of Personality, 59,* 355—386. Available from http://dx.doi.org/10.1111/j.1467-6494.1991.tb00253.x.

Broese van Groenou, M., Hoogendijk, E. O., & Van Tilburg, T. G. (2013). Continued and new personal relationships in later life: Differential effects of health. *Journal of Aging and Health, 25,* 274—295. Available from http://dx.doi.org/10.1177/0898264312468033.

Carstensen, L. L. (1991). Selectivity theory: Social activity in life-span context. In K. Schaie (Ed.), *Annual review of gerontology and geriatrics* (pp. 195–217). New York, NY: Springer.

Chapman, B. P., Khan, A., Harper, M., Stockman, D., Fiscella, K., Walton, J., . . . Moynihan, J. (2009). Gender, race/ethnicity, personality, and interleukin-6 in urban primary care patients. *Brain, Behavior, and Immunity*, *23*, 636–642. Available from http://dx.doi.org/10.1016/j.bbi.2008.12.009.

Cukrowicz, K. C., Franzese, A. T., Thorp, S. R., Cheavens, J. S., & Lynch, T. R. (2008). Personality traits and perceived social support among depressed older adults. *Aging & Mental Health*, *12*, 662–669. Available from http://dx.doi.org/10.1080/1360786080 2343258.

Day, A. L., Therrien, D. L., & Carroll, S. A. (2005). Predicting psychological health: Assessing the incremental validity of emotional intelligence beyond personality, Type A behaviour, and daily hassles. *European Journal of Personality*, *19*, 519–536. Available from http://dx.doi.org/10.1002/per.552.

Diehr, P., Williamson, J., Burke, G., & Psaty, B. (2002). The aging and dying processes and the health of older adults. *Journal of Clinical Epidemiology*, *55*, 269–278. Available from http://dx.doi.org/10.1016/S0895-4356(01)00462-0.

Duberstein, P. R., Sörensen, S., Lyness, J. M., King, D. A., Conwell, Y., Seidlitz, L., & Caine, E. D. (2003). Personality is associated with perceived health and functional status in older primary care patients. *Psychology and Aging*, *18*, 25–37. Available from http://dx.doi.org/10.1037/0882-7974.18.1.25.

Federal Interagency Forum on Aging-Related Statistics (2012). *Older Americans 2012: Key indicators of well-being*. Washington, DC: U.S. Government Printing Office.

Fleeson, W., & Jayawickreme, E. (2014). Whole trait theory. *Journal of Research in Personality*, *56*, 82–92. Available from http://dx.doi.org/10.1016/j.jrp.2014.10.009.

Friedman, H. S. (2000). Long-term relations of personality and health: Dynamisms, mechanisms, tropisms. *Journal of Personality*, *68*, 1089–1107. Available from http://dx.doi.org/10.1111/1467-6494.00127.

Gerstorf, D., & Ram, N. (2013). Inquiry into terminal decline: Five objectives for future study. *The Gerontologist*, *53*, 727–737. Available from http://dx.doi.org/10.1093/geront/gnt046.

Gerstorf, D., Ram, N., Lindenberger, U., & Smith, J. (2013). Age and time-to-death trajectories of change in indicators of cognitive, sensory, physical, health, social, and self-related functions. *Developmental Psychology*, *49*, 1805–1821. Available from http://dx.doi.org/10.1037/a0031340.

Graham, E. K., & Lachman, M. E. (2012). Personality stability is associated with better cognitive performance in adulthood: Are the stable more able? *The Journals of Gerontology Series B: Psychological Sciences and Social Sciences*, *67*, 545–554. Available from http://dx.doi.org/10.1093/geronb/gbr149.

Havighurst, R. J. (1972). *Developmental tasks and education*. New York, NY: McKay Company.

Hawthorne, G. (2008). Perceived social isolation in a community sample: its prevalence and correlates with aspects of peoples' lives. *Social Psychiatry and Psychiatric Epidemiology*, *43*, 140–150. Available from http://dx.doi.org/10.1007/s00127-007-0279-8.

Hayman, K. J., Kerse, N. M., La Grow, S. J., Wouldes, T., Robertson, M. C., & Campbell, A. J. (2007). Depression in older people: Visual impairment and subjective ratings of health. *Optometry and Vision Science*, *84*, 1024–1030. Available from https://dx.doi.org/10.1097/OPX.0b013e318157a6b1.

Heckhausen, J., Wrosch, C., & Schulz, R. (2010). A motivational theory of life-span development. *Psychological Review*, *117*, 32–60. Available from http://dx.doi.org/10.1037/a0017668.

Hill, P. L., & Roberts, B. W. (2011). The role of adherence in the relationship between conscientiousness and perceived health. *Health Psychology*, *30*, 797–804. Available from http://dx.doi.org/10.1037/a0023860.

Hill, P. L., Turiano, N. A., Mroczek, D., & Roberts, B. W. (2012). Examining concurrent and longitudinal relations between personality traits and social well-being in adulthood. *Social Psychological and Personality Science*, *3*, 698–705. Available from http://dx.doi.org/10.1177/1948550611433888.

Hogan, R., & Roberts, B. W. (2004). A socioanalytic model of maturity. *Journal of Career Assessment*, *12*, 207–217. Available from http://dx.doi.org/10.1177/1069072703255882.

Hoth, K. F., Christensen, A. J., Ehlers, S. L., Raichle, K. A., & Lawton, W. J. (2007). A longitudinal examination of social support, agreeableness and depressive symptoms in chronic kidney disease. *Journal of Behavioral Medicine*, *30*, 69–76. Available from http://dx.doi.org/10.1007/s10865-006-9083-2.

Hülür, G., Ram, N., & Gerstorf, D. (in press). Terminal decline of function. In V. L. Bengtson & R. A. Settersten, Jr. (Eds.), *Handbook of theories of aging* (3rd ed.). New York, NY: Springer.

Human, L., Whillans, A., Hoppmann, C., Klumb, P., Dickerson, S., & Dunn, E. (2015). Finding the middle ground: Curvilinear associations between positive affect variability and daily cortisol profiles. *Emotion*, *15*, 705–720. Available from http://dx.doi.org/10.1037/emo0000071.

Hutteman, R., Hennecke, M., Orth, U., Reitz, A. K., & Specht, J. (2014). Developmental tasks as a framework to study personality development in adulthood and old age. *European Journal of Personality*, *28*, 267–278. Available from http://dx.doi.org/10.1002/per.1959.

Ironson, G. H., O'Cleirigh, C., Schneiderman, N., Weiss, A., & Costa, P. T. (2008). Personality and HIV disease progression: Role of NEO-PI-R openness, extraversion, and profiles of engagement. *Psychosomatic Medicine*, *70*, 245–253. Available from http://dx.doi.org/10.1097/PSY.0b013e31816422fc.

Jokela, M., Hakulinen, C., Singh-Manoux, A., & Kivimäki, M. (2014). Personality change associated with chronic diseases: pooled analysis of four prospective cohort studies. *Psychological Medicine*, *44*, 2629–2640. Available from http://dx.doi.org/10.1017/S0033291714000257.

Kleemeier, R. W. (1962). Intellectual change in the senium. *Proceedings of the Social Statistics Section of the American Statistical Association*, *1*, 290–295.

Köhncke, Y., Laukka, E. J., Brehmer, Y., Kalpouzos, G., Li, T.-Q., Fratiglioni, L., & Lövdén, M. (2016). Three-year changes in leisure activities are associated with concurrent changes in white matter microstructure and perceptual speed in individuals aged 80 years and older. *Neurobiology of Aging*, *41*, 173–186. Available from https://dx.doi.org/10.1016/j.neurobiolaging.2016.02.013.

Korten, A. E., Jorm, A. F., Jiao, Z., Letenneur, L., Jacomb, P. A., Henderson, A. S., & Rodgers, B. (1999). Health, cognitive, and psychosocial factors as predictors of mortality in an elderly community sample. *Journal of Epidemiology and Community Health*, *53*, 83–88. Available from http://dx.doi.org/10.1136/jech.53.2.83.

Lang, F. R., & Carstensen, L. L. (1994). Close emotional relationships in late life: Further support for proactive aging in the social domain. *Psychology and Aging*, *9*, 315–324. Available from http://dx.doi.org/10.1037/0882-7974.9.2.315.

Lißmann, I. (2003). *Intraindividuelle Veränderungen von Extraversion und Neurotizismus im hohen Alter: Die Bedeutung sensorischer Beeinträchtigung* [Intraindividual change of extraversion and neuroticism in old age: The role of sensory impairment]. Unpublished doctoral dissertation, Free University of Berlin. Retrieved November 1, 2015, from http://www.diss.fu-berlin.de/diss/receive/FUDISS_thesis_000000001242.

Löckenhoff, C. E., Sutin, A. R., Ferrucci, L., & Costa, P. T. (2008). Personality traits and subjective health in the later years: The association between NEO-PI-R and SF-36 in advanced age is influenced by health status. *Journal of Research in Personality, 42*, 1334−1346. Available from http://dx.doi.org/10.1016/j.jrp.2008.05.006.

Malouff, J. M., Thorsteinsson, E. B., & Schutte, N. S. (2006). The five-factor model of personality and smoking: A meta-analysis. *Journal of Drug Education, 36*, 47−58. Available from http://dx.doi.org/10.2190/9EP8-17P8-EKG7-66AD.

Mõttus, R., Johnson, W., & Deary, I. J. (2012). Personality traits in old age: Measurement and rank-order stability and some mean-level change. *Psychology and Aging, 27*, 243−249. Available from http://dx.doi.org/10.1037/a0023690.

Mõttus, R., Johnson, W., Starr, J. M., & Deary, I. J. (2012). Correlates of personality trait levels and their changes in very old age: The Lothian Birth Cohort 1921. *Journal of Research in Personality, 46*, 271−278. Available from http://dx.doi.org/10.1016/j.jrp.2012.02.004.

Mroczek, D. K., & Spiro, A. (2003). Modeling intraindividual change in personality traits: Findings from the Normative Aging Study. *The Journals of Gerontology: Series B: Psychological Sciences and Social Sciences, 58*, 153−165. Available from http://dx.doi.org/10.1093/geronb/58.3.P153.

Mroczek, D., & Spiro, A. (2007). Personality change influences mortality in older men. *Psychological Science, 18*, 371−376. Available from http://dx.doi.org/10.1111/j.1467-9280.2007.01907.x.

Nater, U. M., Hoppmann, C. A., & Klumb, P. L. (2010). Neuroticism and conscientiousness are associated with cortisol diurnal profiles in adults—Role of positive and negative affect. *Psychoneuroendocrinology, 35*, 1573−1577. Available from http://dx.doi.org/10.1016/j.psyneuen.2010.02.017.

Quinn, M. E., Johnson, M. A., Poon, L. W., & Martin, P. (1999). Psychosocial correlates of subjective health in sexagenarians, octogenarians, and centenarians. *Issues in Mental Health Nursing, 20*, 151−171. Available from http://dx.doi.org/10.1080/016128499248727.

Ram, N., & Gerstorf, D. (2009). Time-structured and net intraindividual variability: Tools for examining the development of dynamic characteristics and processes. *Psychology and Aging, 24*, 778−791. Available from http://dx.doi.org/10.1037/a0017915.

Ram, N., Gerstorf, D., Fauth, E., Zarit, S., & Malmberg, B. (2010). Aging, disablement, and dying: Using time-as-process and time-as-resources metrics to chart late-life change. *Research in Human Development, 7*, 27−44. Available from http://dx.doi.org/10.1080/15427600903578151.

Read, S., Vogler, G. P., Pedersen, N. L., & Johansson, B. (2006). Stability and change in genetic and environmental components of personality in old age. *Personality and Individual Differences, 40*, 1637−1647. Available from http://dx.doi.org/10.1016/j.paid.2006.01.004.

Rhodes, R. E., & Smith, N. E. I. (2006). Personality correlates of physical activity: A review and meta-analysis. *British Journal of Sports Medicine, 40*, 958−965. Available from http://dx.doi.org/10.1136/bjsm.2006.028860.

Roberts, B. W., Smith, J., Jackson, J. J., & Edmonds, G. (2009). Compensatory conscientiousness and health in older couples. *Psychological Science*, 20, 553–559. Available from http://dx.doi.org/10.1111/j.1467-9280.2009.02339.x.

Roberts, B. W., & Wood, D. (2006). Personality development in the context of the Neo-Socioanalytic Model of Personality. In D. K. Mroczek, & T. D. Little (Eds.), *Handbook of personality development* (pp. 11–39). Mahwah, NJ: Lawrence Erlbaum Associates Publishers.

Robins Wahlin, T.-B., & Byrne, G. J. (2011). Personality changes in Alzheimer's disease: A systematic review. *International Journal of Geriatric Psychiatry*, 26, 1019–1029. Available from http://dx.doi.org/10.1002/gps.2655.

Röcke, C., Li, S.-C., & Smith, J. (2009). Intraindividual variability in positive and negative affect over 45 days: Do older adults fluctuate less than young adults? *Psychology and Aging*, 24, 863–878. Available from http://dx.doi.org/10.1037/a0016276.

Russell, D., & Booth, B. (1997). Personality, social networks, and perceived social support among alcoholics: A structural equation analysis. *Journal of Personality*, 65, 649–692. Available from http://dx.doi.org/10.1111/j.1467-6494.1997.tb00330.x.

Scheier, M. F., & Bridges, M. W. (1995). Person variables and health: Personality predispositions and acute psychological states as shared determinants for disease. *Psychosomatic Medicine*, 57, 255–268. Available from http://dx.doi.org/10.1097/00006842-199505000-00007.

Schulz, R., Bookwala, J., Knapp, J. E., Scheier, M., & Williamson, G. M. (1996). Pessimism, age, and cancer mortality. *Psychology and Aging*, 11, 304–309. Available from http://dx.doi.org/10.1037/0882-7974.11.2.304.

Segerstrom, S. C. (2000). Personality and the immune system: Models, methods, and mechanisms. *Annals of Behavioral Medicine*, 22, 180–190. Available from http://dx.doi.org/10.1007/BF02895112.

Siegler, I. C. (1975). The terminal drop hypothesis: Fact or artifact? *Experimental Aging Research*, 1, 169–185. Available from http://dx.doi.org/10.1080/03610737508257957.

Smith, B. W., & Zautra, A. J. (2002). The role of personality in exposure and reactivity to interpersonal stress in relation to arthritis disease activity and negative affect in women. *Health Psychology*, 21, 81–88. Available from http://dx.doi.org/10.1037/0278-6133.21.1.81.

Smith, J., & Ryan, L. H. (2016). Psychological vitality in the oldest old. In K. W. Schaie, & S. L. Willis (Eds.), *Handbook of the psychology of aging* (8th ed., pp. 303–319). San Diego: Academic Press.

Smith, T. W. (2006). Personality as risk and resilience in physical health. *Current Directions in Psychological Science*, 15, 227–231. Available from http://dx.doi.org/10.1111/j.1467-8721.2006.00441.x.

Smith, T. W., & Spiro, A. (2002). Personality, health, and aging: Prolegomenon for the next generation. *Journal of Research in Personality*, 36, 363–394. Available from http://dx.doi.org/10.1016/S0092-6566(02)00014-4.

Staudinger, U. M., & Fleeson, W. (1996). Self and personality in old and very old age: A sample case of resilience? *Development and Psychopathology*, 8, 867–885. Available from http://dx.doi.org/10.1017/S0954579400007471.

Staudinger, U. M., & Kunzmann, U. (2005). Positive adult personality development. *European Psychologist*, 10, 320–329. Available from http://dx.doi.org/10.1027/1016-9040.10.4.320.

Steinhagen-Thiessen, E., & Borchelt, M. (1999). Morbidity, medication, and functional limitations in very old age. In P. B. Baltes, & K. Mayer (Eds.), *The Berlin Aging Study: Aging from 70 to 100* (pp. 131–166). Cambridge: Cambridge University Press.

Suls, J., & Martin, R. (2005). The daily life of the garden-variety neurotic: reactivity, stressor exposure, mood spillover, and maladaptive coping. *Journal of Personality*, *73*, 1485−1509. Available from http://dx.doi.org/10.1111/j.1467-6494.2005.00356.x.

Sutin, A. R., Costa, P. T., Uda, M., Ferrucci, L., Schlessinger, D., & Terracciano, A. (2010). Personality and metabolic syndrome. *Age*, *32*, 513−519. Available from http://dx.doi.org/10.1007/s11357-010-9153-9.

Sutin, A. R., Zonderman, A. B., Ferrucci, L., & Terracciano, A. (2013). Personality traits and chronic disease: Implications for adult personality development. *The Journals of Gerontology: Series B: Psychological Sciences and Social Sciences*, *68*, 912−920. Available from http://dx.doi.org/10.1093/geronb/gbt036.

Wagner, J., Lüdtke, O., Roberts, B. W., & Trautwein, U. (2014). Who belongs to me? Social relationship and personality characteristics in the transition to young adulthood. *European Journal of Personality*, *603*, 586−603. Available from http://dx.doi.org/10.1002/per.1974.

Wagner, J., Ram, N., Smith, J., & Gerstorf, D. (2016). Personality trait development at the end of life: Antecedents and correlates of mean-level trajectories. *Journal of Personality and Social Psychology*, *111*, 411−429. Available from https://doi.org/10.1037/pspp0000071.

Wahl, H. W., Heyl, V., Drapaniotis, P. M., Hormann, K., Jonas, J. B., Plinkert, P. K., & Rohrschneider, K. (2013). Severe vision and hearing impairment and successful aging: A multidimensional view. *The Gerontologist*, *53*, 950−962. Available from http://dx.doi.org/10.1093/geront/gnt013.

Watson, D., & Hubbard, B. (1996). Adaptational style and dispositional structure: Coping in the context of the Five-Factor Model. *Journal of Personality*, *64*, 737−774. Available from http://dx.doi.org/10.1111/j.1467-6494.1996.tb00943.x.

Weiss, A., & Costa, P. T. (2005). Domain and facet personality predictors of all-cause mortality among Medicare patients aged 65 to 100. *Psychosomatic Medicine*, *67*, 724−733. Available from http://dx.doi.org/10.1097/01.psy.0000181272.58103.18.

Wilson, R. S., Krueger, K. R., Gu, L., Bienias, J. L., Mendes de Leon, C. F., & Evans, D. A. (2005). Neuroticism, extraversion, and mortality in a defined population of older persons. *Psychosomatic Medicine*, *67*, 841−845. Available from http://dx.doi.org/10.1097/01.psy.0000190615.20656.83.

Wilson, R. S., Segawa, E., Buchman, A. S., Boyle, P. A., Hizel, L. P., & Bennett, D. A. (2012). Terminal decline in motor function. *Psychology and Aging*, *27*, 998−1007. Available from http://dx.doi.org/10.1037/a0028182.

Wrosch, C., Scheier, M. F., Carver, C. S., & Schulz, R. (2003). The importance of goal disengagement in adaptive self-regulation: When giving up is beneficial. *Self and Identity*, *2*, 1−20. Available from http://dx.doi.org/10.1080/15298860309021.

Wrzus, C., Hänel, M., Wagner, J., & Neyer, F. J. (2013). Social network changes and life events across the life span: A meta-analysis. *Psychological Bulletin*, *139*, 53−80. Available from http://dx.doi.org/10.1037/a0028601.

Ziegler, M., Cengia, A., Mussel, P., & Gerstorf, D. (2015). Openness as a buffer against cognitive decline: The Openness-Fluid-Crystallized-Intelligence (OFCI) model applied to late adulthood. *Psychology and Aging*, *30*, 573−588. Available from http://dx.doi.org/10.1037/a0039493.

# Part Three

# Theoretical Perspectives on Personality Development

# Five-Factor Theory and personality development

**7**

*René Mõttus*
University of Edinburgh, Edinburgh, United Kingdom

## Five-Factor Theory and personality development

Five-Factor Theory (FFT; McCrae & Costa, 2008) is one of the grand theories of current personality psychology. Its foundations are built on empirical evidence and the interpretation of this evidence is guided by some time-tested hypotheses from earlier theorists such as Allport, Cattell, and Eysenck. It is a comprehensive theory in that it covers most of what personality researchers are typically looking into such as traits, behavior, social-cognitive constructs, and their connections. And FFT is an evolving theory in that it attempts to keep up with new evidence and expand to new territories (McCrae, 2015, 2016). As it stands, however, FFT is rather limited in what it explicitly says about personality development. FFT does not have a subtheory specifically dedicated to this aspect of personality. Despite this, what the theory does say about individual differences in personality has also implications for what constitutes and drives personality development.

### Basic dispositions and personality development

Most notably, FFT resides on decades-long factor analytic research on the covariation structure of personality characteristics in groups, which has yielded the Five-Factor Model (FFM; McCrae & John, 1992). The five FFM traits—Neuroticism, Extraversion, Openness (to Experience), Agreeableness, and Conscientiousness—are thought to constitute a particularly important level in the hierarchy of personality traits (Markon, Krueger, & Watson, 2005). Accumulating evidence shows that the structure of the FFM traits can be replicated across a variety of environments (McCrae & Terracciano, 2005; Schmitt, Allik, McCrae, & Benet-Martinez, 2007) and that individual differences in the scores of these traits are relatively stable over decades (Roberts & DelVecchio, 2000), agreed on by different raters (Connelly & Ones, 2010) and associated with a range of important variables outside personality domain (Ozer & Benet-Martínez, 2006), and that genetically more similar individuals also tend to have more similar trait scores (Vukasović & Bratko, 2015).

A parsimonious way to interpret these findings has been to hypothesize that the five covariation patterns reflect real, unobserved but causally potent

Personality Development Across the Lifespan. DOI: http://dx.doi.org/10.1016/B978-0-12-804674-6.00007-7

attributes—trait-specific structures within human brain that generate their observable manifestations. As a result, these traits should constitute central units of personality psychology: they can tell us something about causality—traits cause or guide behavior, thoughts, and feelings—and, unlike their context-specific manifestations, may provide information that is generalizable across people and contexts. This is how Allport (1931), Cattell (1946), and Eysenck (1991), among others, conceptualized traits and this is how FFT conceptualizes them. The five traits are called basic tendencies in the FFT (McCrae & Costa, 2008).[1]

Cattell (1946), for example, suggested that traits constitute of constitutional parts, reflecting genetic influences, and environmental mold, representing the contributions of any environmental factors. FFT (McCrae & Costa, 2008) defines basic tendencies as endogenous dispositions that are completely uncoupled from environmental influences, unless these act directly on the brain (e.g., pharmacological interventions or injuries). However, it must be emphasized that FFT does not specify what the endogenous underpinnings of the basic tendencies are—they remain hypothetical constructs, or placeholders for any biological influences (but for an attempt to provide these underpinnings, see DeYoung, 2015). The postulate that individuals' life experiences generally have no influence on their basic personality dispositions is perhaps one of the most important and distinctive features of the FFM. This seems to fly in the face of our everyday experiences. For example, many of us have seen people behaving increasingly assertively as they progress through their careers or, in contrast, decreasing in self-esteem and social activity as a result of being fired. This postulate also contradicts other personality theories such as the neo-socioanalytic (Lodi-Smith & Roberts, 2007) and sociogenomic (Roberts & Jackson, 2008) approaches. However, FTT does not defy common sense: it simply filters those aspects of personality that are malleable by environment into other components of personality system. These other components will be addressed later.

The postulate of basic tendencies being isolated from environment has inevitable implications for how personality development occurs according to FFT. Any change in these tendencies at whatever point of life has to result from endogenous processes and personality development must therefore reflect intrinsic maturation, much like "development" of height largely reflects genetically driven maturation—in normal circumstances and within fairly homogeneous populations, at least (Johnson, 2010).

## Evidence for the lack of external influence on basic tendencies: Cultural comparisons

One line of evidence for the FFM traits—and therefore their development—being driven by intrinsic rather than external influences comes from cross-cultural studies

---

[1] In fact, FFT postulates that personality characteristics are organized hierarchically with the FFM traits constituting the highest level of the hierarchy (McCrae & Costa, 2008). The traits at lower levels of personality hierarchy such as facets (Costa & McCrae, 1992) and nuances (McCrae, 2015) can also be considered as basic tendencies (Mõttus et al., 2016).

on their structure. FFM questionnaires such as the NEO Personality Inventory (Costa & McCrae, 1992) and Big Five Inventory (John, Donahue, & Kentle, 1991) have been translated into dozens of languages and administered in a wide range of cultures spanning most of the world. In most cultures, the covariations among the items or subscales (facets) of these inventories can be interpreted as being similar to the covariations found in the culture of where the tests were initially developed (McCrae & Terracciano, 2005; Schmitt et al., 2007). These findings suggest that, structure-wise, FFM may be a human universal and therefore a result of biological factors (supposedly more or less universal to all humans) rather than environmental factors that ostensibly vary across cultures to large extents. However, it must be noted that studies that have not been based on predesigned FFM questionnaires (Saucier et al., 2014) or rely on more rigorous statistical tests (Thalmayer & Saucier, 2014) have offered somewhat less convincing support for the replicability of the FFM structure.

Furthermore, differences in the FFM scores across world regions are generally smaller than could be expected if environment was a powerful contributor to personality variance, given the ostensibly large cultural diversity. For example, Schmitt et al. (2007) compared FFM scores across 10 regions from North- and South-America, Europe, Africa, and Asia and found that region could explain only 1% to 6% of variability in scores. It is possible, however, that cross-cultural (regional) differences in self-report-based FFM scores are confounded by rating biases such as reference group effect (Heine, Lehman, Peng, & Greenholtz, 2002) or extreme responding (Mõttus, Allik et al., 2012), especially given that these differences are not particularly meaningfully correlated with relevant criterion variables (Mõttus, Allik, & Realo, 2010). Furthermore, there is some evidence that moving to a Western culture may be related to people's FFM trait scores becoming more Western-like, suggesting that environment can, after all, have some impact on these traits (Güngör et al., 2013; McCrae, Yik, Trapnell, Bond, & Paulhus, 1998).

Of direct relevance for personality development is the finding that age differences in the FFM scores appear to be more or less similar in a range of cultures: on average, older people tend to be lower in Neuroticism, Extraversion, and Openness and higher in Agreeableness and Conscientiousness than younger people, regardless of the cultural and economic conditions in which they live (McCrae & Terracciano, 2005; McCrae et al., 1999). Of course, there are exceptions to these trends: for example, older Germans have been found to be higher in Neuroticism than their younger counterparts (Donnellan & Lucas, 2008). If environmental factors had a substantial influence on personality traits and their development, one would expect to see age differences to be more culture-specific. But then there is evidence that sex differences in FFM personality traits vary systematically across cultures, with differences being larger in more prosperous countries with higher average educational level (Schmitt, Realo, Voracek, & Allik, 2008). This would point to the role of environment, if only as a facilitator or inhibitor of intrinsic dispositions.

Bleidorn et al. (2013) found that normative age-related changes in the FFM traits were somewhat more pronounced in cultures where compulsory education was shorter and lower proportions of population had tertiary education (the two culture-level variables were aggregated into a composite "job index"). However, two of the associations were only "marginally significant" (i.e., the likelihood of these findings being false positives was slightly larger than psychologists usually accept) and the rest were similar to the marginally significant ones in terms of effect size (i.e., these associations bordered marginal significance). Authors' other prediction that normative age-related changes would be more pronounced in cultures where people take family roles on earlier received even more modest empirical support. Overall, although the study (Bleidorn et al., 2013) offered some support for environmental effects on personality development, the findings were far from robust and definitely need further replications.

## Further evidence for the lack of external influence on basic tendencies

Cultural comparisons aside, there is further evidence—or more precisely, relative lack of it—consistent with the FFM traits being more or less isolated from environmental influences. Attempts to find environmental factors that could possibly contribute to variability and changes in the FFM traits have yielded numerous associations, but they are often weak, generally not well replicated and sometimes even contradictory. For example, one study (Roberts, Helson, & Klohnen, 2002) found that divorce was associated with increases in dominance, a manifestation of Extraversion, whereas another study (Costa, Herbst, McCrae, & Siegler, 2000) reported an association between divorce and decreases in Extraversion; relatedly, van Aken, Denissen, Branje, Dubas, and Goossens (2006) failed to find a significant association between Extraversion and perceived partner support. Recently, however, one replication was reported: Hudson and Roberts (2016) directly replicated the results of a previous study linking investment in work with increases in Conscientiousness.

Individual studies have often reported tens of associations between personality traits and specific environmental factors hypothesized to contribute to their variance. Unless stringent control over type I error (a false positive finding) rate is exercised, at least a some of the findings may reflect random fluctuations in data (better still when the findings are replicated in an independent sample). For example, Mõttus, Johnson, Starr, and Deary (2012) investigated the associations of cognitive ability, physical fitness, and level of independent functioning with changes in the FFM personality traits in the ninth decade of life. They hypothesized that these three predictors represented some of the most important domains at that stage of life and could therefore be linked to changes in personality traits. Overall, 30 associations were tested—15 between trait changes and the baseline levels of predictors and 15 between trait changes and changes in the predictors. Although four of the five traits changed significantly over the 6-year testing interval, only two significant associations appeared at 5% alpha level (which means that on average every 20th association is allowed to be a type I error): higher baseline cognitive ability and smaller declines in fitness were correlated with smaller declines in Conscientiousness. Both of these findings could have been false positives, especially because the inferential statistics were not adjusted for multiple testing as researchers wanted to retain maximum statistical power. Multiple testing increases type I error rate. For example, had the authors adjusted the findings even for fairly liberal false discovery rate (Benjamini & Hochberg, 1995), no significant findings would have emerged. Importantly, neither of these two findings were replicated in a larger cohort tested on three occasion from ages 70 to 76 years (Mõttus, Marioni, & Deary, in press).

As another example, Specht, Egloff, and Schmukle (2011) used data from a large sample of Germans to investigate possible associations between 12 major life events such as marriage, divorce, childbirth, first job and retirement and the FFM trait scores: their baseline levels and changes over 4 years. These analyses yielded 60 associations for baseline FFM scores and another 60 for their changes. For baseline scores, authors found 10 statistically significant associations (main effects) at 5% alpha level (which means that on average every 20th association is allowed to be a type I error), but they did not adjust the inferential statistics for multiple testing. Had they used an adjustment such false discovery rate, only one association—between moving in with partner and higher Extraversion—had remained statistically significant. For changes in trait scores, 12 of the 60 associations (main effects) were significant without adjustment, whereas controlling for false discovery rate would have reduced this number to 5. These five associations vary in terms of their intuitiveness: for example, decreases in Conscientiousness after retirement seem to make sense, whereas decreases in the same trait after childbirth and increases after divorce seem less obvious. The study also found decreases in Extraversion and Openness after marriage and, among a few significant interactions, a sex-specific effect of the death of spouse on Conscientiousness (increases in men and decreases in women). Another study, however, found that these two events were associated with changes in Neuroticism in men: marriage/remarriage was related with greater and spousal death smaller declines in this trait (Mroczek & Spiro, 2003).

Admittedly, these are just two more or less randomly picked studies, but they illustrate the current state of art: researchers have invested considerable efforts in attempting to identify the environmental contributors to personality variation and change, but the findings have been far less robust than many of them had probably expected. Specht et al. (2014) have summarized the available evidence as follows: "changes in personality that can be traced back to experience of life events beyond general age trends are of limited impact" (p. 223). The likelihood that specific environmental variables can, at least individually, only account for small proportions of variance in personality characteristics was also pointed out by Turkheimer and Waldron (2000). Eventually, of course, it is quite possible that some specific classes of external influences turn out to be consequential for basic personality tendencies. However, as yet there is not much robust evidence for this.

## Set like plaster

An earlier version of the FFT suggested that almost all of the intrinsic personality development happened before age 30, after which personality would become "set like plaster" (Costa & McCrae, 1994), whereas this claim seems to be somewhat softened in the later descriptions of the theory (Terracciano, Costa, & McCrae, 2006). Indeed, although mean-level personality change continues into very old age (Specht et al., 2014), there is remarkable evidence for very high rank-order stability even in the latest decades of life, regardless of often notable changes and individual differences in people's health, cognitive functioning, and abilities to independently cope with life (Mõttus, Johnson, & Deary, 2012; Mõttus et al., in press; but see evidence for decreasing rank-order stability in older age in Ardelt, 2000; Specht et al., 2011). Furthermore, mean-level changes may represent intrinsic maturation throughout life: for example, declining Conscientiousness in later life may reflect some sort of general functional decline that is characteristic of most people at that age. Likewise, individual differences in the rates of change may reflect intrinsic differences throughout life. On the other hand, high rank-order stability may also result from increasingly stable environmental influences (Briley & Tucker-Drob, 2014). Thus although the idea of personality be set like plaster after age 30 does not seem to be entirely correct—people, on average, do keep changing and individual differences are never perfectly stable—this does not seem to have major implications for the principal suggestion of the FFT—the development of the basic tendencies reflects intrinsic maturation rather than external influences.

## Person–environment transactions and age differences in variance

As personality characteristics are conceptualized as disposing people to particular behaviors, thoughts, and feelings, it would seem natural to assume that people and environmental experiences do not become matched randomly. Instead, different trait levels and thereby different behaviors, thoughts, and feelings would sort people to different environments, make them evoke different responses from the environment, and perceive environments in distinct ways. These are called person–environment transactions (Caspi & Roberts, 2001). Indeed, there is evidence that people with different trait levels report, on average, different situational experiences and that trait levels and situation experiences are often matched: for example, more agreeable people are more likely to encounter positive situations and less deception—or at least perceive situations as more positive and less deceitful (Sherman, Rauthmann, Brown, Serfass, & Jones, 2015). To the extent that people tend to actively construct or passively perceive their environments in ways that match their characteristics, it would also make sense to hypothesize that the self-induced experiences back-influence the characteristics that predisposed people to these experiences—if environmental factors indeed contribute to personality change. This is called the corresponsive principle: "the most likely effect of life experience on personality development is to deepen the characteristics that lead people to those experiences in the first place" (Roberts, Caspi, & Moffitt, 2003, p. 583). This reasoning is consistent with increases of rank-order stability (stability of individual differences) until older adulthood (Roberts & DelVecchio, 2000; but see also Ardelt, 2000; Specht et al., 2011) that seems to be at least partly related to increasing environmental stability (Briley & Tucker-Drob, 2014).

If so, individual differences in trait scores should increase over time (McCrae, 1993; Mõttus, Allik, Hřebíčková, Kööts-Ausmees, & Realo, 2015). Extraverted people should seek out social experiences and other extraverted people, which should make them even more extraverted (e.g., by developing social skills). Introverts, in contrast, should shy away from social encounters and thereby deprive themselves from developing social competence and, as a result, become even more introverted. However, this is not consistent with available evidence. Mõttus and colleagues (2015) studied age differences in the variance of the FFM traits in multiple cultures and found no systematic differences across age groups. Of course, this finding does not constitute direct evidence for the lack of environmental influences on basic tendencies, but is consistent with this proposition.

## Observed age differences may or may not pertain to the basic tendencies

Studies that break the scores of the FFM traits into more specific components such as facets or even individual questionnaire items and study age differences in these often find that these specific components display rather different age trends (e.g., Lucas & Donnellan, 2009; Terracciano, McCrae, Brant, & Costa, 2005). For example, Soto and John (2012) found that the gregariousness facet of Extraversion declined over time, whereas assertiveness and social confidence facets increased. Furthermore, Mõttus and colleagues (2015) found that more often than not even the items of the same facets differed in their age differences, never mind facets of the same FFM traits.

Such findings suggest that whatever mechanisms are driving personality development, they may not operate at the level of the basic tendencies. Instead, they may to some or perhaps even to a large extent pertain to the specific manifestations of the traits that have happened to be included in trait operationalizations (questionnaires). If so, the same may be true for external influences on trait scores. For example, if or when marriage is associated with decreases in Extraversion, it may not be Extraversion as the basic tendency that reacts to this external influence but one or more specific manifestations of the trait. For example, the commitments related to marriage may contribute to cutbacks in going to parties or visiting sporting events, whereas marriage may have no effect whatsoever on friendliness or tendency to feel positive emotions; in fact, marriage may even contribute to happiness (Lucas, Clark, Georgellis, & Diener, 2003). Likewise, decreases in Conscientiousness as a result of retirement may reflect decreased scores in the work-related content of the trait questionnaires, but not necessarily in all manifestations to this basic tendency.

In order to address this possibility, studies that aim to identify potential environmental contributors to personality change should examine the degrees to which these contributors are linked to all manifestations of the trait (Mõttus, 2016). Unfortunately, this has been rarely done so far. One exception is a study by Jackson and colleagues (2012) that investigated the effect of cognitive training in Openness; the observed effect of training was reported to be consistent across all facets of

Openness (footnote 3). It must be noted, however, that Openness was defined very narrowly in this study, mostly in terms of cognitively engaging activities, so the generalizability of the effect of cognitive training across the manifestations of the trait needs further testing. Unless such "sensitivity" analyses are carried out, the correlations between potential environmental causes and personality trait levels, or changes in them, are difficult to interpret. Even if associations are observed, they may not point to influences on basic tendencies.

This takes us to the task of addressing other aspects of FFT because the theory is not only about basic tendencies. As it stands, FFT holds that environment has no effect of basic tendencies in personality (unless they directly change brain) and therefore their development also reflects intrinsic maturation. However, FFT also holds that basic tendencies become manifest through more specific components of personality system[2] and these can indeed be subject to external influences.

## Characteristic adaptations and personality development

According to FFT, basic tendencies are decontextualized, unobserved neuropsychic structures that generate behavioral patterns. They are qualitatively the same for every individual and only differ in terms of the quantity of their "output." The more powerful one's Extraversion generator (basic tendency), the more extraverted behavior it generates, regardless of whether the person is a child, adolescent, or adult or whether he or she lives in New York or New Delhi. But surely the specific behavioral patterns that are being generated by basic tendencies should not be expected to be the same for every individual, regardless of their age or cultural background. How a 12-year old manifests its Extraversion might be quite different from the extraverted behavior of a 70-year old. The manifestations of Openness might be quite different among the Bororo in Brazil than among *des Parisiens*.

FFT holds that basic tendencies become manifest as characteristic adaptations: relatively stable goals, attitudes, self-schema, personal strivings, personal myths, and the likes. In contrast to basic tendencies, characteristic adaptations are suited to particular cultural, social, or developmental contexts. Furthermore, "FFT holds that these causal influences work jointly: [characteristic] adaptations are not simply the sum of trait influences plus life experience influences, but mental structures that evolve as individuals with particular traits interact over time with particular life experiences" (McCrae, 2016, p. 9). Characteristic adaptations, in turn, interact with external influences to produce specific and potentially observable

[2] It should be acknowledged that this is, of course, only an assumption that there exist underlying basic tendencies that cause their purported manifestations. We would only be able to test this assumption by manipulating the basic tendencies and observing resultant changes in their manifestations (Markus & Borsboom, 2013), but such tests are currently hard to carry out because of our limited understanding of the basic tendencies (cf. Jackson et al., 2012). However, this assumption is not specific to FFT and pertains to most of personality psychology (e.g., this is a tacit assumption in latent trait modeling or estimating test reliability on the basis of internal consistency). Yet there are alternative accounts for how specific components of personality system may relate to each other (Cramer et al., 2012; Wood, Gardner, & Harms, 2015; Mõttus, 2016).

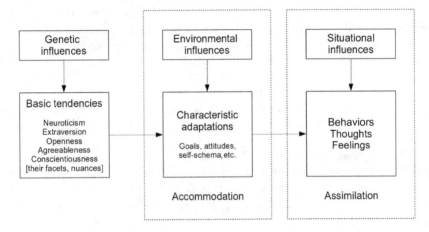

**Figure 7.1** Schematic representation of personality development according to FFT.

manifestations of personality such as behaviors, thoughts, and feelings. McCrae (2016) has termed these two interactive processes as accommodation—the creation of new mental structures, characteristic adaptations, that accommodate both basic tendencies and environmental inputs—and assimilation—the generation of specific personality manifestations that fit the characteristic adaptations into particular situations (Fig. 7.1). As a result, FFT is consistent with the above-described proposal of person—environment transactions (Caspi & Roberts, 2001)—as long as the transactions pertain to characteristic adaptations and not to basic tendencies.

Therefore, according to FFT external factors can and do influence personality differences and thereby their development but this happens at the level of characteristic adaptations rather than at the level of basic tendencies. This sets FFT apart from Cybernetic Big Five Theory (DeYoung, 2015), which also differentiates between traits and characteristic adaptations: according to this theory, environment can influence both classes of personality constructs.

## Telling the difference between basic tendencies and characteristic adaptations

Few studies on personality development have attempted to explicitly distinguish between basic tendencies and characteristic adaptations. There is an obvious reason for this: because basic tendencies are operationalized (e.g., in questionnaires) through characteristic adaptations, our inferences about the two classes of personality constructs are confounded. Personality questionnaire items simultaneously represent both basic tendencies and characteristic adaptations. This has been called the duality principle (Costa & McCrae, 2015), similarly to how quantum physics conceives elementary particles as simultaneously having both wave- and particle-like properties. Therefore, it is important to bear in mind that findings pertaining to the development of FFM traits may reflect both—development of basic tendencies and development of characteristic adaptations. The findings that different constituents of trait operationalizations (facets of the same traits or items of the same facets) demonstrate different developmental patterns (Mõttus, Realo et al., 2015; Soto & John, 2012) may suggest that the observed changes at least sometimes pertain to characteristic adaptations rather than to basic tendencies.

In order to tease apart development of basic tendencies and characteristic adaptations, it may help to decompose personality trait scores into the variance shared by items, ostensibly pertaining to basic tendencies (or facets), and item-specific variance that is potentially more infused with characteristic adaptations. One can then separately examine their developmental trends or correlations with possible external influences. For example, this can and has been done using structural equation modeling (Mõttus, Realo et al., 2015). Of course, even the shared variance of items depends on which particular items happen to be included in the model and is thereby to some extent infused by characteristic adaptations, but at least some of the unique variance of the latter is filtered out, especially if a large number of diverse items is employed. Ideally, the development of basic tendencies should be investigated using multiple operationalizations (questionnaires) of them at the same time, in order to further reduce the likelihood of findings pertaining to characteristic adaptations.

## Conclusion

On one hand, FFT makes a bold claim that flies in the face of common sense: personality dispositions (basic tendencies) are completely isolated from external influences and therefore develop only according to their intrinsic, genetically driven program. But, as other good scientific proposals, this claim is testable and, surprising as it may seem, it has generally been backed by empirical evidence. At least, there is not much robust evidence that lends support to the contrary. On the other hand, however, FFT allows common sense to prevail. It postulates that external influences *can* contribute to personality development, but this happens at the level of characteristic adaptations—mental structures that develop when basic tendencies interact with, or attempt to fit into, particular environmental conditions (accommodation). There are simply two different layers to personality, which are distinguished exactly on the basis of the malleability of their development. This conceptual distinction is reminiscent to Cattell's (1946) constitutional traits and environmental mold. However, empirically it is difficult to separate these layers of personality because basic tendencies cannot be directly observed and have to be operationalized through characteristic adaptations.

## Acknowledgment

I am grateful to Jeff McCrae for his comments on a draft of this chapter.

# References

Allport, G. W. (1931). What is a trait of personality? *The Journal of Abnormal and Social Psychology*, *25*, 368–372.

Ardelt, M. (2000). Still stable after all these years? Personality stability theory revisited. *Social Psychology Quarterly*, *63*, 392–405.

Benjamini, Y., & Hochberg, Y. (1995). Controlling the false discovery rate: A practical and powerful approach to multiple testing. *Journal of the Royal Statistical Society. Series B*, *57*, 289–300.

Bleidorn, W., Klimstra, T. A., Denissen, J. J. A., Rentfrow, P. J., Potter, J., & Gosling, S. D. (2013). Personality maturation around the world: A cross-cultural examination of social-investment theory. *Psychological Science*, *24*, 2530–2540.

Briley, D. A., & Tucker-Drob, E. M. (2014). Genetic and environmental continuity in personality development: A meta-analysis. *Psychological Bulletin*, *140*, 1303–1331.

Caspi, A., & Roberts, B. W. (2001). Personality development across the life course: The argument for change and continuity. *Psychological Inquiry*, *12*, 49–66.

Cattell, R. B. (1946). Personality structure and measurement. *British Journal of Psychology. General Section*, *36*, 88–103.

Connelly, B. S., & Ones, D. S. (2010). An other perspective on personality: Meta-analytic integration of observers' accuracy and predictive validity. *Psychological Bulletin*, *136*, 1092–1122.

Costa, P. T., Herbst, J. H., McCrae, R. R., & Siegler, I. C. (2000). Personality at midlife: Stability, intrinsic maturation, and response to life events. *Assessment*, *7*, 365–378.

Costa, P. T., & McCrae, R. R. (2015). The NEO Inventories as instruments of psychological Theory. In T. A. Widiger (Ed.), *Oxford handbook of the Five-Factor Model*. New York, NY: Oxford University Press.

Costa, P. T., & McCrae, R. R. (1992). *Revised NEO Personality Inventory (NEO PI-R) and NEO Five-Factor Inventory (NEO-FFI) professional manual*. Odessa, FL: Psychological Assessment Resources.

Costa, P. T., & McCrae, R. R. (1994). Set like plaster: Evidence for the stability of adult personality. In T. Heatherton, & J. Weinberger (Eds.), *Can personality change?* (pp. 21–40). Washington, DC: American Psychological Association.

Cramer, A. O. J., van der Sluis, S., Noordhof, A., Wichers, M., Geschwind, N., Aggen, S. H., … Borsboom, D. (2012). Dimensions of normal personality as networks in search of equilibrium: You can't like parties if you don't like people. *European Journal of Personality*, *26*, 414–431.

DeYoung, C. G. (2015). Cybernetic Big Five Theory. *Journal of Research in Personality*, *56*, 33–58.

Donnellan, M. B., & Lucas, R. E. (2008). Age differences in the Big Five across the life span: Evidence from two national samples. *Psychology and Aging*, *23*, 558–566.

Eysenck, H. J. (1991). Dimensions of personality: 16, 5 or 3?—Criteria for a taxonomic paradigm. *Personality and Individual Differences*, *12*, 773–790.

Güngör, D., Bornstein, M. H., Leersnyder, J. D., Cote, L., Ceulemans, E., & Mesquita, B. (2013). Acculturation of personality: A three-culture study of Japanese, Japanese Americans, and European Americans. *Journal of Cross-Cultural Psychology*, *44*, 701–718.

Heine, S. J., Lehman, D. R., Peng, K., & Greenholtz, J. (2002). What's wrong with cross-cultural comparisons of subjective Likert scales? The reference-group effect. *Journal of Personality and Social Psychology*, *82*, 903–918.

Hudson, N. W., & Roberts, B. W. (2016). Social investment in work reliably predicts change in conscientiousness and agreeableness: A direct replication and extension of Hudson, Roberts, and Lodi-Smith (2012). *Journal of Research in Personality, 16*, 12–23.

Jackson, J. J., Hill, P. L., Payne, B. R., Roberts, B. W., & Stine-Morrow, E. A. L. (2012). Can an old dog learn (and want to experience) new tricks? Cognitive training increases openness to experience in older adults. *Psychology and Aging, 27*, 286–292.

John, O. P., Donahue, E. M., & Kentle, R. L. (1991). *The Big Five Inventory—versions 4a and 54*. Berkeley, CA: University of California, Berkeley, Institute of Personality and Social Research.

Johnson, W. (2010). Understanding the genetics of intelligence: Can height help? Can corn oil? *Current Directions in Psychological Science, 19*, 177–182.

Lodi-Smith, J., & Roberts, B. W. (2007). Social investment and personality: A meta-analysis of the relationship of personality traits to investment in work, family, religion, and volunteerism. *Personality and Social Psychology Review, 11*, 68–86.

Lucas, R. E., Clark, A. E., Georgellis, Y., & Diener, E. (2003). Reexamining adaptation and the set point model of happiness: Reactions to changes in marital status. *Journal of Personality and Social Psychology, 84*, 527–539.

Lucas, R. E., & Donnellan, M. B. (2009). Age differences in personality: Evidence from a nationally representative Australian sample. *Developmental Psychology, 45*(5), 1353–1363. https://doi.org/10.1037/a0013914

Markon, K. E., Krueger, R. F., & Watson, D. (2005). Delineating the structure of normal and abnormal personality: An integrative hierarchical approach. *Journal of Personality and Social Psychology, 88*, 139–157.

Markus, K. A., & Borsboom, D. (2013). *Frontiers of test validity theory: Measurement, causation, and meaning*. New York, NY: Routledge/Taylor & Francis Group.

McCrae, R. R. (2016). Integrating trait and process approaches to personality: A sketch of an agenda. In U. Kumar (Ed.), *Wiley handbook of personality assessment*. Hoboken, NJ: Wiley.

McCrae, R. R. (1993). Curiouser and curiouser! Modifications of a paradoxical theory of personality coherence. *Psychological Inquiry, 4*, 300–303.

McCrae, R. R. (2015). A more nuanced view of reliability: Specificity in the trait hierarchy. *Personality and Social Psychology Review, 19*, 97–112.

McCrae, R. R., & Costa, P. T. (2008). The Five-Factor Theory of personality. In O. P. John, R. W. Robins, & L. A. Pervin (Eds.), *Handbook of personality: Theory and research* (3rd ed., pp. 159–181). New York, NY: Guilford Press.

McCrae, R. R., Costa, P. T., de Lima, M. P., Simões, A., Ostendorf, F., Angleitner, A., ... Piedmont, R. L. (1999). Age differences in personality across the adult life span: Parallels in five cultures. *Developmental Psychology, 35*, 466–477. Available from http://dx.doi.org/10.1037/0012-1649.35.2.466.

McCrae, R. R., & John, O. P. (1992). An introduction to the five-factor model and its applications. *Journal of Personality, 60*, 175–215.

McCrae, R. R., & Terracciano, A. (2005). Universal features of personality traits from the Observer's Perspective: Data from 50 cultures. *Journal of Personality and Social Psychology, 88*, 547–561.

McCrae, R. R., Yik, M. S., Trapnell, P. D., Bond, M. H., & Paulhus, D. L. (1998). Interpreting personality profiles across cultures: Bilingual, acculturation, and peer rating studies of Chinese undergraduates. *Journal of Personality and Social Psychology, 74*, 1041–1055.

Mõttus, R. (2016). Towards more rigorous personality trait-outcome research. *European Journal of Personality, 303*, 292–303.

Mõttus, R., Allik, J., Hřebíčková, M., Kööts-Ausmees, L., & Realo, A. (2015). Age differences in the variance of personality characteristics. *European Journal of Personality*.

Mõttus, R., Allik, J., & Realo, A. (2010). An attempt to validate national mean scores of Conscientiousness: No necessarily paradoxical findings. *Journal of Research in Personality*, *44*, 630–640.

Mõttus, R., Allik, J., Realo, A., Rossier, J., Zecca, G., Ah-Kion, J., ... Johnson, W. (2012). The effect of response style on self-reported Conscientiousness across 20 countries. *Personality & Social Psychology Bulletin*, *38*, 1423–1436.

Mõttus, R., Johnson, W., & Deary, I. J. (2012). Personality traits in old age: Substantial structural and rank-order stability, and some mean-level change. *Psychology and Aging*, *27*, 243–249.

Mõttus, R., Johnson, W., Starr, J. M., & Deary, I. J. (2012). Correlates of personality trait levels and their changes in very old age: The Lothian Birth Cohort 1921. *Journal of Research in Personality*, *46*, 271–278.

Mõttus, R., Kandler, C., Bleidorn, W., Riemann, R., & McCrae, R. R. (2016, April 28). Personality Traits Below Facets: The Consensual Validity, Longitudinal Stability, Heritability, and Utility of Personality Nuances. Journal of Personality and Social Psychology. Advance online publication. http://dx.doi.org/10.1037/pspp0000100.

Mõttus, R., Marioni, R., & Deary, I. J. (in press). Markers of psychological differences and social and health inequalities: Possible genetic and phenotypic overlaps. *Journal of Personality*.

Mõttus, R., Realo, A., Allik, J., Esko, T., Metspalu, A., & Johnson, W. (2015). Within-trait heterogeneity in age group differences in personality domains and facets: Implications for the development and coherence of personality traits. *PLoS ONE*, *10*, e0119667.

Mroczek, D. K., & Spiro, A. (2003). Modeling intraindividual change in personality traits: Findings from the normative aging study. *The Journals of Gerontology: Series B: Psychological Sciences and Social Sciences*, *58*, P153–165.

Ozer, D. J., & Benet-Martínez, V. (2006). Personality and the prediction of consequential outcomes. *Annual Review of Psychology*, *57*, 401–421.

Roberts, B. W., Caspi, A., & Moffitt, T. E. (2003). Work experiences and personality development in young adulthood. *Journal of Personality and Social Psychology*, *84*, 582–593.

Roberts, B. W., & DelVecchio, W. F. (2000). The rank-order consistency of personality traits from childhood to old age: A quantitative review of longitudinal studies. *Psychological Bulletin*, *126*, 3–25.

Roberts, B. W., Helson, R., & Klohnen, E. C. (2002). Personality development and growth in women across 30 years: Three perspectives. *Journal of Personality*, *70*, 79–102.

Roberts, B. W., & Jackson, J. J. (2008). Sociogenomic personality psychology. *Journal of Personality*, *76*, 1523–1544.

Saucier, G., Thalmayer, A. G., Payne, D. L., Carlson, R., Sanogo, L., Ole-Kotikash, L., ... Zhou, X. (2014). A basic bivariate structure of personality attributes evident across nine languages. *Journal of Personality*, *82*, 1–14.

Schmitt, D. P., Allik, J., McCrae, R. R., & Benet-Martinez, V. (2007). The geographic distribution of big five personality traits: Patterns and profiles of human self-description across 56 nations. *Journal of Cross-Cultural Psychology*, *38*, 173–212.

Schmitt, D. P., Realo, A., Voracek, M., & Allik, J. (2008). Why can't a man be more like a woman? Sex differences in Big Five personality traits across 55 cultures. *Journal of Personality and Social Psychology*, *94*, 168–182.

Sherman, R. A., Rauthmann, J. F., Brown, N. A., Serfass, D. G., & Jones, A. B. (2015). The independent effects of personality and situations on real-time expressions of behavior and emotion. *Journal of Personality and Social Psychology*, *109*, 872–888.

Soto, C. J., & John, O. P. (2012). Development of Big-Five domains and facets in adulthood: Mean-level age trends and broadly versus narrowly acting mechanisms. *Journal of Personality*, *80*, 881–914.

Specht, J., Bleidorn, W., Denissen, J. J. A., Hennecke, M., Hutteman, R., Kandler, C., ... Zimmermann, J. (2014). What drives adult personality development? A comparison of theoretical perspectives and empirical evidence. *European Journal of Personality*, *28*, 216–230.

Specht, J., Egloff, B., & Schmukle, S. C. (2011). Stability and change of personality across the life course: The impact of age and major life events on mean-level and rank-order stability of the Big Five. *Journal of Personality and Social Psychology*, *101*, 862–882.

Terracciano, A., Costa, P. T., & McCrae, R. R. (2006). Personality plasticity after age 30. *Personality & Social Psychology Bulletin*, *32*, 999–1009.

Terracciano, A., McCrae, R. R., Brant, L. J., & Costa, P. T., Jr. (2005). Hierarchical linear modeling analyses of the NEO-PI-R scales in the Baltimore Longitudinal Study of Aging. *Psychology and Aging*, *20*(3), 493–506. https://doi.org/10.1037/0882-7974.20.3.493.

Thalmayer, A. G., & Saucier, G. (2014). The questionnaire Big Six in 26 nations: Developing cross-culturally applicable Big Six, Big Five and Big Two inventories. *European Journal of Personality*, *28*, 482–496.

Turkheimer, E., & Waldron, M. (2000). Nonshared environment: A theoretical, methodological, and quantitative review. *Psychological Bulletin*, *126*, 78–108.

van Aken, M. A. G., Denissen, J. J. A., Branje, S. J. T., Dubas, J. S., & Goossens, L. (2006). Midlife concerns and short-term personality change in middle adulthood. *European Journal of Personality*, *20*, 497–513.

Vukasović, T., & Bratko, D. (2015). Heritability of personality: A meta-analysis of behavior genetic studies. *Psychological Bulletin*, *141*, 769–785.

Wood, D., Gardner, M. H., & Harms, P. D. (2015). How functionalist and process approaches to behavior can explain trait covariation. *Psychological Review*, *122*, 84–111.

# Theoretical perspectives on the interplay of nature and nurture in personality development

**8**

*Christian Kandler[1,2] and Alexandra Zapko-Willmes[1,2]*
[1]Bielefeld University, Bielefeld, Germany, [2]Medical School Berlin, Berlin, Germany

## Genetic and environmental variance in personality characteristics

The claim that "all human behavioral traits are heritable" (Turkheimer, 2000, p. 160) is known as the first law of behavior genetics and means that genetic differences matter regarding individual differences in all human characteristics. In their meta-analysis of the genetic and environmental influences on individual differences in 17,804 human traits based on 50 years of twin studies, Polderman et al. (2015) reported that the average heritability across all complex traits is 49%. Consequently, about one half of individual differences across all focused traits was attributable to genetic differences (see Kandler & Papendick, Chapter 29). On average, only about 17% of variance in human traits were due to environmental influences that act to increase the similarity of same-aged siblings (i.e., monozygotic and dizygotic twins) reared together.

These findings have two important implications. First, the similarity of biologically related family members in complex human behavioral traits is primarily attributable to their genetic relatedness. This has been formulated as the second law of behavior genetics: "The effect of being raised in the same family is smaller than the effect of genes" (Turkheimer, 2000, p. 160). Second, a substantial residual portion of individual differences in complex human behavioral traits can be accounted for by factors that are not shared by family members and act to make them dissimilar. The latter has come to be known as the third law of behavior genetics: "A substantial portion of the variation in complex human behavioral traits is not accounted for by the effects of genes or families" (Turkheimer, 2000, p. 160).

Despite some variation in the size of heritability estimates, the average heritability of psychological features commonly termed "personality characteristics" also amounts to 50% (Bouchard, 2004; Johnson, Vernon, & Feiler, 2008). Additionally, both little evidence for significant environmental influences shared by family members and strong influences of individual environmental factors apply to personality traits. These findings do not exclusively stem from aggregates of self-rated personality-descriptive adjectives or statements, but also from behavioral

Personality Development Across the Lifespan. DOI: http://dx.doi.org/10.1016/B978-0-12-804674-6.00008-9

observations (Borkenau, Riemann, Angleitner, & Spinath, 2001) and reports from well-informed raters such as peers (Kandler, Bleidorn, & Riemann, 2012; Kandler, Bleidorn, Riemann, Angleitner, & Spinath, 2011). Beyond descriptive personality traits, equal portions of genetic and environmental variance have been found for individual differences in specific motivational and socio-cognitive personality characteristics, such as basic human motives, value priorities, sociopolitical orientations, interests, control beliefs, or self-esteem (see Kandler, Zimmermann, & McAdams, 2014, for an overview).

The empirical support of the first two laws of behavior genetics regarding personality characteristics suggests a triumph of nature over nurture in personality development. However, this would constitute an oversimplification. Even though being raised in the same family (apparently) makes few differences in people's personality, the importance of familial environments should not be disregarded. Most families provide equal sufficiently supportive and enriched environments, which represent the toolbox necessary for the children's development of their individual genetic differences (Scarr, 1992). Most rearing environments fall within the limits of a normal environment, are thus crucial to normal development, and have little impact on actual differences among children's personality. The same applies to genetic effects. Saying that 50% of individual differences in personality traits are attributable to genetic differences does not signify that 50% of a person's personality is determined by his or her genetic makeup.

Ultimately, estimates of heritability and environmental contributions basically represent genetic and environmental components of individual differences in a specific trait within a specific group or population at a specific point in time. They have few implications for particular individuals, causations, or developmental processes. For a deeper understanding of the genetic and environmental variation and contributions to the development, it is crucial to apprehend how genetic and environmental factors can unfold their impact.

## Genetic and environmental causation inside and outside the organism

The complex cofunctioning of the genetic makeup (i.e., the genotype) and the environment have led behavior geneticists (Gottlieb, 2003; Kendler, 2001) to describe pathways—inside and outside the organism—through which genes and environments can influence personality characteristics and associated behavior (i.e., the phenotype). In the following, two models describing functioning, interacting, and intertwining of genotypes and environments will be outlined.

### The traditional model of genotype–environment additivity

In the traditional view (Kendler, 2001), gene expression solely takes place inside the organism (i.e., within the individual's physiological internal milieu).

Genetic factors of psychological traits unfold their effects via individual differences in the protein synthesis, neuroanatomic structures and neural as well as hormonal mechanisms. Equally, we can think of environmental influences solely acting outside the organism through cultural and social mediators (e.g., family, peers, and neighborhood) or individual experiences of major life events (e.g., accidents, illnesses, successes, or failures). Both genetic and environmental factors can affect individual differences in personality characteristics (see Fig. 8.1).

The endogenous physiological pathway can account for the specific associations between gene variants and personality differences. Whereas specific genes have been successfully identified for various disorders whose symptoms include personality change (e.g., Alzheimer disease), it has emerged as exceedingly difficult to identify single gene responsible for the substantial heritability of complex personality traits. There is a large discrepancy between the aforementioned substantial and robust heritability estimates for personality traits and the rather small as well as less replicable effects of specific gene variants, which could only account for a trivial

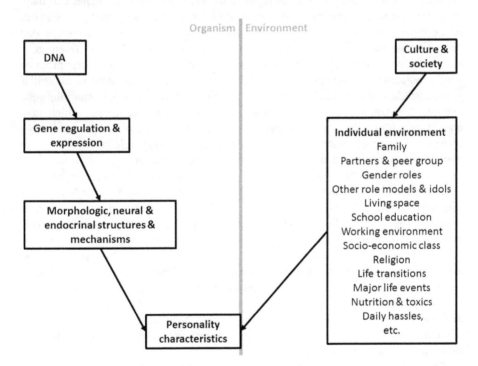

**Figure 8.1** This simplistic model is based on the traditional assumption that genetic and environmental factors additively contribute to individual differences in personality characteristics. *Solid lines with arrows* represent causal relationships between factors. There is no direct connection between genetic activity and personality. Genes unfold their influences on personality variation within the organism via protein synthesis, anatomic structures, neurophysiological mechanisms, and hormones, whereas environments act outside the organism via culture, society, immediate social contexts, and physical experiences.

proportion of personality differences (<1%; based on molecular genetic population studies; Terracciano et al., 2010).

This discrepancy—known as the *missing heritability problem*—may have various reasons (Plomin, 2013). On the one hand, a small number of specific gene variants, which rarely occur in a population and are thus difficult to detect, may show large effects. On the other hand, a large number of gene variants, each of which accounts for a very small percentage of personality differences, may be involved. In line with the latter consideration, a recent study found evidence that the additive combination of multiple single nucleotide polymorphisms (i.e., the smallest gene units that vary among individuals) explained 12% of the variance in extraversion and 6% of the variance in neuroticism (Vinkhuyzen et al., 2012). Those estimates of additive gene influences are still not comparable to the estimates of substantial heritability derived from twin and family studies.

An additional explanation for the missing heritability problem might be gene × gene interaction (i.e., epistasis). Gene variants can interact in multiple ways between gene loci. Some genes can regulate the expression of other genes and may, thus, increase or decrease the effect of these genes. As a consequence, two carriers of the same gene variant within one gene locus may differ in the expression of that gene, because they differ in the gene regulation. Likewise, carriers of different gene variants may show similar gene expression by virtue of regulations that promote similar outcomes. Those epistatic gene interactions are not considered in molecular genetic studies, which exclusively focus on the additive effect of multiple gene variants. Substantial heritability estimates often stem from twin studies, which have consistently found that monozygotic (genetically identical) twins are considerably more similar to each other on personality traits than are dizygotic twins, who share approximately half the genes varying among humans, whereas studies on the similarity among other first-degree relatives (e.g., parents and offspring) or between adoptees and their biological relatives have frequently reported lower heritability estimates (Loehlin, Neiderhiser, & Reiss, 2003; Plomin, Corley, Caspi, Fulker, & DeFries, 1998). This discrepancy indicates the presence of epistatic interaction effects contributing to the phenotypic similarity between monozygotic twins and the dissimilarity between other biological relatives, because gene × gene interaction effects are only shared by genetically identical individuals. Accordingly, a recent meta-analysis on the heritability of personality traits (Vukasović & Bratko, 2015) found that twin studies yielded higher estimates (about 47%) compared to family and adoption studies (about 22%). As a consequence, epistatic gene interaction could account for about half of the genetic variance and about a fourth of individual differences in personality traits.

The meta-analysis by Vukasović and Bratko (2015) also revealed that a large portion of individual differences in personality traits cannot be explained by genetic factors. Since environmental factors shared by family members turned out to merely account for a small proportion of the variability in personality traits, environmental factors must act individually, indicating that the family environment—if it matters—would primarily amplify the differences between siblings reared together. In other words, objectively shared environmental factors may be effectively not shared (Plomin & Daniels, 1987). Similar to the missing heritability problem, however, the effects of specific measured nonshared environmental factors (different peers, parenting, schooling, life events, etc.) on personality traits have been found to be relatively small. A meta-analysis provided evidence that measured environmental differences accounted for less than 2% of the differences in the siblings' developmental outcomes (Turkheimer & Waldron, 2000). This again may have several reasons. To some degree, error of measurement can reflect estimates of environmental contributions not shared by individuals. However, environmental influences play a substantial role beyond random and nonrandom error variance (Kandler, 2012a).

Analogous to a polygenic model comprising a large number of gene variants with very small effects on personality differences, the cumulative effect of multiple events may cause detectable personality differences and changes. In line with this suggestion, aggregates of several environmental variables can account for up to, or even more than, 10% of the variance in individual attributes (Plomin & Daniels, 2011; Turkheimer & Waldron, 2000). In addition, very extreme and rare events beyond the normal range might have a detectable direct influence (Caspi et al., 2002; Löckenhoff, Terracciano, Patriciu, Eaton, & Costa, 2009).

As a parallelism to the role of epistatic gene interactions, several environmental variables may trans- and interact in multiple ways. The experience of some events may increase the probability of another event. For example, promotion in the workplace is often accompanied with financial improvements. The same event may affect some but not all individuals who experienced that event, or different experiences may have the same effect on different people depending on other effective experiences they had. For example, mother—child closeness can buffer the adverse effects of negative life events on negative emotionality (Ge, Natsuaki, Neiderhiser, & Reiss, 2009), or the critical influence of the accumulation of negative events may depend on the absence of positive experiences (Luhmann, Orth, Specht, Kandler, & Lucas, 2014).

In sum, the traditional model ascribes individual differences in personality traits to both genetic and environmental effects. While genetic factors endogenously affect individual differences via molecular biological and physiological processes, environmental factors act exogenously through social and cultural surroundings and experienced major life events. Albeit acknowledging an existent additivity of genetic and environmental factors, an interplay of genes and environment is neglected. Findings on rather low additive influences of multiple gene variants and several measured environmental factors cast doubt on whether this model can sufficiently explain the sources of individual differences in personality traits.

## The revisionist model of genotype—environment interplay

A modern revisionist view (Gottlieb, 2003; Kendler, 2001) abolishes the simple additivity of genetic and environmental factors and the idea that genetic factors can only act inside the organism, whereas environmental factors solely represent the individual's external milieu (see Fig. 8.2). Environmental factors can also unfold

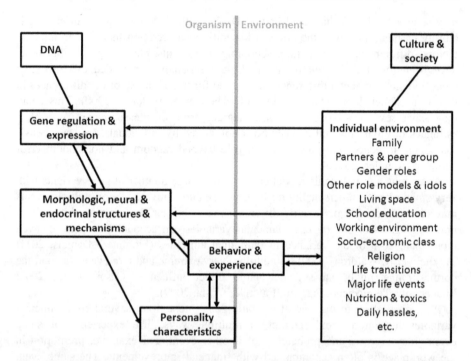

**Figure 8.2** This simplistic model of genotype−environment interplay inside and outside the organism is loosely based on Kendler's (2001) and Gottlieb's (2003) extensions of the traditional model (see Fig. 8.1). Gene regulation and expression can be affected by cytoplasmic factors, which can be triggered by neural and hormonal activity. The external environment of the organism can directly influence genetic activity or via morphological, neural, and endocrinal changes. Individual genotypes can influence the environment via specific and occasional behavior, which is more or less the individual expression of personality traits (reflecting relatively stable tendencies to specific behavior) and increases the probability of exposure to individual environments. The environment, in turn, provides opportunities of personality expression and thus the basis of personality reinforcement or even change. Environmental factors act through the filter of the individual construction of experiences which are more or less associated with personality traits. Note that the more the definition of personality includes the entire spectrum of tendencies to "behavior & experience," the more "personality characteristics" mediate the genetic and biological effects on "behavior & experience."

their impact inside the organism. For example, nutrition, drugs, toxics, mental stress, and so on can affect biological processes such as hormonal regulation and neurotransmitter release. Moreover, environmental factors can switch on and off the gene expression. This is referred to as epigenetic influences. In fact, each step in the process from gene regulation to observable behavior can be influenced by the environment. Thus the environment can affect the physiological and molecular biological bases of an organism that, in turn, can affect personality traits (Roberts & Jackson, 2008).

Conversely, genetic factors can act outside the organism via specific and occasional behavior which is more or less associated with the individual personality (i.e., more associated with one trait and less with another or vice versa). Behavior can affect an individual's external milieu by increasing or decreasing the probability of exposure to certain environments (i.e., genotype—environment correlation). In other words, differences in people's genotypes promote differing behavior, such as the diversity of the selection or evocation of situations and environments that are consistent with an individual's personality trait. For example, genetic factors may contribute to individual differences in friendliness (associated with agreeableness). More friendly behavior evokes more positive social reactions and support from others. Individual genotypes may also affect modification or avoidance of situations and environments that are inconsistent with an individuals' personality trait. For example, genetic influences may affect orderly behavior (associated with conscientiousness) such as cleaning one's own living space and trying to avoid chaos. As a consequence, each seeming environmental factor may be caused to some degree by the individual genotype navigating the behavior.

Genotype—environment correlation can account for the intriguing finding that virtually everything is heritable. This is not only true for complex behavioral traits (first law of behavior genetics) but also for experiences of individual events and social contexts, such as familial SES, parental support, and major life events. And that does not just apply to the subjective perception of the individual environment. Individual differences in reports on events, which are sufficiently salient, and objective measures of the environment have been found to be genetically influenced as well (Kendler & Baker, 2007). These genetic influences may reflect heritable personality traits, which may affect the way people experience events and the probability of exposure to certain environments by evoking social reactions, selecting and seeking out settings, changing and creating situations. For instance, the link between personality and the propensity to marry was found to be primarily mediated by genetic factors (Johnson, McGue, Krueger, & Bouchard, 2004). Further, genetic factors can account for the link between personality and divorce risk (Jockin, McGue, & Lykken, 1996). And there have been many other examples of genetic links between heritable traits and life events or other environmental measures. For example, genetic variance in personality traits accounted for about two-third of the genetic influences on individual differences in perceived parental support (Kandler, Riemann, & Kämpfe, 2009).

Beyond the genetic control of the construction of experiences and the exposure to individual environments, the impact of genes may depend on environmental factors to some degree (i.e., genotype $\times$ environment interaction; see Fig. 8.3). For instance, the genetic influences on individual differences in positive and negative emotionality at age 17 have been found to be lower for adolescents who experienced lower levels of parental regard (Krueger, South, Johnson, & Iacono, 2008). Religious upbringing appears to moderate the heritability of neuroticism (Willemsen & Boomsma, 2008), since genetic influences on individual differences in neuroticism are lower for people with religious upbringing. The other way round, genetic differences may affect variation in the sensitivity to environmental stressors.

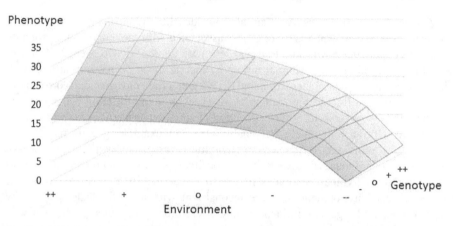

**Figure 8.3** This hypothetical reaction surface shows a positive linear effect of the genotype on the phenotype (i.e., additive genetic influences), a positive nonlinear effect of the environment on the phenotype (i.e., a strong effect of poor environments [between "-" and "--"], whereas median and rich environmental opportunities show smaller effects), and genotype × environment interaction (i.e., the genetic influence declines with decreasing environmental opportunities and is very small in the range of very poor environments).

For example, genetic differences can explain why some children who are maltreated grow up to develop antisocial behavior, whereas others do not (Caspi et al., 2002). Hence, genetic factors can interact with environments on many different levels in many different ways.

In sum, the revisionist model incorporates genetic and environmental interplay and claims that the environment can affect gene regulation through epigenetic mechanisms and genetic effects can be expressed outside the organism through behavior and the individual construction of experiences. Genetic and environmental influences are closely and multifariously interwoven to drive the development of individual differences in personality traits. Indeed, one could argue that it makes no sense to disentangle genetic from environmental variance. However, each specific pathway, through which genes and environments can contribute, is a small puzzle piece of the complex picture which portrays the etiology of personality differences and development. In particular, genotype−environment correlation and genotype × environment interaction can act in isolation or together as truly developmental mechanisms (Bleidorn, Kandler, & Caspi, 2014).

# Genotype−environment interplay in personality development

## Theory of genotype−environment effects

The genetically driven effect on the environment via individual behavior does not only explain why monozygotic twins—even when reared apart—select and create similar environmental settings or evoke similar environmental responses, but it also clarifies why monozygotic twins do that in a more similar way than dizygotic twins, and why biological siblings do that more similarly than adopted siblings (Wright, 1997). If genotypes drive experiences, then the degree to which relatives make similar experiences will depend upon their degree of genetic resemblance. Moreover, the genetic control of the construction of experiences and the exposure to certain environments can act as propulsive mechanism of personality development if the experiences within or of these environments, in turn, reinforce or even change personality.

Scarr and McCartney (1983) described this developmental mechanism in their theory of genotype→environment effects. In this theory, genes are the driving force behind the individual development. This does not imply that development is predetermined in genes or that environmental influences on the development are entirely induced by the individual genotype. Rather, it alludes to the fact that some experiences are not random, but prompted by the individual genotype. That is, the genotype affects, to some degree, which and how environments are actually experienced and what (form of) influences these experiences have on the development. According to Plomin, DeFries, and Loehlin (1977), Scarr and McCartney described three kinds of genotype→environment effects: an active, an evocative, and a passive kind.

The active kind represents the people's attraction to, avoidance and manipulation of their environments that are driven by their genetically influenced preferences or personality characteristics. These environments may in turn enhance the stability of personality traits. For example, as we know, individual differences in extraversion are partly genetically influenced. Extraverts are attracted to parties and larger social networks that may reinforce extraversion, whereas introverts and shy people are attracted to smaller social networks and rather avoid parties that maintain introversion and shyness.

The evocative kind refers to situations, in which the individuals receive responses from the social environment that are influenced by their genotypes. For instance, genetically affected low agreeableness may increase the probability to experience more major conflicts and serious disputes with others, which may consequently reinforce low agreeableness. Consistent with this example, a longitudinal twin study by Kandler, Bleidorn, Riemann, Angleitner, and Spinath (2012) found that the effect from low agreeableness to negative life events was genetically mediated and that these events negatively retroacted to agreeableness.

The passive kind reflects situations, in which the biologically related parents provide a rearing environment that is correlated both with their genotype and the genotype of their offspring. Passive genotype→environment effects can only arise in biologically related families, since biological parents provide both genes and family environments for their biological offspring. For example, individual differences in value priorities are partly genetically influenced and parents, who cherish self-direction, may provide a liberal parenting style that supports a similar priority of self-direction in their offspring. A recent study found that about 6% of reliable individual differences in the prioritization of self-direction values were attributable to passive genotype−environment correlation (Kandler, Gottschling, & Spinath, 2016).

Genotype→environment effects are expressions of the genotype in the environment via behavioral tendencies that are reflected by or associated with personality traits. The environments, in turn, can elaborate, reinforce, and sometimes change the traits. Personality change is probable in the case of negative genotype→environment effects. And there are some opportunities of environmental enrichments or deprivations and other successful interventions that provide negatively correlated experiences for the individual's genotype and, eventually, may alter relevant characteristics from those that would be predicted by the genotype. For example, a less agreeable and criminal person may evoke social exclusion and punishment. These experiences can in turn affect the development to more agreeable and less criminal behavior. Or in a more active way, people with a genetic diathesis to psychopathological symptoms may seek psychotherapeutic help that reduces their symptoms. Scarr and McCartney (1983), however, maintained that "in the usual course of development beyond early childhood, individuals select and evoke experiences that are [...] positively correlated with their own phenotypic characteristics" (p. 430). In particular, the active kind of genotype→environment effects, also described as niche-picking, refers to the selection, creation, manipulation, and avoidance of environments on the basis of people's genotypes. It is the most direct expression of the genotype in the environment. The positively correlated environments reinforce and strengthen the behavioral tendencies and personality characteristics that have initially led to them.

Genotype→environment effects represent the developmental expression of genotype−environment correlations, which describe components of individual differences. Negative genotype−environment correlation would act to decrease the genetic influence on individual differences, whereas positive genotype−environment correlation would act to increase the effect of the genotype on individual differences. If not explicitly modeled in quantitative genetic designs, the variance due to genotype−environment correlations is confounded with the variance attributable to genetic factors. Or in other words, the similarity between individuals in the exposure to environmental influences and in the reinforcement of their genetically influenced personality characteristics depends on their genetic relatedness. Thus the theory of genotype→environment effects provides an alternative explanation for the genetic variance in personality traits and for higher heritability estimates derived from twin studies compared to family and adoption studies.

Scarr (1992) proposed that the balance of the three kinds of genotype→environment effects changes across the lifespan. The influence of the passive kind declines from infancy to adolescence, whereas the importance of the active kind increases with the individuals' growing self-determination. She also claims that the general degree to which experience is influenced by individual genotypes increases across the lifespan. The rising importance of active genotype→environment effects would be expected to manifest in increasing heritability and stability of genetic influences on personality with age that, in turn, would lead to an increasing stabilization of personality differences. Although recent research provides support for the stabilization of individual differences in personality characteristics due to stabilizing genetic differences from childhood to adulthood (Briley & Tucker-Drop, 2014;

Kandler, 2012b), the heritability of personality traits in fact declines across the lifespan, while the environmental contribution increases (cf. Kandler & Papendick, Chapter 29). Therefore, the theory of genotype→environment effects describes a developmental mechanism that accounts for substantial genetic influences on individual differences in individuals' experiences and increasing stability of genetic variance in personality traits. The theory, however, cannot explain the entire picture of the patterns and sources of personality development throughout the entire lifespan.

## Genotype × environment interaction across the lifespan

Variation of genotype × environment interactions across age can also explain age-related changes in heritability as a function of changing environmental contexts with age (e.g., leaving the parental home) or as a result of ontogenetic changes (e.g., puberty). When siblings grow up in their shared familial environment, they may differently respond to the same environment provided by their parents on the basis of their differing genotypes. With increasing genetic similarity of individuals they respond in a more similar way to the shared environment and thus may become more similar. In other words, genotype × shared environment interaction would act like genetic influences and would be confounded with estimates of heritability if not explicitly modeled in behavior genetic studies (Purcell, 2002).

With the child's increasing autonomy during the first two decades of life, more unique environments (e.g., romantic relationships, own friends), as opposed to those shared with their siblings, emerge. Interactions between genetic influences and those nonshared environments will have an individually unique impact on the development. In other words, genotype × nonshared environment interactions would have the effect of making genetically related individuals less similar, regardless of their genetic relatedness, and would be confounded with estimates of individual environmental effects not shared with family members if not explicitly modeled in behavior genetic studies (Purcell, 2002).

The shift from the importance of genotype × shared environment interactions early in life to the importance of genotype × nonshared environment interactions with increasing maturation can explain larger estimates of heritability in childhood and the decrease of heritability across the lifespan (Briley & Tucker-Drop, 2014). Moreover, as the variance due to genotype × nonshared environment interactions is confounded with variance attributable to individual environmental influences, the cumulative influences of genotype × nonshared environment interactions across the lifespan would result in an increasing variance component due to environmental influences not shared by individuals.

## The epigenetic drift over time

Epigenetic mechanisms may potentially portray a further explanation for the increasing environmental differences among individuals and between siblings across the lifespan. The environmentally triggered differences in gene expression (i.e., epigenetic differences inside the organism) between people with the same genotype (e.g., monozygotic twins) may appear as differences due to environmental influences not shared by twins. If those epigenetic effects accumulate within an individual's lifetime, then increases in (environmental) differences between genetically identical individuals over the lifespan may be attributable to an epigenetic drift (Kandler & Bleidorn, 2015).

In line with the epigenetic drift hypothesis, Fraga et al. (2005) reported that twins are epigenetically indistinguishable during the early years of life. However, they found that older monozygotic twins exhibited substantial epigenetic differences (e.g., in their overall content and genomic distribution of 5-methylcytosine DNA and histone acetylation), affecting their gene expression portrait. Epigenomic profiling of monozygotic as well as dizygotic twin pairs across the lifespan is helpful to quantify the developmental consequences of an epigenetic drift (Kaminsky et al., 2008, 2009). Future longitudinal epigenetically informative twin studies on personality development will provide more insight into the role of cumulative environmental manifestations inside the organism for increasing individual differences in complex personality traits over time.

## Conclusion

That genetic differences account for personality differences is no longer controversial. In line with the three laws of behavior genetics, studies have found that about 50% of individual differences in personality traits are genetically influenced. The remaining variance is primarily due to individual environmental influences not shared by family members. However, as we have shown, this does not mean that 50% of personality traits are caused by genes and that the other 50% are caused by the environment. Genetic and environmental sources unfold their impact through many different pathways—from the biological micro to the sociological macro (McAdams, 2015). The influences of genes and environments are difficult to disentangle, because they trans- and interact in many complex ways. Nevertheless, the analysis of the net effects of genetic and environmental sources provides interesting insights into their roles for personality development. The proportions of genetic and environmental components in personality traits change across the lifespan. Heritability steadily declines as people get older, whereas environmental influences mount.

Whereas genes are located inside the organic cell, they can also unfold their influence outside the organism. Similarly, environmental influences can also act under the skin, affecting hormonal regulation, neurotransmitter release, or DNA methylation. Genotypes can drive experiences. People select and create their niches, they construct their own experiences, and they influence the course of their development through genetically driven choices across time. These experiences and choices, however, depend on the access to or the limitation of opportunities afforded by the environment and people are differently sensitive to same environments depending upon their genotypes. Personality is a product of the genetic makeup and experiences, which are individually filtered and constructed from the opportunities provided by the environment (Scarr, 1993). A more plausible model of genetic and environmental sources of personality differences and development would consider genotype—environment interplays as propulsive mechanisms of personality development. In this sense, genetic variance in personality traits primarily reflects genotype—environment correlations, and individual environmental variance mainly mirrors genotype × environment interactions. Personality development is an intriguingly complex and multilevel affair that we can only understand if we gain more insight into how genetic and environmental sources work together on many different levels in dynamic, synergetic, and interdependent ways.

# Funding

The authors received support from the Deutsche Forschungsgemeinschaft KA 4088/2-1.

# References

Bleidorn, W., Kandler, C., & Caspi, A. (2014). The behavioural genetics of personality development in adulthood—Classic, contemporary, and future trends. *European Journal of Personality*, *28*, 244—255.

Borkenau, P., Riemann, R., Angleitner, A., & Spinath, F. (2001). Genetic and environmental influences on observed personality: Evidence from the German observational study of adult twins. *Journal of Personality and Social Psychology*, *80*, 655—668.

Bouchard, T. J., Jr. (2004). Genetic influence on human psychological traits: A survey. *Current Directions in Psychological Science*, *13*, 148—151.

Briley, D., & Tucker-Drop, E. M. (2014). Genetic and environmental continuity in personality development: A meta-analysis. *Psychological Bulletin*, *140*, 1303—1331.

Caspi, A., McClay, J., Moffitt, T. E., Mill, J., Martin, J., Craig, I. W., ... Poulton, R. (2002). Role of genotype in the cycle of violence in maltreated children. *Science*, *297*, 851—854.

Fraga, M. F., Ballestar, E., Paz, M. F., Ropero, S., Setien, F., Ballestar, M. L., ... Esteller, M. (2005). Epigenetic differences arise during the lifetime of monozygotic twins. *PNAS*, *106*, 10604—10609.

Ge, X., Natsuaki, M. N., Neiderhiser, J. M., & Reiss, D. (2009). The longitudinal effects of stressful life events on adolescent depression are buffered by parent-child closeness. *Development and Psychopathology*, *21*, 621—635.

Gottlieb, G. (2003). On making behavioral genetics truly developmental. *Human Development*, *46*, 337—355.

Jockin, V., McGue, M., & Lykken, D. T. (1996). Personality and divorce: A genetic analysis. *Journal of Personality and Social Psychology*, *71*, 288—299.

Johnson, A. M., Vernon, P. A., & Feiler, A. R. (2008). Behavioral genetic studies of personality: An introduction and review of the results of 50+ years of research. In G. J. Boyle, G. Matthews, & D. H. Saklofske (Eds.), *The Sage handbook of personality theory and assessment. Vol. 1: Personality theories and models* (pp. 145–173). London, England: Sage.

Johnson, W., McGue, M., Krueger, R. F., & Bouchard, T. J., Jr. (2004). Marriage and personality: A genetic analysis. *Journal of Personality and Social Psychology, 86*, 285–294.

Kaminsky, Z. A., Petronis, A., Wang, S.-C., Levine, B., Ghaffar, O., Floden, D., & Feinstein, A. (2008). Epigenetics of personality traits: An illustrative study of identical twins discordant for risk-taking behavior. *Twin Research and Human Genetics, 11*, 1–11.

Kaminsky, Z. A., Tang, T., Wang, S.-C., Ptak, C., Oh, G. H. T., Wong, A. H. C., ... Petronis, A. (2009). DNA methylation profiles in monozygotic and dizygotic twins. *Nature Genetics, 41*, 240–245.

Kandler, C. (2012a). Knowing your personality is knowing its nature: The role of information accuracy of peer assessments for heritability estimates of temperamental and personality traits. *Personality and Individual Differences, 53*, 387–392.

Kandler, C. (2012b). Nature and nurture in personality development: The case of neuroticism and extraversion. *Current Directions in Psychological Science, 21*, 290–296.

Kandler, C., & Bleidorn, W. (2015). Personality differences and development: Genetic and environmental contributions. In J. D. Wright (Ed.), *International Encyclopedia of the Social & Behavioral Sciences* (2nd ed., Vol. 17). Oxford: Elsevier.

Kandler, C., Bleidorn, W., & Riemann, R. (2012). Left or right? Sources of political orientation: The roles of genetic factors, cultural transmission, assortative mating, and personality. *Journal of Personality and Social Psychology, 102*, 633–645.

Kandler, C., Bleidorn, W., Riemann, R., Angleitner, A., & Spinath, F. M. (2011). The genetic links between the big five personality traits and general interest domains. *Personality and Social Psychology Bulletin, 37*, 1633–1643.

Kandler, C., Bleidorn, W., Riemann, R., Angleitner, A., & Spinath, F. M. (2012). Life events as environmental states and genetic traits and the role of personality: A longitudinal twin study. *Behavior Genetics, 42*, 57–72.

Kandler, C., Gottschling, J., & Spinath, F. M. (2016). Genetic and environmental parent child transmission of value orientations: An extended twin family study. *Child Development, 87*, 270–284.

Kandler, C., Riemann, R., & Kämpfe, N. (2009). Genetic and environmental mediation between measures of personality and family environment in twins reared together. *Behavior Genetics, 39*, 24–35.

Kandler, C., Zimmermann, J., & McAdams, D. P. (2014). Core and surface characteristics for the description and theory of personality differences and development. *European Journal of Personality, 28*, 231–243.

Kendler, K. S. (2001). Twin studies of psychiatric illness: An update. *Archives of Genetic Psychiatry, 58*, 1005–1014.

Kendler, K. S., & Baker, J. H. (2007). Genetic influences on measures of the environment: A systematic review. *Psychological Medicine, 37*, 615–626.

Krueger, R. F., South, S., Johnson, W., & Iacono, W. G. (2008). The heritability of personality is not always 50%: Gene–environment interactions and correlations between personality and parenting. *Journal of Personality, 76*, 1485–1522.

Löckenhoff, C. E., Terracciano, A., Patriciu, N. S., Eaton, W. W., & Costa, P. T., Jr. (2009). Self-reported extremely adverse life events and longitudinal changes in five-factor model personality traits in an urban sample. *Journal of Traumatic Stress, 22*, 53–59.

Loehlin, J. C., Neiderhiser, J. M., & Reiss, D. (2003). The behavior genetics of personality and the NEAD study. *Journal of Research in Personality, 37*, 373–387.

Luhmann, M., Orth, U., Specht, J., Kandler, C., & Lucas, R. E. (2014). Studying changes in life circumstances and personality: It's about time. *European Journal of Personality, 28*, 256−266.

McAdams, D. P. (2015). *The art and science of personality development.* New York, NY: Guilford.

Plomin, R. (2013). Child development and molecular genetics: 14 years later. *Child Development, 84*, 104−120.

Plomin, R., & Daniels, D. (1987). Why are children in the same family so different from one another? *Behavioral and Brain Sciences, 10*, 1−60.

Plomin, R., & Daniels, D. (2011). Why are children in the same family so different from one another? *International Journal of Epidemiology, 40*, 563−582.

Plomin, R., Corley, R., Caspi, A., Fulker, D. W., & DeFries, J. (1998). Adoption results for self-reported personality: Evidence for nonadditive genetic effects? *Journal of Personality and Social Psychology, 75*, 211−218.

Plomin, R., DeFries, J. C., & Loehlin, J. C. (1977). Genotype−environment interaction and correlation in the analysis of human behavior. *Psychological Bulletin, 84*, 309−322.

Polderman, T. J. C., Benyamin, B., De Leeuw, C. A., Sullivan, P. F., Van Bochoven, A., ... Posthuma, D. (2015). Meta-analysis of the heritability of human traits based on fifty years of twin studies. *Nature Genetics, 47*, 702−709.

Purcell, S. (2002). Variance components models for gene−environment interaction in twin analysis. *Twin Research and Human Genetics, 5*, 554−571.

Roberts, B. W., & Jackson, J. J. (2008). Sociogenomic personality psychology. *Journal of Personality, 76*, 1523−1544.

Scarr, S. (1992). Developmental theories for the 1990s: Development and individual differences. *Child Development, 63*, 1−19.

Scarr, S. (1993). Biological and cultural diversity: The legacy of Darwin for development. *Child Development, 64*, 1333−1353.

Scarr, S., & McCartney, K. (1983). How people make their own environments: A theory of genotype→environment effects. *Child Development, 54*, 424−435.

Terracciano, A., Sanna, S., Uda, M., Deiana, B., Usala, G., Busonero, F., ... Costa, P. T., Jr. (2010). Genome-wide association scan for five major dimensions of personality. *Molecular Psychiatry, 15*, 647−656.

Turkheimer, E. (2000). Three laws of behavior genetics and what they mean. *Current Directions in Psychological Science, 9*, 160−164.

Turkheimer, E., & Waldron, M. (2000). Nonshared environment: a theoretical, methodological, and quantitative review. *Psychological Bulletin, 126*, 78−108.

Vinkhuyzen, A. A. E., Pedersen, N. L., Yang, J., Lee, S. H., Magnusson, P. K. E., Iacono, W. G., ... Wray, N. R. (2012). Common SNPs explain some of the variation in the personality dimensions of neuroticism and extraversion. *Translational Psychiatry, 2*, e102.

Vukasović, T., & Bratko, D. (2015). Heritability of personality: A meta-analysis of behavior genetic studies. *Psychological Bulletin, 141*, 769−785.

Willemsen, G., & Boomsma, D. I. (2008). Religious upbringing and neuroticism in Dutch twin families. *Twin Research and Human Genetics, 10*, 327−333.

Wright, L. (1997). *Twins: And what they tell us about who we are.* New York, NY: Wiley.

# Set-Point Theory and personality development: Reconciliation of a paradox

*Johan Ormel[1], Michael VonKorff[2], Bertus F. Jeronimus[1], and Harriëtte Riese[1]*
[1]University Medical Center Groningen, University of Groningen, Groningen, The Netherlands, [2]Group Health Research Institute, Group Health Cooperative, Seattle, WA, United States

## Personality: Developmental perspectives

Personality is defined as enduring differences between individuals in thoughts, feelings, and behaviors that are not situation-specific (Specht, 2015). Personality reflects the often unconscious, reflexive ways in which people respond to environmental cues (Allport & Odbert, 1936; Magidson, Roberts, Collado-Rodriguez, & Lejuez, 2014). Conventionally five high-order personality characteristics are identified (the "Big Five"): extraversion, neuroticism, agreeableness, conscientiousness, and openness to experience (Kotov, Gamez, Schmidt, & Watson, 2010). Personality is typically assessed by self-report questionnaire or interview (John, Robins, & Pervin, 2008) using items with nonspecific descriptors of frequency, intensity, and duration. For example, in the NEO-PI-3 (McCrae, Costa, Paul, & Martin, 2005) neuroticism is assessed with items like "I often worry about things that might happen" or "sometimes I feel completely worthless." Designed to capture the unique ways in which people think, feel, and interact with others, these questionnaires indicate an individual's general level on a particular personality trait.

### Developmental models

A popular developmental model is McCrae and Costa's Five-Factor Theory (FFT) of personality traits. It posits that personality traits follow a common life course trajectory, viz. traits emerge early in life, reach maturity in young adulthood, followed by a gradual change in response to age-related brain maturation, and changes in gene expression (McCrae & Costa, 2003; McCrae, 2010). However, longitudinal evidence indicates that people can differ substantially in these trajectories of personality development and change across the lifespan (Luhmann, Orth, Specht, Kandler, & Lucas, 2014; Roberts & DelVecchio, 2000; Roberts, Walton, & Viechtbauer, 2006).

Personality Development Across the Lifespan. DOI: http://dx.doi.org/10.1016/B978-0-12-804674-6.00009-0

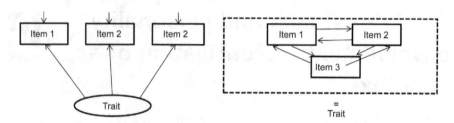

**Figure 9.1** Schematic presentation of two models of traits: the latent factor model (left) and the dynamic system (or network) model (right).

Nowadays theorists convene that personality trait changes are driven by both genes and experiences (Plomin, DeFries, & Loehlin, 1977; Scarr & McCartney, 1983), but the exact processes underlying adult personality development remain controversial (Cramer et al., 2012b; Roberts, Wood, & Caspi, 2008; Specht et al., 2014). Several theories stress the significance of life experiences in personality stability and change (Jeronimus, Riese, Sanderman, & Ormel, 2014). The best known is the neosocioanalytic theory or social investment principle, which emphasizes the impact of social roles on personality, and posits that environmentally driven personality changes may occur throughout life (Roberts & Wood, 2006, Roberts, Wood, & Smith, 2005).

Another perspective emphasizing environmental influences is the set-point (or dynamic equilibrium) model of traits, recently proposed by Ormel, Riese, and Rosmalen (2012; but see also Fleeson & Gallagher, 2009; Fraley & Roberts, 2005; Luhmann et al., 2014). According to this perspective, personality traits have a person-specific set-point around which trait levels fluctuate in response to life experiences. Thus personality levels can temporarily be changed by life experiences, but eventually people return to their characteristic set-point level. Importantly, major life events or enduring changes in social circumstances may also change the set-point of personality traits for long periods of time or even permanently.

Another alternative, proposed by Cramer et al. (2012b), conceives personality as a system (or network) of affective, cognitive, and behavioral elements. Rather than a shared underlying factor producing covariance among these elements (as assumed in the latent factor model of personality traits), the network model suggests that these elements are causally interdependent (see Fig. 9.1). Personality dimensions "emerge out of the connectivity structure that exists between the various components of personality" (Cramer et al., 2012a, p. 414). The components are jointly influenced by genetic and environmental forces, and therefore develop synchronously. In factor analysis, the interconnectedness "produces" the latent factors.

## Personality development and life experiences

That life experiences can be followed by small but meaningful changes in personality is well established (Jeronimus et al., 2014; Luhmann et al., 2014;

Riese et al., 2014; Specht, Egloff, & Schmukle, 2011; Sutin, Costa, Wethington, & Eaton, 2010). Changes in personality are also observed subsequent to age-related developmental role transitions (Bleidorn et al., 2013; Lodi-Smith & Roberts, 2007; Roberts & Mroczek, 2008). For example, Specht et al. (2011) found that individuals who got married became more introverted while those who separated from a poor marriage became more agreeable and conscientious. Men, but not women, became more open after separation. Conscientiousness declined after having a baby and after retirement, whereas it increased after starting a first job. After death of a spouse, conscientiousness declined among women whereas it increased among men. Marriage, remarriage, and experiencing satisfying and engaging employment are all associated with decreases in neuroticism. In contrast, conflict, poor relationship quality, and chronic or repeated unemployment have been found to associate with increases in neuroticism (Lucas, Clark, Georgellis, & Diener, 2004; Lüdtke, Trautwein, & Husemann, 2009; Robins, Caspi, & Moffitt, 2000). Exposure to personal illness or injury reduced concordance of neuroticism among monozygotic twins (Middeldorp, Cath, Beem, Willemsen, & Boomsma, 2008). Jeronimus and colleagues (2013, 2014) found small but persistent decreases in neuroticism after positive life events.

## Subjective well-being and set-point theory

Subjective Well-Being (SWB) is a well-studied construct that refers to how people feel and think about their lives (Diener, 1984). Popular measures of SWB include items like: "How satisfied are you with your life as a whole?" The SWB construct involves a hybrid of affective judgments (how do I usually feel) and cognitive assessments of satisfaction with life and its main domains (such as work and relationships). There is an important distinction between the feelings people experience and the judgments they make about their lives. In SWB research, happiness, life satisfaction, and well-being are often conceptualized as enduring traits (Cummins, 2015; Davern, Cummins, & Stokes, 2007). People asked to assess happiness or life satisfaction tend to use their moods as information (Cummins, 2015), in a process that Kahneman (2011) calls the "affect heuristic." It is not surprising, then, that SWB is highly correlated with neuroticism, extraversion, and, although less, conscientiousness (DeNeve & Cooper, 1998; Steel, Schmidt, & Shultz, 2008; Weiss, Bates, & Luciano, 2008).

Like personality traits, SWB shows substantial continuity over time (Lucas & Donnellan, 2007). Long-term studies of SWB have yielded data that permit evaluation of key hypotheses about the development of SWB and its determinants. While research on dynamic changes in personality traits is limited, there are relevant theoretical constructs and empirical studies pertaining to SWB that can help evaluate the stable and changing components of personality traits. Stability may be due to genetic factors and other enduring influences, while change may be influenced by the social environment and by shifts in a person's physical or psychological health. Research has not evaluated these dynamic processes for personality per se, but it has for SWB. An important theoretical model that explains the relationship between the stability and change of SWB is the set-point theory.

## History of set-point theory

Set-point theory has its roots in the concept of physiological homeostasis. In Canon's (1932) classic essay, "The Wisdom of the Body," set-point refers to steady states of the body that are actively maintained by corrective physiological and behavioral mechanisms (also referred to as negative feedback loops). This active defense mechanism or dynamic compensation, generates a degree of stability in the factor it regulates, such as blood pressure, body temperature, blood glucose level, or weight (Keesey & Powley, 1986). Before that, psychologists Wundt and James had transformed the then-dominant humor theory of temperament into a concept of dimensional psychological traits, a theory that incorporated the principle of a fixed internal milieu: a set-point with homeostasis (Dumont, 2010; Jeronimus, 2015). The key feature of a set-point is that it defies change via compensatory mechanisms that regulate short-term fluctuations caused by internal or external events back to their typical state (i.e., set-point). Importantly, physiological set-points (e.g., blood pressure) often change with age.

Set-point theory played a prominent role in SWB research over the past 40 years because this idea of adaptation to changing environments could explain counterintuitive properties of SWB. For example, that gains in health, income, and relationships only had temporary effects on SWB. This kind of adaptive processes also explained the observation that people with substantial resources are, on average, not much happier than those with limited resources. Original SWB theories became therefore founded on the idea that people's levels of SWB change temporarily in anticipation and response to life experiences, but do not permanently change (Brickman, Coates, & Janoffbulman, 1978). This led some to conclude that "trying to be happier [may be] as futile as trying to be taller" (Lykken & Tellegen, 1996, p. 189).

Cummins (2010, 2015) explicitly argued that a set of psychological processes actively control and maintain SWB in a manner analogous to the homeostatic maintenance of blood pressure or body temperature. These homeostatic processes apply particularly to the affective component of SWB. The dynamic equilibrium theory of SWB posits that this continuity in SWB is based on personality, especially neuroticism and extraversion, whereas change is attributed to life experiences (Headey & Wearing, 1989; Headey, 2006).

## Recent revisions of set-point theory for SWB

The results from major longitudinal panel studies led to at least six significant revisions in SWB set-point theory (Diener, Lucas, & Scollon, 2006; Headey, 2006,

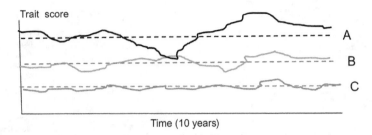

**Figure 9.2** Trajectories of SWB of three individuals (A, B, C) with person-specific set-points and susceptibilities.

2010; Luhmann, Hofmann, Eid, & Lucas, 2012) that merit discussion when implementing a set-point theory for personality traits:

1. *Personal set-point.* Person-specific levels of SWB can be accurately predicted from personality traits. Fig. 9.2 illustrates three trajectories of SWB with personalized individual set-points.
2. *Persistent negativity.* The major components of SWB differ in terms of their set-point and stability, most saliently that "negative affect" is more stable over increasing time intervals than "positive affect" or "life satisfaction."
3. *Cultural differences.* SWB levels and composition differ substantially between countries, partly due to economic, social, and political characteristics (Diener & Diener, 1995; Minkov, 2009).
4. *Persistent changes in SWB.* About 15−30% of the population shows long-lasting changes in SWB following life experiences and typically do not return to their previous baseline levels within 3−5 years (Anusic, Yap, & Lucas, 2014; Luhmann et al., 2012). This holds true in particular for major negative experiences such as disability, widowhood, unemployment, or divorce.
5. *Differences in adaptability.* Initially SWB theorists assumed that people adapted in similar ways. For example, Diener et al. (2006, p. 310) observed that, "If adaptation results from automatic and inevitable homeostatic processes, then all individuals should return to neutrality or at least to their own unique baseline." However, studies observed significant individual differences in the rate and extent of adaptation after experiencing "objectively" similar life events (see Fig. 9.2).
6. *Differences in susceptibility.* Trait stability is partly driven by the tendency of people to repeatedly experience specific events (cf. corresponsive principle). So, life experiences may not only cause disequilibrium in SWB, but personality−environment correlations may also maintain stability (Headey & Wearing, 1989; Jeronimus et al., 2014; Ormel & Schaufeli, 1991). Persistent within-subject changes in SWB may be partially explained by individual differences in susceptibility to life experiences (see Fig. 9.3). For example, people who combine high extraversion with low neuroticism levels may increase in SWB whereas introverted but highly neurotic people may tend to decrease in SWB.

## Personality psychology and set-point theory

Despite the popularity of set-point theory in the psychology of SWB, it has only occasionally been applied in personality psychology (Costa & McCrae, 1980;

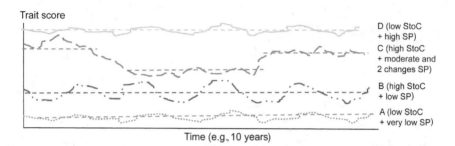

Time (e.g., 10 years)

**Figure 9.3** Four different within-subject trajectories of personality trait scores. *Note*: Capital letters A, B, C, and D refer to each of the individuals; StoC = sensitivity to context; SP = set-point.

Jeronimus et al., 2013; Lykken & Tellegen, 1996; Lykken, 2007; Ormel et al., 2013; Vachon & Krueger, 2015). For example, Williams (1993) proposed a set-point hypothesis to explain the stability of personality traits: "In this set-point hypothesis, psychological function is treated as having a substantial basis in physiology with a specified level and a surrounding 'bandwidth' of typical behavior for a given individual [...] it is necessary to determine whether a prevailing personality pattern, stable or otherwise, is actively defended by appropriate behavioral or psychological adjustments" (p. 52).

Also the network perspective on personality traits describes people as functioning within a relatively fixed region of a potentially large behavioral space, resulting in stable states. The causally interconnected affective, cognitive, and behavioral elements are "in relative equilibrium with themselves and their environments" (Cramer et al., 2012a, p. 416), suggesting sort of trait set-point. In the network perspective, life experiences may support trait stability (as they influence the total complex of elements) but can also induce personality change as the system finds an alternative stable state (see "Alternative Explanations for Homeostatic Stable States" section).

Provided that SWB may be a manifestation of underlying personality traits, as assumed in set-point theory, it seems timely to consider whether set-point theory can help explain stability and change in personality traits over the lifespan.

## Immutable, experience-dependent, and mixed set-point models

In considering the application of set-point theory to research on stability and change of personality traits, it is useful to differentiate three set-point models (Ormel & Rijsdijk, 2000; Ormel et al., 2012): (1) *the immutable set-point model*; (2) *the experience-dependent set-point model*; and (3) *the mixed set-point model*. Fig. 9.4 depicts these three models. The time scale describing stability and change in these models is measured in years, rather than days or weeks.

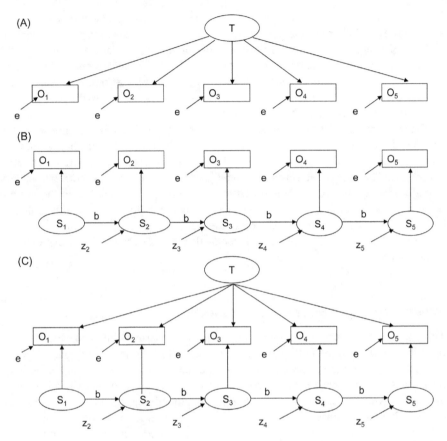

**Figure 9.4** (A) Immutable set-point model. *Note*: T = latent trait factor; $O_i$ = observed trait scores at 5 waves. (B) Experience-dependent set-point model. *Note*: $O_i$ = observed trait scores at 5 waves; $S_i$ = latent changing component; $z_i$ = influence of unobserved determinants of change; b (if intervals are equal, these will typically be equal as well); e = time-specific and measurement error variance. (C) Mixed set-point model. *Note*: T = latent trait factor; $O_i$ = observed trait scores at 5 waves; $S_i$ = latent changing component; e = measurement error variance; $z_i$ = influence of unobserved determinants of change in changing component; b = autoregression coefficient (if intervals are equal, these will typically be equal as well).

## Immutable set-point model

The immutable set-point model posits that individual set-points of personality traits are "set like plaster" (James, 1890). This notion of an immutable person-characteristic set-point of personality traits is compatible with the "basic tendencies" in Costa and McCrae's classical (FFT) trait model (1990; McCrae, 2010), being both internally determined and largely independent of environmental influences. In this model, homeostatic forces keep an individual's trait set-point constant over time. Deviations from the set-point, which may be due to life experiences, are assumed to be temporal, and levels eventually return to the set-point. Thus the immutable set-point model fits both the FFT and genotype—environment theory of personality development.

The "environment perspectives" of personality development (e.g., neo-socioanalytic model) are incompatible with an immutable set-point model, which permits only temporary experience-driven changes. Also the "network perspective" is definitely inconsistent with the immutable set-point model.

The statistical model that corresponds with the immutable set-point model is the common factor model, which asserts that items on a trait scale and their summary scores correlate over time because of underlying latent traits, which are essentially immutable. The immutable set-point model predicts that test—retest correlations are virtually independent of the length of time between assessments. While the notion of an immutable set-point fits the evidence of high stability of personality traits, it is inconsistent with a large body of evidence showing a gradual but persistent decline in the differential stability of personality traits over time and experience-driven change.

## Experience-dependent set-point model

The experience-dependent set-point model posits that set-points can change over the lifespan when impelled by life experiences with long-term behavioral conse-quences. The experience-dependent model assumes that these consequences can result in set-point change (see person C in Fig. 9.3) through three mechanisms, viz. cognitive, biological, and environmental embedding. Cognitive embedding occurs when such consequences lead to persistent alterations in beliefs about the self and others and changes in the approach to appraising and coping with stress-ful events (Laceulle, Jeronimus, Van Aken, & Ormel, 2015; Ormel & Rijsdijk, 2000). An example of biological embedding is when environmental factors trigger chemic changes that activate or silence genes via epigenetic processes such as DNA methylation and chromatin remodeling (Van der Knaap et al., 2015; Weaver et al., 2004; Zhang & Meaney, 2010). Such epigenetic changes occur most frequently early in life but continue to occur throughout the lifespan (Fraga et al., 2005; Kanherkar, Bhatia-Dey, & Csoka, 2014). Biological embedding may follow cognitive embedding if cognitive alterations bring about persistent changes in the regulatory neurophysiological systems, e.g., via epigenetic processes (McEwen, 2012; Zhang & Meaney, 2010). Environmental embedding occurs when changes in behavioral repertoires become maintained by correspondingly changed environments.

The statistical model that corresponds with environmentally dependent set-points is the autoregressive (or simplex) model, which asserts ongoing cumulative differ-ential change. That is, traits change continuously at a very slow rate. The autore-gressive model predicts that test—retest correlations decrease gradually over time, theoretically declining toward a correlation of zero (Ormel & Rijsdijk, 2000; Roberts & Jackson, 2008; Roberts & Mroczek, 2008).

## Mixed set-point model

The mixed set-point model combines the previous two models and basically extends on the experience-dependent set-point model by incorporating features of an immutable set-point. The mixed model seeks to differentiate variation in personality traits into a stable trait component (T, in Fig. 9.4C) and an in time varying component (Si). In contrast to the experience-dependent model, the mixed model allows for two possibilities. The first is that some people have (virtually) immutable set-points but that other people's set-points change. The second possibility is that the trait set-point is complex, and has partly an immutable component and partly a changing component. Thus changes in the set-point itself are possible in the mixed model, for example, in response to long-term difficulties and marked altered life circumstances. In contrast to the immutable set-point model, the mixed set-point model assumes that differential stability correlations will fall with time but, due to the enduring influence of stable personality components, will never reach zero, something which is possible with the experience-dependent model.

## Between-subject and within-subject models

These set-point models have been used primarily to analyze between-subject differences and cannot be directly generalized to understand within-subject changes (Barlow & Nock, 2009; Molenaar, 2008; Van der Krieke et al., 2015). The mixed model may provide a better fit to longitudinal data compared to either the immutable or experience-dependent set-point models, because at the population level, it is more flexible for modeling within-subject change. New statistical approaches have been developed to formally test the differences in person-specific developmental trajectories (Borsboom et al., 2016).

It remains complex to account for within-subject changes in analyses of stability and change in personality traits. Fig. 9.3 displays the hypothetical development of a personality trait during adulthood in four individuals who differ in terms of both their trait set-point and sensitivity to context. The trait set-point is highest for D (blue), followed by C (purple), B (red), and then A (green). Low sensitivity to context is characteristic of A and D. High sensitivity to context is characteristic of B and C, evident as relatively low and high amplitudes of deviation from the set-point, respectively. If individuals differ in sensitivity to context the most sensitive may experience enduring changes in personality in response to major life experiences and long-term difficulties (Boyce & Ellis, 2005). Individuals with low sensitivity to context may resist the effects of environmental events on personality traits; person A and D respond more or less the same way to the same events. In addition, individual C is exposed to far-reaching positive and negative experiences which change C's set-point twice.

# Theories to explain set-point change

Two theories may help explain the association between personality trait change and life experiences or (age-graded) role transitions: the social investment principle and the social production function (SPF) theory, which are outlined later. Roberts et al. (2005) introduced the social investment principle explicitly to explain why role transitions and associated life events can change personality. The social production theory, in contrast, has been developed to explain individual differences in SWB, especially the impact of life experiences on SWB (Ormel, Lindenberg, Steverink, & Vonkorff, 1997). Note that neither of these theories preclude genetic effects on personality change; rather, they address in particular the transactional and random factors that contribute to personality development.

## Social investment principle

According to the social investment principle, people build identities through commitments to age-graded social roles, such as work, marriage, family, and community. Each role comes with a set of expectations and contingencies that create a reward structure that promotes becoming more socially dominant, agreeable, and conscientious, and less neurotic. These expectations and contingencies induce and maintain altered behavior patterns and these, in turn, may change personality traits in a bottom-up fashion. A growing body of evidence supports the social investment principle (Bleidorn et al., 2013; Hudson & Roberts, 2016). However, the evidence is largely limited to crude, epidemiological measures of role experiences as presented above, rather than psychological experiences. Thus it is still necessary to demonstrate that role expectations drive personality development and not vice versa.

## Social production function theory

Whereas the social investment principle seems particularly suited to understand *how* role transitions may change personality traits, SPF theory might help explain *why* particular experiences have long-term behavioral consequences that might, in turn, alter self-perception and hence personality. In addition, SPF theory seems better suited to clarify non-normative personality change compared to the social investment principle. However, the evidence supporting the utility of SPF theory in understanding personality development is lacking and SPF remained limited to SWB. SPF theory holds that people seek physical and social well-being (Lindenberg, 1996; Ormel et al., 1999; Steverink, Lindenberg, & Ormel, 1998), which they achieve through behaviors that enhance status, affection, and behavioral confirmation. Physical well-being is achieved by behaviors that are stimulating or activating, and that enhance physical comfort. Over an adult's lifespan, having work, being happily married, and having good friends and family gives a person status, behavioral confirmation, affection, and comfort.

The SPF perspective suggests that the initial magnitude and persistence of personality change is likely to depend on how the consequences of altered life circumstances affect one's ability to achieve physical and social well-being. For example, a harmonious intimate relationship provides opportunities for activities that produce comfort, affection, and behavioral confirmation. Moreover, SPF theory holds that enduring impairments of the resources and ability to produce physical or social well-being should have unfavorable effects on personality development. Empirical evidence regarding how social production influences personality comes entirely from research linking changes in SWB to major life events. Therefore, it is unclear what effects social circumstances have on traits other than those that are associated with SWB (neuroticism, extraversion, and, to a lesser extent, conscientiousness).

## Life events and depression

Research into the effects of life events and major role transitions on personality development is still limited, especially regarding SPF theory. This is in contrast to the enormous amount of research into the relationship between life events and psychological states, especially depression. Core symptoms of major depressive disorder are depressed mood and loss of interest that last for at least 2 weeks. Depression is strongly associated with low levels of SWB and high neuroticism.

Importantly, the onset and remission of major depressive illnesses are often accompanied by alterations in neuroticism, extraversion, and conscientiousness. Often these alterations are temporary, in that they wax and wane in parallel with depression status (Ormel, Oldehinkel, Nolen, & Vollebergh, 2004). Although limited in quantity, some recent research indicates that psychotherapeutic interventions are associated with more persistent personality change (Clark, Vittengl, Kraft, & Jarrett, 2003; De Fruyt, Van Leeuwen, Bagby, Rolland, & Rouillon, 2006; Tang et al., 2009). For instance, Tang and colleagues found that the combination of cognitive therapy and antidepressant medication not only associated with remission of depression but reduced neuroticism as well. Importantly, the improvements in depression seemed driven by decreases in neuroticism. De Fruyt et al. (2006), investigating a similar combined treatment, reported more extraversion, openness to experience, agreeableness, conscientiousness, and substantially less neuroticism after treatment. Therefore, life events involved in the onset and remission of major depressive episodes may yield important insights into what kind of experiences might change personality traits.

Brown and Harris and their colleagues have contributed much to our insights into the life events that can induce depressive illness and significant decreases in SWB. These events include loss events, humiliating events, and entrapment events (Brown, Harris, & Hepworth, 1995). They also explored the specific experiences that are likely to reduce depression and enhance SWB, including anchoring, a fresh start, and events that neutralize a long-term environmental difficulty (Brown, Lemyre, & Bifulco, 1992). Loss includes not only loss of a person but also loss of a social role (becoming unemployed). Most loss events involve core roles and relationships, with a substantial proportion linked to events likely to produce a sense of defeat. Entrapment events occur in the context of a prolonged and marked difficulty, emphasizing that the difficulty may last much longer than initially thought. Anchoring events involved increased security, increased hope, or amelioration of a difficulty. It would be interesting to determine whether loss, humiliation, or entrapment events produce enduring negative changes in personality, and whether anchoring, fresh start, and difficulty-neutralizing events yield enduring positive changes in personality.

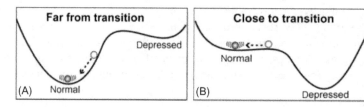

**Figure 9.5** Ball-in-a-cup diagram (A vs B). *Note*: This example assumes two stable states normal and depressed. The stability of a healthy person may become more fragile close to a transition toward depression, which can intuitively be understood from these two ball-in-a-cup diagram.
*Source:* With permission from Van de Leemput, I. A., Wichers, M., Cramer, A. O. J., Borsboom, D., Tuerlinckx, F.,Kuppens, P., . . . Scheffer, M. (2014). Critical slowing down as early warning for theonset and termination of depression. PNAS, doi:10.1073/pnas.1312114110, p. 88.

### Alternative explanations for homeostatic stable states

Cramer et al. (2012aand 2012b) have proposed that dynamic systems have alternative homeostatic stable states, also called "dynamic regimes" (Scheffer et al., 2009) or "mechanistic property clusters" (Kendler, Zachar, & Craver, 2011). Marked transitions from one dynamic regime to another have been observed for diverse complex dynamic systems such as lake ecosystems, climate, financial markets, and also mood (Van de Leemput et al., 2014). Positive-feedback loops among related elements within a major trait domain might yield alternative stable states. This has consequences for how complex dynamic systems respond to deviations from homeostasis. Fig. 9.5 illustrates that when a system approaches a tipping point (due to a major shock or cumulative incremental changes), the system becomes vulnerable. It loses resilience and becomes unstable. Small perturbations may then cause a shift to an alternative stable state.

How can this perspective help the modeling of stability and change in personality? If there are specific stable trait positions on a distribution one expects a multimodal distribution of population scores, with relatively high frequencies at stable state positions and low frequencies at regions in between. In existing databases, multimodal trait score distributions are not observed (Van der Krieke et al., 2015). At the individual level, the question becomes whether someone can have two or more person-characteristic stable trait levels? Currently we lack the data to test this question. Nonetheless, we do know that personality trait change scores tend to be normally distributed, with frequent small changes and fewer marked changes. However, this does neither falsify nor confirm the idea of multiple person-characteristic stable trait levels if these levels differ between individuals (Fig. 9.3).

## Future directions

Databases with sufficient participants, assessments, and time coverage to formally test expected differences in set-point models have not been available. Optimal research designs are needed to: (1) compare between-subject set-point models; (2) determine the impact of major life events and altered social circumstances on personality, both in terms of the magnitude of change and rate of adaptation; and (3) identify typical within-subject trajectories before and after major life events or changes in social circumstances. But first it is important to consider how long a change in personality trait score must persist to indicate set-point change.

## Identifying set-point change

Trait set-points are theoretical constructs that cannot be measured directly. Identifying a set-point involves inference from repeated measurements. In order to distinguish measurement error, temporary deviation from the set-point, and enduring change in trait set-point, personality needs to be measured multiple times. The key question remains what true set-point change is and what that interpretation implies for the time scale of assessments.

One operational definition might depart from the assumption that personality trait set-points are immutable and determined entirely by an individual's genetic make-up. In this view, all change is temporary. According to this view, the best operational definition of set-point would be the average observed trait score across multiple assessments over an extended period of time, at least decade.

An alternative is to identify the time scale over which an observed change in trait score may indicate a true change in set-point. One approach could be based on the adaptation period plus a few months. In this approach, it is crucial to establish when the adaption process has entirely leveled off. If the trait level has not returned to its pre-event level, say a few months after leveling off, we could define the difference as a change in set-point. Some evidence suggests that the leveling off period may last as long as 1 year (e.g., retirement, marriage) to more than 5 years (e.g., disability, widowhood), depending on the specifics of the event and contextual factors, such as age (Diener et al., 2006; Luhmann et al., 2012). For personality traits, these dynamics require further study (Jeronimus, 2015; Ormel et al. 2013).

## Optimal research designs

### Compare the between-subject set-point models

In this chapter, we distinguished three fundamental set-point models that have different implications which can be empirically tested. First, the immutable set-point model predicts a constant differential stability, independent of the time interval. Conversely, the experience-dependent model predicts an ongoing drop, even after intervals of 10−20 years. The mixed set-point model predicts that the drop in differential stability levels off over time. Second, because the mixed model assumes that part of the trait score variance is not influenced by life events, the prospective association between major life events and trait scores at successive follow-ups is predicted to drop faster in the mixed model than in the experience-dependent model. Third, if the trait is entirely plastic, which implies there is no trait component, the experience-dependent model should fit longitudinal data better than a mixed model with a large immutable variance component.

However, sufficient statistical power is needed to distinguish the experience-dependent and mixed set-point models. Assuming a steady drop of test–retest trait correlations with time and a 25-year test–retest correlation of between 0.40 and 0.50, a sample of at least 1200 individuals would be necessary to differentiate the models (Ormel & Rijsdijk, 2000). Moreover, multiple assessments (at least four) over a long time period (preferably >10 years) are needed (see also Kenny & Zautra, 1995; Ormel & Rijsdijk, 2000).

## Determine the impact of major life events and altered social circumstances on personality, both in terms of the magnitude of change and rate of adaptation

Since the average occurrence rate of major life events and importantly altered social circumstances is low in most segments of the population-at-large, evaluation of their effects on personality traits may require novel research designs. For example, studies of the impact of the planned closure of a large employer could assess changes in personality traits before and after closure relative to a similar population that did not experience job displacement. To obtain reliable and valid data for modeling nonlinear change, the interval between the postevent assessments should gradually increase from 1–2 to 3–6 months and continue for at least 5 years. The timing of measurement intervals is important and, ideally, should match theory-based predictions on trajectories of personality development, the impact of events, and the rate of adaptation (Luhmann et al., 2014). With a sufficient frequency of measurements, it is possible to estimate measurement error variance, and short-term and long-term mean-level and rank-order stability and change adjusted for measurement error.

### Identification of typical within-subject trajectories

The designs proposed above, with 10–25 assessments during at least 5 years would not only allow for diverse between-subject analyses but within-subject panel regression analyses as well. The latter could address a variety of questions. For instance, whether typical trajectories exist, in terms of set-point bandwidth and adaptation rate, and the associated individual characteristics. This would address important sensitivity-to-context issues (Boyce & Ellis, 2005) and help to identify the kinds of environmental changes and personal events that have the potential to change personality trait set-points. Another possibility would be to examine whether changes in personality traits relate to simultaneous changes in level of life event exposure (Heady, 2006). Another advantage of so many assessments across an extended period is the potential to examine hypotheses about both event and individual characteristics that determine the effects of major life events on personality.

# Conclusion

Set-point theory has been productively applied in studies of SWB, but not in research on stability and change in personality. This divergence may be explained by the traditional but wrong assumptions that SWB responds to environmental influences, whereas personality traits do not. The experience-dependent and mixed set-point models provide a promising framework for future research to better understand stability and change in adult personality development because they fit available evidence. A significant challenge will be integrating research that concerns between-subject differences in personality traits with longitudinal studies assessing within-subject stability and change.

# References

Allport, G. W., & Odbert, H. S. (1936). Traitnames. A psycho-lexical study. *Psychological Monographs*, *47*(211), 171.

Anusic, I., Yap, S. Y., & Lucas, R. (2014). Testing set-point theory in a Swiss national sample: Reaction and adaptation to major life events. *Social Indicators Research*, *119* (3), 1265−1288. Available from http://dx.doi.org/10.1007/s11205-013-0541-2.

Barlow, D. H., & Nock, M. K. (2009). Why can't we be more idiographic in our research? *Perspectives on Psychological Science*, *4*(1), 19−21. Available from http://dx.doi.org/ 10.1111/j.1745-6924.2009.01088.x.

Bleidorn, W., Klimstra, T. A., Denissen, J. J. A., Rentfrow, P. J., Potter, J., & Gosling, S. D. (2013). Personality maturation around the world—A cross-cultural examination of the social investment principle. *Psychological Science*, *24*(12), 2530. Available from http:// dx.doi.org/10.1177/0956797613498396.

Borsboom, D., Rhemtulla, M., Cramer, A. O. J., van der Maas, H. L. J., Scheffer, M., & Dolan, C. V. (2016). Kinds versus continua: A review of psychometric approaches to uncover the structure of psychiatric constructs. *Psychological Medicine*, *46*(8), 1567−1579. Available from http://dx.doi.org/10.1017/S0033291715001944.

Boyce, W., & Ellis, B. (2005). Biological sensitivity to context: I. An evolutionary-developmental theory of the origins and functions of stress reactivity. *Development and Psychopathology*, *17*(2), 271−301. Available from http://dx.doi.org/10.1017/ S0954579405050145.

Brickman, P., Coates, D., & Janoffbulman, R. (1978). Lottery winners and accident victims —Is happiness relative. *Journal of Personality and Social Psychology*, *36*(8), 917−927. Available from http://dx.doi.org/10.1037/0022-3514.36.8.917.

Brown, G. W., Harris, T. O., & Hepworth, C. (1995). Loss, humiliation and entrapment among women developing depression: A patient and non-patient comparison. *Psychological Medicine*, *25*(1), 7−21.

Brown, G. W., Lemyre, L., & Bifulco, A. (1992). Social-factors and recovery from anxiety and depressive-disorders—A test of specificity. *British Journal of Psychiatry*, *161*, 44−54. Available from http://dx.doi.org/10.1192/bjp.161.1.44.

Cannon, W. B. (1932). *The wisdom of the body*. New York, NY: W.W. Norton.

Clark, L., Vittengl, J., Kraft, D., & Jarrett, R. (2003). Separate personality traits from states to predict depression. *Journal of Personality Disorders, 17*(2), 152−172. Available from http://dx.doi.org/10.1521/pedi.17.2.152.23990.

Costa, P. T., & McCrae, R. R. (1980). Influence of extraversion and neuroticism on subjective well-being: Happy and unhappy people. *Journal of Personality and Social Psychology, 38*(4), 668.

Cramer, A. O. J., Van der Sluis, S., Noordhof, A., Wichers, M., Geschwind, N., Aggen, S. H., ... Borsboom, D. (2012a). Dimensions of normal personality as networks in search of equilibrium: You can't like parties if you don't like people. *European Journal of Personality, 26*(4), 414−431. Available from http://dx.doi.org/10.1002/per.1866.

Cramer, A. O. J., Van der Sluis, S., Noordhof, A., Wichers, M., Geschwind, N., Aggen, S. H., ... Borsboom, D. (2012b). Measurable like temperature or mereological like flocking? On the nature of personality traits. *European Journal of Personality, 26*(4), 451−459. Available from http://dx.doi.org/10.1002/per.1879.

Cummins, R. A. (2010). Subjective wellbeing, homeostatically protected mood and depression: A synthesis. *Journal of Happiness Studies, 11*(1), 1−17.

Cummins, R. A. (2015). Understanding quality of life in medicine: A new approach. *Journal of the American College of Nutrition, 34*(Suppl. 1), 4−9. Available from http://dx.doi.org/10.1080/07315724.2015.1080099.

Davern, M., Cummins, R., & Stokes, M. (2007). Subjective wellbeing as an affective-cognitive construct. *Journal of Happiness Studies, 8*(4), 429−449. Available from http://dx.doi.org/10.1007/s10902-007-9066-1.

De Fruyt, F., Van Leeuwen, K., Bagby, R. M., Rolland, J., & Rouillon, F. (2006). Assessing and interpreting personality change and continuity in patients treated for major depression. *Psychological Assessment, 18*(1), 71−80. Available from http://dx.doi.org/10.1037/1040-3590.18.1.71.

DeNeve, K., & Cooper, H. (1998). The happy personality: A meta-analysis of 137 personality traits and subjective well-being. *Psychological Bulletin, 124*(2), 197−229. Available from http://dx.doi.org/10.1037//0033-2909.124.2.197.

Diener, E. (1984). Subjective well-being. *Psychological Bulletin, 95*(3), 542−575. Available from http://dx.doi.org/10.1037//0033-2909.95.3.542.

Diener, E., & Diener, M. (1995). Cross-cultural correlates of life satisfaction and self-esteem. *Journal of Personality and Social Psychology, 68*(4), 653−663. Available from http://dx.doi.org/10.1037/0022-3514.69.1.120.

Diener, E., Lucas, R., & Scollon, C. (2006). Beyond the hedonic treadmill—Revising the adaptation theory of well-being. *American Psychologist, 61*(4), 305−314. Available from http://dx.doi.org/10.1037/0003-066X.61.4.305.

Dumont, F. (2010). *A history of personality psychology: Theory, science, and research from hellenism to the twenty-first century.* New York, NY: Cambridge University Press.

Fleeson, W., & Gallagher, P. (2009). The implications of Big Five standing for the distribution of trait manifestation in behavior: Fifteen experience-sampling studies and a meta-analysis. *Journal of Personality and Social Psychology, 97*(6), 1097−1114. Available from http://dx.doi.org/10.1037/a0016786.

Fraga, M. F., Ballestar, E., Paz, M. F., Ropero, S., Setien, F., Ballestar, M. L., ... Esteller, M. (2005). Epigenetic differences arise during the lifetime of monozygotic twins. *Proceedings of the National Academy of Sciences of the United States of America, 102*(30), 10604−10609. Available from http://dx.doi.org/10.1073/pnas.0500398102.

Fraley, R. C., & Roberts, B. W. (2005). Patterns of continuity: A dynamic model for conceptualizing the stability of individual differences in psychological constructs across the life
course. *Psychological Review*, *112*(1), 60−74. Available from http://dx.doi.org/10.1037/
0033-295X.112.1.60.

Headey, B. (2006). Subjective well-being: Revisions to dynamic equilibrium theory using
national panel data and panel regression methods. *Social Indicators Research*, *79*(3),
369−403. Available from http://dx.doi.org/10.1007/s11205-005-5381-2.

Headey, B. (2010). The set point theory of well-being has serious flaws: On the eve of a
scientific revolution? *Social Indicators Research*, *97*(1), 7−21. Available from http://dx.
doi.org/10.1007/s11205-009-9559-x.

Headey, B., & Wearing, A. (1989). Personality, life events, and subjective well-being:
Toward a dynamic equilibrium model. *Journal of Personality and Social Psychology*, *57*
(4), 731−739. Available from http://dx.doi.org/10.1037/0022-3514.57.4.731.

Hudson, N. W., & Roberts, B. W. (2016). Social investment in work reliably predicts change
in conscientiousness and agreeableness: A direct replication and extension of Hudson,
Roberts, and Lodi-Smith (2012). *Journal of Research in Personality*, *60*, 12−23.
Available from http://dx.doi.org/10.1016/j.jrp.2015.09.004.

James, W. (1890). *The principles of psychology.*

Jeronimus, B. F. (2015). *Environmental influences on neuroticism: A story about emotional
(in)stability*. PhD thesis, Groningen, the Netherlands: University of Groningen. http://dx.
doi.org/10.13140/2.1.3452.2407, ISBN: 978-94-6299-035-7.

Jeronimus, B. F., Ormel, J., Aleman, A., Penninx, B. W. J. H., & Riese, H. (2013). Negative
and positive life events predict small but long-term change in neuroticism.
*Psychological Medicine*, *43*(11), 2403−2415. Available from http://dx.doi.org/10.1017/
S0033291713000159.

Jeronimus, B. F., Riese, H., Sanderman, R., & Ormel, J. (2014). Mutual reinforcement
between neuroticism and life stressors: A five-wave, sixteen-year study to test reciprocal
causation. *Journal of Personality and Social Psychology*, *107*(4), 751.

John, O. P., Robins, R., & Pervin, L. A. (2008). *Handbook of personality: Theory and
research* (3rd ed.). New York, NY: Guilford.

Kahneman, D. (2011). *Thinking, fast and slow.* London: Penguin Books.

Kanherkar, R. R., Bhatia-Dey, N., & Csoka, A. B. (2014). Epigenetics across the human
lifespan. *Frontiers in Cell and Developmental Biology*, *2*, 49. Available from http://dx.
doi.org/10.3389/fcell.2014.00049.

Keesey, R. E., & Powley, T. L. (1986). The regulation of body weight. *Annual Review of
Psychology*, *37*(1), 109−133. Available from http://dx.doi.org/10.1146/annurev.
ps.37.020186.000545.

Kendler, K. S., Zachar, P., & Craver, C. (2011). What kinds of things are psychiatric
disorders? *Psychological Medicine*, *41*, 1143−1150.

Kenny, D. A., & Zautra, A. (1995). The trait-state-error model for multiwave data. *Journal
of Consultancy and Clinical Psychology*, *63*(1), 52−59.

Kotov, R., Gamez, W., Schmidt, F., & Watson, D. (2010). Linking "big" personality traits to
anxiety, depressive, and substance use disorders: A meta-analysis. *Psychological
Bulletin*, *136*(5), 768−821. Available from http://dx.doi.org/10.1037/a0020327.

Laceulle, O. M., Jeronimus, B. F., Van Aken, M. A. G., & Ormel, J. (2015). Why not every-
body gets their fair share of stress: Adolescent's perceived relationship affection
mediates associations between temperament and subsequent stressful social events.
*European Journal of Personality*, *29*(2), 125−137. Available from http://dx.doi.org/
10.1002/per.1989.

Lindenberg, S. (1996). Continuities in the theory of social production functions. In H. Ganzeboom, & S. Lindenberg (Eds.), *Verklarende sociologie: Opstellen voor reinhard wippler*. Amsterdam: Thela Thesis.

Lodi-Smith, J., & Roberts, B. W. (2007). Social investment and personality: A meta-analysis of the relationship of personality traits to investment in work, family, religion, and volunteerism. *Personality and Social Psychology Review, 11*(1), 68−86. Available from http://dx.doi.org/10.1177/1088868306294590.

Lucas, R. E., Clark, A. E., Georgellis, Y., & Diener, E. (2004). Unemployment alters the set point for life satisfaction. *Psychological Science, 15*(1), 8−13.

Lucas, R. E., & Donnellan, M. B. (2007). How stable is happiness? Using the STARTS model to estimate the stability of life satisfaction. *Journal of Research in Personality, 41*(5), 1091−1098. Available from http://dx.doi.org/10.1016/j.jrp.2006.11.005.

Lüdtke, O., Trautwein, U., & Husemann, N. (2009). Goal and personality trait development in a transitional period: Assessing change and stability in personality development. *Personality and Social Psychology Bulletin, 35*(4), 428−441. Available from http://dx.doi.org/10.1177/0146167208329215.

Luhmann, M., Hofmann, W., Eid, M., & Lucas, R. E. (2012). Subjective well-being and adaptation to life events: A meta-analysis. *Journal of Personality and Social Psychology, 102*(3), 592−615. Available from http://dx.doi.org/10.1037/a0025948.

Luhmann, M., Orth, U., Specht, J., Kandler, C., & Lucas, R. E. (2014). Studying changes in life circumstances and personality: It's about time. *European Journal of Personality, 28*(3), 256−266. Available from http://dx.doi.org/10.1002/per.1951.

Lykken, D. T. (2007). "Beyond the hedonic treadmill: Revising the adaptation theory of well-being": Comment on diener, lucas, and scollon (2006). *American Psychologist, 62*(6), 611−612. Available from http://dx.doi.org/10.1037/0003-066X62.6.611.

Lykken, D., & Tellegen, A. (1996). Happiness is a stochastic phenomenon. *Psychological Science, 7*(3), 186−189. Available from http://dx.doi.org/10.1111/j.1467-9280.1996.tb00355.x.

Magidson, J. F., Roberts, B. W., Collado-Rodriguez, A., & Lejuez, C. W. (2014). Theory-driven intervention for changing personality: Expectancy value theory, behavioral activation, and conscientiousness. *Developmental Psychology, 50*(5), 1442−1450. Available from http://dx.doi.org/10.1037/a0030583.

McCrae, R. R. (2010). The place of the FFM in personality psychology. *Psychological Inquiry: An International Journal for the Advancement of Psychological Theory, 21*(1), 57.

McCrae, R. R., & Costa, P. T. (1990). *Personality in adulthood*. New York, NY: Guilford Press.

McCrae, R. R., & Costa, P. T. (2003). *Personality in adulthood: A five-factor theory perspective* (2nd ed.). New York, NY: Guilford Press.

McCrae, R. R., Costa, J., Paul, T., & Martin, T. A. (2005). The NEO-PI-3: A more readable revised NEO personality inventory. *Journal of Personality Assessment, 84*(3), 261−270. Available from http://dx.doi.org/10.1207/s15327752jpa8403_05.

McEwen, B. S. (2012). Brain on stress: How the social environment gets under the skin. *Proceedings of the National Academy of Sciences, 109*(Suppl. 2), 17180−17185. Available from http://dx.doi.org/10.1073/pnas.1121254109.

Middeldorp, C. M., Cath, D. C., Beem, A. L., Willemsen, G., & Boomsma, D. I. (2008). Life events, anxious depression and personality: A prospective and genetic study. *Psychological Medicine, 38*(11), 1557−1565. Available from http://dx.doi.org/10.1017/S0033291708002985.

Minkov, M. (2009). Predictors of differences in subjective well-being across 97 nations. *Cross-Cultural Research*, *43*(2), 152−179. Available from http://dx.doi.org/10.1177/1069397109332239.

Molenaar, P. C. M. (2008). On the implications of the classical ergodic theorems: Analysis of developmental processes has to focus on intra-individual variation. *Developmental Psychobiology*, *50*(1), 60−69. Available from http://dx.doi.org/10.1002/dev.20262.

Ormel, J., Jeronimus, B. F., Kotov, R., Riese, H., Bos, E. E., Hankin, B., & Rosmalen, J. G. M. (2013). Neuroticism and common mental disorders: Meaning and utility of a complex relationship. *Clinical Psychology Review*, *33*(5), 686−697.

Ormel, J., Lindenberg, S., & Steverink, N. (1999). *Social Indicators Research*, *46*, 61. Available from http://dx.doi.org/10.1023/A:1006907811502.

Ormel, J., Lindenberg, S., Steverink, N., & Vonkorff, M. (1997). Quality of life and social production functions: A framework for understanding health effects. *Social Science & Medicine*, *45*(7), 1051−1063. Available from http://dx.doi.org/10.1016/S0277-9536(97)00032-4.

Ormel, J., Oldehinkel, A. J., Nolen, W. A., & Vollebergh, W. (2004). Psychosocial disability before, during, and after a major depressive episode—A 3-wave population-based study of state, scar, and trait effects. *Archives of General Psychiatry*, *61*(4), 387−392.

Ormel, J., Riese, H., & Rosmalen, J. G. M. (2012). Interpreting neuroticism scores across the adult life course: Immutable or experience-dependent set points of negative affect? *Clinical Psychology Review*, *32*(1), 71−79. Available from http://dx.doi.org/10.1016/j.cpr.2011.10.004.

Ormel, J., & Rijsdijk, F. V. (2000). Continuing change in neuroticism during adulthood: Structural modelling of a 16-year, 5-wave community study. *Personality and Individual Differences*, *28*(3), 461−478. Available from http://dx.doi.org/10.1016/S0191-8869(99)00112-9.

Ormel, J., & Schaufeli, W. B. (1991). Stability and change in psychological distress and their relationship with self-esteem and locus of control: A dynamic equilibrium model. *Journal of Personality and Social Psychology*, *60*(2), 288−299. Available from http://dx.doi.org/10.1037/0022-3514.60.2.288.

Plomin, R., DeFries, J. C., & Loehlin, J. C. (1977). Genotype−environment interaction and correlation in the analysis of human behavior. *Psychological Bulletin*, *84*(2), 309−322. Available from http://dx.doi.org/10.1037/0033-2909.84.2.309.

Riese, H., Snieder, H., Jeronimus, B. F., Korhonen, T., Rose, R. J., Kaprio, J., & Ormel, J. (2014). Timing effects stressful life events on stability and change of neuroticism scores. *European Journal of Personality*, *2*, 193−200. Available from http://dx.doi.org/10.1002/per.1929.

Roberts, B. W., & DelVecchio, W. F. (2000). The rank-order consistency of personality traits from childhood to old age: A quantitative review of longitudinal studies. *Psychological Bulletin*, *126*(1), 3−25. Available from http://dx.doi.org/10.1037/0033-2909.126.1.3.

Roberts, B. W., & Jackson, J. J. (2008). Sociogenomic personality psychology. *Journal of Personality*, *76*(6), 1523−1544. Available from http://dx.doi.org/10.1111/j.1467-6494.2008.00530.x.

Roberts, B. W., & Mroczek, D. (2008). Personality trait change in adulthood. *Current Directions in Psychological Science*, *17*(1), 31−35. Available from http://dx.doi.org/10.1111/j.1467-8721.2008.00543.x.

Roberts, B. W., Walton, K. E., & Viechtbauer, W. (2006). Patterns of mean-level change in personality traits across the life course: A meta-analysis of longitudinal studies.

*Psychological Bulletin*, *132*(1), 1−25. Available from http://dx.doi.org/10.1037/0033-2909.132.1.1.

Roberts, B. W., & Wood, D. (2006). *Personality development in the context of the neo-socioanalytic model of personality. Handbook of personality development* (pp. 11−39). Mahwah, NJ: Lawrence Erlbaum Associates Publishers.

Roberts, B. W., Wood, D., & Caspi, A. (2008). The development of personality traits in adulthood. In O. P. John, R. W. Robins, & L. A. Pervin (Eds.), *Handbook of personality psychology: Theory and research* (3rd ed., pp. 375−398). New York, NY: Guilford Press.

Roberts, B. W., Wood, D., & Smith, J. L. (2005). Evaluating five factor theory and social investment perspectives on personality trait development. *Journal of Research in Personality*, *39*(1), 166−184. Available from http://dx.doi.org/10.1016/j.jrp.2004.08.002.

Robins, R. W., Caspi, A., & Moffitt, T. E. (2000). Two personalities, one relationship: Both partners' personality traits shape the quality of their relationship. *Journal of Personality and Social Psychology*, *79*(2), 251−259.

Scarr, S., & McCartney, K. (1983). How people make their own environments: A theory of genotype→environment effects. *Child Development*, *54*(2), 424−435.

Scheffer, M., Bascompte, J., Brock, W. A., Brovkin, V., Carpenter, S. R., Dakos, V., ... Sugihara, G. (2009). Early-warning signals for critical transitions. *Nature*, *461*(7260), 53−59.

Specht, J. (2015). Personality beyond generalization and traits: An oxymoron. *European Journal of Personality*, *29*(3), 349−350.

Specht, J., Bleidorn, W., Denissen, J. J. A., Hennecke, M., Hutteman, R., Kandler, C., ... Zimmermann, J. (2014). What drives adult personality development? A comparison of theoretical perspectives and empirical evidence. *European Journal of Personality*, *28*(2), 216−230. Available from http://dx.doi.org/10.1002/per.1966.

Specht, J., Egloff, B., & Schmukle, S. C. (2011). Stability and change of personality across the life course: The impact of age and major life events on mean-level and rank-order stability of the Big Five. *Journal of Personality and Social Psychology*, *101*(4), 862−882.

Steel, P., Schmidt, J., & Shultz, J. (2008). Refining the relationship between personality and subjective well-being. *Psychological Bulletin*, *134*(1), 138−161. Available from http://dx.doi.org/10.1037/0033-2909.134.1.138.

Steverink, N., Lindenberg, S., & Ormel, J. (1998). Towards understanding successful ageing: Patterned change in resources and goals. *Ageing & Society*, *18*(04), 441−467.

Sutin, A. R., Costa, P. T., Jr., Wethington, E., & Eaton, W. (2010). Turning points and lessons learned: Stressful life events and personality trait development across middle adulthood. *Psychology and Aging*, *25*(3), 524−533. Available from http://dx.doi.org/10.1037/a0018751.

Tang, T. Z., DeRubeis, R. J., Hollon, S. D., Amsterdam, J., Shelton, R., & Schalet, B. (2009). Personality change during depression treatment: A placebo-controlled trial. *Archives of General Psychiatry*, *66*(12), 1322−1330.

Vachon, D. D., & Krueger, R. F. (2015). Emotion and the joint structure of personality and psychopathology. *Emotion Review*, *7*(3), 265−271. Available from http://dx.doi.org/10.1177/1754073915575403.

Van der Krieke, L., Jeronimus, B. F., Blaauw, F. J., Wanders, R. B. K., Emerencia, A. C., Schenk, H. M., ... Jonge, P. D. (2015). HowNutsAreTheDutch (HoeGekIsNL): A crowdsourcing study of mental symptoms and strengths. *International Journal of Methods in Psychiatric Research*, *25*(2), 123−144. Available from http://dx.doi.org/10.1002/mpr.1495.

Van der Knaap, L. J., Riese, H., Hudziak, J. J., Verbiest, M. M. P. J., Verhulst, F. C., Oldehinkel, A. J., & Van Oort, F. V. A. (2015). Adverse life events and allele-specific methylation of the serotonin transporter gene (SLC6A4) in adolescents: The TRAILS study. *Psychosomatic Medicine*, *77*(3), 246−255. Available from http://dx.doi.org/10.1097/PSY.0000000000000159.

Van de Leemput, I. A., Wichers, M., Cramer, A. O. J., Borsboom, D., Tuerlinckx, F., Kuppens, P., ... Scheffer, M. (2014). Critical slowing down as early warning for the onset and termination of depression. *PNAS*, *111*(1), 87−92. Available from http://dx.doi.org/10.1073/pnas.1312114110.

Weaver, I., Cervoni, N., Champagne, F., D'Alessio, A., Sharma, S., Seckl, J., ... Meaney, M. (2004). Epigenetic programming by maternal behavior. *Nature Neuroscience*, *7*(8), 847−854. Available from http://dx.doi.org/10.1038/nn1276.

Weiss, A., Bates, T. C., & Luciano, M. (2008). Happiness is a personal(ity) thing. *Psychological Science*, *19*(3), 205−210. Available from http://dx.doi.org/10.1111/j.1467-9280.2008.02068.x.

Williams, D. G. (1993). Are personality effects upon average mood due to personality effects upon mood variation. *Personality and Individual Differences*, *14*(1), 199−208. Available from http://dx.doi.org/10.1016/0191-8869(93)90190-E.

Zhang, T., & Meaney, M. J. (2010). Epigenetics and the environmental regulation of the genome and its function. *Annual Review of Psychology*, *61*(1), 439−466.

# Evolutionary aspects of personality development: Evidence from nonhuman animals

10

*Conor G. Smith and Alexander Weiss*
The University of Edinburgh, Edinburgh, United Kingdom

## Personality development in nonhuman animals

At first glance, personality seems to be counterproductive to evolutionary success. An individual from a species where personalities are present will engage in predictable behaviors when exposed to similar situations, limiting its behavioral flexibility. In theory, an individual with greater behavioral flexibility should have an advantage over more inflexible individuals, being able to adapt to a wider range of potential scenarios (Wolf, van Doorn, Leimar, & Weissing, 2007). Instead, we see personality structures of varying degrees in not just humans, but a huge range of species (Gosling, 2001). It follows then that there must be some further processes at work for personality to be as successful and widespread an adaptation as it appears to be. As has been evidenced in earlier chapters, personality in modern humans changes over the course of the lifespan. These developmental arcs have not developed suddenly, but have come about over millions of years through natural selection. When taking into account other factors involved in the passing along of one's genes, such as reproductive strategies and life history, the evolution of personality and its developmental trajectories seems to be inevitable (Figueredo et al., 2005). Here we explore leading theories as to why personality has evolved and how developmental trajectories of personality can be beneficial to the evolutionary fitness of an individual.

### Life history theory

Life history theory, first proposed by MacArthur and Wilson (1963) in their paper "An Equilibrium Theory of Insular Zoogeography," is the idea that different expectations of evolutionary fitness require different systematic behavioral choices to be successful. These systematic behaviors tend to fall into two broad categories of reproductive strategies, r-strategy and K-strategy. The term "r-strategy" refers to a reliance on a high ecological growth rate for success. The term "K-strategy" refers to populations that stay close to the carrying capacity of their habitat. The typical r-strategist has a short lifespan and a high mortality rate while the typical K-strategist has a long lifespan with low mortality. To deal with this predicament and successfully pass on its genes to the next generation, the r-strategist will attempt to have as

Personality Development Across the Lifespan. DOI: http://dx.doi.org/10.1016/B978-0-12-804674-6.00010-7

many offspring as possible as early as possible in the short time available to it. This provides the r-strategist with a numerical advantage against the high mortality rate it is faced with in the hopes that a small percentage of its offspring will in turn grow and reproduce quickly to continue the cycle. The classic example of an r-strategist is the mayfly, *Ephemeroptera* spp., each individual laying and fertilizing millions of eggs during their short lifespan (Brittain, 1990). K-strategists, on the other hand, only have a small number of offspring at much longer intervals than the r-strategists. K-strategists invest a great deal in their few offspring, providing parental support until the young are able to fend for themselves. In relation to the mayfly, humans may be considered K-strategists (Kaplan, Hill, Lancaster, & Hurtado, 2000), having usually only one child at a time and caring for them many years after they are born.

Life history theory can also be applied at the level of individuals within a species (Biro & Stamps, 2008; Figueredo, Vásquez, Brumbach, & Schneider, 2007). Individuals that have high future expectations of success, and therefore a great deal to lose should injury or death befall them, should be more averse to risk-taking behavior than an individual with lower expectations. This risk avoidance is applicable to any number of commonly occurring situations, leading different individuals to consistently respond in different ways to the same stimulus. Eventually, these consistent and predictable patterns of behavior can be reasonably referred to as personalities. As a result of this theory of the evolution of personality, we would expect personality structures in most species to contain some factor related to risk aversion and indeed we do. Timidity/boldness come up time and time again at a fundamental level in the personality structure of a variety of species (Carere & van Oers, 2004; Sinn, Gosling, & Moltschaniwskyj, 2008; Sneddon, 2003).

At its core, what life history theory represents is a strategic allocation of resources to maximize reproductive success. To maximize fitness, a trade-off must take place in regards to how energy is allocated. Where survival is not guaranteed, it is more prudent to invest energy in reaching sexual maturity as quickly as possible and then pouring energy into reproduction at the expense of longevity. However, when safety is more assured, it may be better to invest in one's own longevity and the longevity of a few well-cared-for offspring so that many successful offspring can be produced. These variable reproductive strategies provide us with an explanation of the origins of personality and its prevalence across taxa.

## Balancing selection

Life history theory, however, is only the beginning of the evolution of personality. The five human personality factors that appear to be present in most, if not all, human cultures (McCrae, Terracciano, & 78 Members of the Personality Profiles of Cultures Project, 2005), are more complex than timidity versus boldness. Variation in the levels of personality factors is thought to be maintained by one or more forms of balancing selection (Buss, 2009; Nettle, 2006). Balancing selection occurs when variation in a trait is maintained over generations because different levels of a trait are adaptive in different environments to a similar degree. Balancing selection can maintain variation in personality via several different mechanisms (Penke, Denissen, & Miller, 2007).

One such mechanism is environmental heterogeneity or, putting it more straightforwardly, differences in personality are selected by differences across geographical locations. Different environments select for different personality traits which in turn select for variation in the population. Genetic analysis has shown that people with a migratory ancestry have a higher prevalence of alleles related to novelty seeking or extraversion than those from sedentary populations (Chen, Burton, Greenberger, & Dmitrieva, 1999; Eisenberg, Campbell, Gray, & Sorenson, 2008; Matthews & Butler, 2011). This supports the idea that variation in personality has been selected for by the varying environmental demands of a geographical location. Balancing selection can also interact with the effects of social structure (see Section "Sociability") when social roles are influenced by the environment.

Another, possibly more influential type of balancing selection, is frequency-dependent selection. This form of selection occurs where the evolutionary fitness of a particular strategy or behavior is proportional to the frequency with which it occurs in the population. A prime example of frequency-dependent selection is in the phenomenon of "social loafing" (Latané, Williams, & Harkins, 1979). A social loafer is one who allows others to do a majority of the work required to reach a goal. However, this strategy stops being effective if the frequency of loafers in the population changes. Therefore, for loafing to be a viable strategy, the frequency of loafers in the population must be balanced.

A further possibility is that personality traits each have their own advantages and disadvantages. Neuroticism, for example, may have some benefits from increased vigilance against danger, but ultimately has negative effects on long-term health due to added stress (Nettle, 2006). The same mechanisms can apply to age and development as well. Behavioral plasticity with changing population dynamics and the changing nature of interactions with conspecifics with age can alter the frequencies of trait clusters selected for (Wolf & Weissing, 2012). This provides an ideal situation for individuals whose personality develops in accordance with these changes to use their increased fitness to propagate genetic predispositions toward adaptive developmental arcs of personality factors.

While this idea may provide an explanation for a further evolution of variation in basic personality, it does not fully explain the extent to which this variation follows consistent developmental trajectories within the individual over time (for the case in humans, see Roberts, Walton, & Viechtbauer, 2006, for a review). Complementing the application of life history strategies and frequency-dependent selection to the evolution of personality, another common characteristic of species with complex personalities has contributed to the structure we see today—sociability (Wolf & McNamara, 2012).

## Sociability

A key attribute of any personality trait is consistency. Personality can and does change within an individual over time but the way it changes is consistent and predictable, and thus retest correlations tend to be high (Bell, Hankison, & Laskowski, 2009; Roberts & DelVecchio, 2000). One theory as to why this may be the case has to do with the social contexts that accompany species in which personality has been described. Being part of a community means interacting with conspecifics on a regular basis and some of these individuals are bound to respond differently to stimuli, due to chance, personality, or any number of other plausible reasons. When this involves social interaction, individuals may respond to each other's behaviors and subsequently modify their own behavior based on the information gained through these interactions. This phenomenon is known as social responsiveness and is advantageous because it allows individuals to tailor their responses to each other in a way that may be more beneficial in the future (Dall, Houston, & McNamara, 2004; Johnstone, 2001; Johnstone & Manica, 2011; Wolf, Van Doorn, & Weissing, 2011). For example, if an individual knows that another is less likely to share food if they are aggressive toward it, in the future they may withhold aggression whether food is present or not. This change in behavior increases the chances of cooperation and reduces the negative effects that would arise from competition, thereby benefiting the individual. However, social responsiveness is only possible if the behaviors involved are consistent over time and applicable information can be obtained from previous observations and interactions. In this way, social responsiveness is only valuable if there is consistency in behavior (Dall et al., 2004). By the same token, the value of being consistent in one's behaviors is greatly increased when other individuals are socially responsive (Wolf et al., 2011). This interaction, coupled with frequency-dependent selection, leads to the emergence of consistent behavioral tendencies over time. It should also be noted that, alternatively, social responsiveness can evolve first, giving rise to frequency-dependent selection and, consequently, consistent personalities.

Social responsiveness and the specialization of sociability into specific roles can have a strong influence on personality development as well. With the selective pressure of reducing conflict between social partners, changes in social roles with age and changes in the personality traits most beneficial to success in these roles strongly support the development of personality over the lifespan (Bergmüller & Taborsky, 2010). Through the lens of the theories of frequency-dependent selection and social responsiveness, it becomes clear that personality and personality development are adaptive traits that evolved over millions of years and continue to be adaptive for a large number of species today.

## The comparative method

Up to this point most of the evidence presented for the evolution of personality has been theoretical, simulated, or based on our knowledge of animal behavior. The question remains, how can we more directly study the evolution of human personality? The answer to this question lies in comparative research (Gosling & Graybeal, 2007; Harvey & Pagel, 1991). By studying the personality structures of related species such as chimpanzees (*Pan troglodytes*) and orangutans (*Pongo* spp.), we can, using deductive reasoning, begin to piece together a model of what our early human ancestors' personality may have been like a few million years ago (Gosling & Graybeal, 2007). This approach can also be, and has been, used to address questions about personality development (King, Weiss, & Sisco, 2008; Weiss & King, 2015). Specifically, by comparing how personality develops over the lifespan in great apes and other nonhuman primates with human personality development, we can begin to infer approximately when particular aspects of human personality evolved and what relevant selective pressures may have been influential in the process. Although we cannot yet definitively know whether any similarities reflect a common evolutionary heritage, it is the most parsimonious explanation (Harvey & Pagel, 1991).

## Factor structure in nonhuman primates

The starting point for our own work and that of our collaborators has been the identification of differences and similarities in the covariation (or structure) of a common set of traits. The starting point for this work was the identification of traits in Goldberg's 1990 taxonomy of the Big Five that could be applied to assess personality in chimpanzees (King & Figueredo, 1997). Since then, a questionnaire comprising these traits, as well as later versions of this questionnaire that have included other traits have been used to assess personality in several nonhuman primate species (Adams et al., 2015; Konečná et al., 2008; Konečná, Weiss, Lhota, & Wallner, 2012; Morton et al., 2013; Weiss, Adams, Widdig, & Gerald, 2011; Weiss, King, & Perkins, 2006), and even deer (Bergvall, Schäpers, Kjellander, & Weiss, 2011). Other researchers, beginning at different sets of traits, have also gathered data on a variety of species. The most prominent such example would be the work started by Joan Stevenson-Hinde and her colleagues (see Stevenson-Hinde & Hinde, 2011, for a history and review). To explore the structure of rhesus macaque personality they used a set of traits sampled from Sheldon's studies of personality and somatotypes in humans (Sheldon, 1942). The "Madingley Questionnaire" developed by Joan Stevenson-Hinde and Marion Zunz (1978) has since enjoyed widespread use across multiple taxa.[1]

We do not wish to dwell on differences in the structure of personality across different species. However, it is worth describing some findings to illustrate how interspecies differences allow the opportunity to understand the origins of personality domains. In chimpanzees instead of the five factors typically found in humans (McCrae & Costa, 1997), the most plausible personality structure comprises five human-like factors and a sixth factor labeled dominance (King & Figueredo, 1997). Dominance is a broad factor indicating an individual's propensity to exhibit dominant behavior in social interactions with conspecifics. Individuals high in dominance tend to be more assertive over others when interacting and often rise higher in the social order (King & Figueredo, 1997). Four of these factors, dominance, extraversion, conscientiousness, and agreeableness, have been replicated in other

---

[1] Both the questionnaire based on King and Figueredo's work and the Madingley Questionnaire are available at http://extras.springer.com/2011/978-1-4614-0175-9.

samples measured on these traits (King, Weiss, & Farmer, 2005; Weiss et al., 2009; Weiss, King, & Hopkins, 2007). Moreover, studies of different samples of chimpanzees that were assessed using other sets of traits (Dutton, 2008; Freeman et al., 2013) have identified neuroticism and openness factors similar to those originally identified by King and Figueredo (1997).

A later study of orangutans by Weiss et al. (2006) found evidence for five factors. Of these, extraversion, agreeableness, and neuroticism resembled their human and chimpanzee counterparts, dominance was similar to the chimpanzee dominance factor, and intellect stood out as combining traits related to human conscientiousness and openness to experience. Most recently, a study of personality in bonobos using this same instrument identified six factors (Weiss et al., 2015). These factors included assertiveness, which is comparable to chimpanzee and orangutan dominance, conscientiousness and openness, which resembled the same-named factors in humans and chimpanzees, a narrow variant of the extraversion factor identified in humans, chimpanzees, and orangutans, and attentiveness, which, to date, has only been identified in brown capuchin monkeys (Morton et al., 2013).

These studies, and studies of other species that use overlapping sets of traits, allow us to infer approximately when certain personality factors emerged or disappeared. For example, personality factors labeled dominance, assertiveness, or confidence consistently emerge in studies where nonhuman primate personality is measured using a variety of approaches (Freeman & Gosling, 2010). Although these factors share labels with and are similar to facets of human extraversion (Costa & McCrae, 1995; John, Naumann, & Soto, 2008; Roberts et al., 2006), they typically are broader. For example, these factors in chimpanzees and bonobos, our closest nonhuman relatives, also include traits related to low agreeableness, low neuroticism, and high conscientiousness (King & Figueredo, 1997; Weiss et al., 2015). These findings therefore suggest that dominance emerged as an independent factor early in primate evolution (or even before that) and that its absence in humans can be traced to events that occurred sometime after the ancestors of hominids and the *Pan* species parted some 5 to 7 million years ago (Hobolth, Christensen, Mailund, & Schierup, 2007).

In addition to allowing researchers to understand when personality factors emerged, comparing personality structures enables us to rule out alternative explanations for why they emerged (Gosling & Graybeal, 2007; Harvey & Pagel, 1991). For example, extraversion is nominally related to sociability, and gregariousness, activity. Evolutionary psychologists have thus posited adaptive explanations for extraversion that focus on the social aspect of extraversion (e.g., Nettle, 2006). The fact that extraversion has also been identified in orangutans, a fairly closely related species, which can be described as semisolitary at best (Galdikas, 1985a, 1985b, 1985c), should give these researchers pause.

There has been controversy over the use of ratings as well as basing these studies on items sampled from the Five-Factor Model (Uher, 2013). However, the reliabilities of animal personality ratings are comparable to or exceed those of human ratings and also behavioral measures (Freeman & Gosling, 2010; Gosling, 2001; Vazire, Gosling, Dickey, & Schapiro, 2007), there is little evidence of bias arising from anthropomorphism (Kwan, Gosling, & John, 2008; Weiss, Inoue-Murayama, King, Adams, & Matsuzawa, 2012), and similar inferences can be made by studying personality using other sets of rated traits, such as the Madingley Questionnaire (Stevenson-Hinde & Zunz, 1978), or broadly sampled sets of behaviors (see, e.g., Neumann, Agil, Widdig, & Engelhardt, 2013).

## Personality development in nonhuman primates

The comparative approach has been applied to address the question of why do human personality traits develop in a way that suggests greater maturity, i.e., a decrease in neuroticism, an increase in extraversion, conscientiousness, and agreeableness, and an increase followed by decrease in openness to experience (McCrae & Costa, 2003)? Two theories have been put forward to explain these trends. Five-Factor Theory claims that these developmental trends have biological and genetic origins (McCrae & Costa, 2003). Evidence supporting this theory includes age-related trends, similar in both direction and magnitude, across cultures (McCrae et al., 1999, 2000, 2005), heritabilities of personality domains ranging from 0.4 to 0.6 (Bouchard & Loehlin, 2001), the presence of common genetic underpinnings of personality structure in different cultures (Yamagata et al., 2006), and the presence of common genetic effects that underlie the stability of personality factors as well as their developmental trajectories (Bleidorn, Kandler, Riemann, Angleitner, & Spinath, 2009; McGue, Bacon, & Lykken, 1993; Viken, Rose, Kaprio, & Koskenvuo, 1994).

On the other hand, the social-investment principle states that age-related personality changes are a result of individuals investing in particular social roles that change during the course of people's lives. Examples of social roles believed to be important in this regard, include starting work, becoming married, and becoming a parent (Roberts, Wood, & Smith, 2005; though see van Scheppingen et al., 2016). Evidence has been put forward in support of the social-investment principle. For example, a meta-analysis of cross-sectional studies found that the degree to which people invested in their jobs, families, religions, and volunteerism was associated with higher conscientiousness and agreeableness, and lower neuroticism (Lodi-Smith & Roberts, 2007). Moreover, the associations just described were greater among those who were more committed to these social roles (Lodi-Smith & Roberts, 2007). Further evidence for this theory comes from a recent study of age differences in personality in 62 countries (Bleidorn et al., 2013). This study found that neuroticism declined more steeply and conscientiousness increased more rapidly in countries where the transition to the work force started earlier, and that openness increased less rapidly in countries in which the transition to family life started earlier. Finally, the social-investment principle's proponents cite the same behavioral genetic studies as its opponents do, though they highlight findings that nonshared environmental influences influence personality development (Roberts et al., 2005).

Prior to discussing these theories in light of research on nonhuman primates, it is important to note that these competing theories are not mutually exclusive, and that, to date, the studies conducted do not decisively rule one or the other out. The question therefore remains: which theory provides us with a more complete understanding of human personality development? The comparative method, although still not providing a definitive answer, advances the argument, namely as it enables us to rule out explanations for these trajectories that rely upon present day human social and cultural constraints.

Although other studies have investigated personality development in various species of nonhuman primates (Sussman, Mates, Ha, Bentson, & Crockett, 2014) and other animals (Class & Brommer, 2016), we will turn to two studies that directly compared the developmental trajectories of humans, chimpanzees, and orangutans on comparable personality dimensions. The first study investigated cross-sectional associations between age and personality in chimpanzees and compared these to cross-sectional associations between age and personality in humans (King et al., 2008). After scaling age to compensate for the fact that chimpanzees develop and mature approximately 50% more rapidly than do humans, King and his colleagues found that the magnitudes of the associations between age and the five human-like chimpanzee personality factors were similar to those found in humans. As noted in their discussion, these largely comparable age effects simply cannot be explained as being the products of social roles related to work, family, volunteerism, or religion, and the comparable magnitudes are not what one would predict given the inarguably large impact that culture has on human lives. In addition to these similarities, there were some interesting deviations from this pattern. In particular, although the trajectories were similar in direction to those found in humans, male and female chimpanzees differed in the size of these effects: agreeableness was associated with greater age-related increases in females, activity (a facet of extraversion) was associated with greater age-related decreases in females, and tameness (a facet of conscientiousness) was possibly associated with greater age-related increases in females. As noted by the authors, these differences appeared to reflect a period of prolonged aggressive tendencies in male chimpanzees that would be consistent with the heightened intermale aggression in this species (Wrangham, Wilson, & Muller, 2006).

These results would appear to support Five-Factor Theory, but, of course, they do not rule out the possibility that broader social effects common to humans and chimpanzees play a role. To rule out this explanation, Weiss and King (2015) compared the developmental trajectories of chimpanzee personality factors with those of orangutans, which, as we noted before, are semisolitary as opposed to being highly social like the chimpanzees. Because of the different personality structures, the comparisons were limited to four overlapping personality factors—dominance, extraversion, neuroticism, and agreeableness—of which only the latter three are shared in common with humans. Weiss and King (2015) found that the magnitudes of age effects were comparable to those of humans and chimpanzees. Moreover, like humans and chimpanzees, older orangutans were lower in extraversion and neuroticism (see Figs. 10.1 and 10.2, respectively). On the other hand, in contrast to findings across human societies and in chimpanzees, older orangutans were agreeableness (see Fig. 10.3). Finally, unlike chimpanzees, there was no evidence in orangutans for a prolonged period in males marked by aggression. With the

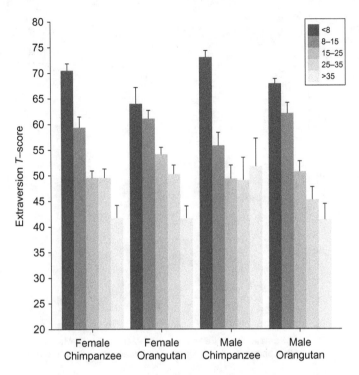

**Figure 10.1** Mean levels ± 1 standard error for extraversion expressed as within-species *T*-scores across five age groups for male and female orangutans and chimpanzees. *Source:* Figure by Weiss, A., & King, J. E. (2015). Great ape origins of personality maturation and sex differences: A study of orangutans and chimpanzees. *Journal of Personality and Social Psychology, 108*, 648–664. Available from http://dx.doi.org/10.1037/pspp0000022 and licensed under a Creative Commons Attribution 3.0 Unported License and published under the terms of this license. For more details, see http://creativecommons.org/licenses/by/3.0/.

exception of agreeableness, the developmental trends for male orangutans resembled those of female orangutans, female chimpanzees, and therefore, both male and female humans.

These findings suggest that the declines seen in extraversion and neuroticism, in both orangutans and chimpanzees, follow trajectories of development that are phylogenetically rooted as opposed to being a result of social pressures. Again, if these development trends were socially instead of evolutionarily based, we would expect changes, and perhaps especially those related to extraversion, to be reduced or even nonexistent in a semisolitary species. The parallels seen here thus rule out the possibility that these changes came about as a result of individuals' investments in their particular social roles within a highly social community (Roberts et al., 2005). They also rule out the influence of social roles related to maintaining a family as, unlike humans, males of both species do not contribute to caring for their offspring (Galdikas, 1985a, 1985b, 1985c; Goodall, 1986).

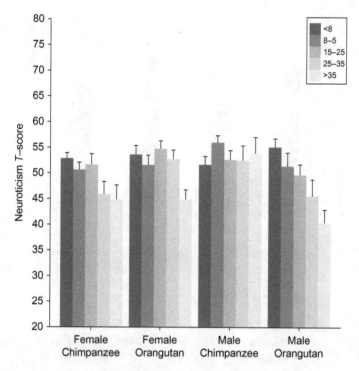

**Figure 10.2** Mean levels ± 1 standard error for neuroticism expressed as within-species *T*-scores across five age groups for male and female orangutans and chimpanzees. *Source:* Figure by Weiss, A., & King, J. E. (2015). Great ape origins of personality maturation and sex differences: A study of orangutans and chimpanzees. *Journal of Personality and Social Psychology, 108*, 648–664. Available from http://dx.doi.org/10.1037/pspp0000022 and licensed under a Creative Commons Attribution 3.0 Unported License and published under the terms of this license. For more details, see http://creativecommons.org/licenses/by/3.0/.

The contrast between the developmental trajectories related to agreeableness may be most straightforwardly explained as indicating that the tendency for agreeableness to increase with age reflects selection against growing disagreeableness in societies where individuals benefit from developing and maintaining cohesive bonds in adulthood. Alternatively, this could reflect the composition of the agreeableness factor, which, in orangutans, includes some traits related to extraversion (Weiss & King, 2015).[2] The finding of similar age-related decreases in agreeableness in white-faced capuchins (Manson & Perry, 2013) contradicts the previous explanation because this species' social structure is similar to that of chimpanzees

---

[2] Of course, this too may be related to the difference between the differences in the sociality of orangutans, chimpanzees, and humans.

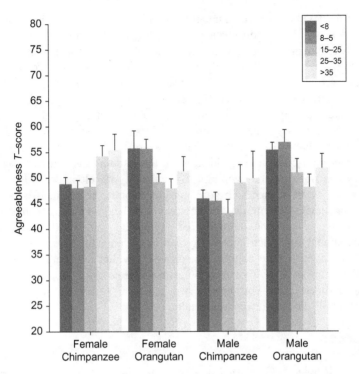

**Figure 10.3** Mean levels ± 1 standard error for agreeableness expressed as within-species *T*-scores across five age groups for male and female orangutans and chimpanzees.
*Source:* Figure adapted from figure 5 in Weiss, A., & King, J. E. (2015). Great ape origins of personality maturation and sex differences: A study of orangutans and chimpanzees. *Journal of Personality and Social Psychology, 108*, 648−664. Available from http://dx.doi.org/10.1037/pspp0000022 and licensed under a Creative Commons Attribution 3.0 Unported License and published under the terms of this license. For more details, see http://creativecommons.org/licenses/by/3.0/.

(Aureli et al., 2008). However, given that white-faced capuchins are a New World monkey species and are thus only distantly related to humans, chimpanzees, and orangutans (Steiper & Young, 2006), more data needs to be collected before we can firmly rule out the possibility that the different social structures of chimpanzees and orangutans are responsible for these differences.

As Weiss and King (2015) noted, the findings concerning chimpanzee and orangutan personality development suggest that frequency-dependent selection may also have played a role in the evolution of developmental trajectories in personality and in the cross-cultural differences observed by Bleidorn et al. (2013). Briefly, selection may disfavor individuals whose personality trajectories differ from those found in the population. At the species level, for example, male chimpanzees who do not maintain a personality profile characterized by intense aggression into adult-hood, are less likely to survive and reproduce than those who do maintain such a profile. At the level of cultures, human men and women who live in a country full of "go-getters" will be at a disadvantage if the rate at which their conscientiousness increases is less than that of their countrymen and women. These men and women, unless they move to more "laid back" pastures, are less likely to leave descendants.

We can see that it is likely developmental arcs in personality are deeply ingrained in our evolutionary past. However, personality development is not likely to be a product of any one evolutionary pressure or set of circumstances. It is a result of a multitude of situations, from as basic a genetic standpoint as life history theory and reproductive success to the subtleties of gradual and nuanced changes in social roles within communities. Identifying the circumstances involved and how much they contribute to the evolution of personality development is a formidable task. However, with advances in nonhuman personality research, it is possible to start moving beyond theoretical frameworks and begin to explore this question using deductive comparisons between the phylogenies and social structures of the nonhuman animals in which personality and developmental trajectories have been identified. Creating a more complete picture of how and why personality develops thus requires further studies of developmental trajectories in nonhuman primates, and in other species, too. Fortunately, such research is underway and we have no doubt that it will produce interesting results.

# References

Adams, M. J., Majolo, B., Ostner, J., Schuelke, O., De Marco, A., Thierry, B., ... Weiss, A. (2015). Personality structure and social style in macaques. *Journal of Personality and Social Psychology*, *109*(2), 338–353. Available from http://dx.doi.org/10.1037/pspp0000041.

Aureli, F., Schaffner, C. M., Boesch, C., Bearder, S. K., Call, J., Chapman, C. A., ... van Schaick, C. P. (2008). Fission–fusion dynamics new research frameworks. *Current Anthropology*, *49*, 627–654. Available from http://dx.doi.org/10.1086/586708.

Bell, A. M., Hankison, S. J., & Laskowski, K. L. (2009). The repeatability of behaviour: A meta-analysis. *Animal Behaviour*, *77*, 771–783. Available from http://dx.doi.org/10.1016/j.anbehav.2008.12.022.

Bergmüller, R., & Taborsky, M. (2010). Animal personality due to social niche specialisation. *Trends in Ecology & Evolution*, *25*, 504–511. Available from http://dx.doi.org/10.1016/j.tree.2010.06.012.

Bergvall, U. A., Schäpers, A., Kjellander, P., & Weiss, A. (2011). Personality and foraging decisions in fallow deer. *Dama dama. Animal Behaviour*, *81*, 101–112. Available from http://dx.doi.org/10.1016/j.anbehav.2010.09.018.

Biro, P. A., & Stamps, J. A. (2008). Are animal personality traits linked to life-history productivity? *Trends in Ecology and Evolution*, *23*, 361–368. Available from http://dx.doi.org/10.1016/j.tree.2008.04.003.

Bleidorn, W., Kandler, C., Riemann, R., Angleitner, A., & Spinath, F. M. (2009). Patterns and sources of adult personality development: Growth curve analyses of the NEO PI-R scales in a longitudinal twin study. *Journal of Personality and Social Psychology*, *97*, 142–155. Available from http://dx.doi.org/10.1037/a0015434.

Bleidorn, W., Klimstra, T. A., Denissen, J. J. A., Rentfrow, P. J., Potter, J., & Gosling, S. D. (2013). Personality maturation around the world: A cross-cultural examination of social-investment theory. *Psychological Science*. Available from http://dx.doi.org/10.1177/0956797613498396.

Bouchard, T. J., Jr., & Loehlin, J. C. (2001). Genes, evolution, and personality. *Behavior Genetics*, *31*, 243−273. Available from http://dx.doi.org/10.1023/A:1012294324713.

Brittain, J. E. (1990). Life history strategies in Ephemeroptera and Plecoptera. In I. C. Campbell (Ed.), *Mayflies and stoneflies: Life histories and biology* (pp. 1−12). Dordrecht, Netherlands: Springer Netherlands.

Buss, D. M. (2009). How can evolutionary psychology successfully explain personality and individual differences. *Perspectives on Psychological Science*, *4*, 359−366. Available from http://dx.doi.org/10.1111/j.1745-6924.2009.01138.x.

Carere, C., & van Oers, K. (2004). Shy and bold great tits (*Parus major*): Body temperature and breath rate in response to handling stress. *Physiology & Behavior*, *82*(5), 905−912. Available from http://dx.doi.org/10.1016/j.physbeh.2004.07.009.

Chen, C. S., Burton, M., Greenberger, E., & Dmitrieva, J. (1999). Population migration and the variation of dopamine D4 receptor (DRD4) allele frequencies around the globe. *Evolution and Human Behavior*, *20*, 309−324, http://dx.doi.org/10.1016/S1090-5138(99)00015-X.

Class, B., & Brommer, J. E. (2016). Senescence of personality in a wild bird. *Behavioral Ecology and Sociobiology*. Available from http://dx.doi.org/10.1007/s00265-016-2096-0.

Costa, P. T., Jr., & McCrae, R. R. (1995). Domains and facets: Hierarchical personality assessment using the Revised NEO Personality Inventory. *Journal of Personality Assessment*, *64*(1), 21−50. Available from http://dx.doi.org/10.1207/s15327752jpa6401_2.

Dall, S. R. X., Houston, A. I., & McNamara, J. M. (2004). The behavioural ecology of personality: Consistent individual differences from an adaptive perspective. *Ecology Letters*, *7*(8), 734−739. Available from http://dx.doi.org/10.1111/j.1461-0248.2004.00618.x.

Dutton, D. M. (2008). Subjective assessment of chimpanzee (*Pan troglodytes*) personality: Reliability and stability of trait ratings. *Primates*, *49*, 253−259. Available from http://dx.doi.org/10.1007/s10329-008-0094-1.

Eisenberg, D. T. A., Campbell, B., Gray, P. B., & Sorenson, M. D. (2008). Dopamine receptor genetic polymorphisms and body composition in undernourished pastoralists: An exploration of nutrition indices among nomadic and recently settled Ariaal men of northern Kenya. *BMC Evolutionary Biology*, *8*, 173. Available from http://dx.doi.org/10.1186/1471-2148-8-173.

Figueredo, A. J., Sefcek, J., Vasquez, G., Brumbach, B. H., King, J. E., & Jacobs, W. J. (2005). Evolutionary personality psychology. In D. M. Buss (Ed.), *Handbook of evolutionary psychology* (pp. 851−877). Hoboken, NJ: Wiley.

Figueredo, A. J., Vásquez, G., Brumbach, B. H., & Schneider, S. M. R. (2007). The K-factor, covitality, and personality: A psychometric test of life history theory. *Human Nature*, *18*, 47−73. Available from http://dx.doi.org/10.1007/BF02820846.

Freeman, H. D., Brosnan, S. F., Hopper, L. M., Lambeth, S. P., Schapiro, S. J., & Gosling, S. D. (2013). Developing a comprehensive and comparative questionnaire for measuring personality in chimpanzees using a simultaneous top-down/bottom-up design. *American Journal of Primatology*, *75*, 1042−1053. Available from http://dx.doi.org/10.1002/ajp.22168.

Freeman, H. D., & Gosling, S. D. (2010). Personality in nonhuman primates: A review and evaluation of past research. *American Journal of Primatology*, *72*, 653−671. Available from http://dx.doi.org/10.1002/ajp.20833.

Galdikas, B. M. F. (1985a). Adult male sociality and reproductive tactics among orangutans at Tanjung Puting. *Folia Primatologica, 45*, 9–24. Available from http://dx.doi.org/10.1159/000156188.

Galdikas, B. M. F. (1985b). Orangutan sociality at Tanjung-Puting. *American Journal of Primatology, 9*, 101–119. Available from http://dx.doi.org/10.1002/ajp.1350090204.

Galdikas, B. M. F. (1985c). Subadult male orangutan sociality and reproductive behavior at Tanjung-Puting. *American Journal of Primatology, 8*, 87–99. Available from http://dx.doi.org/10.1002/ajp.1350080202.

Goldberg, L. R. (1990). An alternative "description of personality": The Big-Five factor structure. *Journal of Personality and Social Psychology, 59*, 1216–1229. Available from http://dx.doi.org/10.1037/0022-3514.59.6.1216.

Goodall, J. (1986). *The chimpanzees of Gombe: Patterns of behavior.* Cambridge, MA: Belknap Press of Harvard University.

Gosling, S. D. (2001). From mice to men: What can we learn about personality from animal research? *Psychological Bulletin, 127*, 45–86. Available from http://dx.doi.org/10.1037/0033-2909.127.1.45.

Gosling, S. D., & Graybeal, A. (2007). Tree thinking: A new paradigm for integrating comparative data in psychology. *The Journal of General Psychology, 134*, 259–277. Available from http://dx.doi.org/10.3200/GENP.134.2.259-278.

Harvey, P. H., & Pagel, M. D. (1991). *The comparative method in evolutionary biology.* Oxford, England: Oxford University Press.

Hobolth, A., Christensen, O. F., Mailund, T., & Schierup, M. H. (2007). Genomic relationships and speciation times of human, chimpanzee, and gorilla inferred from a coalescent hidden Markov model. *PLoS Genetics, 3*, 0294–0304. Available from http://dx.doi.org/10.1371/journal.pgen.0030007.

John, O. P., Naumann, L. P., & Soto, C. J. (2008). Paradigm shift to the integrative Big Five trait taxonomy: History, measurement, and conceptual issues. In O. P. John, R. W. Robins, & L. A. Pervin (Eds.), *Handbook of personality: Theory and research* (pp. 114–158). New York, NY: Guilford Press.

Johnstone, R. A. (2001). Eavesdropping and animal conflict. *Proceedings of the National Academy of Sciences of the United States of America, 98*, 9177–9180. Available from http://dx.doi.org/10.1073/pnas.161058798.

Johnstone, R. A., & Manica, A. (2011). Evolution of personality differences in leadership. *Proceedings of the National Academy of Sciences of the United States of America, 108*, 8373–8378. Available from http://dx.doi.org/10.1073/pnas.1102191108.

Kaplan, H., Hill, K., Lancaster, J., & Hurtado, A. M. (2000). A theory of human life history evolution: Diet, intelligence, and longevity. *Evolutionary Anthropology, 9*, 156–185, http://dx.doi.org/10.1002/1520-6505(2000)9:4 < 156::Aid-Evan5 > 3.0.Co;2-7.

King, J. E., & Figueredo, A. J. (1997). The Five-Factor Model plus Dominance in chimpanzee personality. *Journal of Research in Personality, 31*, 257–271. Available from http://dx.doi.org/10.1006/jrpe.1997.2179.

King, J. E., Weiss, A., & Farmer, K. H. (2005). A chimpanzee (*Pan troglodytes*) analogue of cross-national generalization of personality structure: Zoological parks and an African sanctuary. *Journal of Personality, 73*, 389–410. Available from http://dx.doi.org/10.1111/j.1467-6494.2005.00313.x.

King, J. E., Weiss, A., & Sisco, M. M. (2008). Aping humans: Age and sex effects in chimpanzee (*Pan troglodytes*) and human (*Homo sapiens*) personality. *Journal of Comparative Psychology, 122*, 418–427. Available from http://dx.doi.org/10.1037/a0013125.

Konečná, M., Lhota, S., Weiss, A., Urbánek, T., Adamová, T., & Pluháček, J. (2008). Personality in free-ranging Hanuman langur (*Semnopithecus entellus*) males: Subjective ratings and recorded behavior. *Journal of Comparative Psychology, 122,* 379−389. Available from http://dx.doi.org/10.1037/a0012625.

Konečná, M., Weiss, A., Lhota, S., & Wallner, B. (2012). Personality in Barbary macaques (*Macaca sylvanus*): Temporal stability and social rank. *Journal of Research in Personality, 46,* 581−590. Available from http://dx.doi.org/10.1016/j.jrp.2012.06.004.

Kwan, V. S. Y., Gosling, S. D., & John, O. P. (2008). Anthropomorphism as a special case of social perception: A cross-species social relations model analysis of humans and dogs. *Social Cognition, 26,* 129−142. Available from http://dx.doi.org/10.1521/soco.2008.26.2.129.

Latané, B., Williams, K., & Harkins, S. (1979). Many hands make light the work—Causes and consequences of social loafing. *Journal of Personality and Social Psychology, 37,* 822−832. Available from http://dx.doi.org/10.1037//0022-3514.37.6.822.

Lodi-Smith, J., & Roberts, B. W. (2007). Social investment and personality: A meta-analysis of the relationship of personality traits to investment in work, family, religion, and volunteerism. *Personality and Social Psychology Review, 11,* 68−86. Available from http://dx.doi.org/10.1177/1088868306294590.

MacArthur, R. H., & Wilson, E. O. (1963). An equilibrium theory of insular zoogeography. *Evolution, 17,* 373−387. Available from http://dx.doi.org/10.2307/2407089.

Manson, J. H., & Perry, S. (2013). Personality structure, sex differences, and temporal change and stability in wild white-faced capuchins. *Cebus capucinus. Journal of Comparative Psychology, 127,* 299−311. Available from http://dx.doi.org/10.1037/a0031316.

Matthews, L. J., & Butler, P. M. (2011). Novelty-seeking DRD4 polymorphisms are associated with human migration distance out-of-Africa after controlling for neutral population gene structure. *American Journal of Physical Anthropology, 145,* 382−389. Available from http://dx.doi.org/10.1002/ajpa.21507.

McCrae, R. R., & Costa, P. T., Jr. (1997). Personality trait structure as a human universal. *American Psychologist, 52,* 509−516. Available from http://dx.doi.org/10.1037/0003-066X.52.5.509.

McCrae, R. R., & Costa, P. T., Jr. (2003). *Personality in adulthood: A Five-Factor Theory perspective.* New York, NY: Guilford Press.

McCrae, R. R., Costa, P. T., Jr., de Lima, M. P., Simoes, A., Ostendorf, F., Angleitner, A., ... Piedmont, R. L. (1999). Age differences in personality across the adult life span: Parallels in five cultures. *Developmental Psychology, 35,* 466−477. Available from http://dx.doi.org/10.1037/0012-1649.35.2.466.

McCrae, R. R., Costa, P. T., Jr., Ostendorf, F., Angleitner, A., Hrebickova, M., Avia, M. D., ... Smith, P. B. (2000). Nature over nurture: Temperament, personality, and life span development. *Journal of Personality and Social Psychology, 78,* 173−186. Available from http://dx.doi.org/10.1037/0022-3514.78.1.173.

McCrae, R. R., Terracciano, A., & 78 Members of the Personality Profiles of Cultures Project (2005). Universal features of personality traits from the observer's perspective: Data from 50 cultures. *Journal of Personality and Social Psychology, 88,* 547−561. Available from http://dx.doi.org/10.1037/0022-3514.88.3.547.

McGue, M., Bacon, S., & Lykken, D. T. (1993). Personality stability and change in early adulthood: A behavioral genetic analysis. *Developmental Psychology, 29,* 96−109. Available from http://dx.doi.org/10.1037/0012-1649.29.1.96.

Morton, F. B., Lee, P. C., Buchanan-Smith, H. M., Brosnan, S. F., Thierry, B., Paukner, A., ... Weiss, A. (2013). Personality structure in brown capuchin monkeys (*Sapajus apella*):

Comparisons with chimpanzees (*Pan troglodytes*), orangutans (*Pongo* spp.), and rhesus macaques (*Macaca mulatta*). *Journal of Comparative Psychology*, *127*, 282–298. Available from http://dx.doi.org/10.1037/a0031723.

Nettle, D. (2006). The evolution of personality variation in humans and other animals. *American Psychologist*, *61*, 622–631. Available from http://dx.doi.org/10.1037/0003-066X.61.6.622.

Neumann, C., Agil, M., Widdig, A., & Engelhardt, A. (2013). Personality of wild male crested macaques (*Macaca nigra*). *PLoS ONE*, *8*, e69383. Available from http://dx.doi.org/10.1371/journal.pone.0069383.

Penke, L., Denissen, J. J. A., & Miller, G. F. (2007). The evolutionary genetics of personality. *European Journal of Personality*, *21*, 549–587. Available from http://dx.doi.org/10.1002/per.629.

Roberts, B. W., & DelVecchio, W. F. (2000). The rank-order consistency of personality traits from childhood to old age: A quantitative review of longitudinal studies. *Psychological Bulletin*, *126*, 3–25. Available from http://dx.doi.org/10.1037/0033-2909.126.1.3.

Roberts, B. W., Walton, K. E., & Viechtbauer, W. (2006). Patterns of mean-level change in personality traits across the life course: A meta-analysis of longitudinal studies. *Psychological Bulletin*, *132*, 1–25. Available from http://dx.doi.org/10.1037/0033-2909.132.1.1.

Roberts, B. W., Wood, D., & Smith, J. L. (2005). Evaluating Five Factor Theory and social investment perspectives on personality trait development. *Journal of Research in Personality*, *39*, 166–184. Available from http://dx.doi.org/10.1016/j.jrp.2004.08.002.

Sheldon, W. H. (1942). *The varieties of temperament: A psychology of constitutional differences*. New York, NY: Harper & Brothers.

Sinn, D. L., Gosling, S. D., & Moltschaniwskyj, N. A. (2008). Development of shy/bold behaviour in squid: Context-specific phenotypes associated with developmental plasticity. *Animal Behaviour*, *75*, 433–442. Available from http://dx.doi.org/10.1016/j.anbehav.2007.05.008.

Sneddon, L. U. (2003). The bold and the shy: Individual differences in rainbow trout. *Journal of Fish Biology*, *62*, 971–975. Available from http://dx.doi.org/10.1046/j.1095-8649.2003.00084.x.

Steiper, M. E., & Young, N. M. (2006). Primate molecular divergence dates. *Molecular Phylogenetics and Evolution*, *41*, 384–394. Available from http://dx.doi.org/10.1016/j.ympev.2006.05.021.

Stevenson-Hinde, J., & Hinde, C. A. (2011). Individual characteristics: Weaving psychological and ethological approaches. In A. Weiss, J. E. King, & L. Murray (Eds.), *Personality and temperament in nonhuman primates* (pp. 3–14). New York, NY: Springer.

Stevenson-Hinde, J., & Zunz, M. (1978). Subjective assessment of individual rhesus monkeys. *Primates*, *19*, 473–482. Available from http://dx.doi.org/10.1007/BF02373309.

Sussman, A. F., Mates, E. A., Ha, J. C., Bentson, K. L., & Crockett, C. M. (2014). Tenure in current captive settings and age predict personality changes in adult pigtailed macaques. *Animal Behaviour*, *89*, 23–30. Available from http://dx.doi.org/10.1016/j.anbehav.2013.12.009.

Uher, J. (2013). Personality psychology: Lexical approaches, assessment methods, and trait concepts reveal only half of the story—Why it is time for a paradigm shift. *Integrative Psychological and Behavioral Science*, *47*(1), 1–55. Available from http://dx.doi.org/10.1007/s12124-013-9230-6.

van Scheppingen, M. A., Jackson, J. J., Specht, J., Hutteman, R., Denissen, J. J. A., & Bleidorn, W. (2016). Personality trait development during the transition to parenthood: A test of social investment theory. *Social Psychological and Personality Science.* Available from http://dx.doi.org/10.1177/1948550616630032.

Vazire, S., Gosling, S. D., Dickey, A. S., & Schapiro, S. J. (2007). Measuring personality in nonhuman animals. In R. W. Robins, R. C. Fraley, & R. F. Krueger (Eds.), *Handbook of research methods in personality psychology* (pp. 190−206). New York, NY: The Guilford Press.

Viken, R. J., Rose, R. J., Kaprio, J., & Koskenvuo, M. (1994). A developmental genetic analysis of adult personality: Extraversion and neuroticism from 18 to 59 years of age. *Journal of Personality and Social Psychology, 66*, 722−730. Available from http://dx.doi.org/10.1037/0022-3514.66.4.722.

Weiss, A., Adams, M. J., Widdig, A., & Gerald, M. S. (2011). Rhesus macaques (*Macaca mulatta*) as living fossils of hominoid personality and subjective well-being. *Journal of Comparative Psychology, 125*, 72−83. Available from http://dx.doi.org/10.1037/a0021187.

Weiss, A., Inoue-Murayama, M., Hong, K.-W., Inoue, E., Udono, S., Ochiai, T., ... King, J. E. (2009). Assessing chimpanzee personality and subjective well-being in Japan. *American Journal of Primatology, 71*, 283−292. Available from http://dx.doi.org/10.1002/ajp.20649.

Weiss, A., Inoue-Murayama, M., King, J. E., Adams, M. J., & Matsuzawa, T. (2012). All too human? Chimpanzee and orang-utan personalities are not anthropomorphic projections. *Animal Behaviour, 83*, 1355−1365. Available from http://dx.doi.org/10.1016/j.anbehav.2012.02.024.

Weiss, A., & King, J. E. (2015). Great ape origins of personality maturation and sex differences: A study of orangutans and chimpanzees. *Journal of Personality and Social Psychology, 108*, 648−664. Available from http://dx.doi.org/10.1037/pspp0000022.

Weiss, A., King, J. E., & Hopkins, W. D. (2007). A cross-setting study of chimpanzee (*Pan troglodytes*) personality structure and development: Zoological parks and Yerkes National Primate Research Center. *American Journal of Primatology, 69*, 1264−1277. Available from http://dx.doi.org/10.1002/ajp.20428.

Weiss, A., King, J. E., & Perkins, L. (2006). Personality and subjective well-being in orangutans (*Pongo pygmaeus* and *Pongo abelii*). *Journal of Personality and Social Psychology, 90*, 501−511. Available from http://dx.doi.org/10.1037/0022-3514.90.3.501.

Weiss, A., Staes, N., Pereboom, J. J. M., Inoue-Murayama, M., Stevens, J. M. G., & Eens, M. (2015). Personality in bonobos. *Psychological Science, 26*(9), 1430−1439. Available from http://dx.doi.org/10.1177/0956797615589933.

Wolf, M., & McNamara, J. M. (2012). On the evolution of personalities via frequency-dependent selection. *American Naturalist, 179*, 679−692. Available from http://dx.doi.org/10.1086/665656.

Wolf, M., Van Doorn, G. S., & Weissing, F. J. (2011). On the coevolution of social responsiveness and behavioural consistency. *Proceedings of the Royal Society B: Biological Sciences, 278*, 440−448. Available from http://dx.doi.org/10.1098/rspb.2010.1051.

Wolf, M., van Doorn, S., Leimar, O., & Weissing, F. J. (2007). Life-history trade-offs favour the evolution of animal personalities. *Nature, 447*, 581−585. Available from http://dx.doi.org/10.1038/nature05835.

Wolf, M., & Weissing, F. J. (2012). Animal personalities: Consequences for ecology and evolution. *Trends in Ecology & Evolution, 27*, 452−461. Available from http://dx.doi.org/10.1016/j.tree.2012.05.001.

Wrangham, R. W., Wilson, M. L., & Muller, M. N. (2006). Comparative rates of violence in chimpanzees and humans. *Primates*, *47*, 14—26. Available from http://dx.doi.org/10.1007/s10329-005-0140-1.

Yamagata, S., Suzuki, A., Ando, J., Ono, Y., Kijima, N., Yoshimura, K., … Jang, K. L. (2006). Is the genetic structure of human personality universal? A cross-cultural twin study from North America, Europe, and Asia. *Journal of Personality and Social Psychology*, *90*, 987—998. Available from http://dx.doi.org/10.1037/0022-3514.90.6.987.

# A critical evaluation of the Neo-Socioanalytic Model of personality

Brent W. Roberts and Lauren B. Nickel
University of Illinois, Urbana-Champaign, IL, United States

The field of personality development has experienced a genuine resurgence in the last few decades. At the turn of the 21st century, we saw a huge influx of new longitudinal studies of personality development, with a preponderance coming from Europe. Alongside this critical mass of data came new thinking about, and new models of, personality and personality development. As part of the re-emergence of personality development, we authored several frameworks and theoretical ideas to better capture the empirical patterns quickly coalescing within this new body of research. Specifically, we introduced the Neo-Socioanalytic Model (Roberts & Wood, 2006) to address issues in personality and personality development not captured by other personality frameworks developed at the same time. Enough time has now passed that it is worthwhile spending some time and energy to clarify why we developed this framework and to determine its current relevance. To that end, we will describe how the Neo-Socioanalytic Model differs from other personality frameworks and discuss how well components of the framework, such as the principles of personality development, have held up over time.

## The Neo-Socioanalytic Model

The Neo-Socioanalytic Model consists of four primary, and essentially distinct, domains of personality: traits, motives, abilities, and narratives (for more in-depth descriptions, see Roberts, 2006; Roberts & Wood, 2006; Roberts, Wood, & Caspi, 2008). Fig. 11.1 depicts these four domains in the model, along with the units of analysis, the modes of assessment, and the primary contexts thought to play a role in personality development. Traits, the first domain, are defined as the relatively enduring, automatic patterns of thoughts, feelings, and behaviors that people exhibit in similar situations across time (Roberts, 2009). Values and motives, the second domain, reflect what people find desirable—that is, what people want to do or would like to have in their lives. The third domain consists of abilities and the associated hierarchical models and identifies what people are capable of doing. Abilities are classically viewed through the lens of *cognitive* abilities but could also include abilities in other areas such as emotional and physical (Lubinski, 2000). The fourth and

Personality Development Across the Lifespan. DOI: http://dx.doi.org/10.1016/B978-0-12-804674-6.00011-9

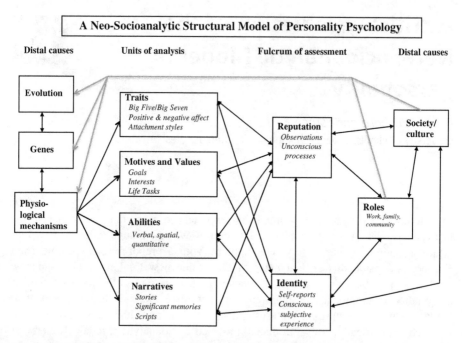

**Figure 11.1** The Neo-Socioanalytic Model of personality.

final domain focuses on the stories and narratives people use to understand themselves, their environments, and the history of their lives (McAdams, 1993).

The domains of personality are both manifested by and organized around two entities, reflecting both the psychological and the methodological: (1) identity, assessed through self-reports, and (2) reputation, assessed through observer reports. From a methodological perspective, self-reports and observer reports represent two privileged, yet flawed, ways of accessing information about people—what they say about themselves and what others say about them, respectively. Personality inventories represent typical self-report methods, whereas observer methods are best exemplified by observer ratings of behavior.

These methods' corresponding global psychological constructs, identity and reputation, have meaning above and beyond the methods themselves. Identity reflects the sum total of opinions cognitively available to a person across the four units of analysis described earlier. Traits, the first domain of these cognitions, are the content of identity—whether people consider themselves shy or creative, for example. Identity also pertains to the meta-cognitive perception of those same self-perceptions. Specifically, people can see themselves as both "outgoing" and a "carpenter" (content) and feel more or less confident and invested (meta-perception) in those self-perceptions.

Reputation is others' perspectives of a person's traits, motives, abilities, and narratives. Consistent with the concept of the "looking glass self," reputation can affect identity; that is, people will come to see themselves differently depending on how others define them. But others' perspectives of a person do not always impact their identity, as underlying dispositions can affect reputation directly without being mediated through identity. This reflects the fact that people are not always aware of their own behavior and that others may see patterns in their behavior that they do not. We also propose that people actively shape their own reputation, seen in Fig. 11.1 with an arrow pointing from identity to reputation. It is a fact of social interaction that people do not share all of their self-perceptions with others and actively attempt to persuade them of their desirable qualities (Goffman, 1959).

When considering the environment, we prefer social roles as the unit of analysis. Social roles tend to fall in two broad domains that correspond closely to two primary motives: (1) status and (2) belongingness. Roles associated with status include work and social-position roles, such as CEO, supervisor, or PTA president. Roles associated with belongingness include friendship, family, and community roles, such as father, mother, or friend. Although work is often associated with status hierarchies, both status and belongingness roles can be found in the workplace. Clearly, the person who aspires for and achieves the CEO position has acquired a high status role. But many friendships are made and fostered through work and serve to provide meaning and support in a situation where status is salient.

# Why did we, and do we, need the Neo-Socioanalytic Model?

At the time of the creation of the Neo-Socioanalytic Model, there were a number of existing frameworks largely dedicated to organizing the units of analysis in the field of personality psychology. The most relevant frameworks to the development of the Neo-Socioanalytic Model were Hogan's socioanalytic theory (Hogan & Blickle, 2013), McAdams' Levels Theory (McAdams & Pals, 2006), and McCrae and Costa's Five Factor Theory (1999). Of these three, the closest system to the Neo-Socioanalytic Model is socioanalytic theory; our framework was intended to be a permutation of Hogan's work. Both frameworks focus on traits, acknowledge the distinctiveness of identity and reputation, and highlight the importance of social roles. But socioanalytic theory lacked a consideration of development, which is part of what prompted the creation of the Neo-Socioanalytic Model. Other significant differences between the two models include the treatment of motivation and the inclusion of abilities and narratives in the Neo-Socioanalytic Model, domains, which are missing from socioanalytic theory.

Another framework that informed the development of the Neo-Socioanalytic Model is the Five Factor Theory (FFT). The two fundamental differences between these two models lie in (1) the organization and prioritization of traits and (2) the factors that lead to the development of traits. In the FFT, traits are considered "basic tendencies," meaning that they cause all other psychological constructs, such as motives. Based on our work on goals and motives, we believe that the domain of motivation is distinct enough from that of traits to warrant considering motivation as a separate domain with its own causal status. When one assesses desires in the form of what people want, rather than what they do, the correlations between motivation and the Big Five are modest at best (Roberts & Robins, 2000). Moreover, the developmental trends for goals lie in stark contrast to traits, as the importance of goals tends to decrease, whereas trait levels tend to increase (Roberts, O'Donnell, & Robins, 2004). The second critical difference between the two models lies in the effects of experiences on traits. The FFT posits that personality traits are functionally unaffected by experience. In contrast, the Neo-Socioanalytic Model assumes that personality is influenced by socialization factors such that experiences can and do render change in personality traits. While there are other differences between the two models, such as the inclusion of cognitive abilities, the organization of personality units and distinctiveness of the domains are the most critical differences.

The third framework closely allied with the Neo-Socioanalytic Model is McAdams' Levels Theory or the "New Big Five" (McAdams & Pals, 2007). These two frameworks are highly similar in the units of analysis considered vital, as well as the inclusion of environmental influences at cultural and role levels. However, three features of the McAdams framework make it problematic for the field of personality development. First, traits are assumed to be relatively developmental—that is, little or no clarity is provided in Levels Theory for explaining why personality traits develop and change throughout adulthood. Second, the units of analysis in Levels Theory have often been conceptualized on different "levels," reflecting different levels of changeability, with motives and narratives assumed to be less consistent and more changeable than traits. In contrast, to reflect the fact that the stability of motives and narrative structures is quite similar to that of traits (McAdams, Bauer, Sakaeda, Anyidoho et al., 2006), we proposed in the Neo-Socioanalytic Model that each domain can be organized from broad to narrow, and each subsumes both stable and changeable aspects of traits, motives, and narratives. Finally, like the other two frameworks discussed, Levels Theory does not include individual differences in abilities, which in our opinion is a serious oversight given the importance of abilities for both individuals and societies.

In sum, we found it necessary to create the Neo-Socioanalytic Model for two main reasons. First, no established personality model organized the units of analysis in a way that matched the empirical literature well. The existing models either omitted major domains of individual differences or structured them in a way that needlessly prioritized certain domains over others (e.g., traits being prioritized over motives). Second, none of the existing models provided an adequate framework for capturing the patterns of continuity and change found across these domains or for identifying the most sensible causes of those changes. We would never argue that the Neo-Socioanalytic Model is qualitatively different than models like the FFM or Levels Theory. We would argue, however, that the small distinctions among the frameworks are profound for how we understand and study both personality and personality development.

# Evaluating the Neo-Socioanalytic Model

The Neo-Socioanalytic Model embodies the structure and content of personality as well as a set of principles of personality development and mechanisms of continuity and change. In terms of the structure of the framework, there is now ample evidence to support the division of the units of analysis, the distinction between identity and reputation, and the importance of social roles in development and personality. First, research testing the relative contribution of some or all of the units of analysis in the framework reliably shows that traits, motives, abilities, and narrative dimensions tend to contribute independently to fundamental outcomes such as educational attainment, health, and relationships (e.g., Damian, Su, Shanahan, Trautwein, & Roberts, 2015; Roberts, Kuncel, Shiner, Caspi, & Goldberg, 2007; Lodi-Smith, Geise, Roberts, & Robins, 2009). Second, the fact that self-reports (associated with identity) and observer ratings (associated with reputation) are not interchangeable has emerged as a fundamental finding in personality psychology, so much so that we now have theories to explain why these two perspectives are not synonymous (Vazire, 2010). Finally, a host of studies have examined relationship, work, and community roles and their association with changes in personality over time (see Roberts et al., 2008, for a review).

The principles of personality development and mechanisms of continuity and change, the other components of the Neo-Socioanalytic Model, are more involved. To aid in evaluating the status of these components, we provided a table of the principles and mechanisms as well as exemplary research on each topic and our estimate of the strength of the evidence for the idea. Table 11.1 shows the seven basic principles of personality trait development put forward in the Neo-Socioanalytic Model. We briefly review the seven principles here, as we have provided an exhaustive evaluation of them elsewhere (Roberts & Damian, in press).

## *The cumulative continuity principle*

The first principle, the cumulative continuity principle, proposes that personality traits increase in rank-order consistency throughout the life span, peaking between the ages of 50 and 60, with a plateau or decrease after that decade (Roberts & DelVecchio, 2000). The accumulated evidence for this principle appears to be more robust than most of the components of the Neo-Socioanalytic Model. Originally derived from a meta-analysis of 152 longitudinal studies examining of the rank-order consistency of personality traits (Roberts & DelVecchio, 2000), the findings were confirmed by a second meta-analysis testing the same idea (Ferguson, 2010). The evidentiary value for the cumulative continuity principle is comparable to the "first law" of behavior genetics (all phenotypes are heritable). In this case, it appears that the first law of personality development should be that at a population level, rank-order consistency increases with age until midlife.

**Table 11.1 Principles of personality development**

| Principle | Definition | Example research | Strength of evidence |
|---|---|---|---|
| Cumulative Continuity Principle | Personality traits increase in rank-order consistency until midlife | Ferguson (2010) | Strong |
| Maturity Principle | People become more socially dominant, agreeable, conscientious, and emotionally stable with age | Donnellan, Conger, and Burzette (2007) | Strong |
| Social Investment Principle | Investing in social institutions, such as age-graded social roles, outside of the self is one of the driving mechanisms of personality development in general and greater maturity in particular | Bleidorn et al. (2013) | Good |
| Correspondive Principle | The effect of life experience on personality development is to deepen the characteristics that lead people to those experiences in the first place | Roberts et al. (2003) | Moderate |
| Plasticity Principle | Personality traits are open systems that can be influenced by the environment at any age | Lodi-Smith and Roberts (2012) | Strong |
| Role Continuity Principle | Consistent roles rather than consistent environments are the cause of continuity in personality over time | | Weak |
| Identity Development Principle | With age, the process of developing, committing to, and maintaining an identity leads to greater personality consistency | Lodi-Smith et al. (in press) | Weak |
| Niche-Picking Principle | Through their personality traits, people create social environments and paths in their lives that help maintain their current trait levels | Roberts and Robins (2004) | Weak |

## The maturity principle

The second principle of personality development is the maturity principle; that is, people become more psychologically mature with age, with maturity being defined as becoming more agreeable, conscientious, and emotionally stable (see Table 11.1). This definition aligns closely with what we observe in the data: as people age, they tend to increase in agreeableness, conscientiousness, and emotional stability (Roberts, Walton, & Viechtbauer, 2006). This meta-analysis also showed robust increases in young adulthood in social dominance, a facet of extraversion that reflects assertiveness, self-confidence, and dominance.

Additional research since 2006, both cross-sectional and longitudinal, has provided support for the argument that people generally increase in agreeableness, conscientiousness, and emotional stability as they grow older. Numerous cross-sectional aging studies show, across cohorts, that older people are more agreeable, conscientious, and emotionally stable than their younger counterparts (Donnellan & Lucas, 2008). The longitudinal evidence in support of the maturity principle is impressive because it encompasses data from many different research teams and multiple longitudinal studies from a variety of countries. For example, a longitudinal study of Iowans found increases in constraint, a form of conscientiousness, and marked decreases in neuroticism during the transition from adolescence to young adulthood (Donnellan, Conger, & Burzette, 2007). Remarkably similar findings have been reported in longitudinal studies from Minnesota (Johnson, Hicks, McGue, & Iacono, 2007), Germany (Lüdtke, Roberts, Trautwein, & Nagy, 2011), Finland (Josefsson et al., 2013), and Italy (Vecchione, Alessandri, Barbaranelli, & Caprara, 2012). Like the cumulative continuity principle, the maturity principle has strong support.

## The social investment principle

The third principle, the social investment principle, was created, in part, to explain *why* people become more mature with age. Specifically, it posits that personality trait change in young adulthood occurs because of new investments in conventional social roles, such as being a parent or an employee, which bring with them experiences and expectations for being nurturing, responsible, and emotionally stable (see Table 11.1; Roberts, Wood, & Smith, 2005). In other words, the personalities of young adults change because they commit to adult social roles (Lodi-Smith & Roberts, 2007). This appears to be a normative process (Helson, Kwan, John, & Jones, 2002) because across most societies, people commit themselves to the adult roles found in the social structures of family, work, and community.

There appears to be good evidence for the social investment principle as longitudinal data has shown that increasing investment in adult social roles correlate with changes in personality traits. For example, Lehnart, Neyer, and Eccles (2010) found that young adults who became increasingly socially invested in romantic relationships experienced simultaneous increases in emotional stability and self-esteem. In a study of age differences in personality traits across 62 countries, people who adopted adult roles earlier showed an accelerated form of personality development consistent with the social investment principle (Bleidorn et al., 2013). Furthermore, a 2-year longitudinal study of students from Finland showed that initiating a career or job for the first time was linked to increases in conscientiousness (Leikas & Salmela-Aro, 2015).

However, two findings from recent research pose a challenge to the social investment principle. First, one study showed that longitudinal changes in psychological investment in work were associated with predicted changes in personality traits, but not only in young adulthood (Hudson, Roberts, & Lodi-Smith, 2012). Although this is only one study, and although it partially supports the social investment principle, the findings are relevant to the age specificity of the principle. There may be nothing special about social investment in young adulthood, and relevant experiences may lead to consonant personality trait changes at any age. If so, it would be incumbent to show that the preponderance of factors associated with the social investment principle occur in young adulthood, an empirical finding yet to be demonstrated.

The second finding that poses a problem for the social investment principle is the lack of personality change associated with becoming a parent (Scheppingen et al., in press; Specht, Egloff, & Schmukle, 2011). Unlike other normative transitions, becoming a parent is not associated with the requisite increases in agreeableness, conscientiousness, or emotional stability that are the basis of the social investment principle. In fact, if anything, becoming a parent is associated with no change or slightly negative changes in personality traits (e.g., Galdiolo & Roskam, 2014). Two possibilities arise as a result of these findings. First, the relevant change may happen well in advance of the acquisition of the role of parent; people who become parents may plan far in advance to have children and do the appropriate work on their identity well before embarking on that path. The second possibility highlights the importance of getting the definition of social investment right and correctly identifying the causal mechanism. For example, the cause of personality trait change may not be the acquisition of the role or even commitment to the role, but rather the sense of mastery that comes with successfully fulfilling the obligations of the role. Future research should attempt to tease these factors apart in researching just what aspects of experiences are associated with normative changes in personality traits in young adulthood.

## The corresponsive principle

The fourth principle, the corresponsive principle, states that people enter specific environments and have specific experiences because of their personality traits, and in turn, those experiences change the personality traits that brought them to the situation in the first place. For example, the corresponsive principle predicts that if a person chooses a job such as sales because they are extraverted, then the experience of being a salesperson will make them even more extraverted than before. The idea is nothing more or less than a reciprocal relationship, a hallmark of self-efficacy theory, for example (Bandura, 1977). It should be noted at the outset that the corresponsive principle was not stated in the extreme, i.e., that all life course person—environment transactions follow this pattern. Rather, it was proposed because it was a notable pattern in many longitudinal studies, albeit not all of them and not all of the time.

The corresponsive principle emerged out of studies testing a wide swath of personality traits alongside an equally wide array of outcomes (e.g., Lüdtke et al., 2011; Roberts & Robins, 2004; Roberts, Caspi, & Moffitt, 2003). Subsequent research has produced findings supporting the original argument that personality and experiential factors are corresponsive. In one case, the relation between goals and personality change was tested within a genetically informed model (Bleidorn et al., 2010). This longitudinal study confirmed the corresponsive relation between traits and goals, such that agentic goals and extraversion were associated; it also showed that this corresponsive relation was both genetic and environmental in origin. Similar findings have shown corresponsive relations between personality and psychopathology (Klimstra, Akse, Hale, Raaijmakers & Meeus, 2010) and between neuroticism and negative life events (Jeronimus, Riese, Sanderman, & Ormel, 2014).

Despite the supportive findings, conceptual and empirical issues have proven to be a challenge to testing the corresponsive principle. Many associations between personality traits and life experiences are noncorresponsive. For example, in the case of life events (Lüdtke et al., 2011), we found that people who were more open tended to have more difficulties in their sex lives, their sleeping and eating habits, and their finances. But experiencing these difficulties did not predict increases in openness; instead they predicted increases in neuroticism. In this study, people who were more open inadvertently made themselves more neurotic by being more open in the first place. Despite these types of findings, we would argue that there is definitely evidence in support of the corresponsive principle, but we would also argue that it has not been articulated in a fashion clear enough to test formally and refute. Our future theoretical work will need to clarify when, where, and just how often this type of pattern should result in order to provide a stronger theoretical edifice to test. Also, there is no elegant way of testing the corresponsive principle. In the past, we have examined overall patterns of predictions and change relations, which is crude. Moreover, there is no clear indication of how much corresponsiveness should exist to either support or refute the idea. Future research should engage with the methodological challenges entailed in testing the corresponsive principle.

## *The plasticity principle*

The fifth principle, the plasticity principle, posits that personality traits can and do change at any age (Table 11.1). While there has been no systematic assessment of the changeability of personality traits across the life course, there are enough studies showing that change does occur at previously unexpected ages (i.e., in middle and old age) and that evidence for this principle appears to be strong. In terms of mean-level changes, there is now robust evidence that personality traits change throughout the life course. It has been found repeatedly that young adulthood is the primary age in which mean-level change in personality occurs and mostly for the better (i.e., higher conscientiousness, lower neuroticism, etc.) (Donnellan et al., 2007; Johnson et al., 2007; Josefsson et al., 2013; Vecchione et al., 2012). But studies also show evidence for mean-level personality trait change in both middle age (Allemand, Gomez, & Jackson, 2010) and old age (Kandler, Kornadt, Hagemeyer, & Neyer, 2015; Wortman, Lucas, & Donnellan, 2012). However, in many cases personality trait change in old age is not for the better, with many traits decreasing as people approach senescence.

Research on individual differences in personality trait change also supports the plasticity principle. Many studies have found associations between personality traits and life experiences such as relationship factors (Lehnart et al., 2010), stressful life events (Jeronimus et al., 2014; Laceulle, Nederhof, Karreman, Ormel, & van Aken, 2012), and work experiences (Le, Donnellan, & Conger, 2014), demonstrating individual differences in personality trait change in adolescence and young adulthood, as well as in middle age (Van Aken, Denissen, Branje, Dubas, & Goossens, 2006) and old age (Mõttus, Johnson, & Deary, 2012). While it was previously thought that personality traits did not change in old age, recent studies indicate that change does indeed occur and can be predicted certain experiential factors. For instance, a recent study showed that changes in perceived social support among older adults (age 60−90) were related to changes in conscientiousness (Hill, Payne, Roberts & Stine-Morrow, 2014). Another study showed that changes in social engagement in old age were associated with changes in conscientiousness and agreeableness (Lodi-Smith & Roberts, 2012). While some studies find less plasticity for specific traits in middle and old age (Allemand et al., 2010), the preponderance of findings would support the argument that personality traits remain plastic throughout the life course.

## The role continuity principle

The sixth principle, the role continuity principle, posits that consistent roles, rather than consistent environments, are the cause of continuity in personality traits over time. For example, a person could move from organization to organization, even moving from one geographic location to another, but their role, which is to be a CEO or professor might remain relatively unchanged. Though this is an intriguing idea, no test for it has been developed so far. In addition, there are some findings contradicting the role continuity principle. For instance, Neyer and Lehnart (2007) found that staying in a relationship longer was related to more personality trait change, but the role continuity principle suggests that the consistency of the relationship would have suggested greater consistency in personality traits.

## The identity development principle

The seventh principle, the identity development principle, proposes that with age, the process of developing, committing to, and maintaining an identity leads to greater personality consistency (Roberts & Caspi, 2003). Identity development is thought to facilitate personality consistency by providing clear reference points for making life decisions; strong identities serve as filters for life experiences and lead individuals to interpret new events in ways consistent with their identities. To date, there is only one study that has examined the relation of identity structure to personality continuity; the results indicate that that self-concept clarity is unrelated to personality consistency (Lodi-Smith, Spain, Cologgi, & Roberts, in press). So, the initial empirical test of the identity development principle failed to support the idea. Nonetheless, one study is not enough to draw firm conclusions from and clearly, more research is necessary to evaluate both the role continuity and identity development principles.

## The niche-picking principle

In our more in-depth review of the principles of personality development (Roberts & Damian, in press), we decided it was necessary to identify a new principle, albeit one with little or no empirical basis, termed the niche-picking principle. This new principle proposes that, through their personality traits, people create social environments and paths in their lives that help maintain their current trait levels; this type of person—environment transaction should lead to greater personality trait consistency because of the selection effects of personality traits (Table 11.1). We identified this as a separate principle largely because many people confused the corresponsive principle with this type of effect. That is, many researchers thought the corresponsive principle referred to selecting environments, which then made people more consistent over time, whereas in reality the corresponsive principle refers to change, not continuity. Thus we have formally proposed a principle that encompasses the similar process—selecting environments as result of one's personality—but through which people remain consistent rather than change.

The niche-picking principle has, to our knowledge, only been tested twice. In the first study, which took place at a highly competitive university, students who were both extraverted and disagreeable fit into that type of college climate better than other students. In turn, better fit was associated with more continuity and less change in personality (Roberts & Robins, 2004). This finding was partially replicated in a second longitudinal study of college students at another highly competitive university (Harms, Roberts, & Winter, 2006). But the overarching idea of niche-picking, despite its appeal, has yet to be tested well or rigorously in longitudinal research. We propose the niche-picking principle as a complement to the corresponsive principle in the hopes that (1) it might help clarify the corresponsive principle and (2) it will provide an impetus to test the niche-picking principle.

These principles of personality development, most of which have strong empirical support, are entirely unique to the Neo-Socioanalytic Model. Nonetheless, some clarity still needs to be brought to principles like the corresponsive principle, and, as always seems to be the case, more data is needed to evaluate all of the principles. Currently, many of the principles capture patterns of development but only imply the existence of mechanisms that would explain the patterns captured therein. In the next two sections, we consider the mechanisms proposed to explain the patterns derived and codified in the principles of personality development.

# Mechanisms of continuity and change

Since we began theorizing about personality development (e.g., Caspi & Bem, 1990; Caspi & Roberts, 1999), we have sought to identify factors that contribute to the stabilization of personality over time. There exists good evidence for some factors, such as genetic factors, and a sparse amount of evidence for others, such as environmental factors, which is surprising given the length of time these ideas have been invoked (see Table 11.2). Quite possibly, genetic factors are the most robust factor contributing to continuity in personality traits; longitudinal data from twins suggest that much of the stability in adult personality is attributable to genetic factors (e.g., McGue, Bacon, & Lykken, 1993). To the extent that the effects of genetic factors might increase with age, they might also be partially responsible for the increase in personality consistency. Conversely, there is relatively little good evidence for the environment's role in promoting continuity, especially as portrayed in our model as manifest in consistent social roles over time. That said, the same genetic studies showing a robust genetic signal for continuity also sometimes find evidence for environmental contributions to continuity in personality traits (e.g., Johnson, McGue, & Krueger, 2005). It would be ideal if investigators began to track social roles or social environments over time to test what aspects of the environment contribute to continuity.

A similar, if less sanguine, story can be told for person–environment transactions and their contribution to continuity (Table 11.2). These are some of the longest-standing but least-tested ideas in personality development. Almost everyone

**Table 11.2 Mechanisms of personality consistency**

| Mechanism | Definition | Evidence |
|---|---|---|
| Genetic effects | Heritable factors fix personality | Strong |
| Role continuity/ environment | Unchanging environments promote personality consistency | Weak |
| Person-by-environment transactions | | |
| Attraction | Being drawn to personality consistent environments | Weak |
| Selection | Choosing or being chosen for personality consistent environments | Weak |
| Reactance | Reacting to experiences or environments in personality consistent fashions | Weak |
| Evocation | Evoking personality consistent reactions from others | Weak |
| Manipulation | Changing one's environment to be more personality consistent | Weak |
| Attrition | Leaving environments so as to avoid changing one's personality | Weak |
| Identity clarity | Having a clear sense of self | Weak |

accepts the fact that selecting into certain environments leads to greater personality consistency, with the same being said for reactance, evocation, manipulation, and attrition, and there are good studies supporting the existence of these mechanisms. For example, people really are attracted to environments that are consistent with their personality traits and interests (e.g., Ackerman & Heggestad, 1997; Botwin, Buss, & Shackelford, 1997). But we as researchers have yet to test the next obvious leg of the implicit path model: research showing that those who more successfully select trait-consistent environments stay more consistent over time. There is a striking dearth of longitudinal research testing whether these mechanisms play out in the expected way, and this constitutes one of the more serious empirical omissions in the field of personality development.

If the evidence for mechanisms of continuity looks poor, the evidence for the mechanisms of change looks even worse (see Table 11.3). This might come as a surprise, given how reasonable many of the mechanisms appear to be—how could anyone doubt that reward and punishment contingencies shape behavior? It is clear that behavior can be shaped with different schedules of reinforcement and punishment, but we have yet to show that actual contingencies shape personality. A similar lack of evidence exists for the remaining putative mechanisms of change, such as watching others, watching ourselves, and listening to others. These mechanisms all emerged out of mechanistic models of behavioral modification that have been tested on proximal behavioral change, but not long-term change.

Instead of directly testing these mechanisms, longitudinal researchers have linked demographic and "experiential" variables with changes in personality traits over time. We now know that being in more satisfying marriages and jobs is linked to increases in emotional stability (e.g., Roberts & Chapman, 2000; Scollon & Diener, 2006; Specht, Egloff, & Schumkle, 2013). Doing drugs and other nonconforming activities is associated with decreases in conscientiousness (Roberts & Bogg, 2004; Littlefield, Sher, & Steinley, 2010), while investing in work in a conventional fashion is associated with increases in conscientiousness (Hudson et al., 2012). While seemingly consistent with many of the mechanisms outlined in the

**Table 11.3 Mechanisms of personality change**

| Mechanism | Definition | Evidence |
|---|---|---|
| Role contingencies | Roles provide reinforcements and punishments for specific behaviors | Weak |
| Watching ourselves | Seeing changes in our own behaviors leads to changes in perceptions of ourselves or changes in reputation | Weak |
| Watching others | Change comes about through modeling other's behavior | Weak |
| Listening to others | People provide feedback on how we should change | Weak |
| Role expectations and demands | Roles communicate behaviors that will be reinforced and punished | Moderate |

Neo-Socioanalytic Model, none of these studies examines if a role model inspired these changes, if listening to someone's feedback changed their personality, or even if these experiences tracked actual changes in contingencies. Even in research that examines the effect of interventions, such as therapy, on personality trait change, the mechanistic features of the intervention go undiagnosed (Roberts, Luo, Chow, Su & Hill, in press).

Moreover, there are data points that call into question the presumed effect of something as widely accepted as social learning through observation. For example, many assume that children learn how to act simply by watching their parents model specific behaviors, eventually resulting in children adopting the behavioral reper-toire of their mother and father—what could be a more consistent model of behav-ior than the personality traits of one's parents? Because of this, one might assume that children end up being more like their parents because they model their parents' personality as they develop throughout childhood. However, the research linking parents' and children's personalities calls into question this assumption. While par-ents' and children's personalities are correlated, the average correlation is remark-ably small—around 0.13 (Loehlin, 2005). This number is far too small to reflect the combined effect of genetics and socialization; in fact, the magnitude of this correla-tion is entirely consistent with the hypothesis that genetics are the sole reason for any similarity between parents and their offspring. Combine this with the near-zero correlation between the personalities of parents and adoptive children, and one may infer that, if modeling does indeed occur, it is not contributing to personality devel-opment. The second fly in the ointment of the socialization models of personality is found in the research on couples and whether their personalities converge over time. Early research set out to show that the personalities of the members of a cou-ple converge but found little or no evidence for it (Caspi & Herbener, 1993). Two decades later, most longitudinal research continues to fail to show any strong con-vergence over time in couples who stay together (Hudson & Fraley, 2014).

In summary, like the mechanisms of continuity, the mechanisms of change have been "understudied." Part of this oversight presumably comes from the fact that so many researchers accept the basic premises behind each mechanism. These wide-spread assumptions seem warranted—we have good evidence that selection and socialization processes work in the short term on outcomes like behavior change in a lab. However, personality development researchers have yet to test the implicit full model in which one follows up on the short-term selection and socialization processes to see if they affect long-term personality continuity and change. Clearly, the next frontier in personality development research is investigations into the mechanistic processes underlying personality continuity and change.

## Clarifying terminological heterogeneity and future directions

We need to apologize to those few individuals who have bothered to keep track of our prior theoretical writings, as it could be said that we have used too many different titles and names for our ideas. Part of this terminological confusion arose because of the development of our thinking. The earliest incarnation of these theoretical ideas was called the "Cumulative Continuity Model," which reflected the emphasis at that time on explanations for greater personality consistency rather than change (Roberts & Caspi, 2003). In other cases, the terminology reflected an effort to adapt the model for an audience who might not be immediately open to the idea of personality change (e.g., the ASTMA model for industrial—organizational psychologists, Roberts, 2006). Additionally, we have theorized about specific components of the Neo-Socioanalytic Model, such as the sociogenomic model of personality traits (Roberts & Jackson, 2008). This could be confusing as some mistakenly equate "personality" with "personality trait." Finally, certain aspects of the framework have taken on a life of their own in the hands of motivated researchers. For example, the social investment principle has been promoted to "social investment theory" in a number of papers.

We see no intrinsic conflict between the overarching model afforded in the Neo-Socioanalytic Model and the identification and creation of more specific theories to be housed within it. Of course, for a theory to be good, it should (1) explain the phenomena of interest, (2) provide testable hypotheses that could lead to the disconfirmation of the theory, (3) be as parsimonious as possible, and (4) generate new ideas. To the extent that these subtheories satisfy the basic necessities of good theorizing, not only should they proceed but also be supported and not confused with the Neo-Socioanalytic Model.

It is appropriate to evaluate the Neo-Socioanalytic Model with these basic criteria for good theorizing in mind. First, the initial motivation for the creation of the Neo-Socioanalytic Model was mostly descriptive. None of the personality theories that existed at the time described the topography of personality or personality development in a way that captured the empirical picture emerging from the data. In this respect, we would argue that the Neo-Socioanalytic Model was, and remains, quite useful—no other framework does as good of a job of capturing the cleavages in personality psychology or the developmental patterns found in each domain. Second, though we have proposed testable hypotheses in the form of the principles of personality development and the mechanisms of continuity and change, the articulation of those ideas could be clearer. Third, the Neo-Socioanalytic Model is admittedly not the least bit parsimonious. This is only made worse by the fact that the theory to date has primarily focused on personality trait development. Once it has expanded to better deal with the unique and particular developmental patterns and etiology of both abilities and motives, it is bound to become more complex. Fourth, we have found the model useful for generating new ideas within personality development. In fact, the number of ideas generated far exceeds the number that has been tested at this point in time. In sum, while useful, the Neo-Socioanalytic Model could be much improved still.

Two areas are clearly in need of attention for the Neo-Socioanalytic Model to be improved in the coming years. First, as the majority of mechanisms of both continuity and change remain untested, simply testing these ideas in well-designed longitudinal research is critical. Many of these putative mechanisms may not be mechanisms at all, which would lead to both a modification in the theory and more parsimony. Second, the Neo-Socioanalytic Model was unabashedly biased toward personality development in adulthood (as are most other frameworks, for that matter). There is a huge theoretical gulf in personality psychology concerning the childhood development of personality. Beautiful research is being conducted on the "what" of childhood personality (e.g., Tackett, Slobodskaya Mar, Deal, Halverson et al., 2012), but comparable research on the "how" is missing—we do not know how children become adults possessing the personalities we study so often in our research. We have recently begun the task of filling in this gulf (e.g., Roberts & Hill, in press), but nonetheless, given the emerging consensus on the importance of personality for leading a successful and fulfilling life, it would be invaluable to know the childhood antecedents of adult personality (see Herzhoff, Kushner, & Tackett, Chapter 2).

In closing, let us pitch for new theorizing. Theories are best improved when they compete with one another to help answer critical questions about a phenomenon. The Neo-Socioanalytic Model does not capture all of emerging empirical patterns, but neither do many of the existing frameworks. This means we need new thinking and theorizing, and it would be best if these ideas were crafted in such a way that they provided viable alternatives to these existing frameworks.

# References

Ackerman, P. L., & Heggestad, E. D. (1997). Intelligence, personality, and interests: Evidence for overlapping traits. *Psychological Bulletin, 121*, 219−245. Available from http://dx.doi.org/10.1037/0033-2909-121.2.219.

Allemand, M., Gomez, V., & Jackson, J. J. (2010). Personality trait development in midlife: Exploring the impact of psychological turning points. *European Journal of Ageing, 7*, 147−155. Available from http://dx.doi.org/10.1007/s10433-010-0158-0.

Bandura, A. (1977). Self-efficacy: Toward a unifying theory of behavioral change. *Psychological Review, 84*(2), 191.

Bleidorn, W., Kandler, C., Hülsheger, U. R., Riemann, R., Angleitner, A., & Spinath, F. M. (2010). Nature and nurture of the interplay between personality traits and major life goals. *Journal of Personality and Social Psychology, 99*, 366−379. Available from http://dx.doi.org/10.1037/a0019982.

Bleidorn, W., Klimstra, T. A., Denissen, J. J., Rentfrow, P. J., Potter, J., & Gosling, S. D. (2013). Personality maturation around the world: A cross-cultural examination of social-investment theory. *Psychological Science, 24*, 2530−2540. Available from http://dx.doi.org/10.1177/0956797613498396.

Botwin, M. D., Buss, D. M., & Shackelford, T. K. (1997). Personality and mate perferences: Five factors in mate selection and marital satisfaction. *Journal of Personality, 65*, 107−136. Available from http://dx.doi.org/10.1111/j.1467-6494.1997.tb00531.x.

Caspi, A., & Bem, D. J. (1990). Personality continuity and change across the life course. In L. Pervin (Ed.), *Handbook of personality theory and research* (pp. 549−575). New York: Guilford Press.

Caspi, A., & Herbener, E. S. (1993). Marital assortment and phenotypic convergence: Longitudinal evidence. *Social Biology*, *40*, 48−60. Available from http://dx.doi.org/10.1080/19485565.1993.9988835.

Caspi, A., & Roberts, B. W. (1999). Personality change and continuity across the life course. In L. A. Pervin, & O. P. John (Eds.), *Handbook of personality theory and research* (Vol. 2, pp. 300−326). New York: Guilford Press.

Damian, R. I., Su, R., Shanahan, M., Trautwein, U., & Roberts, B. W. (2015). Can personality traits and intelligence compensate for background disadvantage? Predicting status attainment in adulthood. *Journal of Personality and Social Psychology*, *109*, 473−489. Available from http://dx.doi.org/10.1037/pspp0000024.

Donnellan, M. B., Conger, R. D., & Burzette, R. G. (2007). Personality development from late adolescence to young adulthood: Differential stability, normative maturity, and evidence for the maturity-stability hypothesis. *Journal of Personality*, *75*, 237−264. Available from http://dx.doi.org/10.1111/j.1467-6494.2007.00438.x.

Donnellan, M. B., & Lucas, R. E. (2008). Age differences in the Big Five across the life span: evidence from two national samples. *Psychology and Aging*, *23*, 558. Available from http://dx.doi.org/10.1037/a0012897.

Ferguson, C. J. (2010). A meta-analysis of normal and disordered personality across the life span. *Journal of Personality and Social Psychology*, *98*, 659−667. Available from http://dx.doi.org/10.1037/a0018770.

Galdiolo, S., & Roskam, I. (2014). Development of personality traits in response to childbirth: A longitudinal dyadic perspective. *Personality and Individual Differences*, *69*, 223−230. Available from http://dx.doi.org/10.1016/j.paid.2014.06.002.

Goffman, E. (1959). *The presentation of self in everyday life*. Garden City, NY: Doubleday.

Harms, P. D., Roberts, B. W., & Winter, D. (2006). Becoming the Harvard man: Person−environment fit, personality development, and academic success. *Personality and Social Psychology Bulletin*, *32*, 851−865. Available from http://dx.doi.org/10.1177/0146167206287720.

Helson, R., Kwan, V. S., John, O. P., & Jones, C. (2002). The growing evidence for personality change in adulthood: Findings from research with personality inventories. *Journal of Research in Personality*, *36*, 287−306. Available from http://dx.doi.org/10.1016/S0092-6566(02)00010-7.

Hill, P. L., Payne, B. R., Roberts, B. W., & Stine-Morrow, E. A. L. (2014). Perceived social support predicts increased conscientiousness during older adulthood. *Journal of Gerontology: Psychological Sciences*, *69*, 543−547. Available from http://dx.doi.org/10.1093/geronb/gbt024.

Hogan, R., & Blickle, G. (2013). Socioanalytic theory. *Handbook of personality at work*, 53−70.

Hudson, N. W., & Fraley, R. C. (2014). Partner similarity matters for the insecure: Attachment orientations moderate the association between similarity in partners' personality traits and relationship satisfaction. *Journal of Research in Personality*, *53*, 112−123. Available from http://dx.doi.org/10.1016/j.jrp.2014.09.004.

Hudson, N. W., Roberts, B. W., & Lodi-Smith, J. (2012). Personality trait development and social investment at work. *Journal of Research in Personality*, *46*, 334−344. Available from http://dx.doi.org/10.1016/j.jrp.2012.03.002.

Jeronimus, B. F., Riese, H., Sanderman, R., & Ormel, J. (2014). Mutual reinforcement between neuroticism and life experiences: A five-wave, 16-year study to test reciprocal causation. *Journal of Personality and Social Psychology*, *107*, 751−764. Available from http://dx.doi.org/10.1037/a0037009.

Johnson, W., Hicks, B. M., McGue, M., & Iacono, W. G. (2007). Most of the girls are alright, but some aren't: Personality trajectory groups from ages 14 to 24 and some associations with outcomes. *Journal of Personality and Social Psychology*, *93*, 266–284. Available from http://dx.doi.org/10.1037/0022-3514.93.2.266.

Johnson, W., McGue, M., & Krueger, R. F. (2005). Personality stability in late adulthood: A behavioral genetic analysis. *Journal of Personality*, *73*, 523–552. Available from http://dx.doi.org/10.1111/j.1467-6494.2005.00319.x.

Josefsson, K., Jokela, M., Cloninger, C. R., Hintsanen, M., Salo, J., Hintsa, T., ... Keltikangas-Järvinen, L. (2013). Maturity and change in personality: Developmental trends of temperament and character in adulthood. *Development and Psychopathology*, *25*, 713–727. Available from http://dx.doi.org/10.1017/S0954579413000126.

Kandler, C., Kornadt, A. E., Hagemeyer, B., & Neyer, F. J. (2015). Patterns and sources of personality development in old age. *Journal of Personality and Social Psychology*, *109*, 175–191. Available from http://dx.doi.org/10.1037/pspp0000028.

Klimstra, T. A., Akse, J., Hale, W. W., III, Raaijmakers, Q. A., & Meeus, W. H. (2010). Longitudinal associations between personality traits and problem behavior symptoms in adolescence. *Journal of Research in Personality*, *44*, 273–284. Available from http://dx.doi.org/10.1016/j.jrp.2010.02.004.

Laceulle, O. M., Nederhof, E., Karreman, A., Ormel, J., & Aken, M. A. G. (2012). Stressful events and temperament change during early and middle adolescence: The TRAILS study. *European Journal of Personality*, *26*, 276–284. Available from http://dx.doi.org/10.1002/per.832.

Le, K., Donnellan, M. B., & Conger, R. (2014). Personality development at work: Workplace conditions, personality changes, and the correspondive principle. *Journal of Personality*, *82*, 44–56. Available from http://dx.doi.org/10.1111/jopy.12032.

Lehnart, J., Neyer, F. J., & Eccles, J. (2010). Long-term effects of social investment: The case of partnering in young adulthood. *Journal of Personality*, *78*, 639–670. Available from http://dx.doi.org/10.1111/j.1467-6494.2010.00629.x.

Leikas, S., & Salmela-Aro, K. (2015). Personality trait changes among young Finns: The role of life events and transitions. *Journal of Personality*, *83*, 117–126. Available from http://dx.doi.org/10.1111/jopy.12088.

Littlefield, A. K., Sher, K. J., & Steinley, D. (2010). Developmental trajectories of impulsivity and their association with alcohol use and related outcomes during emerging and young adulthood I. *Alcoholism: Clinical and Experimental Research*, *34*, 1409–1416. Available from http://dx.doi.org/10.1111/j.1530-0277.2010.01224.x.

Lodi-Smith, J. L., Geise, A. C., Roberts, B. W., & Robins, R. W. (2009). Narrating personality change. *Journal of Personality and Social Psychology*, *96*, 679–689. Available from http://dx.doi.org/10.1037/a0014611.

Lodi-Smith, J., & Roberts, B. W. (2007). Social investment and personality: A meta-analytic analysis of the relationship of personality traits to investment in work, family, religion, and volunteerism. *Personality and Social Psychology Review*, *11*, 68–86. Available from http://dx.doi.org/10.1177/1088868306294590.

Lodi-Smith, J., & Roberts, B. W. (2012). Concurrent and prospective relationships between social engagement and personality traits in older adulthood. *Psychology and Aging*, *27*, 720–727. Available from http://dx.doi.org/10.1037/a0027044.

Lodi-Smith, J., Spain, S. M., Cologgi, K., & Roberts, B. W. (in press). The development of self-concept clarity in adulthood. *Journal of Personality and Social Psychology*.

Loehlin, J. C. (2005). Resemblance in personality and attitudes between parents and their children. In S. Bowles, H. Gintis, & M. O. Groves (Eds.), *Unequal chances: Family background and economic success* (pp. 192–207). New York, NY: Russell Sage Foundation.

Lubinski, D. (2000). Scientific and social significance of assessing individual differences: "Sinking shafts at a few critical points." *Annual Review of Psychology, 51*, 405–444. Available from http://dx.doi.org/10.1146/annurev.psych.51.1.405.

Lüdtke, O., Roberts, B. W., Trautwein, U., & Nagy, G. (2011). A random walk down university avenue: Life paths, life events, and personality trait change at the transition to university life. *Journal of Personality and Social Psychology, 101*, 620–637. Available from http://dx.doi.org/10.1037/a0023743.

McAdams, D. P. (1993). *The stories we live by: Personal myths and the making of the self.* New York, NY: Guilford.

McAdams, D. P., Bauer, J. J., Sakaeda, A. R., Anyidoho, N. A., Machado, M. A., Magrino-Failla, K., ... Pals, J. L. (2006). Continuity and change in the life story: A longitudinal study of autobiographical memories in emerging adulthood. *Journal of personality, 74*, 1371–1400.

McAdams, D. P., & Pals, J. L. (2006). A new Big Five: fundamental principles for an integrative science of personality. *American Psychologist, 61*, 204.

McAdams, D. P., & Pals, J. L. (2007). The role of theory in personality research. In R. W. Robins, R. C. Fraley, & R. F. Krueger (Eds.), *Handbook of research methods in personality psychology* (pp. 3–20). New York, NY: Guilford Press.

McCrae, R. R., & Costa, P. T., Jr. (1999). A Five-Factor Theory of personality. In L. A. Pervin, & O. P. John (Eds.), *Handbook of personality: Theory and research* (pp. 139–153). New York, NY: Guilford Press.

McGue, M., Bacon, S., & Lykken, D. T. (1993). Personality stability and change in early adulthood: A behavioral genetic analysis. *Developmental Psychology, 29*, 96–109. Available from http://dx.doi.org/10.1037/0012-1649.29.1.96.

Mõttus, R., Johnson, W., & Deary, I. J. (2012). Personality traits in old age: Measurement and rank-order stability and some mean-level change. *Psychology and Aging, 27*, 243–249. Available from http://dx.doi.org/10.1037/a0023690.

Neyer, F. J., & Lehnart, J. (2007). Relationships matter in personality development: Evidence from an 8-year longitudinal study across young adulthood. *Journal of Personality, 75*, 535–568. Available from http://dx.doi.org/10.1111/j.1467-6494.2007.00448.x.

Roberts, B. W. (2006). Personality development and organizational behavior. *Research in Organizational Behavior, 27*, 1–40. Available from http://dx.doi.org/10.1016/S0191-3085(06)27001-1.

Roberts, B. W. (2009). Back to the future: Personality and assessment and personality development. *Journal of Research in Personality, 43*, 137–145. Available from http://dx.doi.org/10.1016/j.jrp.2008.12.015.

Roberts, B. W., & Bogg, T. (2004). A longitudinal study of the relationships between conscientiousness and the social–environmental factors and substance-use behaviors that influence health. *Journal of Personality, 72*, 325–354. Available from http://dx.doi.org/10.1111/j.0022-3506.2004.00264.x.

Roberts, B. W., & Caspi, A. (2003). The cumulative continuity model of personality development: Striking a balance between continuity and change in personality traits across the life course. In R. M. Staudinger, & U. Lindenberger (Eds.), *Understanding human development: Lifespan psychology in exchange with other disciplines* (pp. 183–214). Dordrecht, NL: Kluwer Academic Publishers.

Roberts, B. W., & Chapman, C. N. (2000). Change in dispositional well-being and its relation to role quality: A 30-year longitudinal study. *Journal of Research in Personality, 34*, 26–41. Available from http://dx.doi.org/10.1006/jrpe.1999.2259.

Roberts, B. W., & DelVecchio, W. F. (2000). The rank-order consistency of personality from childhood to old age: A quantitative review of longitudinal studies. *Psychological Bulletin, 126*, 3—25. Available from http://dx.doi.org/10.1037/0033-2909.126.1.3.

Roberts, B. W., & Jackson, J. J. (2008). Sociogenomic personality psychology. *Journal of Personality, 76*, 1523—1544. Available from http://dx.doi.org/10.1111/j.1467-6494.2008.00530.x.

Roberts, B. W., & Robins, R. W. (2000). Broad dispositions, broad aspirations: The intersection of the Big Five dimensions and major life goals. *Personality and Social Psychology Bulletin, 26*, 1284—1296. Available from http://dx.doi.org/10.1177/0146167200262009.

Roberts, B. W., & Robins, R. W. (2004). Person—environment fit and its implications for personality development: A longitudinal study. *Journal of Personality, 72*, 89—110. Available from http://dx.doi.org/10.1111/j.0022-3506.2004.00257.x.

Roberts, B. W., & Wood, D. (2006). Personality development in the context of the Neo-Socioanalytic Model of personality. In D. Mroczek, & T. Little (Eds.), *Handbook of personality development* (pp. 11—39). Mahwah, NJ: Lawrance Erlbaum Associates.

Roberts, B. W., Caspi, A., & Moffitt, T. E. (2003). Work experiences and personality development in young adulthood. *Journal of Personality and Social Psychology, 84*, 582—593. Available from http://dx.doi.org/10.1037/0022-3514.84.3.582.

Roberts, B. W., & Damian, R. I. (in press). The principles of personality trait development and their relation to psychopathology. In D. Lynam (Ed.), *Personality and clinical psychology: Purdue series on behavior*.

Roberts, B. W., & Hill, P. L. (in press). The sourdough model of conscientiousness. In J. Burrus & R. Roberts (Eds.), *Building better students*.

Roberts, B. W., Kuncel, N. R., Shiner, R., Caspi, A., & Goldberg, L. R. (2007). The power of personality: The comparative validity of personality traits, socio-economic status, and cognitive ability for predicting important life outcomes. *Perspectives in Psychological Science, 2*, 313—345. Available from http://dx.doi.org/10.1111/j.1745-6916.2007.00047.x.

Roberts, B. W., Luo, J., Chow, P., Su, R., & Hill, P. L. (in press). A systematic review of personality trait change through intervention. *Psychological Bulletin*.

Roberts, B. W., O'Donnell, M., & Robins, R. W. (2004). Goal and personality trait development in emerging adulthood. *Journal of Personality and Social Psychology, 87*, 541—550. Available from http://dx.doi.org/10.1037/0022-3514.87.4.541.

Roberts, B. W., Walton, K. E., & Viechtbauer, W. (2006). Patterns of mean-level change in personality traits across the life course: A meta-analysis of longitudinal studies. *Psychological Bulletin, 132*, 1—25. Available from http://dx.doi.org/10.1037/0033-2909.132.1.1.

Roberts, B. W., Wood, D., & Caspi, A. (2008). The development of personality traits in adulthood. In O. P. John, R. W. Robins, & L. A. Pervin (Eds.), *Handbook of personality: Theory and research* (pp. 375—398). New York, NY: Guilford.

Roberts, B. W., Wood, D., & Smith, J. L. (2005). Evaluating Five Factor Theory and social investment perspectives on personality trait development. *Journal of Research in Personality, 39*, 166—184. Available from http://dx.doi.org/10.1016/j.jrp.2004.08.002.

Scheppingen, M. A. V., Jackson, J. J., Specht, J., Hutteman, R., Denissen, J. J. A., Bleidorn, W. (in press). Personality trait development during the transition to parenthood: A test of social investment theory. *Social Psychology and Personality Science*.

Scollon, C. N., & Diener, E. (2006). Love, work, and changes in extraversion and neuroticism over time. *Journal of Personality and Social Psychology, 91*, 1152—1165. Available from http://dx.doi.org/10.1037/0022-3514.91.6.1152.

Specht, J., Egloff, B., & Schmukle, S. C. (2011). Stability and change of personality across the life course: The impact of age and major life events on mean-level and rank-order stability of the Big Five. *Journal of Personality and Social Psychology, 101*(4), 862.

Specht, J., Egloff, B., & Schmukle, S. C. (2013). Examining mechanisms of personality maturation: The impact of life satisfaction of the development of the Big Five personality traits. *Social Psychological & Personality Science, 4*, 181−189. Available from http://dx.doi.org/10.1177/1948550612448197.

Tackett, J. L., Slobodskaya, H. R., Mar, R. A., Deal, J., Halverson, C. F., Baker, S. R., ... Besevegis, E. (2012). The hierarchical structure of childhood personality in five countries: Continuity from early childhood to early adolescence. *Journal of Personality, 80* (4), 847−879.

Van Aken, M. A. G., Denissen, J. J. A., Branje, S. J. T., Dubas, J. S., & Goossens, L. (2006). Midlife concerns and short-term personality change in middle adulthood. *European Journal of Personality, 20*, 497−513. Available from http://dx.doi.org/10.1002/per.603.

Vazire, S. (2010). Who knows what about a person? The self-other knowledge asymmetry (SOKA) model. *Journal of Personality and Social Psychology, 98*, 281−300. Available from http://dx.doi.org/10.1037/a0017908.

Vecchione, M., Alessandri, G., Barbaranelli, C., & Caprara, G. (2012). Gender differences in the Big Five personality development: A longitudinal investigation from late adolescence to emerging adulthood. *Personality and Individual Differences, 53*, 740−746. Available from http://dx.doi.org/10.1016/j.paid.2012.05.033.

Wortman, J., Lucas, R. E., & Donnellan, M. B. (2012). Stability and change in the Big Five personality domains: Evidence from a longitudinal study of Australians. *Psychology and Aging, 27*, 867−874. Available from http://dx.doi.org/10.1037/a0029322.

# Part Four

# Important Personality Characteristics and Their Development

# The lifespan development of self-esteem

**12**

*Ulrich Orth*
University of Bern, Bern, Switzerland

The question of whether self-esteem—which is defined as an "individual's subjective evaluation of his or her worth as a person" (Donnellan, Trzesniewski, & Robins, 2011, p. 718; see also Harter, 2006)—shows normative change across the lifespan has been debated for decades (see, e.g., Demo, 1992; Huang, 2010; Pullmann, Allik, & Realo, 2009; Robins, Trzesniewski, Tracy, Gosling, & Potter, 2002; Wylie, 1979). Fortunately, in recent years a growing number of longitudinal studies have yielded converging evidence on the general pattern of the lifespan development of self-esteem. Moreover, during the past decade, longitudinal research has tackled additional issues—such as the stability of individual differences in self-esteem—that should be resolved to gain a more complete understanding of the development of self-esteem. This chapter provides an overview of this field, by addressing the following questions: What is the normative lifespan trajectory of self-esteem? To which degree is self-esteem a stable trait like extraversion and neuroticism? Is the development of self-esteem consequential, that is, does self-esteem influence success and well-being in important life domains? Although previous reviews are available (Orth & Robins, 2014; Robins & Trzesniewski, 2005; Trzesniewski, Donnellan, & Robins, 2013), the field currently develops quickly, supporting the need for an up-to-date review.

## The self-esteem trajectory across the lifespan

As yet, three longitudinal studies are available that have tracked the self-esteem trajectory across the lifespan (Orth, Maes, & Schmitt, 2015; Orth, Robins, & Widaman, 2012; Orth, Trzesniewski, & Robins, 2010). All three studies used data from large and diverse samples, which had been assessed multiple times for periods of 4–16 years. The samples included broad age ranges from adolescence, or young adulthood, to old age. The analyses were based on cohort-sequential growth modeling, which allowed using the information from all participants simultaneously to model the trajectory across the complete observed age range (Duncan, Duncan, & Strycker, 2006; Preacher, Wichman, MacCallum, & Briggs, 2008). In all studies, competing growth models were tested, such as models without any change (i.e., intercept-only), and linear, quadratic, and cubic models. In all studies, an inverted U-shaped trajectory fit the data best, suggesting that self-esteem increases

Personality Development Across the Lifespan. DOI: http://dx.doi.org/10.1016/B978-0-12-804674-6.00012-0

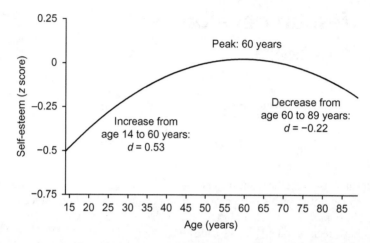

**Figure 12.1** Average predicted trajectory of self-esteem from age 14 to 89 years (Orth et al., 2015). Self-esteem increased from adolescence to age 60 years and then decreased into old age. Effect sizes are reported as *d* values, indicating that the increase from age 14 to 60 years corresponded to a medium effect size, and the decrease from age 60 to 89 years to a small effect size.
Copyright 2015 by the American Psychological Association (APA). Adapted with permission. Orth, U., Maes, J., & Schmitt, M. (2015). Self-esteem development across the life span: A longitudinal study with a large sample from Germany. *Developmental Psychology, 51*, 248−259.

continuously from adolescence to middle adulthood, peaks at about age 50−60 years, and then decreases into old age. Fig. 12.1 illustrates this pattern using findings from Orth et al. (2015). Across studies, the increase from adolescence to middle adulthood corresponded to an effect size ranging from about 0.30 to 0.50 (expressed as *d*; Cohen, 1992), whereas the decrease from middle adulthood to old age ranged from about −0.20 to −0.70 (thus, varying more strongly across studies). In sum, there is now robust evidence on the average, normative pattern of changes in self-esteem across the lifespan.

In addition, an increasing number of longitudinal studies has focused on specific developmental stages, such as adolescence (Birkeland, Melkevik, Holsen, & Wold, 2012; Erol & Orth, 2011; Hutteman, Nestler, Wagner, Egloff, & Back, 2015; Kuzucu, Bontempo, Hofer, Stallings, & Piccinin, 2014; Morin, Maiano, Marsh, Nagengast, & Janosz, 2013), young adulthood (Chung et al., 2014; Kiviruusu, Huurre, Aro, Marttunen, & Haukkala, 2015; Wagner, Lang, Neyer, & Wagner, 2014; Wagner, Lüdtke, Jonkmann, & Trautwein, 2013; Zeiders, Umaña-Taylor, & Derlan, 2013), and old age (Wagner, Gerstorf, Hoppmann, & Luszcz, 2013; Wagner, Hoppmann, Ram, & Gerstorf, 2015; Wagner et al., 2014). Generally, the findings of these studies converge with the lifespan trajectory described earlier, suggesting that self-esteem increases in adolescence and young adulthood and decreases in old age. Moreover, von Soest, Wichstrom, and Kvalem (2016) examined trajectories of domain-specific self-esteem (such as self-evaluations with regard to physical appearance, academic competence, and social acceptance) in adolescence and young adulthood. For most dimensions of domain-specific self-esteem, the trajectory was consistent with the developmental pattern of global self-esteem depicted above (see also Cole et al., 2001).

Importantly, the longitudinal studies showed that individuals differ in the particular lifespan trajectory they follow, as indicated by significant variances of growth factors. Likewise, studies using growth mixture modeling (see, e.g., Ram & Grimm, 2009) indicate that distinct classes of self-esteem development can be identified (Birkeland et al., 2012; Morin et al., 2013). The heterogeneity of self-esteem trajectories raises the question of which factors explain why individuals deviate from the average trajectory.

A first set of factors includes demographic variables such as gender, socio-economic status (as indicated by education and income), and ethnicity. Across studies, men and women differed only slightly, or not all, in the self-esteem trajectory (Erol & Orth, 2011; Orth et al., 2010, 2012, 2015; Wagner, Lüdtke et al., 2013), which is consistent with meta-analytic findings based on cross-sectional data suggesting that the gender difference in self-esteem is small (Kling, Hyde, Showers, & Buswell, 1999; Major, Barr, Zubek, & Babey, 1999). Individuals with high socioeconomic status showed higher self-esteem than individuals with low socioeconomic status at each point of the lifespan, corresponding to a small- to medium-sized effect (Orth et al., 2010, 2012, 2015; Wagner, Gerstorf et al., 2013; Wagner et al., 2014). Finally, longitudinal studies have tested for the moderating effect of ethnicity on the self-esteem trajectory using data from US samples (Erol & Orth, 2011; Orth et al., 2010; Shaw, Liang, & Krause, 2010). For example, the findings suggested that African Americans experienced a stronger increase of self-esteem in young adulthood and also showed a stronger decline in old age. It is important to note that these ethnic differences in self-esteem could not be explained by differences in socioeconomic status and health (Orth et al., 2010) and that the factors that account for the diverging lifespan trajectories of European Americans and African Americans are not yet understood.

A second set of factors that might influence the lifespan trajectory of self-esteem includes personality characteristics and life experiences. For example, research suggests that extraversion, emotional stability, and conscientiousness explain why some individuals experience more positive trajectories (Erol & Orth, 2011; Wagner, Lüdtke et al., 2013). Moreover, stressful life experiences such as serious accidents and illnesses, criminal victimization, and unemployment account for negative change in self-esteem (Orth & Luciano, 2016; Pettit & Joiner, 2001). The available evidence also suggests that transitions in romantic relationships such as beginning a relationship and separating (Luciano & Orth, 2016; Wagner, Becker, Lüdtke, & Trautwein, 2015), as well as the quality of romantic relationships (Mund, Finn, Hagemeyer, Zimmermann, & Neyer, 2015; Schaffhuser, Wagner, Lüdtke, & Allemand, 2014), influence the development of self-esteem. However, it should be noted that several longitudinal studies failed to find evidence that factors such as work success, social network size, and closeness to one's parents predict change in self-esteem (Harris et al., 2015; Kuster, Orth, & Meier, 2013; Marshall, Parker,

Ciarrochi, & Heaven, 2014; Orth et al., 2012). Thus an important goal of future research will be to gain a better understanding of the factors that influence the individual trajectory of self-esteem.

More evidence is needed also with regard to the extent of the self-esteem decline in old age. As noted above, whereas in some studies the decline was strong (Orth et al., 2010, 2012), other studies suggest relatively small decreases (Orth et al., 2015; Wagner, Gerstorf et al., 2013; Wagner, Hoppmann et al., 2015; Wagner et al., 2014). It is possible that sociocultural and economic differences between countries—such as attitudes toward the elderly, pension schemes, and availability of health care—contribute to cross-cultural differences in the old-age decline in self-esteem. In fact, empirical evidence suggests that differences in socioeconomic status and health moderate the trajectory in old age; that is, the decline in self-esteem was much smaller when older adults had stable income and good health (Orth et al., 2010). Moreover, longitudinal research shows that declines in cognitive abilities and perceived control, as well as increasing loneliness, may contribute to lower self-esteem in old age (Wagner, Gerstorf et al., 2013; Wagner, Hoppmann et al., 2015).

Research has tested whether there are developmental trends in other aspects of self-esteem, besides its level (i.e., high vs low), such as instability (Kernis, 2005) and contingency (Crocker & Wolfe, 2001). Self-esteem instability is defined as the degree to which people experience short-term fluctuations in self-esteem in daily life (i.e., intraindividual variability), and self-esteem contingency, a related but distinct concept, can be defined as the degree to which a person's self-esteem depends on external feedback. The findings from a study with a large sample including participants from age 13 to 72 years suggested that self-esteem becomes better adjusted across adolescence and adulthood—that is, not only higher but also less fluctuating and less contingent (Meier, Orth, Denissen, & Kühnel, 2011). It should be noted, however, that this study included only few participants at age 60 years and older. Thus future research should test whether self-esteem continues to become more stable and less contingent in old age, or whether this trend reverses at the end of middle adulthood, similar to the developmental trend for the level of self-esteem.

An interesting question is whether there have been secular changes in the self-esteem trajectory across the lifespan during the past decades (Trzesniewski & Donnellan, 2009; Twenge & Campbell, 2001). More precisely, did sociocultural changes in Western countries result in higher levels of self-esteem, or steeper increases in self-esteem, among more recent generations compared to older generations? In fact, an increasing cultural focus on self-esteem in parenting, education, in the media, and at the workplace might have contributed to more positive self-esteem trajectories among cohorts born since about the 1970s (Gentile, Twenge, & Campbell, 2010). As a side note, it is also possible that the same sociocultural changes have been ineffective and have rather led to the development of maladaptive personality characteristics such as narcissism (for the debate see, e.g., Trzesniewski, Donnellan, & Robins, 2008; Twenge, Konrath, Foster, Campbell, & Bushman, 2008). With regard to self-esteem, however, the findings from cohort-sequential longitudinal studies—which allow disentangling age and cohort effects (Baltes, Cornelius, & Nesselroade, 1979)—suggest that the normative trajectory has not changed across the cohorts born during the 20th century, with regard to both level and shape of the trajectory (Erol & Orth, 2011; Orth et al., 2010, 2012, 2015). These null findings are meaningful given that the samples in these cohort-sequential studies were large (ranging from 1800 to 7100 participants), increasing the power to test for cohort effects. Moreover, two of the samples were nationally representative, which strengthens the validity of the findings.

Research suggests that cultures shape the prototypical self-concept among their members (Heine, Lehman, Markus, & Kitayama, 1999; Markus & Kitayama, 1991), potentially affecting the normative self-esteem trajectory. Thus it is important to test whether the lifespan trajectory found in Western samples, as reviewed above, replicates in samples from other cultural contexts (Henrich, Heine, & Norenzayan, 2010). Recently, Bleidorn et al. (2016) tested for cross-cultural differences in the age trends in self-esteem from age 16 to 45 years, using data from nearly 1 million participants from about 50 countries. The general pattern of increasing self-esteem in adolescence and young adulthood replicated in almost all countries. Importantly, however, cross-cultural differences with regard to socioeconomic, demographic, and cultural-value indicators moderated the increase in self-esteem. For example, the results suggested that women from countries with greater gender equality experience steeper increases during adolescence and young adulthood than women from countries with more traditional gender roles and stronger discrimination of women.

As yet, no theory is available that focuses specifically on self-esteem development across the life course (for a review of theories from the broader context of personality development, see Specht et al., 2014). Sociometer theory (Leary, 2004, 2012; Leary & Baumeister, 2000) might be a promising starting point for developing a theory of the lifespan development of self-esteem. Sociometer theory states that self-esteem reflects a person's relational value as subjectively perceived by the person him- or herself. Relational value is defined as "the degree to which other people regard their relationships with the individual as valuable or important" (Leary, 2004, p. 375). Consequently, whether an individual perceives that he or she has high or low relational value depends on the degree to which the individual thinks that he or she is, and will be in the long term, sought after for inclusion in desired relationships and groups. Thus sociometer theory predicts that self-esteem changes whenever the individual perceives that his or her relational value rises or falls (note that most of these processes are automatic, effortless, and preconscious; Leary & Baumeister, 2000).

On the one hand, a person's perceived relational value—and, consequently, his or her self-esteem—will be influenced by changes in the objective standing on social attributes that contribute to the true relational value of individuals, such as competence, friendliness, trustworthiness, social status, and physical attractiveness (Leary & Baumeister, 2000). If most people improve in many of these attributes during adolescence and young adulthood (as suggested by the maturity principle of personality development; Roberts, Wood, & Caspi, 2008), this might explain why individuals tend to increase in self-esteem during these developmental periods.

On the other hand, a person's perceived relational value can also be altered if the individual changes the way how he or she habitually processes existing and new information on the social attributes mentioned earlier. For example, if an individual reevaluates his or her beliefs about the centrality of specific attributes (e.g., if the individual starts to believe that trustworthiness is more important for being a valued romantic partner than attractiveness), this might lead to changes in his or her perceived relational value. Other factors that influence how information on relational value is processed include selective attention to positive versus negative information about the self and choice of reference group. During adolescence and young adulthood, people tend to select social contexts that match their personality (i.e., niche picking; see Roberts et al., 2008), which likely leads to adaptive changes in the standards by which they evaluate themselves and, consequently, to higher self-esteem.

Thus, building on sociometer theory, I propose that age-related changes in both the objective standing on valued social attributes and in the processing of self-related information might explain why self-esteem shows normative change across the lifespan as observed in the empirical studies reviewed earlier. Moreover, these processes might not only explain the normative trajectory of self-esteem but might also explain individual deviations from the average trajectory in the population. In future research, it would be interesting to explore these hypotheses in more detail.

## The stability of individual differences in self-esteem

Although the average level of self-esteem changes in systematic ways across the life course, research suggests—as will be reviewed in this section—that individual differences in self-esteem are relatively stable across long periods. As early as at the end of the 19th century, William James pointed to the stability of self-esteem by observing that "there is a certain average tone of self-feeling which each one of us carries about with him" (James, 1890, p. 306). Later, empirical studies have tested for the rank-order stability of self-esteem. Typically, estimates of stability were based on test–retest correlations between two assessments of the same sample, where the second assessment is conducted some time—e.g., 1 or 2 years—after the first assessment (note that a test–retest correlation of 1 indicates perfect stability and a correlation of 0 indicates complete absence of stability). Generally, these studies suggested that the stability of self-esteem is high (Alsaker & Olweus, 1992; Block & Robins, 1993; Marsh, Craven, & Debus, 1998; O'Malley & Bachman, 1983). Trzesniewski, Donnellan, and Robins (2003) meta-analyzed the findings of 50 published studies and, in addition, examined data from 4 large nationally representative samples. Their findings suggested that stability is low during childhood, increases in adolescence, is highest in young and middle adulthood, and decreases during old age. For intervals of 3 years (i.e., the average observed time interval across studies), the rank-order stability of self-esteem was estimated as 0.64 when corrected for the effect of measurement error. Moreover, Trzesniewski et al. (2003) found that the pattern of findings replicated across gender, ethnicity, measure of self-esteem, and year of publication.

However, although estimates of rank-order stability provide some information about the stability of constructs such as self-esteem, a complete understanding requires information about the pattern of stability estimates across intervals of different length (Fraley & Roberts, 2005). Clearly, rank-order stability decreases, as the interval between assessments increases. But as Fraley and Roberts (2005) have demonstrated, the crucial question is whether the stability of a construct asymptotically approaches zero or a nonzero, positive value when intervals become very long. A nonzero asymptote has important theoretical implications, because it indicates that constant factors—such as genetic influences, formative experiences in early childhood, or stable environmental conditions—contribute to the maintenance of individual differences in the construct. In contrast, a zero asymptote suggests that only transient factors shape the individuals' standing on the construct.

Therefore, in a study with a large sample that was assessed multiple times across 29 years, Kuster and Orth (2013) examined the time-dependent decline of stability in self-esteem and tested alternative functions that might explain the pattern of stability across time. The results showed that the decline in stability followed an exponential decay function with a nonzero asymptote at about 0.40. Thus, as the time interval increased, stability first quickly declined but in the long run leveled off at a medium-sized value. Moreover, the pattern of results held across gender and across age groups from adolescence to old age. The findings suggest that individual differences in self-esteem are relatively stable across very long periods and that constant factors that account for the long-term stability of self-esteem must be present. The time-dependent pattern of stability in self-esteem was similar to findings on the Big Five personality traits (Fraley & Roberts, 2005), although the asymptotic value might be somewhat smaller for self-esteem than for the Big Five (Anusic & Schimmack, 2016; Kandler, Zimmermann, & McAdams, 2014). Nevertheless, the results overall suggest that self-esteem exhibits trait-like stability. Thus individuals who have relatively high (or low) self-esteem at one developmental stage are likely to have high (or low) self-esteem 10, 20, or even 30 years later.

Another approach to gain information about the stability of a construct is to test latent trait-state models, using structural equation modeling (Cole, 2012; Kenny & Zautra, 1995, 2001). These models allow disentangling stable and unstable variance components (i.e., trait and state factors) of a construct over time. Three recent longitudinal studies have used this approach to examine the stability of individual differences in self-esteem across long periods (Donnellan, Kenny, Trzesniewski, Lucas, & Conger, 2012; Kuster & Orth, 2013; Wagner, Lüdtke, & Trautwein, 2016). The findings of these studies showed that a stable trait factor is needed to explain the patterns of change and stability in the data. Across the three studies, about 70% to 85% of the variance in self-esteem was accounted for by trait factors, whereas only 15% to 30% was state variance or measurement error. A short-term longitudinal study that used data from four assessments across 18 months yielded similar estimates of trait and state components of self-esteem, which strengthens the generalizability of the conclusions from the long-term studies (Orth & Luciano, 2016).

Taken together, the studies reviewed in this section suggest that self-esteem shows trait-like stability, even across very long periods. Put differently, the findings suggest that self-esteem is a relatively enduring personality characteristic rather than a state-like construct such as mood.

# The effects of self-esteem on important life outcomes

Does it matter whether people develop high or low self-esteem as they grow up and go through life? Does self-esteem influence what people experience in their relationships, at work, and in the health domain, or are high versus low self-esteem mere epiphenomena of a person's successes versus failures in important life domains? The question of whether self-esteem influences life outcomes has been hotly debated (Baumeister, Campbell, Krueger, & Vohs, 2003; Krueger, Vohs, & Baumeister, 2008; Orth & Robins, 2014; Swann, Chang-Schneider, & McClarty, 2007, 2008).

Since the past decade, a growing number of longitudinal studies have suggested that self-esteem does have consequences for people's lives. Specifically, the studies indicated that self-esteem predicts relationship satisfaction and relationship quality (Johnson & Galambos, 2014; Mund et al., 2015; Orth et al., 2012; for a review, see Erol & Orth, 2016), social support (Marshall et al., 2014), better education (Trzesniewski et al., 2006; von Soest et al., 2016), job satisfaction and job success (Kuster et al., 2013; Orth et al., 2012; Trzesniewski et al., 2006; von Soest et al., 2016), physical health (Orth et al., 2012; Trzesniewski et al., 2006), less stressful life events (Orth & Luciano, 2016), and less criminal behavior (Trzesniewski et al., 2006). Moreover, a large number of longitudinal studies suggest that low self-esteem contributes to the development of depression (Orth, Robins, Meier, & Conger, 2016; Orth, Robins, & Roberts, 2008; Rieger, Göllner, Trautwein, & Roberts, 2016; Sowislo & Orth, 2013; Steiger, Allemand, Robins, & Fend, 2014; von Soest et al., 2016; Wouters et al., 2013; for a review, see Orth & Robins, 2013).

Importantly, the studies cited above used study designs that allow for relatively strong conclusions about the effects of self-esteem. For example, many studies used data from large community samples (with about 1000 participants or more), aggregated the estimates across several waves of data, and controlled for previous levels of self-esteem and life outcomes. Moreover, many studies controlled the effects of self-esteem for relevant third variables, which helps ruling out alternative hypotheses about the potentially confounding effects of other influential factors. Specifically, longitudinal studies controlled for third variables such as gender (Johnson & Galambos, 2014; Marshall et al., 2014; Orth, Robins, Trzesniewski, Maes, & Schmitt, 2009; Orth, Robins, Widaman, & Conger, 2014; Trzesniewski et al., 2006; von Soest et al., 2016; Wouters et al., 2013), socioeconomic status (Marshall et al., 2014; Trzesniewski et al., 2006; von Soest et al., 2016), level of education (Johnson & Galambos, 2014; Orth, Robins, Trzesniewski et al., 2009), intelligence (Marshall et al., 2014; Trzesniewski et al., 2006), grades (Steiger et al., 2014; von Soest et al., 2016), popularity among peers (Steiger et al., 2014), body mass index (Steiger et al., 2014; Trzesniewski et al., 2006), stressful life events

(Orth, Robins, & Meier, 2009; Orth et al., 2014), the Big Five personality traits (Sowislo, Orth, & Meier, 2014), and narcissism (Orth & Luciano, 2016).

In sum, recent longitudinal research suggests that people's level of self-esteem influences their success and well-being in important life domains such as relationships, work, and health. It is important to note that, in most studies, the prospective effects were not large but of small to medium size (see, e.g., Orth et al., 2012; Sowislo & Orth, 2013; Trzesniewski et al., 2006; von Soest et al., 2016) and that, clearly, many factors influence the outcomes in a person's life. Nevertheless, the evidence suggests that self-esteem is one of these factors.

# Concluding remarks

Although research on the development of self-esteem across the lifespan has made considerable progress in the past decade, many aspects remain insufficiently understood. For example, future research should continue to examine the factors that lead to change in self-esteem. Although research provides some evidence on influential factors, such as life events and experiences in romantic relationships, a better understanding is needed with regard to the causes of self-esteem change across the life course. Also, longitudinal research is needed to identify the mechanisms that account for the effects of self-esteem on life outcomes. Likely, these mechanisms differ across domains, although some general processes might account for effects on several outcomes. For example, a possible intrapersonal process is that low self-esteem increases rumination and depression (Kuster, Orth, & Meier, 2012; Orth & Robins, 2013), which, in turn, may impair functioning in the relationship and work domain. A possible interpersonal process is that low self-esteem may motivate social avoidance, which reduces the availability of social support and may negatively influence relationships, job performance, and health. Finally, the field would benefit from developing a comprehensive theory of self-esteem development, explaining how self-esteem first emerges in childhood and why self-esteem changes across the lifespan the way it does. Although the growing body of longitudinal research provides important information that strongly contributes to our understanding of self-esteem development, a good theoretical model allows for a more parsimonious interpretation of empirical findings and for generating testable hypotheses about insufficiently understood aspects.

The research reviewed in this chapter has important implications. First, there is now robust evidence that self-esteem changes in systematic ways across the life course. For the average person, self-esteem increases during adolescence and young adulthood, peaks in middle adulthood at about age 50—60 years, and declines in old age. Second, despite these normative developmental changes, long-term studies show that individual differences in self-esteem are relatively stable across long periods, indicating that self-esteem is a personality trait. Thus, if individuals have relatively high (or low) self-esteem compared to their age group, research predicts that they will continue having relatively high (or low) self-esteem even decades later. Third, research suggests that self-esteem has consequences for the person's well-being and success in important life domains such as relationships, work, and health. The latter finding is particularly important from a practical perspective because if self-esteem influences life outcomes then interventions aimed at increasing self-esteem should prove beneficial for the individual. In fact, the evidence suggests that it is possible to improve self-esteem through interventions and that effective interventions do not only lead to improvements in self-esteem but also in other areas of functioning (Haney & Durlak, 1998; O'Mara, Marsh, Craven, & Debus, 2006).

# References

Alsaker, F. D., & Olweus, D. (1992). Stability of global self-evaluations in early adolescence: A cohort longitudinal study. *Journal of Research on Adolescence, 2*, 123–145.

Anusic, I., & Schimmack, U. (2016). Stability and change of personality traits, self-esteem, and well-being: Introducing the meta-analytic stability and change model of retest correlations. *Journal of Personality and Social Psychology, 110*, 766–781.

Baltes, P. B., Cornelius, S. W., & Nesselroade, J. R. (1979). Cohort effects in developmental psychology. In J. R. Nesselroade, & P. B. Baltes (Eds.), *Longitudinal research in the study of behavior and development* (pp. 61–87). New York, NY: Academic Press.

Baumeister, R. F., Campbell, J. D., Krueger, J. I., & Vohs, K. D. (2003). Does high self-esteem cause better performance, interpersonal success, happiness, or healthier life-styles? *Psychological Science in the Public Interest, 4*, 1–44.

Birkeland, M. S., Melkevik, O., Holsen, I., & Wold, B. (2012). Trajectories of global self-esteem development during adolescence. *Journal of Adolescence, 35*, 43–54.

Bleidorn, W., Arslan, R. C., Denissen, J. J. A., Rentfrow, P. J., Gebauer, J. E., Potter, J., & Gosling, S. D. (2016). Age and gender differences in self-esteem: A cross-cultural window. *Journal of Personality and Social Psychology, 111*, 396–410.

Block, J., & Robins, R. W. (1993). A longitudinal study of consistency and change in self-esteem from early adolescence to early adulthood. *Child Development, 64*, 909–923.

Chung, J. M., Robins, R. W., Trzesniewski, K. H., Noftle, E. E., Roberts, B. W., & Widaman, K. F. (2014). Continuity and change in self-esteem during emerging adult-hood. *Journal of Personality and Social Psychology, 106*, 469–483.

Cohen, J. (1992). A power primer. *Psychological Bulletin, 112*, 155–159.

Cole, D. A. (2012). Latent trait-state models. In R. H. Hoyle (Ed.), *Handbook of structural equation modeling* (pp. 585–600). New York, NY: Guilford.

Cole, D. A., Maxwell, S. E., Martin, J. M., Peeke, L. G., Seroczynski, A. D., Tram, J. M., Maschman, T., et al. (2001). The development of multiple domains of child and adolescent self-concept: A cohort sequential longitudinal design. *Child Development, 72*, 1723–1746.

Crocker, J., & Wolfe, C. T. (2001). Contingencies of self-worth. *Psychological Review, 108*, 593–623.

Demo, D. H. (1992). The self-concept over time: Research issues and directions. *Annual Review of Sociology, 18*, 303–326.

Donnellan, M. B., Kenny, D. A., Trzesniewski, K. H., Lucas, R. E., & Conger, R. D. (2012). Using trait-state models to evaluate the longitudinal consistency of global self-esteem from adolescence to adulthood. *Journal of Research in Personality, 46*, 634–645.

Donnellan, M. B., Trzesniewski, K. H., & Robins, R. W. (2011). Self-esteem: Enduring issues and controversies. In T. Chamorro-Premuzic, S. von Stumm, & A. Furnham (Eds.), *The Wiley-Blackwell handbook of individual differences* (pp. 718–746). Chichester, UK: Wiley-Blackwell.

Duncan, T. E., Duncan, S. C., & Strycker, L. A. (2006). *An introduction to latent variable growth curve modeling: Concepts, issues, and applications*. Mahwah, NJ: Erlbaum.

Erol, R. Y., & Orth, U. (2016). Self-esteem and the quality of romantic relationships. *European Psychologist, 21*, 274–283.

Erol, R. Y., & Orth, U. (2011). Self-esteem development from age 14 to 30 years: A longitudinal study. *Journal of Personality and Social Psychology, 101*, 607–619.

Fraley, R. C., & Roberts, B. W. (2005). Patterns of continuity: A dynamic model for conceptualizing the stability of individual differences in psychological constructs across the life course. *Psychological Review, 112*, 60–74.

Gentile, B., Twenge, J. M., & Campbell, W. K. (2010). Birth cohort differences in self-esteem, 1988–2008: A cross-temporal meta-analysis. *Review of General Psychology, 14*, 261–268.

Haney, P., & Durlak, J. A. (1998). Changing self-esteem in children and adolescents: A meta-analytic review. *Journal of Clinical Child Psychology, 27*, 423–433.

Harris, M. A., Gruenenfelder-Steiger, A. E., Ferrer, E., Donnellan, M. B., Allemand, M., Fend, H., Conger, R. D., & Trzesniewski, K. H. (2015). Do parents foster self-esteem? Testing the prospective impact of parent closeness on adolescent self-esteem. *Child Development, 86*, 995–1013.

Harter, S. (2006). Developmental and individual difference perspectives on self-esteem. In D. K. Mroczek, & T. D. Little (Eds.), *Handbook of personality development* (pp. 311–334). Mahwah, NJ: Erlbaum.

Heine, S. J., Lehman, D. R., Markus, H. R., & Kitayama, S. (1999). Is there a universal need for positive self-regard? *Psychological Review, 106*, 766–794.

Henrich, J., Heine, S. J., & Norenzayan, A. (2010). The weirdest people in the world? *Behavioral and Brain Sciences, 33*, 61–83.

Huang, C. (2010). Mean-level change in self-esteem from childhood through adulthood: Meta-analysis of longitudinal studies. *Review of General Psychology, 14*, 251–260.

Hutteman, R., Nestler, S., Wagner, J., Egloff, B., & Back, M. D. (2015). Wherever I may roam: Processes of self-esteem development from adolescence to emerging adulthood in the context of international student exchange. *Journal of Personality and Social Psychology, 108*, 767–783.

James, W. (1890). *The principles of psychology*. New York, NY: Henry Holt and Company.

Johnson, M. D., & Galambos, N. L. (2014). Paths to intimate relationship quality from parent-adolescent relations and mental health. *Journal of Marriage and Family, 76*, 145–160.

Kandler, C., Zimmermann, J., & McAdams, D. P. (2014). Core and surface characteristics for the description and theory of personality differences and development. *European Journal of Personality, 28*, 231–243.

Kenny, D. A., & Zautra, A. (1995). The trait-state-error model for multiwave data. *Journal of Consulting and Clinical Psychology, 63*, 52–59.

Kenny, D. A., & Zautra, A. (2001). Trait-state models for longitudinal data. In L. M. Collins, & A. G. Sayer (Eds.), *New methods for the analysis of change* (pp. 243–263). Washington, DC: American Psychological Association.

Kernis, M. H. (2005). Measuring self-esteem in context: The importance of stability of self-esteem in psychological functioning. *Journal of Personality, 73*, 1569–1605.

Kiviruusu, O., Huurre, T., Aro, H., Marttunen, M., & Haukkala, A. (2015). Self-esteem growth trajectory from adolescence to mid-adulthood and its predictors in adolescence. *Advances in Life Course Research, 23*, 29−43.

Kling, K. C., Hyde, J. S., Showers, C. J., & Buswell, B. N. (1999). Gender differences in self-esteem: A meta-analysis. *Psychological Bulletin, 125*, 470−500.

Krueger, J. I., Vohs, K. D., & Baumeister, R. F. (2008). Is the allure of self-esteem a mirage after all? *American Psychologist, 63*, 64−65.

Kuster, F., & Orth, U. (2013). The long-term stability of self-esteem: Its time-dependent decay and nonzero asymptote. *Personality and Social Psychology Bulletin, 39*, 677−690.

Kuster, F., Orth, U., & Meier, L. L. (2012). Rumination mediates the prospective effect of low self-esteem on depression: A five-wave longitudinal study. *Personality and Social Psychology Bulletin, 38*, 747−759.

Kuster, F., Orth, U., & Meier, L. L. (2013). High self-esteem prospectively predicts better work conditions and outcomes. *Social Psychological and Personality Science, 4*, 668−675.

Kuzucu, Y., Bontempo, D. E., Hofer, S. M., Stallings, M. C., & Piccinin, A. M. (2014). Developmental change and time-specific variation in global and specific aspects of self-concept in adolescence and association with depressive symptoms. *Journal of Early Adolescence, 34*, 638−666.

Leary, M. R. (2004). The sociometer, self-esteem, and the regulation of interpersonal behavior. In R. F. Baumeister, & K. D. Vohs (Eds.), *Handbook of self-regulation* (pp. 373−391). New York, NY: Guilford.

Leary, M. R. (2012). Sociometer theory. In P. A. M. Van Lange, A. W. Kruglanski, & E. T. Higgins (Eds.), *Handbook of theories of social psychology* (pp. 141−159). Thousand Oaks, CA: Sage.

Leary, M. R., & Baumeister, R. F. (2000). The nature and function of self-esteem: Sociometer theory. In M. P. Zanna (Ed.), *Advances in experimental social psychology* (Vol. 32, pp. 1−62). San Diego, CA: Academic Press.

Luciano, E. C., & Orth, U. (2016). Transitions in romantic relationships and development of self-esteem. *Journal of Personality and Social Psychology*. Advance online publication.

Major, B., Barr, L., Zubek, J., & Babey, S. H. (1999). Gender and self-esteem: A meta-analysis. In W. B. Swann, J. H. Langlois, & L. A. Gilbert (Eds.), *Sexism and stereotypes in modern society: The gender science of Janet Taylor Spence* (pp. 223−253). Washington, DC: American Psychological Association.

Markus, H. R., & Kitayama, S. (1991). Culture and the self: Implications for cognition, emotion, and motivation. *Psychological Review, 98*, 224−253.

Marsh, H. W., Craven, R., & Debus, R. (1998). Structure, stability, and development of young children's self-concepts: A multicohort-multioccasion study. *Child Development, 69*, 1030−1053.

Marshall, S. L., Parker, P. D., Ciarrochi, J., & Heaven, P. C. L. (2014). Is self-esteem a cause or consequence of social support? A 4-year longitudinal study. *Child Development, 85*, 1275−1291.

Meier, L. L., Orth, U., Denissen, J. J. A., & Kühnel, A. (2011). Age differences in instability, contingency, and level of self-esteem across the life span. *Journal of Research in Personality, 45*, 604−612.

Morin, A. J. S., Maiano, C., Marsh, H. W., Nagengast, B., & Janosz, M. (2013). School life and adolescents' self-esteem trajectories. *Child Development, 84*, 1967−1988.

Mund, M., Finn, C., Hagemeyer, B., Zimmermann, J., & Neyer, F. J. (2015). The dynamics of self-esteem in partner relationships. *European Journal of Personality, 29*, 235−249.

O'Malley, P. M., & Bachman, J. G. (1983). Self-esteem: Change and stability between ages 13 and 23. *Developmental Psychology, 19*, 257—268.

O'Mara, A. J., Marsh, H. W., Craven, R. G., & Debus, R. L. (2006). Do self-concept interventions make a difference? A synergistic blend of construct validation and meta-analysis. *Educational Psychologist, 41*, 181—206.

Orth, U., & Luciano, E. C. (2016). Self-esteem, narcissism, and stressful life events: Testing for selection and socialization. *Journal of Personality and Social Psychology, 109*, 707—721.

Orth, U., Maes, J., & Schmitt, M. (2015). Self-esteem development across the life span: A longitudinal study with a large sample from Germany. *Developmental Psychology, 51*, 248—259.

Orth, U., & Robins, R. W. (2013). Understanding the link between low self-esteem and depression. *Current Directions in Psychological Science, 22*, 455—460.

Orth, U., & Robins, R. W. (2014). The development of self-esteem. *Current Directions in Psychological Science, 23*, 381—387.

Orth, U., Robins, R. W., & Meier, L. L. (2009). Disentangling the effects of low self-esteem and stressful events on depression: Findings from three longitudinal studies. *Journal of Personality and Social Psychology, 97*, 307—321.

Orth, U., Robins, R. W., Meier, L. L., & Conger, R. D. (2016). Refining the vulnerability model of low self-esteem and depression: Disentangling the effects of genuine self-esteem and narcissism. *Journal of Personality and Social Psychology, 110*, 133—149.

Orth, U., Robins, R. W., & Roberts, B. W. (2008). Low self-esteem prospectively predicts depression in adolescence and young adulthood. *Journal of Personality and Social Psychology, 95*, 695—708.

Orth, U., Robins, R. W., Trzesniewski, K. H., Maes, J., & Schmitt, M. (2009). Low self-esteem is a risk factor for depressive symptoms from young adulthood to old age. *Journal of Abnormal Psychology, 118*, 472—478.

Orth, U., Robins, R. W., & Widaman, K. F. (2012). Life-span development of self-esteem and its effects on important life outcomes. *Journal of Personality and Social Psychology, 102*, 1271—1288.

Orth, U., Robins, R. W., Widaman, K. F., & Conger, R. D. (2014). Is low self-esteem a risk factor for depression? Findings from a longitudinal study of Mexican-origin youth. *Developmental Psychology, 50*, 622—633.

Orth, U., Trzesniewski, K. H., & Robins, R. W. (2010). Self-esteem development from young adulthood to old age: A cohort-sequential longitudinal study. *Journal of Personality and Social Psychology, 98*, 645—658.

Pettit, J. W., & Joiner, T. E. (2001). Negative life events predict negative feedback seeking as a function of impact on self-esteem. *Cognitive Therapy and Research, 25*, 733—741.

Preacher, K. J., Wichman, A. L., MacCallum, R. C., & Briggs, N. E. (2008). *Latent growth curve modeling*. Los Angeles, CA: Sage.

Pullmann, H., Allik, J., & Realo, A. (2009). Global self-esteem across the life span: A cross-sectional comparison between representative and self-selected internet samples. *Experimental Aging Research, 35*, 20—44.

Ram, N., & Grimm, K. J. (2009). Growth mixture modeling: A method for identifying differences in longitudinal change among unobserved groups. *International Journal of Behavioral Development, 33*, 565—576.

Rieger, S., Göllner, R., Trautwein, U., & Roberts, B. W. (2016). Low self-esteem prospectively predicts depression in the transition to young adulthood: A replication of Orth, Robins, and Roberts (2008). *Journal of Personality and Social Psychology, 110*, e16—e22.

Roberts, B. W., Wood, D., & Caspi, A. (2008). The development of personality traits in adulthood. In O. P. John, R. W. Robins, & L. A. Pervin (Eds.), *Handbook of personality: Theory and research* (pp. 375–398). New York, NY: Guilford.

Robins, R. W., & Trzesniewski, K. H. (2005). Self-esteem development across the lifespan. *Current Directions in Psychological Science, 14*, 158–162.

Robins, R. W., Trzesniewski, K. H., Tracy, J. L., Gosling, S. D., & Potter, J. (2002). Global self-esteem across the life span. *Psychology and Aging, 17*, 423–434.

Schaffhuser, K., Wagner, J., Lüdtke, O., & Allemand, M. (2014). Dyadic longitudinal interplay between personality and relationship satisfaction: A focus on neuroticism and self-esteem. *Journal of Research in Personality, 53*, 124–133.

Shaw, B. A., Liang, J., & Krause, N. (2010). Age and race differences in the trajectory of self-esteem. *Psychology and Aging, 25*, 84–94.

Sowislo, J. F., & Orth, U. (2013). Does low self-esteem predict depression and anxiety? A meta-analysis of longitudinal studies. *Psychological Bulletin, 139*, 213–240.

Sowislo, J. F., Orth, U., & Meier, L. L. (2014). What constitutes vulnerable self-esteem? Comparing the prospective effects of low, unstable, and contingent self-esteem on depressive symptoms. *Journal of Abnormal Psychology, 123*, 737–753.

Specht, J., Bleidorn, W., Denissen, J. J. A., Hennecke, M., Hutteman, R., Kandler, C., Zimmermann, J., et al. (2014). What drives adult personality development? A comparison of theoretical perspectives and empirical evidence. *European Journal of Personality, 28*, 216–230.

Steiger, A. E., Allemand, M., Robins, R. W., & Fend, H. A. (2014). Low and decreasing self-esteem during adolescence predict adult depression two decades later. *Journal of Personality and Social Psychology, 106*, 325–338.

Swann, W. B., Chang-Schneider, C., & McClarty, K. L. (2007). Do people's self-views matter? *American Psychologist, 62*, 84–94.

Swann, W. B., Chang-Schneider, C., & McClarty, K. L. (2008). Yes, cavalier attitudes can have pernicious consequences. *American Psychologist, 63*, 65–66.

Trzesniewski, K. H., & Donnellan, M. B. (2009). Reevaluating the evidence for increasingly positive self-views among high school students: More evidence for consistency across generations (1976–2006). *Psychological Science, 20*, 920–922.

Trzesniewski, K. H., Donnellan, M. B., Moffitt, T. E., Robins, R. W., Poulton, R., & Caspi, A. (2006). Low self-esteem during adolescence predicts poor health, criminal behavior, and limited economic prospects during adulthood. *Developmental Psychology, 42*, 381–390.

Trzesniewski, K. H., Donnellan, M. B., & Robins, R. W. (2003). Stability of self-esteem across the life span. *Journal of Personality and Social Psychology, 84*, 205–220.

Trzesniewski, K. H., Donnellan, M. B., & Robins, R. W. (2008). Is "Generation Me" really more narcissistic than previous generations? *Journal of Personality, 76*, 903–917.

Trzesniewski, K. H., Donnellan, M. B., & Robins, R. W. (2013). Development of self-esteem. In V. Zeigler-Hill (Ed.), *Self-esteem* (pp. 60–79). London, UK: Psychology Press.

Twenge, J. M., & Campbell, W. K. (2001). Age and birth cohort differences in self-esteem: A cross-temporal meta-analysis. *Personality and Social Psychology Review, 5*, 321–344.

Twenge, J. M., Konrath, S., Foster, J. D., Campbell, W. K., & Bushman, B. J. (2008). Egos inflating over time: A cross-temporal meta-analysis of the Narcissistic Personality Inventory. *Journal of Personality, 76*, 875–901.

von Soest, T., Wichstrom, L., & Kvalem, I. L. (2016). The development of global and domain-specific self-esteem from age 13 to 31. *Journal of Personality and Social Psychology, 110*, 592–608.

Wagner, J., Becker, M., Lüdtke, O., & Trautwein, U. (2015). The first partnership experience and personality development: A propensity score matching study in young adulthood. *Social Psychological and Personality Science, 6*, 455−463.

Wagner, J., Gerstorf, D., Hoppmann, C., & Luszcz, M. A. (2013). The nature and correlates of self-esteem trajectories in late life. *Journal of Personality and Social Psychology, 105*, 139−153.

Wagner, J., Hoppmann, C., Ram, N., & Gerstorf, D. (2016). Self-esteem is relatively stable late in life: The role of resources in the health, self-regulation, and social domains. *Developmental Psychology, 51*, 136−149.

Wagner, J., Lang, F. R., Neyer, F. J., & Wagner, G. G. (2014). Self-esteem across adulthood: The role of resources. *European Journal of Ageing, 11*, 109−119.

Wagner, J., Lüdtke, O., Jonkmann, K., & Trautwein, U. (2013). Cherish yourself: Longitudinal patterns and conditions of self-esteem change in the transition to young adulthood. *Journal of Personality and Social Psychology, 104*, 148−163.

Wagner, J., Lüdtke, O., & Trautwein, U. (2016). Self-esteem is mostly stable across young adulthood: Evidence from latent STARTS models. *Journal of Personality 84*, 523−535.

Wouters, S., Duriez, B., Luyckx, K., Klimstra, T., Colpin, H., Soenens, B., & Verschueren, K. (2013). Depressive symptoms in university freshmen: Longitudinal relations with contingent self-esteem and level of self-esteem. *Journal of Research in Personality, 47*, 356−363.

Wylie, R. C. (1979). *The self-concept*. Lincoln, NE: University of Nebraska Press.

Zeiders, K. H., Umaña-Taylor, A. J., & Derlan, C. L. (2013). Trajectories of depressive symptoms and self-esteem in Latino youths: Examining the role of gender and perceived discrimination. *Developmental Psychology, 49*, 951−963.

# The development of subjective well-being

# 13

*Maike Luhmann*
Ruhr University Bochum, Bochum, Germany

Folk wisdom tells us that after a relatively carefree and happy childhood, we experience teenage years full of self-doubt and misery, which are swiftly followed by quarterlife crisis, midlife crisis, and old age which we spend being sick, lonely, and miserable (Buchanan & Holmbeck, 1998; Hummert, Garstka, Shaner, & Strahm, 1994; Wethington, 2000). Scientific research, however, paints a very different picture of the development of subjective well-being (SWB). Generally, SWB is only marginally correlated with age (Diener, Suh, Lucas, & Smith, 1999; Lucas & Gohm, 2000). People can be happy and satisfied at any age and even in the face of health-related, cognitive, and social losses, a phenomenon known as the paradox of well-being (Kunzmann, Little, & Smith, 2000; Mroczek & Kolarz, 1998). Furthermore, SWB is partly heritable (Røysamb, Nes, & Vittersø, 2014) and is characterized by moderate retest stability (Anusic & Schimmack, 2015; Schimmack & Oishi, 2005; Sheldon & Lucas, 2014). Nevertheless, there are some general age trends in SWB; the most significant being a decline in SWB during the last years of life (Gerstorf, Ram, Estabrook et al., 2008). This chapter focuses on describing and explaining these age trends.

This chapter begins with the definition and measurement of SWB. The development of SWB is then described separately for childhood/adolescence and adulthood. Relative to adulthood, considerably fewer studies have examined SWB in childhood and adolescence and mainly focused on predictors of SWB in early life. In line with the focus of this volume on life-span development, this chapter will therefore focus on adults and only briefly cover development of SWB during childhood and adolescence. The chapter concludes with theoretical explanations of potential developmental mechanisms.

## Defining and measuring SWB

According to the widely adopted definition by Diener (1984), SWB is a multifaceted construct encompassing both cognitive and affective components. Cognitive well-being refers to how people evaluate their lives overall (life satisfaction) and specific life domains (e.g., job satisfaction, marital satisfaction). Life satisfaction is typically measured with multi-item self-report scales such as the Satisfaction With

Personality Development Across the Lifespan. DOI: http://dx.doi.org/10.1016/B978-0-12-804674-6.00013-2

Life Scale (Diener, Emmons, Larsen, & Griffin, 1985) or with single items asses-sing the global satisfaction with one's lives (Diener, Inglehart, & Tay, 2013). Affective well-being refers to the frequency and intensity with which people experience positive affect (PA) and negative affect (NA). PA and NA encompass both specific emotions and general mood states. Affective well-being is typically measured by asking people to rate the extent to which they experienced different affective states over a specified time frame (e.g., the past 2 weeks) or right now (Diener et al., 2010; Watson, Clark, & Tellegen, 1988). The latter approach is often used in experience sampling studies or daily-diary studies that provide repeated measures of affective well-being which are then aggregated within individuals to provide a more valid estimate of people's habitual level of affective well-being (Kahneman, 1999; Stone, Shiffman, & DeVries, 1999).

Several studies suggest that cognitive and affective well-being are conceptually, structurally, and functionally distinct (Lucas, Diener, & Suh, 1996; Luhmann, Hawkley, Eid, & Cacioppo, 2012; Luhmann, Hofmann, Eid, & Lucas, 2012). Cognitive and affective well-being also differ in their predictors. External life cir-cumstances tend to be more strongly associated with cognitive than with affective well-being whereas personality characteristics tend to be more strongly associated with affective than with cognitive well-being (Schimmack, Schupp, & Wagner, 2008). In this chapter, the development of SWB will therefore be discussed separately for these components.

# SWB in childhood and adolescence

Although research on SWB in children and adolescents has largely been conducted separately from research on SWB in adults, the findings on children and adolescents parallel those for adults. First, just like adults, most children and adolescents are satisfied with their lives (Proctor, Linley, & Maltby, 2009). Second, similar effects have been found with respect to predictors of SWB (for reviews, see Gilman & Huebner, 2003; Proctor et al., 2009). For instance, SWB is moderately to strongly associated with personality characteristics such as neuroticism, extraversion, and self-esteem, and only weakly correlated with sociodemographic variables such as family income, parental education, or parental marital status (Proctor et al., 2009). Some important predictors of SWB in children and adolescents are unique to that age group, in particular school-related variables such as school satisfaction (Huebner & Diener, 2008). Third, SWB tends to be moderately stable across time. For adolescents, the retest correlation of life over 1 year or more was substantial (Antaramian & Huebner, 2009; Huebner, Funk, & Gilman, 2000) and comparable in size with those found for adults (Anusic & Schimmack, 2015). Rank-order stabil-ity can be found even for very long time spans. In one study, the level of observed PA among infants correlated positively with self-reported life satisfaction in early adulthood (Coffey, Warren, & Gottfried, 2015).

Only a few studies have examined age differences in SWB in adolescence systematically. A consistent cross-sectional finding is that life satisfaction is lower (Goldbeck, Schmitz, Besier, Herschbach, & Henrich, 2007; Moksnes, Løhre, & Espnes, 2013; Weber, Ruch, & Huebner, 2013) and depressive mood is higher (Costello, Swendsen, Rose, & Dierker, 2008) in mid-adolescence than in early adolescence. However, in a longitudinal study of American 6th to 12th graders followed over 2 years, average levels of life satisfaction did not change significantly over this period (Lyons, Huebner, Hills, & Van Horn, 2013). Furthermore, a longitudinal study of Finnish highschool students found increasing average life satisfaction levels from 9th grade until 2 years later (Salmela-Aro & Tuominen-Soini, 2010). In sum, any conclusions about the average trajectories of SWB in children and adolescents are premature given the lack of studies that follow large-scale samples of children and adolescents over multiple years. The remainder of this chapter therefore focuses on the development of SWB from early adulthood to old age, on which more and better studies are available.

# SWB in adulthood

## *Life satisfaction*

The trajectory of life satisfaction across the life span has been described as U-shaped (Stone, Schwartz, Broderick, & Deaton, 2010), inversely U-shaped (Mroczek & Spiro, 2005), or flat (Hamarat, Thompson, Steele, Matheny, & Simons, 2002). Evidence for a U-shaped trajectory stems mostly from cross-sectional studies (for an overview of central studies on the development of life satisfaction, see Table 13.1). For instance, Stone et al. (2010) used a cross-sectional sample representative of the US American population and found that average levels of life satisfaction decrease with increasing age during early adulthood, reach the minimum around the age of 50, and increase again with age during late adulthood. Similar findings have been obtained from cross-sectional data collected in other Western nations (Blanchflower & Oswald, 2008; Fukuda, 2013; Steptoe, Deaton, & Stone, 2015). Additional support for the U-shaped trajectory comes from a longitudinal study of older adults (62−95 years) in which life satisfaction increased linearly with age (Gana, Bailly, Saada, Joulain, & Alaphilippe, 2013).

In contrast, Mroczek and Spiro (2005) found an inversely U-shaped trajectory for life satisfaction. Using longitudinal data from the Veterans Affairs Normative Aging Study covering up to 22 waves, they found that life satisfaction levels of adults aged 40+ increase up to age of 65 and decrease thereafter. Similarly, in the Midlife in the United States (MIDUS) study, participants in their 40s and 50s experienced a significant increase in life satisfaction in the following 8−10 years whereas participants in their 60s and 70s experienced a significant decrease during

**Table 13.1 Overview of selected studies on the development of life satisfaction**

| Authors | Design | Sample | Country | N | Age range | Measure | Main findings on the development of life satisfaction |
|---|---|---|---|---|---|---|---|
| Baird et al. (2010) | Cross-sectional and longitudinal | Socioeconomic Panel Study (SOEP) | Germany | 20,696 | 16–91 years | Single item | Flat trajectory across most of adulthood, decline in old age |
| | | British Household Panel Study (BHPS) | Great Britain | 21,448 | 16–91 years | | Declining levels among younger adults, increasing levels between age 50 and 70, declining levels in old age |
| Berg et al. (2009) | Longitudinal | Swedish Origins of Variance in the Old-Old (OCTO)-Twin-study | Sweden | 412 | 80+ | Multiple items | Linear decline |
| Blanchflower and Oswald (2008) | Cross-sectional | U.S. General Social Surveys (GSS) | United States | 41,193 | 20+ | Single items | U-shaped age distribution with a minimum at age 45 |
| | | Eurobarometer Surveys | Western European countries | 422,475 | 20+ | | U-shaped age distribution with a minimum at age 47 |
| | | World Values Surveys (WVS) | Cross-cultural study | 151,298 | 20+ | | U-shaped age distribution found in most, but not all countries |
| Freund and Baltes (1998) | Cross-sectional | Berlin Aging Study (BASE) | Germany | 200 | 72.6–102.7 | Multiple items | Decline among the oldest-old |
| Fukuda (2013) | Cross-sectional | General Social Survey (GSS) | United States | 46,898 | 18–88 | Single item | U-shaped trajectory with a minimum around age 50 |
| Gana et al. (2013) | Longitudinal | Adjustment to Retirement study | France | 899 | 62–95 | Multiple items | Linear increase |
| Gerstorf, Ram, Estabrook et al. (2008) | Longitudinal | Socioeconomic Panel (SOEP) | Germany | 1637 | 70–100 | Single item | Decline among the oldest-old |

| Study | Design | Sample | Country | N | Age | Measure | Findings |
| --- | --- | --- | --- | --- | --- | --- | --- |
| Gerstorf, Ram, Röcke et al. (2008) | Longitudinal | Berlin Aging Study (BASE) | Germany | 414 | 70–103 | Multiple items | Decline among the oldest-old |
| Koivumaa-Honkanen et al. (2005) | Longitudinal | Nationwide sample of adult Finnish twins | Finland | 9679 | 18–45 | Multiple items | Stable during early and mid-adulthood, decline in old age |
| Lachman et al. (2008) | Longitudinal | Midlife in the United States (MIDUS) study | United States | 3793 | 24–74 | Single item | No significant changes over 8 years except among participants aged 40–50 (significant increase) and participants aged 60–70 (significant decline) |
| Lang and Heckhausen (2001) | Cross-sectional | German adult sample | Germany | 480 | 20–90 | Multiple items | Age is unrelated with life satisfaction in early adulthood, positively associated in midlife, negatively associated in old age |
| Mroczek and Spiro (2005) | Longitudinal | Veterans Affairs (VA) Normative Aging Study (NAS) | United States | 1927 | 33–92 | Multiple items | Inversely U-shaped trajectory with a maximum around 65 |
| Realo and Dobewall (2011) | Longitudinal | European Value Survey (EVS) World Values Survey (WVS) European Social Survey (ESS) | Cross-cultural study | 39,420 | 15–100 | Single item | U-shaped trajectory in Estonia and Latvia, stable levels in Finland and Sweden |
| Steptoe et al. (2015) | Cross-sectional | Gallup World Poll | Cross-cultural study | ~25,000 | 18+ | Single item | Age distribution varies between countries |
| Stone et al. (2010) | Cross-sectional | Gallup-Healthways Wellbeing Index | United States | 340,847 | 18–85 | Single item | U-shaped trajectory with a minimum around age 50 |

this time period (Lachman, Röcke, Rosnick, & Ryff, 2008). Both of these studies, however, covered only midlife to old age. Studies including participants of all adult age groups provide a more nuanced picture of the trajectory of life satisfaction. Baird, Lucas, and Donnellan (2010) used longitudinal data from the British Household Panel Study (BHPS) and replicated the inverse U-shaped trajectory among adults aged 50+. Among younger adults, however, they found slightly decreasing levels of life satisfaction, consistent with the U-shaped trajectory documented in cross-sectional studies. A similar picture emerged in a cross-sectional study in which age was unrelated with life satisfaction in early adulthood, positively associated with life satisfaction in midlife, and negatively associated with age in old age (Lang & Heckhausen, 2001).

Finally, some studies failed to find any association between age and life satisfaction (Hamarat et al., 2002) or found that life satisfaction was stable during early and mid-adulthood (e.g., Koivumaa-Honkanen, Kaprio, Honkanen, Viinamäki, & Koskenvuo, 2005) and only decreased in old age (e.g., in the German Socioeconomic Panel [SOEP]; Baird et al., 2010).

Together, these studies do not provide a clear answer on how life satisfaction changes over the life span. One reason for the diverse findings may be that the studies discussed above included both cross-sectional and longitudinal samples. Cross-sectional studies confound age, cohort, and period effects (Schaie, 1965). It is therefore not possible to infer whether the observed age differences are due to developmental processes or to generational differences and whether these age differences would replicate in earlier or later time periods. Indeed, there is evidence that cohort and time period effects account at least partially for cross-sectional age differences in life satisfaction (de Ree & Alessie, 2011; Fukuda, 2013; Realo & Dobewall, 2011; Twenge, Sherman, & Lyubomirsky, 2015). For instance, the U-shaped age distribution found among Germans in one study is driven by cohort effects, and the distribution becomes flat (except for a persisting decline in old age) after controlling for cohort (Gwozdz & Sousa-Poza, 2010).

Another reason for the divergent findings may be that life satisfaction trajectories differ among cultures. Even with cross-sectional data, the U-shaped distribution has only been found in Western countries but could not be replicated in studies conducted in non-Western countries (Blanchflower & Oswald, 2008; Steptoe et al., 2015). Similarly, trajectories estimated with longitudinal data vary among countries (Baird et al., 2010; Realo & Dobewall, 2011). To further complicate things, even studies using the same longitudinal data (e.g., the SOEP or the BHPS) sometimes come to different conclusions because of details of the statistical procedures (Frijters & Beatton, 2012; López Ulloa, Møller, & Sousa-Poza, 2013; Wunder, Wiencierz, Schwarze, & Kuchenhoff, 2013).

Despite these limitations, two central findings were replicated in most studies. First, life satisfaction tends to increase from midlife to early old age (Lachman et al., 2008; Mroczek & Spiro, 2005; Stone et al., 2010). Second, life satisfaction tends to decline among the oldest-old (Baird et al., 2010; Berg, Hoffman, Hassing, McClearn, & Johansson, 2009; Freund & Baltes, 1998; Gerstorf, Ram, Estabrook et al., 2008; Gerstorf, Ram, Röcke, Lindenberger, & Smith, 2008; Lang & Heckhausen, 2001; Mroczek & Spiro, 2005). This decline can be predicted better by how many years people still have to live (distance to death) than by how old people are (chronological age) and has therefore been termed *terminal decline* (Mroczek & Spiro, 2005; Mueller, Wagner, & Gerstorf, Chapter 6).

## Positive and negative affect

Similarly to life satisfaction, the development of PA and NA has been studied using both cross-sectional and longitudinal data (see Table 13.2). The methodological reservations about cross-sectional studies discussed above apply here as well. Overall, cross-sectional and longitudinal studies converge on the conclusion that the quality of affective experiences tends to improve with age and deteriorates only in very old age. The exact shape of these trajectories, however, is disputed.

Mroczek and Kolarz (1998) were among the first to examine the age distribution of PA and NA in a large cross-sectional sample (MIDUS). They found somewhat divergent distributions for PA and NA such that PA is stable in early adulthood and then increases into old age whereas NA declines linearly with increasing age. At a follow-up 10 years later (Lachman, Teshale, & Agrigoroaei, 2015), participants who were in their 30s and 70s at baseline reported lower levels whereas participants who were in their 50s at baseline reported higher levels of PA than at baseline. No significant within-person changes were observed for the other age groups. These general age trends were replicated in other studies. For instance, Charles, Reynolds, and Gatz (2001) examined changes in PA and NA using longitudinal data spanning up to 23 years and found that PA was stable among younger participants but declined among older participants whereas NA declined in all age groups. In another longitudinal study, happiness (measured with a single item and assumed to be an indicator of PA) increased over time even among young adults (Galambos, Fang, Krahn, Johnson, & Lachman, 2015).

Despite the general upward trend across the life span, affective well-being appears to deteriorate in the last years of life. Several longitudinal studies have found declining levels of PA (Gana, Saada, & Amieva, 2015; Kunzmann et al., 2000; Kunzmann, Richter, & Schmukle, 2013; Schilling, Wahl, & Wiegering, 2013) and stable (Kunzmann et al., 2000) or increasing levels of NA (Schilling et al., 2013; Vogel, Schilling, Wahl, Beekman, & Penninx, 2013) among the oldest-old. Similarly to the late-life decrease in life satisfaction, these changes can often be better explained with distance to death than with chronological age (Schilling et al., 2013; Vogel et al., 2013) and are at least partially due to declining health (Kunzmann et al., 2000).

Whereas the studies discussed so far examined general affective well-being, others have focused on specific emotions (for an overview, see Kunzmann, Kappes, & Wrosch, 2014). In a large cross-sectional study of Americans, levels of stress and anger decreased linearly with age, worry decreased only after age 50, and sadness was stable across age except for somewhat elevated levels around age 50 (Stone et al., 2010).

**Table 13.2 Overview of selected studies on the development of PA and NA**

| Reference | Design | Sample | Country | N | Age range | Measure | Main findings on the development of PA | Main findings on the development of NA |
|---|---|---|---|---|---|---|---|---|
| Carstensen et al. (2000, 2011) | Experience sampling study | Adult sample | United States | 184 | 18–94 | Experience sampling of 8 positive and 11 negative emotions | No significant cross-sectional association between age and PA, but increasing levels of positive affective experiences until age 60s in longitudinal data | Cross-sectional data: NA decreases until age 60 |
| Charles et al. (2001) | Longitudinal | The Longitudinal Study of Generations | United States | 8804 | 64–102 | Bradburn Affect Balance Scale | Stable among younger and middle-aged adults but decline among older adults | Declining levels with age |
| Galambos et al. (2015) | Longitudinal | Edmonton Transitions Study | Canada | 968 | 18–43 | Single items | Increasing levels | |
| Gana et al. (2015) | Longitudinal | College graduates PAQUID | Canada France | 589 3777 | 23–37 62–101 | PA subscale of the CES-D | Nonlinear declining trajectory | |
| Kunzmann et al. (2000) | Cross-sectional Longitudinal | Berlin Aging Study (BASE) | Germany | 516 | 70–103 | PANAS | Negative association with age Declining levels | No significant association with age Stable levels |
| Kunzmann et al. (2013) | Longitudinal | Socioeconomic Panel (SOEP) | Germany Germany | 203 20,850 | 18–87 | Single item-measures of specific emotions | Decline in happiness in old age | Anger increases in young adulthood and declines thereafter. Sadness is stable across adulthood but increases in old age |

| Study | Design | Study name | Country | N | Age | Measure | PA | NA |
|---|---|---|---|---|---|---|---|---|
| Lachman et al. (2015) | Longitudinal | Midlife in the United States (MIDUS) study | United States | 7100 | 25–75 | MIDI affect scales | Declining levels among participants aged young and old adults but increasing levels among mid-aged adults | Declining levels |
| Mroczek and Kolarz (1998) | Cross-sectional | Midlife in the United States (MIDUS) study | United States | 2727 | 25–74 | MIDI affect scales | Stable in early adulthood, then increases into old age | Increasing levels |
| Schilling et al. (2013) | Longitudinal | German subsample of the European ENABLE-AGE Project & LateLine study | Germany | 140 | 80–90 | PANAS | Declining levels | Increasing levels |
| Stone et al. (2010) | Cross-sectional | Gallup-Healthways Wellbeing Index | United States | 340,847 | 18–85 | Single item-measures of specific emotions | U-shaped trajectory with a minimum around age 50 | Stress and anger decrease with age, worry decreases only after age 50, mostly stable levels for sadness |
| Vogel et al. (2013) | Longitudinal | Longitudinal Aging Study Amsterdam (LASA) | Netherlands | 1671 | 55–85 | CES-D | Declining levels | Increasing levels |

PA, positive affect; NA, negative affect; PANAS, Positive Affect Negative Affect Schedule; CES-D, Center for Epidemiologic Studies-Depression Scale.

Using longitudinal data of the SOEP, Kunzmann et al. (2013) came to similar conclusions about the development of anger and sadness. Similarly to the cross-sectional study, they found declining levels of anger across most of adulthood but, contrary to the cross-sectional data, increasing levels in early adulthood. Moreover, levels of sadness were relatively stable across adulthood except for an increase in old age. In sum, both studies found divergent trajectories for different emotions.

Most studies used retrospective measures of PA and NA, for instance by asking people to rate how often they experienced specific affective states within the last 30 days. One limitation of these measures is that people might misremember or misrepresent their actual affective experiences (Kahneman, 1999). This limitation is particularly concerning when age differences are of interest because older people tend to rate past autobiographic events more positively than younger people, regardless of their actual valence (Schryer & Ross, 2012). Retrospective biases can be reduced by measuring affective experiences as they happen. Carstensen, Pasupathi, Mayr, and Nesselroade (2000) measured PA and NA in a 1-week experience sampling study in a small, age-heterogeneous sample. In a measurement burst design, this experience sampling study was repeated among the same participants 5 and 10 years later. At the first occasion, age was unrelated to the frequency of PA and nonlinearly related to the frequency of NA such that the frequency of NA decreased until about age 60 after which the distribution leveled off (Carstensen et al., 2000). These patterns were corroborated by the longitudinal data which showed increasing levels of positive affective experiences (defined as the frequency of PA minus the frequency of NA) into the 60s and no significant changes thereafter (Carstensen et al., 2011).

Individuals vary substantially in their trajectories of PA and NA over time (Hoppmann, Gerstorf, Willis, & Schaie, 2011). Despite these interindividual variations, the studies reviewed here consistently indicate that on average, affective experiences improve over most of adulthood. These findings stand in contrast to the ones on life satisfaction which appears to be stable or follow a nonlinear trajectory across most of adulthood. Hence, the development of life satisfaction and affective well-being is asynchronous and probably driven by different factors. A notable exception is terminal decline which can be observed for both life satisfaction and affective well-being.

# Mechanisms of the development of SWB

The determinants of SWB can broadly be categorized into three groups: personality traits, life circumstances, and intentional activities (Lyubomirsky, Sheldon, & Schkade, 2005). This trichotomy guides the following discussion of potential mechanisms of the development of SWB.

## *Personality*

Personality, particularly neuroticism and extraversion, accounts for a substantial proportion of the variance in PA and NA and, to a lesser degree, in LS (DeNeve &

Cooper, 1998; Steel, Schmidt, & Shultz, 2008). Personality has long been considered the driving stabilizing factor for SWB. According to set-point theory, long-term levels of SWB are characterized by a stable set point which is determined by heritable factors such as personality traits (Headey & Wearing, 1989; Lykken & Tellegen, 1996). In early versions of this theory, it was assumed that this set point is fixed. However, in the light of studies showing that people can experience long-term changes in life satisfaction (Fujita & Diener, 2005), in particular in the context of life events such as unemployment (Lucas, Clark, Georgellis, & Diener, 2004) and disability (Lucas, 2007b), this strong assumption is no longer tenable (Diener, Lucas, & Scollon, 2006; for a detailed discussion of this theory, see Ormel, VonKorff, Jeronimus & Riese, Chapter 9). In addition, we now know that even personality can change throughout adulthood and particularly in old age (Roberts, Wood, & Caspi, 2008; Specht et al., 2014).

Can changes in personality explain changes in SWB? Neuroticism, which is positively correlated with NA and negatively correlated with PA, tends to decrease over the life span (Roberts, Walton, & Viechtbauer, 2006). The mean-level trajectory of neuroticism therefore matches the trajectories of PA and NA. Two studies examined the link between personality change and SWB directly and found that changes in personality correlate with changes in SWB. Specifically, increases in neuroticism and decreases in extraversion, conscientiousness, agreeableness, and, in one study, openness to experiences over a 4-year period were correlated with decreases in life satisfaction during the same period (Boyce, Wood, & Powdthavee, 2013; Magee, Miller, & Heaven, 2013). Together, these findings suggest that age-related changes in SWB may partially be due to age-related changes in personality. Note, however, that the causal direction of this association may be bidirectional such that changes in personality may both precede and succeed changes in SWB (Specht, Egloff, & Schmukle, 2013).

## Life circumstances

Life circumstances vary systematically with age. For instance, social networks change over the life span in terms of both size and composition (Wrzus, Hänel, Wagner, & Neyer, 2013). Although health problems can arise at any age, average health levels decline with increasing age. Social relationships, health, and other life circumstances are important determinants of SWB (Diener et al., 1999). Can age-related changes in these life circumstances explain age differences in SWB?

Overall, most changes in life circumstances have only small and short-term effects on SWB (Lucas, 2007a; Luhmann, Hofmann et al., 2012). For instance, marriage is associated with a short boost in life satisfaction and a return to premarriage levels within a few years (Lucas, Clark, Georgellis, & Diener, 2003), although people getting married end up more satisfied than their unmarried counterparts (Yap, Anusic, & Lucas, 2012). Income is positively correlated with SWB on the between-person level, but within-person changes in income are only weakly related to within-person changes in SWB (Luhmann, Schimmack, & Eid, 2011), possibly because rising income is associated with rising aspirations for income (Di Tella, Haisken-De New, & MacCulloch, 2010). Health, in contrast, seems to have more persistent effects on SWB. For instance, average life satisfaction levels remain low over many years after becoming disabled (Lucas, 2007b). Moreover, declining levels of perceived health partially account for the terminal decline in SWB (Berg et al., 2009; Kunzmann et al., 2000). In sum, life circumstances may account for some age differences in SWB, but their effects are probably weak because people adapt to changes in their life circumstances (for a review of mechanisms, see Sheldon, Boehm, & Lyubomirsky, 2013).

In addition, the relative impact of life circumstances on SWB varies across the life span (George, Okun, & Landerman, 1985). These effects can be explained with developmental life-span theories (Baltes & Baltes, 1990; Haase, Heckhausen, & Wrosch, 2013; Heckhausen, Wrosch, & Schulz, 2010). According to the motivational theory of life-span development (Heckhausen et al., 2010), different life stages are associated with unique developmental goals. People are therefore motivated to invest their resources in those life domains which are particularly relevant or normative in their life stage (Nurmi, 1992). Consistent with these perspectives, the effect of income on SWB is stronger among mid-aged adults, for whom acquiring and accumulating income and wealth is a central developmental task, than among both younger and older adults (Cheung & Lucas, 2015).

In summary, age-related differences in both actual and desired life circumstances may account for some age differences in SWB. However, their effects are probably weak and short-lived. In addition, similar to personality, the relationship between life circumstances and SWB may be bidirectional such that changes in SWB may both precede and succeed changes in various life domains such as work, family, and health (Diener & Chan, 2011; Luhmann, Lucas, Eid, & Diener, 2013; Lyubomirsky, King, & Diener, 2005).

## Intentional activities

SWB is also influenced by so-called intentional activities which refer to the "things that people do and think in their daily lives" (Lyubomirsky, Sheldon et al., 2005, p. 118). This category includes cognitions (e.g., attitudes and values), motivation and volition (e.g., goal setting and goal pursuit), and behaviors (e.g., socializing with friends).

Developmental life-span theories have outlined in detail how people's priorities and goals change over the life span. Socioemotional selectivity theory (Carstensen, Isaacowitz, & Charles, 1999) is particularly relevant for explaining age-related changes in PA and NA in old age. According to this theory, older people are more likely to perceive their time as bounded and are therefore more likely to set emotional goals instead of goals related to preparing for the future. As a consequence, older people are more likely to attend to and remember positive aspects of stimuli (positivity effect; Carstensen & Mikels, 2005). Furthermore, socioemotional selectivity theory predicts that older people are more likely to spend their time with close friends rather than with peripheral members of their social network (Lang & Carstensen, 2002). Consistent with this prediction, older adults tend to derive less well-being from activities with families than from activities with friends, compared to mid-aged adults (Huxhold, Miche, & Schüz, 2014). Hence, one explanation for why PA increases and NA decreases with age is that older people think and behave in ways that are associated with more PA and less NA.

According to the theory of selection, optimization, and compensation (Baltes & Baltes, 1990), younger people are more likely to pursue goals that are associated with growth whereas older people are more likely to pursue goals that are associated with maintenance and avoidance of loss (Ebner, Freund, & Baltes, 2006). Similarly, according to the dual process model of assimilative and accommodative coping (Brandtstädter & Renner, 1990; Brandtstädter & Rothermund, 2002), older people are more likely than younger people to pursue goals in flexible ways and to disengage from goals and instead adjust their aspirations (accommodation). Younger people, in contrast, are more likely to pursue their goals tenaciously and cope with challenges by attempting to change their circumstances (assimilation). Tenacious goal pursuit is generally positively associated with SWB, but this association is weaker among older adults, suggesting that flexible goal adjustment and goal disengagement can be adaptive in this age group (Rothermund & Brandtstädter, 2003; Wrosch & Heckhausen, 1999). Indeed, Cheng (2004) found that perceived discrepancies between people's current conditions in and their aspirations for specific life domains changed with age such that older people were more likely to report discrepancies in the health domain and less likely to report discrepancies in social and other life domains than younger people. Health discrepancies, however, had a weaker effect on SWB than discrepancies in other domains. These findings indicate that older people may compensate for losses in one domain (here: health) by perceived gains in other domains (see also Kunzmann, 2008). In short, age differences in motivation and goal pursuit may explain why SWB does not decrease across most of adulthood.

Finally, many of these theories highlight the central role of perceived control in life-span development (Haase et al., 2013; Heckhausen et al., 2010). Perceived control determines whether and how people select and pursue specific goals. Higher levels of perceived control are generally associated with greater SWB (Lachman, 2006) and may buffer the terminal decline in SWB (Berg, Hassing, Thorvaldsson, & Johansson, 2011; Gerstorf et al., 2014).

In sum, age-related changes in motivation and goal setting may account for stability and change in SWB. To understand how SWB develops over the life span, the development of these intentional activities must be taken into consideration.

# Conclusion

If common stereotypes were true, we could only be happy if we were fit, lean, healthy, attractive, and above all, young. Luckily for those of us who grow older year by year, these stereotypes do not have much empirical support. If anything, the opposite is true: Different components of SWB are either stable across the life span or improve with age, particularly from midlife into early old age. It is only the last years before death that a significant downward trend in SWB can reliably be detected.

Presumably, these age-related changes in SWB are partially attributable to changes in personality and life circumstances. Developmental life-span theories, however, suggest that change and stability of SWB is probably primarily driven by motivational, socio-cognitive, and behavioral changes, which Lyubomirsky, Sheldon, et al. (2005) dubbed "intentional activities." Note, however, that longitudinal studies investigating all three sets of predictors simultaneously are absent to date. It is therefore not yet possible to quantify the relative impact of personality, life circumstances, and intentional activities on the development of SWB.

Two additional caveats about this field of research need to be mentioned. First, most studies have been conducted in Western countries. In fact, most of what we know today about the development of SWB is based on only a couple of datasets such as the SOEP, BHPS, or MIDUS. Cross-cultural studies indicate that the development of SWB may differ among cultures. For instance, in one study, the positivity effect for older adults was only found for US participants but not for Japanese participants (Grossmann, Karasawa, Kan, & Kitayama, 2014). Furthermore, the age distribution of SWB varies between countries, and this variation can partially be explained by the level of affluence of a country (Blanchflower & Oswald, 2008; Morgan, Robinson, & Thompson, 2015).

Second, age may not only affect the level of SWB itself but also how people define SWB and the good life more generally (McMahan & Estes, 2012; Oishi, Graham, Kesebir, & Galinha, 2013). These idiosyncratic definitions of SWB may affect how people respond to questions about their life satisfaction and affective well-being.

In sum, this chapter has shown that the influence of sagging skin and bulging bellies on our SWB is probably overestimated. Whether or not we become and stay happy as we grow old depends substantially on our own thoughts and actions.

# References

Antaramian, S. P., & Huebner, E. S. (2009). Stability of adolescents' multidimensional life satisfaction reports. *Journal of Psychoeducational Assessment, 27*(5), 421–425. Available from http://dx.doi.org/10.1177/0734282909331744.

Anusic, I., & Schimmack, U. (2015). Stability and change of personality traits, self-esteem, and well-being: Introducing the meta-analytic stability and change model of retest correlations. *Journal of Personality and Social Psychology*, Available from http://dx.doi.org/10.1037/pspp0000066 10.1037/pspp0000066 (Supplemental).

Baird, B. M., Lucas, R. E., & Donnellan, M. B. (2010). Life satisfaction across the lifespan: Findings from two nationally representative panel studies. *Social Indicators Research, 99*(2), 183–203. Available from http://dx.doi.org/10.1007/s11205-010-9584-9.

Baltes, P. B., & Baltes, M. M. (1990). Psychological perspectives on successful aging: The model of selective optimization with compensation. In P. B. Baltes, & M. M. Baltes (Eds.), *Successful aging: Perspectives from the behavioral sciences* (pp. 1–34). New York, NY: Cambridge University Press.

Berg, A. I., Hassing, L. B., Thorvaldsson, V., & Johansson, B. (2011). Personality and personal control make a difference for life satisfaction in the oldest-old: Findings in a longitudinal population-based study of individuals 80 and older. *European Journal of Ageing*, *8*(1), 13−20. Available from http://dx.doi.org/10.1007/s10433-011-0181-9.

Berg, A. I., Hoffman, L., Hassing, L. B., McClearn, G. E., & Johansson, B. (2009). What matters, and what matters most, for change in life satisfaction in the oldest-old? A study over 6 years among individuals 80 +. *Aging & Mental Health*, *13*(2), 191−201. Available from http://dx.doi.org/10.1080/13607860802342227.

Blanchflower, D. G., & Oswald, A. J. (2008). Is well-being U-shaped over the life cycle? *Social Science & Medicine*, *66*(8), 1733−1749. Available from http://dx.doi.org/10.1016/j.socscimed.2008.01.030.

Boyce, C. J., Wood, A. M., & Powdthavee, N. (2013). Is personality fixed? Personality changes as much as "variable" economic factors and more strongly predicts changes to life satisfaction. *Social Indicators Research*, *111*(1), 287−305. Available from http://dx.doi.org/10.1007/s11205-012-0006-z.

Brandtstädter, J., & Renner, G. (1990). Tenacious goal pursuit and flexible goal adjustment: Explication and age-related analysis of assimilative and accommodative strategies of coping. *Psychology and Aging*, *5*(1), 58−67. Available from http://dx.doi.org/10.1037/0882-7974.5.1.58.

Brandtstädter, J., & Rothermund, K. (2002). The life-course dynamics of goal pursuit and goal adjustment: A two-process framework. *Developmental Review*, *22*(1), 117−150. Available from http://dx.doi.org/10.1006/drev.2001.0539.

Buchanan, C. M., & Holmbeck, G. N. (1998). Measuring beliefs about adolescent personality and behavior. *Journal of Youth and Adolescence*, *27*(5), 607−627. Available from http://dx.doi.org/10.1023/A:1022835107795.

Carstensen, L. L., Isaacowitz, D. M., & Charles, S. T. (1999). Taking time seriously: A theory of socioemotional selectivity. *American Psychologist*, *54*(3), 165−181. Available from http://dx.doi.org/10.1037/0003-066x.54.3.165.

Carstensen, L. L., & Mikels, J. A. (2005). At the intersection of emotion and cognition. *Current Directions in Psychological Science*, *14*(3), 117−121.

Carstensen, L. L., Pasupathi, M., Mayr, U., & Nesselroade, J. R. (2000). Emotional experience in everyday life across the adult life span. *Journal of Personality and Social Psychology*, *79*(4), 644−655. Available from http://dx.doi.org/10.1037/0022-3514.79.4.644.

Carstensen, L. L., Turan, B., Scheibe, S., Ram, N., Ersner-Hershfield, H., Samanez-Larkin, G. R., & Nesselroade, J. R. (2011). Emotional experience improves with age: Evidence based on over 10 years of experience sampling. *Psychology and Aging*, *26*(1), 21−33. Available from http://dx.doi.org/10.1037/a0021285.

Charles, S. T., Reynolds, C. A., & Gatz, M. (2001). Age-related differences and change in positive and negative affect over 23 years. *Journal of Personality and Social Psychology*, *80*(1), 136−151. Available from http://dx.doi.org/10.1037/0022-3514.80.1.136.

Cheng, S.-T. (2004). Age and subjective well-being revisited: A discrepancy perspective. *Psychology and Aging*, *19*(3), 409−415. Available from http://dx.doi.org/10.1037/0882-7974.19.3.409.

Cheung, F., & Lucas, R. E. (2015). When does money matter most? Examining the association between income and life satisfaction over the life course. *Psychology and Aging*, *30*(1), 120−135. Available from http://dx.doi.org/10.1037/a0038682.

Coffey, J. K., Warren, M. T., & Gottfried, A. W. (2015). Does infant happiness forecast adult life satisfaction? Examining subjective well-being in the first quarter century of life. *Journal of Happiness Studies*, *16*(6), 1401−1421. Available from http://dx.doi.org/10.1007/s10902-014-9556-x.

Costello, D. M., Swendsen, J., Rose, J. S., & Dierker, L. C. (2008). Risk and protective factors associated with trajectories of depressed mood from adolescence to early adulthood. *Journal of Consulting and Clinical Psychology*, 76(2), 173–183. Available from http://dx.doi.org/10.1037/0022-006X.76.2.173.

DeNeve, K. M., & Cooper, H. (1998). The happy personality: A meta-analysis of 137 personality traits and subjective well-being. *Psychological Bulletin*, 124(2), 197–229. Available from http://dx.doi.org/10.1037/0033-2909.124.2.197.

de Ree, J., & Alessie, R. (2011). Life satisfaction and age: Dealing with underidentification in age-period-cohort models. *Social Science & Medicine*, 73(1), 177–182. Available from http://dx.doi.org/10.1016/j.socscimed.2011.04.008.

Diener, E. (1984). Subjective well-being. *Psychological Bulletin*, 95(3), 542–575. Available from http://dx.doi.org/10.1037/0033-2909.95.3.542.

Diener, E., & Chan, M. Y. (2011). Happy people live longer: Subjective well-being contributes to health and longevity. *Applied Psychology: Health and Well-Being*, 3(1), 1–43. Available from http://dx.doi.org/10.1111/j.1758-0854.2010.01045.x.

Diener, E., Emmons, R. A., Larsen, R. J., & Griffin, S. (1985). The Satisfaction With Life Scale. *Journal of Personality Assessment*, 49(1), 71–75. Available from http://dx.doi.org/10.1207/s15327752jpa4901_13.

Diener, E., Inglehart, R., & Tay, L. (2013). Theory and validity of Life Satisfaction Scales. *Social Indicators Research*, 112(3), 497–527. Available from http://dx.doi.org/10.1007/s11205-012-0076-y.

Diener, E., Lucas, R. E., & Scollon, C. N. (2006). Beyond the hedonic treadmill—Revising the adaptation theory of well-being. *American Psychologist*, 61(4), 305–314. Available from http://dx.doi.org/10.1037/0003-066x.61.4.305.

Diener, E., Suh, E. M., Lucas, R. E., & Smith, H. L. (1999). Subjective well-being: Three decades of progress. *Psychological Bulletin*, 125(2), 276–302. Available from http://dx.doi.org/10.1037/0033-2909.125.2.276.

Diener, E., Wirtz, D., Biswas-Diener, R., Tov, W., Kim-Prieto, C., Chi, D. W., & Oishi, S. (2010). New well-being measures: Short scales to assess flourishing and positive and negative feelings. *Social Indicators Research*, 97(2), 143–156. Available from http://dx.doi.org/10.1007/s11205-009-9493-y.

Di Tella, R., Haisken-De New, J., & MacCulloch, R. (2010). Happiness adaptation to income and to status in an individual panel. *Journal of Economic Behavior & Organization*, 76(3), 834–852. Available from http://dx.doi.org/10.1016/j.jebo.2010.09.016.

Ebner, N. C., Freund, A. M., & Baltes, P. B. (2006). Developmental changes in personal goal orientation from young to late adulthood: From striving for gains to maintenance and prevention of losses. *Psychology and Aging*, 21(4), 664–678. Available from http://dx.doi.org/10.1037/0882-7974.21.4.664.

Freund, A. M., & Baltes, P. B. (1998). Selection, optimization, and compensation as strategies of life management: Correlations with subjective indicators of successful aging. *Psychology and Aging*, 13(4), 531–543. Available from http://dx.doi.org/10.1037/0882-7974.13.4.531.

Frijters, P., & Beatton, T. (2012). The mystery of the U-shaped relationship between happiness and age. *Journal of Economic Behavior & Organization*, 82(2–3), 525–542. Available from http://dx.doi.org/10.1016/j.jebo.2012.03.008.

Fujita, F., & Diener, E. (2005). Life satisfaction set point: Stability and change. *Journal of Personality and Social Psychology*, 88(1), 158–164. Available from http://dx.doi.org/10.1037/0022-3514.88.1.158.

Fukuda, K. (2013). A happiness study using age—period—cohort framework. *Journal of Happiness Studies*, *14*(1), 135—153. Available from http://dx.doi.org/10.1007/s10902-011-9320-4.

Galambos, N. L., Fang, S., Krahn, H. J., Johnson, M. D., & Lachman, M. E. (2015). Up, not down: The age curve in happiness from early adulthood to midlife in two longitudinal studies. *Developmental Psychology*, *51*(11), 1664—1671. Available from http://dx.doi.org/10.1037/dev0000052.

Gana, K., Bailly, N., Saada, Y., Joulain, M., & Alaphilippe, D. (2013). Does life satisfaction change in old age: Results from an 8-year longitudinal study. *The Journals of Gerontology Series B: Psychological Sciences and Social Sciences*, *68B*(4), 540—552. Available from http://dx.doi.org/10.1093/geronb/gbs093.

Gana, K., Saada, Y., & Amieva, H. (2015). Does positive affect change in old age? Results from a 22-year longitudinal study. *Psychology and Aging*, *30*(1), 172—179. Available from http://dx.doi.org/10.1037/a0038418.

George, L. K., Okun, M. A., & Landerman, R. (1985). Age as a moderator of the determinants of life satisfaction. *Research on Aging*, *7*(2), 209—233. Available from http://dx.doi.org/10.1177/0164027585007002004.

Gerstorf, D., Heckhausen, J., Ram, N., Infurna, F. J., Schupp, J., & Wagner, G. G. (2014). Perceived personal control buffers terminal decline in well-being. *Psychology and Aging*, *29*(3), 612—625. Available from http://dx.doi.org/10.1037/a0037227.

Gerstorf, D., Ram, N., Estabrook, R., Schupp, J., Wagner, G. G., & Lindenberger, U. (2008). Life satisfaction shows terminal decline in old age: Longitudinal evidence from the German Socio-Economic Panel Study (SOEP). *Developmental Psychology*, *44*(4), 1148—1159. Available from http://dx.doi.org/10.1037/0012-1649.44.4.1148.

Gerstorf, D., Ram, N., Röcke, C., Lindenberger, U., & Smith, J. (2008). Decline in life satisfaction in old age: Longitudinal evidence for links to distance-to-death. *Psychology and Aging*, *23*(1), 154—168.

Gilman, R., & Huebner, S. (2003). A review of life satisfaction research with children and adolescents. *School Psychology Quarterly*, *18*(2), 192—205. Available from http://dx.doi.org/10.1521/scpq.18.2.192.21858.

Goldbeck, L., Schmitz, T. G., Besier, T., Herschbach, P., & Henrich, G. (2007). Life satisfaction decreases during adolescence. *Quality of Life Research: An International Journal of Quality of Life Aspects of Treatment, Care & Rehabilitation*, *16*(6), 969—979. Available from http://dx.doi.org/10.1007/s11136-007-9205-5.

Grossmann, I., Karasawa, M., Kan, C., & Kitayama, S. (2014). A cultural perspective on emotional experiences across the life span. *Emotion*, *14*(4), 679—692. Available from http://dx.doi.org/10.1037/a0036041.

Gwozdz, W., & Sousa-Poza, A. (2010). Ageing, health and life satisfaction of the oldest old: An analysis for Germany. *Social Indicators Research*, *97*(3), 397—417. Available from http://dx.doi.org/10.1007/s11205-009-9508-8.

Haase, C. M., Heckhausen, J., & Wrosch, C. (2013). Developmental regulation across the life span: Toward a new synthesis. *Developmental Psychology*, *49*(5), 964—972. Available from http://dx.doi.org/10.1037/a0029231 10.1037/a0029231 (Supplemental).

Hamarat, E., Thompson, D., Steele, D., Matheny, K., & Simons, C. (2002). Age differences in coping resources and satisfaction with life among middle-aged, young-old, and oldest-old adults. *The Journal of Genetic Psychology: Research and Theory on Human Development*, *163*(3), 360—367. Available from http://dx.doi.org/10.1080/00221320209598689.

Headey, B., & Wearing, A. J. (1989). Personality, life events and subjective well-being: Toward a dynamic equilibrium model. *Journal of Personality and Social Psychology*, *57*, 731−739. Available from http://dx.doi.org/10.1037/0022-3514.57.4.731.

Heckhausen, J., Wrosch, C., & Schulz, R. (2010). A motivational theory of life-span development. *Psychological Review*, *117*(1), 32−60. Available from http://dx.doi.org/10.1037/a0017668.

Hoppmann, C. A., Gerstorf, D., Willis, S. L., & Schaie, K. W. (2011). Spousal interrelations in happiness in the Seattle Longitudinal Study: Considerable similarities in levels and change over time. *Developmental Psychology*, *47*(1), 1−8. Available from http://dx.doi.org/10.1037/a0020788.

Huebner, E. S., & Diener, C. (2008). Research on life satisfaction of children and youth: Implications for the delivery of school-related services. In M. Eid, & R. J. Larsen (Eds.), *The science of subjective well-being* (pp. 376−392). New York, NY: Guilford Press.

Huebner, E. S., Funk, B. A., III, & Gilman, R. (2000). Cross-sectional and longitudinal psychosocial correlates of adolescent life satisfaction reports. *Canadian Journal of School Psychology*, *16*(1), 53−64. Available from http://dx.doi.org/10.1177/082957350001600104.

Hummert, M. L., Garstka, T. A., Shaner, J. L., & Strahm, S. (1994). Stereotypes of the elderly held by young, middle-aged, and elderly adults. *Journal of Gerontology*, *49*(5), 240−249. Available from http://dx.doi.org/10.1093/geronj/49.5.P240.

Huxhold, O., Miche, M., & Schüz, B. (2014). Benefits of having friends in older ages: Differential effects of informal social activities on well-being in middle-aged and older adults. *The Journals of Gerontology Series B: Psychological Sciences and Social Sciences*, *69B*(3), 366−375. Available from http://dx.doi.org/10.1093/geronb/gbt029.

Kahneman, D. (1999). Objective happiness. In D. Kahneman, E. Diener, & N. Schwarz (Eds.), *Well-being: Foundations of hedonic psychology* (pp. 3−25). New York, NY: Russell Sage Foundation.

Koivumaa-Honkanen, H., Kaprio, J., Honkanen, R. J., Viinamäki, H., & Koskenvuo, M. (2005). The stability of life satisfaction in a 15-year follow-up of adult Finns healthy at baseline. *BMC Psychiatry*, *5*. Available from http://dx.doi.org/10.1186/1471-244X-5-4.

Kunzmann, U. (2008). Differential age trajectories of positive and negative affect: Further evidence from the Berlin Aging Study. *Journals of Gerontology Series B: Psychological Sciences and Social Sciences*, *63*(5), 261−270. Available from http://dx.doi.org/10.1093/geronb/63.5.P261.

Kunzmann, U., Kappes, C., & Wrosch, C. (2014). Emotional aging: A discrete emotions perspective. *Frontiers in Psychology*, *5*. Available from http://dx.doi.org/10.3389/fpsyg.2014.00380.

Kunzmann, U., Little, T. D., & Smith, J. (2000). Is age-related stability of subjective well-being a paradox? Cross-sectional and longitudinal evidence from the Berlin Aging Study. *Psychology and Aging*, *15*(3), 511−526. Available from http://dx.doi.org/10.1037/0882-7974.15.3.511.

Kunzmann, U., Richter, D., & Schmukle, S. C. (2013). Stability and change in affective experience across the adult life span: Analyses with a national sample from Germany. *Emotion*, *13*(6), 1086−1095. Available from http://dx.doi.org/10.1037/a0033572.

Lachman, M. E. (2006). Perceived control over aging-related declines: Adaptive beliefs and behaviors. *Current Directions in Psychological Science*, *15*(6), 282−286. Available from http://dx.doi.org/10.1111/j.1467-8721.2006.00453.x.

Lachman, M. E., Röcke, C., Rosnick, C., & Ryff, C. D. (2008). Realism and illusion in Americans' temporal views of their life satisfaction: Age differences in reconstructing the past and anticipating the future. *Psychological Science (Wiley-Blackwell)*, *19*(9), 889−897. Available from http://dx.doi.org/10.1111/j.1467-9280.2008.02173.x.

Lachman, M. E., Teshale, S., & Agrigoroaei, S. (2015). Midlife as a pivotal period in the life course: Balancing growth and decline at the crossroads of youth and old age. *International Journal of Behavioral Development*, *39*(1), 20−31. Available from http://dx.doi.org/10.1177/0165025414533223.

Lang, F. R., & Carstensen, L. L. (2002). Time counts: Future time perspective, goals, and social relationships. *Psychology and Aging*, *17*(1), 125−139. Available from http://dx.doi.org/10.1037/0882-7974.17.1.125.

Lang, F. R., & Heckhausen, J. (2001). Perceived control over development and subjective well-being: Differential benefits across adulthood. *Journal of Personality and Social Psychology*, *81*(3), 509−523. Available from http://dx.doi.org/10.1037/0022-3514.81.3.509.

Lucas, R. E. (2007a). Adaptation and the set-point model of subjective well-being: Does happiness change after major life events? *Current Directions in Psychological Science*, *16*(2), 75−79. Available from http://dx.doi.org/10.1111/j.1467-8721.2007.00479.x.

Lucas, R. E. (2007b). Long-term disability is associated with lasting changes in subjective well-being: Evidence from two nationally representative longitudinal studies. *Journal of Personality and Social Psychology*, *92*(4), 717−730. Available from http://dx.doi.org/10.1037/0022-3514.92.4.717.

Lucas, R. E., Clark, A. E., Georgellis, Y., & Diener, E. (2003). Reexamining adaptation and the set point model of happiness: Reactions to changes in marital status. *Journal of Personality and Social Psychology*, *84*(3), 527−539. Available from http://dx.doi.org/10.1037/0022-3514.84.3.527.

Lucas, R. E., Clark, A. E., Georgellis, Y., & Diener, E. (2004). Unemployment alters the set point for life satisfaction. *Psychological Science*, *15*(1), 8−13. Available from http://dx.doi.org/10.1111/j.0963-7214.2004.01501002.x.

Lucas, R. E., Diener, E., & Suh, E. (1996). Discriminant validity of well-being measures. *Journal of Personality and Social Psychology*, *71*(3), 616−628. Available from http://dx.doi.org/10.1037/0022-3514.71.3.616.

Lucas, R. E., & Gohm, C. L. (2000). Age and sex differences in subjective well-being across cultures. In E. Diener, & E. M. Suh (Eds.), *Culture and subjective well-being* (pp. 291−317). Cambridge, MA: MIT Press.

Luhmann, M., Hawkley, L. C., Eid, M., & Cacioppo, J. T. (2012). Time frames and the differences between affective and cognitive well-being. *Journal of Research in Personality*, *46*(4), 431−441. Available from http://dx.doi.org/10.1016/j.jrp.2012.04.004.

Luhmann, M., Hofmann, W., Eid, M., & Lucas, R. E. (2012). Subjective well-being and adaptation to life events: A meta-analysis. *Journal of Personality and Social Psychology*, *102*(3), 592−615. Available from http://dx.doi.org/10.1037/a0025948.

Luhmann, M., Lucas, R. E., Eid, M., & Diener, E. (2013). The prospective effect of life satisfaction on life events. *Social Psychological and Personality Science*, *4*(1), 39−45. Available from http://dx.doi.org/10.1177/1948550612440105.

Luhmann, M., Schimmack, U., & Eid, M. (2011). Stability and variability in the relationship between subjective well-being and income. *Journal of Research in Personality*, *45*(2), 186−197. Available from http://dx.doi.org/10.1016/j.jrp.2011.01.004.

Lykken, D., & Tellegen, A. (1996). Happiness is a stochastic phenomenon. *Psychological Science, 7*(3), 186–189. Available from http://dx.doi.org/10.1111/j.1467-9280.1996.tb00355.x.

Lyons, M. D., Huebner, E. S., Hills, K. J., & Van Horn, M. L. (2013). Mechanisms of change in adolescent life satisfaction: A longitudinal analysis. *Journal of School Psychology, 51*(5), 587–598. Available from http://dx.doi.org/10.1016/j.jsp.2013.07.001.

Lyubomirsky, S., King, L., & Diener, E. (2005). The benefits of frequent positive affect: Does happiness lead to success? *Psychological Bulletin, 131*(6), 803–855. Available from http://dx.doi.org/10.1037/0033-2909.131.6.803.

Lyubomirsky, S., Sheldon, K. M., & Schkade, D. (2005). Pursuing happiness: The architecture of sustainable change. *Review of General Psychology, 9*(2), 111–131. Available from http://dx.doi.org/10.1037/1089-2680.9.2.111.

López Ulloa, B., Møller, V., & Sousa-Poza, A. (2013). How does subjective well-being evolve with age? A literature review. *Journal of Population Ageing, 6*(3), 227–246. Available from http://dx.doi.org/10.1007/s12062-013-9085-0.

Magee, C. A., Miller, L. M., & Heaven, P. C. L. (2013). Personality trait change and life satisfaction in adults: The roles of age and hedonic balance. *Personality and Individual Differences, 55*(6), 694–698. Available from http://dx.doi.org/10.1016/j.paid.2013.05.022.

McMahan, E. A., & Estes, D. (2012). Age-related differences in lay conceptions of well-being and experienced well-being. *Journal of Happiness Studies, 13*(1), 79–101. Available from http://dx.doi.org/10.1007/s10902-011-9251-0.

Moksnes, U. K., Løhre, A., & Espnes, G. A. (2013). The association between sense of coherence and life satisfaction in adolescents. *Quality of Life Research: An International Journal of Quality of Life Aspects of Treatment, Care & Rehabilitation, 22*(6), 1331–1338. Available from http://dx.doi.org/10.1007/s11136-012-0249-9.

Morgan, J., Robinson, O., & Thompson, T. (2015). Happiness and age in European adults: The moderating role of gross domestic product per capita. *Psychology and Aging, 30*(3), 544–551. Available from http://dx.doi.org/10.1037/pag0000034.

Mroczek, D. K., & Kolarz, C. M. (1998). The effect of age on positive and negative affect: A developmental perspective on happiness. *Journal of Personality and Social Psychology, 75*(5), 1333–1349. Available from http://dx.doi.org/10.1037/0022-3514.75.5.1333.

Mroczek, D. K., & Spiro, A., III (2005). Change in life satisfaction during adulthood: Findings from the Veterans Affairs Normative Aging Study. *Journal of Personality and Social Psychology, 88*(1), 189–202. Available from http://dx.doi.org/10.1037/0022-3514.88.1.189.

Nurmi, J.-E. (1992). Age differences in adult life goals, concerns, and their temporal extension: A life course approach to future-oriented motivation. *International Journal of Behavioral Development, 15*(4), 487–508. Available from http://dx.doi.org/10.1177/016502549201500404.

Oishi, S., Graham, J., Kesebir, S., & Galinha, I. C. (2013). Concepts of happiness across time and cultures. *Personality and Social Psychology Bulletin, 39*(5), 559–577. Available from http://dx.doi.org/10.1177/0146167213480042.

Proctor, C. L., Linley, P. A., & Maltby, J. (2009). Youth life satisfaction: A review of the literature. *Journal of Happiness Studies, 10*(5), 583–630. Available from http://dx.doi.org/10.1007/s10902-008-9110-9.

Realo, A., & Dobewall, H. (2011). Does life satisfaction change with age? A comparison of Estonia, Finland, Latvia, and Sweden. *Journal of Research in Personality, 45*(3), 297–308. Available from http://dx.doi.org/10.1016/j.jrp.2011.03.004.

Roberts, B. W., Walton, K. E., & Viechtbauer, W. (2006). Patterns of mean-level change in personality traits across the life course: A meta-analysis of longitudinal studies. *Psychological Bulletin, 132*(1), 1−25. Available from http://dx.doi.org/10.1037/0033-2909.132.1.1.

Roberts, B. W., Wood, D., & Caspi, A. (2008). The development of personality traits in adulthood. In O. P. John, R. W. Robins, & L. A. Pervin (Eds.), *Handbook of personality: Theory and research* (3rd ed., pp. 375−398). New York, NY: Guilford Press.

Rothermund, K., & Brandstädter, J. (2003). Coping with deficits and losses in later life: From compensatory action to accommodation. *Psychology and Aging, 18*(4), 896−905. Available from http://dx.doi.org/10.1037/0882-7974.18.4.896.

Røysamb, E., Nes, R. B., & Vittersø, J. (2014). Well-being: Heritable and changeable. In K. M. Sheldon, & R. E. Lucas (Eds.), *Stability of happiness: Theories and evidence on whether happiness can change* (pp. 9−36). San Diego, CA: Elsevier Academic Press.

Salmela-Aro, K., & Tuominen-Soini, H. (2010). Adolescents' life satisfaction during the transition to post-comprehensive education: Antecedents and consequences. *Journal of Happiness Studies, 11*(6), 683−701. Available from http://dx.doi.org/10.1007/s10902-009-9156-3.

Schaie, K. W. (1965). A general model for the study of developmental problem. *Psychological Bulletin, 64*(2), 92−107. Available from http://dx.doi.org/10.1037/h0022371.

Schilling, O. K., Wahl, H.-W., & Wiegering, S. (2013). Affective development in advanced old age: Analyses of terminal change in positive and negative affect. *Developmental Psychology, 49*(5), 1011−1020. Available from http://dx.doi.org/10.1037/a0028775.

Schimmack, U., & Oishi, S. (2005). The influence of chronically and temporarily accessible information on life satisfaction judgments. *Journal of Personality and Social Psychology, 89*(3), 395−406. Available from http://dx.doi.org/10.1037/0022-3514.89.3.395.

Schimmack, U., Schupp, J., & Wagner, G. G. (2008). The influence of environment and personality on the affective and cognitive component of subjective well-being. *Social Indicators Research, 89*(1), 41−60. Available from http://dx.doi.org/10.1007/s11205-007-9230-3.

Schryer, E., & Ross, M. (2012). Evaluating the valence of remembered events: The importance of age and self-relevance. *Psychology and Aging, 27*(1), 237−242. Available from http://dx.doi.org/10.1037/a0023283.

Sheldon, K. M., Boehm, J., & Lyubomirsky, S. (2013). Variety is the spice of happiness: The hedonic adaptation prevention model. In S. A. David, I. Boniwell, & A. Conley Ayers (Eds.), *The Oxford handbook of happiness* (pp. 901−914). New York, NY: Oxford University Press.

Sheldon, K. M., & Lucas, R. E. (2014). *Stability of happiness: Theories and evidence on whether happiness can change*. San Diego, CA: Elsevier Academic Press.

Specht, J., Bleidorn, W., Denissen, J. J. A., Hennecke, M., Hutteman, R., Kandler, C., & Zimmermann, J. (2014). What drives adult personality development? A comparison of theoretical perspectives and empirical evidence. *European Journal of Personality, 28*(3), 216−230. Available from http://dx.doi.org/10.1002/per.1966.

Specht, J., Egloff, B., & Schmukle, S. C. (2013). Examining mechanisms of personality maturation: The impact of life satisfaction on the development of the Big Five personality traits. *Social Psychological and Personality Science, 4*(2), 181−189. Available from http://dx.doi.org/10.1177/1948550612448197.

Steel, P., Schmidt, J., & Shultz, J. (2008). Refining the relationship between personality and subjective well-being. *Psychological Bulletin, 134*(1), 138−161. Available from http://dx.doi.org/10.1037/0033-2909.134.1.138.

Steptoe, A., Deaton, A., & Stone, A. A. (2015). Subjective wellbeing, health, and ageing. *The Lancet*, *385*(9968), 640−648. Available from http://dx.doi.org/10.1016/S0140-6736 (13)61489-0.

Stone, A. A., Schwartz, J. E., Broderick, J. E., & Deaton, A. (2010). A snapshot of the age distribution of psychological well-being in the United States. *Proceedings of the National Academy of Sciences*, *107*(22), 9985−9990. Available from http://dx.doi.org/ 10.1073/pnas.1003744107.

Stone, A. A., Shiffman, S. S., & DeVries, M. W. (1999). Ecological momentary assessment. In D. Kahneman, E. Diener, & N. Schwarz (Eds.), *Well-being: The foundations of hedonic psychology* (pp. 26−39). New York, NY: Russell Sage Foundation.

Twenge, J. M., Sherman, R. A., & Lyubomirsky, S. (2015). More happiness for young people and less for mature adults: Time period differences in subjective well-being in the United States, 1972−2014. *Social Psychological and Personality Science*. Available from http://dx.doi.org/10.1177/1948550615602933.

Vogel, N., Schilling, O. K., Wahl, H.-W., Beekman, A. T. F., & Penninx, B. W. J. H. (2013). Time-to-death-related change in positive and negative affect among older adults approaching the end of life. *Psychology and Aging*, *28*(1), 128−141. Available from http://dx.doi.org/10.1037/a0030471.

Watson, D., Clark, L. A., & Tellegen, A. (1988). Development and validation of brief measures of positive and negative affect: The PANAS scales. *Journal of Personality and Social Psychology*, *54*(6), 1063−1070. Available from http://dx.doi.org/10.1037/0022-3514.54.6.1063.

Weber, M., Ruch, W., & Huebner, E. S. (2013). Adaptation and initial validation of the German version of the Students' Life Satisfaction Scale (German SLSS). *European Journal of Psychological Assessment*, *29*(2), 105−112. Available from http://dx.doi.org/ 10.1027/1015-5759/a000133.

Wethington, E. (2000). Expecting stress: Americans and the "midlife crisis." *Motivation and Emotion*, *24*(2), 85−103. Available from http://dx.doi.org/10.1023/A:1005611230993.

Wrosch, C., & Heckhausen, J. (1999). Control processes before and after passing a developmental deadline: Activation and deactivation of intimate relationship goals. *Journal of Personality and Social Psychology*, *77*(2), 415−427. Available from http://dx.doi.org/ 10.1037/0022-3514.77.2.415.

Wrzus, C., Hänel, M., Wagner, J., & Neyer, F. J. (2013). Social network changes and life events across the life span: A meta-analysis. *Psychological Bulletin*, *139*(1), 53−80. Available from http://dx.doi.org/10.1037/a0028601.

Wunder, C., Wiencierz, A., Schwarze, J., & Kuchenhoff, H. (2013). Well-being over the life span: Semiparametric evidence from British and German longitudinal data. *Review of Economics and Statistics*, *95*(1), 154−167. Available from http://dx.doi.org/10.1162/ REST_a_00222.

Yap, S. C. Y., Anusic, I., & Lucas, R. E. (2012). Does personality moderate reaction and adaptation to major life events? Evidence from the British Household Panel Survey. *Journal of Research in Personality*, *46*(5), 477−488. Available from http://dx.doi.org/ 10.1016/j.jrp.2012.05.005.

# Getting older, getting better? Toward understanding positive personality development across adulthood

## 14

*Anne K. Reitz[1,2] and Ursula M. Staudinger[1]*
[1]Columbia University, New York, NY, United States,
[2]New York University, New York, NY, United States

Personality is the only domain of psychological functioning that is linked with a positive old-age stereotype. In contrast to the domain of cognitive functioning, there is a general expectation that our personality gets better as we get older. Does this stereotype capture the truth—do we "get better" as we get older? And if that was the case, what does getting better mean; which kind of personality is better than another? It is easier to determine whether a person's cognitive functioning is better than another's, as thinking faster and solving problems seems more desirable than thinking slowly and making mistakes. But there is no simple analogy with personality functioning.

The terms that are often used in the context of personality research are "personality maturity" and "personality growth." Defining "personality maturity" is challenging given the manifold conceptualizations stemming from different traditions in psychology. Some approaches are mainly rooted in personality psychology and conceptualize personality maturation as the age-related increase of desirable characteristics across the lifespan, such as becoming emotionally more stable, more agreeable, conscientious, and satisfied with one's life; in short, becoming more competent in dealing with life-course challenges. Other approaches, mainly rooted in lifespan psychology, define "personality maturity" and "personality growth" more specifically, in terms of reaching the ideal endpoint of human development, which, by definition, is a rare quality and does not automatically come with age.

This chapter aims to clarify the terminology and to integrate the different notions of positive personality development in an overarching framework. This framework proposes that there are two types of positive personality development across the adult lifespan: one is linked with adjustment and the other one with growth. Adjustment involves desirable change toward an individual's greater functionality (or success) in the face of developmental tasks and societal norms and expectations. Growth, in contrast, refers to growing beyond functionality for oneself and others; it involves transcending one's own limitations and interests, embracing complexity and differentiation, and striving toward insight and wisdom. This may often imply

Personality Development Across the Lifespan. DOI: http://dx.doi.org/10.1016/B978-0-12-804674-6.00014-4

to transcend given societal rules and structures for the greater good at the cost of jeopardizing personal well-being.

This framework maintains that not all positive age-related trajectories are indicative of maturation in terms of growth. While the majority of people develop a personality that helps them to be well adjusted and more competent in dealing with developmental tasks and tasks of everyday life across the lifespan, not everyone (in fact, only a minority) experiences personality growth as defined here. By separating the two types of positive personality development conceptually and by delineating the different antecedents and processes underlying their lifespan trajectories, this framework provides a helpful guideline for future research on positive personality development.

In the first section, we outline definitions and indicators of these two types of positive personality development. Next, we provide an overview of the current evidence for their age trajectories. Subsequently, we review research concerning their predictors and underlying processes. Finally, we discuss avenues for future research and provide concluding remarks.

# An integrative framework for studying two types of positive personality development

## Adjustment

Maturation as adjustment is a form of positive personality development that has an adaptive value and functionality for the individual and for society. It involves the mastery of everyday life, productivity, and maintenance of subjective well-being. As the success of a society depends, among other factors, on a high prevalence of individuals that function effectively (Helson & Wink, 1987), the adjustment of individuals is highly desirable and executed by socializing institutions (e.g., schools) and social norms (e.g., age-related expectations; see Staudinger & Kessler, 2009). The tenet that most people's personality changes in similar ways in the face of mastering developmental tasks defined by society is widely shared among personality researchers (Havighurst, 1972; Helson & Kwan, 2000; Hutteman, Hennecke, Orth, Reitz, & Specht, 2014; Masten et al., 2005).

Social investment theory (SIT; Roberts, Wood, & Smith, 2005) applied these notions to the development of the Big Five traits and proposed that the investment in age-graded social roles is a key influence on the positive trajectories of personality development. Research following this approach has particularly focused on the Big Five personality traits (Costa & McCrae, 1980; John & Srivastava, 1999). Conscientiousness, Agreeableness, Emotional Stability, and to some degree social dominance/assurance (one facet of Extraversion) qualify as personality adjustment according to our conception. In the same vein, it is noteworthy that Conscientiousness, Agreeableness, and Emotional Stability share a considerable amount of common variance in the sense of a second-order factor (DeYoung, 2006).

The trait approach to personality is based on the interindividual differences tradition and focuses on describing rather stable characteristics that allow distinguishing between individuals. There is a complementary approach to studying personality that is based on the developmental tradition of personality research (cf. Baltes, Lindenberger, & Staudinger, 2006). This approach is exemplified by Ryff's (1989) dimensions of psychological well-being such as Self-Acceptance (i.e., a positive attitude toward the self), Positive Social Relations, and Environmental Mastery (i.e., the capacity to manage effectively one's life and surrounding world). Environmental Mastery was found to be strongly correlated with Conscientiousness, Agreeableness, and Emotional Stability (see Ryff, 2013). Strong associations have also been found for Self-acceptance and Positive Relations With Others (Wink & Staudinger, 2015), which supports the idea that they are all part of personality adjustment.

Thirdly, there has been a tradition in personality research that focuses on the self-concept system such as the stage model of Loevinger (1976). The earlier stages of her model on ego development, i.e., stages 3–6, are indicative of personality maturation toward adjustment: self-protective (i.e., the first step toward self-control; stage 3), conformist (i.e., conforming to socially approved norms; stage 4), self-aware (i.e., conscientious-conformist; stage 5), and conscientious (i.e., internalization of rules, sense of responsibility; stage 6).

We propose that personality change that is linked to the mastery of developmental tasks and to becoming a well-functioning member of society is, albeit essential and highly functional, only one type of positive personality development. What is missing from this approach to personality maturation is personality change that transcends the well-being of the self and given societal expectations, i.e., personality maturation toward growth.

## Growth

Maturation as growth is a form of positive personality development that refers to transcending social structures within which we have been socialized for the sake of increasing the greater good. The prevalence for maturation as growth is smaller than for maturation as adjustment, which may partly be due to the weaker socialization pressure to achieve growth than adjustment and partly due to the fact that maturation as growth implies costs for the maturing individuals. Maturation as growth is indexed by personality qualities that reflect the ideal endpoint of human development as described in the prototype of personality growth, wisdom. Two types of wisdom were distinguished: general wisdom and personal wisdom. General wisdom is based on the ancient wisdom literature and lifespan theory. It is defined as insight into life from an observer's point of view; as expert-level knowledge and judgment about difficult problems related to the meaning and conduct of life (see "Berlin Wisdom Paradigm"; Baltes, Smith, & Staudinger, 1992). Personal wisdom is based on the personality literature (Helson & Srivastava, 2001, 2002) and is defined as good judgment about the self and deep insights into one's own life, which makes personal wisdom the ideal prototype of personality growth (Mickler & Staudinger, 2008). Personal and general wisdom are related, but not synonymous.

Wisdom is understood as the perfect integration of mind and character for the greater good (Staudinger & Glück, 2011). It concerns mastering the basic dialetics shaping human existence, such as the dialectic between good and bad, positivity and negativity, dependence and independence, certainty and doubt, control and lack of control, finiteness and eternity, strength and weakness, selfishness and altruism. Rather than considering them as a decision between either/or, wisdom embraces these contradictions of life and draws insights from them. In terms of psychological functioning, three facets need to be integrated: a cognitive, an emotional, and a motivational facet, i.e., (1) deep and broad insight into self, others, and the world, (2) complex emotion regulation (in the sense of tolerance of ambiguity), and (3) a motivational orientation that is transcending self-interest and is investing in the well-being of others and the world (cf. Staudinger & Kessler, 2009). A previous study that used several observer-scored wisdom measures supported the notion of wisdom as the perfect integration of mind and character for the greater good. The authors found that, like creativity, wisdom was associated with a sense of personal growth in Openness and complexity, but unlike creativity, wisdom was also associated with tolerance and benevolence in terms of being open to and skillful in appraising the feelings of others (Helson & Srivastava, 2002).

Related but narrower notions of growth that focus either on affect or self-conceptualization have been described by Labouvie-Vief (1982) (affect complexity, the amplification of affect in the search for differentiation) and Loevinger (1976) (the highest stages of ego development, the most complex ways of perceiving oneself in relation to the world). Indicators of growth are also part of Ryff's approach to psychological well-being. In particular, the dimensions of Personal Growth (i.e., a sense of continued growth and development), Autonomy (i.e., independence, ability to resist social pressures), and Purpose in Life (i.e., the belief that one's life is purposeful; Ryff & Keyes, 1995) are associated with personality maturation in terms of growth.

Growth indicators within the Big Five paradigm of personality assessment (McCrae & Costa, 2008) are Openness to new Experience (i.e., to have wide interests and to seek new experiences) and possibly social vitality (a subfacet of Extraversion; see Roberts, Walton, & Viechtbauer, 2006). Openness has been found to be an important correlate of other indicators of personality growth, such as wisdom (Helson & Srivastava, 2002; Staudinger, Lopez, & Baltes, 1997), purpose in life (Hill, Turiano, Spiro, & Mroczek, 2015), higher ego development (Vincent, 2013), making sense of one's life (McAdams et al., 2004), a sense of continued development (Ryff, 2013), and mature affective responses and self-knowledge (Pals, 2006). Personal wisdom correlates with general wisdom and other growth indicators such as Generativity, Psychological Mindedness, Creativity, or Judiciousness (Mickler & Staudinger, 2008; Wink & Staudinger, 2015). These correlations demonstrate the conceptual overlap and convergent validity of the different growth indicators.

Apart from the benefits of personality growth in terms of personal wisdom for the greater good of society, there is also evidence that suggests beneficial effects of growth-related personality characteristics in later life. Openness, for instance, was found to predict life satisfaction in retired adults above and beyond subjective health and financial satisfaction (Stephan, 2009). One explanation for this link is that Openness may facilitate the development of a fulfilled life after retirement, such as seeking new activities, pursuing interests, and using available opportunities for growth (see also Van Solinge & Henkens, 2008). Openness was also found to be related to preserved higher cognitive ability in older adults, which was partly mediated by higher activity levels (Hogan, Staff, Bunting, Deary, & Whalley, 2012).

Concerning health, there is some evidence that Openness is related to decreased mortality (Jonassaint et al., 2007). One explanation is the greater stress resilience of open individuals, as they were found to show less blood pressure reactivity in stressful situations (Williams, Rau, Cribbet, & Gunn, 2009). Other research has provided related evidence underlying the role of adaptive processing styles of difficult life experiences. Openness in young adulthood predicted maturity (i.e., affective response, self-knowledge, and integrity) in late midlife, which was mediated by an exploratory, reflected, analytical way of processing difficult life experiences (Pals, 2006). Hence, being open to learn from life experiences and to incorporate a sense of change into the life story can support maturity and insight in later life.

Table 14.1 lists the key differences between personality adjustment and growth, which underscore the importance to treat these two notions of personality maturation separately.

## Adjustment and growth: comparison with other theoretical approaches

The distinction between adjustment and growth relates to similar two-dimensional conceptualizations, such as two facets of optimal human functioning that are recently receiving increasing attention: hedonic and eudaimonic well-being. Although specific definitions vary, hedonic well-being ("happiness") relates to the evaluation of one's feelings toward life, such as life satisfaction. Eudaimonic well-being involves the pursuit of self-realization and living in accordance with one's values, such as meaning in life (Bauer & McAdams, 2010; Ryan & Deci, 2001; Ryff & Singer, 1998). Despite similarities, competence, relatedness, and self-acceptance are not sufficient to qualify as growth; they are rather a sign of being well adjusted. In a similar vein, the notion of eudaimonic well-being, Maslow's notion of self-actualization (Maslow, 1968), and Helson and Wink's (1987) notion of intrapsychic differentiation differ from our notion of personality growth. These approaches encompass concepts relating to productive self-actualization, whereas maturation in terms of growth also involves seeking to balance one's own good with that of others in order to advance the common good (cf. Law & Staudinger, 2016).

**Table 14.1  Two types of positive personality development:
adjustment and growth**

|  | Adjustment | Growth |
|---|---|---|
| *Definition* | Desirable change toward greater functionality | Ideal endpoint of human development: embracing complexity, striving toward insight and improving the common good |
| *Main focus of subdiscipline* | Personality psychology | Lifespan psychology |
| *Developmental tasks* | Adjusting to developmental tasks | Transcending beyond developmental tasks |
| *Social expectations* | Desired or obligatory | Optional |
| *Age trajectory* | Increase across most of adulthood, but not in late old adulthood | Age-related stability/decline starting in middle adulthood |
| *Individual differences* | Moderate | Large |
| *Biological basis* | Serotonergic | Dopaminergic |
| **Indicators** | | |
| *Big Five personality traits (Costa, McCrae)* | Emotional stability, Agreeableness, Conscientiousness, Social dominance (facet of Extraversion) | Openness, social vitality (facet of Extraversion) |
| *Well-being (Ryff)* | Environmental mastery | Personal growth, Purpose in life |
| *Ego development (Loevinger)* | Stages 3–6 (conformist, self-aware, conscientious) | Stages 7–8 (individualistic, autonomous) |
| *Affect development (Labouvie-Vief)* | Affect optimization | Affect complexity |
| *Other indicators* | Life satisfaction | Personal wisdom |
| **Predictors and mechanisms** | | |
| *Contextual* | Life transitions, developmental tasks, social role investments | Opportunity structures to stay engaged and explore, old-age stereotypes |
| *Personal* | Self-regulatory strategies, emotion regulation goals (positive affect) | Cognitive abilities; growth goals and need to explore |

Another related two-dimensional framework proposes that maintaining and enhancing levels of subjective well-being (affect optimization) does not provide a complete picture of personality development (Labouvie-Vief, 2003). A person's ability and willingness to understand, differentiate, and integrate emotional experiences is an important second part of personality development. This distinction maps well on the distinction of adjustment and growth, but it is more narrow as it only focuses on affect regulation.

A structural factor-analytically informed model that makes a similar distinction is the higher order factor solution of the Big Five traits (*Big Two*; Digman, 1997). Conscientiousness, Agreeableness, and Emotional Stability are subsumed under the factor "Stability," which is regarded as a socialization factor, whereas Extraversion and Openness are subsumed under the factor "Plasticity," which is considered a factor of personal growth (DeYoung, 2006; DeYoung, Peterson, & Higgins, 2002). The correlation between Extraversion and Openness was attenuated when using mini-markers, which may be higher for the vitality facet of Extraversion. Whereas Stability and Plasticity were positively correlated when using self-ratings, they were uncorrelated when the variance associated with specific informants was removed, which may be due to a desirability bias in self-reports (DeYoung, 2006). In contrast to the present framework, the Big Two solution is solely based on the Big Five traits and does not make predictions about lifespan trajectories. Based on a lifespan perspective, we have assumed, for instance, that a certain level of adjustment is a necessary but not sufficient condition for maturing toward personality growth. This is an assumption that awaits empirical support based on longitudinal analyses.

In sum, the presented framework shows meaningful overlap with other two-dimensional frameworks but is more comprehensive in combining an interindividual difference approach with a developmental approach to personality. Also, in contrast to most notions of personality maturation, the notion of personality growth presented here necessitates a value orientation geared toward promoting the common good, which is missing from other approaches to personality growth. The distinction between maturation toward personality adjustment and growth is linked with a unique constellation of differences in terms of personal motivation, individual characteristics, and contextual experiences (see Table 14.1). In the following, we review evidence showing that the two types of positive personality development follow different age trajectories that are influenced by different factors and mechanisms.

# Lifespan trajectories of personality adjustment and growth

## Adjustment

Most empirical evidence for stability and change in personality traits comes from research on the Big Five personality traits. There is consistent evidence from a number of longitudinal studies that Emotional Stability, Conscientiousness, Agreeableness, and social dominance (a facet of Extraversion) show mean-level increases across the adult lifespan (for a meta-analysis, see Roberts et al. 2006). This positive change pattern was found for most of adulthood, beginning in adolescence (Klimstra, Hale, Raaijmakers, Branje, & Meeus, 2009), whereas it was not consistently found in very old age. The few longitudinal studies that have covered the end of life mostly demonstrated a reversed trend, as Conscientiousness, Agreeableness, and Emotional Stability were found to decrease (Kandler, Kornadt, Hagemeyer, & Neyer, 2015; Mõttus, Johnson, & Deary, 2012). There are, however, also some findings suggesting stability or further increases toward the end of life in Conscientiousness, Agreeableness, and Emotional Stability (Lucas & Donnellan, 2011; Noftle & Fleeson, 2010). The positive change pattern over most of adulthood has sometimes been labeled *maturation* (Roberts & Wood, 2006). We call it the *adjustment-type of maturation* as it denotes mastering developmental tasks and one's well-being regulation.

Less longitudinal evidence exists for other adjustment indicators. With regard to the adjustment dimension of psychological well-being, it has been shown that Environmental Mastery, Self-acceptance, and Positive Social Relations increase during most of adulthood and show stability after midlife (Ryff & Keyes, 1995; see also Diener & Suh, 1998). Similar findings were found for the development of emotional functioning, as growth curve analyses revealed a positive trajectory for affect optimization (e.g., dampening negative affect, reframing stressful situations) up to late middle age, which subsequently leveled off (Labouvie-Vief, Diehl, Jain, & Zhang, 2007). Similar to adjustment indicators of the Big Five, some studies also found a decline in life satisfaction (Mroczek & Spiro, 2003) and emotional well-being (Kunzmann, Little, & Smith, 2000), particularly for individuals with functional health problems.

In sum, research on indicators of adjustment both native to classical personality and developmental psychology revealed mean-level increases from young to the beginning of late adulthood; findings for very old age are mixed but point to a reversed trend. There is a consistent pattern of desirable age trajectories for indicators of adjustment: Conscientiousness, Agreeableness, Environmental Mastery, Self-Acceptance, Positive Social Relations, affect optimization, identity certainty, and confident power. These constructs are all considered as highly functional for mastering developmental tasks and everyday life (Hutteman et al., 2014; Roberts & Wood, 2006); and thus, they are supportive of adjustment and social mastery (Staudinger, 2005). Longitudinal evidence generally supports this assumption. For instance, Conscientiousness during college years was found to have positive long-term effects on commitment to duties in the context of family and work (George, Helson, & John, 2011). Neuroticism in young adulthood predicted worse physical health and subjective well-being in old age and extraversion predicted social competence (Friedman, Kern, & Reynolds, 2010). In another study, increases in Agreeableness, Emotional Stability, and Conscientiousness in adulthood were found to affect health (Turiano et al., 2011).

## Growth

Maturation toward growth does, in contrast to adjustment, not normatively occur across adulthood. With regard to the Big Five traits, Openness to experience does not follow the pattern of positive lifespan trajectories described earlier. Openness was found to increase somewhat from early adolescence until age 20, then it remains stable, and subsequently declines by one standard deviation starting in mid-life (Roberts et al., 2006; Wortmann, Lucas, & Donnellan, 2012). Constructs that are related to Openness, such as Novelty seeking and Self-transcendence, show similar decreases from young to middle adulthood (Josefsson et al., 2013). Hence, with increasing age, adults become on average less behaviorally flexible, less intellectually curious, and they have a decreasing motivation to explore and actively seek out new and varied experiences and ideas. Social vitality was found to decline starting in midlife, which parallels the Openness trajectory.

Growth indicators derived from other traditions also showed stability or declines after middle adulthood, such as Ryff's Personal Growth and Purpose in Life (Ryff & Keyes, 1995). A meta-analysis demonstrated a highly consistent pattern: older adults reported lower levels of Purpose in Life than younger adults (Pinquart, 2002). This is in line with findings from a longitudinal study that reported mean-level decreases in Purpose in Life across a 3-year interval in late adulthood (Hill et al. 2015). These findings seem to be linked to the loss of work and social roles in later adulthood (see also Staudinger, 2005). Such declines in later life are in line with findings for personal wisdom. Older adults were found to show less personal wisdom, which was partially mediated by declines in Openness (Mickler & Staudinger, 2008).

Affect complexity, another marker of growth, was found to increase up to age 45 and to decrease thereafter (Labouvie-Vief et al., 2007). With regard to Loevinger's stages of ego development, it was found that progress decelerated once individuals became self-aware (Westenberg & Gjerde, 1999), which suggests that stabilization depends on the level, rather than a particular age. This finding also suggests that the stages following self-awareness, which increasingly shift away from adjustment toward growth, are harder to achieve.

In sum, in contrast to the increase of adjustment across adulthood, growth indicators remain stable or even decrease in later life, such as for Openness, emotional complexity, personal wisdom, high ego levels, Personal Growth, and Purpose in Life. Hence, adjustment and growth indicators follow different lifespan trajectories: growth is less likely to come automatically with age than adjustment. This differential pattern of age trajectories supports the notion that adjustment and growth are two clearly distinguishable types of positive personality.

# Antecedents and mechanisms of change in personality adjustment and growth

Several theoretical perspectives have addressed causes and processes of normative personality change (for an overview of trait theories, see, e.g., Specht et al., 2014). Although most theories agree that there are both biological and contextual factors at play, they place differential emphasis on the two factors. The most prominent theory that argues that personality development is mainly driven by genetic factors is the five-factor theory (McCrae & Costa, 2008). Genetic studies have, however, consistently shown that heritability explains only about half of the variance in personality traits in adulthood (Bouchard & Loehlin, 2001). There is evidence for a large overlap in the genetic effects operating on personality expression at different ages (i.e., stability), but at each point in time they account for not more than half of the variance (Pedersen & Reynolds, 1998).

Environmental influences and the interaction between genetic predispositions and contextual influences ought to be better understood. Furthermore, from a lifespan perspective, it is indispensable to not only account for genetic and contextual characteristics but also for the developing person him or herself (Staudinger, 2005). In the following, we thus review evidence concerning the role of different levels of social contexts in adult personality development (Hogan & Roberts, 2004; Reitz, Zimmermann, Huttemann, Specht, & Neyer, 2014a) and show evidence that elucidates the role of individuals as active agents in co-constructing their personality development (Brandtstädter, Wentura, & Rothermund, 1999; Freund, 2008; Heckhausen, Wrosch, & Schulz, 2010).

## Adjustment

**Contextual factors**. Socialization processes in terms of continuously adapting to socially approved behavior by means of model learning, instrumental conditioning, or the internalization of behavioral norms have been suggested as drivers of mean-level increases of adjustment across adulthood (Digman, 1997). The social investment principle (Roberts et al., 2005) also proposes that increased investment in normative roles of adult life (e.g., career, committed relationship, parenthood) predict the above-mentioned mean-level increases. Empirical evidence generally supports these notions. For instance, starting the first romantic relationship led to increases in emotional stability (Neyer & Lehnart, 2007), entering the first job led to increases (Denissen, Asendorpf, & van Aken, 2008) and retirement to decreases in Conscientiousness (Specht, Egloff & Schmukle; 2011), and an earlier onset of adult-role responsibilities was related to an earlier onset of mean-level increases in Conscientiousness, Agreeableness, and Emotional Stability (Bleidorn et al., 2013).

Beyond basic principles of model learning or instrumental conditioning, the processes that promote the mastery of age-salient tasks and thus, promote normative personality change, are not yet well understood. Adopting group norms has been suggested as an important mechanism that may shape personality in a norm-consistent way (Reitz et al., 2014a): they guide thoughts, feelings, and behaviors (see also Deaux, 1996; Harris, 1995) that lead to typical perceptual and reactive patterns across time (i.e., normative personality change; Roberts & Jackson, 2008). Peer group effects may be a particularly important driver of such effects, as they are omnipresent, serve important functions across the entire lifespan, and communicate social norms (see Reitz et al., 2014a). It was consistently found that the developmental task of adolescence to build positive relationships with peers had a particularly strong effect on personality development in groups that shared similar peer norms (Reitz, Motti-Stefanidi, & Asendorpf, 2014b, 2016). Such relationship effects on personality development are more likely in normative and highly scripted as compared to non-normative life transitions (Neyer, Mund, Zimmermann, & Wrzus, 2014), and as such, play a key role in increasing adjustment.

Transitions into social roles of adult life are most salient in young adulthood, which is why this developmental mechanism underlying increasing adjustment is assumed to mainly apply to young adults (Bleidorn et al., 2013; Roberts et al., 2005). Most evidence for role investments comes from research on young adulthood and the magnitude of the correlated change in Neuroticism, Conscientiousness, and Agreeableness is greatest in young adulthood (Klimstra, Bleidorn, Asendorpf, van Aken, & Denissen, 2013). There are some social role changes that may drive personality adjustment beyond young adulthood (e.g., maintaining a romantic relationship, retirement; see Huttemann et al., 2014). These transitions, however, do not fully explain the increase in adjustment up until the beginning of later old age. It may be that they are less scripted than in young adulthood or that behavioral patterns have been strongly habituated by this age.

**Personal factors**. Other mechanisms that may explain the continuous increase in adjustment across the adult lifespan relate to continuously improving regulatory abilities. This has been put forward by lifespan theories that view, more than SIT does, the individual as active developmental agent. With age, people become better at actively maintaining and regaining levels of subjective well-being in the face of challenges (Brandtstädter & Greve, 1994; Heckhausen et al., 2010; Kunzmann et al., 2000; Staudinger, Marsiske, & Baltes, 1995).

For instance, it has been suggested that the coordinated use of strategies, such as selection of goals (selection), investment in the pursuit of selected goals (optimization), and compensatory efforts to maintain a goal state in the face of losses (compensation), can help maintain functioning in the face of age-related losses of resources (SOC; Baltes & Baltes, 1990). In line with this theory, research has shown that employing more SOC-related behaviors predicted higher levels of well-being and adjustment in adulthood (Freund, 2008; Wiese, Freund, & Baltes, 2002).

Concerning age differences, it has been found that there are age-related increases of optimization and compensation from young to middle adulthood (Freund & Baltes, 2002). Adults were found to become increasingly better at adjusting to losses by using strategies such as disengaging from blocked goals (Wrosch, Scheier, Carver, & Schulz, 2003), rescaling personal expectations to the given (Rothermund & Brandtstädter, 2003), letting go of self-images that do not fit the actual self anymore (Freund & Smith, 1999; Greve & Wentura, 2003), and adopting more adaptive (e.g., intellectualization) and less maladaptive (e.g., doubt) coping and defense strategies (Diehl et al., 2014). Similar results were reported for emotion regulation, as the experience of negative emotions was found to decrease after young adulthood (Carstensen, Pasupathi, Mayr, & Nesselroade, 2000). This is in line with socioemotional selectivity theory suggesting that the more the future is perceived as limited, the more emotion-regulatory goals are prioritized, which in turn is linked with increased social satisfaction (Lang & Carstensen, 2002).

This adaptation process however seems to reach its limit in very old age, when adjustment, as described earlier, levels off or even decreases. A recent longitudinal study found that the positive trajectory of coping and defense mechanisms from young to early old adulthood is reversed for late old age (Diehl et al., 2014). In line with lifespan psychology (Baltes & Smith, 2003; Freund & Baltes, 2002), these findings suggest that toward the end of life the severity of losses in social and cognitive resources eventually hamper personality adjustment. A main risk factor of personality adjustment in very old age is declining health. A prospective study has found that the onset of chronic disease predicted decreases in Emotional Stability and Conscientiousness (Jokela, Hakulinen, Singh-Manoux, & Kivimäki, 2014). Hence, across adulthood, people tend to adopt more adaptive coping and self-regulatory strategies that promote positive changes in personality adjustment, which however reaches its limit in very old age.

Concerning the biological foundations of personality adjustment, the Stability factor (i.e., Agreeableness, Conscientiousness, Emotional Stability) has been linked to the serotonergic neurobiological system (DeYoung et al., 2002), which is involved in behavioral inhibition (Crockett, Clark, & Robbins, 2009). A recent study has consistently demonstrated a link between the serotonergic system and age-related patterns for correlated change in Agreeableness, Conscientiousness, and Emotional Stability (Klimstra et al., 2013). Hence, changes in the serotonergic system may be another source of the age-related change in adjustment.

## Growth

**Contextual factors**. What contributes to the age-related decline in maturation toward growth? In contemporary society, the likelihood to be exposed to or to have the motivation to expose oneself to new contexts declines with age, which may contribute to the declining trajectory of growth across adulthood. Less exposure to new contexts implies a lower likelihood to be faced with new challenges, new people, and experiences that contradict expectations and opportunities to transcend them (Cohn, 1998; Staudinger & Kunzmann, 2005).

Opportunities in people's environment to stay active and gain new experiences should thus help maintain growth. Findings from intervention studies have supported this idea. For instance, an intervention that asked participants to think about and discuss life problems with a confidant facilitated general wisdom-related knowledge and judgment in solving life dilemmas, particularly for middle to old adults (Staudinger & Baltes, 1996). Another study found that a life-review intervention that involved reminiscence alongside an analysis of personal life problems facilitated personal wisdom in both younger and older adults (Staudinger & Reitz, 2016). Positive intervention effects were also reported for Openness in older adults (Jackson, Hill, Payne, Roberts, & Stine-Morrow, 2012; Mühlig-Versen, Bowen, & Staudinger, 2012). Openness increased in older volunteers who had received a training to prepare them for the new volunteering tasks as compared to volunteers on the waiting list for this training (Mühlig-Versen et al., 2012). These findings suggest that growth can be promoted by providing challenging contextual experiences and by empowering older adults to be successful in new contexts. It can, however, not be denied that the age-related decline in Openness can have functional value with regard to increases in adjustment. It is functional because it saves resources, which are shrinking with age.

The finding that the majority of people in our societies decrease in growth (i.e., Openness, Purpose in Life, Personal Growth, Ego Level) despite this potential for plasticity reflects a lack of contextual resources that support the potential for continued growth (Settersten, 2009; Staudinger & Kessler, 2009). From middle to later adulthood, rights and responsibilities to engage are getting increasingly limited in most societies, which is particularly problematic as the need for cultural resources increases when biological potential wanes with age (Baltes et al., 2006). This constrains options for different life avenues and the individuals' opportunities to achieve personality growth. A recent study provided further support for this idea. Using a population-based cross-country design, the study found that societal opportunity structures to participate in work, volunteering, and education attenuated negative age differences·in Openness after midlife (Reitz, Shrout, Weiss, & Staudinger, 2016). The decline of Openness seemed to be less extreme in societies that provided older adults with opportunities to stay engaged rather than with constraints that force them to give up participation and social roles.

In addition to structural influences, the findings of this study also suggest that negative social expectations and stereotypes toward older adults can accelerate the decline of Openness in adulthood by turning into self-fulfilling prophecies (Reitz et al., 2016). Negative perceptions of old age are prevalent in most societies (see North & Fiske, 2015). For instance, there is a cross-cultural consensus in the perception of older adults as decreasing in their ability to perform everyday tasks and to learn (Löckenhoff et al., 2009) and as increasing in incompetence, inactivity, and rigidity (Cuddy et al., 2009). The internalization of these negative perceptions of old age may be one driver of the normative decrease of growth across adulthood.

**Personal factors**. As growth involves the striving toward insight and wisdom, a certain level of cognitive abilities is a necessary yet not sufficient precondition of growth. The cognitive decline observed across late adulthood that accelerates after around the age of 60 (Salthouse, 2009) is one potential driver of the declining trajectories of growth indicators. In line with this idea, previous research has shown that cognitive performance is not only a correlate (Sharp, Reynolds, Pedersen, & Gatz, 2010) but also a predictor of Openness (Wagner, Ram, Smith, & Gerstorf, 2015). It was also found that controlling for fluid intelligence and Openness attenuated negative age differences in personal wisdom (Mickler & Staudinger, 2008). Furthermore, an inductive reasoning intervention designed to improve cognitive functioning in old age resulted in concomitant changes in Openness (Jackson et al., 2012).

Previous research has related the cognitive decline across old adulthood with the decline of dopaminergic modulation, a transmitter that is involved in motivational processes, exploratory behavior, and cognitive flexibility (Braver & Barch, 2002; Li, Lindenberger, & Sikström, 2001). There is also evidence for a link between the Plasticity factor of the Big Two (e.g., Openness) and the dopaminergic system (DeYoung et al., 2002; Klimstra et al., 2013), suggesting that changes in the dopaminergic system may contribute to the age-related decrease of growth. These findings illustrate the biological basis of personality growth (cf. Staudinger & Pasupathi, 2000). Together, the finding that adjustment indicators seem to be linked to the serotonergic system, whereas growth indicators seem to be linked to the dopaminergic system underlines the distinctiveness of the two types of positive personality change (see Table 14.1).

It needs to be noted, however, that cognitive and biological resources are not a sufficient condition for growth to occur; a motivation to grow toward a specific goal is decisive. It has been found that an intellectual and reflective growth motivation predicts ego development and psychosocial maturity (Bauer & McAdams, 2010; Bauer, Park, Montoya, & Wayment, 2015). Similarly, endorsement of universal rather than hedonic values was found to be associated with personal wisdom (Kunzmann & Baltes, 2005; Mickler & Staudinger, 2008). The age-related changes in goals that are helpful for achieving adjustment are not necessarily helpful for achieving growth. The normative increase in goal selection across adulthood supports personality adjustment, but it constrains the possible range of new and challenging experiences, which is necessary for continued growth. Similarly, striving to optimize positive emotions conflicts with questioning oneself and exposing oneself to flaws and failures which may, however, help to derive new insights about oneself (Staudinger & Glück, 2011).

Young adults experience a high need to explore the different pathways of life and strive for new information, whereas middle and particularly older adults tend to pursue their established pathways and improve regulation (Carstensen, Isaacowitz, & Charles, 1999; Freund & Baltes, 2002). Resources are less invested in growth and more in maintenance and later also repair across adulthood (Staudinger et al., 1995). Research has consistently demonstrated that older adults show decreases in total network size, in preference for knowledgeable partners, and in seeking out new interaction partners (Lang & Carstensen, 2002; Wrzus, Hänel, Wagner, & Neyer, 2013). These normative changes in goals limit possibilities of exploration and growth in later adulthood.

In sum, a number of contextual and personal factors influence the different trajectories of personality adjustment and growth during adulthood. A mayor influence on the normative increase of adjustment, particularly in young adulthood, is the transitioning into adult roles. The continuous increase of adjustment beyond young adulthood is linked with improving regulatory abilities that support the adjustment to losses, which is however limited in the face of increased losses toward the end of life. The decline of growth across adulthood is associated with sociocultural factors that limit opportunities to stay engaged and to make new experiences. Personal influences on the growth trajectories involve declining cognitive, health-related, and dopaminergic functioning, and decreasing goals for exploration.

# Conclusion and outlook

Research describing personality trajectories across the lifespan is constantly growing due to increasing availability of longitudinal data sets and methodological developments. We have reviewed the literature along the lines of the framework of positive personality development, delineated the lifespan trajectories for adjustment and growth, and discussed some of the main predictors and change mechanisms. The next important step for current research is to better understand what drives these two types of positive personality development and their interplay. We have reviewed current evidence that delineates a number of factors that contribute to the normative lifespan changes. We propose that a stronger integration of personality and lifespan approaches would help to identify the contextual and personal factors and how they operate to propel the development of adjustment and growth throughout adulthood. This is particularly important for old age, as a combination of contextual and personal resources is needed to accommodate the increasing need for resources to maintain high levels of functioning.

Two factors are particularly promising and deserve more attention in future research: sociocultural and self-regulatory influences on personality development. First, there is a need to account not only for the immediate environment but also for sociocultural influences, as societies differ in the resources (and limitations) for positive personality development. Initial evidence shows that sociocultural factors influence both adjustment (Bleidorn et al., 2013) and growth (Reitz et al., 2016). Studies on societal influences are especially needed for growth, as research is scarce and growth implies benefits not only for individuals (e.g., mental health: Webster, Westerhof, & Bohlmeijer, 2012; mortality: Turiano, Spiro, & Mroczek, 2012) but also for societies. As we have reviewed, research has shown that growth can be promoted, which opens up the possibility for interventions. Interventions could for instance be implemented in work settings (e.g., to increase Openness as a resource for creativity), in educational settings (e.g., to promote ego development and divergent thinking), or in programs to promote successful aging (e.g., to increase wisdom and openness to cope with age-related losses such as retirement).

Another promising avenue for future research is the role of self-regulation. Research needs to consider individuals as active agents in their development. This will not only help to understand age trajectories of adjustment (Freund, 2008) and growth (Staudinger & Glück, 2011), but also individual differences in change. Research on individual differences in growth is particularly important, as it is not well understood why most people decrease in growth, whereas some remain stable or even increase (see Hill et al., 2015; Noftle & Fleeson, 2010). Initial evidence has demonstrated a link between individual differences in goals and individual differences in positive personality development. Several studies demonstrated that growth-related goals (e.g., exploration goals) predicted personality growth (e.g., socio-cognitive maturity); whereas adjustment-related goals (e.g., intrinsic interests such as feeling good) predicted personality adjustment (e.g., environmental mastery; Bauer & McAdams, 2004a, 2004b; Bauer et al., 2015; Helson & Srivastava, 2001, 2002). A recent study has even demonstrated that people are able to change their personality traits through volitional means (Hudson & Fraley, 2015). Future research that accounts for goals thus seems to be a promising approach to better understand personality adjustment and growth across adulthood.

In conclusion, positive personality development is a multidimensional phenomenon. We have presented a framework that distinguishes between two types: adjustment and growth. We demonstrated that this distinction is useful as the two types show different lifespan trajectories, which are driven by different factors. This distinction helps to illuminate the question we posed at the beginning, whether personality matures as we grow older. The answer is *yes* and *no*: as we age, we optimize adjustment but not necessarily growth. We tend to show increasing personality adjustment across most of the adult lifespan, as we become, on average, better able to master developmental and environmental challenges; become more agreeable, reliable, emotionally stable, and satisfied. Only toward the very end of life, when faced with too many challenges and losses of resources, we encounter limits to this mastery. This positive trajectory is however not the case for personality growth. We stagnate or even decrease in growth after midlife, as we do, on average, become less open, wise, and insightful, experience less emotional complexity, and purpose in life. This negative outlook on growth is however not set in stone: individuals *can* experience continued growth across adulthood when contextual and personal resources are available. In sum, evidence shows that adjustment comes with aging but growth does not.

# References

Baltes, P. B., & Baltes, M. M. (1990). Psychological perspectives on successful aging: The model of selective optimization with compensation. In P. B. Baltes, & M. M. Baltes (Eds.), *Successful aging: Perspectives from the behavioral sciences* (pp. 1–34). New York, NY: Cambridge University Press.

Baltes, P. B., & Smith, J. (2003). New frontiers in the future of aging: From successful aging of the young old to the dilemmas of the fourth age. *Gerontology, 49*, 123–135.

Baltes, P. B., Lindenberger, U., & Staudinger, U. M. (2006). Lifespan theory in developmental psychology. *Handbook of Child Psychology, 1*, 569–664.

Baltes, P. B., Smith, J., & Staudinger, U. M. (1992). Wisdom and successful aging. In T. Sonderegger (Ed.), *Nebraska symposium on motivation* (Vol. 39, pp. 123–167). Lincoln, NE: University of Nebraska Press.

Bauer, J., & McAdams, D. P. (2004a). Growth goals, maturity, and well-being. *Developmental Psychology, 40*, 114–127.

Bauer, J. J., & McAdams, D. P. (2004b). Personal growth in adults' stories of life transitions. *Journal of Personality, 72*, 573–602.

Bauer, J. J., & McAdams, D. P. (2010). Eudaimonic growth: Narrative growth goals predict increases in ego development and subjective well-being 3 years later. *Developmental Psychology, 46*(4), 761.

Bauer, J. J., Park, S. W., Montoya, R. M., & Wayment, H. A. (2015). Growth motivation toward two paths of eudaimonic self-development. *Journal of Happiness Studies*, *16*(1), 185–210.

Bleidorn, W., Klimstra, T. A., Denissen, J. J. A., Rentfrow, P. J., Potter, J., & Gosling, S. (2013). Personality maturation around the world—A cross-cultural examination of social investment theory. *Psychological Science*, *24*, 2530–2540.

Bouchard, T. J., & Loehlin, J. C. (2001). Genes, evolution and personality. *Behavior Genetics*, *31*, 243–273.

Brandtstädter, J., & Greve, W. (1994). The aging self: Stabilizing and protective processes. *Developmental Review*, *14*, 52–80.

Brandtstädter, J., Wentura, D., & Rothermund, K. (1999). Intentional self development through adulthood and later life: Tenacious pursuit and flexible adjustment of goals. In J. Brandtstädter, & R. M. Lerner (Eds.), *Action and self development: Theory and research through the life span* (pp. 373–400). Thousand Oaks, CA: Sage.

Braver, T. S., & Barch, D. M. (2002). A theory of cognitive control, aging cognition, and neuromodulation. *Neuroscience and Biobehavioral Reviews*, *26*, 809–817.

Carstensen, L. L., Isaacowitz, D. M., & Charles, S. T. (1999). Taking time seriously: A theory of socioemotional selectivity. *American Psychologist*, *54*, 165–181.

Carstensen, L. L., Pasupathi, M., Mayr, U., & Nesselroade, J. R. (2000). Emotional experience in everyday life across the adult life span. *Journal of Personality and Social Psychology*, *79*(4), 644.

Cohn, L. D. (1998). Age trends in personality development: A quantitative review. In P. M. Westenberg, A. Blasi, & L. D. Cohn (Eds.), *Personality development: Theoretical, empirical, and clinical investigations of Loevinger's conception of ego development* (pp. 133–143). Mahwah, NJ: Erlbaum.

Costa, P. T., Jr., & McCrae, R. R. (1980). Still stable after all these years: Personality as a key to some issues in adulthood and old age. In P. B. Baltes, & J. O. G. Brim (Eds.), *Life-span development and behavior* (Vol. 3, pp. 66–102). New York, NY: Academic Press.

Crockett, M. J., Clark, L., & Robbins, T. W. (2009). Reconciling the role of serotonin in behavioral inhibition and aversion: Acute tryptophan depletion abolishes punishment-induced inhibition in humans. *The Journal of Neuroscience*, *29*(38), 11993–11999.

Cuddy, A. J., Fiske, S. T., Kwan, V. S., Glick, P., Demoulin, S., Leyens, J. P., ... Htun, T. T. (2009). Stereotype content model across cultures: Towards universal similarities and some differences. *British Journal of Social Psychology*, *48*(1), 1–33.

Deaux, K. (1996). Social identification. In E. Higgins, & A. W. Kruglanski (Eds.), *Social psychology: Handbook of basic principles* (pp. 777–798). New York, NY: Guilford Press.

Denissen, J. J. A., Asendorpf, J. B., & van Aken, M. A. G. (2008). Childhood personality predicts long-term trajectories of shyness and aggressiveness in the context of demographic transitions in emerging adulthood. *Journal of Personality*, *76*, 67–99.

DeYoung, C. G. (2006). Higher-order factors of the Big Five in a multi-informant sample. *Journal of Personality and Social Psychology*, *91*(6), 1138–1151.

DeYoung, C. G., Peterson, J. B., & Higgins, D. M. (2002). Higher-order factors of the Big Five predict conformity: Are there neuroses of health? *Personality and Individual Differences*, *33*(4), 533–552.

Diehl, M., Chui, H., Hay, E. L., Lumley, M. A., Grühn, D., & Labouvie-Vief, G. (2014). Change in coping and defense mechanisms across adulthood: Longitudinal findings in a European American sample. *Developmental Psychology*, *50*(2), 634–648.

Diener, E., & Suh, E. (1998). Subjective well-being and age: An international analysis. *Annual Review of Gerontology and Geriatrics, 17*, 304–324.

Digman, J. M. (1997). Higher-order factors of the Big Five. *Journal of Personality and Social Psychology, 73*(6), 1246–1256.

Freund, A. M. (2008). Successful aging as management of resources: The role of selection, optimization, and compensation. *Research in Human Development, 5*(2), 94–106.

Freund, A. M., & Baltes, P. B. (2002). Life-management strategies of selection, optimization, and compensation: Measurement by self-report and construct validity. *Journal of Personality and Social Psychology, 82*, 642–662.

Freund, A. M., & Smith, J. (1999). Content and function of the self-definition in old and very old age. *Journals of Gerontology, 54B*, P55–P67.

Friedman, H. S., Kern, M. L., & Reynolds, C. A. (2010). Personality and health, subjective well-being, and longevity. *Journal of Personality, 78*(1), 179–216.

George, L. G., Helson, R., & John, O. P. (2011). The "CEO" of women's work lives: How Big Five Conscientiousness, Extraversion, and Openness predict 50 years of work experiences in a changing sociocultural context. *Journal of Personality and Social Psychology, 101*(4), 812.

Greve, W., & Wentura, D. (2003). Immunizing the self: Self-concept stabilization through reality-adaptive self-definitions. *Personality and Social Psychology Bulletin, 29*(1), 39–50.

Harris, J. (1995). Where is the child's environment? A group socialization theory of development. *Psychological Review, 102*, 458–489.

Havighurst, R. J. (1972). *Developmental tasks and education.* New York, NY: McKay Company.

Heckhausen, J., Wrosch, C., & Schulz, R. (2010). A motivational theory of life-span development. *Psychological Review, 117*, 32–60.

Helson, R., & Kwan, V. S. Y. (2000). Personality development in adulthood: The broad picture and processes in one longitudinal sample. In S. Hampson (Ed.), *Advances in personality psychology* (Vol. 1, pp. 77–106). London: Routledge.

Helson, R., & Srivastava, S. (2001). Three paths of adult development: Conservers, seekers, and achievers. *Journal of Personality and Social Psychology, 80*, 995–1010.

Helson, R., & Srivastava, S. (2002). Creative and wise people: Similarities, differences, and how they develop. *Personality and Social Psychology Bulletin, 28*(10), 1430–1440.

Helson, R., & Wink, P. (1987). Two conceptions of maturity examined in the findings of a longitudinal study. *Journal of Personality and Social Psychology, 53*, 531–541.

Hill, P. L., Turiano, N. A., Spiro, A., III, & Mroczek, D. K. (2015). Understanding interindividual variability in purpose: Longitudinal findings from the VA Normative Aging Study. *Psychology and Aging, 30*(3), 529–533.

Hogan, M. J., Staff, R. T., Bunting, B. P., Deary, I. J., & Whalley, L. J. (2012). Openness to experience and activity engagement facilitate the maintenance of verbal ability in older adults. *Psychology and Aging, 27*(4), 849.

Hogan, R., & Roberts, B. W. (2004). A socioanalytic model of maturity. *Journal of Career Assessment, 12*(2), 207–217.

Hudson, N. W., & Fraley, R. C. (2015). Volitional personality trait change: Can people choose to change their personality traits? *Journal of Personality and Social Psychology, 109*(3), 490.

Hutteman, R., Hennecke, M., Orth, U., Reitz, A. K., & Specht, J. (2014). Developmental tasks as a framework to study personality development in adulthood and old age. *European Journal of Personality, 28*, 268–279.

Jackson, J. J., Hill, P. L., Payne, B. R., Roberts, B. W., & Stine-Morrow, E. A. L. (2012). Can an old dog learn (and want to experience) new tricks? Cognitive training increases openness to experience in older adults. *Psychology and Aging, 27*(2), 286−292.

John, O. P., & Srivastava, S. (1999). The Big Five Trait taxonomy: History, measurement, and theoretical perspectives. In L. A. Pervin, & O. P. John (Eds.), *Handbook of personality: Theory and research* (2nd ed., pp. 102−139). New York, NY: Guilford.

Jonassaint, C. R., Boyle, S. H., Williams, R. B., Mark, D. B., Siegler, I. C., & Barefoot, J. C. (2007). Facets of openness predict mortality in patients with cardiac disease. *Psychosomatic Medicine, 69*, 319−322.

Jokela, M., Hakulinen, C., Singh-Manoux, A., & Kivimaki, M. (2014). Personality change associated with chronic diseases: Pooled analysis of four prospective cohort studies. *Psychological Medicine, 44*(12), 2629−2640.

Josefsson, K., Jokela, M., Cloninger, C. R., Hintsanen, M., Salo, J., Hintsa, T., ... Keltikangas-Järvinen, L. (2013). Maturity and change in personality: Developmental trends of temperament and character in adulthood. *Development and Psychopathology, 25*(3), 713−727.

Kandler, C., Kornadt, A. E., Hagemeyer, B., & Neyer, F. J. (2015). Patterns and sources of personality development in old age. *Journal of Personality and Social Psychology, 109* (1), 1−56.

Klimstra, T. A., Bleidorn, W., Asendorpf, J. B., van Aken, M. A. G., & Denissen, J. J. A. (2013). Correlated change of Big Five personality traits across the lifespan: A search for determinants. *Journal of Research in Personality, 47*(6), 768−777.

Klimstra, T. A., Hale, W. W., Raaijmakers, Q. A. W., Branje, S. J. T., & Meeus, W. H. (2009). Maturation of personality in adolescence. *Journal of Personality and Social Psychology, 96*(4), 898−912.

Kunzmann, U., & Baltes, P. B. (2005). The psychology of wisdom: Theoretical and empirical challenges. In R. J. Sternberg, & J. Jordan (Eds.), *Handbook of wisdom: Psychological perspective* (pp. 110−135). New York, NY: Cambridge University Press.

Kunzmann, U., Little, T. D., & Smith, J. (2000). Is age-related stability of subjective well-being a paradox? Cross-sectional and longitudinal evidence from the Berlin Aging Study. *Psychology and Aging, 15*, 511−526.

Labouvie-Vief, G. (1982). Dynamic development and mature autonomy: A theoretical prologue. *Human Development, 25*, 161−191.

Labouvie-Vief, G. (2003). Dynamic integration: Affect, cognition, and the self in adulthood. *Current Directions in Psychological Science, 12*, 201−206.

Labouvie-Vief, G., Diehl, M., Jain, E., & Zhang, F. (2007). Six-year change in affect optimization and affect complexity across the adult life span: A further examination. *Psychology and Aging, 22*(4), 738.

Lang, F. R., & Carstensen, L. L. (2002). Time counts: Future time perspective, goals, and social relationships. *Psychology & Aging, 17*, 125−139.

Law, A., & Staudinger, U. M. (2016). Eudaimonia and wisdom. In J. Vittersø (Ed.), *Handbook of eudaimonic well-being, 2016*, New York, NY: Springer, 135−146.

Li, S. C., Lindenberger, U., & Sikström, S. (2001). Aging cognition: From neuromodulation to representation. *Trends in Cognitive Sciences, 5*(11), 479−486.

Löckenhoff, C. E., De Fruyt, F., Terracciano, A., McCrae, R. R., De Bolle, M., Costa, P. T., Jr, ... Allik, J. (2009). Perceptions of aging across 26 cultures and their culture-level associates. *Psychology and Aging, 24*(4), 941.

Loevinger, J. (1976). *Ego development: Conception and theory*. San Francisco, CA: Jossey Bass.

Lucas, R. E., & Donnellan, M. B. (2011). Personality development across the life span: Longitudinal analyses with a national sample from Germany. *Journal of Personality and Social Psychology*, *101*(4), 847.

Maslow, A. H. (1968). *Toward a psychology of being*. New York, NY: Van Nostrand Reinhold Company.

Masten, A. S., Roisman, G. I., Long, J. D., Burt, K. B., Obradović, J., Riley, J. R., ... Tellegen, A. (2005). Developmental cascades: Linking academic achievement and externalizing and internalizing symptoms over 20 years. *Developmental Psychology*, *41*(5), 733.

McAdams, D. P., Anyidoho, N. A., Brown, C., Huang, Y. T., Kaplan, B., & Machado, M. A. (2004). Traits and stories: Links between dispositional and narrative features of personality. *Journal of Personality*, *72*(4), 761−784.

McCrae, R. R., & Costa, P. T., Jr. (2008). The Five-Factor Theory of personality. In O. P. John, R. W. Robins, & L. A. Pervin (Eds.), *Handbook of personality: Theory and research* (3rd ed., pp. 159−181). New York, NY: Guilford Press.

Mickler, C., & Staudinger, U. M. (2008). Personal wisdom: Validation and age-related differences of a performance measure. *Psychology and Aging*, *23*(4), 787−799.

Mõttus, R., Johnson, W., & Deary, I. J. (2012). Personality traits in old age: Measurement and rank-order stability and some mean-level change. *Psychology and Aging*, *27*(1), 243−249.

Mroczek, D. K., & Spiro, R. A., III (2003). Modeling intraindividual change in personality traits: Findings from the Normative Aging Study. *Journals of Gerontology*, *58B*, P153−P165.

Mühlig-Versen, A., Bowen, C. E., & Staudinger, U. M. (2012). Personality plasticity in later adulthood: Contextual and personal resources are needed to increase openness to new experiences. *Psychology and Aging*, *27*(4), 855−866.

Neyer, F. J., & Lehnart, J. (2007). Relationships matter in personality development. Evidence from an 8-year longitudinal study across young adulthood. *Journal of Personality*, *75*, 535−568.

Neyer, F. J., Mund, M., Zimmermann, J., & Wrzus, C. (2014). Personality-relationship transactions revisited. *Journal of Personality*, *82*(6), 539−550.

Noftle, E. E., & Fleeson, W. (2010). Age differences in Big Five behavior averages and variabilities across the adult life span: Moving beyond retrospective, global summary accounts of personality. *Psychology and Aging*, *25*(1), 95.

North, M. S., & Fiske, S. T. (2015). Modern attitudes toward older adults in the aging world: A cross-cultural meta-analysis. *Psychological Bulletin*, *141*(5), 993−1021.

Pals, J. L. (2006). Narrative identity processing of difficult life experiences: Pathways of personality development and positive self-transformation in adulthood. *Journal of Personality*, *74*(4), 1079−1110.

Pedersen, N. L., & Reynolds, C. A. (1998). Stability and change in adult personality: Genetic and environmental components. *European Journal of Personality*, *12*, 365−386.

Pinquart, M. (2002). Creating and maintaining purpose in life in old age: A meta-analysis. *Ageing International*, *27*, 90−114.

Reitz, A. K., Motti-Stefanidi, F., & Asendorpf, J. B. (2014b). Mastering developmental transitions in immigrant adolescents: The longitudinal interplay of family functioning, developmental and acculturative tasks. *Developmental Psychology*, *50*, 754−765.

Reitz, A. K., Zimmermann, J., Hutteman, R., Specht, J., & Neyer, F. J. (2014a). How peers make a difference: The role of peer groups and peer relationships in personality development. *European Journal of Personality*, *28*, 280−289.

Reitz, A. K., Motti-Stefanidi, F., & Asendorpf, J. B. (2016). Me, us, and them: Testing socio-meter theory in a socially diverse real-life context. *Journal of Personality and Social Psychology, 110*(6), 908–920.

Reitz, A. K., Shrout, P., Weiss, D., & Staudinger, U. M. (2016). Is openness decline after midlife inevitable? A cross-national study and its replication. *Journal of Personality and Social Psychology. Manuscript under review.*

Roberts, B. W., & Jackson, J. J. (2008). Sociogenomic personality psychology. *Journal of Personality, 76,* 1523–1544.

Roberts, B. W., Walton, K. E., & Viechtbauer, W. (2006). Patterns of mean-level change in personality traits across the life course: A meta-analysis of longitudinal studies. *Psychological Bulletin, 132,* 1–25.

Roberts, B. W., & Wood, D. (2006). Personality development in the context of the neo-socioanalytic model of personality. In D. K. Mroczek, T. D. Little, D. K. Mroczek, & T. D. Little (Eds.), *Handbook of personality development* (pp. 11–39). Mahwah, NJ: Lawrence Erlbaum Associates Publishers.

Roberts, B. W., Wood, D., & Smith, J. L. (2005). Evaluating Five Factor theory and social investment perspectives on personality trait development. *Journal of Research in Personality, 39*(1), 166–184.

Rothermund, K., & Brandtstädter, J. (2003). Depression in later life: Cross-sequential patterns and possible determinants. *Psychology and Aging, 18*(1), 80.

Ryan, M. R., & Deci, E. L. (2001). On happiness and human potential: A review of research on hedonic and eudaimonic well-being. *Annual Review of Psychology, 52,* 141–166.

Ryff, C. D. (1989). Happiness is everything, or is it? Explorations on the meaning of psychological well-being. *Journal of Personality and Social Psychology, 57*(6), 1069.

Ryff, C. D. (2013). Eudaimonic well-being and health: Mapping consequences of self-realization. In A. S. Waterman (Ed.), *The best within us: Positive psychology perspectives on eudaimonia* (pp. 77–98). Washington, DC: American Psychological Association.

Ryff, C. D., & Keyes, C. L. M. (1995). The structure of psychological well-being revisited. *Journal of Personality and Social Psychology, 69,* 719–727.

Ryff, C. D., & Singer, B. (1998). The contours of positive human health. *Psychological Inquiry, 9,* 1–28.

Salthouse, T. A. (2009). When does age-related cognitive decline begin? *Neurobiology of Aging, 30*(4), 507–514.

Settersten, R. A. (2009). It takes two to tango: The (un)easy dance between life-course sociology and life-span psychology. *Advances in Life Course Research, 14*(1), 74–81.

Sharp, E. S., Reynolds, C. A., Pedersen, N. L., & Gatz, M. (2010). Cognitive engagement and cognitive aging: Is openness protective? *Psychology and Aging, 25*(1), 60.

Specht, J., Bleidorn, W., Denissen, J. J. A., Hennecke, M., Hutteman, R., Kandler, C., ... Zimmermann, J. (2014). What drives adult personality development? A comparison of theories and empirical evidence. *European Journal of Personality, 28*(3), 216–230.

Specht, J., Egloff, B., & Schmukle, S. C. (2011). Stability and change of personality across the life course: The impact of age and major life events on mean-level and rank-order stability of the Big Five. *Journal of Personality and Social Psychology, 101,* 862–882.

Staudinger, U. M. (2005). Personality and aging. In M. Johnson, V. L. Bengtson, P. G. Coleman, & T. Kirkwood (Eds.), *Handbook of age and ageing* (pp. 237–244). Cambridge: Cambridge University Press.

Staudinger, U. M., & Baltes, P. B. (1996). Interactive minds: A facilitative setting for wisdom-related performance? *Journal of Personality and Social Psychology, 71*(4), 746.

Staudinger, U. M., & Glück, J. (2011). Psychological wisdom research: Commonalities and differences in a growing field. *Annual Review of Psychology, 62*, 215−241.

Staudinger, U. M., & Kessler, E.-M. (2009). Adjustment and growth—Two trajectories of positive personality development across adulthood. In M. C. Smith, & N. DeFrates-Densch (Eds.), *Handbook of research on adult learning and development* (pp. 241−268). New York, NY: Routledge.

Staudinger, U. M., & Kunzmann, U. (2005). Positive adult personality development: Adjustment and/or growth? *European Psychologist, 10*(4), 320−329.

Staudinger, U. M., Lopez, D. F., & Baltes, P. B. (1997). The psychometric location of wisdom-related performance. *Personality and Social Psychology Bulletin, 23*, 1200−1214.

Staudinger, U. M., Marsiske, M., & Baltes, P. B. (1995). Resilience and reserve capacity in later adulthood: Potentials and limits of development across the life span. In D. Cicchetti, & D. Cohen (Eds.), *Developmental Psychopathology, Risk, disorder, and adaptation* (Vol. 2, pp. 801−847). New York, NY: Wiley.

Staudinger, U. M., & Pasupathi, M. (2000). Lifespan perspectives on self, personality, and social cognition. In T. Salthouse, & F. Craik (Eds.), *Handbook of cognition and aging* (pp. 633−688). Mahwah, NJ: Erlbaum.

Staudinger, U. M. & Reitz, A. K. (2016). Improving personal wisdom: Is life review a key? *Journal of Personality and Social Psychology.* Manuscript in preparation.

Stephan, Y. (2009). Openness to experience and active older adults' life satisfaction: A trait and facet-level analysis. *Personality and Individual Differences, 47*(6), 637−641.

Turiano, N. A., Pitzer, L., Armour, C., Karlamangla, A., Ryff, C. D., & Mroczek, D. K. (2011). Personality trait level and change as predictors of health outcomes: Findings from a national study of Americans (MIDUS). *The Journals of Gerontology Series B: Psychological Sciences and Social Sciences, 67B*(1), 4−12.

Turiano, N. A., Spiro, A., & Mroczek, D. K. (2012). Openness to experience and mortality in men: Analysis of trait and facets. *Journal of Aging and Health, 24*(4), 654−672.

Van Solinge, H., & Henkens, K. (2008). Adjustment to and satisfaction with retirement: Two of a kind? *Psychology and Aging, 23*(2), 422.

Vincent, N., Ward, L., & Denson, L. (2013). Personality preferences and their relationship to ego development in Australian Leadership Program participants. *Journal of Adult Development, 20*(4), 197−211.

Wagner, J., Ram, N., Smith, J., & Gerstorf, D. (2015). Personality trait development at the end of life: Antecedents and correlates of mean-level trajectories. *Journal of Personality and Social Psychology*, Online first publication.

Westenberg, P. M., & Gjerde, P. F. (1999). Ego development during the transition from adolescence to young adulthood: A 9-year longitudinal study. *Journal of Research in Personality, 33*, 233−252.

Webster, J. D., Westerhof, G. J., & Bohlmeijer, E. T. (2012). Wisdom and mental health across the lifespan. *The Journals of Gerontology Series B: Psychological Sciences and Social Sciences, 69*(2), 209−218. http://dx.doi.org/10.1093/geronb/gbs121.

Wiese, B. S., Freund, A. M., & Baltes, P. B. (2002). Subjective career success and emotional well-being: Longitudinal predictive power of selection, optimization, and compensation. *Journal of Vocational Behavior, 60*(3), 321−335.

Williams, P. G., Rau, H. K., Cribbet, M. R., & Gunn, H. E. (2009). Openness to experience and stress regulation. *Journal of Research in Personality, 43*(5), 777−784.

Wink, P., & Staudinger, U. M. (2015). Wisdom and psychosocial functioning in later life. *Journal of Personality*, Online first publication.

Wortmann, J., Lucas, R. E., & Donnellan, M. B. (2012). Stability and change in the Big Five personality domains: Evidence from a longitudinal study of Australians. *Psychology and Aging*, *27*, 867–874.

Wrosch, C., Scheier, M. F., Carver, C. S., & Schulz, R. (2003). The importance of goal disengagement in adaptive self-regulation: When giving up is beneficial. *Self and Identity*, *2*(1), 1–20.

Wrzus, C., Hänel, M., Wagner, J., & Neyer, F. J. (2013). Social network changes and life events across the life span: A meta-analysis. *Psychological Bulletin*, *139*, 53–80.

# The development of perceived control

**15**

*Frank J. Infurna[1] and Charles J. Infurna[2,3]*
[1]Arizona State University, Tempe, AZ, United States, [2]Children's Institute, Rochester, NY, United States, [3]St. John Fisher College, Rochester, NY, United States

Perceived control is broadly defined as individuals' beliefs in their ability to exert influence over their life circumstances (Pearlin & Schooler, 1978; Skinner, 1996). Perceived control is a widely studied construct that has transcended disciplines and has a long history, dating back to the 1960s, with Rotter's influential paper on locus of control (Reich & Infurna, 2016; Rotter, 1966). The influence and interest of perceived control spans disciplines (i.e., psychology, sociology, economics, etc.) and across the lifespan, with studies examining antecedents and outcomes of perceived control in children and adolescence and young adulthood to midlife and old age. Most research centered on perceived control has been on its effects on various outcomes across the lifespan, including academic achievement, employment, well-being, cognition, and health. Despite the accumulation of research showing perceived control being instrumental in influencing developmental outcomes across the lifespan, much less research has focused on how this important construct develops and changes across the lifespan. The following chapter is devoted to exploring further the origins of perceived control across the lifespan with an emphasis on how antecedents of perceived control likely differ depending on one's stage in the lifespan. The specific setup of this chapter is as follows: (1) what is perceived control; (2) why is it important to study perceived control; (3) how does perceived control change across the lifespan; and (4) what leads to the development of perceived control.

## What is perceived control?

Constructs encompassing perceptions of control range from locus of control to constraints, fatalism, mastery, agency, competence, learned helplessness, and self-efficacy. This set of constructs represents an integral general-purpose belief system that has diverse effects across the lifespan. Perceived control in this chapter is considered a catch-all term that encompasses many different constructs relating to control, such as locus of control (Rotter, 1966), self-efficacy (Bandura, 1997), learned helplessness (Seligman, 1975), constraints (Lachman & Weaver, 1998), and

Personality Development Across the Lifespan. DOI: http://dx.doi.org/10.1016/B978-0-12-804674-6.00015-6

mastery (Pearlin & Schooler, 1978). At the very heart of the various definitions and constructs of perceived control are *competence* and *contingency*. Competence is defined as one's ability or capacity to interact effectively with its environment and effectiveness in carrying out goals (White, 1959). Contingency refers to the belief that performing a particular behavior will then lead to the desired outcome or belief that there are obstacles or factors beyond one's control that interfere with reaching goals (Skinner, 1996). Generally speaking, the collective measures of perceived control can be broadly defined as (1) the belief that one's own actions, efforts, and choices can exert influence over and shape life circumstances and (2) one's ability to attain desired outcomes (Infurna & Mayer, 2015; Krause, 2003; Levenson, 1981; Pearlin & Schooler, 1978; Skinner, 1996).

More broadly, we believe that perceived control can be construed as one's *orientation* toward life circumstances. That is, perceived control refers to how individuals orient themselves with their life circumstances; do individuals believe they have the means and abilities for attaining desired outcomes or do they view their life as being determined by external factors (fatalistically ruled), to which their actions have no way of attaining desired outcomes? Also, does one's orientation function to assist in adaptation by protection against the adverse effects of stressors through soliciting support from their social network or engaging in the wrong goals, leading to negative outcomes? In sum, perceived control is a general-purpose belief system that consists of a toolbox for success, which has downstream effects on key outcomes across the lifespan.

As this is a chapter on the development of perceived control, we strongly believe that perceived control does not reflect innate attributes that are fixed in personality, but instead are malleable or have the capacity to change. The construct of perceived control should be considered as a flexible set of interrelated beliefs that are organized around interpretations of prior interactions in specific domains or learned appraisals of one's capabilities (Pearlin, 2010; Skinner, 1995).

Fig. 15.1 graphically illustrates data from the Americans' Changing Lives (ACL) study showing the developmental trajectory of perceived control across the adult lifespan (for details on the measure of perceived control in this study, see Infurna & Okun, 2015; Infurna, Ram, & Gerstorf, 2013). The ACL study consists of four assessments, spanning 16 years on individuals ranging in age from 24 to 100. In Fig. 15.1, data are shown for a subset of 250 participants (gray lines) and the solid black line is the model implied trajectory from a multilevel model (see Grimm, Ram, & Estabrook, 2016; Singer & Willett, 2003) examining change in perceived control across chronological age. We observe that, on average, the developmental trajectory of perceived control is one of stability in young adulthood and midlife, but declines in old age. However, the raw data from individuals in the study (gray lines) indicate that there is a great deal of heterogeneity in the extent to which perceived control changes across the adult lifespan. As shown, from the wave-to-wave data, some participants show stability, whereas others show substantial increases or decreases. This chapter focuses on reasons *why* perceived control changes across the adult lifespan, or put differently, what are the possible reasons why some

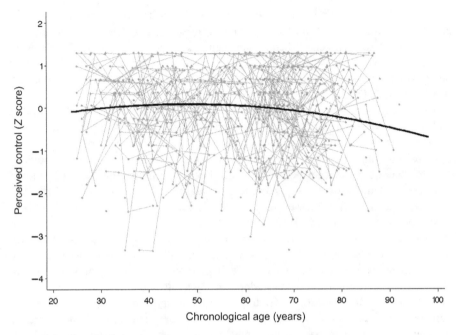

**Figure 15.1** Developmental change in perceived control across the adult lifespan. Perceived control shows a curvilinear trend across the adult lifespan, showing relative stability in young adulthood and midlife and declines in old age. Data are taken from the Americans' Changing Lives Study and a multilevel model with linear and quadratic components were applied to four assessments of perceived control that cover 16 years of time.

individuals show substantial changes in perceived control? The emphasis is on examining developmental change across different time metrics and how antecedents likely differ by one's stage in the lifespan. Before doing so, we next discuss the numerous beneficial effects that have been observed of perceived control across the lifespan.

## Why is it important to study perceived control?

Perceived control has wide-ranging ramifications across the lifespan. Numerous studies have documented how reporting higher levels of perceived control are associated with beneficial outcomes. In childhood and adolescence, early research showed that children who reported higher levels of perceived control were more likely to achieve better academically in the classroom (Skinner, Wellborn, & Connell, 1990). Furthermore, during the transition from elementary school to middle school, more consistent beliefs were associated with better academic and social competence (Molloy, Ram, & Gest, 2011). Perceived control and its related constructs have been shown to be instrumental during the transition from adolescence to adulthood, with those reporting stronger control beliefs in adolescence being more likely to report better well-being and employment opportunities in young adulthood (Evans, 2002; Haase, Heckhausen, & Köller, 2008), as well as being associated with engaging in healthier behaviors and feeling in better health (Gale, Batty, & Deary, 2008).

Depending on one's work situation, perceptions of control can transfer to other colleagues or in the specific instance that we highlight, teachers, this can transfer to the development of students. Characteristics of the teacher, in particular, perceptions of control, are shown to have tremendous effects on children. Previous research has linked teacher perceived control with teaching behaviors, the amount of effort exerted and extent of persistence that are passed onto the students' abilities (Fantuzzo et al., 2012; Klassen & Tze, 2014). For example, teachers with lower perceived control are more likely to criticize students who responded incorrectly to problem questions, whereas higher control teachers instead praised students for trying to solve the problems (Gibson & Dembo, 1984). Thus teachers with more developmentally oriented beliefs provide higher quality learning opportunities in their classrooms through greater student engagement and classroom management (Wang, Hall, & Rahimi, 2015), leading to eliciting more positive development of perceived control and higher achievement from their students. Higher efficacy teachers also tended to persist more with students who were struggling academically and engaged in monitoring and observing student's time spent working on activities in their seats. Thus this shows that in specific contexts, such as work, individuals' levels of perceived control can transfer or have effects on those who they interact most with.

In adulthood and old age, perceived control is shown to be associated with preserved cognitive abilities, maintenance of well-being, and better physical health and longevity. Research in adulthood has utilized longitudinal panel surveys that involve participants from across the adult lifespan to those in old age, as well as patient populations to document the beneficial effects of perceived control. For example, Agrigoroari and Lachman (2011) found that individuals who reported higher levels of perceived control were more likely to exhibit better memory, executive functioning, and processing speed. Multiple studies have found similar protective effects longitudinally with individuals who report higher levels of perceived control exhibiting more positive 4-year changes in memory, processing speed, and verbal intelligence (Infurna & Gerstorf, 2013; Windsor & Anstey, 2008). The link between perceived control and well-being has been extensively studied, dating back to the learned helplessness literature (Peterson & Seligman, 1984). Higher levels of perceived control are linked to lower levels of negative affect, better positive affect, and being more satisfied with one's life (see Infurna & Mayer, 2015; Lang & Heckhausen, 2001; Windsor & Anstey, 2010). The outcome that has been most extensively studied is health. Many studies have documented that individuals who report higher levels of perceived control are protected against declines in physical functioning over time periods ranging from 2.5 to 20 years of time, as well as being associated with longevity (see Caplan & Schooler, 2003;

Gerstorf, Röcke, & Lachman, 2011; Infurna & Okun, 2015; Infurna et al., 2011, 2013; Lachman & Agrigoroaei, 2010; Surtees, Wainwright, Luben, Khaw, & Day, 2006;Surtees et al., 2010).

It is also worth mentioning that perceived control is a protective resource that can be drawn upon in times of distress to protect against declines across a wide range of domains. This has been extensively studied in the caregiving literature, with research documenting that caregivers who report higher levels of perceived control show fewer declines in mental and physical health (Aneshensel et al., 1995; Harmell, Chattillion, Roepke, & Mausbach, 2011; Wrosch, Amir, & Miller, 2011). Furthermore, in the context of chronic conditions, the enactment of control processes is shown to buffer from declines in mental health (Wrosch, Heckahusen, & Lachman, 2000; Wrosch, Schulz & Heckhausen, 2004).

We want to also make note that there are certain instances when lower levels of perceived control are adaptive and result in more positive outcomes (e.g., Kunzmann, Little, & Smith, 2002). For example, in children whose parents are divorcing, reporting lower levels of perceived control are associated with better psychological adjustment and school performance, because of the uncontrollable situation of parental divorce (Skinner, 1995). Specht et al. (2011) found that in the context of spousal loss, surviving spouses who reported lower levels of perceived control reported less steep declines in life satisfaction following spousal loss. Therefore, in certain life circumstances, possibly those where individuals have less control over, higher levels of perceived control are less adaptive.

Based on the aforementioned research, it is evident that perceived control has important implications for pertinent outcomes across the lifespan. What is less known is what contributes to the development of perceived control across the lifespan. We next discuss the development of and antecedents of perceived control, with a focus on how its antecedents likely differ depending on one's stage in the lifespan.

## How does perceived control develop and change across the lifespan?

Developmental change is not a static enterprise but occurs across a dynamical, moving force called time. Change in relation to developmental processes tied to age (e.g., time since birth), pathology (e.g., disability and morbidity), and mortality, as well as non-normative processes (e.g., caregiving) are instrumental in shaping perceived control, its corresponding antecedents and outcomes and their across-domain interplay. We first review research showing the developmental course of perceived control across the lifespan and then focus on pertinent antecedents at each stage of the lifespan.

Aging-, pathology-, and mortality-related, as well as non-normative processes (for discussions, see Baltes & Nesselroade, 1979; Birren & Cunningham, 1985) can operate as contextual systematical influences on developmental change processes involving perceived control. Targeting aging-related processes, initial work examining age differences in perceived control showed that older adults reported lower levels of perceived control when compared to individuals in midlife and young adulthood (Lachman & Firth, 2004; Mirowsky, 1995). Recent longitudinal evidence echoes cross-sectional findings such that changes in perceived control across adulthood and old age is characterized by a curvilinear (quadratic) trend, peaking in late midlife and displaying accelerated declines in older ages (Gerstorf, Ram, Lindenberger, & Smith, 2013; Lachman, Rosnick, & Röcke, 2009; Lewis, Ross, & Mirowski, 1999; Mirowsky & Ross, 2007; Ross & Mirowsky, 2002; Specht, Egloff, & Schmukle, 2013). This quadratic trend is observed in Fig. 15.1, with individuals showing a great deal of between- and within-person variability in how perceived control changes across the adult lifespan.

Development may not be best characterized by chronological age but through developmental changes in relation to processes beyond that of age, such as pathology, mortality, and non-normative events. This could account for sudden changes (declines or increases) in perceived control observed for some participants in Fig. 15.1. Pathology-related processes include assessing within-person changes in functioning in relation to disease or disability and the role of pathology-related burdens such as incidence of chronic illness or disability as between-person difference variables (Infurna et al., 2011; Ram, Gerstorf, Fauth, Zarit, & Malmberg, 2010; Verbrugge & Jette, 1994). Perceived control shows stability across adulthood but declines in older ages (Lachman et al., 2009; Mirowsky & Ross, 2007), whereas in relation to cancer diagnosis (pathology) control may display a differential pattern. For example, Ranchor et al. (2010) examined change in control in relation to cancer diagnosis and found that individuals, on average, experienced significant declines in control immediately following diagnosis followed by stability. Therefore, the onset of disability or health declines may limit individuals' ability to exert influence over their immediate environment, become more dependent on others for help, leading to accelerated declines in perceived control.

Mortality-related processes may rise to the forefront and drive developmental changes occurring in old age (Bäckman & MacDonald, 2006; Gerstorf et al., 2008). There is little research examining how perceived control changes in relation to mortality. One scenario is that the pervasiveness and cascade of mortality-related processes would result in steeper changes in feelings of perceived control (declines) as compared to changes over chronological age. A contrasting scenario is that as individuals are approaching death and perceive time as being restrictive they will turn to (unconsciously or not) domains of functioning that are controllable, preserving one's feelings of control. Recent evidence from the Berlin Aging Study provides support for perceived control showing steeper declines in relation to death, as compared to chronological age (Gerstorf et al., 2013).

Nonnormative processes refer to events whose occurrence, patterning, and sequencing are not applicable to many individuals, nor are they clearly tied to a dimension of developmental time (Baltes, 1987; Bandura, 1982). Examples of such events include incidence of cancer in childhood and caregiving for someone with dementia. Caregiving for someone with dementia is a significant stressful experience that challenges and constrains systemic functioning across a myriad of domains (Aneshensel, Pearlin, Mullan, Zarit, & Whitlatch, 1995; Pearlin, Menaghan, Lieberman, & Mullan, 1981). Research on perceived control in the context of caregiving has primarily focused on its role as a protective resource, showing that it is associated with fewer depressive symptoms (see Aneshensel, Botticello, & Yamamoto-Mitani, 2004). Empirical evidence has studied changes in perceived control with the duration of caregiving and suggests that that perceived control increases in caregivers post bereavement of their care recipient (Skaff, Pearlin, & Mullan, 1996). More recently, Infurna et al. (2013) found that perceived control declines during the course of caregiving, but increases at the time of and in the years following placement of a care recipient in a nursing home or similar institution. Placement and bereavement of the loved one with dementia may result in a relief for caregivers and a restoration of a caregiver's sense of control over the events in his/her own life.

# Antecedents of perceived control

Now that we have discussed the developmental course of perceived control across the lifespan, as well as in relation to processes beyond that of age, such as pathology, mortality, and non-normative events, we turn our attention to specific factors that contribute to levels of and rates of change in perceived control across the lifespan. We reiterate that we believe perceived control is not an innate personality trait that is fixed, but is considered an important self-concept that grows out of experiences and is shaped by or can be challenged with different contexts and experiences (Pearlin, Nguyen, Schieman, & Milkie, 2007). We divide our discussion into specific stages in the lifespan, namely, childhood and adolescence and adulthood and old age.

**Childhood and adolescence**. Contexts and experiences in childhood and adolescence are the foundation for shaping perceptions of control. This stems from conceptual models of perceived control that have long argued the importance of one's context, whether it be familial or societal in contributing to the development of perceived control (see Heckhausen, Wrosch, & Schulz, 2010). Areas that we feel are especially important for shaping perceived control early in development include family relationships and the school environment. Focusing on the family, parents can especially have a tremendous influence on the development of perceived control in their children, through teaching them what they can do for themselves and not being overly restrictive or do too much for them. This can be done through parents helping with the promotion of volitional functioning and independence (Soenens & Beyers, 2012). For example, greater participation in family decision making and positive relationships with parents and family members is linked to indicators of school motivation and perceptions of control in adolescence and into adulthood (Eccles et al., 1993; Shaw, Krause, Chatters, Connell, & Ingersoll-Dayton, 2004; Uchino, 2009). Conversely, a family environment characterized by maltreatment can have detrimental consequences for the development of perceived control in childhood and adolescence that can potentially extend into adulthood (Infurna, Rivers, Reich, & Zautra, 2015).

School environments that provide structure, predictability, and focus on developing children's actions, efforts, and competence systems contribute most to developing perceived control (Eccles et al., 1993; Skinner, 1995). Skinner et al. (1990) found in elementary schools (grades 3−6) that teacher context or perceptions of teacher contingency was associated with better grades and achievement and this was mediated by perceptions of perceived control and teacher-rated engagement. Furthermore, as discussed earlier, specific characteristics of the teacher, such as their levels of perceived control have the potential to be passed onto the students' abilities (Fantuzzo et al., 2012; Klassen & Tze, 2014).

**Adulthood and old age**. Moving from childhood to the adult lifespan, influences on perceived control may shift from the school and parent context to social relationship quality with family and friends, as well as work and adult roles, such as a work environment that is not overly rigid or caregiving for a loved one with dementia, in addition to health status. In this section, we discuss the role of the social context and health status as contributing to the development of perceived control in adulthood and old age.

Theoretical and conceptual models of control have long acknowledged the instrumental role of one's social context in contributing to the development of perceived control (Antonucci & Jackson, 1987; Bandura, 1997). The effect of parenting in childhood and adolescence does not cease its effects on perceived control in adulthood. For example, over parenting in adolescence can lead to children not developing a sense of control over life due to too much instrumental or tangible support and shielding children from perceived obstacles and negative outcomes (Padilla-Walker & Nelson, 2012). Emotional support and social participation have shown to play an important role for perceived control in adulthood and old age. Research from Gerstorf et al. (2011) found that more emotional support was associated with more 9-year changes in perceived control in midlife and old age. Infurna and Okun (2015) examined the effect of emotional support on perceived control across midlife and old age and found that higher levels were associated with more perceived control across midlife and old age, with emotional support showing stronger effects of being protective against declines in old age, compared to midlife. Not only have levels of support been linked to perceived control, but more consistent support or participation in one's social network is beneficial for maintenance of perceived control (Infurna et al., 2011). In older ages, residing in assisted living or a nursing home can provide a context that especially influences perceived control. As shown in seminal research by Langer and Rodin (1976), nursing home residents who were given the opportunity to exert more control over everyday activities and given responsibilities within their environment had a greater likelihood of survival and reported more positive mental health. Institutional workers must not do everything for their residents, because this hinders their experiences of control and in the long run residents may rely on staff more (for discussion, see Baltes, 1995, 1996). Assisted living and nursing homes need to emphasize independence, motivation, competence, and contingency for everyday activities. For example, if someone has trouble opening a jar of honey or cutting their food, it may be best to let them struggle a little and in the end succeed in the action, whereas helping them may make them feel helpless for eating, which may carry over into other areas of life. In conclusion, one's social context, including social relationships and living context, can have a tremendous impact on perceived control. Components of one's social network may influence perceived control through interactions and availability of support, and can enhance or erode one's own sense of efficacy to carry out and persist with behaviors to attain the desired outcome, which can have downstream effects on beliefs of control to become internalized and eventually increase.

Health plays a strong role in shaping the course of perceived control across the adult lifespan as there are multiple facets that are associated with perceived control. Greater disease burden as measured through the number of chronic conditions and degree to which they are limited by their conditions constrains feelings of perceived control (Penninx et al., 1996). Infurna and Okun (2015) found that functional limitations have a differential effect on perceived control in midlife and old age, such that reporting more functional limitations in midlife was more detrimental to perceived control, as compared to old age. The onset of functional limitations or declines in health in midlife may be considered an "off-time" event, leading to stronger effects on perceived control in midlife, compared to old age (Neugarten & Hagestad, 1976; Wurm, Tomasik, & Tesch-Römer, 2008). Incidence and accumulation of functional limitations may undermine perceptions of control through perceiving more external constraints that interfere with day-to-day living and experiencing daily (un)desirable events (Zautra, Reich, & Guarnaccia, 1990). Health declines may lead the inability of striving for and maintaining independence, leading to interference with making a change or adapting to a challenging life situation. Difficulties with daily physical functioning may impede success in carrying out desired activities, as a result of limited access to network members and community resources. In sum, changes in health during adulthood and old age have the potential to considerably effect the development of perceived control, with the impact differing across the adult lifespan.

# Conclusion

Perceived control has wide-ranging implications across the lifespan and as we have argued has the capacity to change. Perceived control is shaped by one's social context and health changes across the adult lifespan, with classroom and family context being prominent antecedents in childhood and adolescence and health and social relationship quality rising to the forefront in adulthood and old age to shape the course of changes in perceived control. Although this was not the focus of this chapter, but it is worth briefly mentioning nonetheless, the capacity for perceived control to change makes it a good target for interventions across the lifespan to be an initiator of better outcomes (Reich, 2015). The construct of perceived control is instrumental for shaping the course of numerous outcomes and is shaped by numerous forces across the lifespan, making clear its importance for further study.

# References

Agrigoroari, S., & Lachman, M. E. (2011). Cognitive functioning in midlife and old age: Combined effects of psychosocial and behavioral factors. *The Journals of Gerontology, Series B: Psychological Sciences and Social Sciences, 66B*(S1), i130–i140.

Aneshensel, C. S., Botticello, A. L., & Yamamoto-Mitani, N. (2004). When caregiving ends: The course of depressive symptoms after bereavement. *Journal of Health and Social Behavior, 45*, 422–440.

Aneshensel, C. S., Pearlin, L. I., Mullan, J. T., Zarit, S. H., & Whitlatch, C. J. (1995). *Profiles in caregiving: The unexpected career*. San Diego, CA: Academic Press.

Antonucci, T. C., & Jackson, J. S. (1987). Social support, interpersonal efficacy and health. In L. L. Carstensen, & B. A. Edelstein (Eds.), *Handbook of clinical gerontology* (pp. 291–311). New York, NY: Pergamon.

Bäckman, L., & MacDonald, S. W. S. (2006). Death and cognition: Synthesis and outlook. *European Psychologist, 11*, 224–235.

Baltes, M. M. (1995). Dependency in old age: Gains and losses. *Current directions in psychological science, 4*(1), 14–19.

Baltes, M. M. (1996). *The many faces of dependency in old age*. Cambridge University Press.

Baltes, P. B., & Nesselroade, J. R. (1979). History and rationale of longitudinal research. In J. R. Nesselroade, & P. B. Baltes (Eds.), *Longitudinal research in the study of behavior and* development (pp. 1–39). New York, NY: Academic Press.

Bandura, A. (1997). *Self-efficacy: The exercise of control*. New York, NY: Freeman.

Bandura, A. (1982). The psychology of chance encounters and life paths. *American Psychologist, 37*, 747–755.

Birren, J. E., & Cunningham, W. (1985). Research on the psychology of aging: Principles, concepts, and theory. In J. E. Birren, & K. W. Schaie (Eds.), *Handbook of the psychology of aging* (2nd ed., pp. 3–34). New York, NY: Van Nostrand Reinhold.

Caplan, L. J., & Schooler, C. (2003). The roles of fatalism, self-confidence, and intellectual resources in the disablement process in older adults. *Psychology and Aging, 18*, 551–561.

Eccles, J. S., Midgley, C., Wigfield, A., Buchanan, C. M., Reuman, D., Flanagan, C., et al. (1993). Development during adolescence: The impact of stage-environment fit on young adolescents' experiences in schools and in families. *American Psychologist, 48*, 90–101.

Evans, K. (2002). Taking control of their lives? Agency in young adult transitions in England and the new Germany. *Journal of Youth Studies, 5*, 245–269.

Fantuzzo, J., Perlman, S., Sproul, F., Minney, A., Perry, M. A., & Li, F. (2012). Making visible teacher reports of their teaching experiences: The early childhood teacher experiences scale. *Psychology in the Schools, 49*, 194–205.

Gale, C. R., Batty, G. D., & Deary, I. J. (2008). Locus of control at age 10 years and health outcomes and behaviors at age 30 years: The 1970 British Cohort Study. *Psychosomatic Medicine, 70*, 397–403.

Gerstorf, D., Ram, N., Estabrook, R., Schupp, J., Wagner, G. G., & Lindenberger, U. (2008). Life satisfaction shows terminal decline in old age: Longitudinal evidence from the Germany Socio-Economic Panel Study (SOEP). *Developmental Psychology, 44*, 1148–1159.

Gerstorf, D., Ram, N., Lindenberger, U., & Smith, J. (2013). Age and time-to-death trajectories of change in indicators of cognitive, sensory, physical, health, social, and self-related functions. *Developmental Psychology, 49,* 1805−1821.

Gerstorf, D., Röcke, C., & Lachman, M. E. (2011). Antecedent-consequent relations of perceived control to health and social support: Longitudinal evidence for between-domain associations across adulthood. *Journals of Gerontology: Psychological Sciences, 66B,* 61−71.

Gibson, S., & Dembo, M. (1984). Teacher efficacy: A construct validation. *Journal of Educational Psychology, 76,* 569−582.

Grimm, K. J., Ram, N., & Estabrook, R. (2016). *Growth modeling: Structural equation and multilevel modeling approaches.* New York, NY: Guilford.

Haase, C. M., Heckhausen, J., & Köller, O. (2008). Goal engagement during the school-work transition: Beneficial for all, particularly for girls. *Journal of Research on Adolescence, 18,* 671−698.

Harmell, A. L., Chattillion, E. A., Roepke, S. K., & Mausbach, B. T. (2011). A review of the psychobiology of dementia caregiving: A focus on resilience factors. *Current Psychiatry Reports, 13,* 219−224.

Heckhausen, J., Wrosch, C., & Schulz, R. (2010). A motivational theory of life-span development. *Psychological Review, 117,* 32−60.

Infurna, F. J., & Gerstorf, D. (2013). Linking perceived control, physical activity, and biological health to memory change. *Psychology and Aging, 28,* 1147−1163.

Infurna, F. J., Gerstorf, D., Ram, N., Schupp, J., & Wagner, G. G. (2011). Long-term antecedents and outcomes of perceived control. *Psychology and Aging, 26,* 559−575.

Infurna, F. J., Gerstorf, D., & Zarit, S. H. (2013). Substantial changes in mastery perceptions of dementia caregivers with the placement of a care recipient. *The Journals of Gerontology, Series B: Psychological Sciences and Social Sciences, 68,* 202−214.

Infurna, F. J., & Mayer, A. (2015). The effects of constraints and mastery on mental and physical health: Conceptual and methodological considerations. *Psychology and Aging, 30,* 432−448.

Infurna, F. J., & Okun, M. A. (2015). Antecedents and outcomes of levels and rates of change in perceived control: The moderating role of age. *Developmental Psychology, 51,* 1420−1437.

Infurna, F. J., Ram, N., & Gerstorf, D. (2013). Level and change in perceived control predict 19-year mortality: Findings from the Americans' Changing Lives Study. *Developmental Psychology, 49,* 1833−1847.

Infurna, F. J., Rivers, C. T., Reich, J., & Zautra, A. J. (2015). Childhood trauma and personal mastery: Their influence on emotional reactivity to everyday events in a community sample of middle-aged adults. *PLoS ONE, 10,* e0121840.

Klassen, R. M., & Tze, V. M. C. (2014). Teachers' self-efficacy, personality, and teaching effectiveness: A meta-analysis. *Educational Research Review, 12,* 59−76.

Krause, N. (2003). The social foundations of personal control in late life. In S. H. Zarit, L. I. Pearlin, & K. W. Schaie (Eds.), *Personal control in social and life course contexts* (pp. 45−70). New York, NY: Springer.

Kunzmann, U., Little, T. D., & Smith, J. (2002). Perceiving control: A double-edged sword in old age. *Journals of Gerontology Series B-Psychological Sciences & Social Sciences, 57,* P484−P491.

Lachman, M. E., & Agrigoroaei, S. (2010). Promoting functional health in midlife and old ages: Long-term protecting effects of control beliefs, social support, and physical exercise. *PLoS ONE, 5,* e13297.

Lachman, M. E., & Firth, K. M. (2004). The adaptive value of feeling in control during midlife. In O. G. Brim, Jr., C. D. Ryff, & R. C. Kessler (Eds.), *How healthy are we? A national study of well-being at midlife* (pp. 320–349). Chicago, IL: University of Chicago Press.

Lachman, M. E., Rosnick, C. B., & Röcke, C. (2009). The rise and fall of control beliefs and life satisfaction in adulthood: Trajectories of stability and change over ten years. In H. B. Bosworth, & C. Hertzog (Eds.), *Aging and cognition: Research methodologies and empirical advances. Decade of behavior (2000–2010)* (pp. 143–160). Washington, DC: American Psychological Association.

Lachman, M. E., & Weaver, S. L. (1998). The sense of control as a moderator of social class differences in health and well-being. *Journal of Personality and Social Psychology, 74,* 763–773.

Lang, F. R., & Heckhausen, J. (2001). Perceived control over development and subjective well-being: Differential benefits across adulthood. *Journal of Personality and Social Psychology, 81,* 509–523.

Langer, E. J., & Rodin, J. (1976). The effects of choice and enhanced personal responsibility for the aged: A field experiment in an institutional setting. *Journal of Personality and Social Psychology, 34,* 191–198.

Lewis, S. K., Ross, C. E., & Mirowsky, J. (1999). Establishing a sense of personal control in the transition to adulthood. *Social Forces, 77*(4), 1573–1599.

Levenson, H. (1981). Differentiating among internality, powerful others, and chance. In H. M. Lefcourt (Ed.), *Research with the locus of control construct* (Vol. 1, pp. 15–63). New York, NY: Academic Press.

Mirowsky, J. (1995). Age and the sense of control. *Social Psychology Quarterly, 58,* 31–43.

Mirowsky, J., & Ross, C. E. (2007). Life course trajectories of perceived control and their relationship to education. *American Journal of Sociology, 112,* 1139–1382.

Molloy, L. E., Ram, N., & Gest, S. D. (2011). The storm and stress (or calm) of early adolescent self-concepts: Within- and between-person variability. *Developmental Psychology, 47,* 1589–1607.

Neugarten, B. L., & Hagestad, G. O. (1976). Age and the life course. In R. E. Binstock, & E. Shanas (Eds.), *Handbook of aging and social sciences.* New York: Van Nostrand Reinhold.

Padilla-Walker, L. M., & Nelson, L. J. (2012). Black hawk down? Establishing helicopter parenting as a distinct construct from other forms of parental control during emerging adulthood. *Journal of Adolescence, 35*(5), 1177–1190.

Pearlin, L. I. (2010). The life course and the stress process: Some conceptual comparisons. *Journal of Gerontology: Social Sciences, 65B,* 207–215.

Pearlin, L. I., Nguyen, K. B., Schieman, S., & Milkie, M. A. (2007). The life-course origins of mastery among older people. *Journal of Health and Social Behavior, 48*(2), 164–179.

Pearlin, L. I., Menaghan, E. G., Lieberman, M. A., & Mullan, J. T. (1981). The stress process. *Journal of Health and Social Behavior, 22,* 337–356.

Pearlin, L. I., & Schooler, C. (1978). The structure of coping. *Journal of Health and Social Behavior, 19,* 2–21.

Penninx, B. W. J. H., Beekman, A. T. F., Ormel, J., Kriegsman, D. M. W., Boeke, A. J. P., van Eijk, J., et al. (1996). Psychological status among elderly people with chronic diseases: Does type of disease play a part? *Journal of Psychosomatic Research, 40,* 521–534.

Peterson, C., & Seligman, M. E. P. (1984). Causal explanations as a risk factor for depression: Theory and evidence. *Psychological Review, 91*, 347–374.

Ram, N., Gerstorf, D., Fauth, B., Zarit, S. H., & Malmberg, B. (2010). Aging, disablement, and dying: Using time-as-process and time-as-resources metrics to chart late-life change. *Research in Human Development, 7*, 27–44.

Ranchor, A. V., Wardle, J., Steptoe, A., Henselmans, I., Ormel, J., & Sanderman, R. (2010). The adaptive role of perceived control before and after cancer diagnosis: A prospective study. *Social Science & Medicine, 70*, 1825–1831.

Reich, J. W. (2015). *Mastering your self, mastering your world: Living by the serenity prayer.* Psyche Books.

Reich, J. W. & Infurna, F. J. (Eds.) (2016). *Perceived control: Theory, research, and practice in the first 50 years.* New York, NY: Oxford Publishing.

Ross, C. E., & Mirowsky, J. (2002). Family relationships, social support and subjective life expectancy. *Journal of Health and Social Behavior*, 469–489.

Rotter, J. B. (1966). Generalized expectancies for internal versus external control reinforcement. *Psychological Monographs, 80*, 1–28.

Seligman, M. E. P. (1975). *Helplessness: On depression, development, and death.* San Francisco, CA: Freeman.

Shaw, B. A., Krause, N., Chatters, L. M., Connell, C. M., & Ingersoll-Dayton, B. (2004). Emotional support from parents early in life, aging, and health. *Psychology and Aging, 19*, 4–12.

Singer, J. D., & Willett, J. B. (2003). *Applied longitudinal data analysis: Modeling change and event occurrence.* Oxford University Press.

Skaff, M. M., Pearlin, L. L., & Mullan, J. I. (1996). Transitions in the caregiving career: Effects on sense of mastery. *Psychology and Aging, 11*, 247–257.

Skinner, E. A. (1995). *Perceived control, motivation, and coping.* Thousand Oaks, CA: Sage.

Skinner, E. A. (1996). A guide to constructs of control. *Journal of Personality and Social Psychology, 71*, 549–570.

Skinner, E. A., Wellborn, J. G., & Connell, J. P. (1990). What it takes to do well in school and whether I've got it: A process model of perceived control and children's engagement and achievement in school. *Journal of Educational Psychology, 82*, 22–32.

Soenens, B., & Beyers, W. (2012). The cross-cultural significance of control and autonomy in parent–adolescent relationships. *Journal of Adolescence, 35*, 243–248.

Specht, J., Egloff, B., & Schmukle, S. C. (2011). Stability and change of personality across the life course: The impact of age and major life events on mean-level and rank-order stability of the Big Five. *Journal of Personality and Social Psychology, 101*(4), 862–882.

Specht, J., Egloff, B., & Schmukle, S. C. (2013). Everything under control? The effects of age, gender, and education on trajectories of perceived control in a nationally representative German sample. *Developmental Psychology, 49*(2), 353–364.

Surtees, P. G., Wainwright, N. W. J., Luben, R., Khaw, K.-T., & Day, N. E. (2006). Mastery, sense of coherence, and mortality: Evidence of independent associations from the EPIC Norfolk Prospective Cohort Study. *Health Psychology, 25*, 102–110.

Surtees, P. G., Wainwright, W. J., Luben, R., Wareham, N. J., Bingham, S., & Khaw, K.-T. (2010). Mastery is associated with cardiovascular disease mortality in men and women at apparently low risk. *Health Psychology, 29*, 412–420.

Uchino, B. N. (2009). Understanding the links between social support and physical health: A life-span perspective with emphasis on the separability of perceived and received support. *Perspectives on Psychological Science, 4*, 236–255.

Verbrugge, L. M., & Jette, A. M. (1994). The disablement process. *Social Science & Medicine, 38*, 1—14.

Wang, H., Hall, N. C., & Rahimi, S. (2015). Self-efficacy and causal attributions in teachers: Effects on burnout, job satisfaction, illness, and quitting intentions. *Teaching and Teacher Education, 47*, 120—130.

White, R. (1959). Motivation reconsidered: The concept of competence. *Psychological Review, 66*, 297—333.

Windsor, T. D., & Anstey, K. J. (2008). A longitudinal investigation of perceived control and cognitive performance in young, midlife and older adults. *Aging, Neuropsychology, and Cognition, 15*, 744—763.

Windsor, T. D., & Anstey, K. J. (2010). Age differences in psychosocial predictors of positive and negative affect: A longitudinal investigation of young, midlife, and older adults. *Psychology and Aging, 25*, 641—652.

Wrosch, C., Amir, E., & Miller, G. E. (2011). Goal adjustment capacities, coping, and subjective well-being: The sample case of caregiving for a family member with mental illness. *Journal of Personality and Social Psychology, 100*, 934—946.

Wrosch, C., Heckahusen, J., & Lachman, M. E. (2000). Primary and secondary control strategies for managing health and financial stress across adulthood. *Psychology and Aging, 15*, 387—399.

Wrosch, C., Schulz, R., & Heckhausen, J. (2004). Health stresses and depressive symptomatology in the elderly: A control-process approach. *Current Directions in Psychological Science, 13*, 17—20.

Wurm, S., Tomasik, M. J., & Tesch-Römer, C. (2008). Serious health events and their impact on changes in subjective health and life satisfaction: The role of age and a positive view on ageing. *European Journal of Ageing, 5*, 117—127.

Zautra, A. J., Reich, J. W., & Guarnaccia, C. A. (1990). Some everyday life consequences of disability and bereavement for older adults. *Journal of Personality and Social Psychology, 59*, 550—561.

# The development of goals and motivation

# 16

*Marie Hennecke and Alexandra M. Freund*
University of Zurich, Zurich, Switzerland

## Introduction

Since the beginnings of personality psychology, goals have been viewed as the building blocks of personality (Allport, 1937) and they have also played a central role for understanding personality development (Freund & Riediger, 2006; Hennecke, Bleidorn, Denissen, & Wood, 2014; Hudson & Fraley, Chapter 33). First, goals provide consistency across situations, a central aspect of personality. Second, people differ with regard to *what* they want to achieve, maintain, or avoid (their goals), as well as *why* they pursue certain goals (their motives). Consequently, goals and motives contribute to individual differences in behavior, another central aspect of personality. Whereas in the past, goals and traits (e.g., the Big Five) have been viewed as more or less independent aspects of personality (Allport, 1937; McAdams, 2009; McCrae & Costa, 1996, 2008; Roberts & Robins, 2000), recent developments have begun to emphasize the role of goals in determining people's traits (Denissen, Van Aken, Penke, & Wood, 2013; Fleeson & Jayawickreme, 2015; Heller, Komar, & Lee, 2007; Hudson & Roberts, 2014; Nikitin & Freund, 2015; McCabe & Fleeson, 2012). Third and finally, goals structure and organize behavior over time into meaningful action units (e.g., dressing nicely, going on dates, sending text messages might all serve the goal of "finding a partner"), thereby allowing to study central aspects of human development (e.g., when are certain behaviors more likely and why).

Goals and motives play a double role in human development. On the one hand, they are subject to development as our goals and motives change as we age. On the other hand, goals and motives also drive development. They provide our lives with direction, and shape our behavior, feelings, and thoughts (Freund, 2007); for instance, they affect our health (Mann, De Ridder, & Fujita, 2013), our relationships (Fitzsimons & Finkel, 2011; Impett et al., 2010; Nikitin, Schoch, & Freund, 2014), our work life (Latham & Yukl, 1975; Lee, Locke, & Latham, 1989; Wiese & Freund, 2000, 2002), and our well-being (Brunstein, 1993; Diener & Fujita, 1995; Elliot & Sheldon, 1998; Freund & Baltes, 2002).

In line with other goal researchers (Elliot & Fryer, 2008; Fishbach & Ferguson, 2007; Higgins & Kruglanski, 2000), we define goals as cognitive representations of desired (or dreaded) endstates that the individual commits to attain (or avoid)

Personality Development Across the Lifespan. DOI: http://dx.doi.org/10.1016/B978-0-12-804674-6.00016-8

through action. They can be understood as knowledge structures that cognitively link information about ends to information about means (Kruglanski et al., 2002). Goals may be more or less specific and contextualized (e.g., "finishing a marketing report") or abstract and spanning across contexts and time (e.g., "having a success-ful career"). Often, goals are described as forming a hierarchy, with abstract goals on higher levels that are served by more specific goals on lower levels (Carver & Scheier, 1998). In this hierarchy, subgoals represent the means to superordinate goals. Most research on goals has focused on midlevel goals (e.g., personal projects, current concerns, life tasks), most likely because they provide a useful level of anal-ysis where they can be directly linked to observable behaviors while still being experienced as valuable and meaningful (Little, 1989).

The goal concept is closely related to processes of self-regulation and self-control (Carver & Scheier, 1998). Self-regulation entails the broad range of processes that are involved in goal setting, pursuit, disengagement, and goal re-engagement (Heckhausen & Gollwitzer, 1987; Wrosch, Scheier, Miller, Schulz, & Carver, 2003). The term self-control is often used to describe the pro-cess by which persons align their behavior, thoughts, and feelings with their personal standards or goals, often with a specific focus on the inhibition of unwanted impulses or desires (Baumeister, Vohs, & Tice, 2007; but see Kuhl, 2000; for different definitions of the two concepts). Self-control failures are frequently observed whenever people, despite their best intentions, eat too much, procrastinate studying, or exercise less than they want to. However, many people lead a satisfying life, finish an education, get a job, have a family, and good social relations. We argue that goals are essential in this regard (Freund & Riediger, 2006) as they guide attention and behavior in ways that support peo-ple's long-term interests, thereby focusing them on possible opportunities for goal pursuit (Kruglanski et al., 2002) and helping them to inhibit the disturbing influences of temptations (Fishbach, Friedman, & Kruglanski, 2003) and compet-ing goals (Shah, Friedman, & Kruglanski, 2002).

Whereas goals are usually conceived of as accessible to people's conscious reports, motivation is also fueled by sources inaccessible to self-report. Such implicit motives have been defined as clusters of cognitions with affective over-tones that are organized around preferred experiences and goals (McClelland, 1984) or recurrent preferences for particular kinds of affective experiences (McAdams & Vaillant, 1982). The motivation literature mostly agrees in distin-guishing four implicit motives: power (a preference for experiences of having impact on others), achievement (a preference for experiences of performing well in comparison to some standard or others), affiliation (a preference for establish-ing and maintaining positive relationships to others), and intimacy (a preference for experiencing warm, close relationships with others) (McAdams, 1980; McClelland, 1984). Not much research has looked at the development of motives across the life span (but see exceptions below). This chapter will therefore focus on the development of goals.

## Age-related expectations as guidelines for managing one's life across the life span

Development is often described as resulting from the interplay of "nature," i.e., genetic and biological preconditions, and "nurture," i.e., environmental influences and learning histories (Lerner, 1978; Plomin, 1994). On an analytical level, it seems useful to also acknowledge the active role that individuals play in their development (Baltes, 1997; Lerner & Busch-Rossnagel, 1981). From this perspective, persons shape their environment and place themselves into certain physical, cultural, and social contexts. Moreover, they continuously adapt to these contexts.

One important way in which persons play an active role in their development is by committing to and pursuing personal goals (Freund, 2007). Goals, however, do not develop in a vacuum but are themselves subject to influences like biological conditions and social expectations. For example, the concept of a "social clock" (Neugarten, 1968) emphasizes the role of social expectations about when certain transitions (e.g., finishing an education) are age appropriate. These expectations set a standard against which individuals compare their own lives and decide whether their lives are "on time" (Cohler & Boxer, 1984). Similarly, Erikson's (1963) developmental model proposes a normative sequence of eight developmental stages covering the entire life span, each of which is characterized by a specific theme or, in Erikson's terms a "psycho-social crisis." According to Erikson, progression to a higher stage can only occur after having successfully solved the previous crises. Examples for such crises are "identity versus identity diffusion" in adolescence and "generativity versus stagnation" in middle adulthood. In this framework, development can be viewed as solving a sequence of problems occurring at particular phases in life.

Similarly, the concept of developmental tasks suggests age-graded normative life tasks that are based on societal expectations about developmental milestones that should be mastered in different life phases (Freund & Baltes, 2005; Havighurst, 1972; Hutteman, Hennecke, Orth, Reitz, & Specht, 2014; McCormick, Kuo, & Masten, 2011). Whereas the successful achievement of developmental tasks such as "starting a family" in young adulthood or "adjustment to retirement" in old age should lead to happiness and to success with later tasks, failure to master a developmental task should lead to "unhappiness in the individual, disapproval by society, and difficulty with later tasks" (Havighurst, 1972, p. 2).

Given the influence of a person's socio-cultural background, personal goals may not be so "personal" after all (Sheldon & Elliot, 1998). Nevertheless, stage theories or the idea of a social clock may overestimate how clearly ordered the course of development really is and tend to neglect individual differences in developmental pathways (Cohler, Hostetler, & Boxer, 1998). In the following, we will review the data and what it so far has told us about how goal content changes across the life span and whether it changes along developmental tasks and expectations.

# Goal content across adulthood

The question of how many and which content classes should be considered to represent the broad variety of people's goals has so far been approached in different ways. One tradition has categorized goals in line with their assumed underlying implicit motives into the three (or four) content classes of achievement, power, affiliation (and sometimes intimacy; e.g., Emmons & McAdams, 1991; McClelland, 1985). Other traditions have contrasted two higher level classes of goals, such as agency versus communion (Bleidorn et al., 2010; Sheldon & Cooper, 2008) or extrinsic versus intrinsic goals (Kasser & Ryan, 1996; Vansteenkiste, Lens, & Deci, 2006). Another tradition has taken a more data-driven approach and distinguished content domains like work, education, friends, family, health, generativity, or spirituality (Emmons & Diener, 1986; Emmons, 1999; Little, 1983; Salmela-Aro, Aunola, & Nurmi, 2007). Despite different classifications, the available research suggests that goals often reflect the developmental transitions, roles, and tasks that adults face across the life span.

For example, in a study by Nurmi, Pulliainen, and Salmela-Aro (1992), 19- to 71-year-old participants were asked to name their personal goals which were then placed into content categories, such as occupation, family, education, health, travel, children, and leisure activities. Whereas education-related goals were frequent among young adults, the frequency of these goals decreased across the life span. The goals of older as compared to younger adults reflected an increased interest in their health, their children's lives, as well as politics and global issues. In another sample covering 371 adults between 19 and 64 years, Nurmi (1992) found similar and additional patterns. Whereas younger adults most frequently reported goals in the domains of education and family, middle-aged adults' goals reflected that they cared about their children's lives and property. Older adults were mostly interested in their health, retirement, leisure, and the world.

In one of the few longitudinal studies, 300 university students between 18 and 28 years reported their current goals repeatedly over a 10-year time span (Salmela-Aro et al., 2007). Goals were coded into 13 content categories, among them the categories of education, travel, work, health, and hobbies. Over time, younger adults reported a decrease in the number of education-, friendship-, and travel-related goals. At the same time, the number of work-related goals first increased strongly and then leveled off again. Moreover, family- and health-related goals became more prevalent over time. Other goals, such as hobby- or lifestyle-related goals, remained pretty stable across time. Overall, these studies support the idea that goals reflect a normative developmental pathway. As adults progressed through university, work, family, and health became more important while pursuing fewer education goals.

Sheldon and Kasser (2001) content coded adults' self-reported personal strivings and analyzed them on the basis of Erikson's (1963) stage model of personality development. As expected, older adults' strivings more often referred to intrinsic values like self-acceptance, emotional intimacy, and community contribution, reflecting increased maturity and personality integration. In contrast, younger adults' strivings more often referred to more extrinsic values like an interest in money, popularity, and physical attractiveness. Older adults were moreover more concerned with generativity and ego integrity than with identity. Apparently, during adulthood, people first strive for consolidating or establishing their identity, and then are increasingly concerned with the creation and nurturance of things that will outlast them. Intimacy strivings toward forming and maintaining reciprocal and meaningful interpersonal relationships remained stable across the life span.

Recently, Dunlop, Bannon, and McAdams (2015) presented a systematic analysis of both the rank-order consistency and the mean-level stability of goals across time. Young and middle-aged adults repeatedly reported their goals within a 3- and 4-year period. Goals were coded according to motives (i.e., whether they referred to achievement, affiliation, intimacy, power), and to content (i.e., generativity, health, finance, travel). Younger and middle-aged adults' goals showed a moderate degree of rank-order consistency across time, i.e., the within-domain correlations of the frequencies by which goals were named over time were small to moderate. The mean-level consistency of goals was analyzed using latent growth curve modeling. For younger adults, goals remained remarkably stable as no-growth models provided the best fit for each of the eight conceptual goal categories. For middle-aged adults, there was a linear increase in the frequency of affiliation goals over time, a finding the authors interpret as consistent with Socioemotional Selectivity Theory (SST; Carstensen, Isaacowitz, & Charles, 1999; see the next section on "Increasing selectivity in old age"). There was also a linear decrease in the frequency of generativity goals over time. According to Dunlop et al. (2015), this finding is in line with Erikson's stage model which assumes that generativity concerns are most prevalent in midlife but become less important afterward (but see Penningroth & Scott, 2012; Sheldon & Kasser, 2001). For the other conceptual goal categories, no-growth models again provided the best fit to the data. While this research points to a moderate to high stability of goals across adulthood, it is important to note that the observed time spans of 3 or 4 years were still relatively short. It is likely that the rank-order stability and the mean-level consistency of goals are reduced if longer time spans are considered and individuals transition through middle adulthood and old age.

Together, the data support that goals are useful to understand lifespan development. Moreover, there is considerable between-person variance regarding personal goals (Dunlop et al., 2015; Salmela-Aro et al., 2007), a fact that further corroborates the usefulness of goals for describing a person's personality. However, the content of personal goals reflects developmental tasks and normative expectations. The increasing importance of health goals furthermore reflects biologically-based, health-related, and cognitive declines in middle and old adulthood (Baltes, 1997).

# Increasing selectivity in old age

Whereas developmental changes in goal content have largely been explained by age-graded norms and biological resources, SST (Carstensen et al., 1999) focuses on the subjective extension of future time. According to SST puts forth that when adults see their future as increasingly limited, this changes the goals they pursue. Healthy young adults, who face a future that seems almost unlimited, are assumed to pursue what Carstensen, Fung, and Charles (2003) consider "expansive goals," i.e., goals with benefits that extend into the distant future, such as acquiring knowledge. Older adults who face a more limited future are assumed to pursue goals that have more immediate benefits, such as the experience of meaningful positive emotions in the "here and now" (Lang & Carstensen, 2002). According to SST, social preferences also change in line with these changing goals: younger adults prefer more extended social networks and are generally interested in getting acquainted with novel interaction partners. In contrast, older adults tend to prefer smaller social networks composed of well-known and close social partners (Fung, Carstensen, & Lang, 2001; Lang & Carstensen, 1994; Lang, Staudinger, & Carstensen, 1998) who are more likely to provide adults with the emotionally meaningful and positive social experiences and the feeling of being socially connected.

Not only with regard to social networks, but with regard to goals in general, people become more selective across the life span. Generally, people pursue more than just one goal at a time. A typical middle-aged adult might, for example, hold a number of both career- as well as family-related goals, while at the same time trying to maintain a healthy weight. The number of goals that a person can pursue at any given time is limited by the availability of resources such as time, energy, attention, money, or social support. Resource limitations become even more severe in old age, when cognitive and physical abilities decline. As a consequence, older adults have been found to be more selective in their adoption of goals and report pursuing fewer goals at a time (Cross & Markus, 1991; Lawton, Moss, Winter, & Hoffman, 2002; Nurmi, 1992; Riediger & Freund, 2006; but see Ogilvie, Rose, & Heppen, 2001; Penningroth & Scott, 2012). The increased selectivity is also reflected in the way that goals relate to one another. Intergoal facilitation occurs when the pursuit of one goal also helps to accomplish of another goal. In contrast, intergoal conflict occurs when the pursuit of one goal impairs the accomplishment of another goal. Riediger, Freund, and Baltes (2005) found that older adults show a higher degree of intergoal facilitation and, as a consequence, more goal engagement than younger adults. These age-related differences in goal relations come about because older adults focus and restrict their goal pursuit to a few important life domains (Riediger & Freund, 2006). Older adults also experience fewer want— should conflicts than younger adults, i.e., the feeling that they want to or should do something else in a given situation, a factor likely contributing to higher emotional well-being in old age (Riediger & Freund, 2008).

## Goal orientation: from achieving gains to preventing losses

One of the central tenets of life span developmental psychology holds that at all points in life development encompasses both gains and losses (Baltes, 1987).

However, the ratio of gains and losses changes dramatically across the life span, whereas developmental gains are predominant in childhood, adolescence, and young adulthood, with increasing age and particularly when entering old age, people face more and more developmental losses (Baltes, 1997). Many of the losses are biologically based and include health-related and cognitive declines, but they also encompass a reduction in social status through retirement or the loss of social partners (Baltes, Lindenberger, & Staudinger, 2006). This change in gains and losses is also reflected in social expectations; adults of different ages share the view that young adulthood is a phase in life when we can expect gains in many areas of life, while later adulthood is characterized by losses in various functional domains (Heckhausen, Dixon, & Baltes, 1989; Mustafic & Freund, 2013). Motivationally, this change in the opportunity for gains and the likelihood of losses is reflected in a primary orientation of personal goals toward gains in young adulthood and increase in goal orientation toward maintenance and the avoidance of losses across middle adulthood and into old age (Staudinger, Marsiske, & Baltes, 1995).

As we have argued in more detail elsewhere (Freund & Ebner, 2005; Freund, Hennecke, & Mustafic, 2012), the motivation to gain and accumulate resources seems particularly important in young adulthood when there is a lot of potential for gains and in order to build a basis for further successful development. Young adulthood is the phase in life when the developmental tasks concern gaining education or professional skills, founding a family, building a home, and establishing a career. With increasing age, people are more likely to have accumulated resources (e.g., material belongings, social relations) that are both worth and, when facing increasing losses, also need to be protected. This is also reflected in developmental tasks for older adulthood that concern the maintenance of functioning and the prevention of losses (Freund & Baltes, 2005).

Empirical evidence supports this notion of a change in goal orientation across adulthood (Ebner, Freund, & Baltes, 2006; Heckhausen, 1999). Moreover, this change seems to be adaptive both regarding subjective well-being and persistence in goal pursuit. Ebner et al. (2006) showed an age-differential association of goal focus and subjective well-being that suggests that a stronger maintenance orientation is associated with positive well-being for middle-aged and older adults but not for younger adults. For younger adults, it even seems detrimental to orient their personal goals toward the prevention of losses. Moreover, Freund (2006) demonstrated that younger adults are more persistent when pursuing the same goal is framed as being oriented toward achieving gains than toward counteracting losses, whereas the opposite pattern is true for older adults.

Taken together, this line of research suggests that not only the content of goals changes across the life span but also their orientation toward gains and losses. Goal orientation seems to shift in sync with the changing ratio of developmental gains to losses. This shift in goal orientation might foster the acquisition of resources in young adulthood and their maintenance in later phases of the life span.

## Goal focus: the path or the end?

Goal representations entail both the desired endstates and the means that are functional for attaining them (Kruglanski et al., 2002). Both aspects are integral to the definition of goals as representations of desired endstates only denote wishes, dreams, or fantasies, whereas the representations of means only refer to actions. However, within a given goal, people may focus more on the means (process focus) or the ends (outcome focus) (Freund & Hennecke, 2015). In a process focus, a person focuses primarily on the way a goal can be pursued and the experience of this process. In an outcome focus, a person focuses primarily on the benefits and positive consequences of goal attainment (Freund & Hennecke, 2015).

In typical self-control situations where temptations and goals collide, a focus on higher level goals may help to reframe the temptation at hand. A piece of cake is less likely to be eaten if it is viewed in the context of a weight loss (Fujita, Trope, Liberman, & Levin-Sagi, 2006). Nevertheless, self-regulation can benefit from a focus on the process of goal pursuit. As shown in our own research, focusing on the process of dieting during a low-calorie diet was related to more successful weight loss as well as fewer deviations from the diet. An outcome focus, in contrast, was associated with more disinhibited eating after dieting lapses (Freund & Hennecke, 2012). These effects can probably be explained by the fact that process-focused goal pursuers might be better planners. Instead of thinking about the distant ends, their dieting can accomplish, they take precautions that allow them to follow through with the diet and fully instrumentalize their eating behavior. A process focus also increases dental flossing, exercising adherence (Fishbach & Choi, 2012; Freund, Hennecke, & Riediger, 2010), and hours spent on studying for an exam (Pham & Taylor, 1999). As Fishbach and Choi have proposed, a focus on outcomes may also devalue the intrinsic appeal of an activity, as it is seem primarily as a means to an end and not as an end in itself.

In response to successful goal pursuit, a process focus might have additional benefits: In dieters who strongly identified their dieting successes on the level of means (e.g., as having dieted well or as having changed their eating behavior), weight loss in 1 week was not as strongly negatively related to weight loss in the next week (Hennecke & Freund, 2014). It could be that focusing on the process rather than on outcome attainment lacks the demotivating qualities that come with the attainment of desired outcomes (see Amir & Ariely, 2008; De Witt Huberts, Evers, & De Ridder, 2012). In contrast, identifying success as something that relies on the appropriate implementation of dieting means, informs the person that the chosen path to the goal was right and should be maintained.

Across adulthood, people shift their goal focus from the outcome to an increasingly stronger process focus. Freund et al. (2010) found that younger adults reported to focus more on the outcomes of exercising (e.g., losing weight, becoming more physically attractive) whereas older adults reported to focus more on its process (e.g., having fun, socializing with friends). In a different study, young but not older adults preferred outcome- over process-related descriptions of goals.

This preference was also supported in another study where young and older adults were asked to choose a thinking exercise that either focused on the desired outcomes of personal goals or on the means to pursue these goals. Again younger but not older adults favored the outcome-focused exercise (Freund et al., 2010). The more concrete representation of goals in terms of the more proximal process rather than the more distant outcome might be due to a shorter future time perspective that, as Construal Level Theory posits, is related to more concrete representation of goals (Trope & Liberman, 2010).

# The importance of goal disengagement

So far, our review has emphasized the importance of goal engagement for adaptive development. In fact, persistent goal pursuit usually has positive consequence for goal attainment, health, and well-being (Bandura, 1997; Freund & Baltes, 1998; Mann et al., 2013). Vince Lombardi's famous adage "Winners never quit and quitters never win" reflects the popular belief that persistence is the key to success. However, being able to disengage from goals may just be as important given that goals have become unattainable (Wrosch et al., 2003).

Across adulthood, goals may become difficult or impossible to attain for different reasons like socio-structural conditions, biological constraints, or age-graded norms. Studies have supported that in the face of blocked goals, the ability to disengage and to re-engage in other goals is crucial for the maintenance of subjective well-being (Wrosch et al., 2003).

The importance of goal disengagement has been further investigated in research on "developmental deadlines." After passing such a deadline, accomplishing a goal becomes increasingly difficult or impossible. Bearing children, for example, becomes dramatically more different for women after a certain age (Heckhausen, Wrosch, & Fleeson, 2001). Childless women between 27 and 33 more often reported actively pursuing the goal, whereas childless women older than 40 usually did not report a childbearing goal but focused more on developing their self, their social network, and their health. Interestingly, predeadline women also remembered baby-related sentences from an incidental memory task better than postdeadline women. Women who, despite having passed the deadline, where highly receptive to baby-relevant sentences furthermore reported higher levels of negative affect, indicating that the inability to cognitively disengage from an unattainable goal has negative consequences for well-being. In a second study, predeadline women also reported being more involved in active strategies of goal pursuit whereas postdeadline women valued goal disengagement and self-protection. Active goal pursuit after having passed the deadline was positively related to depression whereas it was negatively related depression for predeadline women.

Given that in old age there may be fewer opportunities for goal attainment while, at the same time, difficulties due to losses may increase, goal disengagement might be of increasing importance for older adults. In fact, older adults find it easier to let go of unattainable goals and to reengage in different goals (Wrosch et al., 2003). As expected, goal disengagement buffered the association of functional disability in old age with increases in depressive symptoms (Dunne, Wrosch, & Miller, 2011).

## Implicit motives across the life span

As previously mentioned, people do not only differ with regard to the goals they pursue but also with regard to *why* they want to pursue them, their implicit motives. From a theoretical viewpoint, multiple developmental trajectories seem possible. On the one hand, implicit motives could be chronically more activated in older adults because they perceive the time that remains for the satisfaction of these motives as more limited than younger adults (Valero, Nikitin, & Freund, 2015). On the other hand, older adults become less sensitive to affectively relevant stimuli in general (Keil & Freund, 2009) and show lower variability in their affective experience (Röcke, Li, & Smith, 2009). This developmental pattern might correspond to a decreased identification of incentives, which, in turn, should be reflected in lower motive scores.

To further complicate matters, empirical evidence on implicit motives across the life span has remained contradictory. Some authors report higher implicit motive scores for older than younger adults. For example, Valero et al. (2015) report that older adults score higher on the achievement and the affiliation motive. Contradicting these results, Veroff, Depner, Kulka, and Douvan (1980) report that older women score lower on the achievement and the affiliation motive than younger women. Likewise, in a study of McClelland, Scioli, and Weaver (1998), older participants scored lower on implicit affiliation and power motives. Some studies have included middle-aged adults and yielded contradictory results indicating an increase of the power motive in middle-aged men (Veroff, Reuman, & Feld, 1984) or an increase in the power motive from young to middle-aged college-educated women in some jobs but not in others (Jenkins, 1994), pointing to additional sources of influence on the development of motives. In sum, the current evidence regarding age-trajectories of implicit motives is highly inconclusive and further studies are required.

## Final remarks

Despite the fact that across adulthood ratio of gains and losses becomes less positive across adulthood, studies converge to show a silver lining, namely a corresponding increase in adults' motivational competence (Hennecke & Freund, 2010). Compared to younger adults, older adults report a stronger process focus (Freund et al., 2010), experience less motivational conflict (Riediger & Freund, 2006, 2008), more often chose goals that are aligned with their psychological needs (Sheldon & Kasser, 2001), and more often succeed at disengaging from unattainable goals (Wrosch et al., 2003). Although these results are interesting and promising, the processes that underlie these developmental changes are still under-explored. Age is not "just a number" but the aging process has many implications such as the accumulation of life experiences, the loss of fluid cognitive abilities and physical resources, and the restriction of future time perspective. Moreover, as persons approach the end of their lives, additional processes may take place. Adults who are facing their own death might, for example, show motivational shifts that are more extreme than the ones observed earlier, e.g., an even stronger desire to restrict social contact to the closest family and friends. At the end of life, goals may also revolve around preparations for one's impending death including not only practical concerns such as making the necessary medical and funeral arrangements but also more abstract concerns such as reviewing one's life, resolving conflicts, achieving a sense of completion, or coming to peace with God (Heyland et al., 2006; Steinhauser et al., 2000). In order to gain a deeper understanding of personality development across the life span, a comprehensive developmental theory encompassing different levels and aspects of personality will need to be further elaborated (see Hennecke et al., 2014 for a first step in this direction).

# References

Allport, F. H. (1937). Teleonomic description in the study of personality. *Journal of Personality, 5*, 202–214.

Allport, G. W. (1937). Personality: A psychological interpretation. New York, NY: Holt.

Amir, O., & Ariely, D. (2008). Resting on laurels: The effects of discrete progress markers as subgoals on task performance and preferences. *Journal of Experimental Psychology: Learning, Memory, and Cognition, 34*, 1158–1171.

Baltes, P. B. (1987). Theoretical propositions of life-span developmental psychology: On the dynamics between growth and decline. *Developmental Psychology, 23*, 611–626.

Baltes, P. B. (1997). On the incomplete architecture of human ontogeny: Selection, optimization, and compensation as foundation for developmental theory. *American Psychologist, 52*, 366–380.

Baltes, P. B., Lindenberger, U., & Staudinger, U. M. (2006). Life span theory in developmental psychology. In R. M. Lerner, & W. Damon (Eds.), *Handbook of child psychology: Theoretical models of human development* (pp. 569–664). Hoboken, NJ: Wiley.

Bandura, A. (1997). *Self-efficacy: The exercise of control.* London, England: Macmillan.

Baumeister, R. F., Vohs, K. D., & Tice, D. M. (2007). The strength model of self-control. *Current Directions in Psychological Science, 16*, 351–355.

Bleidorn, W., Kandler, C., Hülsheger, U. R., Riemann, R., Angleitner, A., & Spinath, F. M. (2010). Nature and nurture of the interplay between personality traits and major life goals. *Journal of Personality and Social Psychology, 99*, 366–379.

Brunstein, J. C. (1993). Personal goals and subjective well-being: A longitudinal study. *Journal of Personality and Social Psychology, 65*, 1061–1070.

Carstensen, L. L., Fung, H. H., & Charles, S. T. (2003). Socioemotional selectivity theory and the regulation of emotion in the second half of life. *Motivation and Emotion, 27*, 103–123.

Carstensen, L. L., Isaacowitz, D. M., & Charles, S. T. (1999). Taking time seriously: A theory of socioemotional selectivity. *American Psychologist, 54*, 165–181.

Carver, C. S., & Scheier, M. F. (1998). *On the self-regulation of behavior*. New York, NY: Cambridge University Press.

Cohler, B. J., & Boxer, A. M. (1984). Personal adjustment, well-being, and life events. In C. Z. Malatesta, & C. E. Izard (Eds.), *Emotion in adult development* (pp. 85–100). Beverly Hills, CA: Sage.

Cohler, B. J., Hostetler, A. J., & Boxer, A. M. (1998). Generativity, social context, and lived experience: Narratives of gay men in middle adulthood. In D. P. McAdams, & E. de St. Aubin (Eds.), *Generativity and adult development: How and why we care for the next generation* (pp. 265–309). Washington, DC: American Psychological Association.

Cross, S., & Markus, H. (1991). Possible selves across the life span. *Human Development, 34*, 230–255.

De Witt Huberts, J. C., Evers, C., & De Ridder, D. T. D. (2012). License to sin: Self-licensing as a mechanims underlying hedonic consumption. *European Journal of Social Psychology, 42*, 190–496.

Denissen, J. J., Aken, M. A., Penke, L., & Wood, D. (2013). Self-regulation underlies temperament and personality: An integrative developmental framework. *Child Development Perspectives, 7*, 255–260.

Diener, E., & Fujita, F. (1995). Resources, personal strivings, and subjective well-being: A nomothetic and idiographic approach. *Journal of Personality and Social Psychology, 68*, 926–935.

Dunlop, W. L., Bannon, B. L., & McAdams, D. P. (2015). Studying the motivated agent through time: Personal goal development during the adult life span. *Journal of Personality, 12*, 1–13.

Dunne, E., Wrosch, C., & Miller, G. E. (2011). Goal disengagement, functional disability, and depressive symptoms in old age. *Health Psychology, 30*, 763–770.

Ebner, N. C., Freund, A. M., & Baltes, P. B. (2006). Developmental changes in personal goal orientation from young to late adulthood: From striving for gains to maintenance and prevention of losses. *Psychology and Aging, 21*, 664–678.

Elliot, A. J., & Fryer, J. W. (2008). The goal construct in psychology. In J. Y. Shah, & W. L. Gardner (Eds.), *Handbook of motivation science* (pp. 235–250). New York, NY: Guilford Press.

Elliot, A. J., & Sheldon, K. M. (1998). Avoidance personal goals and the personality–illness relationship. *Journal of Personality and Social Psychology, 75*, 1282–1299.

Emmons, R. A. (1999). *The psychology of ultimate concerns: Motivation and spirituality in personality*. New York, NY: Guilford Press.

Emmons, R. A., & Diener, E. (1986). A goal–affect analysis of everyday situational choices. *Journal of Research in Personality, 20*, 309–326.

Emmons, R. A., & McAdams, D. P. (1991). Personal strivings and motive dispositions: Exploring the links. *Personality and Social Psychology Bulletin, 17*, 648–654.

Erikson, E. H. (1963). *Childhood and society* (pp. 5–56). New York, NY: Norton.

Fishbach, A., & Choi, J. (2012). When thinking about goals undermines goal pursuit. *Organizational Behavior and Human Decision Processes, 118*, 99–107.

Fishbach, A., & Ferguson, M. J. (2007). The goal construct in social psychology. In A. W. Kruglanski, & E. T. Higgins (Eds.), *Social psychology: Handbook of basic principles* (pp. 490–515). New York, NY: Guilford Press.

Fishbach, A., Friedman, R. S., & Kruglanski, A. W. (2003). Leading us not into temptation: Momentary allurements elicit overriding goal activation. *Journal of Personality and Social Psychology, 84*, 296–309.

Fitzsimons, G. M., & Finkel, E. J. (2011). The effects of self-regulation on social relationships. In K. D. Vohs, & R. F. Baumeister (Eds.), *Handbook of self-regulation: Research, theory, and applications* (pp. 407–421). New York, NY: Guildford Press.

Fleeson, W., & Jayawickreme, E. (2015). Whole trait theory. *Journal of Research in Personality, 56*, 82–92.

Freund, A. M. (2006). Age-differential motivational consequences of optimization versus compensation focus in younger and older adults. *Psychology and Aging, 21*, 240–252.

Freund, A. M. (2007). Differentiating and integrating levels of goal representation: A life-span perspective. In B. R. Little, K. Salmela-Aro, & S. D. Phillips (Eds.), *Personal project pursuit: Goals, action and human flourishing* (pp. 247–270). Mahwah, NJ: Erlbaum.

Freund, A. M., & Baltes, P. B. (1998). Selection, optimization, and compensation as strategies of life management: Correlations with subjective indicators of successful aging. *Psychology and Aging, 13*, 531–543.

Freund, A. M., & Baltes, P. B. (2002). Life-management strategies of selection, optimization and compensation: Measurement by self-report and construct validity. *Journal of Personality and Social Psychology, 82*, 642–662.

Freund, A. M., & Baltes, P. B. (2005). Entwicklungsaufgaben als Organisationsstrukturen von Entwicklung und Entwicklungsoptimierung. [Developmental tasks as organizing structures of development]. In S. H. Filipp, & U. M. Staudinger (Eds.), *Entwicklungspsychologie des mittleren und höheren Erwachsenenalters* (pp. 35–78). Göttingen, Germany: Hogrefe.

Freund, A. M., & Ebner, N. C. (2005). The aging self: Shifting from promoting gains to balancing losses. In W. Greve, K. Rothermund, & D. Wentura (Eds.), *The adaptive self: Personal continuity and intentional self-development* (pp. 185–202). Ashland, OH: Hogrefe & Huber.

Freund, A. M., & Hennecke, M. (2012). Changing eating behaviour vs. losing weight: The role of goal focus for weight loss in overweight women. *Psychology & Health, 27*, 25–42.

Freund, A. M., & Hennecke, M. (2015). On means and ends the role of goal focus in successful goal pursuit. *Current Directions in Psychological Science, 24*, 149–153.

Freund, A. M., Hennecke, M., & Mustafić, M. (2012). On gains and losses, means and ends: Goal orientation and goal focus across adulthood. In R. M. Ryan (Ed.), *The Oxford handbook of human motivation* (pp. 280–300). New York, NY: Oxford University Press.

Freund, A. M., Hennecke, M., & Riediger, M. (2010). Age-related differences in outcome and process goal focus. *European Journal of Developmental Psychology, 7*, 198–222.

Freund, A. M., & Riediger, M. (2006). Goals as building blocks of personality and development in adulthood. In D. K. Mroczek, & T. D. Little (Eds.), *Handbook of personality development* (pp. 353–372). Mahwah, NJ: Erlbaum.

Fujita, K., Trope, Y., Liberman, N., & Levin-Sagi, M. (2006). Construal levels and self-control. *Journal of Personality and Social Psychology, 90*, 351–367.

Fung, H. H., Carstensen, L. L., & Lang, F. R. (2001). Age-related patterns in social networks among European Americans and African Americans: Implications for socioemotional selectivity across the life span. *The International Journal of Aging and Human Development, 52*, 185–206.

Havighurst, R. J. (1972). *Developmental tasks and education.* New York, NY: David McKay Co.

Heckhausen, J. (1999). *Developmental regulation in adulthood: Age-normative and socio-structural constraints as adaptive challenges.* New York, NY: Cambridge University Press.

Heckhausen, H., & Gollwitzer, P. M. (1987). Thought contents and cognitive functioning in motivational versus volitional states of mind. *Motivation and Emotion, 11*, 101–120.

Heckhausen, J., Dixon, R. A., & Baltes, P. B. (1989). Gains and losses in development throughout adulthood as perceived by different adult age groups. *Developmental Psychology, 25*, 109–121.

Heckhausen, J., Wrosch, C., & Fleeson, W. (2001). Developmental regulation before and after a developmental deadline: The sample case of "biological clock" for childbearing. *Psychology and Aging, 16*, 400–413.

Heller, D., Komar, J., & Lee, W. B. (2007). The dynamics of personality states, goals, and well-being. *Personality and Social Psychology Bulletin, 33*, 898–910.

Hennecke, M., Bleidorn, W., Denissen, J. J., & Wood, D. (2014). A three-part framework for self-regulated personality development across adulthood. *European Journal of Personality, 28*, 289–299.

Hennecke, M., & Freund, A. M. (2010). Staying on and getting back on the wagon: Age-related improvement in self-regulation during a low-calorie diet. *Psychology and Aging, 25*, 876–885.

Hennecke, M., & Freund, A. M. (2014). Identifying success on the process level reduces negative effects of prior weight loss on subsequent weight loss during a low-calorie diet. *Applied Psychology: Health and Well-Being, 6*, 48–66.

Heyland, D. K., Dodek, P., Rocker, G., Groll, D., Gadni, A., Pichora, D., & Lam, M. (2006). What matters most in end-of-life care: Perceptions of seriously ill patients and their family members. *Canadian Medical Association Journal, 174*, 627–633.

Higgins, E. T., & Kruglanski, A. W. (2000). Motivational science: The nature and functions of wanting. In E. T. Higgins, & A. W. Kruglanski (Eds.), *Motivational science: Social and personality perspectives* (pp. 1–20). Philadelphia, PA: Psychological Press.

Hudson, N. W., & Roberts, B. W. (2014). Goals to change personality traits: Concurrent links between personality traits, daily behavior, and goals to change oneself. *Journal of Research in Personality, 53*, 68–83.

Hutteman, R., Hennecke, M., Orth, U., Reitz, A. K., & Specht, J. (2014). Developmental tasks as a framework to study personality development in adulthood and old age. *European Journal of Personality, 28*, 267–278.

Impett, E. A., Gordon, A. M., Kogan, A., Oveis, C., Gable, S. L., & Keltner, D. (2010). Moving toward more perfect unions: Daily and long-term consequences of approach and avoidance goals in romantic relationships. *Journal of Personality and Social Psychology, 99*, 948–963.

Jenkins, S. R. (1994). Need for power and women's careers over 14 years: Structural power, job satisfaction, and motive change. *Journal of Personality and Social Psychology, 66*, 155–165.

Kasser, T., & Ryan, R. M. (1996). Further examining the American dream: Differential correlates of intrinsic and extrinsic goals. *Personality and Social Psychology Bulletin, 22*, 280–287.

Keil, A., & Freund, A. M. (2009). Changes in the sensitivity to appetitive and aversive arousal across adulthood. *Psychology and Aging, 24*, 668–680.

Kruglanski, A. W., Shah, J. Y., Fishbach, A., Friedman, R., Chun, W. Y., & Sleeth-Keppler, D. (2002). A theory of goal systems. *Advances in Experimental Social Psychology, 34*, 331–378.

Kuhl, J. (2000). A functional-design approach to motivation and self-regulation: The dynamics of personality systems and interactions. In M. Boekaerts, P. R. Pintrich, & M. Zeidner (Eds.), *Handbook of self-regulation* (pp. 111–169). San Diego, CA: Academic Press.

Lang, F. R., & Carstensen, L. L. (1994). Close emotional relationships in late life: Further support for proactive aging in the social domain. *Psychology and Aging, 9*, 315–324.

Lang, F. R., & Carstensen, L. L. (2002). Time counts: Future time perspective, goals, and social relationships. *Psychology and Aging, 17*, 125–139.

Lang, F. R., Staudinger, U. M., & Carstensen, L. L. (1998). Perspectives on socioemotional selectivity in late life: How personality and social context do (and do not) make a difference. *The Journals of Gerontology Series B: Psychological Sciences and Social Sciences, 53*, 21–30.

Latham, G. P., & Yukl, G. A. (1975). A review of research on the application of goal setting in organizations. *Academy of Management Journal, 18*, 824–845.

Lawton, M. P., Moss, M. S., Winter, L., & Hoffman, C. (2002). Motivation in later life: Personal projects and well-being. *Psychology and Aging, 17*, 539–547.

Lee, T. W., Locke, E. A., & Latham, G. P. (1989). Goal setting theory and job performance. In L. A. Pervin (Ed.), *Goal concepts in personality and social psychology* (pp. 291–326). Hillsdale, NJ: Lawrence Erlbaum Associates, Inc.

Lerner, R. M. (1978). Nature, nurture, and dynamic interactionism. *Human Development, 21*, 1–20.

Lerner, R. M., & Busch-Rossnagel (1981). Individuals as producers of their own development: Conceptual and empirical bases. In R. M. Lerner, & N. A. Busch-Rossnagel (Eds.), *Individuals as producers of their development: A life-span perspective* (pp. 1–36). New York, NY: Wiley.

Little, B. R. (1983). Personal projects a rationale and method for investigation. *Environment and Behavior, 15*, 273–309.

Little, B. R. (1989). Personal projects analysis: Trivial pursuits, magnificent obsessions, and the search for coherence. In D. M. Buss, & N. Cantor (Eds.), *Personality psychology: Recent trends and emerging directions* (pp. 15–31). New York, NY: Springer.

Mann, T., De Ridder, D., & Fujita, K. (2013). Self-regulation of health behavior: Social psychological approaches to goal setting and goal striving. *Health Psychology, 32*, 487.

McAdams, D. P. (1980). A thematic coding system for the intimacy motive. *Journal of Research in Personality, 14*, 413–432.

McAdams, D. P. (2009). *The person: An introduction to the science of personality psychology* (5th ed.). New York, NY: Wiley.

McAdams, D. P., & Vaillant, G. E. (1982). Intimacy motivation and psychosocial adjustment: A longitudinal study. *Journal of Personality Assessment, 46*, 586–593.

McCabe, K. O., & Fleeson, W. (2012). What is extraversion for? Integrating trait and motivational perspectives and identifying the purpose of extraversion. *Psychological Science, 23*, 1498–1505.

McClelland, D. C. (1984). *Motives, personality, and society: Selected papers*. Westport, CT: Praeger Publishers.

McClelland, D. C. (1985). *Human motivation*. Glenview, IL: Scott, Foresman.

McClelland, D. C., Scioli, A., & Weaver, S. (1998). The effect of implicit and explicit motivation on recall among old and young adults. *International Journal of Aging & Human Development, 46*, 1–20.

McCormick, C. M., Kuo, S. I. C., & Masten, A. S. (2011). Developmental tasks across the lifespan. In K. L. Fingerman, C. A. Berg, J. Smith, & T. C. Antonucci (Eds.), *The handbook of lifespan development* (pp. 117–140). Berlin, Germany: Springer Verlag.

McCrae, R. R., & Costa, P. T. (1996). Toward a new generation of personality theories: Theoretical contexts for the five-factor model. In J. S. Wiggins (Ed.), *The five-factor model of personality: Theoretical perspectives* (pp. 51–87). New York, NY: Guilford Press.

McCrae, R. R., & Costa, P. T. (2008). Empirical and theoretical status of the five-factor model of personality traits. In G. J. Boyle, G. Matthews, & D. H. Saklofske (Eds.), *The SAGE handbook of personality theory and assessment* (pp. 273–294). Los Angeles, CA: Sage.

Mustafić, M., & Freund, A. M. (2013). Age-related differences in evaluating developmental stability. *International Journal of Behavioral Development, 37*, 376–386.

Neugarten, B. L. (1968). Adult personality. In B. L. Neugarten (Ed.), *Middle age and aging* (pp. 137–147). Chicago, IL: University Chicago Press.

Nikitin, J., Schoch, S., & Freund, A. M. (2014). The role of age and motivation for the experience of social acceptance and rejection. *Developmental Psychology, 50*, 1943–1950.

Nikitin, J., & Freund, A. M. (2015). The indirect nature of social motives: The relation of social approach and avoidance motives with likability via extraversion and agreeableness. *Journal of Personality, 83*, 97–105.

Nurmi, J. E. (1992). Age differences in adult life goals, concerns, and their temporal extension: A life course approach to future-oriented motivation. *International Journal of Behavioral Development, 15*, 487–508.

Nurmi, J. E., Pulliainen, H., & Salmela-Aro, K. (1992). Age differences in adults' control beliefs related to life goals and concerns. *Psychology and Aging, 7*, 194–196.

Ogilvie, D. M., Rose, K. M., & Heppen, J. B. (2001). A comparison of personal project motives in three age groups. *Basic and Applied Social Psychology, 23*, 207–215.

Penningroth, S. L., & Scott, W. D. (2012). Age-related differences in goals: Testing predictions from selection, optimization, and compensation theory and socioemotional selectivity theory. *The International Journal of Aging and Human Development, 74*, 87–111.

Pham, L. B., & Taylor, S. E. (1999). From thought to action: Effects of process- versus outcome-based mental simulations on performance. *Personality and Social Psychology Bulletin, 25*, 250–260.

Plomin, R. (1994). *Genetics and experience: The interplay between nature and nurture.* Los Angeles, CA: Sage Publications, Inc.

Riediger, M., & Freund, A. M. (2006). Focusing and restricting: Two aspects of motivational selectivity in adulthood. *Psychology and Aging, 21*, 173–185.

Riediger, M., & Freund, A. M. (2008). Me against myself: Motivational conflicts and emotional development in adulthood. *Psychology and Aging, 23*, 479–494.

Riediger, M., Freund, A. M., & Baltes, P. B. (2005). Managing life through personal goals: Intergoal facilitation and intensity of goal pursuit in younger and older adulthood. *The Journals of Gerontology Series B: Psychological Sciences and Social Sciences, 60*, 84–91.

Roberts, B. W., & Robins, R. W. (2000). Broad dispositions, broad aspirations: The intersection of personality traits and major life goals. *Personality and Social Psychology Bulletin, 26*, 1284–1296.

Röcke, C., Li, S. C., & Smith, J. (2009). Intraindividual variability in positive and negative affect over 45 days: Do older adults fluctuate less than young adults? *Psychology and Aging, 24*, 863–878.

Salmela-Aro, K., Aunola, K., & Nurmi, J. E. (2007). Personal goals during emerging adulthood: A 10-year follow up. *Journal of Adolescent Research, 22*, 690–715.

Shah, J. Y., Friedman, R., & Kruglanski, A. W. (2002). Forgetting all else: On the antecedents and consequences of goal shielding. *Journal of Personality and Social Psychology, 83*, 1261–1280.

Sheldon, K. M., & Cooper, M. L. (2008). Goal striving within agentic and communal roles: Separate but functionally similar pathways to enhanced well-being. *Journal of Personality, 76*, 415–448.

Sheldon, K. M., & Elliot, A. J. (1998). Not am personal goals are personal: Comparing autonomous and controlled reasons for goals as predictors of effort and attainment. *Personality and Social Psychology, 24*, 546–557.

Sheldon, K. M., & Kasser, T. (2001). Getting older, getting better? Personal strivings and psychological maturity across the life span. *Developmental Psychology, 37*, 491–501.

Staudinger, U. M., Marsiske, M., & Baltes, P. B. (1995). Resilience and reserve capacity in later adulthood: Potentials and limits of development across the life span. In D. Cicchetti, & D. J. Cohen (Eds.), *Developmental psychopathology* (pp. 801–847). New York, NY: Wiley.

Steinhauser, K. E., Christakis, N. A., Clipp, E. C., McNeilly, M., McIntyre, L., & Tulsky, J. A. (2000). Factors considered important at the end of life by patients, family, physicians, and other care providers. *Journal of the American Medical Association, 284*, 2476–2482.

Trope, Y., Liberman, N., & Freund, A. M. (2010). Construal-level theory of psychological distance. *Psychological Review, 117*, 440–463.

Valero, D., Nikitin, J., & Freund, A. M. (2015). The effect of age and time perspective on implicit motives. *Motivation and Emotion, 39*, 175–181.

Vansteenkiste, M., Lens, W., & Deci, E. L. (2006). Intrinsic versus extrinsic goal contents in self-determination theory: Another look at the quality of academic motivation. *Educational Psychologist, 41*, 19–31.

Veroff, J., Depner, C., Kulka, R., & Douvan, E. (1980). Comparison of American motives: 1957 versus 1976. *Journal of Personality and Social Psychology, 39*, 1249–1262.

Veroff, J., Reuman, D., & Feld, S. (1984). Motives in American men and women across the adult life span. *Developmental Psychology, 20*, 1142–1158.

Wiese, B. S., Freund, A. M., & Baltes, P. B. (2000). Selection, optimization, and compensation: An action-related approach to work and partnership. *Journal of Vocational Behavior, 57*, 273–300.

Wiese, B. S., Freund, A. M., & Baltes, P. B. (2002). Subjective career success and emotional well-being: Longitudinal predictive power of selection, optimization, and compensation. *Journal of Vocational Behavior, 60*, 321–335.

Wrosch, C., Scheier, M. F., Miller, G. E., Schulz, R., & Carver, C. S. (2003). Adaptive self-regulation of unattainable goals: Goal disengagement, goal reengagement, and subjective well-being. *Personality and Social Psychology Bulletin, 29*, 1494–1508.

# The development of attachment styles

## 17

R. Chris Fraley[1] and Nathan W. Hudson[2]
[1]University of Illinois at Urbana-Champaign, Champaign, IL, United States,
[2]Michigan State University, East Lansing, MI, United States

There are vast individual differences in the ways in which people relate to significant others in their lives. For example, some adults are relatively secure in their relationships with friends, family members, and romantic partners. They are able to provide support for others, resolve conflict effectively, and, more generally, they find their relationships satisfying and rewarding. Other people, in contrast, are relatively insecure in the way they relate to others. They are uncomfortable opening up to others and being dependent on them. They may also worry that, if push comes to shove, significant others will not be there for them.

Attachment researchers refer to these kinds of individual differences as "attachment patterns" or "attachment styles." A large body of research has accumulated over the past 30 years that examines the implications of attachment patterns for psychological and interpersonal functioning (see Mikulincer & Shaver, 2007; Gillath, Karantzas, & Fraley, 2016). Research has shown, for example, that people who are relatively secure in their attachment styles report fewer depressive symptoms, adapt to stressful events in constructive ways, and report more commitment and satisfaction in their romantic relationships (Mikulincer, Florian, & Weller, 1993; Muris, Meesters, van Melick, & Zwambag, 2001; Simpson, 1990).

Many of the enduring questions in attachment theory and research concern the origins of individual differences in attachment. Specifically, what makes some people more secure than others? How are those differences sustained across time? And what leads people to change? The purpose of this chapter is to review briefly theory and research on how attachment patterns develop and the processes that give rise to continuity and change.[1]

---

[1] We note from the outset that attachment theory is a theory of lifespan development: it focuses on individual differences in both children and adults and attempts to explain how those differences emerge. But, as with research on temperament and personality, research on attachment in early childhood and adulthood is typically conducted in different research traditions (e.g., developmental and social/personality), and these traditions are more likely to intersect in theory than in practice. In this chapter, we review theory and work that is relevant to child and adult domains, but, due to space constraints, we deliberately blur the lines and do not always do justice to important theoretical distinctions.

Personality Development Across the Lifespan. DOI: http://dx.doi.org/10.1016/B978-0-12-804674-6.00017-X

# The basics of attachment theory

Attachment theory was originally developed by the British psychologist, John Bowlby (1907–90), as a way to understand the intense distress expressed by young children who had been separated from their primary caregivers (e.g., their mothers). Bowlby observed that infants would go to extraordinary lengths (e.g., crying, clinging, frantically searching) to prevent separation from their caregivers or to reestablish proximity to a missing parent (Bowlby, 1969/1982). To explain these responses, Bowlby (1969/1982) proposed that infants are equipped with an *attachment behavioral system*—a motivational system designed by natural selection to keep immature infants in close proximity to people who can provide them with care. He argued that the attachment system would be adaptive for species, such as humans, who are born without the ability to feed or protect themselves. He reviewed a broad array of research suggesting that infants of altricial species are more likely to die to predation when they lack the protection of a caregiver (Bowlby, 1969/1982).

How does the attachment system work? According to the theory, the system essentially "asks" the following question: Is the attachment figure nearby, accessible, and attentive? If the child perceives the answer to this question to be "yes," he or she feels loved, secure, and confident, and, behaviorally, is likely to explore his or her environment and be sociable. If, however, the child perceives the answer to this question to be "no," the child experiences anxiety and is likely to exhibit proximity seeking behaviors ranging from simple visual searching for the attachment figure on the low extreme to active following and vocal signaling on the other extreme. These behaviors are often referred to as *attachment behaviors* because they reflect the operation of the attachment system and function to maintain proximity between the child and his or her attachment figure.

The way a child regulates his or her attachment behavior is driven largely by exogenous factors (e.g., physical separation) early in life. But as infants develop, the way they come to regulate their affect and behavior is based increasingly on the mental representations they construct concerning themselves and their caregivers. These representations, often referred to as *internal working models* (Bretherton & Munholland, 2008), are theorized to reflect the child's experiences with primary caregivers. That is, when primary caregivers are available and responsive to a child's needs, the child learns that he or she can count on others to be there. In short, the child develops a *secure* attachment pattern. In contrast, when the attachment figure is unresponsive or inconsistently available, the child develops *insecure* attachment representations. In short, the quality of the experiences that the child has with his or her primary caregivers is believed to shape the representations that the child develops about him or herself and the social world. These working models are assumed to underlie individual differences in the ways in which people (both children and adults) relate to important people in their lives (i.e., the attachment patterns or styles they exhibit).[2]

---

[2] The way researchers conceptualize individual differences in attachment patterns is more nuanced that what is implied here by a simple secure versus insecure distinction. There is not adequate space in this chapter, however, to review these taxonomies carefully and how they have evolved across time. We refer interested readers to the following: Crowell, Fraley, and Shaver (2008), Solomon and George (2008).

Although there are different ways of partitioning individual differences in attachment patterns in childhood and adulthood, one common approach conceptualizes individual differences within a two-dimensional space. One axis in this space is referred to as *attachment anxiety* (or "anxious attachment") and captures the extent to which people (children or adults) are insecure versus secure in their perceptions of the availability and responsiveness of close others. The other axis is sometimes referred to as *attachment avoidance* (or "avoidant attachment") and refers to the extent to which people are uncomfortable opening up to others, depending on them, and using them as a secure base. A prototypically secure person is low on both of these dimensions; he or she is not worried about the responsiveness of others and is comfortable using others as a safe haven and secure base.

This particular taxonomic system has been useful for a number of reasons. First, it provides a way to ground individual differences in attachment in childhood and adulthood in a common framework (see Fraley & Spieker, 2003). Second, it emphasizes the notion that individual differences can vary continuously. Finally, it recognizes that security and insecurity are multidimensional constructs. A highly avoidant person, for example, could be motivated to avoid close relationships either because he or she fears being hurt (is also anxious; what Bartholomew and Horowitz (1991) referred to as *fearful-avoidance*) or because he or she is compulsively self-reliant (is not anxious; what Bartholomew and Horowitz (1991) referred to as *dismissing-avoidance*).[3]

# How do individual differences develop in early childhood? Theory and research

One of the important goals of developmental research is to uncover the antecedents of attachment patterns (see Belsky & Fearon, 2008, for a review). One of the most significant studies in the history of attachment theory is Mary Ainsworth's (1913−99) observational research on a sample of approximately 25 infants and their caregivers in Baltimore in the 1970s (Ainsworth, Blehar, Waters, & Wall, 1978). Although this sample size seems small in light of modern standards, what made Ainsworth's research unique was her emphasis on in-depth, naturalistic behavioral observations. Specifically, Ainsworth and her team visited the homes of the parents and their children multiple times over the course of the child's first year. They were able to take careful, detailed notes of the interactions between parents and children in their lived environments and not merely in laboratory visits. These interactions were coded on a number of dimensions, most notably the extent

---

[3] Attachment styles, as studied among adults, tend to correlate with other dispositional variables, such as those captured by the Big Five (see Noftle & Shaver, 2006). Attachment-related anxiety tends to correlate moderately with Neuroticism. Attachment-related avoidance tends to correlate weakly (and negatively) with Agreeableness and Extraversion. Despite empirical overlap, most scholars tend to treat attachment styles as being relational, psychodynamic, or social-cognitive dispositional variables rather than traditional trait-like dispositional variables (John, Robins, & Pervin, 2008).

to which the parent provided what has come to be known as *sensitive responsive* caregiving—being in tune with a child's needs and responsive in ways that were appropriate in light of the situation (see Colin, 1996).

When the children were 12 months of age, they visited the laboratory for task called the *strange situation*. In the strange situation, infants and their primary care-giver (most often, mothers) are brought to the laboratory and, systematically, sepa-rated from and reunited with one another. In the strange situation, most children (i.e., about 60%) become upset when the mother leaves the room, but, when she returns, they actively seek the parent and are easily comforted by her. Children who exhibit this pattern of behavior are often called *secure*. Other children (about 20% or less) are ill-at-ease initially, and, upon separation, become extremely distressed. Importantly, when reunited with their parents, these children have a difficult time being soothed, and often exhibit conflicting behaviors that suggest they want to be comforted, but that they also want to "punish" the parent for leaving. These chil-dren are often called *anxious-ambivalent*. The third pattern of attachment that Ainsworth and her colleagues documented is called *anxious-avoidant*. Avoidant children (about 20%) do not appear overly distressed by the separation, and, upon reunion, actively avoid seeking contact with their mother, sometimes turning their attention to play objects.

Ainsworth and her colleagues found that children who had a history of sensi-tively responsive care in the first year of life were more likely that those who did not to be classified as secure in the strange situation. Children who were classified as anxious-ambivalent or avoidant were more likely to have mothers who were inconsistently responsive, intrusive, or negligent in the months leading up to the strange situation.

Ainsworth's classic findings have been replicated by Grossmann, Grossmann, Spanger, Suess, and Unzner (1985) who studied parent—child interactions in the homes of 54 families, up to 3 times during the first year of the child's life. Grossmann et al. found that children who classified as secure in the strange situation at 12 months of age were more likely than children classified as insecure to have mothers who provided sensitive and responsive care to their children in the home environment. Experimental research on nonhuman primates (Suomi, 2008) and inter-vention research on children also indicate that sensitive responsiveness may shape attachment security. van den Boom (1990, 1994), for example, developed an interven-tion that was designed to enhance maternal sensitive responsiveness in mothers whose infants had been identified as irritable. At 12 months of age, children in the interven-tion group were more likely to be classified as secure than insecure (anxious or avoidant) in the strange situation compared with the control group (see Bakermans-Kranenburg, van IJzendoorn, & Juffer, 2003, and van IJzendoorn, Juffer, & Duyvesteyn, 1995, for an in-depth discussion of intervention research).

The early research conducted by Ainsworth and her students has been important for a number of reasons. First, their work led to a procedure, the strange situation, for studying individual differences in attachment behavior that could be (and was) widely adopted by investigators across the world. Second, the observational system led to the development of a taxonomy (secure, ambivalent, and avoidant) of individual differences in child attachment. Although this taxonomy has been modified and elaborated over the years (see Solomon & George, 2008), this system, much like the Big Five in personality research, provided a useful way to organize individual differences in child behavior. Moreover, it provided a common language with which to discuss attachment patterns. Finally, Ainsworth's research revealed some of the developmental antecedents, such as sensitive responsiveness, of individual differences in attachment, thereby facilitating our understanding of the factors that promote and inhibit secure attachment.

We should note that although attachment theorists focus on the quality of the relationship between infants and their primary caregivers as being one of the reasons why some children are more secure than others, researchers have studied a number of etiological factors, including temperament and genetics (Roisman & Fraley, 2006, 2008), maternal depression (Teti, Gelfand, Messinger, & Isabella, 1995), family conflict (Davies & Cummings, 1994), and economic well-being (van IJzendoorn & Kroonenberg, 1988). We emphasize sensitive responsive caregiving here partly because it is one of the factors that is emphasized the most in the attachment literature and because of space limitations; we encourage interested readers to consult Belsky and Fearon (2008) for broader coverage.

# Processes that promote continuity: Theory and research

One reason that researchers have invested so much attention in studying the development of attachment in the context of infant—caregiver relationships is that, theoretically, those early attachment bonds serve as the *foundation* for subsequent interpersonal experiences. That is, early caregiving experiences help to seed the way in which interpersonal interactions unfold. As children navigate new social relationships (e.g., relationships with siblings, peers, teachers), they draw upon the experiences they have had in previous attachment relationships. Thus when a secure child enters into a relationship with a new person (e.g., a teacher), the child may assume that this new person will be warm and encouraging rather than threatening or punitive. In short, although socialization processes are thought to help give rise to whether children construct secure or insecure working models, those developing models are thought to play a self-sustaining role in shaping the interpersonal environment itself through selection effects.

Bowlby (1973) called attention to two broad pathways through which people may construct or shape their environments. The most salient of these are psychodynamic in nature. Namely, individuals are likely to interpret the behavior of others in ways that are consistent with the expectations they already hold. A secure person, for example, may be more likely to give others the benefit of the doubt. An insecure person, in contrast, may be more likely to construe ambiguous social signals as signs of exclusion. This dynamic process is likely to lead people to have interpersonal experiences that confirm, rather than disconfirm, the assumptions they hold about themselves and their social worlds (Dykas & Cassidy, 2011).

Collins (1996) conducted a study on adult attachment which illustrates these processes nicely. In her research, people were asked to imagine a variety of scenarios in which the behavior of a loved one was potentially ambiguous—the behavior could be harmless or could represent a threat to the relationship. Although each participant read identical scenarios, the way participants reacted to the scenarios differed dramatically. Some people, for example, believed that the ambiguous behavior of their partner represented an attempt to make them feel jealous; other people wrote the behavior off as if it represented the partner's friendly and outgoing disposition. Importantly, Collins (1996) found that how people responded—the attributions they made about their partner's behavior—was a function of their attachment styles. People who were relatively insecure, for example, were more likely than those who were secure to construe the partner's ambiguous behavior as a threat to the relationship.

Collin's research shows that, even when different people are exposed to the same information, the way they interpret that information is biased by their working models. Thus what people "see" and what they experience tend to reinforce rather than challenge the assumptions they already hold about the world. This dynamic provides one potential mechanism of continuity. It is difficult for people to modify their assumptions about the availability and responsiveness of other people in their lives if they are predisposed to view the behavior of others as negligent or insensitive.

The second broad pathway that Bowlby highlighted is person-driven effects on social context (e.g., selection effects, niche picking, and interpersonal influence). In short, people are likely to select themselves into environments that are consistent with their existing dispositions. For example, Frazier, Byer, Fischer, Wright, and DeBord (1996) demonstrated that adults who were secure were more likely to be attracted to potential mates who were also secure (see also Pietromonaco & Carnelley, 1994). Research also suggests that insecure people may drive secure partners away in dating contexts. In a striking demonstration of this process, McClure and Lydon (2014) studied people in a speed-dating paradigm and found that individuals who were insecure-anxious with respect to attachment were more likely to come across in undesirable ways, expressing greater verbal disfluencies and interpersonal awkwardness. These interpersonal behaviors, in turn, have the potential to undermine the formation of intimate relationships, potentially reinforcing the insecurities that highly anxious people already have.

## Processes that promote change: Theory and research

On the surface, the presence of selection effects would seem to suggest that attachment patterns established in early childhood would be relatively enduring—that secure infants would also be highly likely to be secure in adolescence or as young adults. And, although there is some evidence for continuity in attachment patterns across time (see Fraley, 2002), the overall stability from infancy to early adulthood is relatively weak (see Groh et al., 2014; Pinquart, Feußner, & Ahnert, 2013).

It is important to keep in mind that attachment theory emphasizes both selection and socialization effects. That is, part of the explanation for why some children are more secure than others has to do with the quality of their caregiving experiences. But these influences do not necessarily remain homogenous over time (Pianta, Sroufe, & Egeland, 1989). Thus, to the extent to which working models capture variation in people's interpersonal experiences, those working models should change to some degree. The consequence of such processes, when considered over long periods of time, is that those changes should gradually diminish the stability of individual differences in attachment styles (see Fraley, 2002; Fraley & Roberts, 2005).

What kinds of factors lead to change in attachment patterns? There has been an enormous amount of work on this topic over the decades and, as such, there is not adequate space to review it here (see Gillath et al., 2016). Suffice to say, there are multiple factors that have been linked to changes in attachment organization in adulthood alone, including the transition to parenthood (Feeney, Alexander, Noller, & Hohaus, 2003; Simpson, Rholes, Campbell, & Wilson, 2003), relationship break-ups (Kirkpatrick & Hazan, 1994; Sbarra & Hazan, 2008), the experience of war-related trauma (Mikulincer, Ein-Dor, Solomon, & Shaver, 2011), intimate relationship conflict and support (Chow, Ruhl, & Buhrmester, 2014; Green, Furrer, & McAllister, 2011; La Guardia, Ryan, Couchman, & Deci, 2000), the meaning or construal of life events (Davila & Sargent, 2003), stable vulnerability factors (Davila, Burge, & Hammen, 1997), and therapy (Taylor, Rietzschel, Danquah, & Berry, 2015).

One of the big questions in the literature concerns the extent to which various experiences have the potential to lead to enduring versus transient changes in attachment patterns (Fraley & Brumbaugh, 2004; Fraley & Roisman, 2015; Fraley, Roisman, & Haltigan, 2013). It is possible, for example, that the experience of a breakup has the potential to undermine a person's sense of security, at least temporarily. But, with a bit of time and some corrective experiences, it is likely that the person will return to his or her prebreakup attachment pattern. Researchers are currently trying to tackle these kinds of issues by examining how early experiences might shape social adaptation (Fraley et al., 2013) and how transitions in adulthood shape state- and trait-level forms of security (Karantzas, Deboeck, Gillath, & Fraley, 2017).

# New directions

We have provided a broad overview of theory and research on some of the factors that shape a person's attachment style and the mechanisms that might promote both continuity and change across time. Many of the themes emphasized in the attachment literature mirror those that are emphasized in the broader literature on personality development, such as the interplay of socialization and selection effects (see Caspi & Roberts, 2001). We close this chapter with a brief discussion of some themes (i.e., canalization, differentiation) that are pertinent to the study of individual differences in attachment that, in our view, have not received much attention in the recent literature on personality traits (cf. Murphy, 1947). We also discuss some recent work on age-related changes in attachment—research that fits well with recent efforts in personality psychology to understand mean-level changes in personality traits (Lucas & Donnellan, 2011; Specht, Egloff, & Schmukle, 2011). We hope this discussion will be useful not only for inspiring future research on attachment, but in calling attention to some of the ways in which developmental models on attachment and personality can mutually inform one another.

## Canalization

Bowlby believed that the transactions that take place between children and their social environments have a reinforcing effect on the working models that children construct. Drawing on Waddington's (1957) ideas about cell development (see Fraley & Brumbaugh, 2004, for a review), Bowlby argued that an individual's developmental pathway becomes increasingly canalized or buffered over time, such that experiences that are incompatible with a person's working models are likely to nudge the individual off his or her developmental course, but only temporarily; the individual will gradually revert to the trajectory that was previously established.

There are two implications of this process that researchers have only recently begun to explore. First, this dynamic suggests that the "same" experience can have a more enduring effect on a person when it takes place early in development rather than later in development. Second, this dynamic suggests that the stability of individual differences in attachment may be weaker in childhood than they are in adulthood. We review each of these points in more depth below.

### Developmental timing: Early versus later

The canalization model implies that specific experiences that take place early in development have the potential to leave a greater mark on personality functioning than similar experiences that take place later in time (Fraley & Brumbaugh, 2004).

Fraley and Heffernan (2013) examined parental divorce as a case in point. Parental divorce is a prototypical example of the disruption of family and attachment relationships, one that has the potential to have complex and negative consequences for child development. Does the timing of parental divorce matter in shaping interpersonal functioning? Namely, are the downstream consequences of parental divorce greater if the divorce takes place early in a child's life as opposed to later? A traditional way of addressing this question is to study a sample of children of a common age (e.g., 14−16 years old) and split children from divorced families into two groups: those whose parents divorced when the child was under the age of 5, and those whose parents divorced when the child was 5 or older. The key limitation of this approach is that the two groups not only differ in the age at which their parents divorced (i.e., the *timing* of parental divorce), but the amount of time that has transpired since the divorce. The first group, for example, has had more time for the potential negative consequences of divorce to manifest and accumulate. Although the accumulation of negative consequences is a legitimate pathway through which early parental divorce could have its effects on developmental outcomes, one might expect such effects to exist regardless of whether the divorce took place early or later in the child's life. The evidence for canalization effects per se would be stronger if the timing of the event (age of parental divorce) could be separated from the effects of time per se (i.e., the amount of time that has transpired since the event).

One way to untangle these distinct effects is by studying people who vary in the age at which their parents divorced (i.e., developmental timing) and the length of time that has transpired since the divorce took place (i.e., time). Fraley and Heffernan (2013) examined this issue by assessing the attachment security of adults in their current relationships with their parents. They found that people who reported their parents had divorced when they were younger were more insecure in their parental relationships than people whose parents had divorced when they were older. Importantly, this association was observed when statistically controlling the amount of time that had passed since the divorce. This suggests that the same event (i.e., parental divorce) has the potential to leave a stronger mark on attachment security when it takes place early rather than later in development.

## Is stability weaker in childhood than adulthood?

Yes. There are now a variety of longitudinal studies that have examined the stability of attachment patterns across a variety of ages and varying test—retest intervals. These studies were meta-analyzed by Fraley (2002) and, more recently, by Pinquart et al. (2013). What these meta-analyses reveal is that, when the length of the test—retest interval is held constant, the overall test—retest stability of attachment is higher in adulthood than it is in childhood. Fraley and Brumbaugh (2004), for example, estimated that the test—retest of attachment over a 10-year period in childhood was approximately 0.30, whereas for adults the test—retest over a 10-year period is approximately 0.50 (see Fig. 17.1).

## Differentiation

Historically, attachment researchers have treated attachment style as a trait-like or **global** variable—one that captures the way people think about themselves and others across relationships. One reason for this emphasis is that researchers studying adult attachment dynamics have been interested in the ways in which interpersonal experiences, such as those that take place in childhood and adolescence, are generalized and applied to novel experiences, such as those that take place in romantic relationships (Hazan & Shaver, 1987).

But attachment theory also posits that people develop *relationship-specific attachment representations* for important people in their lives (Collins & Read, 1994; Collins, Guichard, Ford, & Feeney, 2004). Collins and Read (1994) formalized these ideas in their *hierarchical model* of attachment representations (see Fig. 17.2). Specifically, they argued that attachment representations vary within a

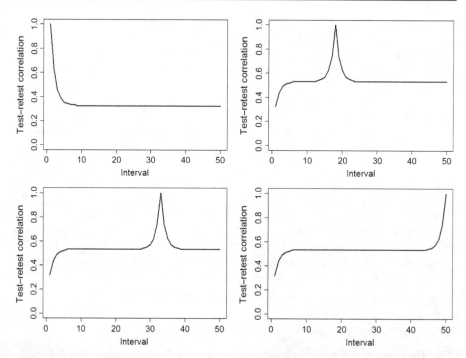

**Figure 17.1** Model-predicted test—retest correlations in attachment security across varying temporal intervals. The first panel shows the predicted stability from age 1 to all subsequent ages (1—50). The second panel shows the predicted stability between age 18 and all ages that precede it (1—17) and all ages that follow it (19—50). Likewise, the third panel shows the predicted stability between age 33 and all prior and subsequent ages. The last panel shows the predicted stability between age 50 and all ages that precede it. What these graphs demonstrate is that the overall degree of stability expected in childhood is lower than that expected in adulthood.

person in at least two crucial ways. First, attachment representations vary in their *generality versus specificity*. Thus people have attachment models that are relevant to how they see themselves and others in general (e.g., "People are trustworthy"). But people also have models that represent the way they understand and relate to specific people in their lives (e.g., "My spouse is trustworthy"). Although it is assumed that general and specific attachment representations tend to be aligned in most individuals, there is no theoretical requirement that they be perfectly aligned.

Second, attachment representations can vary in quality and content *across specific relational domains*. That is, the way a person relates to her mother might be different than the way she relates to her best friend. Because each relationship has the potential to have its own unique history and interpersonal signature, the expectations a person constructs about whether her romantic partner is likely to be available and supportive might differ in important ways from the expectations she has constructed about whether her parents will be available and supportive.

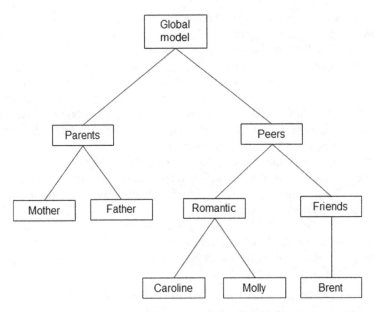

**Figure 17.2** The hierarchical model of attachment (Collins & Read, 1994). According to this model, attachment representations vary both in terms of their (1) generality versus specificity (as aligned vertically in the figure) and (2) their relational domain (e.g., parents vs peers, as aligned horizontally in the figure).

Recent research has emphasized the value of these distinctions. Global attachment security, for example, tends to correlate 0.30 to 0.50 with attachment security measured in specific relationship domains (i.e., relationships with mothers, fathers, romantic partners, and best friends) (Fraley, Hudson, Heffernan, & Segal, 2015). Thus although people who are secure in general also tend to be secure across various relationships (i.e., there is a general factor), there are exceptions to this trend. Recent research also reveals that there is considerable heterogeneity across specific relationships. Although people who are secure in their parental relationships are also more likely to be secure in their romantic relationships, these associations are relatively modest, typically averaging around $r = 0.20$ (Fraley, Heffernan, Vicary, & Brumbaugh, 2011; Klohnen, Weller, Luo, & Choe, 2005; Sibley & Overall, 2010). Taken together, these data suggest that, although there are commonalities in the attachment patterns that people experience across their relationships, there can also be discontinuities in the way in which an individual relates to important people in his or her life. Stated differently, not everyone who is secure in their relationship with their spouse is also secure in their relationships with their parents (even if they are secure more generally).

According to attachment theory, differentiation in working models should be a function of interpersonal experience. Unfortunately, there has been little empirical research designed to directly examine these issues. We outline some specific ideas here in an effort to help set the tone for future research in this area.

One way to pursue this theme from a developmental angle is to examine the ways in which working models in different relationships diverge across time. Because the socialization assumption in attachment theory holds that attachment representations are a function of people's interpersonal experiences (e.g., repeated experiences of feeling accepted and secure vs unloved or misunderstood), the representations that people construct of specific relationship partners should come to diverge from the representations of other people (e.g., parents) over time. This is not to say that security across relational contexts should dramatically diverge, nor is it to say that such divergence will continue unabated across time.

Another way to examine these themes is by studying the ways in which changes to representations in one domain affect representations in other domains. When people experience breakups in their romantic relationships, it appears that they become more insecure (Kirkpatrick & Hazan, 1994; Ruvolo, Fabin, & Ruvolo, 2001; Scharfe & Cole, 2006). But do they become more insecure specifically in the romantic domain? Or does that experience also undermine—even temporarily—the sense of trust they have in others more generally, including, for example, their parents?

## Age-related shifts in attachment

Up to this point, our discussion of continuity and change has largely concerned the stability of individual differences—whether people who are relatively secure at one point in time are also likely to be relatively secure at another point in time. This is often referred to as "rank-order stability" in the personality literature because the primary concern is whether the relative ordering of people is the same across time. Another important form of stability, however, concerns mean-level or absolute stability. This is relevant to understanding whether, on average, people tend to increase (or decrease) in security across time. These two forms of stability are conceptually and mathematically independent of one another because people could preserve their rank-ordering perfectly across two time points even if everyone became more secure, on average. And, similarly, even if the average levels of security were the same across two time points, if the people who were most secure at time 1 became the least secure at time 2 (and vice versa), mean-level stability could be perfect despite rank-order stability being zero.

Several studies have now examined the ways in which attachment varies across the lifecycle, using cross-sectional methods (Chopik, Edelstein, & Fraley, 2013; Konrath, Chopik, Hsing, & O'Brien, 2014; Magai et al., 2001). One recent study has examined both global and relationship-specific attachment in the ways discussed previously (Hudson, Fraley, Chopik, & Heffernan, 2016). Hudson and his colleagues assessed people's general attachment pattern in addition to attachment in the context of relationships with parents, romantic partners, and best friends. They found that people generally became less anxious with respect to attachment across time. That is, younger adults reported greater attachment anxiety than older adults. In contrast, there were few age differences in avoidance. For the most part, global avoidance tended to be relatively stable across age groups.

The patterns of age-related differences varied across specific relational contexts, however. Younger people, for example, were generally more anxious in romantic and friendship relationships than older people. But the reverse was true in parental relationships: in parental relationships, younger people were less anxious than older people. Why might this be the case? One possibility is that, as people's parents age, people become less confident in the availability and responsiveness of their parents, potentially heightening the sense of anxiety people feel in those relationships.

In both peer (romantic and friendship relationships) and parental relationships, people seemed to become more avoidant across time. That is, older people were more avoidant toward their partners, friends, and parents than younger adults. One potential reason for this shift is that role norms for adults typically emphasize a greater need for autonomy and independence as people make the transition from young to middle adulthood. It is also possible that the increase in avoidance in romantic relationships mirrors shifts in martial satisfaction that are commonly observed in long-term marriages. It is important to note that global avoidance, however, did not show systematic, replicable age differences across time. This suggests that, as a general rule, people do not become more avoidant across time, but the dynamics of specific relationships may create a press for greater degrees of independence with age.

## Summary

The purpose of this chapter was to review briefly theory and research on what makes some people more secure in their attachment patterns than others. We highlighted some of the classic work that has examined the role of sensitive responsiveness as an antecedent to infant attachment patterns. We also reviewed some of the processes that may lead early attachment patterns to be sustained across time. However, we also emphasized the fact that attachment theory is not only a theory of selection, but a theory of socialization and, as such, attachment representations should be open to change over time. The consequence of this emphasis is that continuity in attachment should be considered an empirical issue rather than a strong assumption of the theory per se. Having said that, we should note that there is evidence of weak stability from infancy to adulthood (Fraley, 2002; Pinquart et al., 2013). And, as expected on the basis of canalization principles, there is evidence of higher levels of stability in adulthood than childhood. We believe that some promising research directions include examining canalization processes in more detail and exploring the implications of the hierarchical model of attachment for how we understand the dynamics of stability and change.

There were many issues we did not have space to discuss. For one, we know that individual differences in adult attachment styles are multidetermined. In other words, what makes someone secure is not simply a matter of what his or her early experiences were like with caregivers. There is a growing body of work suggesting that working models are sensitive to ongoing experiences and that the cumulative history—not just the origins—of a person's interpersonal experiences is important for understanding who they become (Fraley, Roisman, Booth-LaForce, Owen, & Holland, 2013). We believe that there is still a lot of work that remains to be done at the interface of personality development and attachment theory.

# References

Ainsworth, M. D. S., Blehar, M., Waters, E., & Wall, S. (1978). *Patterns of attachment: A psychological study of the strange situation.* Hillsdale, NJ: Erlbaum.

Bakermans-Kranenburg, M. J., Van Ijzendoorn, M. H., & Juffer, F. (2003). Less is more: Meta-analyses of sensitivity and attachment interventions in early childhood. *Psychological Bulletin, 129,* 195–215.

Bartholomew, K., & Horowitz, L. (1991). Attachment styles among young adults: A test of a four category model. *Journal of Personality and Social Psychology, 61,* 226–244.

Belsky, J., & Fearon, R. M. P. (2008). Precursors of attachment security. In J. Cassidy, & P. R. Shaver (Eds.), *Adult attachment: Theory, research, and clinical applications* (2nd ed., pp. 295–316). New York, NY: Guilford Press.

Bowlby, J. (1969/1982). *Attachment and loss: Vol. 1. Attachment* (2nd ed.). New York, NY: Basic Books.

Bowlby, J. (1973). *Attachment and loss: Vol. 2. Separation: Anxiety and anger.* New York, NY: Basic Books.

Bretherton, I., & Munholland, K. A. (2008). Internal working models in attachment relationships: Elaborating a central construct in attachment theory. In J. Cassidy, & P. R. Shaver (Eds.), *Handbook of attachment: Theory, research, and clinical applications* (2nd ed., pp. 102–127). New York, NY: Guilford Press.

Caspi, A., & Roberts, B. W. (2001). Personality development across the life course: The argument for change and continuity. *Psychological Inquiry, 12,* 49–66.

Chopik, W. J., Edelstein, R. S., & Fraley, R. C. (2013). From the cradle to the grave: Age differences in attachment from early adulthood to old age. *Journal of Personality, 81,* 171–183.

Chow, C. M., Ruhl, H., & Buhrmester, D. (2014). Reciprocal associations between friendship attachment and relational experiences in adolescence. *Journal of Social and Personal Relationships, 33,* 122–146.

Colin, V. L. (1996). *Human attachment.* New York, NY: McGraw Hill.

Collins, N. L. (1996). Working models of attachment: Implications for explanation, emotion, and behavior. *Journal of Personality and Social Psychology, 71,* 810–832.

Collins, N. L., Guichard, A. C., Ford, M. B., & Feeney, B. C. (2004). Working models of attachment: New developments and emerging themes. In W. S. Rholes, & J. A. Simpson (Eds.), *Adult attachment: Theory, research, and clinical implications* (pp. 196–239). New York, NY: Guilford.

Collins, N., & Read, S. (1994). Cognitive representations of attachment: The structure and function of working models. In K. Bartholomew, & D. Perlman (Eds.), *Attachment processes in adulthood: Advances in personal relationships* (Vol. 5, pp. 53–90). London: Kingsley.

Crowell, J., Fraley, R. C., & Shaver, P. R. (2008). Measures of individual differences in adolescent and adult attachment. In J. Cassidy, & P. R. Shaver (Eds.), *Handbook of attachment: Theory, research, and clinical applications* (2nd ed., pp. 599–634). New York, NY: Guilford Press.

Davies, P. T., & Cummings, E. M. (1994). Marital conflict and child adjustment: An emotional security hypothesis. *Psychological Bulletin, 116*, 387–411.

Davila, J., Burge, D., & Hammen, C. (1997). Why does attachment style change? *Journal of Personality and Social Psychology, 73*, 826–838.

Davila, J., & Sargent, E. (2003). The meaning of life (events) predicts changes in attachment security. *Personality and Social Psychology Bulletin, 29*, 1383–1395.

Dykas, M. J., & Cassidy, J. (2011). Attachment and the processing of social information across the life span: Theory and evidence. *Psychological Bulletin, 137*, 19–46.

Feeney, J., Alexander, R., Noller, P., & Hohaus, L. (2003). Attachment insecurity, depression, and the transition to parenthood. *Personal Relationships, 10*, 475–493.

Fraley, R. C. (2002). Attachment stability from infancy to adulthood: Meta-analysis and dynamic modeling of developmental mechanisms. *Personality and Social Psychology Review, 6*, 123–151.

Fraley, R. C., & Brumbaugh, C. C. (2004). A dynamical systems approach to understanding stability and change in attachment security. In W. S. Rholes, & J. A. Simpson (Eds.), *Adult attachment: Theory, research, and clinical implications* (pp. 86–132). New York, NY: Guilford Press.

Fraley, R. C., & Heffernan, M. E. (2013). Attachment and parental divorce: A test of the diffusion and sensitive period hypotheses. *Personality and Social Psychology Bulletin, 39*, 1199–1213.

Fraley, R. C., Heffernan, M. E., Vicary, A. M., & Brumbaugh, C. C. (2011). The Experiences in Close Relationships–Relationship Structures questionnaire: A method for assessing attachment orientations across relationships. *Psychological Assessment, 23*, 615–625.

Fraley, R. C., & Roberts, B. W. (2005). Patterns of continuity: A dynamic model for conceptualizing the stability of individual differences in psychological constructs across the life course. *Psychological Review, 112*, 60–74.

Fraley, R. C., Hudson, N. W., Heffernan, M. E., & Segal, N. (2015). Are adult attachment styles categorical or dimensional? A taxometric analysis of general and relationship-specific attachment orientations. *Journal of Personality and Social Psychology, 109*, 354–368.

Fraley, R. C., & Roisman, G. I. (2015). Do early caregiving experiences leave an enduring or transient mark on developmental adaptation? *Current Opinion in Psychology, 1*, 101–106.

Fraley, R. C., Roisman, G. I., Booth-LaForce, C., Owen, M. T., & Holland, A. S. (2013). Interpersonal and genetic origins of adult attachment styles: A longitudinal study from infancy to early adulthood. *Journal of Personality and Social Psychology, 104*, 8817–8838.

Fraley, R. C., Roisman, G. I., & Haltigan, J. D. (2013). The legacy of early experiences in development: Formalizing alternative models of how early experiences are carried forward over time. *Developmental Psychology, 49*, 109–126.

Fraley, R. C., & Spieker, S. J. (2003). What are the differences between dimensional and categorical models of individual differences in attachment? Reply to Cassidy (2003), Cummings (2003), Sroufe (2003), and Waters and Beauchaine (2003). *Developmental Psychology, 39*, 423–429.

Frazier, P. A., Byer, A. L., Fischer, A. R., Wright, D. M., & DeBord, K. A. (1996). Adult attachment style and partner choice: Correlational and experimental findings. *Personal Relationships*, *3*, 117—136.

Gillath, O, Karantzas, G, & Fraley, RC (2016). *Adult attachment: A concise guide to theory and research*. New York, NY: Academic Press.

Green, B. L., Furrer, C. J., & McAllister, C. L. (2011). Does attachment style influence social support or the other way around? A longitudinal study of Early Head Start mothers. *Attachment & Human Development*, *13*, 27—47.

Groh, A. M., Roisman, G. I., Booth-LaForce, C., Fraley, R. C., Owen, M. T., Cox, M. J., & Burchinal, M. R. (2014). Stability of attachment security from infancy to late adolescence. In C. Booth-LaForce & G. I. Roisman (Eds.), The Adult Attachment Interview: Psychometrics, stability and change from infancy, and developmental origins. *Monographs of the Society for Research in Child Development*, 79, 51—66.

Grossmann, K., Grossmann, K. E., Spangler, G., Suess, G., & Unzner, L. (1985). Maternal sensitivity and newborns' orientation responses as related to quality of attachment in northern Germany. *Monographs of the Society for Research in Child Development*, 233—256.

Hazan, C., & Shaver, P. R. (1987). Romantic love conceptualized as an attachment process. *Journal of Personality and Social Psychology*, *52*, 511—524.

Hudson, N. W., Fraley, R. C., Chopik, W. J., & Heffernan, M. E. (2016). Not all attachment relationships change alike: Normative cross-sectional age trajectories in attachment to romantic partners, best friends, and parents across the lifespan. *Journal of Research in Personality*, *59*, 44—55.

John, O. P., Robins, R. W., & Pervin, L. A. (2008). *Handbook of personality: Theory and research* (3rd ed.). New York, NY: Guilford.

Karantzas, G., Deboeck, P. R., Gillath, O., & Fraley, R. C. (2017). *Stability and change in attachment anxiety and avoidance over time*. Manuscript in preparation.

Kirkpatrick, L. A., & Hazan, C. (1994). Attachment styles and close relationships: A four-year prospective study. *Personal Relationships*, *1*, 123—142.

Klohnen, E. C., Weller, J. A., Luo, S., & Choe, M. (2005). Organization and predictive power of general and relationship-specific attachment models: One for all, and all for one? *Personality and Social Psychology Bulletin*, *31*, 1665—1682.

Konrath, S. H., Chopik, W. J., Hsing, C. K., & O'Brien, E. (2014). Changes in adult attachment styles in American College students over time a meta-analysis. *Personality and Social Psychology Review*, *18*, 326—348.

La Guardia, J. G., Ryan, R. M., Couchman, C. E., & Deci, E. L. (2000). Within-person variation in security of attachment: A self-determination theory perspective on attachment, need fulfillment, and well-being. *Journal of Personality and Social Psychology*, *79*, 367—384.

Lucas, R. E., & Donnellan, M. B. (2011). Personality development across the life span: Longitudinal analyses with a national sample from Germany. *Journal of Personality and Social Psychology*, *101*, 847—861.

Magai, C., Cohen, C., Milburn, N., Thorpe, B., McPherson, R., & Peralta, D. (2001). Attachment styles in older European American and African American adults. *The Journals of Gerontology Series B: Psychological Sciences and Social Sciences*, *56*, S28—S35.

McClure, M. J., & Lydon, J. E. (2014). Anxiety doesn't become you: How attachment anxiety compromises relational opportunities. *Journal of Personality and Social Psychology*, *106*, 89—111.

Mikulincer, M., Ein-Dor, T., Solomon, Z., & Shaver, P. R. (2011). Trajectories of attachment insecurities over a 17-year period: A latent growth curve analysis of the impact of war captivity and posttraumatic stress disorder. *Journal of Social and Clinical Psychology*, *30*, 960–984.

Mikulincer, M., Florian, V., & Weller, A. (1993). Attachment styles, coping strategies, and posttraumatic psychological distress: The impact of the Gulf War in Israel. *Journal of Personality and Social Psychology*, *64*, 817–826.

Mikulincer, M., & Shaver, P. R. (2007). *Attachment in adulthood: Structure, dynamics, and change*. New York, NY: Guilford Press.

Muris, P., Meesters, C., van Melick, M., & Zwambag, L. (2001). Self-reported attachment style, attachment quality, and symptoms of anxiety and depression in young adolescents. *Personality and Individual Differences*, *30*, 809–818.

Murphy, G. (1947). *Personality: A biosocial approach to origins and structure*. New York, NY: Harper.

Noftle, E. E., & Shaver, P. R. (2006). Attachment dimensions and the Big Five personality traits: Associations and comparative ability to predict relationship quality. *Journal of Research in Personality*, *40*, 179–208.

Pianta, R. C., Sroufe, L. A., & Egeland, B. (1989). Continuity and discontinuity in maternal sensitivity at 6, 24, and 42 months in a high-risk sample. *Child Development*, 481–487.

Pietromonaco, P. R., & Carnelley, K. B. (1994). Gender and working models of attachment: Consequences for perceptions of self and romantic relationships. *Personal Relationships*, *1*, 63–82.

Pinquart, M., Feußner, C., & Ahnert, L. (2013). Meta-analytic evidence for stability in attachments from infancy to early adulthood. *Attachment & Human Development*, *15*, 189–218.

Roisman, G. I., & Fraley, R. C. (2006). The limits of genetic influence: A behavior–genetic analysis of infant-caregiver relationship quality and temperament. *Child Development*, *77*, 1656–1667.

Roisman, G. I., & Fraley, R. C. (2008). A behavior–genetic study of parenting quality, infant attachment security, and their covariation in a nationally representative sample. *Developmental Psychology*, *44*, 831–839.

Ruvolo, A. P., Fabin, L. A., & Ruvolo, C. M. (2001). Relationship experiences and change in attachment characteristics of young adults: The role of relationship breakups and conflict avoidance. *Personal Relationships*, *8*, 265–281.

Sbarra, D. A., & Hazan, C. (2008). Coregulation, dysregulation, self-regulation: An integrative analysis and empirical agenda for understanding adult attachment, separation, loss, and recovery. *Personality and Social Psychology Review*, *12*, 141–167.

Scharfe, E., & Cole, V. (2006). Stability and change of attachment representations during emerging adulthood: An examination of mediators and moderators of change. *Personal Relationships*, *13*, 363–374.

Sibley, C. G., & Overall, N. C. (2010). Modeling the hierarchical structure of personality–attachment associations: Domain diffusion versus domain differentiation. *Journal of Social and Personal Relationships*, *27*, 47–70.

Simpson, J. A. (1990). Influence of attachment styles on romantic relationships. *Journal of Personality and Social Psychology*, *59*, 971–980.

Simpson, J. A., Rholes, W. S., Campbell, L., & Wilson, C. L. (2003). Changes in attachment orientations across the transition to parenthood. *Journal of Experimental Social Psychology*, *39*, 317–331.

Specht, J., Egloff, B., & Schmukle, S. C. (2011). Stability and change of personality across the life course: The impact of age and major life events on mean-level and rank-order stability of the Big Five. *Journal of Personality and Social Psychology*, *101*, 862–882.

Solomon, J., & George, C. (2008). The measurement of attachment security and related constructs in infancy and early childhood. In J. Cassidy, & P. R. Shaver (Eds.), *Handbook of attachment: Theory, research, and clinical applications* (2nd ed., pp. 383–416). New York, NY: Guilford Press.

Suomi, S. J. (2008). Attachment in Rhesus monkeys. In J. Cassidy, & P. R. Shaver (Eds.), *Handbook of attachment: Theory, research, and clinical applications* (2nd ed., pp. 173–191). New York, NY: Guilford Press.

Taylor, P., Rietzschel, J., Danquah, A., & Berry, K. (2015). Changes in attachment representations during psychological therapy. *Psychotherapy Research*, *25*, 222–238.

Teti, D. M., Gelfand, D. M., Messinger, D. S., & Isabella, R. (1995). Maternal depression and the quality of early attachment: An examination of infants, preschoolers, and their mothers. *Developmental Psychology*, *31*, 364–376.

Van den Boom, D. (1990). Preventive intervention and the quality of mother–infant interaction and infant exploration in irritable infants. In W. Koops, H. J. G. Soppe, J. L. van der Linden, P. C. M. Molenaar, & J. J. F. Schroots (Eds.), *Developmental psychology behind the dikes: An outline of developmental psychological research in the Netherlands*. Delft, Netherlands: Uitgeverij Eburon.

van den Boom, D. C. (1994). The influence of temperament and mothering on attachment and exploration: An experimental manipulation of sensitive responsiveness among lower-class mothers with irritable infants. *Child Development*, *65*, 1457–1477.

van IJzendoorn, M. H., & Kroonenberg, P. M. (1988). Cross-cultural patterns of attachment: A meta-analysis of the strange situation. *Child Development*, *59*, 147–156.

van IJzendoorn, M. H., Juffer, F., & Duyvesteyn, M. G. (1995). Breaking the intergenerational cycle of insecure attachment: A review of the effects of attachment-based interventions on maternal sensitivity and infant security. *Journal of Child Psychology and Psychiatry and Allied Disciplines*, *36*, 225-225.

Waddington, C. H. (1957). *The strategy of the genes: A discussion of some aspects of theoretical biology*. London: Allen & Unwin.

# Identity formation in adolescence and young adulthood

# 18

*Theo A. Klimstra and Lotte van Doeselaar*
Tilburg University, Tilburg, The Netherlands

Adolescence is among the most confusing periods in the lifespan, largely because it is when we start to doubt whatever our parents taught us while we struggle with finding something new to hold onto and guide us through life. In other words, a process known as identity formation starts in adolescence.

Contemporary psychological research on identity was initiated by Erikson (1950, 1968), who described identity formation as a search for a new sense of sameness and continuity in order to avoid role confusion. Forming a stable identity is important, because role confusion might manifest itself in the form of "delinquent and outright psychotic episodes" (Erikson, 1950). Although identity formation itself only starts in adolescence because it requires cognitive capacities that are only available by then, it should be noted that the concept of adolescent identity formation is embedded in lifespan theory of psychosocial development. This theory divides the lifespan into several stages, and in each of these, a certain ego quality needs to be developed. Because the successful development of ego qualities in later stages in life is dependent on the development of ego qualities in previous life stages, adolescent identity formation is for example affected by the development of trust in the first years of life. Thus, although identity formation itself might begin in adolescence, part of its foundation is already formed earlier in life.

Erikson's writings on identity were not specific enough to be empirically tested. Therefore, Marcia (1966) provided an empirical definition of identity by distinguishing processes of commitment and exploration. Commitment reflects whether individuals have made choices in certain life domains and engage in activities to implement these choices. Exploration refers to comparing different possible commitments before making a choice. Marcia's model has inspired numerous studies, but has been criticized for lacking in detail regarding the exact underlying processes of identity formation (Bosma, 1985; Grotevant, 1987). To overcome this problem, new models of identity formation were developed.

Two of these models are currently particularly prominent. The three-dimension model by Meeus and Crocetti (Crocetti, Rubini, & Meeus, 2008) distinguishes commitment (reflecting the confidence derived from identity choices), in-depth exploration (reflecting on current commitments without necessarily looking for alternatives), and reconsideration (questioning current commitments and considering alternatives). The second model, by Luyckx and colleagues (Luyckx, Goossens,

Soenens, & Beyers, 2006; Luyckx, Schwartz, Berzonsky et al., 2008), distinguishes five dimensions. Commitment is split into dimensions of commitment making (the degree to which commitments to follow a certain direction in life are made) and identification with commitment (the degree to which commitments contribute to a sense of self and provide certainty in life). Exploration is trichotomized into exploration in depth, exploration in breadth, and ruminative exploration. Exploration in depth is the same as in-depth exploration. Exploration in breadth is somewhat similar to reconsideration, but emphasizes looking for new commitments without necessarily comparing these to existing commitments. Ruminative exploration refers to endlessly mulling over what direction to pursue in life, without coming to a satisfying solution.

These two new models partly overlap with each other and with Marcia's (1966) original model, as can be seen in Table 18.1. What is new compared to Marcia's model, is that both new models capture identity formation as a dual-cycle process (Luyckx, Goossens, & Soenens, 2006; Meeus, 2011) with an identity formation cycle and an identity evaluation cycle. In the identity formation cycle, individuals try to (re-)establish stable commitments. Processes fitting this cycle are reconsideration (Crocetti et al., 2008; Meeus, 2011), and commitment making and exploration in breadth (Luyckx, Soenens, & Goossens, 2006). The identity evaluation cycle is characterized by in-depth exploration (Crocetti et al., 2008; Meeus, 2011) and identification with commitment (Luyckx, Schwartz, Berzonsky et al., 2008). As Meeus and Crocetti's commitment dimension is highly similar to Luyckx' identification with commitment dimension (Waterman, 2015), it also fits the best in this cycle. Ruminative exploration may occur in any cycle (Luyckx, Teppers, Klimstra, & Rassart, 2014).

**Table 18.1 Conceptual overlap and specificities between Marcia's identity status model, the five-dimension model by Luyckx, and the three-dimension model by Meeus and Crocetti**

| Identity models | | |
|---|---|---|
| *Marcia's original model* | *Luyckx's five-dimension model* | *Meeus/Crocetti's three-dimension model* |
| Commitment | Commitment making<br>Identification with commitment | Commitment |
| Exploration | Exploration in breadth<br>Ruminative exploration<br>Exploration in depth | Reconsideration<br><br>In-depth exploration |

*Note*: Dimensions that overlap between the models have cells that overlap in the table. For example, Marcia's commitment, Meeus/Crocetti's commitment, and Luyckx's identification with commitment overlap, whereas Luyckx' commitment making overlaps with Marcia's commitment, but not with Meeus/Crocetti's commitment.

## Identity development: General trends, developmental heterogeneity, and possible mechanisms

Until recently, relatively few studies focused on developmental changes in identity formation and even fewer of these had a longitudinal research design (Meeus, 1996). A meta-analysis on studies using Marcia's (1966) classic approach to identity formation (Kroger, Martinussen, & Marcia, 2010) seemed to confirm a basic hypothesis of identity development, stating that individuals' sense of identity strengthens as they grow older (Waterman, 1982).

With the newly developed models (Crocetti et al., 2008; Luyckx, Schwartz, Berzonsky et al., 2008), a more detailed perspective on identity formation has been attained. A longitudinal study covering ages 12−20 (Klimstra, Hale, Raaijmakers, Branje, & Meeus, 2010) uncovered that levels of commitment hardly changed throughout adolescence. However, levels of reconsideration, which is a negative indicator (i.e., low levels reflect a stable identity) of identity formation, decreased between ages 12 and 16. Between ages 16 and 20, there were small increases in in-depth exploration, which is a positive indicator (i.e., high levels reflect a stronger identity) of identity evaluation and maintenance. These findings were in line with theoretical predictions stating that establishing an initial sense of stability is more of a task for younger adolescents, and that a thorough reflection on one's identity is only initiated when individuals approach late adolescence (Bosma & Kunnen, 2008). Increases in in-depth exploration toward late adolescence were replicated in another longitudinal study (Luyckx et al., 2014), but that study also found increases in exploration in breadth suggesting that the identity formation cycle is also still quite active in late adolescence. Overall, it seems clear that identities are increasingly reflected upon when adolescents grow older, while there are few changes in commitment strength in adolescence.

Identity formation continues in young adulthood. In the first year of college, commitment making, exploration in breadth, and exploration in depth were shown to decrease, whereas mean levels of ruminative exploration and identification with commitment remained stable (Luyckx, Klimstra, Schwartz, & Duriez, 2013). Across the college period as a whole (ages 18−22), Luyckx, Schwartz, Goossens, Soenens, and Beyers (2008) found increases in commitment making, exploration in depth, and exploration in breadth. Identification with commitment first decreased, but increased again toward age 22. Working young adults (mean age of 29) have also been shown to exhibit increases in commitment dimensions. In addition, they exhibited decreases in ruminative exploration and exploration in breadth (Luyckx et al., 2013). Thus there appears to be a general pattern of progressive developmental changes in identity formation, but there are temporary regressive changes too.

A study covering ages 14−30 clearly points out that age trends in identity development are not linear (Luyckx, Klimstra, Duriez, Van Petegem, & Beyers, 2013). Overall trends are linear or curvilinear, but deviations from these patterns may occur at any age. For example, levels of commitment making increase toward late adolescence decrease from age 19 into the early 20s and increase again after that.

Overall, there is an increasing trend regarding commitment dimensions. Developmental trends for all exploration dimensions (i.e., exploration in breadth, exploration in depth, and ruminative exploration) are curvilinear, with increasing trends toward the early 20s followed by decreases in the late 20s.

There are also a few studies on identity formation in adulthood. One study found that parents were more committed and exhibited less ruminative exploration than their adolescent children (Luyckx, Schwartz, & Klimstra, 2016). Other studies focused on development within adulthood using configurations of identity dimensions (i.e., statuses). Fadjukoff, Kokko, and Pulkkinen (2010) found substantial heterogeneity in the direction of change before age 36. After that age (i.e., toward age 50), there was increasing stability. Interestingly, more progressive changes in identity (toward a more committed identity) were found in periods of economic growth, whereas regressive changes (toward a less committed identity) were more common during economic crises. This nicely demonstrates the impact of contextual factors on identity formation. Another study found progressive changes in identity from early adulthood (ages 30−37) to middle adulthood (ages 40−47), after which mean levels of identity seemed to stabilize in late middle adulthood (ages 54−61) (Cramer, 2004). Together with another study, showing progressive changes from late adolescence (age 18) to middle adulthood (age 38) (Cramer, 2012), these findings suggest that most of the changes in identity occur before age 40. Thus developmental trends in identity formation are quite complex. Furthermore, identity formation is a highly idiosyncratic process (cf. Lichtwarck-Aschoff, van Geert, Bosma, & Kunnen, 2008), which may lead to large individual differences in developmental trends.

Several studies have attempted to capture this heterogeneity. Meeus, van de Schoot, Keijsers, and Branje (2012) showed that half of their total sample had a quite advantageous identity profile throughout adolescence. However, about half of the individuals reflected relatively high levels of reconsideration and relatively low levels of commitment in early adolescence. Half of this latter subgroup experienced large decreases in reconsideration toward the end of the study and thus recovered well. The other half of this subgroup did not recover from their disadvantageous state of identity within the 4 years of the study. Therefore, this study strongly suggests that a weak sense of identity can be temporary (i.e., a "crisis") or chronic (i.e., "characterological").

Individual differences in identity formation processes were relatively stable across time in one study on young adults (Luyckx, Schwartz, Goossens et al., 2008), as differences that were present at the beginning of the study were largely preserved across time. However, another study (Luyckx et al., 2013) found more evidence for individual differences in developmental trends. For example, exploration in breadth appeared to decrease more strongly in individuals who initially had a so-called carefree diffused profile (i.e., relatively low commitment, combined with low scores on ruminative exploration and exploration in depth and breadth) when compared to individuals with other profiles.

A potential problem with the just-mentioned studies is that they rely on statistical techniques that assume that there is only a limited number of possible developmental pathways. Especially with a highly idiosyncratic process such as identity formation, this may not be a realistic assumption. To capture all developmental heterogeneity, Meeus, van de Schoot, Keijsers, Schwartz, and Branje (2010) examined transitions between identity statuses (i.e., profiles based upon scores on commitment, reconsideration, and in-depth exploration) across 5 yearly measurements. Given that they identified five profiles, many different developmental patterns were possible. Obviously, some of these never occurred and most of these rarely occurred. In fact, over 60% of the sample remained in the same identity status, and over 30% only made one transition from one status to another. Less than 10% made two or more transitions. Thus identity formation as captured by profiles of exploration and commitment dimensions does not change as much as one might expect. The changes that do occur are mostly toward more advantageous identity statuses (i.e., more commitment, less reconsideration), but regressive changes toward a less advanced state of identity are not uncommon.

Little is known about *how* identity change comes about, but identities are thought to take shape in daily life (Kunnen, Bosma, Van Halen, & Van der Meulen, 2001; Lichtwarck-Aschoff et al., 2008). The first studies capturing daily dynamics of identity only emerged recently. These studies show that these daily dynamics can be measured in a reliable and valid manner, and that there are meaningful changes in identity processes on a daily level (Becht et al., 2015; Klimstra et al., 2010). Specifically, there appears to be a spiral process in which reconsideration on one day predicts a weaker sense of commitment the next day, which predicts yet more reconsideration the day thereafter (Klimstra, Luyckx et al., 2010). In addition, greater daily fluctuations in identity processes predict a weaker subsequent sense of identity. Thus daily processes of identity may indeed drive the overall identity formation process.

# Associations of identity with adolescent and young adult functioning

We have now provided an overview of what happens regarding identity development, but it may be unclear why such knowledge is important. In the following section, we provide an overview of the associations of identity processes with adjustment in various domains to show why one should care about identity.

## *Problem behavior symptoms and emotions*

Identity dimensions have clear linkages with symptoms of anxiety and depression (for overviews using the classic approach to identity, see Lillevoll, Kroger, & Martinussen, 2013; Meeus, Iedema, Helsen, & Vollebergh, 1999). Within contemporary models of identity formation, there are consistent negative associations of commitment dimensions with symptoms of both depression and anxiety (Crocetti, Klimstra, Keijsers, Hale, & Meeus, 2009; Crocetti, Schwartz, Fermani, & Meeus,

2010; Luyckx, Duriez, Klimstra, & de Witte, 2010; Luyckx, Schwartz, Berzonsky et al., 2008). For exploration dimensions, the picture is more complex. In Luyckx' model (Luyckx, Schwartz, Berzonsky et al., 2008), ruminative exploration is consistently positively associated with depressive symptoms and anxiety. The associations of internalizing symptoms with exploration in breadth and exploration in depth are a little less consistent (Luyckx, Duriez, Klimstra, & de Witte, 2010; Luyckx et al., 2013; Luyckx, Schwartz, Berzonsky et al., 2008). In the three-dimension model (Crocetti et al., 2008), only positive associations of internalizing symptoms with reconsideration are consistently found (Crocetti et al., 2008; Morsünbül, Crocetti, Çok, & Meeus, 2014). The associations between internalizing symptoms and identity seem to be partly age-dependent (Luyckx, Klimstra, Duriez et al., 2013). Specifically, exploration in breadth was not associated with depressive symptoms in adolescence and early adulthood, whereas it became positively associated with depressive symptoms in individuals above age 26. This suggests that an identity process that is adaptive at one age may not be adaptive at another age.

The linkages of identity formation with externalizing behavior (e.g., aggression, delinquency, and substance use) have been studied less extensively than those with internalizing symptomatology. Studies using the aforementioned three-dimension model of identity formation suggested that in the general population externalizing problem behavior symptoms were associated with high levels of reconsideration, whereas linkages with commitment and in-depth exploration were less clear (Crocetti et al., 2008; Crocetti, Klimstra, Hale, Koot, & Meeus, 2013; Morsünbül et al., 2014). However, a study focusing on convicted juvenile delinquents found that these adolescents scored much lower on educational and relational commitment and educational in-depth exploration, and much higher on relational reconsideration when compared to youth from the general population (Klimstra et al., 2011).

In studies using Luyckx' identity model, substance use tends to be negatively associated with exploration in depth, while there is also some evidence for a positive association with ruminative exploration and negative associations with commitment dimensions (Luyckx et al., 2006; Ritchie et al., 2013). Ritchie and colleagues (2013) found similar associations with other externalizing measures such as rule breaking and aggression. Interestingly, higher levels of commitment were associated with a higher frequency of illicit drug use, sexual risk taking, and risky car-driving behavior. Exploration dimensions predicted a higher prevalence of such behaviors, but a lower frequency. This suggests that individuals that are exploring their identities simply engage in such behaviors to try these out, but do not necessarily commit themselves to a risky lifestyle. In the same dataset applied by Ritchie et al. (2013), Schwartz et al. (2011) studied associations of constellations of identity dimensions with externalizing behaviors and risk taking. Especially individuals who coupled low commitment with low exploration including little ruminative exploration (so-called carefree diffused individuals) were likely to exhibit high levels of rule breaking and aggression, and engage in illicit drug use, unsafe sexual behavior, and impaired driving. Thus considering profiles reflecting constellations of multiple identity dimensions might be very useful for identifying groups vulnerable to externalizing and risky behavior.

The aforementioned studies examined between-person associations indicating that, for example, individuals with higher levels of commitment generally exhibit better adjustment. However, this does not mean that particular individuals also start to feel better once their levels of commitment are on the rise. To examine the latter, studies are needed on within-person associations based on frequent measurement occasions of several processes within the same person. As emotions are thought to be strongly intertwined with identity (Kunnen et al., 2001), a recent study with such a design (i.e., 75 measurement occasions across 5 years) examined within-person associations between identity and mood (Klimstra et al., 2016). On average, commitment appeared to be associated with a less negative mood, whereas in-depth exploration and especially reconsideration seemed to be positively related to a negative mood. Across days, identity and mood seemed to bidirectionally influence each other. In-depth exploration contributed to a more negative mood, and a negative mood induced more educational reconsideration. There were considerable individual differences in the way mood and identity were associated, but it is yet unclear what causes these individual differences. Thus we only just started to gain insight into how mood changes with, affects, and is affected by identity formation processes. The developmental correlates, antecedents, and consequences of identity formation processes definitely warrant further study.

## Personal relationships

Erikson (1950) already emphasized that individuals use relationships as "an attempt to arrive at a definition of one's identity by projecting one's diffused ego image on another and by seeing it thus reflected and gradually clarified." A meta-analysis on studies using the classic approach to identity formation indeed highlighted associations of relationship characteristics such as attachment and intimacy with identity (Arseth, Kroger, Martinussen, & Marcia, 2009).

As parents play a key role in the development of attachment, the meta-analysis by Arseth and colleagues (2009) already suggests an indirect role of parents in identity formation. Schwartz, Mason, Pantin, and Szapoczik (2009) showed this more directly, by demonstrating that identity confusion decreased as family functioning increased. In more specific research, Grotevant and Cooper (1998) showed that parents can promote adaptive exploration in their children if they manage to build a relationship that is characterized by a balance between individuality and connectedness. In line with this, intrusive parenting is associated with higher levels of reconsideration (Crocetti et al., 2008), more ruminative exploration (Pesigan, Luyckx, & Alampay, 2014), and weaker commitments (Luyckx, Soenens, Vansteenkiste, Goossens, & Berzonsky, 2007). However, supportive parenting promotes identification with commitment and lessens exploration in breadth (Beyers & Goossens, 2008; Pesigan et al., 2014). Longitudinal studies (Beyers & Goossens, 2008; Luyckx et al., 2007) suggested not only that parenting affects adolescent identity formation, but also that parents adapt their parenting behavior to the identity formation processes adolescents exhibit.

Within the family, both parents and siblings also seem to function as role models for identity formation. Specifically, parents with stronger (i.e., more committed) identities tended to have children who had stronger commitments and reported less ruminative exploration (Luyckx et al., 2016). Further, the extent to which adolescents commit and explore appears to be affected by the extent to which their older brothers or sisters are approaching the identity formation process (Wong, Branje, VanderValk, Hawk, & Meeus, 2010). How all of these transmission processes within families specifically come about is an open question for now.

Meeus, Iedema, Maassen, and Engels (2002) confirmed Erikson's (1950) idea that the role of peers might be at least as big as the role of parents in identity formation. They showed that associations of identity with peer-relationship quality were indeed stronger than with parent-relationship quality. More specific studies showed that conflicts with friends are associated with more maladaptive identity processes, such as weak commitments (Jones, Vaterlaus, Jackson, & Morrill, 2014) and regressive identity development (Reis & Youniss, 2004). Furthermore, the degree to which adolescents perceive their best friend as accepting their differing opinions and ideas is bidirectionally associated with adaptive educational identity formation (van Doeselaar, Meeus, Koot, & Branje, 2016). Dumas, Ellis, and Wolfe (2012) showed an important function of identity in the peer context, as they found that both high levels of commitment and exploration could serve as a protective factor against peer pressure in the context of substance use and deviant behaviors. Finally, reactions of peers (i.e., same-sex friend or romantic partner) also played an important role when adolescents received feedback on their identity that was incongruent with their self-perceptions (Kerpelman & Pittman, 2001). Specifically, if peers reject incongruent feedback regarding a salient identity domain, they were found to (unwillingly) stimulate identity instability (i.e., exploration). However, with less salient domains, rejection of incongruent feedback seems to serve a protective role and foster identity stability.

Identity development is also positively associated with several aspects of the quality of romantic relationships. In line with Erikson's (1950) theory that identity development precedes the development of intimacy, a profile of high levels of relational exploration and commitment predicted a higher level of intimacy in young adulthood (Beyers & Seiffge-Krenke, 2010). Thus relationships with different individuals (i.e., parents, siblings, friends, and romantic partners) all appear to uniquely contribute to, and be affected by, adolescents' identity formation.

## Academic functioning

Identity formation processes are not only associated with psychosocial functioning but also impact what is arguably the most important objective indicator of adolescent successful functioning: academic success. A meta-analysis (Robbins et al., 2004) and several subsequent studies (Germeijs & Verschueren, 2007; Klimstra, Luyckx, Germeijs, Meeus, & Goossens, 2012) showed that individuals with higher levels of educational commitment are more likely to move through college without study delays. In fact, educational commitment even buffered the adverse effects that living in a disadvantaged neighborhood had on educational attainment (Nieuwenhuis, Hooimeijer, & Meeus, 2015). Collectively, these studies show the importance of identity formation in the early stages of career development.

# Linkages with personality trait development

Erikson (1950) originally defined identity formation as one subtask in personality development. Relatedly, Five-Factor Theory (FFT; McCrae & Costa, 2008) and the core versus surface trait model (Asendorpf & van Aken, 2003) emphasize a distinction between basic tendencies (i.e., personality traits) and characteristic adaptations such as identity processes. Both models would predict that effects from Big Five traits to characteristic adaptations such as identity processes would be larger than in the inverse direction.

McAdams' multilayered model assumes that child behavior is largely driven by basic tendencies (i.e., personality traits; McAdams & Olson, 2010). In late childhood, motivations and goals come to the fore and behavior becomes more goal-directed. From late adolescence onward, individuals' behavior becomes aligned with the way they perceive themselves, as their (narrative) identity starts to play an important role in their behavior. At first, these self-views are largely build upon the way individuals typically behaved up to that point. Hence, traits as well as goals and motivations are likely better predictors of identity at that point. Once identities become solidified, they also start to affect traits. For example, if individuals view themselves as reliable and friendly, they adapt their behavior to fit this self-view. Typically, this should happen from young adulthood onward.

Finally, the Social Investment Principle (Roberts, Wood, & Smith, 2005) poses that the changes in personality that are typically observed in young adulthood (increases in Agreeableness, Conscientiousness, and Emotional Stability) are caused by individuals taking up and committing to roles of adult social life, like getting a stable job and romantic relationship. Specifically, the more committed individuals are to a new role, the more likely they are to adapt their personality to this role. Thus the social investment principle suggests that changes in identity processes (i.e., commitment) predict changes in personality.

A series of longitudinal studies tested these models' predictions. In adolescence, personality traits predicted changes in identity processes, whereas identity processes hardly affected personality traits (Luyckx et al., 2014). In young adulthood, though, associations between personality traits and identity formation processes were bidirectional (Luyckx et al., 2006). Thus these studies seem to confirm aforementioned theoretical predictions.

Two other studies on young adults considered identity dimensions pertaining to specific life domains. In a study on educational identity, personality traits were much more often predictors of identity processes than the other way around (Klimstra et al., 2012). Still, the one effect of identity on personality, with increases in commitment predicting decreases in neuroticism, was in line with the social investment principle. A study focusing on relational identity regarding the romantic partner found rather weak associations with Big Five traits (Klimstra et al., 2013). Still, there was some evidence for bidirectional influences between personality traits and relational identity. Again, one of the strongest longitudinal effects, with increases in commitment predicting increases in conscientiousness, was in line with the Social Investment Principle.

Overall, studies relating personality traits to identity processes provide some support for all aforementioned theories. That is, personality is usually a better predictor of identity than the other way around, identity becomes a better predictor of personality when individuals grow older, and commitment to roles in specific life domains predicts relative changes in at least some personality traits.

## Identity and personality pathology

After the new version of the most commonly used diagnostic manual in mental healthcare (DSM-5; APA, 2013) appeared, a strong renewed interest in identity formation in the context of personality pathology surfaced. This is due to the emphasis in DSM-5 on the importance of personality functioning, which includes identity disturbances (Bender, Morey, & Skodol, 2011), when diagnosing and subsequently treating personality pathology.

Kernberg and Caligor (2005) hypothesized that all personality disorders characterized by a Borderline personality organization (i.e., all DSM-5 personality disorders except for obsessive–compulsive personality disorder) would be accompanied by identity disturbances. Marcia (2006) described patterns of identity formation in terms of combinations of commitment and exploration for all 10 DSM personality disorders. He suggests that both Cluster A (schizotypal, schizoid, and paranoid) and Cluster C (avoidant, dependent, and obsessive–compulsive) personality disorders are accompanied by little exploration and weak commitments, whereas Cluster B (antisocial, borderline, histrionic, and narcissistic) personality disorders are defined by at least some commitment issues. These predictions were confirmed for the role of commitment in Cluster B, but not for Clusters A and C. Specifically, all Cluster B personality disorders, except for histrionic personality disorder, were characterized by a lack of commitment (Westen, Betan, & DeFife, 2011). Empirical evidence regarding the role of other identity processes in personality pathology is minimal. Further investigation of these linkages is important because personality pathology can potentially be treated by focusing on identity.

## Conclusion

This chapter illustrates that research on identity formation has evolved rapidly in recent years. Developmental changes in identity are being mapped, associations with adjustment have repeatedly been found, and the role of identity in the development of the broader personality is increasingly understood. However, little is known about the exact mechanisms involved in identity formation. There is much theorizing regarding these mechanisms (Bosma & Kunnen, 2001; Koepke & Denissen, 2012; Lichtwarck-Aschoff et al., 2008), but testing them is complex. Due to the highly idiosyncratic nature of identity, it may even be delusional to think that general mechanisms can be uncovered. Therefore, it may be more suitable to focus on how identity processes and other variables (e.g., emotions, daily hassles, and social interactions) are related in particular individuals. For example, it could very well be that identity formation is mainly shaped in social interactions in a highly sociable person, whereas it may be more driven by emotions in another person. To examine such individual differences in mechanisms behind identity formation, one way to proceed would be to use within-person research designs with frequent measurements of identity and other processes in large groups of individuals.

It should be emphasized that the identity dimensions we focused on in this chapter (i.e., commitment and exploration processes) capture only a part of the full complexity of identity (van Hoof, 1999). To understand identity formation better, a more comprehensive perspective is needed. That is, we also need to consider identity integration (i.e., associations between identity in different contexts; e.g., van Hoof & Raaijmakers, 2002) and identity distinctiveness (i.e., whether individuals see themselves as unique and different from others; e.g., Pasupathi, 2014). Furthermore, approaches examining individuals' current state of identity need to be complemented by approaches that focus more on individuals' reflections upon the identity formation process. In other words, the quantitative approaches we described need to be complemented with narrative approaches (McLean, Chapter 20).

In addition, more needs to be learned about the exact functions of a stable identity. A core theoretical assumption in identity theory is that a well-developed identity provides individuals with a sense of stability (Erikson, 1950, 1968) and thus protects individuals against adverse effects caused by external influences or conditions. There is now some research showing the protective function of a strong identity in the case of peer pressure (Dumas et al., 2012), and chronic illnesses such as diabetes (Luyckx, Seiffge-Krenke et al., 2008) and chronic heart disease (Luyckx, Goossens, Van Damme, & Moons, 2011). These studies show the potential of identity to help adolescents cope with aversive circumstances, but more potential functions need to be examined. Furthermore, we need to know how and why identity serves as a source of resiliency under adverse circumstances.

Identity formation captures a key aspect of the development of the broader personality. The tools to examine this key process have been reformed and refined, and more knowledge has been gained regarding the development and the functions of identity. Nevertheless, there is still much ground to be covered before identity formation can be fully understood.

# References

American Psychiatric Association (2013). *Diagnostic and Statistical Manual of Mental Disorders* (5th ed.). Washington, DC: Author.

Arseth, A. K., Kroger, J., Martinussen, M., & Marcia, J. E. (2009). Meta-analytic studies of identity status and the relational issues of attachment and intimacy. *Identity, 9*, 1−32.

Asendorpf, J. B., & van Aken, M. A. G. (2003). Personality−relationship transaction in adolescence: Core versus surface personality characteristics. *Journal of Personality, 71*, 629−666.

Becht, A. L., Branje, S. T. J., Vollebergh, W. A. M., Maciejewski, D. F., Lier, P. A. C., van, Koot, H. M., ... Meeus, W. H. J. (2015). Assessment of identity during adolescence using daily diary methods: Measurement invariance across time and sex. *Psychological Assessment*. Available from http://dx.doi.org/10.1037/pas0000204.

Bender, D. S., Morey, L. C., & Skodol, A. E. (2011). Toward a model for assessing level of personality functioning in *DSM-5*, Part I: A review of theory and methods. *Journal of Personality Assessment, 93*, 332−346.

Beyers, W., & Goossens, L. (2008). Dynamics of perceived parenting and identity formation in late adolescence. *Journal of Adolescence, 31*, 165−184.

Beyers, W., & Seiffge-Krenke, I. (2010). Does identity precede intimacy? Testing Erikson's theory on romantic development in emerging adults of the 21st century. *Journal of Adolescent Research, 25*, 387−415.

Bosma, H. A. (1985). Identity development in adolescence: Coping with commitments. *Unpublished doctoral dissertation*, University of Groningen.

Bosma, H. A., & Kunnen, E. S. (2001). Determinants and mechanisms in ego identity development: A review and synthesis. *Developmental Review, 21*, 39−66.

Bosma, H. A., & Kunnen, E. S. (2008). Identity-in-context is not yet identity development-in-context. *Journal of Adolescence, 31*, 281−289.

Cramer, P. (2004). Identity change in adulthood: The contribution of defense mechanisms and life experiences. *Journal of Research in Personality, 38*, 280−316.

Cramer, P. (2012). Psychological maturity and change in adult defense mechanisms. *Journal of Research in Personality, 46*, 306−316.

Crocetti, E., Klimstra, T., Keijsers, L., Hale, W. W., & Meeus, W. (2009). Anxiety trajectory classes and identity development in adolescence: A five-wave longitudinal study. *Journal of Youth and Adolescence, 38*, 839−849.

Crocetti, E., Klimstra, T. A., Hale, W. W., Koot, J. M., & Meeus, W. H. J. (2013). Impact of early adolescent externalizing problem behaviors on identity development in middle to late adolescence: A prospective seven-year longitudinal study. *Journal of Youth and Adolescence, 42*, 1745−1758.

Crocetti, E., Rubini, M., & Meeus, W. H. J. (2008). Capturing the dynamics of identity formation in various ethnic groups: Development and validation of a three-dimensional model. *Journal of Adolescence, 31*, 207−222.

Crocetti, E., Schwartz, S., Fermani, A., & Meeus, W. (2010). The Utrecht-Management of Identity Commitments Scale (U-MICS): Italian validation and cross-national comparisons. *European Journal of Psychological Assessment, 26*, 169−183.

Dumas, T. M., Ellis, W. E., & Wolfe, D. A. (2012). Identity development as a buffer of adolescent risk behaviors in the context of peer group pressure and control. *Journal of Adolescence, 35*, 917−927.

Erikson, E. H. (1950). *Childhood and society*. New York, NY: Norton.

Erikson, E. H. (1968). *Identity: Youth and crisis*. New York, NY: Norton.

Fadjukoff, P., Kokko, K., & Pulkkinen, L. (2010). Changing economic conditions and identity formation in adulthood. *European Psychologist, 15*, 293–303.

Germeijs, V., & Verschueren, K. (2007). High school adolescents' career decision-making process: Consequences for choice implementation in higher education. *Journal of Vocational Behavior, 70*, 223–241.

Grotevant, H. D. (1987). Toward a process model of identity formation. *Journal of Adolescent Research, 2*, 203–222.

Grotevant, H. D., & Cooper, C. R. (1998). Individuality and connectedness in adolescent development. Review and prospects for research on identity, relationships, and context. In E. E. A. Skoe, & A. L. Von Der Lippe (Eds.), *Personality development in adolescence. A cross national and life span perspective*. London: Routledge.

Jones, R. M., Vaterlaus, J. M., Jackson, M. A., & Morrill, T. B. (2014). Friendship characteristics, psychosocial development, and adolescent identity formation. *Personal Relationships, 21*, 51–67.

Kernberg, O. F., & Caligor, E. (2005). A psychoanalytic theory of personality disorders. In M. F. Lenzenweger, & J. F. Clarkin (Eds.), *Major theories of personality disorders* (2nd ed.). New York, NY: The Guilford Press.

Kerpelman, J. L., & Pittman, J. F. (2001). The instability of possible selves: Identity processes within late adolescent's close peer relationships. *Journal of Adolescence, 24*, 491–512.

Klimstra, T. A., Crocetti, E., Hale, W. W., Kolman, A. I. M., Fortanier, E. L., & Meeus, W. H. J. (2011). Identity formation in juvenile delinquents and clinically referred youth. *European Review of Applied Psychology, 61*, 123–130.

Klimstra, T. A., Hale, W. W., Raaijmakers, Q. A. W., Branje, S. J. T., & Meeus, W. H. J. (2010). Identity formation in adolescence: Change or stability? *Journal of Youth and Adolescence, 39*, 150–162.

Klimstra, T. A., Kuppens, P., Luyckx, K., Branje, S., Hale, W. W., Oosterwegel, A., & Meeus, W. H. J. (2016). Daily dynamics of adolescent mood and identity. *Journal of Research on Adolescence, 26*, 459–473.

Klimstra, T. A., Luyckx, K., Branje, S. J. T., Teppers, E., Goossens, L., & Meeus, W. H. J. (2013). Personality traits, interpersonal identity, and relationship stability: Longitudinal linkages in late adolescence and young adulthood. *Journal of Youth and Adolescence, 42*, 1661–1673.

Klimstra, T. A., Luyckx, K., Germeijs, V., Meeus, W. H. J., & Goossens, L. (2012). Personality traits and educational identity formation in late adolescents: Longitudinal associations and academic progress. *Journal of Youth and Adolescence, 41*, 346–361.

Klimstra, T. A., Luyckx, K., Hale, W. W., Frijns, T., van Lier, P. A. C., & Meeus, W. H. J. (2010). Short-term fluctuations in identity: Introducing a micro-level approach to identity formation. *Journal of Personality and Social Psychology, 99*, 191–202.

Koepke, S., & Denissen, J. J. A. (2012). Dynamics of identity development and separation-individuation in parent–child relationships during adolescence and emerging adulthood —A conceptual integration. *Developmental Review, 32*, 67–88.

Kroger, J., Martinussen, M., & Marcia, J. (2010). Identity status change during adolescence and young adulthood: A meta-analysis. *Journal of Adolescence, 33*, 683–698.

Kunnen, E. S., Bosma, H. A., Van Halen, C. P. M., & Van der Meulen, M. (2001). A self-organizational approach to identity and emotions: An overview and implications. In H. A. Bosma, & E. S. Kunnen (Eds.), *Identity and emotion*. Cambridge: Cambridge University Press.

Lichtwarck-Aschoff, A., van Geert, P. L. C., Bosma, H. A., & Kunnen, E. S. (2008). Time and identity: A framework for research and theory formation. *Developmental Review*, *28*, 370–400.

Lillevoll, K. R., Kroger, J., & Martinussen, M. (2013). Identity status and anxiety: A meta-analysis. *Identity*, *13*, 214–227.

Luyckx, K., Duriez, B., Klimstra, T. A., & de Witte, H. (2010). Identity statuses in young adult employees: Prospective relations with work engagement and burnout. *Journal of Vocational Behavior*, *77*, 339–349.

Luyckx, K., Goossens, E., Van Damme, C., & Moons, P. (2011). Identity formation in adolescents with congenital cardiac disease: A forgotten issue in the transition to adulthood. *Cardiology in the Young*, *21*, 411–420.

Luyckx, K., Goossens, L., & Soenens, B. (2006). A developmental–contextual perspective on identity construction in emerging adulthood: Change dynamics in commitment formation and commitment evaluation. *Developmental Psychology*, *42*, 366–380.

Luyckx, K., Goossens, L., Soenens, B., & Beyers, W. (2006). Unpacking commitment and exploration: Preliminary validation of an integrative model of late adolescent identity formation. *Journal of Adolescence*, *29*, 361–378.

Luyckx, K., Klimstra, T. A., Duriez, B., Van Petegem, S., & Beyers, W. (2013). Personal identity processes from adolescence through the late twenties: Age differences, functionality, and depressive symptoms. *Social Development*, *22*, 701–721.

Luyckx, K., Klimstra, T. A., Schwartz, S. J., & Duriez, B. (2013). Personal identity in college and the work context: Developmental trajectories and psychosocial functioning. *European Journal of Personality*, *27*, 222–237.

Luyckx, K., Schwartz, S. J., Berzonsky, M. D., Soenens, B., Vansteenkiste, M., Smits, I., & Goossens, L. (2008). Capturing ruminative exploration: Extending the four-dimensional model of identity formation in late adolescence. *Journal of Research in Personality*, *42*, 58–82.

Luyckx, K., Schwartz, S. J., Goossens, L., Soenens, B., & Beyers, W. (2008). Developmental typologies of identity formation and adjustment in female emerging adults: A latent class growth analysis approach. *Journal of Research on Adolescence*, *18*, 595–619.

Luyckx, K., Schwartz, S. J., & Klimstra, T. A. (2016). Intergenerational associations linking identity styles and processes in adolescents and their parents. *European Journal of Developmental Psychology*, *13*, 67–83. Available from http://dx.doi.org/10.1080/17405629.2015.1066668.

Luyckx, K., Seiffge-Krenke, I., Schwartz, S. J., Goossens, L., Weets, I., Hendrieckx, C., & Groven, C. (2008). Identity development, coping, and adjustment in emerging adults with a chronic illness: The sample case of Type I diabetes. *Journal of Adolescent Health*, *43*, 451–458.

Luyckx, K., Soenens, B., & Goossens, L. (2006). The personality–identity interplay in emerging adult women: Convergent findings from complementary analyses. *European Journal of Personality*, *20*, 195–215.

Luyckx, K., Soenens, B., Vansteenkiste, M., Goossens, L., & Berzonsky, M. (2007). Parental psychological control and dimensions of identity formation in emerging adulthood. *Journal of Family Psychology*, *21*, 546–550.

Luyckx, K., Teppers, E., Klimstra, T. A., & Rassart, J. (2014). Identity processes and personality traits and types in adolescence: Directionality of effects and developmental trajectories. *Developmental Psychology*, *50*, 2144–2153.

Marcia, J. E. (1966). Development and validation of ego-identity status. *Journal of Personality and Social Psychology*, *3*, 551–558.

Marcia, J. E. (2006). Ego identity and personality disorders. *Journal of Personality Disorders*, *20*, 577–596.

McAdams, D. P., & Olson, B. D. (2010). Personality development: Continuity and change over the life course. *Annual Review of Psychology*, *61*, 517–542.

McCrae, R. R., & Costa, P. T., Jr. (2008). The Five-Factor Theory of personality. In O. P. John, R. W. Robins, & L. A. Pervin (Eds.), *Handbook of personality: Theory and research* (3rd ed., pp. 159–181). New York, NY: Guilford Press.

Meeus, W. (2011). The study of adolescent identity formation 2000–2010: A review of longitudinal research. *Journal of Research on Adolescence*, *21*, 75–94.

Meeus, W., Iedema, J., Helsen, M., & Vollebergh, W. (1999). Patterns of adolescent identity development: Review of literature and longitudinal analysis. *Developmental Review*, *19*, 419–461.

Meeus, W., Iedema, J., Maassen, G., & Engels, R. (2002). Relaties met ouders en leeftijds-genoten en identiteitsontwikkeling in de adolescentie [Relationships with parents and peers and identity development in adolescence]. *Nederlands Tijdschrift voor Psychologie*, *57*, 42–57.

Meeus, W., van de Schoot, R., Keijsers, L., & Branje, S. (2012). Identity statuses as developmental trajectories. A Five-Wave Longitudinal Study in early to middle and middle to late adolescents. *Journal of Youth and Adolescence*, *41*, 1008–1021.

Meeus, W., van de Schoot, R., Keijsers, L., Schwartz, S. J., & Branje, S. (2010). On the progression and stability of adolescent identity formation: A five-wave longitudinal study in early-to-middle and middle-to-late adolescence. *Child Development*, *81*, 1565–1581.

Meeus, W. H. J. (1996). Studies on identity development in adolescence: An overview of research and some new data. *Journal of Youth and Adolescence*, *25*, 569–598.

Morsünbül, U., Crocetti, E., Çok, F., & Meeus, W. (2014). Brief report: The Utrecht-Management of Identity Commitments Scale (U-MICS): Gender and age measurement invariance and convergent validity of the Turkish version. *Journal of Adolescence*, *37*, 799–805.

Nieuwenhuis, J., Hooimeijer, P., & Meeus, W. (2015). Neighbourhood effects on educational attainment of adolescents, buffered by personality and educational commitment. *Social Science Research*, *50*, 100–109.

Pasupathi, M. (2014). Identity: Commentary. Identity development: Dialogue between normative and pathological developmental approaches. *Journal of Personality Disorders*, *28*, 113–120.

Pesigan, I. J. A., Luyckx, K., & Alampay, L. P. (2014). Brief report: Identity processes in Filipino late adolescents and young adults: Parental influences and mental health outcomes. *Journal of Adolescence*, *37*, 599–604.

Reis, O., & Youniss, J. (2004). Patterns in identity change and development in relationships with mothers and friends. *Journal of Adolescent Research*, *19*, 31–44.

Ritchie, R. A., Meca, A., Madrazo, V. L., Schwartz, S. J., Hardy, S. A., Zamboanga, B. L., & Weisskrich, R. S. (2013). Identity dimensions and related processes in emerging adulthood: Helpful or harmful? *Journal of Clinical Psychology*, *69*, 415–432.

Robbins, S. B., Lauver, K., Le, H., Davis, D., Langley, R., & Carlstrom, A. (2004). Do psychosocial and study skill factors predict college outcomes? A meta-analysis. *Psychological Bulletin*, *130*, 261–288.

Roberts, B. W., Wood, D., & Smith, J. L. (2005). Evaluating Five Factor Theory and social investment perspectives on personality trait development. *Journal of Research in Personality*, *39*, 166–184.

Schwartz, S., Mason, C., Pantin, H., & Szapoczik, J. (2009). Longitudinal relationships between family functioning and identity development in Hispanic adolescents: Continuity and change. *Journal of Early Adolescence, 29*, 177–211.

Schwartz, S. J., Beyers, W., Luyckx, K., Soenens, B., Zamboanga, B. L., Forthun, L. F., ... Waterman, A. S. (2011). Examining the light and dark sides of emerging adults' identity: A study of identity status differences in positive and negative psychosocial functioning. *Journal of Youth and Adolescence, 40*, 839–859. Available from http://dx.doi.org/10.1007/s10964-010-9606-6.

van Doeselaar, L., Meeus, W., Koot, H. M., & Branje, S. (2016). The role of best friends in educational identity formation in adolescence. *Journal of Adolescence, 47*, 28–37. Available from http://dx.doi.org/10.1016/j.adolescence.2015.12.002.

van Hoof, A. (1999). The identity status field re-reviewed: An update of unresolved and neglected issues with a view on some alternative approaches. *Developmental Review, 19*, 497–556.

Van Hoof, A., & Raaijmakers, Q. A. W. (2002). The spatial integration of adolescent identity: Its relation to age, education, and subjective well-being. *Scandinavian Journal of Psychology, 43*, 201–212.

Waterman, A. S. (1982). Identity development from adolescence to adulthood: An extension of theory and a review of research. *Developmental Psychology, 18*, 342–358.

Waterman, A. S. (2015). What does it mean to engage in identity exploration and to hold identity commitments? A methodological critique of multidimensional measures for the study of identity processes. *Identity, 15*, 309–349.

Westen, D., Betan, E., & DeFife, J. A. (2011). Identity disturbance in adolescence: Associations with borderline personality disorder. *Development and Psychopathology, 23*, 305–313.

Wong, T. M. L., Branje, S., VanderValk, I. E., Hawk, S. T., & Meeus, W. (2010). The role of siblings on identity development in adolescence and emerging adulthood. *Journal of Adolescence, 33*, 673–682.

# Development of cognition and intelligence

19

*Florian Schmiedek*
German Institute for International Educational Research (DIPF), Frankfurt am Main, Germany

Human cognitive development across the lifespan is constrained by biological processes of maturation and senescence and shaped by environmental conditions, societal factors, and individual histories of learning and experience. From the overarching conceptual view of lifespan psychology, general propositions can be made regarding cognitive development, including the multidirectionality of changes for different cognitive functions, the importance of individual differences, and the experience-based yet constrained plasticity of cognitive performance (Baltes, Lindenberger, & Staudinger, 2006). Multidirectionality follows from general considerations about the biological and environmental determinants of cognitive development and can be divided, at a conceptual level, into the *mechanics* (i.e., humans' biologically based information-processing systems) and the *pragmatics* (i.e., knowledge and skills acquired through learning and experience) of cognition (Baltes, 1987), which can be further differentiated and linked to operationally measurable cognitive abilities as well as to skills, knowledge, and expertise in all kinds of real-life domains. Individual differences in the genetic basis of cognition as well as in the multitude of environmental and experiential factors that shape development lead to large heterogeneity in the levels of performance observable at each age throughout the lifespan, as well as in the shapes of the trajectories of growth and decline that connect these points of age. This heterogeneity in change indicates the possibility of experience-dependent malleability of individual cognitive development due to education, lifestyle, practice, and training.

## Multidirectionality of normative change in cognition across the lifespan

Lifespan cognitive development can be decomposed into the two theoretical components of the *mechanics* and the *pragmatics* of cognition (Baltes, 1987). The mechanics subsume all the basic information-processing functions that humans are equipped with, like e.g. perception, attention functions, different kinds of memory, and basic language- and number-processing capacities. These are characterized by genetic predispositions, a relative independence of specific content, and a strong

Personality Development Across the Lifespan. DOI: http://dx.doi.org/10.1016/B978-0-12-804674-6.00019-3

reliance on the functionality of their biological substrates. The pragmatics include all the domain-specific expertise that manifests in skills and knowledge that can be acquired through experience, be it in formal education or in everyday practice. Skills are closely tied to specific content and thereby also more strongly shaped by cultural influences than the mechanics. General considerations about the architecture of lifespan development (Baltes, 1997) lead to the proposition that the biological functions supporting cognition have been shaped by evolutionary selection processes that generally have most angle for the phase of high reproduction rates (e.g., young adulthood) and declining influence throughout adulthood—because of decreasing reproduction as well as the fact that the historical time since when substantial percentages of a population reach higher age has to be considered very short from an evolutionary perspective. This is the basis for the expectation that selection advantages reduce across the adult lifespan, leading to decreasing biological functionality in general and of the cognitive system in particular. As a result of this, the dependence on culture increases, that is, reaching and maintaining high levels of functioning in all kinds of domains increasingly depends on factors like environmental support, specialized knowledge and skills, and strategies of adaptation. It has to be further acknowledged, though, that with age, the efficiency of such cultural factors and interventions for cognitive functionality and performance decreases—due to the biologically determined constraints on the mechanics. This becomes apparent, for example, in the decreased effectiveness and efficiency of cognitive training interventions in older age (see "Malleability of Cognitive Development Across the Lifespan" section).

Taking these lifespan dynamics into account, peak cognitive performance in specific domains is the result of a balance of experience-dependent improvements and deteriorating mechanics and can be observed throughout extended ranges of the lifespan (Lindenberger, 2014). For cognitive performance in real life, both mechanics and pragmatics always play a role. Once applied to any real-life content, "mechanical" performance can be influenced by task-specific knowledge, strategies, and cultural factors. Conversely, it is hard to imagine "pragmatic" behavior that does not depend on some kind of information processing—like for example retrieval processes from long-term memory in the use of semantic knowledge. When applied to performance in real life and addressed by empirical investigations, the theoretical concepts of mechanics and pragmatics therefore need to be transferred to less sharply separable concepts of cognitive abilities, skills, and knowledge. Notwithstanding, cognitive *abilities* are characterized by a relative independence of the content they are applied to. For example, fluid intelligence—the ability of abstract thinking—is necessary for inductive and deductive reasoning and can be investigated with corresponding tasks of verbal, numerical, or figural–spatial content. Other broad abilities, as identified by Cattell and Horn (Cattell, 1971; Horn & Cattell, 1966), or in the review of factor-analytic studies on human intelligence by Carroll (1993), include, for example, visual processing, short-term memory, and processing speed, all of which can be applied to a broad range of contents and thereby are of high relevance for everyday cognitive performance in academic, vocational, and avocational settings.

Cognitive *skills*, like for example computer programming or chess playing, are based on declarative and procedural knowledge and therefore more strongly depend on experience and learning processes. The acquisition and the execution of skills and knowledge, however, are also dependent on cognitive abilities, as for instance proposed in skill acquisition theories (Ackerman, 1988) and in the investment theory by Cattell (1987). Conversely, practice on tasks used to measure abilities will typically allow for the improvement of task-specific skills and strategies. Therefore, individual and age-related differences in measurable cognitive performance always reflect some combination of cognitive abilities and experience-dependent skill.

Regarding normative lifespan trajectories of cognitive abilities, the interpretation of average cross-sectional age-related differences or of longitudinal age-related changes faces methodological issues. Cross-sectional age-related differences are potentially influenced by cohort effects, that is, historical differences in environmental influences that characterize whole birth cohorts. For example, curricular changes and the availability of calculators might be responsible for observed cohort differences in arithmetic ability favoring older birth cohorts (Schaie, Willis, & Pennak, 2005). Longitudinal findings can also paint a biased picture of true age-related change, however, because of selective study drop out or because of retest effects when cognitive tasks are repeatedly applied (Salthouse, 2014b). Evidence from large cohort-sequential studies, like the Seattle Longitudinal Study (Schaie, 1996), which allow disentangling age-related changes from retest and cohort effects, shows historical increases in several cognitive abilities, most prominently for fluid intelligence (i.e., the so-called Flynn effect; Dickens & Flynn, 2001). When cross-sectional differences are corrected for such cohort effects, and longitudinal changes are corrected for retest effects, both show better convergence with each other (Salthouse, 1991). Overall, the picture painted by longitudinal studies like the Betula Study (Nilsson et al., 2004) is one of substantial adult age decreases in performance levels, which differ in extent across abilities. For example, changes in memory recall are more pronounced in older age than changes in verbal fluency (de Frias, Lövdén, Lindenberger, & Nilsson, 2007). These changes in psychometric abilities can be mapped onto changes in the underlying mechanisms, that is, resources investigated by cognitive psychologists, like information-processing speed in simple decisions or working memory functions, that show similar inversed u-shape functions of age differences (Jenkins, Myerson, Hale, & Fry, 1999; Kail & Salthouse, 1991). Similarly, at the neurophysiological and neuroanatomical levels, the picture is mirrored by changes in neurotransmitter levels (Bäckman, Nyberg, Lindenberger, Li, & Farde, 2006), volumes of brain regions (Raz et al., 2005), and measures of neuronal connectivity (Raz & Rodrigue, 2006).

The ubiquitous finding of inverted u-shaped curves for lifespan development (see Fig. 19.1 for the example of episodic memory) and apparently similar patterns of deficits in childhood and old age—as compared to younger adults—invites hypotheses of similar mechanisms being responsible for these at both ends of the lifespan. Such hypotheses should be subjected to close scrutiny, however, as different cognitive processes and developmental adaptation mechanisms may be operating, yet producing comparable levels of observed performance (for a compilation of

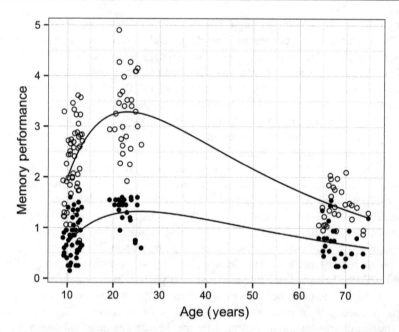

**Figure 19.1** Performance differences in episodic memory across the lifespan before and after training.

In the study by Brehmer et al. (2007), groups of 50 children (9–12 years), 29 younger (20–25 years), and 29 older adults (65–78 years) were intensively trained with a mnemonic technique using a visualization strategy that supports the encoding and retrieval of location-word pairs. The figure illustrates (1) the characteristic "inverted u-shape" function of average age-related memory performance differences across the lifespan, (2) large individual differences in performance, which are magnified by the training (filled circles = before training; open circles = after training), and (3) age-related differences in the effect of the training, which make apparent limitations in the possible range of experience-based improvements. The fitted curves are biexponential functions. *Source*: The figure was produced using raw data from the study by Brehmer and colleagues, kindly made available by the first author.

comparisons between developmental processes in childhood versus old age regarding different cognitive functions, see Bialystok & Craik, 2006). Formal mathematical modeling of simple decision processes, for example, shows that the pattern of age differences in processing parameters responsible for reduced speed and accuracy of responding differs between comparisons of children versus older adults with younger adults (Ratcliff, Love, Thompson, & Opfer, 2012; Ratcliff, Thapar, & McKoon, 2010). Regarding more complex cognitive tasks, two-component frameworks of episodic and working memory explain lifespan differences in performance in terms of underlying associative and strategic components, which show different courses of maturation and senescence (Sander, Lindenberger, & Werkle-Bergner, 2012; Shing et al., 2010). Performance on episodic memory tasks, for example, is proposed to depend on an associative component of binding features into compound representations (e.g., names and telephone numbers) and a strategic component of control mechanisms that support encoding and retrieval of information (e.g., a mnemonic visualization strategy). Because the neuronal substrates of the associative component (i.e., mediotemporal/hippocampal structures) mature earlier than those of the strategic component (i.e., prefrontal structures), children's performance, in comparison to younger adults (see Fig. 19.1), is mainly limited because helpful strategies cannot yet be applied in a way that fully exploits the potential of the associative component. In contrast, older adults' performance deficits seem to be due to the double disadvantage of a reduced strategic component working on a less effective associative component (Shing et al., 2010).

Regarding the lifespan development of the cognitive pragmatics, the standard psychometric assessment of crystallized intelligence (i.e., with tests of general knowledge or vocabulary) only indicates the breadth of potential knowledge that individuals can acquire during their life course. As proposed in the investment theory (Cattell, 1987), crystallized intelligence is mainly determined by individual differences in fluid cognitive ability, which can be invested in the acquisition of knowledge, with this process also being influenced by learning opportunities, motivation, interests, and personality factors like openness to experience. While the complex interplay of such a multitude of individual and environmental factors can potentially lead to very idiosyncratic patterns of knowledge and skill at the individual level, it nevertheless produces a structuring of individual differences in interests, personality factors, and cognitive abilities that can be summarized by broad trait complexes (Ackerman & Heggestad, 1997). For example, a science/math trait complex encompasses mathematical and spatial skills as well as realistic and investigative interests. Regarding the developmental dynamics that produce such complexes, however, the scientific basis is still limited. Also, the large potential for age-related increases in domain-specific knowledge across the whole lifespan and the supportive role that existing knowledge thereby can play for the acquisition of new knowledge so far has been explored only very little. Findings of positive adult age relations for a number of specific domains of knowledge, like law, literature, and history (Ackerman, 2000), and positive associations of older adults' crystallized intelligence with knowledge gains in new subject matters (Beier & Ackerman, 2005) suggest a much more optimistic view on the fate of cognitive development in adulthood than a mere focus on basic cognitive functions.

A very optimistic view on the potentials for acquiring very high skill is taken in propositions that deliberate practice even is the decisive factor for achieving expert levels of performance in all kinds of domains, implying that the cumulated amount of intense practice is what determines the level of performance among experts (Ericsson, Krampe, & Tesch-Römer, 1993). Such a view is challenged, however, by findings showing that even among highly skilled experts, individual differences in cognitive abilities still play an important role (Hambrick & Meinz, 2011). A more balanced view on the sometimes attempted confrontation of innate talent versus deliberate practice (or nature versus nurture) therefore suggests a developmental perspective in which affective, motivational, and cognitive traits influence the direction, intensity, and effectiveness of learning and both, biological and environmental factors potentially constrain levels of expert performance (Ackerman, 2014).

# Individual differences of cognitive development across the lifespan

While stability of cognitive ability in early childhood is difficult to estimate, due to the need to use different tests for different age groups, there exists empirical evidence for substantial stability from mid-childhood to old age. Most impressively, retesting participants from the Scottish Mental Surveys, who did intelligence tests at age 11, after almost 70 years with the same tests, yielded correlation coefficients above 0.70 (Deary, Whiteman, Starr, Whalley, & Fox, 2004). This implies that about half of the variance of individual differences in general cognitive ability is stable across almost the entire human lifespan. Conversely, it also implies that the other half is not—so the stage is set for personality and lifespan developmental researchers alike to investigate the factors responsible for stability and change.

Regarding factors producing stability, the high heritability coefficients estimated for cognitive abilities (Bouchard, 2004) point to the important role of the genetic endowment in determining individual differences around the average normative trends. That is, the interindividual variability of cognitive performance levels observable at different ages throughout the lifespan can to a considerable extent be explained by genetic differences (e.g., by comparisons of monozygotic with dizygotic twins). Interestingly from a developmental perspective, however, heritability estimates themselves show age-related differences. Across childhood and adolescence, the contribution of genetic differences increases from about 0.25 to 0.70 (Tucker-Drob, Briley, & Harden, 2013). As one possibility, this could be due to new genes becoming active and influencing cognitive performance across these age periods. Behavioral genetic analyses of longitudinal studies indicate that this indeed is likely to be a contributing factor in early childhood, while in mid-childhood, adolescence, and adulthood, the more important mechanisms seems to be evocative and active processes leading to increasingly better matches of genetic predispositions and environmental conditions (i.e., gene—environment correlations; Briley & Tucker-Drob, 2013). Put simply, across development, individuals are selected into, or can freely choose, environments that fit their genetically dispositions and magnify the impact of these dispositions on observable behavior by supporting the exploitation of the genetic potential. Importantly, these processes may be constrained by environments that are not responsive or cannot provide the resources necessary to foster genetic potential. An increase in heritability of cognitive ability in early childhood, for example, has been found to interact with socioeconomic status—with only children from families of high status showing the increase (Tucker-Drob, Rhemtulla, Harden, Turkheimer, & Fask, 2011).

While it has been found difficult to identify reliable interindividual differences in the rates of change of cognitive performance and their correlates in young and middle adulthood (Salthouse, 2014a), toward the end of the lifespan, individual differences in change of cognitive abilities tend to grow larger (de Frias et al., 2007), likely indicating the increasing importance of non-normative factors like diseases and terminal decline processes. Such individual differences in change have been shown to be moderately to strongly correlated across different abilities, with a general factor being able to explain a large share of variance of changes in the different abilities (Ghisletta, Rabbitt, Lunn, & Lindenberger, 2012). This picture alluding to common sources of change is reflected in correlated changes at the brain level, for example, for reductions in volumes of different brain regions (Raz et al., 2005).

# Malleability of cognitive development across the lifespan

What about the approximately 50% of interindividual difference variance in cognitive abilities that is not stable from childhood to old age? Similar discussions as visited above regarding skill acquisition have been led regarding the role of genetic versus environmental factors for individual differences in intelligence (i.e., fluid or general cognitive ability). As reviewed by Nisbett et al. (2012), there is abundant empirical evidence that the environment can and does play an important role for the development of individual differences in cognitive ability. Though difficult to separate from effects that are genetically transmitted, there is evidence for effects of risk factors, like preterm birth (Kerr-Wilson, Mackay, Smith, & Pell, 2012) as well as supporting factors, like breastfeeding (Kramer et al., 2008), already in the very early cognitive development of infants. A large study comparing children with siblings to children whose siblings have died in their first year of life indicated that the presence of siblings (rather than the later position in birth order) on average has a negative effect on intelligence (Kristensen & Bjerkedal, 2008), pointing to the importance of intellectual stimulation provided by parents. Notably, adoption studies with children being moved into families with higher socioeconomic status highlight the importance of environmental factors by identifying substantial increases in general cognitive ability (van IJzendoorn, Juffer, & Klein Poelhuis, 2005). Methodologically, it is a tough challenge, however, to disentangle the causal impact of different environmental factors that might contribute to such effects. Those factors include effects of the home environment as well as of neighborhood, peer, and school environments, the quality of which often will be related to each other as well as to socioeconomic status.

Regarding the effects of early education on cognitive development, some intensive programs, like the *Abecedarian Project*, have produced substantial gains in cognitive ability, which were maintained to some degree into adulthood (Campbell, Ramey, Pungello, Sparling, & Miller-Johnson, 2002). The finding that these effects on cognitive ability tend to fade during elementary school may be more than compensated by positive, enduring, and reciprocally reinforcing effects on school achievement and motivation, rendering particularly early interventions targeting children from disadvantaged socioeconomic backgrounds beneficial from a long-term perspective (Heckman, 2006). Evidence from natural experiments that influence the amount of regular schooling (like mandatory cutoff dates for school entry or policy changes regarding school duration) shows that mandatory schooling can have substantial effects on intelligence (Brinch & Galloway, 2012; Ceci, 1991).

In sum, there is broad evidence that the environmental factors and educational offers can have beneficial effects not only on the acquisition of skills and knowledge but also on the development of broad cognitive abilities throughout childhood and adolescence.

Moving forward into the adult lifespan, an active lifestyle has been hypothesized to positively influence cognitive ability development. The "use-it-or-lose-it hypothesis," which suggests that cognitively stimulating work, leisure, and social activities can prevent brain and cognitive deterioration, is difficult to demonstrate empirically because of possible reciprocal causation between cognitive ability and cognitive activity, and because the extensive everyday behavior that the hypothesis puts forward as a cause cannot be experimentally manipulated. A comprehensive review of the evidence regarding effects of enriched cognitive, social, and physical activities on adult cognitive development (Hertzog, Kramer, Wilson, & Lindenberger, 2009) identified leading and maintaining an intellectually stimulating lifestyle as well as physical activity as beneficial for cognitive functioning in older age. While evidence for a stimulating lifestyle mainly comes from longitudinal studies showing relations of intellectual activity on subsequent changes in cognition, the effects of physical activity are more rigorously demonstrated by experimental studies, primarily with different kinds of "aerobic exercise" (e.g., running, jogging, bicycling). The positive effects of physical activity fit into the emerging picture that health factors that are relevant for general well-being and longevity, like hypertension, also have substantial impact on cognitive functioning (Raz & Rodrigue, 2006). While the evidence for nutrition supplements that are advertised to improve cognition in older age is weak, treating risk factors for general health therefore seems to be of high importance for successful cognitive aging (Daffner, 2010).

Another line of research has worked on targeted interventions for improving cognitive abilities, i.e., cognitive training programs. To evaluate their effectiveness and usefulness as a means to counter the effects of cognitive aging, the distinction of skill and ability becomes important again. Trainings that aim at teaching and practicing specific skills in the service of improving cognitive performance can be quite effective. For example, mnemonic strategies, like the method of loci, can lead to substantial improvements of episodic memory performance from childhood to old age (Brehmer, Li, Müller, von Oertzen, & Lindenberger, 2007; see Fig. 19.1). Findings also show, however, that the use of such strategies is less efficient in older age. That is, the same amount of practice does not lead to comparable amounts of improvement for younger and older adults. Also, maximum performance levels after intensive practice are lower for older adults, indicating constraints to practice-induced plasticity due to the above-mentioned losses in the cognitive control mechanisms supporting strategy use together with losses of the associative component (Shing et al., 2010).

Another limitation of practicing specific strategies is their circumscribed applicability regarding everyday cognitive competency. Cognitive strategies are typically tailored to specific cognitive tasks and show little transfer to other tasks. Similarly, while practice on tasks of fluid intelligence leads to improved performance, patterns of transfer to other tasks indicate that improvements are likely due to gains in task-specific skills, rather than gains in the broad cognitive ability of reasoning (Ball et al., 2002; Baltes, Dittman-Kohli, & Kliegl, 1986).

New hope for achieving such far transfer in adults as well as in children and adolescents comes from training interventions that either focus on the assumed cognitive basis of cognitive abilities, like working memory capacity for fluid intelligence, or that intensely train multifaceted heterogeneous batteries of cognitive tasks, thereby mimicking a cognitive stimulating lifestyle. Demonstrations of far transfer are complicated by conceptual and methodological challenges, however, like the creation of appropriate control conditions and the psychometric operationalization of far transfer (Noack, Lövdén, & Schmiedek, 2014), which might be one reason why even meta-analyses on far transfer effects working memory training come to different conclusions (Karbach & Verhaeghen, 2014; Melby-Lervag, Redick, & Hulme, 2016). Based on general considerations about the potential for plastic changes as a result of a mismatch between cognitive demands (e.g., of a cognitive training) and functional supply of the individual (Lövdén, Bäckman, Lindenberger, Schaefer, & Schmiedek, 2010), however, substantial improvements in broad cognitive abilities seem unlikely for short-term training interventions with restricted dosage (of typically some dozen hours) and might require more fundamental and enduring interventions. The generalization of improvements on psychometric transfer tasks to real-life performance criteria also is still relatively open. Even if transfer tasks are strongly correlated with outcomes (like school achievement) at pretest, this does not ensure that *changes* in transfer task performance show equally strong relations to *changes* in the outcomes (Rode, Robson, Purviance, Geary, & Mayr, 2014).

Such a lack of agreement of between-person relations and relations of within-person changes hints to a general conceptual problem that researchers who are interested in individual differences as well as in development and change at different time scale levels are facing. It has been argued theoretically and shown empirically that structures of between-person differences, which build the basis of differential and much of personality psychology, are not necessarily informative about structures of within-person changes (Borsboom, Mellenbergh, & van Heerden, 2003; Molenaar, 2004). Within-person structures can differ from each other as well as from between-person structures and putting them into a unified framework requires the consideration of different sources of variation at these different levels of investigation (Voelkle, Brose, Schmiedek, & Lindenberger, 2014). From such a perspective, research on the malleability of cognitive functions is not only of applied relevance but also a strong means to better understand the factors that shape individual development across the lifespan and the meta-mechanisms that possibly support successful cognitive aging. Besides the experience-based plasticity just reviewed, several such meta-mechanisms have been proposed, including the preservation or *maintenance* of functions, the *compensation* for loss, as well as *selection* processes (Lindenberger, 2014). An emphasis on trying to support *maintenance* of youth-like functioning, on the one hand, is based on findings that brain structure and function of high-performing older adults is more alike that of younger adults than it is the case for older adults with more deficient performance

(Nyberg, Lövdén, Ricklund, Lindenberger, & Bäckman, 2012). *Compensation*, on the other hand, is describing structural or functional reorganizations as a reaction to losses in functionality (e.g., a stroke), that is, the replacement of a function that has been lost with a different function (Bäckman & Dixon, 1992). Finally, *selection* processes may profit from the fact that cognitive performance on certain tasks typically can be achieved in different ways, for example, using different strategies. Regarding such strategies, a general age-related shift from self-initiated processing to reliance on environmental support has been suggested (Craik, 1983), which helps explaining why, for example, recognition memory is less affected by aging than free recall (La Voie & Light, 1994). Such a trend bears the potential of adaptive technology (e.g., smartphone-based applications) by providing environmental support that is tailored to older individuals' natural environmental circumstances and selective behavioral repertoires, which have developed in tandem over extended periods of time. However, such technology also bears the risk of unnecessarily giving up control and opportunities for beneficial cognitive engagement (Lindenberger & Mayr, 2014).

## Conclusion and future directions

There are a huge and ever-growing number of studies comparing cognitive performance and performance-related neurophysiological parameters across groups of children and adults of different ages, documenting a complex picture of more or less pronounced differences across the lifespan. There are also more and more longitudinal studies that allow relating changes in cognitive abilities to changes in potentially related variables, like lifestyle or health, at the time scale of long-term changes. And there is a lot of age-comparative research being conducted on the effectiveness of cognitive trainings and interventions. Together, this large empirical basis underscores the central tenets of lifespan developmental psychology (Baltes et al., 2006), particularly the multidirectionality, the importance of individual differences, and the malleability of cognitive development. Research still is, and will keep, facing great challenges regarding the complexities of the interplay between biological processes of maturation, senescence, and environmental influences that produce the individual differences and create as well as constrain opportunities for the optimization of development. These challenges include getting from the highly interesting findings in behavioral genetics, that investigate individual differences (e.g., of mono- and dizygotic twins) and suggest correlations and interactions of genes and environment, to understanding the underlying processes at the level of individuals. The finding that even genetically identical mice reared in the same environment develop substantial individual differences in exploratory behavior and brain regions associated with memory (Freund et al., 2013) gives a hint at the complexities lifespan developmental researchers ultimately are confronted with. Understanding these will require advancement in the theoretical development of dynamic models as well as the collection of data with study designs of high temporal resolution (Nesselroade & Molenaar, 2010), which in combination allow getting at individual differences in the processes at different time scale levels that underlie individual differences in the developmental trajectories across the lifespan.

# References

Ackerman, P. L. (1988). Determinants of individual differences during skill acquisition: Cognitive abilities and information processing. *Journal of Experimental Psycholog: General, 117*, 288−318.

Ackerman, P. L. (2000). Domain-specific knowledge as the "dark matter" of adult intelligence: Gf/Gc, personality and interest correlates. *Journal of Gerontology: Psychological Sciences, 55B*, P69−P84.

Ackerman, P. L. (2014). Nonsense, common sense, and science of expert performance: Talent and individual differences. *Intelligence, 45*, 6−17. Available from http://dx.doi.org/10.1016/j.intell.2013.04.009.

Ackerman, P. L., & Heggestad, E. D. (1997). Intelligence, personality, and interests: Evidence for overlapping traits. *Psychological Bulletin, 121*, 219−245.

Bäckman, L., & Dixon, R. A. (1992). Psychological compensation: A theoretical framework. *Psychological Bulletin, 112*, 259−283.

Bäckman, L., Nyberg, L., Lindenberger, U., Li, S.-C., & Farde, L. (2006). The correlative triad among aging, dopamine, and cognition: Current status and future prospects. *Neuroscience and Biobehavioral Reviews, 30*, 791−807. Available from http://dx.doi.org/10.1016/j.neubiorev.2006.06.00.

Ball, K. K., Berch, D. B., Helmers, K. F., Jobe, J. B., Leveck, M. D., Marsiske, M., et al. (2002). Effects of cognitive training interventions with older adults—A randomized controlled trial. *Journal of the American Medical Association, 288*, 2271−2281. Available from http://dx.doi.org/10.1001/jama.288.18.2271.

Baltes, P. B. (1987). Theoretical propositions of life span develop-mental psychology: On the dynamics between growth and decline. *Developmental Psychology, 23*, 611−626.

Baltes, P. B. (1997). On the incomplete architecture of human ontogeny: Selection, optimization, and compensation as foundation of developmental theory. *American Psychologist, 52*, 366−380.

Baltes, P. B., Dittmann-Kohli, F., & Kliegl, R. (1986). Reserve-capacity of the elderly in aging-sensitive tests of fluid intelligence: Replication and extension. *Psychology and Aging, 1*, 172−177. Available from http://dx.doi.org/10.1037/0882-7974.1.2.172.

Baltes, P. B., Lindenberger, U., & Staudinger, U. M. (2006). Life span theory in developmental psychology. In W. Damon, & R. M. Lerner (Eds.), *Handbook of child psychology: Vol. 1. Theoretical models of human development* (6th ed., pp. 569−664). New York, NY: Wiley.

Beier, M. E., & Ackerman, P. L. (2005). Age, ability, and the role of prior knowledge on the acquisition of new domain knowledge: Promising results in a real-world learning environment. *Psychology and Aging, 2*, 342−355. Available from http://dx.doi.org/10.1037/0882-7974.20.2.341.

Bialystok, E., & Craik, F. I. M. (Eds.), (2006). *Lifespan cognition: Mechanisms of change* New York, NY: Oxford University Press.

Borsboom, D., Mellenbergh, G. J., & van Heerden, J. (2003). The theoretical status of latent variables. *Psychological Review*, *110*, 203−219. Available from http://dx.doi.org/10.1037/0033-295X.110.2.203.

Bouchard, T. J. (2004). Genetic influence on human psychological traits. *Current Directions in Psychological Science*, *13*, 148−151.

Brehmer, Y., Li, S.-C., Müller, V., von Oertzen, T., & Lindenberger, U. (2007). Memory plasticity across the life span: Uncovering children's latent potential. *Developmental Psychology*, *43*, 465−478. Available from http://dx.doi.org/10.1037/0012-1649.43.2.465.

Briley, D. A., & Tucker-Drob, E. M. (2013). Explaining the increasing heritability of cognitive ability across development: A meta-analysis of longitudinal twin and adoption studies. *Psychological Science*, *24*, 1704−1713. Available from http://dx.doi.org/10.1177/0956797613478618.

Brinch, C. N., & Galloway, T. A. (2012). Schooling in adolescence raises IQ scores. *Proceedings of National Academy of Sciences*, *109*, 425−430. Available from http://dx.doi.org/10.1073/pnas.1106077109.

Campbell, F. A., Ramey, C. T., Pungello, E., Sparling, J., & Miller- Johnson, S. (2002). Early childhood education: Young adult outcomes from the Abecedarian Project. *Applied Developmental Science*, *6*, 42−57. Available from http://dx.doi.org/10.1207/S1532480XADS0601_05.

Carroll, J. B. (1993). *Human cognitive abilities*. Cambridge: Cambride University Press.

Cattell, R. B. (1971). *Abilities: Their structure growth and action*. Boston: Houghton-Mifflin.

Cattell, R. B. (1987). *Intelligence: Its structure, growth and action*. New York, NY: North-Holland.

Ceci, S. J. (1991). How much does schooling influence general intelligence and its cognitive components? A reassessment of the evidence. *Developmental Psychology*, *27*, 703−722. Available from http://dx.doi.org/10.1037/0012-1649.27.5.703.

Craik, F. I. M. (1983). On the transfer of information from temporary to permanent memory. *Philosophical Transactions of Royal Society London B: Biological Science*, *302*, 341−359.

Daffner, K. R. (2010). Promoting successful cognitive aging: A comprehensive review. *Journal of Alzheimer's Disease*, *19*, 1101−1121. Available from http://dx.doi.org/10.3233/JAD-2010-1306.

Deary, I. J., Whiteman, M. C., Starr, J. M., Whalley, L. J., & Fox, H. C. (2004). The impact of childhood intelligence on later life: Following up the Scottish Mental Surveys of 1932 and 1947. *Journal of Personality and Social Psychology*, *86*, 130−147. Available from http://dx.doi.org/10.1037/0022-3514.86.1.130.

de Frias, C. M., Lövdén, M., Lindenberger, U., & Nilsson, L.-G. (2007). Revisiting the dedifferentiation hypothesis with longitudinal multi-cohort data. *Intelligence*, *35*, 381−392. Available from http://dx.doi.org/10.1016/j.intell.2006.07.011.

Dickens, W. T., & Flynn, J. R. (2001). Heritability estimates versus large environmental effects: The IQ paradox resolved. *Psychological Review*, *108*, 346−369. Available from http://dx.doi.org/10.1037//0033-295X, 108.2.346

Ericsson, K. A., Krampe, R. Th, & Tesch-Römer, C. (1993). The role of deliberate practice in the acquisition of expert performance. *Psychological Review*, *100*, 363−406. Available from http://dx.doi.org/10.1037/0033-295X.100.3.363.

Freund, J., Brandmaier, A. M., Lewejohann, L., Kirste, I., Kritzler, M., Krüger, A., ... Kempermann, G. (2013). Emergence of individuality in genetically identical mice. *Science*, *340*(6133), 756−759. Available from http://dx.doi.org/10.1126/science.1235294.

Ghisletta, P., Rabbitt, P., Lunn, M., & Lindenberger, U. (2012). Two thirds of the age-based changes in fluid and crystallized intelligence, perceptual speed, and memory in adulthood are shared. *Intelligence*, *40*, 260−268. Available from http://dx.doi.org/10.1016/j. intell.2012.02.008.

Hambrick, D. Z., & Meinz, E. J. (2011). Limits on the predictive power of domain-specific experience and knowledge in skilled performance. *Current Directions in Psychological Science*, *20*, 275−279. Available from http://dx.doi.org/10.1177/0963721411422061.

Heckman, J. J. (2006). Skill formation and the economics of investing in disadvantaged children. *Science*, *312*, 1900−1902. Available from http://dx.doi.org/10.1126/science.1128898.

Hertzog, C., Kramer, A. F., Wilson, R. S., & Lindenberger, U. (2009). Enrichment effects on adult cognitive development: Can the functional capacity of older adults be preserved and enhanced? *Psychological Science in the Public Interest*, *9*, 1−65. Available from http://dx.doi.org/10.1111/j.1539-6053.2009.01034.x.

Horn, J. L., & Cattell, R. B. (1966). Refinement and test of the theory of fluid and crystallized general intelligences. *Journal of Educational Psychology*, *57*, 253−270.

Jenkins, L., Myerson, J., Hale, S., & Fry, A. F. (1999). Individual and developmental differences in working memory across the life span. *Psychonomic Bulletin and Review*, *6*, 28−40.

Karbach, J., & Verhaeghen, P. (2014). Making working memory work: A meta-analysis of executive-control and working memory training in older adults. *Psychological Science*, *25*, 2027−2037. Available from http://dx.doi.org/10.1177/0956797614548725.

Kail, R., & Salthouse, T. A. (1991). Processing speed as a mental capacity. *Acta Psychologica*, *86*, 199−225.

Kerr-Wilson, C. O., Mackay, D. F., Smith, G. C., & Pell, J. P. (2012). Meta-analysis of the association between preterm delivery and intelligence. *Journal of Public Health*, *34*, 209−216. Available from http://dx.doi.org/10.1093/pubmed/fdr024.

Kramer, M. S., et al. (2008). Breastfeeding and child cognitive development. *Archives of General Psychiatry*, *65*, 578−584. Available from http://dx.doi.org/10.1001/ archpsyc.65.5.578.

Kristensen, P., & Bjerkedal, T. (2008). Explaining the relation between birth order and intelligence. *Science*, *316*, 1717. Available from http://dx.doi.org/10.1126/science.1141493.

La Voie, D., & Light, L. L. (1994). Adult age differences in repetition priming: A meta-analysis. *Psychology and Aging*, *9*, 539−553.

Lindenberger, U. (2014). Human cognitive aging: *Corriger la fortune*? *Science*, *346*, 572−578. Available from http://dx.doi.org/10.1126/science.1254403.

Lindenberger, U., & Mayr, U. (2014). Cognitive aging: Is there a dark side to environmental support? *Trends in Cognitive Science*, *18*, 7−15. Available from http://dx.doi.org/ 10.1016/j.tics.2013.10.006.

Lövdén, M., Bäckman, L., Lindenberger, U., Schaefer, S., & Schmiedek, F. (2010). A theoretical framework for the study of adult cognitive plasticity. *Psychological Bulletin*, *136*, 659−676. Available from http://dx.doi.org/10.1037/a0020080.

Melby-Lervåg, M., Redick, T., & Hulme, C. (2016). Working memory training does not improve performance on measures of intelligence or other measures of "far transfer": Evidence from a meta-analytic review. *Perspectives on Psychological Science*, *11*, 512−534. Available from http://dx.doi.org/10.1177/1745691616635612.

Molenaar, P. C. M. (2004). A manifesto on psychology as idiographic science: Bringing the person back into scientific psychology, this time forever. *Measurement: Interdisciplinary Research & Perspective*, *2*, 201−218. Available from http://dx.doi.org/ 10.1207/s15366359mea0204_1.

Nesselroade, J. R., & Molenaar, P. C. M. (2010). Emphasizing intraindividual variability in the study of development over the lifespan. In W. F. Overton (Ed.), *The handbook of life-span development: Cognition, biology, and methods across the lifespan* (1st ed., pp. 30−54). Hoboken, NJ: Wiley.

Nilsson, L.-G., Adolfsson, R., Bäckman, L., de Frias, C. M., Molander, B., & Nyberg, L. (2004). Betula: A prospective cohort study on memory, health, and aging. *Aging, Neuropsychology, and Cognition, 11*, 134−148. Available from http://dx.doi.org/10.1080/13825580490511026$16.00.

Nisbett, R. E., Aronson, J., Blair, C., Dickens, W., Flynn, J., Halpern, D. F., & Turkheimer, E. (2012). Intelligence: New findings and theoretical developments. *American Psychologist, 67*, 130−159. Available from http://dx.doi.org/10.1037/a0026699.

Noack, H., Lövdén, M., & Schmiedek, F. (2014). On the validity and generality of transfer effects in cognitive training research. *Psychological Research, 78*, 773−789. Available from http://dx.doi.org/10.1007/s00426-014-0564-6.

Nyberg, L., Lövdén, M., Riklund, K., Lindenberger, U., & Bäckman, L. (2012). Memory aging and brain maintenance. *Trends in Cognitive Science, 16*, 292−305. Available from http://dx.doi.org/10.1016/j.tics.2012.04.005.

Ratcliff, R., Love, J., Thompson, C. A., & Opfer, J. (2012). Children are not like older adults: A diffusion model analysis of developmental changes in speeded responses. *Child Development, 83*, 367−381. Available from http://dx.doi.org/10.1111/j.1467-8624.2011.01683.x.

Ratcliff, R., Thapar, A., & McKoon, G. (2010). Individual differences, aging, and IQ in two-choice tasks. *Cognitive Psychology, 60*, 127−157. Available from http://dx.doi.org/10.1016/j.cogpsych.2009.09.001.

Raz, N., Lindenberger, U., Rodrigue, K. M., Kennedy, K. M., Head, D., Williamson, A., ... Acker, J. D. (2005). Regional brain changes in aging healthy adults: General trends, individual differences and modifiers. *Cerebral Cortex, 15*, 1676−1689. Available from http://dx.doi.org/10.1093/cercor/bhi044.

Raz, N., & Rodrigue, K. M. (2006). Differential aging of the brain: Patterns, cognitive correlates and modifiers. *Neuroscience and Biobehavioral Reviews, 30*, 730−748. Available from http://dx.doi.org/10.1016/j.neubiorev.2006.07.001.

Rode, C., Robson, R., Purviance, A., Geary, D. C., & Mayr, U. (2014). Is working memory training effective? A study in a school setting. *PLoS ONE, 9*, e104796. Available from http://dx.doi.org/10.1371/journal.pone.0104796.

Salthouse, T. A. (1991). *Theoretical perspectives on cognitive aging*. Hilsdale, NJ: Lawrence Erlbaum Associates.

Salthouse, T. A. (2014a). Correlates of cognitive change. *Journal of Experimental Psychology: General, 143*, 1026−1048. Available from http://dx.doi.org/10.1037/a0034847.

Salthouse, T. A. (2014b). Why are there different age relations in cross-sectional and longitudinal comparisons of cognitive functioning? *Current Directions in Psychological Science, 23*, 252−256. Available from http://dx.doi.org/10.1177/0963721414535212.

Sander, M. C., Lindenberger, U., & Werkle-Bergner, M. (2012). Lifespan age differences in working memory: A two-component framework. *Neuroscience and Biobehavioral Reviews, 36*, 2007−2033. Available from http://dx.doi.org/10.1016/j.neubiorev.2012.06.004.

Schaie, K. W. (1996). *Intellectual development in adulthood: The Seattle longitudinal study*. New York, NY: Cambridge University Press.

Schaie, K. W., Willis, S. L., & Pennak, S. (2005). An historical framework for cohort differences in intelligence. *Research in Human Development, 2*, 43−67.

Tucker-Drob, E. M., Rhemtulla, M., Harden, K. P., Turkheimer, E., & Fask, D. (2011). Emergence of a gene-by-socioeconomic status interaction on infant mental ability between 10 months and 2 years. *Psychological Science*, *22*, 125–133. Available from http://dx.doi.org/10.1177/0956797610392926.

Tucker-Drob, E. M., Briley, D. A., & Harden, K. P. (2013). Genetic and environmental influences on cognition across development and context. *Current Directions in Psychological Science*, *22*, 349–355. Available from http://dx.doi.org/10.1177/0963721413485087.

Shing, Y.-L., Werkle-Bergner, M., Brehmer, Y., Müller, V., Li, S.-C., & Lindenberger, U. (2010). Episodic memory across the lifespan: The contributions of associative and strategic components. *Neuroscience and Biobehavioral Reviews*, *34*, 1080–1091. Available from http://dx.doi.org/10.1016/j.neubiorev.2009.11.002.

Van IJzendoorn, M. H., Juffer, F., & Klein Poelhuis, C. W. (2005). Adoption and cognitive development: A meta-analytic comparison of adopted and nonadopted children's IQ and school performance. *Psychological Bulletin*, *131*, 301–316. Available from http://dx.doi.org/10.1037/0033-2909.131.2.301.

Voelkle, M. C., Brose, A., Schmiedek, F., & Lindenberger, U. (2014). Toward a unified framework for the study of between-person and within-person structures: Building a bridge between two research paradigms. *Multivariate Behavioral Research*, *49*, 193–213. Available from http://dx.doi.org/10.1080/00273171.2014.889593.

# And the story evolves: The development of personal narratives and narrative identity

*Kate C. McLean*
Western Washington University, Bellingham, WA, United States

In the early 1990s, Dan McAdams (e.g., 1993) proposed that personality had more to it than traits. McAdams was not the first person to say this; the history of personality psychology is full of approaches beyond traits (Carlson, 1971). However, this was the first attempt to describe a personality psychology that included not only traits but also other personality constructs in one integrative model (see also McAdams & Pals, 2006). As part of this integrative model, the third level of personality was introduced (see also McAdams, 1988): the life story, now often called *narrative identity* (McAdams & McLean, 2013; Singer, 2004; see also Murray, 1938; Tompkins, 1979). Since McAdams' initial writings, the study of narrative identity has taken off and is now a robust field with much to offer scholars interested in personality development.

## Personality development at three levels

McAdams' three levels include traits, characteristic adaptations, and the life story. More recently, McAdams (2015) has argued that these three levels can be understood as increasingly sophisticated layers of development, subsumed under the metaphors of actor, motivated agent, and author. This developmental progression encompasses a "whole person" perspective as it takes into account multiple aspects of persons and includes the context of development in these layers. Further, each layer represents a unique aspect of personality; none is a derivative of the other (but see DeYoung, 2015).

*Actor.* The actor self emerges early in the form of temperament, unfolding over time to eventually represent adult personality traits. McAdams discusses the earliest form of the actor self as represented by emotional communication, such as social smiles, and increasing emotional expression (e.g., from distress moving from sadness, anger, or fear) (Izard et al., 1995). These early expressions of emotions foreshadow some of the more emotion-based traits such as extraversion and neuroticism (Shiner & DeYoung, 2013). Still later, we see the

Personality Development Across the Lifespan. DOI: http://dx.doi.org/10.1016/B978-0-12-804674-6.00020-X

emergence of self-regulation, a component of the actor self that relates to conscientiousness. Thus very early in development individual differences in behavior and emotional expression appear and portend later trait development, showing the enduring, relatively stable, and relatively biologically based layer of personality (Asendorph, Denisson, & van Aken, 2008; Caspi et al., 2003; McCrae & Costa, 2008).

*Agent.* The motivated agent emerges toward the end of early childhood when children become more intentional, and more independently goal-directed as they begin to experience a feeling of self-efficacy with their growing skills, coinciding with the time that they also begin school in contemporary industrialized societies (McAdams, 2015). McAdams pays particular attention to motives in the articulation of level 2 of personality. Motivations are a component of personality that has been dominated by measures of unconscious needs (McClelland, 1961; Murray, 1938) such as agency and communion (see McAdams, 1988). Though there is an evolutionary adaptation to needs (e.g., for functioning hierarchies; Hogan, 1982), as well as for well-being (e.g., Deci & Ryan, 2012), contemporary research is rather silent on whether these motives are learned or hardwired, though early theorists fell on the side of learning (McClelland, 1961; Murray, 1938). Regardless, what occurs during middle childhood is the development of the layer of personality that reveals differences in human needs, needs that locate the self in an interpersonal web of society, making this layer more contextualized and responsive to cultural and environmental presses (see also DeYoung, 2015).

*Author.* The author-self emerges in adolescence with the skills for abstract reasoning and the personal and social demand to develop an identity (Habermas & Reese, 2015; McAdams, 2015; McAdams & McLean, 2013). The life story, or narrative identity, is a story of how the person came to be the person she currently is: how did I get here, who am I, and where am I going? There are many experiences in a life, but only some are remembered, and only some of those are particularly salient and connected to self-understanding. Beginning in adolescence it is the job of the individual to select the events that can be strung together to create a narrative arc of one's life, and in so doing, constructing that story brings a sense of coherence, integration, and purpose to the individual (McAdams, 1993).

Compared to the first two levels, narrative identity is more contextual and more idiographic. Further, this story (and the episodes that comprise it) is a subjective construction built by the individual, in interaction with his or her proximal and distal surrounds (McAdams, 2006; McLean, 2015; McLean & Syed, 2016; Nelson & Fivush, 2004; Pasupathi, 2001; Thorne, 2000). And this story is not static. It evolves with new experiences and new ways of understanding the self (Josselson, 2009). Thus, though there is some stability to narrative identity, discussed later, narrative identity is not as stable as traits, nor is there extant evidence that it is as biologically rooted as traits. Indeed, it is largely a level of personality that is defined by the dynamics of individual development and contextual interchange.

# The development of narrative identity: Childhood through adolescence

Although McAdams' (2015) recent work has provided a developmental *framework* for the three levels, the thrust of the *theory* is about understanding adult personality integration. I find this to be an important point because, at the same time that McAdams was developing his model, developmental psychologists were developing a theory to explain the early emergence of the autobiographical self, scholarship rooted in both cognitive theories of memory, as well as sociocultural theories of development (Nelson & Fivush, 2004). Some 30 years later, these two fields are beginning to merge (see McAdams & Zapata-Gietl, 2015; McLean, 2008; Reese, Chen, Jack, & Hayne, 2010; Thorne, 2000), revealing a full palate of scholarship in the development of narrative identity, as well as its consequences as an individual difference.

The parallel work done by developmental psychologists has focused not on personality but also on the development of the early skills that turn out to be quite important in constructing a life story in adolescence and emerging adulthood. This research is rooted in a Vygotskian (1978) approach, in which participation in culturally valued activities is the engine of development (see also Rogoff, 2003). The activity of interest here is the *past-event conversations* that parents have with their children as soon as they are verbally able (see Fivush, Haden, & Reese, 2006, for a review). In these daily, natural conversations about a trip to the zoo, to a grandparent's house, or what happened at day care, parents scaffold the development of early narration skills (e.g., the format and content of culturally valued stories), as well as the value of telling stories for social connection and to define and understand the self through time (Fivush, Bohanek, & Duke, 2008).

Although individual differences from a personality perspective have not been the focus of this work (cf. Laible, Murphy, & Augustine, 2013), variability in parental reminiscing is evident and meaningful. Researchers have identified variability in how parents talk to their children about these past events (Fivush & Fromhoff, 1988), variability that predicts different kinds of narrative patterns in children's own narratives in cross-sectional, longitudinal, and experimental designs (see Fivush et al., 2006, for a review). In short, parents who *elaborate* more with their children in these conversations have children with more elaborative narratives themselves. Intriguingly, parent–child reminiscing is also a predictor of the *volume* of memories that adolescents recall from early childhood (Reese, Jack, & White, 2010), suggesting that the more parents engage with their children in these reminiscing contexts the more material adolescents have to work with once the narrative identity task is engaged. Further, parents may be more important than the children themselves in some cases. Reese, Chen et al. (2010) found that parents' references to emotions in early childhood conversations predicted the ways in which adolescents discussed their own emotions at independent assessments years later. In contrast, the adolescents' *own* references to their own emotions in early childhood did not predict how they discussed past events in adolescence.

Elaborative narratives are particularly important for identity development because it is in the interpretive work where identity is constructed (Habermas, & Köber, 2015; McLean & Pratt, 2006; Pasupathi, Brubaker, & Mansour, 2007; Pasupathi & Wainryb, 2010). Indeed, there are marked increases in measures of narrative interpretation, or autobiographical reasoning (Habermas & Bluck, 2000), in adolescence (Habermas & de Silveira, 2008; McLean, Breen, & Fournier, 2010; Pasupathi & Wainryb, 2010), the stage when the developmental task turns toward the development of identity (Erikson, 1968). Autobiographical reasoning can take many forms, but at its heart is the narration of stories that elaborate on connections between past events and current self-understanding.

However, it does not seem that it is simply the *style* that parents use in these conversations—elaborative or not—that is important. It is the style used when discussing specific kinds of events. In particular, conversational elaboration in the context of *negative* past events predicts children's self-esteem and self-concept during early childhood (Bird & Reese, 2006). Further, mothers' references to their children's negative emotions in early childhood were especially predictive of those same children's independent narration of their own emotional experiences in adolescence (Reese, Chen et al., 2010). Thus there is something about the engagement of particularly challenging events that seems to stick as children begin the work of developing their narrative identities. This finding is echoed in research on adult narrative identity, where we see the importance of managing negative events for identity and well-being (Pals, 2006), work which is discussed later.

Finally, it is in later adolescence and emerging adulthood that narrative characteristics become more clearly connected to other markers of personality. For example, in a cross-sectional study Reese et al. (2014) found significant relations between traits and narrative characteristics for middle and late adolescents, but not for early adolescents, suggesting that it may take some time for these aspects of personality to become integrated. Emerging adulthood is also the time when narrative characteristics become clearly, and consistently, related to aspects of well-being (see Adler, Lodi-Smith, Phillipe, & Houle, 2015, for a review; see also McAdams & Cox, 2010). In sum, beginning at some point between adolescence and emerging adulthood, it appears that the life story begins to emerge and begins to represent a more stable individual difference in personality.

## Narrative identity in adulthood

We are now at the developmental point where the literature meets its division between the developmentalists—who have documented the change and maturation that occurs in narrative skill across the childhood and adolescent years, as well as potential mechanisms of that change—and the personality psychologists who have documented the nature of individual differences in narrative identity, particularly as they relate to well-being and psychological functioning, often above and beyond traits (see Adler et al., 2015, for a review). What we lack currently is a clear understanding of how these developments in childhood and adolescence connect to adult development. I will speculate on the connections between these parts of the lifespan in closing, but for now I turn to the research on narrative identity in adulthood, and where and why we see development in this level of personality, with particular attention to the development of stories themselves.

# The evolution of the story: Stability or change?

There are at least three ways to think about change over time in narratives: change in "style," change in interpretation, and change in content. I address each of these, but I note at the outset that existing empirical evidence is relative scant. However, I spend some time exploring this question of change and stability because I think it may be a newer frontier in research on narrative identity. Thus I also speculate on whether and why we *should* see changes in stories.

## Changes in style, regardless of event narrated

McAdams (McAdams et al., 2006) and Thorne (Thorne, Cutting, & Skaw, 1998) both conducted longitudinal studies of the stability of coded qualities of stories over time in college student samples. McAdams' study was of a 3-month and 3-year period, and Thorne's study was over a 6-month period. In McAdams' study, rank-order stability coefficients were strongest from 1 to 3 months (not surprisingly), but were notable nonetheless, ranging from 0.35 over 3 years for personal growth to 0.53 for narrative complexity. Emotional tone was also rather stable (0.43), as were themes of agency (0.45). Thorne et al. also found moderate stability in themes and motivations over the 6-month time period.

Yet beyond these markers of stability in the style of telling stories, there was also *expected change* in stories over time at the mean level. McAdams et al. found that indices of personal growth, complexity, and positive valence increased over time, likely reflecting a growing maturity and comfort in self (see also Habermas & Berger, 2011). It is possible that we would continue to see such change across young adulthood, which may asymptote in mid-life as identity becomes more consolidated and integrated (Diehl, Hastings, & Stanton, 2001), and as other aspects of personality mature (Roberts, Walton, & Viechtbauer, 2006; Soto, John, Gosling, & Potter 2011) (see also Pasupathi & Mansour, 2006). Thus there is meaningful cross-time stability to the ways that individuals narrate their experiences but, perhaps particularly during the period of intense development in emerging adulthood, there is also reasonable change and development, reflecting the dynamism of this particular level of personality.

## Changes in interpretation of the same events

When examining the same events over time there is also evidence for change. The best example of this comes from a single case study of the assessment of one woman's life story at 4 time points from 21 to 55 years of age (Josselson, 2009). In this analysis, Josselson showed how the same event is told and reinterpreted in relation to the current life tasks and experiences. For example, the event of a relationship in college is interpreted as a romantic story about individuating from family in her 20s, as the negative contrast to her present husband in her 30s, is untold in her 40s, and in her 50s the story returns to a more positive valence and is told as a reminder of her passionate and sexual self. Thus this same event becomes storied in different ways over time as this woman herself changes over time. In some ways, it serves a different function allowing her to reinterpret the past to serve her needs in the present.

In thinking about how a particularly story *should* change, Habermas and Berger (2011) posit that at first an event may be saturated with detail and emotion as it is being processed. As it is processed and integrated into one's larger story (or let go), the details lessen as the event becomes less emotional and resolved (see also Fivush, Sales, & Bohanek, 2008; Pals, 2006; Pennebaker & Beall, 1986). Indeed, they found that over a 3-month period, repeated narratives of emotional events became less emotionally pressing, more condensed, storied from a more distant perspective, and narrated with higher rates of closure. Together these two studies show normative changes in how the same event is narrated across time, as well as how life stories evolve with developmental context and shifting self-perceptions.

## Changes in content: New stories

The studies on changes in interpretation raise the question of how much content actually remains in our narrative identities? Existing data suggest not much, at least for emerging adults. McAdams et al. (2006) found that about 25% of stories were repeated from 1 to 3 months, and about 13% were repeated from 1 to 3 years. In Thorne et al. (1998) study, only 14% of the stories constituted "twice-told tales" over a 6-month period. In Thorne's study, there were no thematic differences between once-told and twice-told stories, though twice-told stories were older than once-told stories, and showed a reminiscence bump of density in the years 16–20 (Rubin, Rahhal, & Poon, 1998). Thus, across both of these studies repeated, specific content was relatively rare. The participants in these studies were of course in a period of relatively dramatic personal change, represented by experiencing many novel and intense events (Rubin et al., 1998), as well as relatively high trait change (Roberts et al., 2006). Thus we would expect repeated content to be rarer in this developmental stage. Josselson's study suggests that for mid-life, or maybe even older, adults there may be more stability in content, even if interpretation of that content changes, but this is a question that remains to be tested.

## How stable should stories be in adulthood?

Given the inherency of stability in personality trait theories (McCrae & Costa, 2008), it makes sense to examine whether there is stability in story characteristics. Indeed, the data to answer the stability question (McAdams et al., 2006; Thorne et al., 1998) were collected and analyzed from a "traditional" personality lens, in which cross-time stability is a focal piece of evidence for the existence of personality (Block, 1981; Funder, 1983). However, from a different lens it is also the case that this framework about *trait* personality may not apply to the *narrative* level of personality.

Indeed, these are markedly different aspects of personality. Traits center on individual differences in cognition, behavior, and affect. The life story is about identity, and identity is not something that sits on the shelf once developed; it is sensitive to context, to time, to new experiences, to new ways of understanding the self and the world (Erikson, 1968). In fact, narrative identity has *not* necessarily been defined by its stability; it has been defined as an ongoing "project." Thus we expect some aspects of narrative to change over time such as the content of stories as new experiences arise, the understanding of one's past as new insights develop, and the interpretation of stories with growth in maturity or wisdom.

Therefore, it makes sense that in McAdams et al.'s longitudinal study they found stability in personal growth, but less so than other aspects of narrative. We would *expect* increases on personal growth across the college years—that makes sense from the perspective of exploring and integrating an identity (see also Carlsson, Wängqvist, & Frisén, 2015). Conversely, certain aspects of events are more likely to stay the same, such as their temporal ordering (see Schiff, 2014), or perhaps the coherence of a story. This is a reminder that given the diversity of ways that one can analyze narratives, clarity about what narrative characteristics one is investigating is critical (McLean, Pasupathi, Fivush, Greenhoot, & Wainryb, 2015). That is, changes in the emotional hue, coherence, or interpretive processes may each show differential patterns of stability and change.

Finally, in thinking about why some stories *do* retain some markers of stability, Thorne and Nam (2009) suggest that telling same story over time may "enhance personality continuity." Indeed, when we hold on to certain stories the narrative arc may solidify and may integrate with other aspects of personality for greater stability over time. Further, just as with trait development, "evocative forces" may also work to maintain story stability: others may ask us to recount the favorite tale, or we may be drawn to situations that evoke the humorous or the dark tales.

However, Thorne and Nam also suggest that repeated storytelling may also *constrain* personality development. The longer the story has been around, the harder it may be to change it. Indeed, I have recently written about the drive to maintain stability in narrative identity that is both internal and external (McLean, 2015; see also McLean & Syed, 2016). The importance of predictability to reduce uncertainty and anxiety is a part of the human condition, a motive that drives one to maintain homeostasis. This drive can be beneficial, if the story still fits, but can be harmful if the story no longer fits, or constrains meaningful personal growth and development. Further, this is not only an internal drive. Others, too, are also invested in this stability. We want to predict how others will act, and we want to think we know who they are. Others may constrain the evolution of personal stories to maintain their own homeostasis, perhaps especially close others, such as the family (McLean, 2015).

This need to maintain homeostasis may be particularly challenged when external events *demand* a rewriting, or a new story all together. For example, a divorce may change the story of one's relationship arc in rather substantive ways. Just as obtaining a job may demand greater conscientiousness (Roberts, 1997), some experiences may demand a revision of our identities.

# How the story evolves in relation to other levels of personality and earlier developments

Clearly identity narratives do not arise out of thin air. They are deeply based in earlier social—cultural practices, such as parental reminiscence, as well as earlier developing components of personality. That is, this level of personality requires a skill that develops, and they are likely shaped by other parts of ourselves that precede the development of narrative identity.

In terms of connections with traits, Lodi-Smith, Geise, Roberts, and Robins (2009) found that traits at the beginning of college predicted specific characteristics of narratives at the end of college. In a mid-life sample, Pals (2006) found that exploratory processing at age 52 was rooted in the trait of coping openness at age 21. Thus we would expect that traits may shape stories, from their emotional tone, with those high on neuroticism telling more negative stories, to their structure, with those high on openness telling more complex stories (McAdams et al., 2004), to the manner of telling them, with those high on extraversion engaging in more frequent narration (McLean & Pasupathi, 2006).

However, storytelling is a dynamic process and stories have the power to changes selves as well (see McLean, Pasupathi, & Pals, 2007). For example, Adler (2012) documented that, over 12 weeks, changes in narratives *preceded* changes in mental health (see also Cox & McAdams, 2014). In Pals' (2006) longitudinal study, narrative processing served as a mediator between early trait coping openness and later maturity at age 61. Although the focus of this chapter has been on stability and change within stories themselves, these studies also show that stories can also serve as a mechanism for change within the person. Thus as the story evolves so too does the person.

In terms of the social—cultural context, Reese's (Reese et al., 2010) longitudinal study, discussed earlier, is the first to document connections between the early parent—child reminiscing context and narrative identity in adulthood. Here we see that parental reminiscing practices are uniquely important in predicting how their children narrate their own lives independently in adolescence.

Connecting these two areas of research it appears that early reminiscing contexts interact with personality, in both mothers and children. For example, children who are temperamentally more active and less sociable experience more repetition in past-event conversations (Lewis, 1999), and children with more effortful control have mothers who are more elaborative (Laible, 2004; Laible et al., 2013). This suggests that child temperament is an evocative force that can draw out varying styles of reminiscence. Maternal personality may also matter. In one of the few studies on the matter, Laible et al. (2013) found that mothers higher on openness to experience discussed causes of and potential coping strategies for negative emotions more than those lower on openness. Further, genetic similarity between parents and children may underlie some of these effects, as when we see the association between elaboration on the parent's side, and then subsequently on the child's side later in development, which may reflect a passive gene–environment correlation.

## Conclusion

As was articulated in discussing the research on narrative, there are many components to a story. That is, there are many characteristics to examine, such as emotional tone, complexity, and interpretive content, all with different meaning for change, stability, and psychological functioning. One way to organize the many components for analysis is to think about integration (Syed & Mitchell, 2015), such that what may in fact be developing across adulthood is an *integrated identity*.

Syed and McLean (2016) recently argued that there are three types of identity integration—contextual, temporal, and ego integration, or the integration of both time and context—all of which can be accomplished via narrative. Contextual integration is the bringing together of multiple aspects of self, such as various content domains of identity (e.g., politics, religion, and family), as well as other aspects of individuals such as ethnic or gender identity. Temporal integration has been the topic of most of this chapter and addresses making sense of the self across time. The final form of integration is making sense of the self across context *and* time (Lilgendahl, 2015). Syed and McLean (2016) argued that ego integration most closely represents McAdams' (2013) idea of the integrated life story. There is far less research on this type of integration; indeed, it is hard to hold this many variables in mind (see Azmitia, Syed, and Radmacher, 2008).

To add to these layers of complexity, it may also be that an integration of multiple aspects of personality is also what's developing in adulthood. There has been little work as of yet on *conceptualizing how to integrate McAdams' three levels* (see DeYoung, 2015; Lilgendahl, 2015; Syed & McLean, in preparation). There has been a good deal of work examining the incremental validity of various iterations of the three levels (Adler et al., 2015), as well as interactions between various levels in predicting a valued outcome (Lilgendahl & McAdams, 2011). But how do the three levels work together? For example, what does it mean that traits and narratives are not clearly connected until mid to late adolescence (Reese et al., 2014)? How do we conceptualize these levels in interaction? This work on personality integration may be the focal point of narrative development in adulthood.

In closing, I note that there are really two questions threaded throughout this chapter. The first is about the *construction* of a life story, a story that while rooted in earlier narrative developments, did not exist before. The second is about the *evolution* of that story once constructed as the person him or herself is evolving. Given these two issues, at least two clear questions arise from the extant research. What facilitates the construction of that story—clearly reminiscence practices and other aspects of personality are important. What facilitates the evolution of that story? Here we know less, given the paucity of longitudinal work. However, personality traits seem to matter, and changes in that story matter for psychological functioning. This is an exciting new frontier for narrative researchers, and I look forward to the evolution of the story.

# Acknowledgment

I thank Jennifer Lilgendahl for comments on an earlier version of this manuscript.

# References

Adler, J. M. (2012). Living into the story: Agency and coherence in a longitudinal study of narrative identity development and mental health over the course of psychotherapy. *Journal of Personality and Social Psychology, 102*(2), 367−389.

Adler, J. M., Lodi-Smith, J., Phlippe, F. L., & Houle, I. (2015). The incremental validity of narrative identity in predicting well-being: A review of the field and recommendations for the future. *Personality and Social Psychology Review.*

Asendorph, J. B., Denisson, J. J., & Van Aken, M. A. (2008). Inhibited and aggressive preschool children at 23 years of age: Personality and social transitions into adulthood. *Developmental Psychology, 44*, 997−1011.

Azmitia, M., Syed, M., & Radmacher, K. (2008). On the intersection of personal and social identities: Introduction and evidence from a longitudinal study of emerging adults In M. Azmitia, M. Syed, & K. Radmacher (Eds.), *The intersections of personal and social identities. New directions for child and adolescent development* (120, pp. 1−16). San Francisco: Jossey-Bass.

Bird, A., & Reese, E. (2006). Emotional reminiscing and the development of an autobiographical self. *Developmental Psychology, 42*, 613−626.

Block, J. (1981). Some enduring and consequential structures of personality. In A. I. Rabin, J. Arnoff, A. M. Barclay, & R. A. Zucker (Eds.), *Further explorations in personality* (pp. 27−43). New York, NY: Wiley.

Carlson, R. (1971). Where is the person in personality research? *Psychological Bulletin, 75*, 203−219.

Carlsson, J., Wängqvist, M., & Frisén, A. (2015). Identity development in the late twenties: A never ending story. *Developmental psychology, 51*(3), 334.

Caspi, A., Harrington, H. L., Milne, B., Amell, J., Theodore, R. F., & Moffitt, T. E. (2003). Children's behavioral styles at age 3 are linked to their adult personality traits at age 26. *Journal of Personality, 71*, 495−513.

Cox, K., & McAdams, D. P. (2014). Meaning making during high and low point life story episodes predicts emotion regulation two years later: How the past informs the future. *Journal of Research in Personality, 50*, 66−70.

Deci, E. L., & Ryan, R. M. (2012). Self-determination theory In P. A. M. Van Lange, A. W. Kruglanski, & E. T. Higgins (Eds.), *Handbook of theories of social psychology* (Vol. 1, pp. 416−437). Thousand Oaks, CA: Sage.

DeYoung, C. G. (2015). Cybernetic Big Five theory. *Journal of Research in Personality*, *56*, 33–58.

Diehl, M., Hastings, C. T., & Stanton, J. M. (2001). Self-concept differentiation across the adult life span. *Psychology and Aging*, *16*, 643–654.

Erikson, E. (1968). *Identity, youth and crisis*. New York, NY: W W Norton & Co.

Fivush, R., Bohanek, J. G., & Duke, M. (2008). The intergenerational self: Subjective perspective and family history. In F. Sani (Ed.), *Individual and collective self-continuity*. Mahwah, NJ: Erlbaum.

Fivush, R., & Fromhoff, F. (1988). Style and structure in mother–child conversations about the past. *Discourse Processes*, *11*, 337–355.

Fivush, R., Haden, C. A., & Reese, E. (2006). Elaborating on elaborations: Role of maternal reminiscing style in cognitive and socioemotional development. *Child Development*, *77*, 1568–1588.

Fivush, R., Sales, J. M., & Bohanek, J. G. (2008). Meaning making in mothers' and children's narratives of emotional events. *Memory*, *16*(6), 579–594.

Funder, D. C. (1983). Three issues in predicting more of the people: A reply to Mischel and Peake. *Psychological Review*, *90*, 283–290.

Habermas, T., & Berger, N. (2011). Retelling everyday emotional events: Condensation, distancing, and closure. *Memory and Emotion*, *25*, 206–291.

Habermas, T., & Bluck, S. (2000). Getting a life: The development of the life story in adolescence. *Psychological Bulletin*, *126*, 748–769.

Habermas, T., & de Silveira, C. (2008). The development of global coherence in life narratives across adolescence: Temporal, causal, and thematic aspects. *Developmental Psychology*, *44*, 707–721.

Habermas, T., & Köber, C. (2015). Autobiographical reasoning in life narratives buffers the effect of biographical disruptions on the sense of self-continuity. *Memory*, *23*, 564–574.

Habermas, T., & Reese, E. (2015). Getting a life takes time: The development of the life story in adolescence, its precursoes and consequences. *Human Development*, *58*, 172–201.

Hogan, R. (1982). A socioanalytic theory of personality. In M. Paige (Ed.), *Nebraska symposium on motivation* (Vol. 29, pp. 55–89). Lincoln, NE: University of Nebraska Press.

Izard, C. E., Fantauzzo, C. A., Castle, J. M., Haynes, O. M., Rayias, M. F., & Putnam, P. H. (1995). The ontogeny and significance of infants' facial expressions in the first nine months. *Developmental Psychology*, *31*, 997–1013.

Josselson, R. (2009). The present of the past: Dialogues with memory over time. *Journal of Personality*, *77*, 647–668.

Laible, D. (2004). Mother–child discourse in two contexts: Factors that predict differences in the quality and emotional content of the discourse and consequences of those differences for socioemotional development. *Developmental Psychology*, *40*, 979–992.

Laible, D., Murphy, T. P., & Augustine, M. (2013). Predicting the quality of mother-child reminiscing surrounding negative emotional events at 42 and 48 months old. *Journal of Cognition and Development*, *14*, 270–291.

Lewis, K. (1999). Maternal style in reminiscing: Relations to child individual differences. *Cognitive Development*, *14*, 381–399.

Lilgendahl, J. P. (2015). The dynamic role of identity processes in personality development: Theories, patterns, and new directions. In K. C. McLean, & M. Syed (Eds.), *The Oxford handbook of identity development*. New York, NY: Oxford University Press.

Lilgendahl, J. P., & McAdams, D. P. (2011). Constructing stories of self-growth: How individual differences in patterns of autobiographical reasoning relate to well-being in midlife. *Journal of Personality, 79*, 391−428.

Lodi-Smith, J., Geise, A. C., Roberts, B. W., & Robins, R. W. (2009). Narrating personality change. *Journal of Personality and Social Psychology, 96*, 679−689.

McAdams, D. P. (1988). *Power, intimacy, and the life story: Personological inquiries into identity*. New York, NY: Guilford.

McAdams, D. P. (1993). *The stories we live by: Personal myths and the making of the self*. New York, NY: Guilford Press.

McAdams, D. P. (2006). *The redemptive self: Stories Americans live by*. New York, NY: Oxford University Press.

McAdams, D. P. (2015). *The art and science of personality development*. New York, NY: Guilford.

McAdams, D. P., Anyidoho, N. A., Brown, C., Huang, Y. T., Kaplan, B., & Machado, M. A. (2004). Traits and stories: Links between dispositional and narrative features of personality. *Journal of Personality, 72*, 761−784.

McAdams, D. P., Bauer, J. J., Sakaeda, A., Anyidoho, N. A., Machado, M., Magrino, K., … Pals, J. L. (2006). Continuity and change in the life story: A longitudinal study of autobiographical memories in emerging adulthood. *Journal of Personality, 74*, 1371−1400.

McAdams, D. P., & Cox, K. S. (2010). Self and identity across the life span. In R. Lerner, A. Freund, & M. Lamb (Eds.), *Handbook of life span development* (Vol. 2, pp. 158−207). New York, NY: Wiley.

McAdams, D. P., & McLean, K. C. (2013). Narrative identity. *Current Directions in Psychological Science, 22*, 233−238.

McAdams, D. P., & Pals, J. L. (2006). A new Big Five: Fundamental principles for an integrative science of personality. *American Psychologist, 61*, 204−217.

McAdams, D. P., & Zapata-Gietl, C. (2015). Three strands of identity development across the human life course: Reading Erik Erikson in full. In K. C. McLean, & M. Syed (Eds.), *Oxford handbook of identity development* (pp. 81−94). New York, NY: Oxford University Press.

McClelland, D. C. (1961). *The achieving society*. New York, NY: Van Nostrand.

McCrae, R. R., & Costa, P. T., Jr. (2008). The Five Factor Theory of personality. In O. P. John, R. W. Robins, & L. A. Pervin (Eds.), *Handbook of personality: Theory and research* (pp. 159−181). New York, NY: Guilford Press.

McLean, K. C., & Syed, M. (2016). Personal, master, and alternative narratives: An integrative framework for understanding identity development in context. *Human Development, 58*, 318−349.

McLean, K. C. (2008). The emergence of narrative identity. *Social and Personality Compass, 2*, 1−18.

McLean, K. C. (2015). *The co-authored self: Family stories and the construction of personal identity*. New York, NY: Oxford University Press.

McLean, K. C., Breen, A. V., & Fournier, M. A. (2010). Constructing the self in early, midlife and late adolescent boys. *Journal of Research on Adolescence, 20*, 166−187.

McLean, K. C., & Pasupathi, M. (2006). Collaborative narration of the past and extraversion. *Journal of Research in Personality, 40*, 1219−1231.

McLean, K. C., Pasupathi, M., Fivush, R., Greenhoot, A. G., & Wainryb, C. (2015). *Does within person variability in narration matter and for what?* Manuscript submitted for publication.

McLean, K. C., Pasupathi, M., & Pals, J. L. (2007). Selves creating stories creating selves: A process model of narrative self development in adolescence and adulthood. *Personality and Social Psychology Review*, *11*, 262−278.

McLean, K. C., & Pratt, M. W. (2006). Life's little (and big) lessons: Identity statuses and meaning-making in the turning point narratives of emerging adults. *Developmental Psychology*, *42*, 714−722.

Murray, H. A. (1938). *Explorations in personality*. New York, NY: Oxford University Press.

Nelson, K., & Fivush, R. (2004). The emergence of auto-biographical memory: A social cultural developmental theory. *Psychological Review*, *111*, 486−511.

Pals, J. L. (2006). Narrative identity processing of difficult life experiences: Pathways of personality development and positive self-transformation in adulthood. *Journal of Personality*, *74*, 1079−1110.

Pasupathi, M. (2001). The social construction of the personal past and its implications for adult development. *Psychological Bulletin*, *127*, 651−672.

Pasupathi, M., Brubaker, J., & Mansour, E. (2007). Developing a life story: Constructing relations between self and experience in autobiographical narratives. *Human Development*, *50*, 85−110.

Pasupathi, M., & Mansour, E. (2006). Adult age differences in autobiographical reasoning in narratives. *Developmental Psychology*, *42*, 798−808.

Pasupathi, M., & Wainryb, C. (2010). On telling the whole story: Facts and interpretations in autobiographical memory narratives from childhood through midadolescence. *Developmental Psychology*, *46*, 735−746.

Pennebaker, J. W., & Beall, S. K. (1986). Confronting a traumatic event: Toward an understanding of inhibition and disease. *Journal of Abnormal Psychology*, *95*, 274−281.

Reese, E., Chen, Y., Jack, F., & Hayne, H. (2010). Emerging identities: Narrative and self from early child-hood to early adolescence. In K. McLean, & M. Pasupathi (Eds.), *Narrative development in adolescence* (pp. 23−43). New York, NY: Springer.

Reese, E., Jack, F., & White, N. (2010). Origins of adolescents' autobiographical memories. *Cognitive Development*, *25*, 352−367.

Reese, E., Chen, Y., McAnally, H. M., Myftari, E., Neha, T., Wang, Q., & Jack, F. (2014). Narratives and traits in personality development among New Zealand Maori, Chinese, and European adolescents. *Journal of Adolescence*, *37*, 727−737.

Roberts, B. W. (1997). Plaster or plasticity: Are work experiences associated with personality change in women? *Journal of Personality*, *65*, 205−232.

Roberts, B. W., Walton, K. E., & Viechtbauer, W. (2006). Patterns of mean-level change in personality traits across the life course: A meta-analysis of longitudinal studies. *Psychological Bulletin*, *132*, 1−25.

Rogoff, B. (2003). *The cultural nature of human development*. New York, NY: Oxford University Press.

Rubin, D. C., Rahhal, T. A., & Poon, L. W. (1998). Things learned in early adulthood are remembered best. *Memory & Cognition*, *26*, 3−19.

Schiff, B. (2014). Introduction: Development's story in time and place. In B. Schiff (Ed.), *Rereading personal narrative and the life course* (145, pp. 1−13). New Directions for Child and Adolescent Development.

Shiner, R. L., & DeYoung, C. G. (2013). The structure of temperament and personality traits: A developmental perspective. In P. D. Zelazo (Ed.), *The Oxford handbook of developmental psychology* (pp. 113−141). New York, NY: Oxford University Press.

Singer, J. A. (2004). Narrative identity and meaning-making across the adult span: An introduction. *Journal of Personality*, *72*, 437−459.

Soto, C. J., John, O. P., Gosling, S. D., & Potter, J. (2011). Age differences in personality traits from 10 to 65: Big Five domains and facets in a large cross-sectional sample. *Journal of Personality and Social Psychology, 100,* 330−348.

Syed, M., & McLean, K. C. (in preparation). *Integrating the three levels of personality: An empirical test of some possible structures.*

Syed, M., & McLean, K. C. (2016). Understanding identity integration: Theoretical, methodological, and applied issues. *Journal of Adolescence, 47,* 109−118.

Syed, M., & Mitchell, L. L. (2015). Temporal identity integration as a core developmental process. In R. Scott, & S. Kosslyn (Eds.), *Emerging trends in the social and behavioral sciences* (pp. 1−15). San Francisco, CA: Wiley.

Thorne, A. (2000). Personal memory telling and personality development. *Personality and Social Psychology Review, 4,* 45−56.

Thorne, A., Cutting, L., & Skaw, D. (1998). Young adults' relationship memories and the life story: Examples or essential landmarks? *Narrative Inquiry, 8,* 1−32.

Thorne, A., & Nam, V. (2009). The storied construction of personality. In P. J. Corr, & G. Matthew (Eds.), *The Cambridge handbook of personality* (pp. 491−505). Cambridge: Cambridge University Press.

Tompkins, S. S. (1979). Script theory: Differential magnification of affects. In H. E. Howe, & R. A. Dienstbier (Eds.), *Nebraska symposium on motivation.* Lincoln, NE: University of Nebraska Press.

Vygotsky, L. S. (1978). *Mind in society.* Cambridge, MA: Harvard University Press.

# Part Five

# Personality Development in Context

# Personality development in reaction to major life events

*Jule Specht[1,2],* *

[1]Humboldt-Universität zu Berlin, Berlin, Germany, [2]German Institute for Economic Research (DIW Berlin), Berlin, Germany

Life is filled with events that have an impact on the life paths we take, the daily routines we follow, the expectations we are faced with, and the people we are surrounded with. Consequently, major life events are assumed to impact how individuals tend to think, feel, and behave, thus, their personality.

This chapter deals with the question of how life events affect the development of personality in terms of the Big Five personality traits (John, Naumann, & Soto, 2008). In line with a definition introduced by Luhmann, Orth, Specht, Kandler, and Lucas (2014), major life events are considered here as "time-discrete transitions that bring about a major change in status and/or social roles" (p. 256; see also Luhmann, Hofmann, Eid, & Lucas, 2012). Thus major life events have a concrete starting point (and do not evolve continuously) and mark the beginning and/or end of the position an individual has in society like a marital or occupational status.

The following section starts with the question of why personality is expected to change in reaction to major life events by providing an overview on theoretical perspectives that either predict personality change or personality stability even in the face of such events. Then methodological challenges in this area of research are reviewed that need to be resolved to come to trustworthy conclusions. At the center of this chapter is a review on empirical studies on personality changes in reaction to major life events that are either positive or negative and that can each be assigned into one of three domains, namely the occupational, social, and health domain. The chapter closes with future directions within this research area.

## Theoretical perspectives: why should personality change due to major life events?

Major life events play, as the term suggests, a major role in the life of individuals. However, this does not necessarily result in changes in personality in reaction to such events. Indeed, some theoretical perspectives assume that major life events are likely starting points that trigger changes in personality whereas other theoretical

---

* While writing this chapter, Jule Specht was also affiliated at Freie Universität Berlin, Berlin, Universität zu Lübeck, Lübeck, and the German Institute for Economic Research (DIW Berlin), Berlin.

Personality Development Across the Lifespan. DOI: http://dx.doi.org/10.1016/B978-0-12-804674-6.00021-1

perspectives assume less impact or even a stabilizing impact of major life events on personality (for an overview on theoretical perspectives on personality development, see Specht et al., 2014).

The Neo-Socioanalytic Model (Roberts & Nickel, Chapter 11) assumes that personality changes can occur at any age (i.e., plasticity principle) and that individuals change because of investments in social roles (i.e., social investment principle). Thus if a major life event results in an important new social role that comes along with expectations about how to act, think, or feel, which an individual does not yet meet, this is expected to result in personality changes.

However, there are some requirements that need to be complied to trigger personality development: An individual has to be aware of the expectations associated with a new social role and that he or she not yet fulfills these expectations. An individual needs furthermore to be able and willing to change his or her personality in an adaptive way. These requirements may be met if new social roles directly reinforce or punish personality traits (i.e., role contingency mechanism) or communicate which personality traits are more or less adaptive (i.e., role expectation and demand mechanism) or if feedback is given by close others (for more information on issues of processes in personality development, see Geukes, van Zalk, & Back, Chapter 28).

From a developmental perspective, personality changes occur if major life events are accompanied by new developmental tasks (for an overview, see Hutteman, Hennecke, Orth, Reitz, & Specht, 2014). Such tasks confront the majority of individuals within a society with age-graded expectations about how to behave, think, and feel. Because such tasks are normative, most individuals are assumed to aim at mastering these tasks, which oftentimes require personality changes. Developmental tasks have been classified by Hutteman, Hennecke and colleagues (2014) into five different domains (i.e., romantic relationships, family life, social life, job life, and physical changes) and three age groups. In young adulthood, most developmental tasks deal with establishing roles, whereas in middle adulthood, they tend to deal with maintaining these roles and in old age, they oftentimes deal with preventing losses.

In a revision of the transactional paradigm, Neyer, Mund, Zimmermann, and Wrzus (2014) place high importance on transparent role demands. They assume that major life events may impact personality development depending on the type of event. In the context of normative life transitions that offer clear information about how to adapt, personality development is likely to occur. In contrast, the reversed impact from personality to life experiences is more likely in the context of nonnormative life events. Taken together, these theoretical perspectives all assume that personality changes in reaction to life events if these come along with new role demands an individual is aware of.

In contrast to the aforementioned theoretical perspectives, the Dynamic Equilibrium Model (for an overview, see Ormel, VonKorff, Jeronimus, & Riese, Chapter 9) assumes that personality changes only temporarily in reaction to major life events. The model suggests that individuals differ in their set points, i.e., typical levels on each personality trait that are enduring over time. A major life event may impact the level of a trait for a limited amount of time, but individuals are expected to return to their individual set point after some time. Thus lasting personality changes would only occur if the individual set point changes enduringly or if adaptation back to set point takes very long (i.e., multiple years).

Other theoretical perspectives assume that personality is less prone to major life events. For example, Five-Factor Theory of Personality (for an overview, see Mõttus, Chapter 7), assumes that the Big Five personality traits are not determined by major life events but by biological maturation. Theory of Genotype → Environment Effects (for an overview, see Kandler & Zapko-Willmes, Chapter 8) expects that personality changes in reaction to major life events but mainly due to genetic effects that led to experiencing these events but less due to the event itself. Finally the Paradoxical Theory of Personality Coherence (Caspi & Moffitt, 1993) expects that—paradoxically—personality is particularly stable in the face of major life events. If information is lacking on which personality trait levels are adaptive after a major life event occurred, then individuals will accentuate preexisting personality traits (i.e., accentuation hypothesis). Similar to the models introduced at the beginning, this theory assumes that personality does change if clear information on role-appropriate personality trait levels is available (i.e., change hypothesis).

# Methodological perspectives: how can personality changes be traced back to life events?

A variable of central importance for the analysis of personality development in reaction to major life events is time (Luhmann et al., 2014). Thus essential preconditions needed here are longitudinal data with information on personality before and after the occurrence of a major life event as well as a control group that did not experience the event. However, there are a surprisingly small number of studies that fulfill these preconditions.

Most often, only cross-sectional data is available that does not allow differentiating whether individual differences are due to selection effects (i.e., individuals differ in the likelihood to experience specific life events) or socialization effects (i.e., individuals differ in personality development depending on the life experience). The same problem occurs if longitudinal data is available but no information on personality before the event is collected (e.g., Allemand, Gomez, & Jackson, 2010; Allemand, Hill, & Lehmann, 2015; Hagekull & Bohlin, 1998; Headey & Wearing, 1989; Jokela, Alvergne, Pollet, & Lummaa, 2011; Mroczek & Spiro, 2003; Ogle, Rubin, & Siegler, 2014b; Stephan, Sutin, Luchetti, & Terracciano, 2016; Torgersen & Janson, 2002).

Other studies include information on life circumstances like the status of an individual or continuous changes across time but do not provide information on time-discrete status or role transitions (e.g., Berg & Johansson, 2014; Hudson & Roberts, 2016; Hutteman, Bleidorn et al., 2014; Judge, Higgins, Thoresen, & Barrick, 1999; Roberts, Caspi, & Moffitt, 2003; Scollon & Diener, 2006; Sutin & Costa, 2010; Wille, Beyers, & De Fruyt, 2012; Wu, 2016). Even though all of these studies provide important insights into the relationship between personality and environmental characteristics, they offer limited information on personality development in reaction to major life events and are therefore not included in this review.

Despite these essential preconditions, ideal studies that aim at analyzing personality development in reaction to major life events include two or more measurement occasions for personality before as well as after the occurrence of the event under consideration. This allows examining anticipation effects (i.e., whether personality changes before the event) in addition to selection and socialization effects. Furthermore multiple measurement occasions in periods of strong personality changes enable detecting nonlinear changes in personality. However, due to the lack of studies, the following review also includes studies that do not fulfill these ambitious requirements (for more information on an ideal study design in this area of research, see Luhmann et al., 2014).

## Major life event research in the tradition of the stress literature

Most of the studies on personality development in reaction to major life events seem to be conceptualized in the tradition of the stress literature. More specifically, most often, the experience of negative major life events is associated with changes in emotional stability (the opposite pole of neuroticism), which has repeatedly been found to decrease in reaction to different adverse events (e.g., Boals, Southard-Dobbs, & Blumenthal, 2015; Jeronimus, Ormel, Aleman, Penninx, & Riese, 2013; Kandler, Bleidorn, Riemann, Angleitner, & Spinath, 2012; Löckenhoff, Terracciano, Patriciu, Eaton, & Costa, 2009; Lüdtke, Roberts, Trautwein, & Nagy, 2011; Sutin, Costa, Wethington, & Eaton, 2010; Vaidya, Gray, Haig, & Watson, 2002; but see Jeronimus, Riese, Sanderman, & Ormel, 2014; Magnus, Diener, Fujita, & Pavot, 1993; Ogle, Rubin, & Siegler, 2014a; Specht, Egloff, & Schmukle, 2011). In addition, some studies found that experiencing positive events leads to increases in emotional stability (e.g., Jeronimus et al., 2013; Lüdtke et al., 2011; but see Jeronimus et al., 2014; Magnus et al., 1993; Specht et al., 2011; Vaidya et al., 2002).

There are also studies that examined the impact of positive and negative life events on the other Big Five traits. For example, increases in extraversion have been associated with experiencing more positive events (e.g., Lüdtke et al., 2011; Magnus et al., 1993; Vaidya et al., 2002; but see Kandler et al., 2012; Specht et al., 2011) and, less often, with experiencing fewer negative events (e.g., Lüdtke et al., 2011; but see Kandler et al., 2012; Löckenhoff et al., 2009; Magnus et al., 1993; Specht et al., 2011; Vaidya et al., 2002). Some studies found increases in openness to experience in reaction to positive events (e.g., Lüdtke et al., 2011; but see Vaidya et al., 2002) and decreases in reaction to negative events (e.g., Löckenhoff et al., 2009; but see Lüdtke et al., 2011; Vaidya et al., 2002; and see Specht et al., 2011 for gender differences). Agreeableness has also been found to increase in the face of positive life events (e.g., Lüdtke et al., 2011; but see Kandler et al., 2012; Specht et al., 2011; Vaidya et al., 2002) and to decrease in the face of negative events (e.g., Kandler et al., 2012; Löckenhoff et al., 2009; but see Lüdtke et al., 2011; Specht et al., 2011; Vaidya et al., 2002). Similarly some findings suggest that conscientiousness increases in reaction to positive events (e.g., Lüdtke et al., 2011; but see Kandler et al., 2012; Specht et al., 2011; Vaidya et al., 2002).

Taken together, the most consistent finding is that experiencing negative life events leads to decreases of emotional stability. In contrast personality maturation in reaction to adverse events, as assumed in the posttraumatic growth literature (for an overview, see Jayawickreme & Blackie, 2014), received little or even opposing support, at least for an average individual (Kandler & Specht, 2014).

All of the aforementioned studies clustered events with regard to their valence into more positive and more negative, sometimes also more controllable and less controllable life events but did oftentimes not differentiate between single major life events. This makes sense from a stress perspective that conceptualizes major life events as more or less desired disturbances from daily routines (Luhmann et al., 2012) that may increase feelings of insecurity and strain and likely influence trajectories of emotional stability. Because negative life events tend to cooccur to the same people (e.g., Kandler et al., 2012), decreases in emotional stability might be an adaptive strategy to become sensible and prepared for future hassles.

From the personality development perspective, clustering different life events misses central information. If, as hypothesized from, e.g., the Neo-Socioanalytic Model (Roberts & Nickel, Chapter 11), personality changes in reaction to major life events because of social roles that ask for adaptations, then clustering events will combine events that each might stimulate different personality change processes. And indeed Specht and colleagues (2011) showed that clustering events loses important information for the analysis of personality development. Thus the appropriate level of aggregation is essential for the analysis of personality development and remains a topic of empirical investigation to find commonalities between life events that may be clustered and differences between life events that should be examined separately.

# The impact of life events in the occupational, social, and health domain

In the following, studies on personality development in reaction to single major life events are reviewed. Results are sorted into three domains of life, namely the occupational, social, and health domain. For an overview on results, see Table 21.1.

**Table 21.1  The impact of major life events on the Big Five personality traits**

| Domains and major life events | Personality change |
|---|---|
| Occupational domain | |
|   Graduation from school | C + , ES + , E − |
|   Work life entry | C + , ES + |
|   Job change | E and O (direction depends on role demand) |
|   Promotion at work | C + , ES + , O + |
|   Unemployment | C − , O − , A − |
|   Retirement | C − |
| Social domain | |
|   Starting a romantic relationship | ES + , E + , A − |
|   Marriage | ES + , E − , O − , A − |
|   Separation/divorce | O + , A + |
|   Birth of a child | E − , C − |
| Health domain | ES − , E − , O − , C − |

*ES*, emotional stability; *E*, extraversion; *O*, openness to experience; *A*, agreeableness; *C*, conscientiousness; + , tends to increase due to the event; − , tends to decrease due to the event.

## Occupational domain

Changes in personality have repeatedly been found to be associated with life events in the occupational domain. This is particularly true for conscientiousness that tends to increase comparatively strongly in reaction to life events that are associated with occupational role demands.

In a sample of students, Bleidorn (2012) found that those who graduated from school increased more strongly in conscientiousness compared to those a year younger who did not graduate yet. Similarly Specht and colleagues (2011) found increases in conscientiousness in those who started their first job compared to individuals of the same age who did not start their first job in the same time period. Likewise Lüdtke and colleagues (2011) found that conscientiousness increases in students who started a new (not necessarily the first) job at least if the student evaluated this to be a positive event. Also Leikas and Salmela-Aro (2015) found increases in conscientiousness in reaction to entering work life but not to entering university.

Thus individuals tend to increase in conscientiousness in reaction to life events that mark the beginning of a new social role with occupational demands. This is likely due to the fact that the new social role comes along with daily routines that require individuals, among other things, to be reliable and industrious. They also enter a new social network of colleagues that expect them to be conscientious to master their new social role successfully. In terms of the Neo-Socioanalytic Model (Roberts & Nickel, Chapter 11), the plasticity and social investment principle seem to be at work here resulting in changes in conscientiousness in reaction to prevalent investments in the new social role as a student or employee. Also these findings suggest that role demands are sufficiently transparent when entering work life so that young adults are able to adapt to these.

Other traits have also been associated with graduation and starting the first job: Bleidorn (2012) found stronger increases in emotional stability and less increases in extraversion in students who graduated compared to students who did not graduate yet. Similarly Lüdtke and colleagues (2011) found increases in emotional stability in reaction to entering working life if individuals evaluated this event as positive. In contrast they found decreases in emotional stability for individuals who started a new job and evaluated this as a negative event.

Changes in emotional stability seem to depend on how the individual evaluates the occupational event. Individuals may benefit from this life event if they gain confidence in the face of occupational challenges, which may increase their emotional stability. Thus instead of continuous role demands that ask for increases in conscientiousness to which individuals adapt, there might be another mechanism underlying increases in emotional stability. These might rather be due to an affective response to an increased ability to master occupational role demands.

After entering university or work life, life events that result in changes in occupational roles also impact personality development. For example, Lüdtke and colleagues (2011) found that switching university studies accompanied decreases in emotional stability, extraversion, and openness to experience if this was evaluated as a negative event but was associated with increases in agreeableness if this was evaluated as a positive event. Denissen, Ulferts, Lüdtke, Muck, and Gerstorf (2014) found that extraversion and openness to experience were the traits that most consistently selected individuals into jobs (i.e., extraverted/open individuals choose jobs that ask for extraverted/open individuals) and that change over time in reaction to job role demands. Similarly Jackson, Thoemmes, Jonkmann, Lüdtke, and Trautwein (2012) found that young men who perform civilian community service (e.g., working in a hospital or home for the elderly) increase more strongly in agreeableness—a trait likely adaptive in this context—compared to young men who perform military service.

Occupational success and defeat also impact personality development. Lüdtke and colleagues (2011) found increases in emotional stability in reaction to a promotion at work. In contrast Nieß and Zacher (2015) found no significant increases in emotional stability but in openness to experience in reaction to upward job changes into managerial and professional positions. Costa, Herbst, McCrae, and Siegler (2000) found increases in emotional stability and also in conscientiousness in individuals who got promoted compared to individuals who got fired. In a study in which personality changes of those who became unemployed were compared to those of the same age who did not become unemployed, Specht and colleagues (2011) found no effect on personality. However, Boyce, Wood, Daly, and Sedikides (2015) took a closer look at developmental trajectories in the same data and did identify some curvilinear effects (depending on the amount of time of unemployment) with a tendency for decreases in agreeableness, conscientiousness, and openness to experience.

Taken together, changes in personality seem to be more consistent in reaction to job entry and less consistent in reaction to job changes. Being conscientious is probably almost universally valued in work life but once having adapted to this role demand, changes in jobs may result in specific demands that lead to more diverse personality changes. Interestingly when retiring, conscientiousness decreases again (Specht et al., 2011). Thus individuals keep a comparatively high level of conscientiousness during work life but have lower levels on this trait before and afterward (a finding vividly labeled "la dolce vita effect"; Marsh, Nagengast, & Morin, 2013). This again speaks in favor of the Neo-Socioanalytic Model (Roberts & Nickel, Chapter 11) that assumes that individuals invest in social roles and change their personality if they change social roles.

## Social domain

Major life events in the social domain, like starting a romantic relationship or having a baby, have been predicted to have a major influence on personality maturation, i.e., lead to increases in emotional stability, social dominance (a facet of extraversion), agreeableness, and conscientiousness (maturity principle; Roberts & Nickel, Chapter 11). In fact, hypothesized developmental trajectories have sometimes been confirmed for starting a romantic relationship but reactions to childbirth have been quite the opposite of what was expected by, e.g., the Neo-Socioanalytic Model (Roberts & Nickel, Chapter 11).

In a longitudinal study covering eight years and three measurement waves, Neyer and colleagues (Lehnart & Neyer, 2006; Neyer & Asendorpf, 2001; Neyer & Lehnart, 2007) found confirming evidence for personality maturation in individuals who started a romantic relationship. These young adults became more emotionally stable (and increased in self-esteem) as well as more extraverted (and less shy) compared to those who did not start a romantic relationship. Furthermore those who changed their relationship partner during the course of this study increased less in agreeableness compared to those who continued their romantic relationship. No effect was found for conscientiousness and no data was available for openness to experience. Similarly Leikas and Salmela-Aro (2015) found decreases in agreeableness in reaction to starting a new romantic relationship. Despite the high statistical power in their study, Lüdtke and colleagues (2011) found no personality changes at all in reaction to starting or ending a romantic relationship. Taken together, individuals seem to show some predicted desirable personality changes in reaction to starting a new romantic relationship like increases in emotional stability and extraversion.

Personality reactions to marriage are less in line with the maturity principle. Specht and colleagues (2011) found decreases in extraversion in those who moved in with their partner and additionally decreases in openness and agreeableness in individuals who got married compared to those of the same age who did not move in with their partner or got married, respectively. Costa and colleagues (2000) found increases in emotional stability for men who got married (but not for women) and Lüdtke and colleagues (2011) found no effects on personality for marriage, which might be due to insufficient statistical power in their sample of young adults.

In reaction to separation and divorce, individuals tend to increase in some of the traits that decreased due to entering a serious romantic relationship. For example,

Specht and colleagues (2011) found that separation led to increases in agreeableness in both gender and to increases in openness to experience in men (but not women). Similarly agreeableness and conscientiousness increased in individuals who got divorced. Costa and colleagues (2000) instead found that extraversion and openness increased in women who got divorced and that men instead decreased in conscientiousness in reaction to this event. Rammstedt, Spinath, Richter, and Schupp (2013) found that after relationship breakup, the congruence between partners in openness to experience decreases. This might, in part, be explained by the finding that men tend to increase whereas women tend to remain stable in openness after relationship breakup (cf. Specht et al., 2011).

Thus contrary to predictions of the Neo-Socioanalytic Model (Roberts & Nickel, Chapter 11), personality did not mature (but quite the opposite) in reaction to investments in a romantic relationship (i.e., moving together, marrying) but personality did mature to some extent in reaction to ending a romantic relationship. One likely explanation is that mature personality trait levels are more important (or result in more immediate rewards) when looking for a new partner than when already having ensured a committed partner. However, indication of personality maturation was found for individuals who got married if they were satisfied with their lives, which led to increases in agreeableness after this life event (Specht, Egloff, & Schmukle, 2013).

Also the birth of a child lacks a positive impact on personality maturation. Lüdtke and colleagues (2011) found no effect of getting pregnant on personality development. However, due to the young age of the sample, the number of individuals was probably insufficiently small to reliably detect meaningful results. The birth of a child was found to lead to decreases in conscientiousness in a study by Specht and colleagues (2011) and to decreases in extraversion in men in a study by Galdiolo and Roskam (2014). Similar results were found by van Scheppingen and colleagues (2016), who found decreases in conscientiousness for females, and decreases in extraversion for males, who had a baby. In addition, they found that openness tends to increase in men before having a baby even though low values in openness to experience eventually increased the probability to have a baby. Probably, high values in openness are relevant for finding a partner (which is why it increases in parents-to-be first) but low values then predict who of the newly fallen in loved decide to get a baby. Again, personality does not seem to mature on average in reaction to having a baby. However, those who have a baby and are satisfied with their lives do show some personality maturation, namely increases in agreeableness (Specht et al., 2013).

The lack of personality maturation in reaction to childbirth raises the question of why individuals do not adapt—on average—to their new social role as a parent by, e.g., becoming more emotionally stable and agreeable. There might be at least three possible explanations: First, individuals might already have sufficiently high levels in relevant personality traits, which makes additional changes unnecessary. Indeed emotional stability increases already in young adulthood before the average age of having the first child. However, it does not increase in the years preceding childbirth. Also agreeableness does not increase until the second half of life

(Lucas & Donnellan, 2011; Roberts, Walton, & Viechtbauer, 2006; Specht et al., 2011), so even though an average increase in this trait is actually possible later in life, it usually does not happen at the typical age of childbirth.

Second, childbirth marks a period in life that is not only filled with increases in joy and meaning but also with lack of sleep, troubles of combining work and family obligations, and decreases of relationship satisfaction (Luhmann et al., 2012). The lack of personality maturation might thus be a result of a lack of resources that would enable self-regulated personality change toward maturity (cf. Denissen, van Aken, Penke, & Wood, 2013).

Third, most theoretical perspectives assume that changes in personality due to changes in social roles require transparent role demands. However, children (especially at very young age) and probably also spouses might not provide enough, unambiguous, and immediate feedback on which personality traits are more or less adaptive to rear a happy and healthy child or to maintain a stable high-quality relationship.

Despite familial events, the social domain also contains issues associated with friends and acquaintances. However, major life events are less likely in this context because most friendships have a less clear starting and end point compared to, e.g., romantic relationships, in part because friendships are oftentimes not exclusive whereas most romantic relationships are. Furthermore, the role of peers for personality development has received less attention with some notable recent exceptions (for an overview, see Finn, Zimmermann, & Neyer, Chapter 22; Reitz, Zimmermann, Hutteman, Specht, & Neyer, 2014). An empirical example of how peers impact personality development in the context of a major life event is given by Zimmermann and Neyer (2013): In a sample of university students, they found that sojourners increased in openness to experience, agreeableness, and emotional stability during their time abroad compared to students who stayed at home. This personality change could in part be attributed to new social relationships acquired during sojourning. Taken together, friendships might seldom be associated directly with major life events but changes in social networks are certainly oftentimes accompanying major life events and can thereby impact personality development.

## Health domain

Surprisingly little life event research has been done in the domain of health. Most often, studies focus on gradual changes in subjective or objective indicators of health but less on how major life events like disease onset impact personality development (for an overview on the impact of health on personality development, see Jackson, Weston, & Schultz, Chapter 23).

Lüdtke and colleagues (2011) found decreases in emotional stability in young adults who got sexual problems, started psychotherapy (in case they evaluated this to be a negative event, otherwise this led to increases in emotional stability), and the beginning of an illness. In addition, getting sexual problems also led to decreases in extraversion and starting psychotherapy to decreases in openness to experience (if it was evaluated to be a negative event). An illness or injury of a family member or friend, events multiple hundreds of study participants experienced, did not alter personality development.

Only few studies examined the impact of major and/or chronic disease onset on the Big Five personality traits. Leikas and Salmela-Aro (2015) found decreases in emotional stability and extraversion in reaction to chronic disease onset, even though the sample size of diseased was very small due to the young age of study participants. Jokela, Hakulinen, Singh-Manoux, and Kivimäki (2014) found decreases in extraversion, emotional stability, and conscientiousness in reaction to the onset of most of the chronic diseases under investigation. In addition, there were decreases in agreeableness and openness to experience in reaction to having a stroke and having a respiratory disease. Illness does not, however, only impact those directly impaired but also close others. Rohr, Wagner, and Lang (2013) found, e.g., that emotional stability remained stable in individuals who start or continue caregiving but that it increases in those who either do not provide care or stop caregiving.

Taken together, major life events in the health domain oftentimes mean the onset of a disease whereas recovery from a major health issue is oftentimes less abrupt and therefore not a life event as defined here. Disease onset has mainly been associated with declines in most, if not all, of the Big Five personality traits. However, findings on the association between disease onset and personality development remain scarce and future studies might differentiate more diverse developmental trajectories depending on the disease under investigation. At least, several theoretical perspectives would allow for differences across diseases due to different biological changes associated with a disease (e.g., Five-Factor Theory of Personality; cf. Mõttus, Chapter 7) or different social restrictions and expectations associated with a disease (e.g., Neo-Socioanalytic Model; Roberts & Nickel, Chapter 11).

## Conclusion and future directions

This review shows that personality changes in reaction to major life events. As expected by, e.g., the Neo-Socioanalytic Model (Roberts & Nickel, Chapter 11), events that comes along with changes in social role demands can—but not always do—lead to changes in personality. However, the exact mechanism linking life events and personality changes remains speculative. Changes in social networks likely act as mediators by, e.g., providing feedback on role-appropriate behavior or by pure appreciation that increase feelings of confidence to be able to master developmental tasks.

Future research might focus on whether individuals are explicitly aware of which role demands they are faced with and how their current personality deviates from fulfilling these roles or whether more subtle implicit processes are at work here. Furthermore, individuals may differ in their ability to recognize social role demands and likewise social roles may differ in transparency and unambiguousness of demands they come along with.

Also the temporal sequence of changes in personality before and after major life events remains largely unknown (Luhmann et al., 2014). Multiple measurement points before and after event occurrence are necessary to uncover this issue. However, data collection before an individual anticipates a major life event is oftentimes only possible in large-scale panel studies like the Socio-Economic Panel Study (Wagner, Frick, & Schupp, 2007) or the Household, Income, and Labor Dynamics in Australia survey (Summerfield et al., 2011), which oftentimes offer no fine-grained personality assessment both in timing and level of detail.

Major life events may result in different social role demands that need to be taken seriously. For example, entering work life may come along with the need to become more conscientious. However, the exact demands associated with the new role likely differ between someone who became a scientist, model, or trucker. Related to this, major life events and social role demands should be examined as objectively as possible. Subjective ratings may offer important insight into mediation processes between demands and personality but may be seriously biased.

There are major life events that have not been included here but that have been hypothesized to impact personality development. For example, some people place high importance on early life experiences and their impact beyond childhood that may even be stronger than recent life experiences. There is not much research reinforcing this assumption but strict tests based on long-term data are needed to come to firm conclusions. Also most life events only impact single individuals at a time but there are also major life events that impact many individuals at once (e.g., due to natural disasters or terrorist attacks). Such collective events may impact the personality development of groups of people via different mechanisms than single life events and depending on the psychological and/or geographical proximity to this event (e.g., Milojev, Osborne, & Sibley, 2014; Sibley & Bulbulia, 2012).

Taken together, a lot has been discovered with regard to the interplay of personality development and major life events in the last years. Many open questions still remain and their number is rather increasing than decreasing. Thus there is hopefully even more to expect in this area of research within the upcoming years.

## Acknowledgment

I thank Christian Kandler for valuable comments on an earlier version of this chapter.

## References

Allemand, M., Gomez, V., & Jackson, J. J. (2010). Personality trait development in midlife: Exploring the impact of psychological turning points. *European Journal of Ageing, 7*, 147–155.

Allemand, M., Hill, P. L., & Lehmann, R. (2015). Divorce and personality development across middle adulthood. *Personal Relationships, 22*, 122–137.

Berg, A. I., & Johansson, B. (2014). Personality change in the oldest-old: Is it a matter of compromised health and functioning? *Journal of Personality*, *82*, 25−31.

Bleidorn, W. (2012). Hitting the road to adulthood: Short-term personality development during a major life transition. *Personality and Social Psychology Bulletin*, *38*, 1594−1608.

Boals, A., Southard-Dobbs, S., & Blumenthal, H. (2015). Adverse events in emerging adulthood are associated with increases in neuroticism. *Journal of Personality*, *83*, 202−211.

Boyce, C. J., Wood, A. M., Daly, M., & Sedikides, C. (2015). Personality change following unemployment. *Journal of Applied Psychology*, *100*, 991−1011.

Caspi, A., & Moffitt, T. E. (1993). When do individual differences matter? A paradoxical theory of personality coherence. *Psychological Inquiry*, *4*, 247−271.

Costa, P. T., Herbst, J. H., McCrae, R. R., & Siegler, I. C. (2000). Personality at midlife: Stability, intrinsic maturation, and response to life events. *Assessment*, *7*, 365−378.

Denissen, J. J. A., Ulferts, H., Lüdtke, O., Muck, P. M., & Gerstorf, D. (2014). Longitudinal transactions between personality and occupational roles: A large and heterogeneous study of job beginners, stayers, and changers. *Developmental Psychology*, *50*, 1931−1942.

Denissen, J. J. A., van Aken, M. A. G., Penke, L., & Wood, D. (2013). Self-regulation underlies temperament and personality: An integrative developmental framework. *Child Development Perspectives*, *7*, 255−260.

Galdiolo, S., & Roskam, I. (2014). Development of personality traits in response to childbirth: A longitudinal dyadic perspective. *Personality and Individual Differences*, *69*, 223−230.

Hagekull, B., & Bohlin, G. (1998). Preschool temperament and environmental factors related to the five-factor model of personality in middle childhood. *Merrill-Palmer Quarterly*, *44*, 194−215.

Headey, B., & Wearing, A. (1989). Personality, life events, and subjective well-being: Toward a dynamic equilibrium model. *Journal of Personality and Social Psychology*, *57*, 731−739.

Hudson, N. W., & Roberts, B. W. (2016). Social investment in work reliably predicts change in conscientiousness and agreeableness: A direct replication and extension of Hudson, Roberts, and Lodi-Smith (2012). *Journal of Research in Personality*, *60*, 12−23.

Hutteman, R., Bleidorn, W., Kereteš, G., Brković, I., Butković, A., & Denissen, J. J. A. (2014). Reciprocal associations between parenting challenges and parents' personality development in young and middle adulthood. *European Journal of Personality*, *28*, 168−179.

Hutteman, R., Hennecke, M., Orth, U., Reitz, A. K., & Specht, J. (2014). Developmental tasks as a framework to study personality development in adulthood and old age. *European Journal of Personality*, *28*, 267−278.

Jackson, J. J., Thoemmes, F., Jonkmann, K., Lüdtke, O., & Trautwein, U. (2012). Military training and personality trait development: Does the military make the man, or does the man make the military? *Psychological Science*, *23*, 270−277.

Jayawickreme, E., & Blackie, L. E. R. (2014). Post-traumatic growth as positive personality change: Evidence, controversies and future directions. *European Journal of Personality*, *28*, 312−331.

Jeronimus, B. F., Ormel, J., Aleman, A., Penninx, B. W. J. H., & Riese, H. (2013). Negative and positive life events are associated with small but lasting change in neuroticism. *Psychological Medicine*, *43*, 2403−2415.

Jeronimus, B. F., Riese, H., Sanderman, R., & Ormel, J. (2014). Mutual reinforcement between neuroticism and life experiences: A five-wave, 16-year study to test reciprocal causation. *Journal of Personality and Social Psychology*, *107*, 751−764.

John, O. P., Naumann, L. P., & Soto, C. J. (2008). Paradigm shift to the integrative Big Five trait taxonomy: History, measurement, and conceptual issues. In O. P. John, R. W. Robins, & L. A. Pervin (Eds.), *Handbook of personality: Theory and research* (3rd ed., pp. 114–158). New York, NY: The Guilford Press.

Jokela, M., Alvergne, A., Pollet, T. V., & Lummaa, V. (2011). Reproductive behavior and personality traits of the five factor model. *European Journal of Personality, 25*, 487–500.

Jokela, M., Hakulinen, C., Singh-Manoux, A., & Kivimäki, M. (2014). Personality change associated with chronic diseases: Pooled analysis of four prospective cohort studies. *Psychological Medicine, 44*, 2629–2640.

Judge, T. A., Higgins, C. A., Thoresen, C. J., & Barrick, M. R. (1999). The Big Five personality traits, general mental ability, and career success across the life span. *Personnel Psychology, 52*, 621–652.

Kandler, C., Bleidorn, W., Riemann, R., Angleitner, A., & Spinath, F. M. (2012). Life events as environmental states and genetic traits and the role of personality: A longitudinal twin study. *Behavior Genetics, 42*, 57–72.

Kandler, C., & Specht, J. (2014). Unravelling the post-traumatic growth paradox: Can negative experiences drive positive personality maturation? *European Journal of Personality, 28*, 341–342.

Lehnart, J., & Neyer, F. J. (2006). Should I stay or should I go? Attachment and personality in stable and instable romantic relationships. *European Journal of Personality, 20*, 475–495.

Leikas, S., & Salmela-Aro, K. (2015). Personality trait changes among young Finns: The role of life events and transitions. *Journal of Personality, 83*, 117–126.

Löckenhoff, C., Terracciano, A., Patriciu, N. S., Eaton, W., & Costa, P. T. (2009). Self-reported extremely adverse life events and longitudinal changes in Five-Factor Model personality traits in an urban sample. *Journal of Traumatic Stress, 22*, 53–59.

Lucas, R. E., & Donnellan, M. B. (2011). Personality development across the life span: Longitudinal analyses with a national sample from Germany. *Journal of Personality and Social Psychology, 101*, 847–861.

Lüdtke, O., Roberts, B. W., Trautwein, U., & Nagy, G. (2011). A random walk down university avenue: Life paths, life events, and personality trait change at the transition to university life. *Journal of Personality and Social Psychology, 101*, 620–637.

Luhmann, M., Hofmann, W., Eid, M., & Lucas, R. E. (2012). Subjective well-being and adaptation to life events: A meta-analysis. *Journal of Personality and Social Psychology, 102*, 592–615.

Luhmann, M., Orth, U., Specht, J., Kandler, C., & Lucas, R. E. (2014). Studying changes in life circumstances and personality: It's about time. *European Journal of Personality, 28*, 256–266.

Magnus, K., Diener, E., Fujita, F., & Pavot, W. (1993). Extraversion and neuroticism as predictors of objective life events: A longitudinal analysis. *Journal of Personality and Social Psychology, 65*, 1046–1053.

Marsh, H. W., Nagengast, B., & Morin, A. J. S. (2013). Measurement invariance of Big-Five factors over the life span: ESEM tests of gender, age, plasticity, maturity, and la dolce vita effects. *Developmental Psychology, 49*, 1194–1218.

Milojev, P., Osborne, D., & Sibley, C. G. (2014). Personality resilience following a natural disaster. *Social Psychological and Personality Science, 5*, 760–768.

Mroczek, D. K., & Spiro, A. (2003). Modeling intraindividual change in personality traits: Findings from the normative aging study. *Journal of Gerontology: Psychological Sciences, 58B*, 153–165.

Neyer, F. J., & Asendorpf, J. B. (2001). Personality-relationship transaction in young adulthood. *Journal of Personality and Social Psychology*, *81*, 1190−1204.

Neyer, F. J., & Lehnart, J. (2007). Relationships matter in personality development: Evidence from an 8-year longitudinal study across young adulthood. *Journal of Personality*, *75*, 535−568.

Neyer, F. J., Mund, M., Zimmermann, J., & Wrzus, C. (2014). Personality-relationship transactions revisited. *Journal of Personality*, *82*, 539−550.

Nieß, C., & Zacher, H. (2015). Openness to experience as a predictor and outcome of upward job changes into managerial and professional positions. *PLoS ONE*, *10*, e0131115.

Ogle, C. M., Rubin, D. C., & Siegler, I. C. (2014a). Changes in neuroticism following trauma exposure. *Journal of Personality*, *82*, 93−102.

Ogle, C. M., Rubin, D. C., & Siegler, I. C. (2014b). Cumulative exposure to traumatic events in older adults. *Aging & Mental Health*, *18*, 316−325.

Rammstedt, B., Spinath, F. M., Richter, D., & Schupp, J. (2013). Partnership longevity and personality congruence in couples. *Personality and Individual Differences*, *54*, 832−835.

Reitz, A. K., Zimmermann, J., Hutteman, R., Specht, J., & Neyer, F. J. (2014). How peers make a difference: The role of peer groups and peer relationships in personality development. *European Journal of Personality*, *28*, 279−288.

Roberts, B. W., Caspi, A., & Moffitt, T. E. (2003). Work experiences and personality development in young adulthood. *Journal of Personality and Social Psychology*, *84*, 582−593.

Roberts, B. W., Walton, K. E., & Viechtbauer, W. (2006). Patterns of mean-level change in personality traits across the life course: A meta-analysis of longitudinal studies. *Psychological Bulletin*, *132*, 1−25.

Rohr, M. K., Wagner, J., & Lang, F. R. (2013). Effect of personality on the transition into caregiving. *Psychology and Aging*, *28*, 692−700.

Scollon, C. N., & Diener, E. (2006). Love, work, and changes in extraversion and neuroticism over time. *Journal of Personality and Social Psychology*, *91*, 1152−1165.

Sibley, C. G., & Bulbulia, J. (2012). Faith after an earthquake: A longitudinal study of religion and perceived health before and after the 2011 Christchurch New Zealand earthquake. *PLOS ONE*, *7*, e49648.

Specht, J., Bleidorn, W., Denissen, J. J. A., Hennecke, M., Hutteman, R., Kandler, C., . . . . . . Zimmermann, J. (2014). What drives adult personality development? A comparison of theoretical perspectives and empirical evidence. *European Journal of Personality*, *28*, 216−230.

Specht, J., Egloff, B., & Schmukle, S. C. (2011). Stability and change of personality across the life course: The impact of age and major life events on mean-level and rank-order stability of the Big Five. *Journal of Personality and Social Psychology*, *101*, 862−882.

Specht, J., Egloff, B., & Schmukle, S. C. (2013). Examining mechanisms of personality maturation: The impact of life satisfaction on the development of the Big Five personality traits. *Social Psychological and Personality Science*, *4*, 181−189.

Stephan, Y., Sutin, A. R., Luchetti, M., & Terracciano, A. (2016). Allostatic load and personality: A 4-year longitudinal study. *Psychosomatic Medicine*, *78*, 302−310.

Summerfield, M., Dunn, R., Freidin, S., Hahn, M., Ittak, P., Kecmanovic, M., . . . Wooden, M. (2011). *HILDA user manual—Release 10. Melbourne*. Australia: Melbourne Institute of Applied Economic and Social Research, University of Melbourne.

Sutin, A. R., & Costa, P. T. (2010). Reciprocal influences of personality and job characteristics across middle adulthood. *Journal of Personality*, *78*, 257−288.

Sutin, A. R., Costa, P. T., Wethington, E., & Eaton, W. (2010). Turning points and lessons learned: Stressful life events and personality trait development across middle adulthood. *Psychology and Aging, 25*, 524—533.

Torgersen, A. M., & Janson, H. (2002). Why do identical twins differ in personality: Shared environment reconsidered. *Twin Research, 5*, 44—52.

Vaidya, J. G., Gray, E. K., Haig, J., & Watson, D. (2002). On the temporal stability of personality: Evidence for differential stability and the role of life experiences. *Journal of Personality and Social Psychology, 83*, 1469—1484.

van Scheppingen, M. A., Jackson, J. J., Specht, J., Hutteman, R., Denissen, J. J. A., & Bleidorn, W. (2016). Personality trait development during the transition to parenthood: A test of social investment theory. *Social Psychological and Personality Science, 7*, 452—462.

Wagner, G. G., Frick, J. R., & Schupp, J. (2007). The German Socio-Economic Panel Study (SOEP): Scope, evolution and enhancements. *Journal of Applied Social Science Studies, 127*, 139—169.

Wille, B., Beyers, W., & De Fruyt, F. (2012). A transactional approach to person-environment fit: Reciprocal relations between personality development and career role growth across young to middle adulthood. *Journal of Vocational Behavior, 81*, 307—321.

Wu, C.-H. (2016). Personality change via work: A job demand-control model of Big-five personality changes. *Journal of Vocational Behavior, 92*, 157—166.

Zimmermann, J., & Neyer, F. J. (2013). Do we become a different person when hitting the road? Personality development of sojourners. *Journal of Personality and Social Psychology, 105*, 515—530.

# Personality development in close relationships

**22**

*Christine Finn[1], Julia Zimmermann[2], and Franz J. Neyer[1]*
[1]Friedrich Schiller University Jena, Jena, Germany, [2]FernUniversität Hagen, Hagen, Germany

## Introduction

### Personality–relationship transactions

The paradigm of dynamic transactionism (e.g., Magnusson, 1990) proposes that an individual's personality and her or his environment interact continuously and reciprocally across the life span (Neyer & Asendorpf, 2001). As social relationships depict one important vector of one's personal environment (Neyer, Mund, Zimmermann, & Wzrus, 2014), they are assumed to reflect an important source of environmental continuity and change (Caspi, 2000). Consequently, personality–relationship transactions describe how individuals select, maintain, and change their social relationships based on their dispositions; at the same time, these social relationships have the potential to retroactively impact a person's stable patterns of feeling, thinking, and behaving (Neyer et al., 2014).

Personality has been shown to affect the emergence, maintenance, and quality of close relationships, for example, with peers and friends (Asendorpf & Wilpers, 1998; Selfhout et al., 2010), family members (Mund & Neyer, 2014; Wagner, Lüdtke, Roberts, & Trautwein, 2014), and romantic partners (Karney & Bradbury, 1995). At the same time, personality itself develops across the life span (Roberts, Walton, & Viechtbauer, 2006). On the one hand, normative relationship changes have been proven to spur personality maturation (Lang, Reschke, & Neyer, 2006). Normative relationship changes are experienced in the context of age-graded life transitions such as entering school or university, finding a new job, finding a partner, having children, or retiring; these transitions may therefore be best described as relationship transitions (Neyer & Lehnart, 2007). On the other hand, social relationships are also affected by less normative life experiences such as spending a year abroad or the death of a parent or the spouse. All in all, social relationships constitute unique social environments that account for interindividual differences in developmental trajectories.

In general, it is instructive to differentiate between the effects of qualitative relationship characteristics, such as closeness or conflicts, and quantitative relationship changes such as relationship gains and losses (Feld, Suitor, & Hoegh, 2007). The quality of specific relationships, such as close ties to family members or

Personality Development Across the Lifespan. DOI: http://dx.doi.org/10.1016/B978-0-12-804674-6.00022-3

romantic partners, has been shown to have a lasting impact on individual development. For example, the mother—child relationship plays a formative role in the development of attachment in childhood (Ainsworth & Bowlby, 1991), while the experience of a stable and reliable romantic relationship in young adulthood shapes secure romantic attachment (Lehnart & Neyer, 2006), increases in self-esteem (Mund, Finn, Hagemeyer, Zimmermann, & Neyer, 2015), and decreases in neuroticism (Finn, Mitte, & Neyer, 2015). In a similar vein, qualitative changes in individuals' networks (e.g., changes in aggregated relationship closeness or conflict across all peer or family relationships) were found to correspond with the development of all Big Five traits from young adulthood to the midlife transition (Parker, Lüdtke, Trautwein, & Roberts, 2012). Quantitative changes in specific relationships in young adulthood such as finding a partner or the birth of a child have also been shown to influence emotional stability, self-esteem (Lehnart, Neyer, & Eccles, 2010; Neyer & Lehnart, 2007), and conscientiousness (Jokela, Kivimäki, Elovainio, & Keltikangas-Järvinen, 2009; Specht, Egloff, & Schmuckle, 2011). Furthermore, gains of international relationships during students' years abroad mediated changes in openness and neuroticism (Greischel, Noack, & Neyer, 2016; Zimmermann, & Neyer, 2013).

While this brief overview illustrates that personality and different types of relationships such as those with family, peers, or partners interact reciprocally (Mund & Neyer, 2014), a closer look at the reviewed research also indicates that most relationship effects occur within circumscribed phases of an individual's life, reflecting the assumption of age-graded relationship transitions (Neyer et al., 2014). In the following chapter, we adopt a life span perspective and hypothesize that the effect of certain types of close relationships on personality development varies with regard to particular phases of life. To explore this hypothesis, we will summarize the current state of research on specific types of close relationships—family, peer, and romantic partner relationships—and consider their role for personality development across the life span.

## Life span hypothesis

Personal networks change across the life span. According to social convoy theory (Kahn & Antonucci, 1982), a network consists of relationships that accompany the individual throughout his or her life. Core family members, close friends, and spouses fill the very stable inner circle of the convoy, while the periphery consists of less stable ties, such as those with acquaintances, coworkers, and neighbors. Social convoy theory thus describes the flux and flow of relationships across the whole life span. The question of why these changes occur has, however, been addressed more thoroughly by socioemotional selectivity theory (Carstensen, 1995), which proposes that personal goals and relationships change to reflect the perceived amount of time remaining in one's life. In adolescence and young adulthood, when individuals subjectively perceive themselves to have a great deal of time left, their primary goal is information acquisition, a goal that is best met with large and heterogeneous networks. From the transition to adulthood on, one's remaining time is perceived as increasingly limited, and emotional aspects of relationships become more important. In this phase of life, emotion regulation goals come to the fore, which are best met within close relationships.

Socioemotional selectivity theory thus has two important implications. First, it emphasizes age as an important moderator of relationship changes. As outlined in the first paragraph, age may not function as an independent factor, but rather may reflect effects of experiences that most persons make at certain ages (i.e., normative life transitions). As such normative life transitions are strongly intertwined with both quantitative and qualitative changes in relationships, these changes can also be described as normative relationship transitions that follow a similar pattern and timing across all people (Neyer et al., 2014). The second implication of socioemotional selectivity theory is that age effects on relationships are moderated by relationship type. This is reflected in the assumption that, with increasing age, less close relationships lose their meaning and are neglected, to the benefit of emotionally close ties that increase in importance. As a consequence, relationship effects on life span personality development can also be expected to differ according to relationship types. Although previous research has provided evidence on life span changes in social relationships (Wrzus, Hänel, Wagner, & Neyer, 2013), a systematic exploration on such differing effects of different relationship types on personality development across the life span is still missing. In this chapter, we address this issue by providing a comprehensive review of recent findings on the effects of relationships with family members, peers, and romantic partners on personality development. We discuss how these relationships vary with regard to their influence across the life span and offer suggestions for exploring this area more in future research.

# Close relationships

## Family

Although the size of one's family relationship network is highly stable across the life span (Wrzus et al., 2013), quantitative relationship changes occur in terms of gains and losses. Marrying one's partner or having children are two examples of relationship gains, whereas the deaths of family members are relationship losses. While the relative importance of one's parents declines beginning in adolescence, other family members, such as one's own children, become more and more important over time. As these examples illustrate, precisely describing the relationship dynamics within family networks requires distinguishing between one's *family of origin*—consisting of parents, siblings, and grandparents—and one's *family of destination*—consisting of romantic partners, children, and in-laws.

As one's family of origin is determined by genetic kinship, it is not deliberately chosen and is seldom ended deliberately (Lang, 2000). As a consequence, quantitative relationship changes occur rather infrequently. Accordingly, most studies on relationships within one's family of origin have considered only the effects of qualitative relationship characteristics, such as relationship closeness or attachment styles, on development. Mother−child attachment is commonly considered to be the earliest influence that relationship quality has on personality (Ainsworth &

Bowlby, 1991). For example, Hagekull and Bohin (2003) found that infants with secure attachment tended to be more extraverted and open and less neurotic in their childhood. During adolescence, the importance of parents decreases with the rise of emerging individuation processes (Harter, 2012). Although family relationships remain subjectively highly important throughout middle and old age (Lang, 2000; Wrzus et al., 2013; Van Tilburg, 1998), the effects of qualitative family relationship characteristics such as relationship closeness or conflict on personality development were shown to be almost negligible during middle adulthood (Mund & Neyer, 2014). In line with that, the only investigations to date that have looked at the impact of quantitative relationship changes (i.e., the death of one's parents, birth of siblings) revealed no influence on Big Five trait development (Damian & Roberts, 2015; Rohrer, Egloff, & Schmukle, 2015; Specht et al., 2011).

While qualitative changes are the most common source of change in one's family of origin, quantitative changes may play a more prominent role in one's family of destination. For example, finding a partner or having children represent relationship gains that bring important changes to individual social networks. As those structural changes depict classic normative relationship transitions, they are expected to shape personality development in an enduring manner. As romantic partners will be considered in detail in a separate paragraph, we will focus on the effects of children in this section. The birth of children has been shown to decrease conscientiousness (Specht et al., 2011; van Scheppingen et al., 2016), increase emotionality and sociability (Jokela et al., 2009). In accordance with the social investment principle proposed by Wood & Roberts (2006), such developments can be attributed to the fulfillment of age-graded social roles. In addition to such quantitative effects, young adults who had better relationships with their own preschool-age children developed higher extraversion and lower neuroticism (Neyer & Asendorpf, 2001).

## Do findings match the life span hypothesis?

The results presented above suggest that family relationships have the strongest effects on personality development from childhood to young adulthood. The effect of having children in young adulthood therefore reflects a highly age-graded relationship transition that has significant influence on personality development. Other relationship changes, such as the death of a parent, have not been shown to affect personality, and the effects of family relationship quality were found for childhood and young adulthood but not for older ages. However, few studies to date have addressed the effects of family relationships on personality development in middle adulthood and beyond. Hence, further research on the later periods of life is needed to obtain a clearer picture on the impact of family relationships on personality development across the entire life span.

## Peers

In contrast to kinship or romantic partners, the definition of peers as a relationship category is somewhat unclear. This may be due to the fact that peer relationships contain different characteristics and functions across the life span. For example, peer relationships can include peripheral ties to neighbors, classmates, or colleagues, and also very close relationships with friends; each different type of peer relationship fulfills distinct functions of instrumental or emotional support (Kahn & Antonucci, 1982; Trinke & Bartholomew, 1997). In a similar vein, peers may influence the individual at two levels: the group level and the relationship level (Reitz, Zimmermann, Hutteman, Specht, & Neyer, 2014).

*Group-level effects* describe the influence of one's whole network of peers on that individual. According to group socialization theory (Harris, 1995), peer effects on personality development can be explained in terms of assimilation and differentiation processes. *Assimilation* pertains to the adoption of group norms that guide behaviors, thoughts, and feelings, resulting in increased similarity of group members over time. In contrast, *differentiation* pertains to differences in group status and social comparisons, resulting in increased dissimilarity of group members over time. Both types of group-level effects have mainly been assumed to occur from childhood to young adulthood. With regard to assimilation processes, Kerr, Lambert, Stattin, and Klackenberg-Larsson (1994) found that shy boys but not shy girls became more outgoing from age 6 to 16 years; the authors attributed this change to the specific behavioral norms of boys' and girls' respective peer groups. Social inclusion in one's peer network was also shown to affect the development of self-esteem during adolescence (Hutteman, Nestler, Wagner, Egloff, & Back, 2015). However, clear empirical evidence is lacking with regard to the differentiation processes that explain why personality characteristics differ between individuals from the same peer group. Overall, the data on group-level effects are scarce and largely limited to childhood and adolescence.

*Relationship-level effects* may explain individual differences in personality development within peer groups. Specific dyadic relationships such as with one's best friend or roommate have been assumed to be more important from young adulthood on. The social relations model (Kenny & la Voie, 1985) and the personality and social relationships framework (PERSOC; Back et al., 2011) address the influence of relationship-level effects on personality development. Both approaches assume that peer dyad members shape each other's feelings, thoughts, and behaviors through repeated interaction patterns. For example, steeper increases in openness and agreeableness, and decreases in conscientiousness were shown for young adults living with roommates as compared to young adults living with their parents (Jonkmann, Thoemmes, Lüdtke, & Trautwein, 2014). In addition, support provided by one's best friend predicted increases in extraversion from age 17 to 23, whereas higher levels of conflict predicted decreases in extraversion and self-esteem (Sturaro, Denissen, van Aken, & Asendorpf, 2008). With regard to the differentiation between close and peripheral ties, Mund and Neyer (2014) found that less insecurity and higher closeness and conflict with friends predicted decreased neuroticism, whereas more closeness and importance for more peripheral relationships predicted decreased extraversion and conscientiousness from young to middle adulthood. As these examples illustrate, most research on peer influence on personality development has not looked beyond young adulthood, ignoring the role of friends in middle and old age (Wrzus, Zimmermann, Mund, & Neyer, in press). Although it has been established that peer networks decrease in size and importance as family relations become more important in old age (Lang, 2000; Van Tilburg, 1998; Wrzus et al., 2013), the effects of peers on personality development in this phase of life remain unclear.

## Do findings match the life span hypothesis?

The research reviewed in this section at least partly supports the life span perspective. Both group-level (Kerr et al., 1994) and relationship-level effects (Jonkmann et al., 2014; Sturaro et al., 2008) in adolescence and young adulthood may mirror age-graded relationship transitions such as entering school or university, which open up new networks and pave the way to peer influence on personality development. However, peers may also play a role in less normative life transitions such as international mobility experiences. Spending time abroad affected personality development in adolescence and young adulthood by means of social inclusion and the experience of relationship fluctuation (Hutteman et al., 2015; Zimmermann & Neyer, 2013). All in all, the current state of research suggests that peer effects decrease after childhood and adolescence and are only small to negligible during young adulthood (Wrzus & Neyer, in press). However, again, most studies are limited to the younger ages and empirical findings on peer effects in later periods of life are rare.

## Romantic partner

The relationship with one's romantic partner is one of the closest and most intimate relationships an individual has (Berscheid, Snyder, & Omoto, 1989; Neyer, Wrzus, Wagner, & Lang, 2011) and has been shown to profoundly shape an individual's personality. For example, engaging in one's first romantic relationship was associated with decreases in neuroticism and shyness, and increases extraversion, conscientiousness, and self-esteem (Lehnart et al., 2010; Neyer & Lehnart, 2007). In addition, further positive and negative relationship-related experiences such as moving in with one's partner (Jonkmann et al., 2014), marrying, separating, divorcing, or the death of the spouse (Specht et al., 2011) were shown to contribute to personality development.

Apart from such relationship transitions, the experiences made within a stable relationship have also been shown to be particularly important for personality development: For example, positive and negative experiences within relationships such as feeling close, having conflicts, or other indicators of relationship quality predicted both changes in self-esteem (Mund et al., 2015) and negative emotionality in young adulthood (Robins, Caspi, & Moffitt, 2002). A similar pattern was found for the midlife transition, whereby conflicts, closeness, and insecurity affected changes in neuroticism, extraversion, agreeableness, and conscientiousness (Mund & Neyer, 2014). However, it is not yet clear why actually romantic relationships shape the personalities of the individuals involved. With regard to relationship transitions such as engaging in a first relationship, marriage, and moving in together

(Wood & Roberts, 2006), investment in age-graded social roles reflects one plausible explanation. For non-normative transitions such as separation and divorce, one can speculate that these individuals just adapted to the challenges of demanding experiences and then returned to their pretransition levels afterward. However, one recent study explicitly addressed the processes underlying personality development within stable relationships. Finn et al. (2015) showed that decreases in specific interpretation biases predicted subsequent decreases in neuroticism in both partners of romantic couples. Apart from this cognitive component, the studies reviewed in this section suggest that affective experiences in romantic relationships (Mund & Neyer, 2014; Mund et al., 2015; Robins et al., 2002) are also important for personality development across adulthood. All in all, these findings suggest that romantic relationships qualify as key drivers of personality development.

## Do results match the life span hypothesis?

In the results presented here, the life span hypothesis is at least partly supported. Typical events in romantic relationships such as finding a partner, marrying, or moving in together mainly happen during young adulthood, and may therefore be described as age-graded relationship transitions. At the same time, non-normative relationship transitions such as separation and divorce, as well as the nontransition of remaining in a stable relationship enduringly shape each partner's ways of thinking, feeling, and behaving. This means that, while the consequences of quantitative changes associated with finding and establishing a partnership mainly pertain to young adulthood, emotion regulation goals may be best met within stable and reliable romantic relationships, which continue throughout one's life span. Although the presented studies underline the importance of partner relationships for personality development from young adulthood up to the midlife transition, there is again a lack of research covering later periods of life.

## Interactions between relationship types

The preceding paragraphs illustrated the distinct effects of family, peer, and romantic relationships on personality development. At the same time, it is also suggested that these relationship types interact both cross-sectionally and longitudinally in their impact on personality development. Across the life span, certain transitions occur that entail a decreasing importance of one relationship type in favor of an increasing importance of another relationship type. For example, in the transition from childhood to adolescence, parents become less important in favor of peers as socialization agents (Harris, 1995). Hence, personality development during this period of life is likely to be affected by changes in both the family and peer networks. Subsequently, during the years of young adulthood, romantic partners become increasingly important (Fraley & Davis, 1997; Simpson, Collins, Tran, & Haydon, 2007). Although childhood experiences with parents lay the foundation for subsequent romantic relationship experiences, Simpson et al. (2007) showed that there is no direct effect of childhood attachment on the attachment to one's romantic partner in young adulthood. Instead, peer relationship qualities mediated this effect. Although different relationship types seem to predominate in distinct life phases, their influences on personality development are still intertwined, as experiences that take place within one phase of life and with one certain relationship type pave the way for subsequent experiences in other relationship contexts.

## Summary

Based on the paradigm of dynamic transactionism (Magnusson, 1990), in this chapter we outlined how an individual's personality and her or his environment interact continuously and reciprocally across the life span. In particular, we illustrated that relationships change across the life span (Wrzus et al., 2013), and with them their power to shape individual development. While parents exert a particularly strong influence during childhood, the focus shifts to peers and close friends in adolescence (Harris, 1995). These social ties are still important in young adulthood when romantic partners come into play, taking the leading role until one has children. Beginning in young adulthood, the importance of peripheral ties decreases in favor of close relationships such as family or close friends, which appear to constitute important socialization agents throughout the life course (for a summary of findings, see Table 22.1).

In accordance with the life span hypothesis, it seems that each type of relationship (i.e., family, peers, and romantic partner) has a specific life phase in which it is particularly important for personality development (at least with regard to normative transitions such as entering school, leaving one's parents' home, finding a

Table 22.1 Summary of findings on relationship effects on personality development

| Relationship type | Relationship effects on personality development | Affected age range |
|---|---|---|
| Family | Mother−child attachment<br>Birth of children | Childhood<br>Young adulthood |
| Peers | Relationship-level effects (roommate, specific friends)<br>Group-level effects | Adolescence to middle adulthood<br>Childhood to adolescence |
| Romantic Partner | Positive and negative relationship events<br><br>Relationship quality | Young to middle adulthood<br>Young to middle adulthood |

partner, or having a child). However, relationships also play a role in less normative transitions such as spending time abroad, separating from a romantic partner, or divorcing. Apart from transition effects, relationships have also been shown to unfold their influence across long periods of life, as stable relationships with friends or romantic partners affect personality development sustainably from adolescence to middle adulthood. All in all, these relationship effects not only emphasize the importance of personal networks for the individual in general but also illustrate how dynamic transactions between relationships and personality happen in manifold ways that follow distinct patterns. Consequently, we suggest that the quantitative and qualitative characteristics of personal networks must be confirmed through longitudinal studies to understand how relationships actually shape personality.

One suitable research design for this purpose would be a network approach, as comparing the composition of personal networks across time is necessary to disentangle the influence of quantitative changes within the network as a whole and to clarify the effects of stability and change in specific subnetworks such as family or peer relationships. In addition to network structure, different aspects of relationship quality within specific subnetworks such as satisfaction, conflicts, or closeness require consideration, in particular with regard to their effects on personality development during the later periods of life (Milardo, 1992; Wellman, 1983).

Another possible research approach would be the analysis of specific dyadic relationships with important others such as parents, romantic partners, or one's best friend. The influence of these relationships on individuals' personalities may unfold over long periods of time, as they are highly stable across the life span. Researchers studying dyadic constellations need to take into consideration the mutual influence that both interaction partners have on each other over the course of their lives (Kenny & la Voie, 1985).

However, beyond the presented evidence on the impact of different relationship types, several studies have failed to confirm these hypothesized relationship effects on personality development (e.g., Asendorpf & Wilpers, 1998; Neyer & Asendorpf, 2001). This failure may at least be partly attributed to methodological challenges (Mund & Neyer, 2014; Neyer & Asendorpf, 2001). The use of advanced methods, for example, allows change—change effects to be taken into account that explicitly address the influence of prior changes in the relationship domain on subsequent changes in personality (Finn et al., 2015; Mund & Neyer, 2014). Such methods may provide a promising extension of research on the role of relationship experiences in personality development.

## Conclusion

Social relationships show large variability with regard to their specific characteristics as well as with regard to their importance for the individual across the life span. In spite of this variability, all types of social relationships serve as key drivers of individual development. However, in accordance with the life span hypothesis, it seems that each type of relationship has a period during which it is particularly important for personality development. These periods, in turn, are linked to age-graded life transitions that the authors see as mainly defined by relationship transitions (Neyer et al., 2014).

However, few studies have addressed the conditions and consequences of dynamic personality—relationship transactions after middle adulthood. Hence, further research is needed to more thoroughly explore the changing effects of different relationship types across the full life span.

# References

Ainsworth, M. S., & Bowlby, J. (1991). An ethological approach to personality development. *American Psychologist, 46*, 333–341.

Asendorpf, J. B., & Wilpers, S. (1998). Personality effects on social relationships. *Journal of Personality and Social Psychology, 74*, 1531–1544. Available from http://dx.doi.org/10.1037/0022-3514.74.6.1531.

Back, M. D., Baumert, A., Denissen, J. J. A., Hartung, F.-M., Penke, L., Schmukle, S. C., et al. (2011). PERSOC: A unified framework for understanding the dynamic interplay of personality and social relationships. *European Journal of Personality, 25*, 90–107.

Berscheid, E., Snyder, M., & Omoto, A. M. (1989). The relationship closeness inventory: Assessing the closeness of interpersonal relationships. *Journal of Personality and Social Psychology, 57*, 792–807. Available from http://dx.doi.org/10.1037/0022-3514.57.5.792.

Carstensen, L. L. (1995). Evidence for a life-span theory of socioemotional selectivity. *Current Directions in Psychological Science, 4*, 151–156. Available from http://dx.doi.org/10.1111/1467-8721.ep11512261.

Caspi, A. (2000). The child is father of the man: Personality continuity from childhood to adulthood. *Journal of Personality and Social Psychology, 78*, 158–172. Available from http://dx.doi.org/10.1037//0022-3514.781.158.

Damian, R. I., & Roberts, B. W. (2015). The association of birth order with personality and intelligence in a representative sample of US, high school students. *Journal of Research in Personality, 58*, 96–105. Available from http://dx.doi.org/10.1016/j.jrp.2015.05.005.

Feld, S. L., Suitor, J. J., & Hoegh, J. G. (2007). Describing changes in personal networks over time. *Field Methods, 19*, 218–236. Available from http://dx.doi.org/10.1177/1525822X06299134.

Finn, C., Mitte, K., & Neyer, F. J. (2015). Recent decreases in specific interpretation biases predict decreases in neuroticism: Evidence from longitudinal study with young adult couples. *Journal of Personality, 83*, 274–286. Available from http://dx.doi.org/10.1111/jopy.12102.

Fraley, R., & Davis, K. E. (1997). Attachment formation and transfer in young adults' close friendships and romantic relationships. *Personal Relationships, 4*, 131–144. Available from http://dx.doi.org/10.1111/j.1475-6811.1997.tb00135.x.

Greischel, H., Noack, P., & Neyer, F. J. (2016). Sailing uncharted waters: Adolescent personality development and social relationship experiences during a year abroad. *Journal of Youth and Adolescence, 45*, 2307–2320. Available from http://dx.doi.org/10.1007/s10964-016-0479-1.

Hagekull, B., & Bohin, G. (2003). Early temperament and attachment as predictors of the five factor model of personality. *Attachment and Human Development*, *5*, 2–18. Available from http://dx.doi.org/10.1080/1461673031000078643.

Harris, J. (1995). Where is the child's environment? A group socialization theory of development. *Psychological Review*, *102*, 458–489. Available from http://dx.doi.org/10.1037/0033-295X.102.3.458.

Harter, S. (2012). *The construction of the self: Developmental and sociocultural foundations* (2nd ed.). New York, NY: Guilford Press.

Hutteman, R., Nestler, S., Wagner, J., Egloff, B., & Back, M. D. (2015). Wherever I may roam: Processes of self-esteem development from adolescence to emerging adulthood in the context of international student exchange. *Journal of Personality and Social Psychology*, *108*, 767–783. Available from http://dx.doi.org/10.1037/pspp0000015.

Jokela, M., Kivimäki, M., Elovainio, M., & Keltikangas-Järvinen, L. (2009). Personality and having children: A two-way relationship. *Journal of Personality and Social Psychology*, *96*, 218–230. Available from http://dx.doi.org/10.1037/a0014058.

Jonkmann, K., Thoemmes, F., Lüdtke, O., & Trautwein, U. (2014). Personality traits and living arrangements in young adulthood: Selection and socialization. *Developmental Psychology*, *50*, 683–698. Available from http://dx.doi.org/10.1037/a0034239.

Kahn, R. L., & Antonucci, T. C. (1982). Applying social psychology to the aging process: Four examples. In John F. Santos (Ed.), *Psychology and the older adult: Challenges for training in the 1980s* (pp. 207–223). Washington, DC: American Psychological Association. Available from http://dx.doi.org/10.1037/10557-015.

Karney, B., & Bradbury, T. N. (1995). Assesing longitudinal change in marriage: An introduction to the analysis of growth curves. *Journal of Marriage and the Family*, *57*, 1091–1108. Available from http://dx.doi.org/10.2307/353425.

Kenny, D. A., & la Voie, L. (1985). Separating individual and group effects. *Journal of Personality and Social Psychology*, *48*, 339–348. Available from http://dx.doi.org/10.1037/0022-3514.48.2.339.

Kerr, M., Lambert, W. W., Stattin, H., & Klackenberg-Larsson, I. (1994). Stability of inhibition in a swedish longitudinal sample. *Child Development*, *65*, 138–146. Available from http://dx.doi.org/10.2307/1131371.

Lang, F. R. (2000). Endings and continuity of social relationships: Maximizing intrinsic benefits within personal networks when feeling near to death. *Journal of Social and Personal Relationships*, *17*, 155–182. Available from http://dx.doi.org/10.1177/0265407500172001.

Lang, F. R., Reschke, F. S., & Neyer, F. J. (2006). Social relationships, transitions, and personality development across the life span. In D. Mroczek (Ed.), *Handbook of personality development* (pp. 445–466). Mahwah, NJ: Lawrence Erlbaum Associates Publishers.

Lehnart, J., & Neyer, F. J. (2006). Should I stay or should I go? Personality-attachment transaction in stable and instable romantic relationships. *European Journal of Personality*, *20*, 475–495.

Lehnart, J., Neyer, F. J., & Eccles, J. (2010). Long-term effects of social investment: The case of partnering in young adulthood. *Journal of personality*, *78*, 639–670. Available from http://dx.doi.org/10.1111/j.1467-6494.2010.00629.x.

Magnusson, D. (1990). Personality development from an interactional perspective. In L. Pervin (Ed.), *Handbook of personality: Theory and research* (pp. 193–222). New York, NY: Guilford Press.

Milardo, R. M. (1992). Comparative methods for delineating social networks. *Journal of Social and Personal Relationships*, *9*, 447–461. Available from http://dx.doi.org/10.1177/0265407592093007.

Mund, M., Finn, C., Hagemeyer, B., Zimmermann, J., & Neyer, F. J. (2015). The dynamics of self-esteem in partner relationships. *European Journal of Personality, 29,* 235–249. Available from http://dx.doi.org/10.1002/per.1984.

Mund, M., & Neyer, F. J. (2014). Treating personality–relationship transactions with respect: Narrow facets, advanced models, and extended time frames. *Journal of Personality and Social Psychology, 107,* 352–368. Available from http://dx.doi.org/10.1037/a0036719.

Neyer, F. J., & Asendorpf, J. B. (2001). Personality–relationship transaction in young adulthood. *Journal of Personality and Social Psychology, 81,* 1190–1204. Available from http://dx.doi.org/10.1037/0022-3514.81.6.1190.

Neyer, F. J., & Lehnart, J. (2007). Relationships matter in personality development: Evidence from an 8-year longitudinal study across young adulthood. *Journal of Personality, 75,* 535–568. Available from http://dx.doi.org/10.1111/j.1467-6494.2007.00448.x.

Neyer, F. J., Mund, M., Zimmermann, J., & Wrzus, C. (2014). Personality–relationship transactions revisited. *Journal of Personality, 82,* 539–550. Available from http://dx.doi.org/10.1111/jopy.12063.

Neyer, F. J., Wrzus, C., Wagner, J., & Lang, F. R. (2011). Principles of relationship differentiation. *European Psychologist, 16,* 267–277. Available from http://dx.doi.org/10.1027/1016-9040/a000055.

Parker, P. D., Lüdtke, O., Trautwein, U., & Roberts, B. W. (2012). Personality and relationship quality during the transition from high school to early adulthood. *Journal of Personality, 80,* 1061–1089. Available from http://dx.doi.org/10.1111/j.1467-6494.2012.00766.x.

Reitz, A. K., Zimmermann, J., Hutteman, R., Specht, J., & Neyer, F. J. (2014). How peers make a difference: The role of peer groups and peer relationships in personality development. *European Journal of Personality, 28,* 279–288. Available from http://dx.doi.org/10.1002/per.1965.

Roberts, B. W., Walton, K. E., & Viechtbauer, W. (2006). Personality traits change in adulthood: Reply to Costa and McCrae. *Psychological Bulletin, 132,* 29–32. Available from http://dx.doi.org/10.1037/0033-2909.132.1.29.

Robins, R. W., Caspi, A., & Moffitt, T. E. (2002). It's not just who you're with, it's who you are: Personality and relationship experiences across multiple relationships. *Journal of Personality, 70,* 925–964. Available from http://dx.doi.org/10.1111/1467-6494.05028.

Rohrer, J. M., Egloff, B., & Schmukle, S. C. (2015). Examining the effects of birth order on personality. *Proceedings of the National Academy of Sciences in the United States of America, 112,* 14224–14229. Available from http://dx.doi.org/10.1073/pnas.1506451112.

Selfhout, M. H. W., Burk, W. J., Denissen, J. J. A., Branje, S. J. T., van Aken, M. A. G., & Meeus, W. H. J. (2010). Emerging late adolescent friendship networks and Big Five personality traits: A social network approach. *Journal of Personality, 78,* 509–538. Available from http://dx.doi.org/10.1111/j.1467-6494.2010.00625.x.

Simpson, J. A., Collins, W. A., Tran, S., & Haydon, K. C. (2007). Attachment and the experience and expression of emotions in romantic relationships: A developmental perspective. *Journal of Personality and Social Psychology, 92,* 355–367. Available from http://dx.doi.org/10.1037/0022-3514.92.2.355.

Specht, J., Egloff, B., & Schmuckle, S. C. (2011). Stability and change of personality across the life course: The impact of age and major life events on mean-level and rank-order stability of the Big Five. *Journal of Personality and Social Psychology, 101,* 862–882. Available from http://dx.doi.org/10.1037/a0024950.

Sturaro, C., Denissen, J. J. A., van Aken, M. A. G., & Asendorpf, J. B. (2008). Person−environment transactions during emerging adulthood: The interplay between personality characteristics and social relationships. *European Psychologist, 13*, 1−11. Available from http://dx.doi.org/10.1027/1016-9040.13.1.1.

Trinke, S. J., & Bartholomew, K. (1997). Hierarchies of attachment relationships in young adulthood. *Journal of Social and Personal Relationships, 14*, 603−625. Available from http://dx.doi.org/10.1177/0265407597145002.

van Scheppingen, M. A., Jackson, J. J., Specht, J., Hutteman, R., Denissen, J. J. A., & Bleidorn, W. (2016). Personality trait development during the transition to parenthood: A test of social investment theory. *Social Psychological and Personality Science, 7*(5), 452−462.

Van Tilburg, T. (1998). Losing and gaining in old age: Changes in personal network size and social support in a four-year longitudinal study. *Journal of Gerontology, 53B*, 313−323. Available from http://dx.doi.org/10.1093/geronb/53B.6.S313.

Wagner, J., Lüdtke, O., Roberts, B. W., & Trautwein, U. (2014). Who belongs to me? Social relationship and personality characteristics in the transition to young adulthood. *European Journal of Personality, 28*, 586−603. Available from http://dx.doi.org/10.1002/per.1974.

Wellman, B. (1983). Network analysis: Some basic principles. In R. Collins (Ed.), *Sociological theory* (pp. 155−200). San Francisco: Jossey-Bass.

Wood, D., & Roberts, B. W. (2006). The effect of age and role information on expectations for Big Five personality traits. *Personality and Social Psychology Bulletin, 32*, 1482−1496. Available from http://dx.doi.org/10.1177/0146167206291008.

Wrzus, C., Hänel, M., Wagner, J., & Neyer, F. J. (2013). Social network changes and life events across the life span: A meta-analysis. *Psychological Bulletin, 139*, 53−80. Available from http://dx.doi.org/10.1037/a0028601.

Wrzus, C. & Neyer, F.J. (in press). Co-development of personality and friendships across the lifespan: An empirical review on selection and socialization. European Psychologist.

Wrzus, C., Zimmermann, J., Mund, M., & Neyer, F. J. (in press). Friendships in young and middle adulthood: Normative patterns and personality differences. In M. Hojjat & A. Moyer (Eds.), *The psychology of friendship*. New York, NY: Oxford University Press.

Zimmermann, J., & Neyer, F. J. (2013). Do we become a different person when hitting the road? Personality development of sojourners. *Journal of Personality and Social Psychology, 105*, 515−530. Available from http://dx.doi.org/10.1037/a00330.

# Personality development and health

*Joshua J. Jackson, Sara J. Weston, and Leah H. Schultz*
Washington University in St. Louis, St. Louis, MO, United States

**23**

Personality traits are some of the best psychological predictors of physical health. Personality traits serve as risk factors for the onset of disease and illness such as Alzheimer's disease, heart disease, and stroke (e.g., Weston, Hill, & Jackson, 2015; Wilson, Schneider, Arnold, Bienias, & Bennett, 2007) and predict premature mortality with greater accuracy than other psychological predictors like IQ and SES (Jokela et al., 2013; Roberts, Kuncel, Shiner, Caspi, & Goldberg, 2007). These associations persist across the lifespan, as childhood personality traits are associated with adult health and health behaviors decades later (Hampson, Goldberg, Vogt, & Dubanoski, 2006; Moffitt et al., 2011). Further, personality–health associations exist regardless of assessment method. For example, peer reports of twenty-some-things' personalities are associated with their mortality risk up to 75 years later (Jackson, Connolly, Garrison, Levine, & Connolly, 2015).

The numerous studies that link personality traits with health status decades into the future (Hampson, Goldberg, Vogt, & Dubanoski, 2007) predict the onset of new diseases (Weston et al. 2015) and describe potential mechanisms that relate personality to future health (Turiano, Whiteman, Hampson, Roberts, & Mroczek, 2012) all provide a strong claim for personality traits to causally influence physical health. Less discussed, however, is the possibility that health status influences personality. For example, it is possible that detriments in health put constraints on the behaviors one may perform, or may even alter one's self-concept—each of which may lead to changes in personality. If this is the case, the causal arrow between personality and health may not be as clear as it once may have appeared. In this chapter, we describe the existing evidence that health is associated with changes in personality and discuss the potential mechanisms that relate the two. Below we review the various designs used to test questions of whether personality development is related to health status.

## Health interventions

Can health status alter and ultimately change personality traits? The best potential evidence for a causal link between health and personality trait development is through a health intervention, where the intervention has an unintentional effect of changing personality. Unfortunately, studies that are able to successfully intervene

Personality Development Across the Lifespan. DOI: http://dx.doi.org/10.1016/B978-0-12-804674-6.00023-5

to influence physical health status typically do not assess personality before and after the intervention, so few studies of this kind exist. Overall, the limited evidence points to a minimal influence of health interventions on personality. In a meta-analysis of interventions to improve the health of those with coronary heart disease (e.g., behavior modification and health education), there were no subsequent changes in trait anxiety or depression, the only individual difference variables assessed (Dusseldorp, Van Elderen, Maes, Meulman, & Kraaij, 1999).

One difficulty in parsing the health intervention literature (e.g., Glanz & Bishop, 2010) is that many health interventions focus on changing health behaviors (e.g,. exercise, diet) that are conceptually related to personality traits such as conscientiousness (Jackson & Roberts, in press). For example, though health interventions typically are effective at influencing health behaviors related to the trait of conscientiousness (e.g., exercise, Marcus et al., 1998), the above meta-analysis did not assess the trait of conscientiousness; thus, it is unknown whether the intervention had any effects on levels of conscientiousness. Despite the lack of evidence, there exists enthusiasm that personality may change in response to interventions targeted at particular health behaviors (e.g., substance abuse; Magidson, Roberts, Collado-Rodriguez, & Lejuez, 2014). While promising, these studies blur the line between health status, the processes that change health, and indicators of personality.

## Disease or illness onset

Outside of changes in health due to a health intervention, the onset of a major disease or illness (e.g., stroke, cancer) provides the best opportunity to examine how physical health is associated with personality development. Due to the relatively substantial changes in health status over a short period of time, it is easier to tease apart cause and effect in these designs. Unlike interventions, however, there may be an association between predisease personality and the likelihood of developing the disease (e.g., Weston et al., 2015), making it more difficult to assess the directionality between personality and health status.

There is a large literature on the association between neurodegenerative diseases such as dementia and Alzheimer's disease (AD) and personality prior to and during the progression of the disease (e.g., Wilson et al., 2007). In a prospective longitudinal study, cognitive markers of neurodegenerative disease were assessed annually, and caregivers provided annual informant reports of participants' personality traits; those who eventually developed AD became more self-centered and inflexible even before the formal AD diagnosis, indicating that personality change may be an early risk factor of AD (Balsis, Carpenter, & Storandt, 2005). Similarly, a meta-analysis of informant-rated personality change in individuals pre- and post-AD diagnosis found increases in neuroticism and decreases in extraversion, conscientiousness, openness, and agreeableness (Robins Wahlin & Byrne, 2011). The onsets of other forms of dementia exhibit similar patterns of personality change. For example, individuals with behavioral variant fronto-temporal dementia (bvFTD) also show declines in extraversion, conscientiousness, openness, and agreeableness. However, in contrast to those with AD, individuals with bvFTD tend to decrease in neuroticism (Lykou et al., 2013; Torrente et al., 2014).

Parkinson's disease is another neurodegenerative disease which appears to be linked to personality change. Though like AD and bvFTD, Parkinson's often involves cognitive decline, but the hallmark of Parkinson's disease is the degeneration of motor function. Ultimately, Parkinson's inhibits an individual's ability to do many daily functions such as walking, eating, and dressing oneself. In a retrospective study of both individuals and their spouses, personality change was found pre- and postdiagnosis of Parkinson's over a 10-year period (Mendelsohn, Dakof, & Skaff, 1995). Compared to a community sample, patients with Parkinson's disease decreased more in extraversion, agreeableness, conscientiousness, and openness, and increased more in neuroticism. Altogether these studies indicate that both informant- and self-reports of personality demonstrate change as a response to the onset of a variety of neurodegenerative diseases that affect all aspects of functioning.

One issue in interpreting these studies is identifying what is responsible for changes in personality. A challenge in all of these studies is that physical health is not a unitary construct, in that two people may both be described as having poor health but have both qualitatively and quantitatively different symptoms. This equifinality thus makes it difficult to broadly discuss the effects that health has for personality development across all possible health conditions. In the context of neurodegenerative diseases, while the Parkinson's disease study implies that changes in personality are not entirely due to memory issues or changes in cognitive functioning, neurodegenerative diseases directly impact one's psychological functioning, by definition. Furthermore, the literature on neurodegenerative disease highlights the importance of describing how physical health may lead to changes in personality. In the case of neurodegenerative diseases, the cause of the change is most likely through limits or constraints in functioning, rather than through a direct influence on a physical health system, such as the respiratory or immune system. In other words, increases in neuroticism in AD patients are likely a byproduct of the frustration of having a debilitating terminal disease, whereas declines in extraversion and conscientiousness may be a direct result of limitations in activities that one may be able to perform.

In contrast to neurodegenerative diseases, the onset of noncognitively based and terminal diseases may allow researchers to separate the forces responsible for personality change. In one of the few studies that have examined this question, Jokela, Hakulinen, Singh-Manoux, and Kivimäki (2014) investigated whether personality traits change after the onset of a particular disease or illness (e.g., diabetes, heart disease, cancer). Across four large samples spanning from 4 to 10 years in length, pooled analyses revealed that personality trait change related to the onset of disease. Compared to participants who did not develop a major illness, those who did tended to decline in extraversion, conscientiousness, emotional stability, and openness. Personality trait changes were greater for those who experienced multiple health problems, suggesting a dosage effect where the severity of illness may determine the degree of personality trait change. Having a stroke in particular was associated with broad changes in personality. All together, the study makes a strong case that the development of a major illness or disease, like having a heart attack or a stroke, alters one's personality, and that these changes persist across a number of years.

In a follow-up study, Jackson, Weston, Schultz, Hill, and Turiano (2016) recently analyzed new data from the MIDUS (Midlife Development in the United States) data set, which included a new wave of personality and health data in addition to the two waves analyzed by Jokela et al. (2014). This third wave of data provided the ability to better assess personality trait development (Jackson & Allemand, 2014), as well as to obtain higher base rates for disease onset. Furthermore, the study accounted for selection bias, as initial levels of health and personality are associated with the onset of many diseases (Weston et al. 2015), complicating straightforward interpretations about how disease onset alters the course of personality development. Results indicated that there were fewer associations between health events and changes in personality, indicating that personality traits are highly resistant to change even in the face of life-altering events such as being diagnosed with cancer. These results are in line with Sutin, Zonderman, Ferrucci, and Terracciano (2013), who examined personality development within the Baltimore Longitudinal Study of Aging across 10 years. Increases in illness burden, as assessed by the Charlson Comorbidity Index, a weighted sum of 19 conditions (e.g., congenital heart failure, diabetes), were associated only with increases in openness, specifically the aesthetics and feelings facets. Developing diseases across a 10-year period was not associated with any lasting changes in any other personality trait nor personality facet.

Collectively, these studies suggest that not all health events lead directly to changes in personality, nor are there consistent findings regarding which traits are impacted. Outside of having a stroke, there appears to be no illness that is reliably associated with changes in personality. These findings paint a picture of a relatively robust personality system that is resilient to change (Roberts, Wood, & Caspi, 2008). In conjunction with the findings from the neurodegenerative diseases, these findings imply that one of the main causes for the association between personality development and health is through physical limitations imposed by the malady, e.g., the inability to work or do chores in response to a stroke.

Why is the onset of other diseases not associated with widespread changes in personality? Outside of developing a severely life-altering condition, other health events may be interpreted as initial short-term hassles (e.g., increased doctor visits), but not factors that change individuals' self-concepts. Or, perhaps individuals view these health events as something they can overcome over time with treatment and a change in lifestyle (e.g., chemotherapy for cancer, dietary changes for diabetes) and thus there are few long-term effects. A parallel is perhaps found in the well-being literature where people are thought to adapt to major life events (Diener, Suh, Lucas, & Smith, 1999), though this may not occur for majorly debilitating disabilities (Lucas, 2007).

## Naturalistic changes in personality and health

In contrast to focusing on acute health events, like the onset of disease, many studies investigate how naturally occurring personality development relates to health status. A primary concern that motivates much of this research is whether changes in personality serve as a viable individual difference to understand health, above and beyond initial levels. The studies reviewed above focused more on the consequences of health events, whereas these designs ask whether or not changes in personality can inform our understanding of the personality—health relationship. The question is important to ask, as it is possible that changes in personality as assessed by standard personality measures do not manifest in "actual" changes in behavior, thoughts, or feelings characteristic of the trait. Instead, personality trait change may only occur in the mind of rater and result from a number of different sources, e.g., reference bias, measurement noninvariance, and self-concept change (Jackson & Allemand, 2014). If this is the case, then changes in personality would not reflect changes in the processes that link personality with health (e.g., health behaviors). To assess whether this is the case, designs typically associate health measures with assessments of personality trait change.

Designs such as these are helpful in two regards. First, by not focusing on an acute health event (e.g., onset of cancer), health can be measured more subjectively. This subjective versus objective balance may be especially important when considering the processes responsible for changes in personality. Especially in older adulthood when health concerns are more prevalent, individuals will differ in the degree to which they anticipate or adapt to changes in health status, and thus how they rate their overall health. Second, because the design does not focus on a particular health event, the assessment of health may be a more comprehensive assessment of physical health that covers multiple domains (e.g., numerous health-related biomarkers, BMI, IADLs).

One of the first studies to demonstrate that changes in personality are associated with health status above and beyond initial levels was a longitudinal study of veterans, where changes in neuroticism predicted premature mortality risk across a 12-year period (Mroczek & Spiro, 2007). In general, individuals decline in neuroticism over the lifespan. However, those individuals who bucked the normative trend by increasing in neuroticism were at a greater premature mortality risk than those who showed the normative pattern of development. A number of other studies have replicated this same basic pattern of results, that changes in personality are associated with health status (e.g., Magee, Heaven, & Miller, 2013; Stephan, Sutin, & Terraciano, 2015; Turiano, Pitzer et al., 2012). Turiano, Pitzer et al. (2012) found over a 10-year period that increases in conscientiousness and extraversion were associated with better self-reported health. Similarly, Magee et al. (2013) found that increases in conscientiousness, extraversion, and decreases in neuroticism were associated with better health 4 years later, even after controlling for initial levels of health.

However, there are some contradictory findings among these studies. Turiano, Pitzer et al. (2012) did not replicate the finding that changes in neuroticism were related to health over and above initial levels. Furthermore, the same study found that increases in agreeableness were associated with worse health (which is typically opposite the general finding that higher levels of agreeableness are associated with positive health outcomes). Similarly, Magee et al. (2013) found differences across cohorts such that changes in neuroticism were positively associated with health for younger cohorts, but negatively associated with health for older cohorts. These divergent findings highlight two important considerations.

First, the assessment of personality trait change depends on many specifics: number of assessments, time between assessments, total length of time, longitudinal quantitative models, and measurement instrument, all of which can influence estimates in change (Jackson & Allemand, 2014). A possible byproduct is that change in one trait could reflect changes in another, or that the underlying mechanisms driving change in one trait are shared for other traits (Allemand, Zimprich, & Martin, 2008). For example, Human et al. (2013) found only limited evidence that changes in neuroticism and conscientiousness were related to various health markers. However, the same study identified that change collapsed across all of the traits (i.e., change regardless of which trait it came from) was indeed associated with health, suggesting that indicators of single trait change may not be reliable in and of themselves, or that mechanisms of change are shared across multiple traits.

Second, processes responsible for associations between personality development and health are likely different across samples. One of the most important sample characteristics may be age, given that health concerns are more prevalent in older adulthood. Drawing from Baltes's selection—organization—compensation model (Baltes, 1997), older adults differ from younger adults due to an increased focus on health and health behaviors, with the goal to mitigate further declines in health. These adaptation processes could result in personality change through physical limitations such as limiting the affordances to act extraverted, or constraining the number of places one may demonstrate behaviors associated with conscientiousness. Similarly, greater health concerns may also increase levels of worry and health-related anxiety, ultimately increasing neuroticism as well.

Only a few studies have examined personality development in individuals aged 80 and older. One study examined how declines in sensory functioning in a sample of 80-year-olds influenced changes in personality, with the hypothesis that a decreased capacity to interact in and enjoy social interactions would lead to decreases in such interactions (i.e., declines in extraversion) and greater stress from these situations (i.e., increases in neuroticism). Overall, self-rated health, number of diseases, and impaired vision were not associated with changes in neuroticism or extraversion (Berg & Johansson, 2014). However, having troubles with hearing was associated with declines in extraversion across the 6-year study period. Another study of older adults tracked changes in personality up to a 13-year period in the Berlin Aging Study, consisting of people aged 70–103 (Wagner, Ram, Smith, & Gerstrof, 2015). Declines in extraversion and openness were associated with greater health problems, but health problems were not associated with changes in neuroticism. In contrast, using the Lothian Birth Cohort of 1921, Mõttus, Johnson, Starr, and Deary (2012) found that increases in conscientiousness from age 81 to 87 were associated with greater physical fitness during this time span. No other associations were found between health and any other Big Five trait.

# Joint development of personality and health

Both personality traits and health are dynamic processes that change across the lifespan. However, many of the above-reviewed studies do not assess health more than once, or only control for initial levels of health rather than examine longitudinal changes in health. As a result, it remains unclear whether personality change drives health change (e.g., changes in personality lead to changes in health behaviors which could then affect health outcomes) or changes in health drive personality change (e.g., people who develop a disease are limited by their actions or change how they see themselves).

A number of studies have started to examine the joint development between changes in personality traits and changes in health in the hope of teasing apart this complex relationship. Using a large sample of middle-aged adults, Letzring, Edmonds, and Hampson (2014) found that changes in all traits but extraversion (increases in agreeableness, conscientiousness, emotional stability, and openness) were associated with increases in self-rated health across a 2- to 4-year period. Similarly, in a study of young adults across 15 years (Mund & Neyer, 2015), while initial levels of health were not associated with future changes in personality, there were a number of correlated changes between personality and health. Specifically, normative increases in extraversion, conscientiousness, and emotional stability were associated with increases in subjective health. Patterns such as these extend beyond Big Five traits and onto other health-related characteristics like optimism. In a 10-year study of former law students, those who increased in optimism also tended to decrease in chronic health problems (Segerstrom, 2007). These findings were recently replicated in a large-scale study of almost 10,000 people across 4 years, where increases in optimism were associated with increases in self-rated health and fewer chronic illnesses (Chopik, Kim, & Smith, 2015).

As with many of the reported associations described throughout this review, correlated change findings between personality and health do not always replicate. For example, in a large sample of older adults, changes in personality across a 6-year timeline were not associated with changes in self-reported health (Small, Hertzog, Hultsch, & Dixon, 2003). As with all longitudinal studies, advanced questions about the dynamics between these two broad constructs require a greater number of assessments to better tease apart directionality.

# Mechanisms relating personality development and health status

If personality development is responsible for changes in health, then personality traits likely influence these changes through at least four overlapping mediating pathways: biological, cognitive, social, and behavioral. Biologically, neuroticism and agreeableness predict the experience of anxiety, fear, depression, and anger/hostility, which in turn activate regulatory systems (Mayne, 1999). Periodic and acute activation of regulatory systems, such as the sympathetic-adrenal medulla and pituitary-adrenal cortex systems, is largely beneficial, including long-term improvements to the immune system. However, chronic activation of these systems is damaging to health, including wear on the cardiovascular and immune systems. Personality is also known to predict cardiovascular reactivity to stress, which can lead to long-term damage to the cardiovascular system (Habra, Linden, Anderson, & Weinberg, 2003). As a cognitive effect on health, personality traits, especially neuroticism, influence the perception of health-related events (Weston & Jackson, 2016), which could influence perceived stress (Mroczek & Almeida, 2004). Increases in perceived stress lead to increased negative emotionality, including increased anxiety, which again, impacts biological functioning through activation of regulatory systems. Luckily, personality can also impact health through social channels. For example, greater perceived social support allows individuals to better cope with stress (Cohen & Wills, 1985), especially stressful health events (Helgeson & Cohen, 1996), ultimately influencing health outcomes (Hill, Weston, & Jackson, 2014). Perceived social support is greater among individuals who are high in extraversion, agreeableness, conscientiousness, and emotional stability (Asendorpf & Van Aken, 2003; Hill, Turiano, Mroczek, & Roberts, 2012).

Finally, the behavioral pathway is perhaps the route through which personality traits exert the most influence, as behaviors are estimated to account for as much as 40% of the relationship between traits and health outcomes (Mroczek, Spiro, & Turiano, 2009). Personality traits influence health-related behaviors, such as smoking and exercise (Bogg & Roberts, 2004; Weston & Jackson, 2015). In turn, these health behaviors have a direct impact on an individual's health (Hampson & Friedman, 2008; Hampson, 2012). Moreover, these behaviors can be the result of health-related news. Individuals high in extraversion and agreeableness report that they are more likely to seek social support in the face of bad health news, whereas individuals high in conscientiousness are more likely to figure out their options (Weston & Jackson, 2016).

Few studies have tested whether these mediational pathways are altered in the presence of personality development. Biological and cognitive focused studies of health typically examine more short-term processes whereas social and behavioral processes are beginning to be tested. In terms of behavior, changes in conscientiousness across a 10-year time span are associated with future levels of drug use above and beyond initial levels (Turiano, Whiteman et al., 2012). Similarly, increases in neuroticism and openness predicted future levels of alcohol and drug use.

Evidence for social pathways exists too. These findings indicate that declines in personality traits associated with social interactions may result in fewer social interactions, weaker social bonds, and even increased likelihood of encountering social stressors. For example, increases in hostility over a decade are associated with increases in social isolation and declines in social support (Siegler et al., 2003). Similarly, changes in each of the Big Five toward the direction of maturity are associated with increases in social well-being (Hill et al., 2012) and declines in loneliness (Mund & Neyer, 2015).

It is likely that many of these pathways depend on age, though some initial evidence suggests similar effects across the lifespan. While it is more difficult to examine health in younger cohorts given their overall better health status, health behaviors play an important role early on, and contribute toward the cumulative impact that personality has on health. Children who increased in hostility from first to eighth grade were more likely to smoke, drink, and experiment with marijuana than those who did not change or who decreased in hostility (Hampson, Tildesley, Andrews, Luyckx, & Mroczek, 2010). In older adults, changes in personality traits toward the direction of maturity are related to increases in social support from one's spouse, friends, and children (Hill, Weston, & Jackson, in press).

Ultimately, research is needed to tie all three components of this process together (i.e., personality, mediating process, and health outcome). One study took an initial attempt, focusing on the trait of conscientiousness (Takahashi, Edmonds, Jackson, & Roberts, 2013). Using a lifespan sample of community adults, they tested whether the proposed pathway of changes in conscientiousness leads to changes in health behaviors, which, in turn, leads to changes in health. To do so, the authors examined the joint development of conscientiousness, preventative health behaviors such as levels of exercise and perceived physical health. Across a 3-year period, increases in conscientiousness were associated with increases in perceived health. Importantly, these changes were mediated by health behaviors, suggesting that one of the mechanisms by which changes in personality result in better health is through corresponding changes in health behaviors (Takahashi et al., 2013). It should be noted, however, that the changes in each of the three components of the proposed model occurred simultaneously, thus opening up the possibility that exogenous changes in health lead to changes in personality.

One way to strengthen tests of this proposed mediational pathway is to intervene on health behaviors and observe corresponding changes in health and personality. In one of the few studies that have directly attempted to alter health behaviors closely related to personality traits, Friedman et al. (1986) intervened on a large group of postmyocardial infraction patients. The patients were randomly assigned to either cardiac counseling or Type-A behavior modification. Over an almost 5-year period, individuals who were trained to reduce Type-A behaviors (through CBT-related behavior modification paired with relaxation techniques across 40 sessions to reduce Type-A behaviors related to impatience, stress, and hostility) were less likely to have another heart issue and had lower premature mortality risk (Friedman et al., 1986).

Other studies provide further evidence that changes in health behaviors may influence changes in personality traits. One of the best examples comes from a study of participants going through Alcoholics Anonymous (AA) over a 16-year period (Blonigen, Timko, & Moos, 2013). As a result of being in AA, individuals tended to decline in impulsivity, implying that being in AA may not only reduce drinking behaviors, but may change personality, as well. Broad interventions on personality are only beginning to be discussed as ways to change (e.g., Magidson et al., 2014), but the possibility of intervening on mediational processes that influence both personality and health is a promising line of inquiry.

# Future directions for the study of personality development and health

Many unresolved questions remain in the study of personality development and health, most importantly whether or not there is a meaningful association between the two. Despite the numerous studies that find various types of associations, it is still unclear under which conditions, for which traits, diseases, age groups, time-spans, and according to which other factors, this relationship unfolds. Consistent across all designs was an inability to replicate many of the findings; though, this is expected in a relatively new field like personality development and health.

Assuming that a relationship exists, the next important question to address is *how* personality development and health are related. There are at least three nonredundant and overlapping possibilities. First, personality development causally influences health via corresponding changes in biology, cognition, social factors. and/or health behaviors. The best evidence for this comes from studies where changes in health behaviors mediate the relationship between changes in personality and health (e.g., Takahashi et al., 2013), though changes in personality traits did not always relate to corresponding future levels of health behaviors (e.g., Turiano, Whiteman et al., 2012). Here, the primary drivers of personality development are outside the domain of health.

Second, changes in health may limit one's behavior or social surroundings, leading to changes in personality. Conceptually, this is the opposite of the above explanation; here changes in health lead to changes in personality. Examples of this kind of change are best demonstrated by the onset of neurodegenerative disease. However, the onset of other illnesses or diseases was not associated with widespread changes in personality. Many of the associations did not replicate across studies or across diseases (other than having a stroke; Jackson et al., 2016; Jokela et al., 2014). New illness or diseases, especially if manageable, may be short lived; the common cold, chronic allergies, or sleep deprivation could make people moody and disagreeable. But, to what extent do people adapt to health conditions and incorporate these limitations into their self-concept?

A third possibility is that the development of personality and changes in health are influenced by similar processes. This may occur because evidence for joint development (i.e. correlated changes) can simply reflect initial correlations persisting across time. Or, instead, other variables may be capable of influencing both personality traits and health status. The most obvious candidates are social environmental variables such as social support. For example, older adults who perceive stronger social support are more likely to increase in conscientiousness over time (Hill, Payne, Jackson, Stine-Morrow, & Roberts, 2014), but social support itself is not entirely dependent on personality traits and independently influences health status (Hill et al. 2014).

## Conclusion

In sum, the newly emerging field of personality development and health offers a way to inform the association between personality and health. Because the health implications for interventions on personality are potentially profound (e.g., Magidson et al., 2014), the field needs to continue to address some of the difficult questions about the direction of association between personality and health.

# References

Allemand, M., Zimprich, D., & Martin, M. (2008). Long-term correlated change in personality traits in old age. *Psychology and Aging*, *23*(3), 545−557.

Asendorpf, J. B., & Van Aken, M. A. G. (2003). Personality-relationship transaction in adolescence: Core versus surface personality characteristics. *Journal of Personality*, *71*(4), 629−666.

Balsis, S., Carpenter, B. D., & Storandt, M. (2005). Personality change precedes clinical diagnosis of dementia of the Alzheimer type. *The Journals of Gerontology Series B: Psychological Sciences and Social Sciences*, *60*(2), P98−P101.

Baltes, P. B. (1997). On the incomplete architecture of human ontogeny: Selection, optimization, and compensation as foundation of developmental theory. *American Psychologist*, *52*(4), 366−380.

Berg, A. I., & Johansson, B. (2014). Personality change in the oldest-old: Is it a matter of compromised health and functioning? *Journal of Personality*, *82*(1), 25−31.

Blonigen, D. M., Timko, C., & Moos, R. H. (2013). Alcoholics anonymous and reduced impulsivity: A novel mechanism of change. *Substance Abuse*, *34*(1), 4−12.

Bogg, T., & Roberts, B. W. (2004). Conscientiousness and health-related behaviors: A meta-analysis of the leading behavioral contributors to mortality. *Psychological Bulletin*, *130* (6), 887−919.

Chopik, W. J., Kim, E. S., & Smith, J. (2015). Changes in optimism are associated with changes in health over time among older adults. *Social Psychological and Personality Science*, *6*(7), 814−822.

Cohen, S., & Wills, T. A. (1985). Stress, social support, and the buffering hypothesis. *Psychological Bulletin*, *98*(2), 310−357.

Diener, E., Suh, E. M., Lucas, R. E., & Smith, H. L. (1999). Subjective well-being: Three decades of progress. *Psychological Bulletin*, *125*, 276−302.

Dusseldorp, E., Van Elderen, T., Maes, S., Meulman, J., & Kraaij, V. (1999). A meta-analysis of psychoeducational programs for coronary heart disease patients. *Health Psychology*, *18*(5), 506−519.

Friedman, M., Thoresen, C. E., Gill, J. J., Ulmer, D., Powell, L. H., Price, V. A., . . . Bourg, E. (1986). Alteration of type A behavior and its effect on cardiac recurrences in post myocardial infarction patients: Summary results of the recurrent coronary prevention project. *American Heart Journal*, *112*(4), 653−665.

Glanz, K., & Bishop, D. B. (2010). The role of behavioral science theory in development and implementation of public health interventions. *Annual Review of Public Health*, *31*, 399−418.

Habra, M. E., Linden, W., Anderson, J. C., & Weinberg, J. (2003). Type D personality is related to cardiovascular and neuroendocrine reactivity to acute stress. *Journal of Psychosomatic Research*, *55*(3), 235−245.

Hampson, S. E. (2012). Personality processes: Mechanisms by which personality traits "get outside the skin". *Annual review of psychology*, *63*, 315.

Hampson, S. E., & Friedman, H. S. (2008). Personality and health: A lifespan perspective. In O. P. John, R. Robins, & L. Pervin (Eds.), *The handbook of personality: Theory and research* (3rd ed., pp. 770−794). New York, NY: Guilford Press.

Hampson, S. E., Goldberg, L. R., Vogt, T. M., & Dubanoski, J. P. (2006). Forty years on: Teachers' assessments of children's personality traits predict self-reported health behaviors and outcomes at midlife. *Health Psychology*, *25*(1), 57−64.

Hampson, S. E., Goldberg, L. R., Vogt, T. M., & Dubanoski, J. P. (2007). Mechanisms by which childhood personality traits influence adult health status: Educational attainment and healthy behaviors. *Health Psychology, 26*(1), 121−125.

Hampson, S. E., Tildesley, E., Andrews, J. A., Luyckx, K., & Mroczek, D. K. (2010). The relation of change in hostility and sociability during childhood to substance use in mid adolescence. *Journal of Research in Personality, 44*(1), 103−114.

Helgeson, V. S., & Cohen, S. (1996). Social support and adjustment to cancer: Reconciling descriptive, correlational, and intervention research. *Health Psychology, 15*(2), 135−148.

Hill, P. L., Payne, B. R., Jackson, J. J., Stine-Morrow, E. A. L., & Roberts, B. W. (2014). Perceived social support predicts increased conscientiousness during older adulthood. *The Journals of Gerontology Series B: Psychological Sciences and Social Sciences, 69* (4), 543−547.

Hill, P. L., Turiano, N. A., Mroczek, D. K., & Roberts, B. W. (2012). Examining concurrent and longitudinal relations between personality traits and social well-being in adulthood. *Social Psychological and Personality Science, 3*(6), 698−705.

Hill, P. L., Weston, S., & Jackson, J. J. (2014). Connecting social environment variables to the onset of major specific health outcomes. *Psychology and Health, 29*(7), 753−767.

Hill, P.L., Weston, S., & Jackson, J.J. (in press). The joint development of social support and personality in older adulthood. International Journal of Behavioral Development.

Human, L. J., Biesanz, J. C., Miller, G. E., Chen, E., Lachman, M. E., & Seeman, T. E. (2013). Is change bad? Personality change is associated with poorer psychological health and greater metabolic syndrome in midlife. *Journal of Personality, 81*(3), 249−260.

Jackson, J. J., & Allemand, M. (2014). Moving personality development research forward: Applications using structural equation models. *European Journal of Personality, 28,* 300−310.

Jackson, J. J., Connolly, J. J., Garrison, S. M., Levine, M., & Connolly, S. L. (2015). Your friends know how long you will live: A 75-year study of peer-rated personality traits. *Psychological Science, 26,* 335−340.

Jackson, J. J., & Roberts, B. W. (in press). Conscientiousness. In T.A. Widiger (Ed.), *The Oxford handbook of the Five Factor Model of personality.*

Jackson, J. J., Weston, S. J., Schultz, L. H., Hill, P. L., & Turiano, N. A. (2016). Personality development and illness onset: A longitudinal study using propensity score weighting. Unpublished manuscript.

Jokela, M., Batty, G. D., Nyberg, S. T., Virtanen, M., Nabi, H., Singh-Manoux, A., & Kivimäki, M. (2013). Personality and all-cause mortality: Individual-participant meta-analysis of 3,947 deaths in 76,150 adults. *American Journal of Epidemiology, 178*(5), 667−675.

Jokela, M., Hakulinen, C., Singh-Manoux, A., & Kivimäki, M. (2014). Personality change associated with chronic diseases: Pooled analysis of four prospective cohort studies. *Psychological Medicine, 44*(12), 2629−2640.

Letzring, T. D., Edmonds, G. W., & Hampson, S. E. (2014). Personality change at mid-life is associated with changes in self-rated health: Evidence from the Hawaii Personality and Health Cohort. *Personality and Individual Differences, 58,* 60−64.

Lucas, R. E. (2007). Long-term disability is associated with lasting changes in subjective well-being: Evidence from two nationally representative longitudinal studies. *Journal of Personality and Social Psychology, 92*(4), 717−730.

Lykou, E., Rankin, K. P., Chatziantoniou, L., Boulas, C., Papatriantafyllou, O., Tsaousis, I., ... Papatriantafyllou, J. D. (2013). Big 5 personality changes in Greek bvFTD, AD, and MCI patients. *Alzheimer Disease and Associated Disorders, 27*(3), 258−264.

Magee, C. A., Heaven, P. C. L., & Miller, L. M. (2013). Personality change predicts self-reported mental and physical health. *Journal of Personality*, *81*(3), 324−334.

Magidson, J. F., Roberts, B. W., Collado-Rodriguez, A., & Lejuez, C. W. (2014). Theory-driven intervention for changing personality: Expectancy value theory, behavioral activation, and conscientiousness. *Developmental Psychology*, *50*(5), 1442−1450.

Marcus, B. H., Bock, B. C., Pinto, B. M., Forsyth, L. A. H., Roberts, M. B., & Traficante, R. M. (1998). Efficacy of an individualized, motivationally-tailored physical activity intervention. *Annals of behavioral medicine*, *20*(3), 174−180.

Mayne, T. J. (1999). Negative affect and health: The importance of being earnest. *Cognition and Emotion*, *13*(5), 601−635.

Mendelsohn, G. A., Dakof, G. A., & Skaff, M. (1995). Personality change in Parkinson's patients: Chronic disease and aging. *Journal of Personality*, *63*(2), 233−257.

Moffitt, T. E., Arseneault, L., Belsky, D., Dickson, N., Hancox, R., Harrington, H., ... Caspi, A. (2011). A gradient of childhood self-control predicts health, wealth, and public safety. *PNAS*, *108*(7), 2693−2698.

Mõttus, R., Johnson, W., Starr, J. M., & Deary, I. J. (2012). Correlates of personality trait levels and their changes in very old age: The Lothian Birth Cohort 1921. *Journal of Research in Personality*, *46*(3), 271−278.

Mroczek, D. K., & Almeida, D. M. (2004). The effect of daily stress, personality, and age on daily negative affect. *Journal of Personality*, *72*(2), 355−378.

Mroczek, D. K., & Spiro, A. (2007). Personality change influences mortality in older men. *Psychological Science*, *18*(5), 371−376.

Mroczek, D. K., Spiro, A., & Turiano, N. A. (2009). Do health behaviors explain the effect of neuroticism on mortality? Longitudinal findings from the VA Normative Aging Study. *Journal of Research in Personality*, *43*(4), 653−659.

Mund, M., & Neyer, F. J. (2015). The winding paths of the lonesome cowboy: Evidence for mutual influences between personality, subjective health, and loneliness. *Journal of Personality*. Advance online publication.

Roberts, B. W., Kuncel, N. R., Shiner, R., Caspi, A., & Goldberg, L. R. (2007). The power of personality: The comparative validity of personality traits, socioeconomic status, and cognitive ability for predicting important life outcomes. *Perspectives on Psychological Science*, *2*(4), 313−345.

Roberts, B. W., Wood, D., & Caspi, A. (2008). The development of personality traits in adulthood. In O. P. John, R. W. Robins, & L. A. Pervin (Eds.), *Handbook of personality: Theory and research* (3rd ed., pp. 375−398). New York, NY: Guilford Press.

Robins Wahlin, T. B., & Byrne, G. J. (2011). Personality changes in Alzheimer's disease: A systematic review. *International Journal of Geriatric Psychiatry*, *26*(10), 1019−1029.

Segerstrom, S. C. (2007). Optimism and resources: Effects on each other and on health over 10 years. *Journal of Research in Personality*, *41*(4), 772−786.

Siegler, I. C., Costa, P. T., Brummett, B. H., Helms, M. J., Barefoot, J. C., Williams, R. B., ... Day, R. S. (2003). Patterns of change in hostility from college to midlife in the UNC Alumni Heart Study predict high-risk status. *Psychosomatic Medicine*, *65*(5), 738−745.

Small, B. J., Hertzog, C., Hultsch, D. F., & Dixon, R. A. (2003). Stability and change in adult personality over 6 years: Findings from the Victoria Longitudinal Study. *The Journals of Gerontology: Psychological Sciences*, *58B*(3), P166−P176.

Stephan, Y., Sutin, A. R., & Terracciano, A. (2015). Subjective age and personality development: A 10-year study. *Journal of Personality*, *83*(2), 142−154.

Sutin, A. R., Zonderman, A. B., Ferrucci, L., & Terracciano, A. (2013). Personality traits and chronic disease: Implications for adult personality development. *Journals of Gerontology, Series B: Psychological Sciences and Social Sciences*, *68*(6), 912−920.

Takahashi, Y., Edmonds, G. W., Jackson, J. J., & Roberts, B. W. (2013). Longitudinal correlated changes in conscientiousness, preventative health-related behaviors, and self-perceived physical health. *Journal of Personality*, *81*(4), 417−427.

Torrente, F., Pose, M., Gleichgerrcht, E., Torralva, T., López, P., Cetkovich-Bakmas, M., & Manes, F. (2014). Personality changes in dementia: Are they disease specific and universal? *Alzheimer Disease & Associated Disorders*, *28*(3), 261−268.

Turiano, N. A., Pitzer, L., Armour, C., Karlamangla, A., Ryff, C. D., & Mroczek, D. K. (2012). Personality trait level and change as predictors of health outcomes: Findings from a national study of Americans (MIDUS). *Journals of Gerontology, Series B: Psychological Sciences and Social Sciences*, *67*(1), 4−12.

Turiano, N. A., Whiteman, S. D., Hampson, S. E., Roberts, B. W., & Mroczek, D. K. (2012). Personality and substance use in midlife: Conscientiousness as a moderator and the effects of trait change. *Journal of Research in Personality*, *46*(3), 295−305.

Wagner, J., Ram, N., Smith, J., & Gerstrof, D. (2015). Personality trait development at the end of life: Antecedents and correlates of mean-level trajectories. *Journal of Personality and Social Psychology*. Advance online publication.

Weston, S., Hill, P. L., & Jackson, J. J. (2015). Personality traits predict the onset of major disease. *Social Personality Psychological Science*, *6*(3), 309−317.

Weston, S., & Jackson, J. J. (2015). Identification of the Healthy Neurotic: Personality traits predict smoking after disease onset. *Journal of Research in Personality*, *54*, 61−69.

Weston, S. J., & Jackson, J. J. (2016). How do people respond to health news? The role of personality traits. *Psychology & Health*. Advance online publication.

Wilson, R. S., Schneider, J. A., Arnold, S. E., Bienias, J. L., & Bennett, D. A. (2007). Conscientiousness and the incidence of Alzheimer's disease and mild cognitive impairment. *Archives of General Psychiatry*, *64*, 1204−1212.

# Personality development and psychopathology

## 24

*Filip De Fruyt, Barbara De Clercq, Elien De Caluwé, and Lize Verbeke*
Ghent University, Ghent, Belgium

## Preamble

Reviewing the current state of knowledge on personality development and psychopathology is challenging, given that very complex relationships between two sets of constructs have to be considered. The two domains and how these develop in isolation have been the subject of intense debate and research yet, though the study of their interconnection and its development is additionally complicated because both fields also inherently overlap when investigating, for example, the disorders of personality. Another obstacle, observable across the life span, is that different types of psychopathology sometimes co-occur in individuals or are switched on and off across the individual's life course, creating additional challenges for nomothetic developmental research. The good news is that it is today relatively well documented how personality and psychopathology are themselves mainly structured across the life span, making it possible to guide prospective research on their mutual influences across development.

The complexities in this area of research have been recently discussed in a target paper by Durbin and Hicks (2014) published in the *European Journal of Personality*, followed by a series of commentaries, launching a call for more sophisticated designs and ways of analyzing data, to be in a better positon to answer the many questions at stake. This chapter will elaborate on some of these points and integrate these in a broader conceptual model for the study of personality and psychopathology and its developmental course. We will first summarize progress in the fields of taxonomic research on key components in such framework, i.e., personality traits, psychopathology, and environments. Subsequently, we will describe how this knowledge can be built into an integrative model to understand personality—psychopathology relationships from a developmental point of view. Finally, some pending questions in the domain that require our attention in future studies will be discussed.

## Taxonomic work

### Personality

At different occasions in this edited book, the Five-Factor Model (FFM; McCrae & Costa, 1997; Mõttus, in press) has been suggested as the model par excellence to structure the complexities of traits in both adults and elderly, and also in childhood and adolescence (De Fruyt, Van Leeuwen, Bagby, Rolland, & Rouillon, 2006; Tackett, Kushner, De Fruyt, & Mervielde, 2013). Besides consensus on structural issues, also normative development of FFM traits has been well documented in the past decade. Soto, John, Gosling, and Potter (2011), for example, studied self-ratings in an impressive sample of children, adolescents, and adults ($N = 1,267,218$), spanning the age range of 10−65, where all were administered the Big Five Inventory (BFI; John, Donahue, & Kentle, 1991) online. The normative age patterns described by Soto et al. (2011) generally paralleled results reported by McCrae and Terracciano (2005), using a different operationalization of the FFM (NEO-PI-R; Costa & McCrae, 1992) and relying on self- and peer-peer ratings obtained in 50 countries around the world. Sex differences on traits also turned out to be grossly cross-culturally universal, in both adolescence (De Bolle et al., 2015) and adulthood (Costa, Terracciano, & McCrae, 2001), with some sex differences found more pronounced in adolescence (De Bolle et al., 2015) and in Western countries (Costa et al., 2001). These patterns are described in detail elsewhere in this book (for adolescence: Hill & Edmonds, in press; for emerging adulthood: Bleidorn & Schwaba, in press; for adulthood and old age: Specht, in press). Today, traits are understood as constructs showing relative between-individual stability (Roberts & DelVecchio, 2000), demonstrating normative change patterns where many persons follow a similar pattern (McCrae et al., 1999). Traits further show substantial changes across the life course, with a substantial number of individuals following unique developmental trajectories (De Fruyt & Van Leeuwen, 2014; Specht et al., 2014).

The most recent edition of the Diagnostic and Statistical Manual of Mental Disorders (DSM-5; American Psychiatric Association, 2013) describes a new trait model as an alternative to describe personality disorders. This DSM-5 model proposes 25 specific traits (Krueger, Derringer, Markon, Watson, & Skodol, 2012; Krueger & Markon, 2014), grouped into the broader factors of Negative affectivity (vs Emotional Stability), Detachment (vs Extraversion), Antagonism (vs Agreeableness), Disinhibition (vs Conscientiousness), and Psychoticism (vs Lucidity). Its relationships with the FFM have been explored now in several studies (for a review, see Al-Dajani, Gralnick, & Bagby, 2016), suggesting that the first four factors substantially align with Neuroticism, Extraversion, Agreeableness, and Conscientiousness, respectively, though there is only moderate overlap between Psychoticism and Openness to experiences. The DSM-5 trait model also demonstrated to be generally applicable in adolescence (De Clercq et al., 2014). Given its inclusion in DSM-5, this model opens a new window of research to demonstrate how maladaptive traits are connected to psychopathology beyond personality disorders.

## Psychopathology

Although there are very different ways to structure the field of psychopathology, there is growing consensus that the empirical structure of psychopathology can be roughly classified along an internalizing spectrum and an externalizing spectrum

(Carragher, Krueger, Eaton, & Slade, 2015). Alternative classifications rely on various criteria, including developmental stages (e.g., disorders occurring in childhood/adolescence vs (late) adulthood), different diagnostic classification systems [such as the DSM-editions or the International Classification of Diseases (ICD; WHO, 1994)], or represent specific content domains (e.g., disorders in emotion and impulse control). At the broadest level, however, the internalizing and externalizing dimensions turned out to be most useful to accommodate a broad range of disorders observable across development. Røysamb et al. (2011) factor-analytically examined the underlying structure of 25 disorders examined through clinical interviews in adult twins, showing that a four-factor model fitted the data well, distinguishing among clinical (DSM-IV axis-I) versus personality disorders (DSM-IV axis-II), but also grouping internalizing versus externalizing disorders. The genetic factors were moderately correlated across spectra, supporting the importance of the internalizing—externalizing distinction (Kendler, Myers, Maes, & Keyes, 2011). Both dimensions of psychopathology similarly received strong support in the childhood and adolescent literatures (Achenbach, 1991; Achenbach et al., 2008), also showing correlations between internalizing and externalizing at these developmental stages. Reviewing this domain, the internalizing and externalizing spectra seem to be the preferred starting point to learn about the association between personality and psychopathology and their developmental course (De Bolle, Beyers, De Clercq, & De Fruyt, 2012).

A broad range of common and age-specific symptoms of mental disorders can be observed across the life span, with a certain reluctance to use diagnostic labels in childhood and adolescence. Firstly, one tries to avoid describing children's and adolescents' behavior with diagnostic categories suggesting strong impairment or a poor prognosis. For example, personality disorders were only diagnosed from the age of 18 onward in DSM-IV, except for the antisocial personality disorder when there is also a clear history of conduct problems (Widiger, De Clercq, & De Fruyt, 2009). Secondly, childhood and adolescence are developmental time frames in which behaviors, cognitions, and emotions quickly develop, making it sometimes difficult to distinguish pathology signals/symptoms from normal maturational experimenting and developments. Eccentric behavior, for example, is a symptom of oddity or a potential signal of the schizophrenic spectrum, though it is not easily differentiated from normal eccentric behavior manifested in the context of identity formation during adolescence (Verbeke & De Clercq, 2014).

## Environment

The previous sections made clear that empirical psychology made significant progress the past decades to construct models for assessing variability in both personality and psychopathology at the level of the individual. However, human beings do not develop in a vacuum, and there is a dearth of research on how to characterize and describe the environments in which individuals develop. The variable "environment" is a broad container term referring to both more formal and physical attributes but also to various psychological features. For children and adolescents, the parents and direct family, the peer group, and the school setting (De Fruyt & De Clercq, 2014) are probably the three most important social networks affecting development and functioning, whereas the partner relationship and direct family, the individual's interpersonal network, and the job environment are the prime systems in which adults function and develop.

Beyond these more formal environments, defined in terms of significant others (parents, partner, family, friends) or institutions in which we spend considerable time (school or work), also how environments are perceived and experienced by the individual is crucially important for understanding the development and manifestations of psychopathology and its interaction with personality. Indeed, beyond the common physical and formal characteristics described earlier, environments are also "perceived and experienced" by the individual. For example, the family environment may be perceived very differently, even by individuals within the same family, as safe or threatening, challenging or relaxed/leisurely or achievement/reward oriented versus demotivating. In order to guarantee a comprehensive and systematic account and description of environments in longitudinal research, we need a guiding framework. The past decades witnessed several initiatives to build taxonomies of situations (for an overview, see Rauthmann et al., 2014), though none received substantial recognition and brought the necessary standardization to the field in order to cumulate research findings. Relying on extensive empirical work, Rauthmann, Sherman, Nave, and Funder (2015) recently proposed the DIAMONDS model, suggesting that everyday human situations can be broadly described by eight psychologically meaningful dimensions, i.e., Duty, Intellect, Adversity, Mating, pOsitivity, Negativity, Deception, and Sociality, summarized in the acronym DIAMONDS. This taxonomy is currently under further investigation, though holds a lot of promise to study the perceived value of environments, beyond their more formal characteristics described in the previous paragraph. The DIAMONDS taxonomy is both useful to study differences among individuals, and also for describing the more dynamic interaction between environmental features, traits, and symptoms notable within the person (Rauthmann & Sherman, 2016).

## Connecting personality, psychopathology, and environments

From the review above, it is clear that the FFM of general traits has formed the cornerstone of many studies examining how personality is related to psychopathology, distinguishing among very different conceptual models specifying how traits and psychopathology co-occur and mutually affect each other across development. First, traits may predispose an individual to develop specific forms of psychopathology, indicating a personality vulnerability to develop specific psychopathology (sometimes moderated by environmental conditions). Following a community adult cohort ($N = 591$) from 1979 to 2008, Hengartner, Ajdacic-Gross, Wyss, Angst, and Rössler (2016) convincingly demonstrated that Neuroticism formed an independent risk factor for the development of major depressive episodes and the use of corresponding professional treatments. Traits and psychopathology may also have independent causes, though the trait may affect the expression of the disorder, called a pathoplasty effect. The reverse mechanism is explained by the complication/scar model, where the mental disorder affects one or more personality traits more permanently, leaving a scar in the individual's personality. Finally, the continuity model claims that a trait and a disorder/syndrome exist on a continuum ranging from normal traits to psychopathology, whereas the spectrum model also assumes a common mechanism driving variability on this continuum. These complex patterns have been studied by De Bolle et al. (2012) and Tackett (2006) in childhood and adolescence and by Krueger (2005) in adults. Evidence for a continuum relationship between general personality traits and personality pathology in adulthood has been further provided by Samuel, Simms, Clark, Livesley, and Widiger (2010) showing that items of a general personality inventory and a personality disorder measure align on a single continuum considering specific personality disorders.

It is important to underscore that these different models are not mutually exclusive and may operate in conjunction to explain the complex trait—disorder relationships. Moreover, the relationship between personality and psychopathology may also differ across age groups and shift across development. For example, there is inconsistency among studies whether the experiencing of (multiple) major depressive episodes leaves a scar on the personality of the individual, e.g., in terms of heightened Neuroticism scores or increased pathology (Ormel, Oldehinkel, & Vollebergh, 2004: no evidence; Rohde, Lewinsohn, & Seeley, 1994: evidence for scar effects on internalizing behavior problems). Such inconsistent findings may suggest that potential long-term effects of having experienced depressive episodes may be dependent on the life stage in which individuals first manifested their symptoms. Overall, the prominence of the FFM dimensions to understand psychopathology has encouraged some (McCrae, Lockenhoff, & Costa, 2005) to promote general personality assessment as an integral part of standard clinical assessment practice, irrespective of the presence of clear (personality) pathology features.

Finally, also the environment has to be taken into account in the (developmental) study of the personality—pathology relationship. Mann et al. (2016), for example, recently demonstrated with a genetically informative design, that adolescents scoring higher on genetically determined sensation seeking ended up in more deviant peer groups (a gene—environment correlation), but were also more susceptible to deviant peers, indicative of a person—environment interaction. Consistent with the continuum/spectrum hypothesis, genetic influences on the sensation-seeking trait and on delinquency overlapped considerably.

## Work in progress: An integrative developmental framework

De Fruyt and De Clercq (2014) recently introduced a situation—trait interactionist model to describe personality pathology development that can be easily extended to represent personality—psychopathology relationships in general across the life span. To this extend, the model will be slightly expanded by explicitly adding some paths (to keep it readable, with some already explicitly discussed in the text of the original manuscript) and further elaborating on the environmental part to give this model an adult/life span explanatory scope. Expansions are the inclusion of reciprocal influences between traits/biology and the environment to accommodate recent findings on gene—environment correlations, genetically driven selection of environments, and environmental impact on biological factors. The distinguished environments for children and adolescents, i.e., "family," "social (peer network)," and "school" (De Fruyt & De Clercq, 2014), can be extended or replaced by "intimate relationship/family," "social (broader interpersonal network)," and the "work environment." Moreover, very recent work on situational taxonomies such as the DIAMONDS model (Brown, Jones, Serfass, & Sherman, 2016; Rauthmann et al., 2015) can be also helpful to describe the different environments from a more psychological and perceptual angle. Finally, we also describe which elements of the integrative model form the focus of different therapeutic intervention approaches, to illustrate that the proposed model is compatible with a range of different clinical frameworks and orientations.

In 2003, the industrial and organizational psychologists Robert Tett and Dawn Burnett (2003) introduced a personality trait-based interactionist model to explain performance at work. This baseline model was taken as a starting point by De Fruyt and De Clercq (2014) to depict an integrative model to understand the developmental roots of personality pathology. De Fruyt and De Clercq (2014) suggested, however, that this model could be easily turned into a framework to describe trait—psychopathology relationships in general, not only in childhood/adolescence but also across the life span. The key elements of this model, however, remain the same across development (though replace "parents/family" by "partner/family," "peer group" by "interpersonal network," and "school" by "work environment" for children/adolescents and adults, respectively) and also its mechanisms. Fig. 24.1 represents the baseline model provided by Tett and Burnett (2003), which is given a clinical twist by De Fruyt and De Clercq (2014) to understand emerging personality pathology, and that is now further molded to explain general trait—psychopathology associations and their development across the life course.

The core of Tett and Burnett's trait-activation model is built around three pillars. First, latent personality traits (Arrow 1) and environmental factors (Arrow 2) may have independent direct effects on behaviors, feelings, and cognitions, further also called characteristic manifestations. For example, the trait of sensation seeking (personality) and getting along with deviant peer groups (environment—social) are considered as independent risk factors of the characteristic manifestation of delinquent behaviors (Mann et al., 2016). Second, these manifestations may be appraised as either adaptive or dysfunctional, considering the person's developmental stages, his/her functioning as a partner/close relative, in relationships with peers/friends, and finally how s/he functions at work. The key point here for clinical/diagnostic decision making is that a behavioral manifestation is not dysfunctional in itself (except for extreme forms), though has to be evaluated against the individual's functioning in his/her environment, taking into account his developmental stage (Durbin & Hicks, 2014) and societal norms. This evaluation may result in behaviors, feelings,

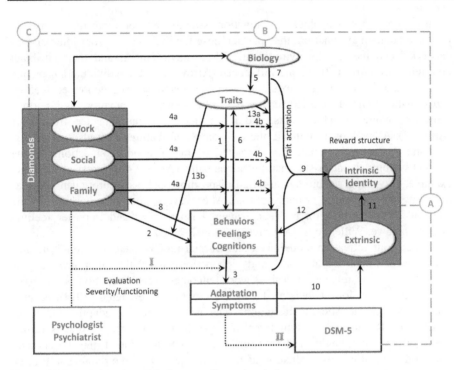

**Figure 24.1** Trait-based model of personality and pathology.

and cognitions, interpreted as symptoms or signals (Arrow 3) of specific disorders. Third and finally, formal/physical environmental factors, and also appraisals of environmental attributes (e.g., assessed by DIAMONDS), may trigger or activate latent personality tendencies expressed in characteristic manifestations (behaviors, feelings, and cognitions), thus acting as moderators of the trait-characteristic manifestations relationship (Arrows 4a).

It is well documented that traits have a genetic origin, and knowledge on their biological basis is steadily increasing (Arrow 5). They represent latent dispositions that have to be observed indirectly assessing people's behaviors, feelings, and cognitions, considered as characteristic manifestations of these underlying traits (Arrow 1). According to this path, traits partially mediate the individual's genetic/biological set up and the characteristic behaviors, emotions, and cognitions. De Fruyt and De Clercq (2014) also specified reciprocal effects (Arrow 6), so more enduring changes in characteristic manifestations are reflected in a changed position on a trait, enabling to model scar effects. Moreover, also a direct path from the biological level to characteristic manifestations is specified (Arrow 7), since there is no full mediation of biological influences on characteristic manifestations by traits. The biology may further affect the environment (not all influences on the environment are mediated via traits: biological-based cognitive impairment, for example, will directly affect school performance and study major options).

In the environmental block, a distinction is made between three main networks in which adults may function: the "partner/close family," the "broader interpersonal network," and the "work environment." These environments and their attributes both influence (Arrow 2) and are influenced (Arrow 8) by the individual's behavior, feelings, and cognitions. For example, a mother demonstrating depressed feelings and showing signs of vital exhaustion is not fully "present" anymore as a partner/caregiver, avoids social contacts, and is on sick leave disconnected from work (Arrow 8). As previously noticed, the environmental features may also act as triggers and moderate the latent trait-characteristic manifestation connection (Arrows 4a) and biology-characteristic manifestations paths (Arrows 4b). Stress at work, for example, may trigger a biological-based disposition such as Neuroticism and lead to feelings of inadequacy or burn-out (4a). Alternatively, good relationships at work may buffer the association between triggered neuroticism and imposter feelings (4a) (Vergauwe, Wille, Feys, De Fruyt, & Anseel, 2015).

In their trait-activation model, Tett and Burnett (2003) make an explicit distinction between "behavior at work" and "job performance," the latter involving an evaluative process relative to desired work outcomes. This distinction is preserved in the clinical version of their model by De Fruyt and De Clercq (2014), because someone's characteristic manifestations may be evaluated as adaptive/functional (dotted line I), but also as symptoms of a psychological disorder, that is further evaluated against a diagnostic framework such as DSM-5 (dotted line II). The current model specifies this evaluation as a distinct step. Once the diagnostic process is accomplished, one can start with defining goals or planning interventions (green line). In addition to the individual her/himself and the psychologist/psychiatrist (inquiring the environment and patient), all main actors involved in the outlined environments (partner, peers, colleagues, etc.) may be valuable informants of the nature of symptoms and the determination of dysfunction severity (indicated by the dotted line).

The trait-activation model also explicitly acknowledges reward structures, connecting this model also with learning theories. The core elements of the model, i.e., latent traits expressed in a set of behaviors, feelings, and cognitions, eventually moderated by the environment, form what Tett and Burnett (2003) called an intrinsic reward structure (Arrow 9). The assumption here is that when people can express their traits, this manifestation is experienced as intrinsically rewarding; when people lack such fulfillment, they get dissatisfied. Contingent rewards accumulate into a characteristic set of behaviors, feelings, and thoughts (depending on the clinical orientation, also called "schemas"), forming the individual's identity or reputation. This identity formation process is continuing across development (and may also change, for example, when an individual loses for example her/his professional identity due to unemployment). The evaluation of behavior, feeling, and cognition patterns, as either adaptive or dysfunctional, also results in extrinsic rewards (Arrow 10), and these may further affect the intrinsic rewards (Arrow 11). For example, behaviors classified as externalizing symptoms may give the individual both positive (e.g., reputation in a gang) and negative (e.g., rejection by loved-ones) extrinsic rewards. Finally, this entire set of reward mechanisms may impact upon change and continuity of behaviors, feelings, and cognitions (Arrow 12), finally forming a feedback loop. De Fruyt and De Clercq (2014) further described in their text direct paths from the environment to the reward structure to incorporate motivational mechanisms.

This trait-activation based model of personality and pathology incorporates all the previously distinguished models to assess the personality–psychopathology relationship (De Bolle et al., 2012), including the vulnerability and continuity models (Arrow 1), the complication or scar model (via the reciprocal path Arrow 6), and pathoplasty effects (Arrows 13a and 13b: traits moderating, respectively, Arrows 7 and 2). In addition, the green arrow depicted at the right side of the model helps to describe the focus of different therapeutic approaches. For example, more cognitive and behavior-oriented clinical approaches (A) will target their interventions at the level of behavior, feelings, and cognitions and the associated reward structures, described in the right part of the model. The clinical–medical approach (B) toward psychopathology will primarily work on the biological basis, trying to affect behaviors, feelings, and cognitions, via medication. Finally, system therapists (C) will chiefly zoom in on the different contexts and networks in which the individual is operating, exploring effects of network positions and relationship features on the patient's characteristic manifestations. Although the attention of the various intervention frameworks is dispersed around different areas in the model, the trait-activation based model functionally integrates key components and developmental mechanisms, tying all perspectives nicely together, showing eclectic roads for intervention.

# Some challenges

## Expending the dynamics agenda

More research on the longitudinal course and reciprocal relationships between personality and psychopathology will inevitably lead to a more dynamic conceptualization and operational use of the trait concept. So far, the field has primarily investigated the personality–psychopathology relationship from a between-person differences angle. Although this viewpoint has considerably advanced our understanding of clinical phenomena and is the dominant perspective used in the diagnostic process, this approach considers short-term within-person variability as irrelevant. Indeed, most personality measures just aggregate raw scores across different items of a scale in an attempt to measure more reliably its underlying core, but variability across items is denied and considered as error. Today, however, it is clear that in addition to between-individual variance, there is also substantial personality state fluctuation (Debusscher, Hofmans, & De Fruyt, 2014; Fleeson & Gallagher, 2009). This state variance can be assumed to affect and interact with pathology symptoms, and both can reciprocally affect each other (Wright, Hopwood, & Simms, 2015). Alternatively, such personality state fluctuations may also form constituting features of different forms of psychopathology, such as for example bipolar disorders or borderline personality pathology (Ebner-Priemer et al., 2015; Fleeson & Gallagher, 2009; Miskewicz et al., 2015). More systematic attention for within-person trait fluctuations in the life course should therefore complement our between-individual focus. The developmental course of within-person trait—psychopathology fluctuations should additionally be investigated. At present, we do not know, for example, whether personality state variability in- or decreases or remains stable across developmental periods.

The empirical study of within-person dynamics is, however, demanding, usually requiring some form of daily-diary or experience sampling design, where people provide ratings on personality states and/or potential situational variables (e.g., stress and threat) and further report on the frequency/severity of particular symptoms. An advantage of some of these designs is that they allow to examine order effects, e.g., personality states (e.g., in the morning) investigated prior to the assessment of symptoms (e.g., assessed in the afternoon), although such analyses are still no proof of causality. Examining within-person variation also provides important opportunities to assess flexibility versus rigidity in behavior/thoughts/cognitions, an important characteristic of several mental disorders and a predictor in itself of a patient's functioning.

There have been major advancements in the assessment of momentary variables (such as personality states or transitory symptoms and their severity) and ambulatory assessments of situational variables (Carpenter, Wycoff, & Trull, 2016; Trull & Ebner-Priemer, 2013), via the increased use of different mobile devices (cell phones, apps, etc.). A key challenge in this field is to optimally combine experience sampling designs with other forms of longitudinal follow-up, combining information from short-time dynamic assessments with more sequenced assessment points to better understand developmental personality—psychopathology trajectories. An interesting feature of experience sampling methodology is that researchers can also direct subsequent assessments relying on preceding ones, introducing adaptive experience sampling assessments to be in a position to adequately monitor the dynamics currently at stake. Such adaptive assessments could be scheduled, for instance, when preceding measurements identified specific triggers in the environment (e.g., particular stressors) and then assess during the subsequent assessment point specific emotional states. Additional research may also want to look at the bandwidth-fidelity dilemma in within-individual fluctuation, where for example specific facets of Neuroticism states may explain within-individual differences in symptoms/psychopathology states beyond the general domain of Neuroticism, either operationalized as a higher order factor or in a bifactor constellation. Debusscher and colleagues (in press), for example, demonstrated that the NEO-facets Self-discipline and Deliberation predicted within-person variance of task performance beyond the general domain of Conscientiousness. One can easily think of similar research with DSM-5 model traits, where one or more of the 25 listed maladaptive traits may show extra within-person predictive value, beyond its broader factor. Finally, the within-individual personality—psychopathology research paradigm provides an interesting angle to examine interpersonal dyads, such as the patient in his/her intimate relationship, or a parent—child dyad examining trait states and symptoms.

## Incorporating the environment and achieving intentional personality change

To advance our understanding of the trait—psychopathology relationship and its development, it is crucial to learn more about the developmental contexts, including the environments in which individuals operate and behave and the key situational attributes they perceive therein. A rudimentary notion of environments is already specified in the model that we described in this chapter. The DIAMONDS model is a first and promising approach to think about an operationalization of the characteristics of the environment, though there is no research so far demonstrating its utility to capture the key features of situations to advance our understanding of patients and the development of symptoms and disorders in particular. The DIAMONDS taxonomy could be used, for example, to examine the effect of situational triggers (e.g., the family situation as being perceived as threatening (Adversity in DIAMONDS) on the trait—psychopathology relationships).

Findings on the dynamics of personality have sometimes been suggested as proof that personality can be intentionally changed. Considering personality dynamics, our current knowledge suggests that beyond a stable part, there are normative (followed by a large group, either determined by biological and/or environmental factors) and also idiosyncratic changes that can be either intentional (e.g., an intended change from a low to a higher level on a trait, due to an intervention or specific action) or nonintentional (e.g., a trait affected by a life event). Although the discussion on intentional personality change is often detoured by a debate on the feasibility of personality change from an ethical point of view, one accepts that the final objective of many psychotherapies is to obtain changes in one or more characteristic (mal)adaptations. To the extent that these changes are permanent and given that a person's standing on a trait is derived from ratings on a set of characteristic adaptation indicators, it is not an absurd idea to assume personality changes. It is an empirical question, however, whether the impact of psychotherapies extends from psychopathology symptoms to personality traits. For example, De Fruyt et al. (2006) examined the impact of six different treatments (2 types of medication × 3 modes of psychotherapy) on depressive symptoms, demonstrating a significant reduction in symptoms, and also affected trait scores, in case decreased Neuroticism and increased Extraversion scores, as reported by the treating clinicians. Compared to a normative sample, however, patients continued to have higher average scores on Neuroticism, in line with the vulnerability hypothesis. It is difficult to judge, however, whether the prior-treatment ratings of personality were not affected by the depressive states of patients at the time of inclusion into the study. An additional challenge is further to go beyond self-reports (or therapist reports, again relying on patient's information) to better examine the effects of intentional personality change.

## Incorporating personality in clinical professional practice

Finally, De Fruyt and Van Leeuwen (2014) recently argued to better integrate personality assessment in clinical professional practice. A description of a patient's standing on the traits of a general personality descriptive model such as the FFM is not a standard part of clinical assessment. This is rather remarkable given the complex interplay between personality traits and psychopathology and the importance of personality to understand an individual's daily functioning. Moreover, personality self- and observer descriptions (partner or parent) can be easily obtained and efficiently scored and normed electronically, without taking psychologist's time. The present review has tried to propose an integrative framework, relying on trait-activation theory, with a focus on explaining the personality—psychopathology relationship. It was further highlighted where the position of psychological assessment and decision making is in this process, and how elements of this framework may form target areas of different types and schools of psychological interventions. We hope that this chapter may contribute to achieve a better integration of personality assessment in the diagnostic process.

# References

Achenbach, T. M. (1991). *Manual for the Child Behavior Checklist/4-18 and 1991 Profile.* Burlington, VT: University of Vermont Department of Psychiatry.

Achenbach, T. M., Becker, A., Dopfner, M., Heiervang, E., Roessner, V., Steinhausen, H. C., et al. (2008). Multicultural assessment of child and adolescent psychopathology with ASEBA and SDQ instruments: Research findings, applications, and future directions. *Journal of Child Psychology and Psychiatry, 49*(3), 251−275. Available from http://dx.doi.org/10.1111/j.1469-7610.2007.01867.x.

AI-Dajani, N., Gralnick, T. M., & Bagby, R. M. (2016). A psychometric review of the personality inventory for DSM-5 (PID-5): Current status and future directions. *Journal of Personality Assessment, 98*(1), 62−81. Available from http://dx.doi.org/10.1080/00223891.2015.1107572.

American Psychiatric Association (2013). *Diagnostic and statistical manual of mental disorders*—Fifth Edition. Arlington, VA.

Bleidorn, W. & Schwaba, T. (in press). Personality trait development in emerging adfulthood. In J. Specht (Ed.), *Personality development across the life-span.* London: Elsevier.

Brown, N. A., Jones, A. B., Serfass, D. G., & Sherman, R. A. Reinvigorating the concept of a situation in situational judgement tests. *Industrial and Organizational Psychology: Perspectives on Science and Practice* **9** (1), 2016, 38−42. Available from https://dx.doi.org/10.1017/iop.2015.113.

Carragher, N., Krueger, R. F., Eaton, N. R., & Slade, T. (2015). Disorders without borders: current and future directions in the meta-structure of mental disorders. *Social Psychiatry and Psychiatric Epidemiology, 50*(3), 339−350. Available from http://dx.doi.org/10.1007/s00127-014-1004-z.

Carpenter, R., Wycoff, A. M., & Trull, T. J. Ambulatory assessment: New adventures in characterizing dynamic processes. *Assessment* **23** (4), 2016, 414−424. Available from http://dx.doi.org/10.1177/1073191116632341.

Costa, P. T., & McCrae, R. R. (1992). *Revised NEO Personality Inventory and Five-Factor Inventory Professional Manual.* Odessa, FL: Psychological Assessment Resources.

Costa, P. T., Terracciano, A., & McCrae, R. R. (2001). Gender differences in personality traits across cultures: Robust and surprising findings. *Journal of Personality and Social Psychology, 81*(2), 322−331. Available from http://dx.doi.org/10.I037/I0022-3514.XI.2.322.

De Bolle, M., Beyers, W., De Clercq, B., & De Fruyt, F. (2012). General personality and psychopathology in referred and non-referred children and adolescents: An investigation of continuity, pathoplasty, and complication models. *Journal of Abnormal Psychology*, *121*(4), 958−970. Available from http://dx.doi.org/10.1037/a0027742.

De Bolle, M., De Fruyt, F., McCrae, R. R., Lockenhoff, C. E., Costa, P. T., Aguilar-Vafaie, M. E., et al. (2015). The emergence of sex differences in personality traits in early adolescence: A cross-sectional, cross-cultural study. *Journal of Personality and Social Psychology*, *108*(1), 171−185. Available from http://dx.doi.org/10.1037/a0038497.

De Clercq, B., De Fruyt, F., De Bolle, M., Van Hiel, A., Markon, K. E., & Krueger, R. F. (2014). The hierarchical structure and construct validity of the PID-5 trait measure in adolescence. *Journal of Personality*, *82*(2), 158−169. Available from http://dx.doi.org/10.1111/jopy.12042.

De Fruyt, F., Bartels, M., Van Leeuwen, K. G., De Clercq, B., Decuyper, M., & Mervielde, I. (2006). Five types of personality continuity in childhood and adolescence. *Journal of Personality and Social Psychology*, *91*(3), 538−552. Available from http://dx.doi.org/10.1037/0022-3514.91.3.538.

De Fruyt, F., & De Clercq, B. (2014). Antecedents of personality disorder in childhood and adolescence: Toward an Integrative Developmental Model. *Annual Review of Clinical Psychology*, *10*(10), 449−476. Available from http://dx.doi.org/10.1146/annurev-clinpsy-032813-153634.

De Fruyt, F., & Van Leeuwen, K. (2014). Advancements in the field of personality development. *Journal of Adolescence*, *37*(5), 763−769. Available from http://dx.doi.org/10.1016/j.adolescence.2014.04.009.

De Fruyt, F., Van Leeuwen, K., Bagby, R. M., Rolland, J. P., & Rouillon, F. (2006). Assessing and interpreting personality change and continuity in patients treated for major depression. *Psychological Assessment*, *18*(1), 71−80.

Debusscher, J., Hofmans, J., & De Fruyt, F. (2014). The curvilinear relationship between state neuroticism and momentary task performance (vol 9, e106989, 2014). *PLoS ONE*, *9*(11). Available from http://dx.doi.org/10.1371/journal.pone.0114538.

Debusscher, J., Hofmans, J., & De Fruyt, F. (in press). The multiple face(t)s of state conscientiousness: Predicting task performance and organizational citizenship behavior. *Journal of Research in Personality*. Available from http://dx.doi.org/10.1016/j.jrp.2016.06.009.

Durbin, C. E., & Hicks, B. M. (2014). Personality and psychopathology: A stagnant field in need of development. *European Journal of Personality*, *28*(4), 362−386. Available from http://dx.doi.org/10.1002/per.1962.

Ebner-Priemer, U. W., Houben, M., Santangelo, P., Kleindienst, N., Tuerlinckx, F., Oravecz, Z., et al. (2015). Unraveling affective dysregulation in borderline personality disorder: A theoretical model and empirical evidence. *Journal of Abnormal Psychology*, *124*(1), 186−198. Available from http://dx.doi.org/10.1037/abn0000021.

Fleeson, W., & Gallagher, P. (2009). The implications of Big Five standing for the distribution of trait manifestation in behavior: Fifteen experience-sampling studies and a meta-analysis. *Journal of Personality and Social Psychology*, *97*(6), 1097−1114. Available from http://dx.doi.org/10.1037/a0016786.

Hengartner, M. P., Ajdacic-Gross, V., Wyss, C., Angst, J., & Rössler, W. (2016). Relationship between personality and psychopathology in a longitudinal community study: A test of the predisposition model. *Psychological Medicine*, *46*(8), 1693−1705. Available from http://dx.doi.org/10.1017/S0033291716000210.

Hill, P. L., & Edmonds, G. W. (in press). Personality development in adolescence. In J. Specht (Ed.), *Personality development across the life-span*. London: Elsevier.

John, O. P., Donahue, E. M., & Kentle, R. L. (1991). *The "Big Five" Inventory—Versions 4a and 54*. Berkeley: University of California/Institute of Personality and Social Research.

Kendler, K. S., Myers, J. M., Maes, H. H., & Keyes, C. L. M. (2011). The relationship between the genetic and environmental influences on common internalizing psychiatric disorders and mental well-being. *Behavior Genetics, 41*(5), 641−650. Available from http://dx.doi.org/10.1007/s10519-011-9466-1.

Krueger, R. F. (2005). Continuity of axes I and II: Toward a unified model of personality, personality disorders, and clinical disorders. *Journal of Personality Disorders, 19*(3), 233−261.

Krueger, R. F., Derringer, J., Markon, K. E., Watson, D., & Skodol, A. E. (2012). Initial construction of a maladaptive personality trait model and inventory for DSM-5. *Psychological Medicine, 42*(9), 1879−1890. Available from http://dx.doi.org/10.1017/S0033291711002674.

Krueger, R. F., & Markon, K. E. (2014). The role of the DSM-5 personality trait model in moving toward a quantitative and empirically based approach to classifying personality and psychopathology. *Annual Review of Clinical Psychology, 10*, 477−501. Available from http://dx.doi.org/10.1146/annurev-clinpsy-032813-153732.

Mann, F. D., Patterson, M. W., Grotzinger, A. D., Kretsch, N., Tackett, J. L., Tucker-Drob, E. M., ... Harden, K. P. (2016). Sensation-seeking, peer deviance, and genetic influences on adolescent delinquency: Evidence of person−environment correlation and interaction. *Journal of Abnormal Psychology 125*(5), 679−691. Available from http://dx.doi.org/10.1037/abn0000160.

McCrae, R. R., & Costa, P. T. (1997). Personality trait structure as a human universal. *American Psychologist, 52*(5), 509−516. Available from http://dx.doi.org/10.1037/0003-066X.52.5.509.

McCrae, R. R., Costa, P. T., de Lima, M. P., Simoes, A., Ostendorf, F., Angleitner, A., et al. (1999). Age differences in personality across the adult life span: Parallels in five cultures. *Developmental Psychology, 35*(2), 466−477. Available from http://dx.doi.org/10.1037//0012-1649.35.2.466.

McCrae, R. R., Lockenhoff, C. E., & Costa, P. T. (2005). A step toward DSM-V: Cataloguing personality-related problems in living. *European Journal of Personality, 19* (4), 269−286. Available from http://dx.doi.org/10.1002/per.564.

McCrae, R. R., & Terracciano, A. (2005). Universal features of personality traits from the observer's perspective: Data from 50 cultures. *Journal of Personality and Social Psychology, 88*(3), 547−561.

Miskewicz, K., Fleeson, W., Arnold, E. M., Law, M. K., Mneimne, M., & Furr, R. M. (2015). A contingency-oriented approach to understanding borderline personality disorder: situational triggers and symptoms. *Journal of Personality Disorders, 29*(4), 486−502. Available from http://dx.doi.org/10.1521/pedi.2015.29.4.486.

Mõttus, R. (in press). Five-Factor Theory and personality development. In J. Specht (Ed.), *Personality development across the life-span*. London: Elsevier.

Ormel, J., Oldehinkel, A. J., & Vollebergh, W. (2004). Vulnerability before, during, and after a major depressive episode—A 3-wave population-based study. *Archives of General Psychiatry, 61*(10), 990−996. Available from http://dx.doi.org/10.1001/archpsyc.61.10.990.

Rauthmann, J. F., Gallardo-Pujol, D., Guillaume, E. M., Todd, E., Nave, C. S., Sherman, R. A., et al. (2014). The situational eight DIAMONDS: A taxonomy of major dimensions of situation characteristics. *Journal of Personality and Social Psychology, 107*(4), 677−718. Available from http://dx.doi.org/10.1037/a0037250.

Rauthmann, J. F., & Sherman, R. A. (2016). Situation change: Stability and change of situation variables between and within persons. *Frontiers in Psychology*, *6*, 1938. Available from http://dx.doi.org/10.3389/fpsyg.2015.01938.

Rauthmann, J. F., Sherman, R. A., Nave, C. S., & Funder, D. C. (2015). Personality-driven situation experience, contact, and construal: How people's personality traits predict characteristics of their situations in daily life. *Journal of Research in Personality*, *55*, 98—111. Available from http://dx.doi.org/10.1016/j.jrp.2015.02.003.

Roberts, B. W., & DelVecchio, W. F. (2000). The rank-order consistency of personality traits from childhood to old age: A quantitative review of longitudinal studies. *Psychological Bulletin*, *126*(1), 3—25. Available from http://dx.doi.org/10.1037//0033-2909.126.1.3.

Rohde, P., Lewinsohn, P. M., & Seeley, J. R. (1994). Are adolescents changed by an episode of major depression? *Journal of the American Academy of Child and Adolescent Psychiatry*, *33*, 289—1298.

Røysamb, E., Kendler, K. S., Tambs, K., Orstavik, R. E., Neale, M. C., Aggen, S. H., et al. (2011). The joint structure of DSM-IV Axis I and Axis II disorders. *Journal of Abnormal Psychology*, *120*(1), 198—209. Available from http://dx.doi.org/10.1037/a0021660.

Samuel, D. B., Simms, L. J., Clark, L. A., Livesley, W. J., & Widiger, T. A. (2010). An item response theory integration of normal and abnormal personality scales. *Personality Disorders—Theory Research and Treatment*, *1*(1), 5—21. Available from http://dx.doi.org/10.1037/a0018136.

Soto, C. J., John, O. P., Gosling, S. D., & Potter, J. (2011). Age differences in personality traits from 10 to 65: Big Five domains and facets in a large cross-sectional sample. *Journal of Personality and Social Psychology*, *100*(2), 330—348. Available from http://dx.doi.org/10.1037/a0021717.

Specht, J. (in press). Personality development in adulthood and old age. In J. Specht (Ed.), *Personality development across the life-span*. London: Elsevier.

Specht, J., Bleidorn, W., Denissen, J. J. A., Hennecke, M., Hutteman, R., Kandler, C., et al. (2014). What drives adult personality development? A comparison of theoretical perspectives and empirical evidence. *European Journal of Personality*, *28*(3), 216—230. Available from http://dx.doi.org/10.1002/per.1966.

Tackett, J. L. (2006). Evaluating models of the personality—psychopathology relationship in children and adolescents. *Clinical Psychology Review*, *26*(5), 584—599.

Tackett, J. L., Kushner, S. C., De Fruyt, F., & Mervielde, I. (2013). Delineating personality traits in childhood and adolescence: Associations across measures, temperament, and behavioral problems. *Assessment*, *20*(6), 738—751. Available from http://dx.doi.org/10.1177/1073191113509686.

Tett, R. P., & Burnett, D. D. (2003). A personality trait-based interactionist model of job performance. *Journal of Applied Psychology*, *88*(3), 500—517. Available from http://dx.doi.org/10.1037/0021-9010.88.3.500.

Trull, T. J., & Ebner-Priemer, U. (2013). Ambulatory assessment. In S. Nolen Hoeksema (Ed.), *Annual review of clinical psychology* (Vol. 9, pp. 151—176). Palo Alto: Annual Reviews.

Verbeke, L., & De Clercq, B. (2014). Integrating oddity traits in a dimensional model for personality pathology precursors. *Journal of Abnormal Psychology*, *123*(3), 598—612. Available from http://dx.doi.org/10.1037/a0037166.

Vergauwe, J., Wille, B., Feys, M., De Fruyt, F., & Anseel, F. (2015). Fear of being exposed: The trait-relatedness of the imposter phenomenon and its relevance in the work context. *Journal of Business and Psychology*, *30*(3), 565—581. Available from http://dx.doi.org/10.1007/s10869-014-9382-5.

Widiger, T. A., De Clercq, B., & De Fruyt, F. (2009). Childhood antecedents of personality disorder: An alternative perspective. *Development and Psychopathology*, *21*(3), 771−791. Available from http://dx.doi.org/10.1017/S095457940900042X.

World Health Organization (1994). International statistical classification of diseases and related health problems.

Wright, A. G. C., Hopwood, C. J., & Simms, L. J. (2015). Daily interpersonal and affective dynamics in personality disorder. *Journal of Personality Disorders*, *29*(4), 503−525. Available from http://dx.doi.org/10.1521/pedi.2015.29.4.503.

# Vocational interests as personality traits: Characteristics, development, and significance in educational and organizational environments

**25**

*Gundula Stoll and Ulrich Trautwein*
University of Tübingen, Tübingen, Germany

## Introduction

When people are first getting acquainted, they usually ask each other about their vocations. Although this is a common process, it is far more than exchanging small talk—it reveals various kinds of information about a person. On the basis of our everyday experiences, we have developed—sometimes inaccurate but nevertheless helpful—knowledge about what people in various occupations are like. And we use these vocational stereotypes to judge people, just as we judge them by their friends, clothing, and actions. Of course stereotypes should be regarded with suspicion, but they also contain valid information, for example, about likes and dislikes, abilities, knowledge, and social status.

There are several models that have attempted to categorize vocational interests and work environments, but the most prominent and frequently investigated theory is John Holland's (1997) *Theory of Vocational Personalities and Work Environments*. This theory offers a framework by which to describe people and environments and can therefore be used to consider associations between people and their work environments. Although the key assumptions of this theory have been investigated frequently, some crucial aspects have garnered only scant attention. Therefore, this chapter has two aims: first, we want to provide an overview of the key assumptions of the theory and summarize empirical findings from educational and organizational contexts. Second, we want to focus on two aspects of the theory that have yet to be intensively investigated: the development of interests across the life span and the relevance of vocational interests for individual life courses.

*Personality Development Across the Lifespan.* DOI: http://dx.doi.org/10.1016/B978-0-12-804674-6.00025-9

# The theory of vocational personalities and working environments

The theory of vocational interests (Holland, 1997) offers a framework by which to characterize people and working environments. Four key assumptions form the body of this theory. The first assumption is that most people can be categorized as one of six interest types[1]: Realistic, Investigative, Artistic, Social, Enterprising, and Conventional. Interest types are characterized by preferences for certain activities, certain skills and abilities, as well as certain attitudes and characteristics. People with the same interest type prefer similar tasks and activities, show abilities in the same areas, and tend to have similar values and life goals.

According to the second assumption, there are six corresponding models of environments: Realistic, Investigative, Artistic, Social, Enterprising, and Conventional. These environmental models are characterized by the demands and opportunities that are dominant in an occupation as well as by the people who typically work in this environment. These demands and opportunities create an atmosphere that influences the behaviors and experiences of the people who work in this occupation. People with the same occupation tend to show similar interests, abilities, characteristics, attitudes, goals, and values. Through demands and opportunities, the environment stimulates people to perform certain tasks, it fosters specific abilities and skills, and—by providing a framework of shared goals and values—it reinforces people's tendencies to display specific values (Holland, 1997).

The third assumption is that individuals search for environments that will let them exercise their skills and abilities, express their attitudes and values, and take on roles that they feel comfortable with. This implies that people strive to choose environments that fit their interests.

Finally, the fourth assumption is that behavior is determined by an interaction between vocational personality and environment. This implies that several outcomes, such as choice of vocation, job changes, vocational or educational achievement, and social behavior, can be predicted by a person's interest type and the model of the environment (Holland, 1997).

## The relatedness of the six interest types

The relations between the six interests can be displayed in a hexagonal model (see Fig. 25.1). In this hexagon, each angle represents one of the six types, and the distance between two angles represents the similarity between the respective interest

---

[1] RIASEC interests are often referred to as "types," but this term is somewhat misleading, as interests are believed to be dimensional constructs rather than distinct categories. The widespread assumption is that each person has interests in all six RIASEC dimensions but to differing degrees—typically displayed in an interest profile. Nevertheless, in many studies, people are assigned to types. In these cases, the RIASEC dimension a person is most interested in defines this person's interest "type." In an alternative approach, three-letter codes are used to indicate the three RIASEC dimensions a person is most interested in (Holland, 1994).

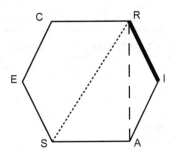

**Figure 25.1** The RIASEC hexagon, representing the postulated order of the R-I-A-S-E-C dimensions and the assumption of equal distances between the six interest dimensions. Line width represents similarity. The strongest relations are expected for adjacent interests (R-I), smaller relations are expected for nonadjacent interest (R-A), and the weakest relations are expected for opposite interests (R-S).

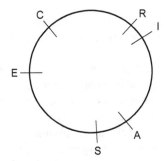

**Figure 25.2** The RIASEC circumplex, representing the postulated order of the R-I-A-S-E-C dimensions without the assumption of equal distances between the six interest dimensions; exemplified demonstration—not based on empirical data.

types (Holland, 1997). Interests with adjacent orientations are postulated to show the strongest relations, and interests with opposite orientations are postulated to show small or negative relations. Research on the structure of vocational interests has demonstrated empirical support for the postulated ordering of the six interest dimensions (R-I-A-S-E-C; Anderson, Tracey, & Rounds, 1997; Darcy & Tracey, 2007; Rounds & Day, 1999) but not for the strong assumption of equal distances between the six angles of the hexagon. A circumplex model (see Fig. 25.2) can therefore best represent the structure of vocational interests. The six interests are located at different points on a circular line, and the different distances between these points represent the different degrees of similarity between the interests. The structure of the RIASEC circumplex has been replicated in numerous samples across gender, ethnicity, and culture. Nevertheless, this does not imply that alternative models (e.g., models with more than six dimensions) would not be able to describe the structure of interests even better. An alternative way to organize the six interest orientations was proposed by Prediger (1982). He showed that the six

**Table 25.1 Characteristics of vocational personalities and working environments**

| | Personality type prefers ... | Environment entails/reinforces ... |
|---|---|---|
| Realistic | ... explicit or systematic manipulation of objects, tools, machines, and animals | |
| Investigative | ... observational, symbolic, systematic, and creative investigation of physical, biological, and cultural phenomena | |
| Artistic | ... manipulation of physical, verbal, or human materials to create art forms or products | |
| Social | ... manipulation of others to inform, train, develop, cure, or enlighten | |
| Enterprising | ... manipulation of others to attain organizational goals or economic gain | |
| Conventional | ... explicit, ordered, systematic manipulation of data | |

*Note*: Summarized from Holland (1997).

interest types could be presented in a two-dimensional space with two orthogonal axes—data versus ideas and people versus things (Prediger, 1982; Rounds & Tracey, 1993).

Table 25.1 summarizes the typical characteristics of the six interest types and environmental models. For example, people with Realistic interests prefer "activities that entail the explicit, ordered, or systematic manipulation of objects, tools, machines, and animals" and show an "aversion to educational or therapeutic activities" (Holland, 1997, p. 21). Realistic environments in turn entail the explicit, ordered, or systematic manipulation of objects, tools, or machines and reinforce the display of realistic attitudes and values (Holland, 1997, p. 43).

By contrast, people with Social interests prefer activities that "entail the manipulation of others to inform, train, develop, cure, or enlighten" (Holland, 1997, p. 25). They value social activities, want to serve others, and are said to have idealistic, altruistic, and somewhat traditional values (Holland, 1997, p. 25). Social environments in turn stimulate people to engage in social activities, foster social competencies, and reward the display of social values and attitudes (Holland, 1997, p. 46).

Vocational interests are usually assessed with interest questionnaires on which people indicate the extent to which they consider different activities to be interesting. Environmental models can be assessed either by aggregating individual interest profiles within a particular environment or with questionnaires on which experts indicate how relevant different activities are in a specific environment.

## The secondary constructs

Holland postulated secondary constructs that moderate the predictions and explanations suggested by his theory: *Consistency, Differentiation, and Congruence*. These secondary constructs help to describe interest profiles and can be applied to both individual interests and environmental models. *Consistency* reflects the extent to which interest types are related within a person or an environment. Individual interest profiles can be more or less consistent. According to the calculus assumption, some pairs of interest domains are more closely related than others. High consistency means that a person's highest interests—or the most important interests in an environment—are closely related (oriented adjacently; e.g., R and I). Research has suggested that people are more likely to have consistent interest profiles than inconsistent profiles. *Differentiation* reflects how clearly a person or environment is defined. Profiles with clear peaks are more differentiated than flat profiles. *Congruence* reflects the fit between an individual's interest profile and the interests reflected by a specific environment. Holland postulated that different interest types require different environments and that people strive for congruence because high congruence is associated with greater stability in career decisions as well as better performance and higher satisfaction in the work environment (Holland, 1997).

# Vocational interests and career choices

## Selection processes and career decisions

Holland (1997) postulated that people actively select environments on the basis of their vocational interests and aim to select congruent environments. But he also postulated that environments tend to attract certain kinds of people who have specific interests. This means that selection processes in the context of vocational interests could be due to people actively selecting an environment, people being selected into an environment by the environment's specific demands and requirements, or a combination of both. Due to these selection processes, vocational interests are expected to predict career decisions. Studies that have focused on selection processes have provided support for Holland's assumption. In an early meta-analysis of six independent studies on the relations between interests and career choices, the overall association between interests and intended choices (e.g., aspirations and expressed choices) was $r = 0.60$ (Lent, Brown, & Hackett, 1994). Since then, several studies investigating the associations between vocational interests and college major choice provided further support for the expected association (Bergmann, 1994; Humphreys & Yao, 2002; Webb, Lubinski, & Benbow, 2002). In a longitudinal study that tracked high school students for 3.5 years, their vocational interests were associated with their career aspirations and the major subject of study that they chose later in college (Bergmann, 1994). In another longitudinal study of high school students, vocational interests—especially social interests—emerged as the most important predictor of whether or not the student would enroll in a teacher education program (Roloff Henoch, Klusmann, Lüdtke, & Trautwein, 2015). Further, in a sample of mathematically precocious 13-year-olds, interests predicted—along with educational experiences and abilities—whether they later attained undergraduate degrees in math-science or non-math—non-science areas (Webb et al., 2002). Vocational interests were also demonstrated to have a higher unique relation to college major choice than several ability measures did (Päßler & Hell, 2012).

With regard to occupational choices, Barak and Meir (1974) showed in a 7-year follow-up study that students' interests in school were highest for the occupational field they entered 7 years later. Congruence analyses in a sample of college alumni revealed a significant fit between interest and occupation at the beginning of their professional career as well as 15 years later (Wille, Tracey, Feys, & De Fruyt, 2014).

Besides the associations between vocational interests and career choices, interest-based selection processes were also found to occur during secondary school. Volodina, Nagy, and Retelsdorf (2015) investigated the role of vocational interests in the transition from lower secondary school to thematic profiles of upper secondary schooling. They showed that the choice of thematic school profiles in Grade 11 was associated with individual interest profile parameters assessed in Grade 9. In addition, they found that the parameters of individual interest profiles independently contributed to the profile choices—even when school grades and gender were controlled for (Volodina et al., 2015).

Although less investigated, vocational interests also show associations with the level of educational achievement and the level of occupational prestige (Tracey & Rounds, 1996). Investigative and Artistic interests, in particular, have been suggested to be associated with higher educational achievement (Holland, 1997), and it seems likely that these associations will manifest themselves in educational decisions (e.g., the choice of different school tracks). There is some empirical evidence for differences in interest between students from different school tracks. For example, in a Swiss sample, secondary students from a school type with advanced academic requirements scored significantly higher on Investigative and Artistic interests than students from a school type with basic academic requirements (Hirschi & Läge, 2007). As these differences could be due to either selection processes or differential socialization effects, longitudinal studies are needed to investigate the role of vocational interests in educational transitions. Von Maurice and Bäumer (2015) investigated vocational interests in primary school children before and after the transition to secondary school. They found that children who later went to the highest secondary school track already showed significantly more Investigative interest in primary school than children who later went to the lowest secondary school track (von Maurice & Bäumer, 2015).

Additional support comes from a longitudinal study that investigated selection and socialization processes in the transition from high school to different types of universities (Kramer et al., 2012). Using propensity score matching, this study revealed that differences between students from three different university types (university, university of applied sciences, and university of cooperative education) were primarily due to selection effects. High school students who chose different types of universities had already differed in their Investigative interests before the transition to university (Kramer et al., 2012).

These findings indicate that vocational interests play an important role in various educational and occupational decisions. Although more research is needed in this area, these findings indicate that interest-driven selection processes may emerge as early as primary school and clearly influence educational decisions at the end of high school.

## Vocational interests and career success

Holland postulated that people will be more likely to choose environments that are congruent with their interests and that people in congruent environments will show more persistence, better performances, and more satisfaction (Holland, 1997). These congruence hypotheses have been tested frequently, but depending on which criteria were investigated, the findings have been mixed.

Empirical studies that have investigated the various criteria that affect the stability of career choice have consistently revealed support for the expected association between congruence and career choice stability, and the effects were supported by two independent meta-analyses (Assouline & Meir, 1987; Hunter & Hunter, 1984). Regarding the relation between interest congruence and performance outcomes, results of an early—and influential—meta-analysis (Hunter & Hunter, 1984) resulted in a long-held common belief that interest congruence shows only weak relations to performance. However, in recent years, two meta-analyses (Nye, Su, Rounds, & Drasgow, 2012; Van Iddekinge, Roth, Putka, & Lanivich, 2011) systematically summarized the findings of newer studies and revealed that interests are substantially related to performance and persistence in work and academic contexts. Interests were shown to predict task performance, organizational citizenship behavior, grades, and persistence in work and academic contexts (Nye et al., 2012). The most frequently investigated relation has been the one between congruence and satisfaction, but the results are still inconsistent to date. Several meta-analyses revealed only small and nonsignificant effects (Assouline & Meir, 1987; Hunter & Hunter, 1984; Tranberg, Slane, & Ekeberg, 1993; Tsabari, Tziner, & Meir, 2005). The failure to generalize significant effects is due not only to small effects but also to the large amount of variability in the effects of the incorporated studies. Several theoretical moderators have been postulated to influence the effects, but most of them could not be replicated. Instead, methodological aspects and the large amount of diversity in operationalization—e.g., the use of a typological or dimensional approach—seem to be the crucial aspects here.

# Development and change in vocational interests across the life span

## Development of interests from childhood to adulthood

Interests develop early in childhood. The first manifestation of individual interests occurs as early as preschool. At that time, children differ in their preferences for different toys (Todt, 2000). Such preferences—described as *universal or general interest*—will continue to change a lot and are oriented toward numerous activities and objects. Before entering school, children develop gender-based preferences—*collective interests*—and tend to ignore activities and objects that are not in line with their own perception of gender (Gottfredson, 1981). In school, individual interests begin to manifest. In elementary school, the gender-specific aspects of students' collective interests are supplemented by the aspect of proximity to and distance from school (Tracey & Ward, 1998; Tracey, 2001, 2002). Further, between the ages of 11 and 13, a re-evaluation of interests takes place, and *individual interests* manifest. In this phase, interests undergo a process of differentiation. Middle school students progressively decide what things they do not like and decrease their level of interest in some areas—resulting in an overall drop in mean levels (see Tracey, 2002). This overall decrease in interests may be associated with a more realistic and more differentiated perception of oneself and one's environment (Osipow, 1983). It is also related to Holland's secondary construct of differentiation. If students reduce their interest levels in some areas and increase their interest levels in other areas, their interests become more differentiated—as postulated (Holland, 1997). Therefore, some researchers regard interest differentiation as an indicator of career-choice readiness and maturation (Hirschi & Läge, 2007).

The development and differentiation of interests also affects the structure of vocational interests. With increasing age, the RIASEC scales adhere to the postulated circular ordering to a larger extent. Tracey and Ward (1998) found no fit with the RIASEC circumplex for elementary school students, only a moderate fit for middle school students, and a good fit for college students. The assumption that the structure of interest changes over time has been confirmed by longitudinal data (Tracey, 2002). A 1-year longitudinal study of elementary school students and middle school students demonstrated that the circular structure became more prominent over time. For ages 14 and older, meta-analytic research (Rounds & Tracey, 1993; Tracey & Rounds, 1993) demonstrated that the circular arrangement of the RIASEC scales is a valid representation.

A meta-analytic study (Low, Yoon, Roberts, & Rounds, 2005) determined that, after much development and change in vocational interests during childhood, such interests become relatively stable during adolescence and young adulthood. The stability of interests remains unchanged during much of adolescence (with estimated population correlations ranging from $\rho = 0.55$ to $0.58$ between the ages of 12 and 17), it increases dramatically during the college years, and peaks between the ages of 25 and 30 ($\rho = 0.83$). Between the ages of 22 and 40, the stability of vocational interests remains at this high level. In addition, vocational interests are markedly more stable than the Big Five personality traits in adolescence and young adulthood (Low et al., 2005). Although the stability of both constructs increases during these life phases, the stability of interests becomes stronger, and vocational interests remain more stable than the Big Five personality traits for ages 22 to 29. From ages 30 to 39, the stability coefficients of the Big Five and vocational interests converge. However, even though vocational interests tend to be remarkably stable, there is still room for change.

To date, there is not much research on normative changes and development in vocational interests across the life span. The existing empirical evidence is mainly based on studies with two time points—originally designed to investigate retest reliabilities for vocational interest scales (Low, 2009). Several of these studies have shown increases on all interest scales during adolescence and emerging adulthood, as individuals begin transitioning into the workforce (Meinster & Rose, 2001;

Tracey, Robbins, & Hofsess, 2005). Other studies have detected the opposite trend for younger people between the ages of 12 and 16. In this life phase, interest scores tend to decline slightly (Lent, Tracey, Brown, Soresi, & Nota, 2006; Tracey, 2002). To date, there is one meta-analysis on mean-level changes in vocational interest (Low, 2009). In this study, Investigative, Artistic, Social, and Enterprising interests were found to increase for both sexes from age 12 to 25. Gender differences in patterns of change were detected for Realistic and Conventional interests. Nevertheless, these findings are mainly based on studies with two time points, and there is little empirical data on longitudinal changes in vocational interests. Thus, more research—especially long-term longitudinal data—is needed to better explore the development of vocational interests and the mechanisms of stability and change —on both the group and individual levels.

Because vocational interests have primarily been investigated in the context of career counseling and career choices, and research on vocational interests has tended to focus on young people and college students, there is to date not much data on vocational interests in middle and older adulthood (but see Costa, McCrae, & Holland, 1984; Rohe & Krause, 1998; Verburg, 1952). In a cross-sectional comparison of vocational interests in different ages groups, Costa et al. (1984) found only small differences between college students and adults (age 25−55) or older adults (age 56−89) and no evidence for linear developmental changes in interests. But as these results are cross-sectional, whether or not these effects represent true changes in interests with age has yet to be determined.

Although it was claimed decades ago that "longitudinal studies are needed to determine if these effects are due to age, retirement, cohort differences, or simply to differences in sampling" (Costa et al., 1984, p. 394), longitudinal data on vocational interests across the life span are still scarce. As a consequence, stability and change in vocational interests in later life phases remains relatively unexplored. The development of vocational interests in later life phases is especially important when dynamic processes of person−environment fit are regarded. Although the existing literature demonstrates high stability in vocational interests up to the age of 40 (Low et al., 2005), there is potential for development and change—even in the later phases of adult life.

## Person−environment fit as a dynamic process

Holland's theory is well known as a theory of occupational *selection*. It is far less known that Holland postulated person−environment fit as a dynamic process of accommodation. He described the theoretical context for his model as follows:

> It [the theory of vocational personalities and working environments] is interactive because it assumes that many career and social behaviors are the outcome of people and environments acting on one another. It is not a one-way street; jobs change people, and people change jobs.
>
> *Holland, 1997, p. 12*

Holland postulated selection processes in which people select environments on the basis of their vocational interests because they want to incorporate their interests and abilities into their work (Holland, 1997, p. 4). He also postulated socialization processes (see Wille & De Fruyt, 2014) by which the selected environments in turn influence how people develop. As environments selectively stimulate behaviors, foster abilities, and reinforce characteristics and attitudes, environmental experiences influence people (see Holland, 1997, p. 43). With time, people become more susceptible to the environmental influences and more attracted to the corresponding occupational roles (see Holland, 1997, p. 44). For example, Realistic environments stimulate people to engage in realistic activities such as using machines and tools, foster technical competencies and achievements, encourage people to see themselves as having mechanical ability, and reward them for displaying traditional values and attitudes (see Holland, 1997, p. 43). Therefore, people in Realistic environments will adapt to these influences and become more pragmatic, materialistic, conforming, and inflexible (see Holland, 1997, p. 44). This means that people change their interests, attitudes, and behaviors in reaction to their working environment because environments reinforce specific behaviors, characteristics, and values.

Holland postulated different processes of accommodation that—over time—will increase person–environment congruence (see Fig. 25.3): If congruence is high, such accommodation processes follow a corresponsive principle (for a further investigation of the corresponsive principle in the context of personality development, see Roberts & Nickel, Chapter 11). This means that the characteristics that determined which environment people selected in the first place will grow stronger. If congruence is low, it could be increased by active or reactive adjustment. Three different processes of accommodation are possible. First, people can change their interests, behaviors, and attitudes to better fulfill the requirements of the environment (reactive adjustment). Second, people can try to reshape and modify their current working environment according to their interests (active adjustment). Third, people can move to a new environment that better corresponds to their interests (quitting). This means that from an intraindividual perspective, interest–environment congruence should increase over time—at least if congruence is low at the

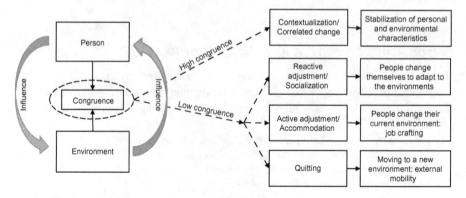

**Figure 25.3** Dynamic processes of accommodation between person and environment.

beginning. If a sufficient level of congruence is present to begin with, the postulated processes might rather lead to stabilizing effects, or as Holland stated, "Incongruent interactions stimulate change in human behavior, conversely, congruent interactions encourage stability of behavior" (Holland, 1997, p. 68).

Although these ideas are crucial for the theory of vocational interests, research on socialization processes and reciprocal effects is scarce. However, a few studies have provided some evidence to support these ideas. For example, Donohue (2006) showed that people who plan to change their careers tend to change toward more congruent careers. In a study involving college alumni, Wille et al. (2014) showed that individual interests and occupational characteristics showed substantial changes (and only moderate stabilities) during the first 15 years of people's professional careers. In addition, changes in interest—occupation congruence were identified (Wille et al., 2014). Reciprocal relations between RIASEC occupational characteristics and Big Five personality traits were investigated by Wille and De Fruyt (2014). Their results provided evidence for all three dynamic mechanisms that had been postulated by Holland (1997). Occupational characteristics influenced changes in personality traits—reflecting reactivity and socialization effects; personality traits influenced changes in occupational characteristics—reflecting active adjustment or accommodation effects; and personality traits changed in association with changes in the occupational characteristics that were relevant for the selection of an occupation in the first place—reflecting correlated change or contextualization effects.

## Vocational interests as personality traits

Although the theory of vocational interests has been very influential in the context of career counseling and vocational psychology, there has yet to be much transfer to other areas of psychological research. In this chapter, we would like to argue for a more integrated view on vocational interests.[2] We think that vocational interests should be considered relevant aspects of individual differences because they direct individuals' goal-oriented behaviors and the decisions they make for their lives. Therefore, vocational interests influence people's lives—beyond the context of work—and should be considered relevant aspects of individual differences (Rounds & Su, 2014).

The approach of viewing vocational interests as personality traits is based on personality models (e.g., the Neo-Socioanalytic Model of Personality; Roberts & Wood, 2006; McAdams & Pals, 2006) that distinguish between personality traits and motivations and consider interests and personality traits to be equivalent or regard interests explicitly as personality characteristics (e.g., Kandler, Zimmermann, & McAdams, 2014). By contrast, several other models of personality view interests as outcomes of personality traits (e.g., McCrae & Costa, 2008).

---

[2] We thank Brent Roberts for relevant suggestions in this context and for inspiring discussions about the nature and potential of vocational interests.

We see three main arguments for why vocational interests could be strong predictors of various life outcomes. First, vocational interests are personality traits. Holland himself stated that vocational interests are "an important aspect of personality" (Holland, 1997, p. 8), and he defined the six interest types as "personality types" (Holland, 1997). As vocational interests contain information about the stable—and therefore the trait-like—characteristics of a person, they should be regarded as trait-like aspects of personality. Nevertheless, vocational interests are not equivalent to the Big Five personality traits. Although vocational interests show some associations with the Big Five personality traits, they are relatively distinct from the Big Five (Larson, Rottinghaus, & Borgen, 2002). This implies that vocational interests contain aspects of the Big Five but also distinct information about individual differences. This view is supported by the high stability of vocational interests. As described earlier, vocational interests are more stable than the Big Five personality traits during adolescence and young adulthood (Low et al., 2005).

Second, vocational interests direct people's behavior and have motivating effects. Interests are defined as trait-like preferences for activities, contexts in which activities occur, or outcomes associated with preferred activities that motivate goal-oriented behaviors and orient people toward certain environments (Rounds, 1995; Su, Rounds, & Armstrong, 2009). Vocational interests contain information about goals and values and therefore reflect what people want out of their lives (Table 25.2). This makes vocational interests potentially strong predictors of various life outcomes—not only in the context of work but in all life domains.

Third, vocational interests might reflect a combination of motivation and ability self-concept. Vocational interests contain information about specific skills and abilities, and people with the same interest type have similar self-concepts about their abilities (Holland, 1997; see Table 25.2). This idea is supported by investment models of cognitive abilities that posit that one's ability in a domain will lead to an increased investment in this area, and this in turn will lead to increased interests (Schmidt, 2014). If a construct combines different aspects of individual differences that each predict concrete behavior and various outcomes, the predictive validity of the combined construct will be higher than that of the single aspects. Vocational interests might be especially strong predictors of life outcomes because they contain different aspects of individual differences.

If the relevance of a psychological construct is considered, it is important to see its relation to other important constructs. Vocational interests show meaningful overlap with the Big Five personality traits (Larson et al., 2002), but the associations are relatively small, ranging from around $r = 0.19$ (Social−Agreeableness) to around $r = 0.48$ (Artistic−Openness), and some interests show only minimal overlap with the Big Five. For cognitive abilities, the picture looks similar. There is some overlap (Armstrong, Day, McVay, & Rounds, 2008), but associations (Realistic/Investigative−quantitative, Artistic−verbal, Conventional−clerical/perceptual speed) are modest and vary by gender, and some interests show overall weak associations with abilities (Ackerman & Heggestad, 1997; Päßler & Hell, 2012). Therefore, vocational interests seem to be relatively distinct constructs that might influence individuals' lives over and above the Big Five personality traits or cognitive abilities.

**Table 25.2 The life goals, self-beliefs, and problem solving styles of the six interest types**

|  | Life goals and values | Self-beliefs | Problem solving |
|---|---|---|---|
| Realistic | Traditional values | Mechanical, technical, and athletic abilities | Concrete, practical, and structured strategies |
| Investigative | Scholarly/scientific achievement, open system of beliefs | Scientific, analytical, and mathematical abilities | Thinking, gathering information, and careful analyses |
| Artistic | Open system of beliefs, liberal goals, and values | Artistic and musical ability, and ability in acting, writing, and speaking | Intuition, expressiveness, and originality |
| Social | Serve others, be helpful and forgiving, values religion, aspires to become a competent parent, teacher, or therapist | Teaching ability and social skills | Seeking mutual interactions and help from others |
| Enterprising | Traditional values, aspires to become a leader in commerce, community, or public affairs | Self-confident, sociable, possessing leadership and speaking abilities, has high self-esteem | Social influence, control over others, traditional beliefs |
| Conventional | Business and economic achievement, traditional virtues | Competent in business, low self-esteem | Follows established rules and procedures, looks for advice, practical solutions, and careful planning |

*Source*: Summarized from Holland, J. L. (1997). *Making vocational choices: A theory of vocational personalities and work environments* (3rd ed., Vol. 14). Odessa, FL: Psychological Assessment Resources.

Although research is scarce in this area, some empirical support has been found. For example, Su (2012) examined the incremental validity of vocational interests beyond cognitive ability and personality for predicting academic achievement and career success. In her study, interests were the most powerful predictor of income and greatly exceeded the contributions of ability and personality. Interests were also found to be powerful predictors of college grades, college persistence, degree attainment, and occupational prestige (see Rounds & Su, 2014). Stoll et al. (2016) investigated the predictive validity of vocational interests using a large-scale, longitudinal data set collected in Germany. They used vocational interests, the Big Five personality traits, cognitive ability, gender, and socioeconomic family background assessed at the end of high school as predictors of life outcomes assessed 10 years later. Vocational interest were important predictors not only of work-related outcomes but also of relationship outcomes (e.g., being married and having children). In addition, for most of the investigated outcomes, vocational interests were stronger predictors than the Big Five personality traits and cognitive ability.

On the basis of these findings and the theoretical assumptions described earlier, we propose that like personality traits, vocational interests have wide-ranging effects on the constitution of people's lives, not only because they affect career outcomes but also because they reflect broader, cross-situational patterns of motivation that affect many different life domains.

# References

Ackerman, P. L., & Heggestad, E. D. (1997). Intelligence, personality, and interests: Evidence for overlapping traits. *Psychological Bulletin, 121*(2), 219–245. Available from http://dx.doi.org/10.1037/0033-2909.121.2.219.

Anderson, M. Z., Tracey, T. J. G., & Rounds, J. (1997). Examining the invariance of Holland's vocational interest model across gender. *Journal of Vocational Behavior, 50* (3), 349–364. Available from http://dx.doi.org/10.1006/jvbe.1996.1550.

Armstrong, P. I., Day, S. X., McVay, J. P., & Rounds, J. (2008). Holland's RIASEC model as an integrative framework for individual differences. *Journal of Counseling Psychology, 55*(1), 1–18. Available from http://dx.doi.org/10.1037/0022-0167.55.1.1.

Assouline, M., & Meir, E. I. (1987). Meta-analysis of the relationship between congruence and well-being measures. *Journal of Vocational Behavior, 31*(3), 319–332. Available from http://dx.doi.org/10.1016/0001-8791(87)90046-7.

Barak, A., & Meir, E. I. (1974). The predictive validity of a vocational interest inventory —"Ramak": Seven year follow-up. *Journal of Vocational Behavior, 4*(3), 377–387. Available from http://dx.doi.org/10.1016/0001-8791(74)90123-7.

Bergmann, C. (1994). Gemessene versus artikulierte Interessen als Prädiktoren der Berufs- bzw. Studienfachwahl und Anpassung im Studium [Assessed vs. expressed interests as predictors of vocational choice and career adjustment]. *Zeitschrift Für Arbeits- Und Organisationspsychologie, 38*(4), 142–151.

Costa, P. T., Jr., McCrae, R. R., & Holland, J. (1984). Personality and vocational interests in an adult sample. *Journal of Applied Psychology, 69*(3), 390–400.

Darcy, M., & Tracey, T. J. G. (2007). Circumplex structure of Holland's RIASEC interests across gender and time. *Journal of Counseling Psychology, 54*(1), 17–31. Available from http://dx.doi.org/10.1037/0022-0167.54.1.17.

Donohue, R. (2006). Person–environment congruence in relation to career change and career persistence. *Journal of Vocational Behavior, 68*(3), 504–515. Available from http://dx.doi.org/10.1016/j.jvb.2005.11.002.

Gottfredson, L. S. (1981). Circumscription and compromise: A developmental theory of occupational aspirations. *Journal of Counseling Psychology, 28*(6), 545–579. Available from http://dx.doi.org/10.1037/0022-0167.28.6.545.

Hirschi, A., & Läge, D. (2007). Holland's secondary constructs of vocational interests and career choice readiness of secondary students: Measures for related but different constructs. *Journal of Individual Differences*, *28*(4), 205−218. Available from http://dx. doi.org/10.1027/1614-0001.28.4.205.

Holland, J. L. (1994). *The self-directed search*. Odessa, FL: Psychological Assessment Resources, Inc.

Holland, J. L. (1997). (3rd ed.). *Making vocational choices: A theory of vocational personalities and work environments*, (Vol. 14Odessa, FL: Psychological Assessment Resources.

Humphreys, L. G., & Yao, G. (2002). Prediction of graduate major from cognitive and self-report test scores obtained during the high school years. *Psychological Reports*, *90*(1), 3−30.

Hunter, J. E., & Hunter, R. F. (1984). Validity and utility of alternative predictors of job performance. *Psychological Bulletin*, *96*(1), 72−98. Available from http://dx.doi.org/ 10.1037/0033-2909.96.1.72.

Kandler, C., Zimmermann, J., & McAdams, D. P. (2014). Core and surface characteristics for the description and theory of personality differences and development. *European Journal of Personality*, *28*(3), 231−243. < https://doi.org/10.1002/per.1952 >

Kramer, J., Zettler, I., Thoemmes, F., Nagy, G., Trautwein, U., & Lüdtke, O. (2012). Stellen Hochschultypen differenzielle Entwicklungsmilieus dar?—Eine Propensity-Score-Analyse zu den Effekten des Hochschulbesuch [Do different types of universities constitute differential developmental milieus?—A propensity score analysis of the effects of university attendance]. *Zeitschrift für Erziehungswissenschaft*, *15*(4), 847−874. Available from http://dx.doi.org/10.1007/s11618-012-0280-1.

Larson, L. M., Rottinghaus, P. J., & Borgen, F. H. (2002). Meta-analyses of Big Six interests and Big Five personality factors. *Journal of Vocational Behavior*, *61*(2), 217−239. Available from http://dx.doi.org/10.1006/jvbe.2001.1854.

Lent, R. W., Brown, S. D., & Hackett, G. (1994). Toward a unifying social cognitive theory of career and academic interest, choice, and performance. *Journal of Vocational Behavior*, *45*(1), 79−122. Available from http://dx.doi.org/10.1006/jvbe.1994.1027.

Lent, R. W., Tracey, T. J. G., Brown, S. D., Soresi, S., & Nota, L. (2006). Development of interests and competency beliefs in Italian adolescents: An exploration of circumplex structure and bidirectional relationships. *Journal of Counseling Psychology*, *53*(2), 181−191. Available from http://dx.doi.org/10.1037/0022-0167.53.2.181.

Low, K. S. D. (2009). *Patterns of mean-level changes in vocational interests: A quantitative review of longitudinal studies* (Unpublished doctoral dissertation). University of Illinois at Urbana-Champaign.

Low, K. S. D., Yoon, M., Roberts, B. W., & Rounds, J. (2005). The stability of vocational interests from early adolescence to middle adulthood: A quantitative review of longitudinal studies. *Psychological Bulletin*, *131*(5), 713−737. Available from http://dx.doi. org/10.1037/0033-2909.131.5.713.

McAdams, D. P., & Pals, J. L. (2006). A new big five: Fundamental principles for an integrative science of personality. *American Psychologist*, *61*(3), 204−217. Available from https://doi.org/10.1037/0003-066X.61.3.204.

McCrae, R. R., & Costa, P. T., Jr. (2008). The Five-Factor Theory of personality. In O. P. John, R. W. Robins, & L. A. Pervin (Eds.), *Handbook of personality: Theory and research* (3rd ed., pp. 159−181). New York, NY: Guilford Press.

Meinster, M. O., & Rose, K. C. (2001). Longitudinal influences of educational aspirations and romantic relationships on adolescent women's vocational interests. *Journal of Vocational Behavior*, *58*(3), 313−327. Available from http://dx.doi.org/10.1006/ jvbe.2000.1772.

Nye, C. D., Su, R., Rounds, J., & Drasgow, F. (2012). Vocational interests and performance: A quantitative summary of over 60 years of research. *Perspectives on Psychological Science*, *7*(4), 384−403. Available from http://dx.doi.org/10.1177/1745691612449021.

Osipow, S. H. (1983). *Theories of career development* (3rd ed.). Englewood Cliffs, NJ: Prentice Hall.

Päßler, K., & Hell, B. (2012). Do interests and cognitive abilities help explain college major choice equally well for women and men? *Journal of Career Assessment, 20*(4), 479−496. Available from http://dx.doi.org/10.1177/1069072712450009.

Prediger, D. J. (1982). Dimensions underlying Holland's hexagon: Missing link between interests and occupations? *Journal of Vocational Behavior, 21*(3), 259−287. Available from http://dx.doi.org/10.1016/0001-8791(82)90036-7.

Roberts, B. W., & Wood, D. (2006). Personality development in the context of the Neo-Socioanalytic Model of Personality. In D. K. Mroczek, & T. D. Little (Eds.), *Handbook of personality development* (pp. 11−39). Mahwah, NJ: Erlbaum.

Rohe, D. E., & Krause, J. S. (1998). Stability of Interests after severe physical disability: An 11-year longitudinal study. *Journal of Vocational Behavior, 52*(1), 45−58. Available from http://dx.doi.org/10.1006/jvbe.1996.1560.

Roloff Henoch, J., Klusmann, U., Lüdtke, O., & Trautwein, U. (2015). Who becomes a teacher? Challenging the "negative selection" hypothesis. *Learning and Instruction, 36*, 46−56. Available from http://dx.doi.org/10.1016/j.learninstruc.2014.11.005.

Rounds, J. (1995). Vocational interests: Evaluating structural hypotheses. In D. J. Lubinski, & R. V. Dawis (Eds.), *Assessing individual differences in human behavior: New concepts, methods, and findings* (pp. 177−232). Palo Alto, CA: Davies-Black Publishing.

Rounds, J., & Day, S. X. (1999). Describing, evaluating, and creating vocational interest structures. In M. L. Savickas, & A. R. Spokane (Eds.), *Vocational interests: Meaning, measurement, and counseling use* (pp. 103−133). Palo Alto, CA: Davies-Black Publishing.

Rounds, J., & Su, R. (2014). The nature and power of interests. *Current Directions in Psychological Science, 23*(2), 98−103. Available from http://dx.doi.org/10.1177/0963721414522812.

Rounds, J., & Tracey, T. J. (1993). Prediger's dimensional representation of Holland's RIASEC circumplex. *Journal of Applied Psychology, 78*(6), 875−890. Available from http://dx.doi.org/10.1037/0021-9010.78.6.875.

Schmidt, F. L. (2014). A general theoretical integrative model of individual differences in interests, abilities, personality traits, and academic and occupational achievement: A commentary on four recent articles. *Perspectives on Psychological Science, 9*(2), 211−218. Available from http://dx.doi.org/10.1177/1745691613518074.

Stoll, G., Rieger, S., Lüdtke, O., Nagengast, B., Trautwein, U., & Roberts, B. W. (2016). Vocational interests as predictors of life outcomes in work, relationship, and health. *Journal of Personality and Social Psychology*. Available from http://dx.doi.org/10.1037/pspp0000117.

Su, R. (2012). *The power of vocational interests and interest congruence in predicting career success* (Unpublished doctoral dissertation). University of Illinois at Urbana-Champaign.

Su, R., Rounds, J., & Armstrong, P. I. (2009). Men and things, women and people: A meta-analysis of sex differences in interests. *Psychological Bulletin, 135*(6), 859−884. Available from http://dx.doi.org/10.1037/a0017364.

Todt, E. (2000). Geschlechtsspezifische Interessen−Entwicklungen und Möglichkeiten der Modifikation [Gender specific interest development and possibilities of modification]. *Empirische Pädagogik, 14*(3), 215−254.

Tracey, T. J. G. (2001). The development of structure of interests in children: Setting the stage. *Journal of Vocational Behavior, 59*(1), 89−104. Available from http://dx.doi.org/10.1006/jvbe.2000.1787.

Tracey, T. J. G. (2002). Development of interests and competency beliefs: A 1-year longitudinal study of fifth- to eighth-grade students using the ICA-R and structural equation modeling. *Journal of Counseling Psychology*, *49*(2), 148−163. Available from http://dx. doi.org/10.1037/0022-0167.49.2.148.

Tracey, T. J. G., Robbins, S. B., & Hofsess, C. D. (2005). Stability and change in interests: A longitudinal study of adolescents from grades 8 through 12. *Journal of Vocational Behavior*, *66*(1), 1−25. Available from http://dx.doi.org/10.1016/j.jvb.2003.11.002.

Tracey, T. J. G., & Rounds, J. (1996). The spherical representation of vocational interests. *Journal of Vocational Behavior*, *48*(1), 3−41. Available from http://dx.doi.org/10.1006/ jvbe.1996.0002.

Tracey, T. J. G., & Rounds, J. B. (1993). Evaluating Holland's and Gati's vocational-interest models: A structural meta-analysis. *Psychological Bulletin*, *113*(2), 229−246. Available from http://dx.doi.org/10.1037/0033-2909.113.2.229.

Tracey, T. J. G., & Ward, C. C. (1998). The structure of children's interests and competence perceptions. *Journal of Counseling Psychology*, *45*(3), 290−303. Available from http:// dx.doi.org/10.1037/0022-0167.45.3.290.

Tranberg, M., Slane, S., & Ekeberg, S. E. (1993). The relation between interest congruence and satisfaction: A metaanalysis. *Journal of Vocational Behavior*, *42*(3), 253−264. Available from http://dx.doi.org/10.1006/jvbe.1993.1018.

Tsabari, O., Tziner, A., & Meir, E. I. (2005). Updated meta-analysis on the relationship between congruence and satisfaction. *Journal of Career Assessment*, *13*(2), 216−232. Available from http://dx.doi.org/10.1177/1069072704273165.

Van Iddekinge, C. H., Roth, P. L., Putka, D. J., & Lanivich, S. E. (2011). Are you interested? A meta-analysis of relations between vocational interests and employee performance and turnover. *Journal of Applied Psychology*, *96*(6), 1167.

Verburg, W. A. (1952). Vocational interests of retired YMCA Secretaries. *Journal of Applied Psychology*, *36*(4), 254−256. Available from http://dx.doi.org/10.1037/h0063450.

Volodina, A., Nagy, G., & Retelsdorf, J. (2015). Berufliche Interessen und der Übergang in die gymnasiale Profiloberstufe: Ihre Struktur und Vorhersagekraft für das individuelle Wahlverhalten [Vocational interests and the transition to the thematic profiles of upper secondary school: Their structure and utility for predicting educational choices]. *Zeitschrift Für Pädagogische Psychologie*, *29*(2), 89−100. Available from http://dx.doi. org/10.1024/1010-0652/a000154.

Von Maurice, J., & Bäumer, T. (2015). Entwicklung allgemeiner Interessenorientierungen beim Übergang von der Grundschule in den Sekundarbereich [Development of general interest orientations in the transition from primary to secondary education]. In C. Tarnai, & F. G. Hartmann (Eds.), *Berufliche Interessen. Beiträge zur Theorie von J. L. Holland* (pp. 63−85). Münster: Waxmann.

Webb, R. M., Lubinski, D., & Benbow, C. P. (2002). Mathematically facile adolescents with math-science aspirations: New perspectives on their educational and vocational develop-ment. *Journal of Educational Psychology*, *94*(4), 785−794. Available from http://dx.doi. org/10.1037/0022-0663.94.4.785.

Wille, B., & De Fruyt, F. (2014). Vocations as a source of identity: Reciprocal relations between Big Five personality traits and RIASEC characteristics over 15 years. *Journal of Applied Psychology*, *99*(2), 262−281. Available from http://dx.doi.org/10.1037/ a0034917.

Wille, B., Tracey, T. J. G., Feys, M., & De Fruyt, F. (2014). A longitudinal and multi-method examination of interest−occupation congruence within and across time. *Journal of Vocational Behavior*, *84*(1), 59−73. Available from http://dx.doi.org/10.1016/j. jvb.2013.12.001.

# Intercultural similarities and differences in personality development

26

*Hyunji Kim and Joni Y. Sasaki*
York University, Toronto, ON, Canada

Based on the research findings from the past two decades, we know that personality changes throughout the life span, from early childhood to early adolescence and from early adolescence to older adulthood. People become more conscientious, agreeable, and less neurotic with age (Roberts, Wood, & Caspi, 2008; Srivastava, John, Gosling, & Potter, 2003). The stability of individual differences in personality also increases across the life course, meaning that traits tend to change together (Roberts et al., 2008). For example, if you become more conscientious in adulthood, you are more likely to change in another trait, such as Agreeableness. However, the vast majority of research in this area has been conducted on North American and Western European samples. Is it then safe to assume that most of these developmental patterns in personality occur universally, or are there differences in personality development between individuals of different cultures? Do East Asians' personalities develop similarly to North Americans? Do East Asians, like North Americans, become more agreeable and conscientious in middle and older adulthood?

In this chapter, we focus on cultural similarities and differences in personality development across the life span. First, we define culture and describe theoretical frameworks that can be used to study personality from a cultural psychological perspective. Next, we focus on parent—child attachment styles and personality, specifically the Big Five traits, across cultures. Third, we discuss empirical cultural evidence for personality development of the Big Five in early, middle, and older adulthood. Lastly, we provide an overview of the current research findings on intercultural similarities and differences in personality development and put forward suggestions for future research to better understand personality development across cultures.

## Integrating research on culture and personality

In this section, we give a brief primer on how culture is studied in cultural psychology before discussing promising existing frameworks for integrating research on culture with personality in psychology.

Personality Development Across the Lifespan. DOI: http://dx.doi.org/10.1016/B978-0-12-804674-6.00026-0

# The cultural psychological perspective

As humans, we are constantly interacting with the world around us in order to create and derive meaning (Bruner, 1990), and this process of "meaning making" is what makes us cultural beings. Culture can be defined as a shared, organized system of beliefs, practices, and artifacts passed on over time. From a cultural psychological perspective, culture can be found publicly via cultural products such as the education system, literature and art, as well as privately in the psychological processes of the human mind, such as in parenting philosophies (Morling & Lamoreaux, 2008). To illustrate, an artist may create a painting of a seascape that survives many generations. Culture, in this case, exists in the painting, in its representation of the ocean and the sky and the implied interests of its creator. But it also exists in the artist herself, in the psychological motives that compelled her to create such a piece in the first place. The constant interplay between the culture that is external, or impressed in the world around us, and internal, or expressed from our internal thoughts and behavior, is what it means to "make meaning." Culture is central to human life, and it is the focus of inquiry in cultural psychology.

Conventionally, culture has been studied in psychology as ethnicity or nationality, yet culture is much more than this. A more inclusive study of culture, one that appreciates its broad definition, examines many forms of culture (A. B. Cohen, 2009). Besides ethnic and national culture, it is possible to conceptualize religion as culture, for instance. Comparing Jewish to Protestant traditions suggests that religious background may shape beliefs about morality (A. B. Cohen & Rozin, 2001). Social class can also be understood as a form of culture, as people from middle-class contexts tend to value uniqueness more than people from working class contexts (Stephens, Markus, & Townsend, 2007). Similarly, region can show meaningful differences between groups, as demonstrated by research on the culture of honor in the Southern United States (D. Cohen, Nisbett, Bowdle, & Schwarz, 1996) and evidence of high independence in Japan's northern frontier, Hokkaido (Kitayama, Ishii, Imada, Takemura, & Ramaswamy, 2006). Research on other forms of culture—such as region, social class, and religion as culture—has been increasing, and there are many other meaningful groups that have yet to be studied in depth (e.g., the culture of academia). However, the most common conceptualization of culture in psychology is still ethnic or national culture, and among studies that examine personality and culture, the vast majority has conceptualized culture as ethnicity or nationality. Thus we use the term "culture" in this chapter to refer to ethnic or national culture for simplicity.

# Frameworks for studying culture and personality

A common assumption is that culture, no matter its form, is a malleable influence working in opposition to more fixed influences such as personality. Yet this assumption may ignore the reality that, first, culture can interact with personality

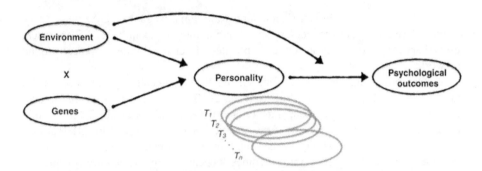

**Figure 26.1** Framework for integrating genes, environment, and personality. *Note*: The model implies direct effects of genes and environmental factors (e.g., cultural, situational, and physical environmental factors, such as early transition into adulthood) and gene-by-environment effects on personality. The relationship between genes and personality change developmentally over time ($T_1$, $T_2$, $T_3$, ..., $T_n$) due to an individual's life experiences. Personality also interacts more proximally with the environment to predict psychological outcomes.

and situations in order to lead to different behaviors (Leung & Cohen, 2011), and second, personality itself can be shaped by environmental and genetic influences to differing degrees over the course of development (Bleidorn, Kandler, & Caspi, 2014). In this section, we discuss two prominent frameworks that can be used to study culture together with personality (see Fig. 26.1).

Culture is composed of shared meanings at the group level, and therefore, cultural differences are not always reducible to individual differences (Na et al., 2010). At the same time, there is often important variability within a culture; some individuals may not share the same meaning as everyone else in their group across situations. Groups and individuals do not always operate under the same rules, and empirical evidence suggests that variables that systematically correlate at the group level may not correlate at the individual level (Na et al., 2010). In order to account for variation both between and within cultures, Leung and Cohen (2011) proposed the Culture × Person × Situation (CuPS) approach, integrating personality with cultural psychology (see also Gebauer et al., 2014, for discussion of the sociocultural motives perspective, or moderation of personality factors depending on sociocultural normativeness). In particular, the CuPS approach highlights the important point that aspects of the person (P) at the level of personality may interact with features of the social situation (S), and furthermore, the nature of this initial interaction (P × S) may differ from one cultural context (Cu) to the next (Cu × P × S). For example, research has shown that mothers in Japan (Cu) are more likely to associate secure attachment of the child (P) with social accommodation, suggesting that they see the context of social relationships (S) as central to the healthy manifestation of secure attachment. Mothers in the United States (Cu), however, are more likely to associate secure attachment (P) with a range of positive personality traits and skills, suggesting that they consider personal attributes of the individual (S) to be central to secure attachment (Rothbaum, Kakinuma, Nagaoka, & Azuma, 2007). By considering how culture, person, and situation interact, as in the CuPS approach, researchers may more fully account for profiles of personality development around the world.

Another promising framework comes from the gene–culture interaction model (G × C; H. S. Kim, Sherman, Sasaki et al., 2010), which is based on the broader framework of gene–environment interactions (G × E; Caspi et al., 2003). Within the broad G × E framework, the same genetic tendency may lead to different outcomes depending on variability in the environment, and conversely, the same environment may lead to different outcomes depending on variability in genetic tendencies. The basic premise of G × C is that culture is a meaningful form of the environment that can shape the expression of genetic tendencies, and there is accumulating evidence that the same genetic tendency seems to be expressed differently depending on culture for a number of psychological processes, including processes of emotion (emotional support seeking: H. S. Kim, Sherman, Sasaki et al., 2010; emotion regulation: H. S. Kim et al., 2011; well-being: Sasaki, Kim, & Xu, 2011) and attention (locus of attention: H. S. Kim, Sherman, Taylor et al., 2010; sensitivity to changes in facial expressions: Ishii, Kim, Sasaki, Shinada, & Kusumi, 2014).[1] To the extent that gene–culture interactions may be implicated in the way people feel and the way they attend to and perceive the world around them, it is likely that G × C processes may be involved in personality development.

One alluring way to integrate the G × C model with personality is to roughly replace G with personality, P. Assuming that G is highly correlated with P, this perspective predicts that personality interacts with culture (P × C) to lead to different psychological outcomes, and genes are the antecedent to personality. By factoring in the situation as well, this perspective would become very similar to the CuPS approach (Leung & Cohen, 2011) and could thus be one possible way to use perspectives from genetics together with personality and cultural psychology. However, one issue with this method of integration is that genes (or more specifically, genotypes) do not change, even if gene expression does. Personality (a collection of phenotypes), although relatively stable, can change to some extent over time (Specht, Egloff, & Schmuckle, 2011). Relatedly, genes do not explain all of the variance in personality: cultural, situational, and physical environmental factors, such as parenting styles or early entry into the labor force, have direct effects on personality (see Fig. 26.1). Correspondence between G and P may also change over time due to life experiences, suggesting a complex interplay between genes and the

---

[1] An important methodological point in G × C research is that if two ethnic groups are used as proxies for culture (the "C" in G × C), then these groups may vary not only in their cultural background but also in their frequencies of alleles for a particular gene. In order to address this issue, some studies (e.g., H. S. Kim, Sherman, Sasaki et al., 2010) have included a third cultural group that shares their cultural context with one group (but not ethnicity) and shares their ethnicity with the other group (but not the cultural context). Using this triangulation method can determine whether a gene is interacting with culture, and not just another set of genes. Other studies that instead considered religious ideas as the cultural environment (e.g., Sasaki et al., 2013) have experimentally manipulated religious salience to determine causal effects of the religio-cultural environment depending on genes.

environment in contributing to personality stability over the course of development. Thus a more useful way to integrate the G $\times$ C model and personality may be to consider personality as one important mediator of G $\times$ C effects on psychological outcomes. When a study shows that a gene interacts with an aspect of the cultural environment to lead to a particular behavior, these effects still require a psychological account of why that effect occurred, and part of that account must include personality.

Research on personality stability suggests a strong genetic foundation for personality traits. According to a recent meta-analysis of data from 134 studies, 40% of individual differences were accounted for by genetic factors (Vukasović & Bratko, 2015). However, the environment plays an important role in a number of ways. First, environmental effects are often nonindependent of genetic effects, and second, genetic and environmental factors interact and can have variable effects on personality at different time points (Bleidorn et al., 2014). In particular, studies seem to suggest a decrease in heritability of personality traits across the life span (McCartney, Harris, & Bernieri, 1990; Viken, Rose, Kaprio, & Koskenvuo, 1994), and these changes in personality seem to result from differences in environmental factors that interact with genes (Kandler et al., 2010; see Caspi, Roberts, & Shiner, 2005, for review). Therefore, frameworks for studying culture and personality may benefit from examining findings at different crucial time points in development, including early childhood and young, middle, and older adulthood.

## Personality development across cultures

Personality development has been studied in various ways in the literature. In this chapter, we review cultural psychological findings on personality development that used any of the three methods at different developmental time points: comparing mean-level differences across different age cohorts and examining intraindividual changes over time (comparing rank-order changes over time or mean-level changes over time; Roberts & DelVecchio, 2000; Soto, John, Gosling, & Potter, 2011; Specht et al., 2011; Terracciano, McCrae, & Costa, 2010). Although these three methods look at personality changes in different ways, recent cross-sectional and longitudinal studies provide convergent evidence on personality development (Roberts, Walton, & Viechtbauer, 2006).

## Early childhood

**Parent—child attachment styles.** Classic work in attachment by Mary Ainsworth classified American infants according to a set of attachment styles, with secure being the most common and insecure variations (avoidant, ambivalent) being relatively less common (Ainsworth, Blehar, Waters, & Wall, 1978). Since then, researchers have set out to replicate these patterns of attachment styles in different cultures, and although there are similarities, there are a number of notable differences in attachment distributions that correspond with differences in cultural practices and values. In some cultures there seem to be differences, not in the proportion of secure attachment, but in the prevalent form of insecure attachment. In Japan, the insecurely attached infants were only insecure-ambivalent (also called insecure-resistant) rather than insecure-avoidant (Miyake, Chen, & Campos, 1985; Takahashi, 1986), and in Israel, there was a high frequency of insecure-ambivalent (Sagi et al., 1985); secure attachment was still the most common attachment style in both cultures. However, in Northern Germany the most common attachment style was insecure-avoidant, followed by secure and then insecure-ambivalent (Grossmann, Grossmann, Spangler, Suess, & Unzner, 1985). The authors of this research suggest that there seem to be differences in the way mothers interact with their infants in Northern Germany, where the culture may emphasize status and interpersonal distance even more than in North America, and these cultural differences may be related to the lower percentage of securely attached infants in Northern Germany.

Some cultural researchers have argued that the tenets of attachment theory, such as sensitivity and competence, are rooted in predominantly North American ideals of personal control and autonomy (Rothbaum, Weisz, Pott, Miyake, & Morelli, 2000), and in particular, the way that secure versus insecure attachment is manifested in children and interpreted by parents may differ depending on cultural values. For instance, mothers in the United States tend to associate secure attachment with a broader range of positive characteristics in personality and social skills, while Japanese mothers focus more on social roles and accommodating others in relationships as correlates of secure attachment (Rothbaum et al., 2007). The general message from these findings of cultural difference is that broader cultural values may be reflected in the relationship between caregivers and infants, leading to different patterns of attachment across cultures. Just as the caregiver—infant bond may change depending on the amount of resources or impending threats in the surrounding environment, it is perhaps unsurprising that different cultural ideals about how to be a good caregiver can have implications for patterns of attachment.

However, there are important similarities in attachment to note as well. While mothers in the United States and Japan may have different ideals for how a "good" infant should behave, mothers in both cultures agreed that secure attachment is related to desirable rather than undesirable child characteristics (Rothbaum et al., 2007). Consistent with this general finding, research comparing descriptions of secure-base behavior from mothers and childcare specialists found marked similarity across seven countries: China, Colombia, Germany, Israel, Japan, Norway, and the United States (Posada et al., 1995). Taking these findings of attachment similarities and differences together, it seems clear that caregivers across cultures are motivated to respond sensitively to their children in order to help them become good, competent members of society, but specific interpretations about what is "sensitive," "competent," or "good" may differ depending on culture. It is likely that the attachment system is attuned to responses from caregivers, which are inevitably shaped by a host of contextual variables, including resources and threats, as well as shared values and norms at the level of culture. Thus it is possible that different attachment styles very early in life (a form of personality) may be in part shaped by cultural information about good ways to interact with caregivers, with preferred attachment styles in a culture becoming relatively more prevalent and nonpreferred styles becoming less prevalent.

**Big Five personality traits**. Research on culture and personality can be traced to the Big Five personality research from the 1990s. The Big Five personality traits—Neuroticism, Extraversion, Openness, Agreeableness, and Conscientiousness—are supposed to capture the core features of personality. The Big Five personality structure appears to be well generalizable across different cultures and age groups (John, Caspi, Robins, Moffitt, & Stouthamer-Loeber, 1994; Schmitt, Allik, McCrae, & Benet-Martínez, 2007; Tackett et al., 2012), although Openness to Experience has not been identified in certain cultures and languages (De Raad et al., 2010).

Childhood is an important developmental period in its own right, especially for the development of personality. Childhood personality predicts a number of crucial future outcomes, including internalizing and externalizing problem behaviors (Denissen, Asendorpf, & van Aken, 2008), success and failure in school and the workplace (Asendorpf, Denissen, & van Aken, 2008), and social and romantic relationships (Ozer & Benet-Martínez, 2006; Simpson, 1999). A few studies have focused on personality development in young children, but most of these have been conducted in Western countries. In one longitudinal study, McCrae et al. (2002) examined personality changes of American and Flemish children from age 12 to 18. The largest age difference was observed for Openness, which increased from childhood to early adulthood in both cultural groups from the United States and Belgium, likely as a result of increased cognitive complexity. Neuroticism increased in girls but not in boys, and no differences were observed in the other three personality traits. Consistent with these findings, other studies provide further evidence that personality development largely follows the same patterns in childhood and adulthood. Individuals' normative increases in maturity occur through their reactions to social and physical environments (Roberts et al., 2006).

Other research including a wide variety of age groups (from 10 to 65 years) provided further support for the U-shaped developmental trend for personality with decreasing maturity during early adolescence and increasing maturity thereafter through mid to late adolescence (Soto et al., 2011). In this study, participants from English-speaking countries provided personality ratings online (72% were residents of the United States). Children's Conscientiousness levels, for instance, dropped in early adolescence but increased in mid to late adolescence. Although only a handful of studies have directly focused on young children from a cross-cultural perspective, many of these studies show evidence of similar developmental patterns for Big Five personality traits in different cultures, at least within North America and parts of Europe.

However, some studies show evidence of cross-cultural differences. One study by Branje, Van Lieshout, and Gerris (2007) compared mean levels of personality between young Dutch children aged 11–15 years and found age and gender differences in personality development. The results were somewhat inconsistent with previous results on American children. Openness increased in girls but not boys.

Furthermore, Extraversion increased for boys, and Extraversion, Agreeableness, and Emotional Stability (reversed Neuroticism) increased for girls. These gender and age differences in the Netherlands may reflect cultural practices and perhaps genetic factors and socio-economic factors in the Netherlands. Compared to the United States, there is a greater gender gap in wages and labor force participation rates, in that men are more likely to be employed compared to women in the Netherlands (see Evertsson et al., 2009). Accordingly, these differences in cultural environments may interact with individuals' personality, values, and beliefs (e.g., child personality and parenting philosophies). Another possible explanation is that there might be differences in genetic tendencies in the two cultures. Even if there are shared cultural values between the Netherlands and the United States, similar cultural environments can interact with the (potentially different) genetic tendencies in the two countries, which may lead to different psychological outcomes.

As most studies on personality development usually start in adolescence, at this time, it is difficult to draw definitive inferences about the contribution of genetic and environmental factors on personality development. Most studies on personality development of young children were predominantly conducted in North America and Western Europe; thus, more research needs to be conducted in cultural groups that are less frequently studied to examine intercultural similarities and differences in personality development among children.

## Personality development in young, middle, and older adulthood

One of the most commonly studied populations in psychological research is young adults (Henrich, Heine, & Norenzayan, 2010). Much psychological research has been conducted on university students mostly for practical reasons. A few large-scale, cross-sectional, and longitudinal studies on personality provide insights into the intercultural similarities and differences in personality development during adulthood. Indeed, one longitudinal study of the Big Five assessed North American university students' personality when they first entered the university and 4 years later (Robins, Fraley, Roberts, & Trzesniewski, 2001). Except for one trait (Extraversion), individuals showed normative changes in their personality, meaning their scores on Conscientiousness, Agreeableness, Openness, and Emotional Stability increased over time. These findings are consistent with a large-scale, cross-cultural investigation with college students from 50 countries (McCrae, Terracciano, & Members of the Personality Profiles of Cultures Project, 2005), suggesting there are similar cross-cultural patterns of personality change in adulthood.

Personality traits continue to change and develop throughout adulthood (Fraley & Roberts, 2005). For example, in one of the first cross-cultural studies on age differences in personality, McCrae et al. (1999) compared personality across various age groups (age group 18−21, 22−29, 30−49, and 50 years and above) in five different cultural groups: Germany, Italy, Portugal, Croatia, and South Korea. This study showed consistent age differences across the cultural groups. College students scored highest on Extraversion and Openness and declined thereafter. The three other traits—Conscientiousness, Agreeableness, and Emotional Stability—increased as people aged from early adulthood to older adulthood. The developmental patterns were consistent across the cultural groups, but a few cultural differences were observed. For instance, Germans experienced relatively steep age-related personality changes, with young Germans (aged 18−21) showing lower levels of Conscientiousness compared to young Portuguese and both cultural groups showing similar levels of Conscientiousness in middle adulthood. Another study by McCrae et al. (2000) observed similar patterns in samples drawn from the United Kingdom, Germany, Spain, the Czech Republic, and Turkey. Perhaps most informative, further studies based on nationally representative data from 50 countries found similar age-related maturation in personality traits (Donnellan & Lucas, 2008; McCrae & Terracciano, 2005). All of these studies support the notion that personality development is likely to have a strong genetic component, but importantly, similarities across cultures can mean either that differences in these cultures did not lead to significant differences in personality traits or that the environments in these studies included similar key factors across cultural groups.

More recent studies may shed some light on the genetic and environmental origins of personality development (Bleidorn et al., 2013; Briley & Tucker-Drob, 2014). Bleidorn et al. (2013) analyzed a large internet-based database of young adults from 62 countries to test two theories providing different explanations for these age effects on personality development. They focused on five different age groups in their cross-sectional study: 16−20, 21−25, 26−30, 31−35, and 36−40. The Five Factor Theory (McCrae et al., 2000), which proposes that maturation is largely determined by genetic factors, would predict similar age differences in personality across various cultural groups. The social investment theory (Roberts, Wood, & Smith, 2005) proposes that personality maturation is influenced by not only genetic factors but (crucial) environmental factors that should matter for personality, such as transition into adult roles, and this theory predicts different patterns of age differences across cultural groups. Indeed, their research findings provided evidence for the latter argument. Individuals from countries that tend to adopt adult roles earlier (i.e., earlier transition into labor force) showed accelerated forms of personality development compared to individuals from countries that have later workforce entry. For instance, individuals from Pakistan, Malaysia, and Brazil enter the workforce sooner than individuals from Argentina (average scores on timing of job transition out of 62 countries) and individuals from the Netherlands, Canada, and the United States (latest transition into labor force). Correspondingly, there were accelerated increases in Emotional Stability, Agreeableness, and Conscientiousness, and decreases in Openness and Extraversion in cultures such as Pakistan, where people take on adult roles earlier. In other words, individuals from Pakistan are more likely to show psychological maturation earlier to fulfill adult-role responsibilities at an earlier age. According to this research, cross-cultural level variables explained 11−25% of the cross-cultural variance in age effects on the Big Five traits. In other words, culture-level variables partially explained the difference in cultural patterns of personality development. Importantly, consistent with previous findings, a mainly universal pattern of personality development was observed across different cultural groups. These results may provide a basis for a more comprehensive understanding of the determinants of personality by elucidating how genetic and nonshared environmental factors are both clearly involved in personality development (Bleidorn et al., 2014).

A few studies focusing on an older age group found an inverted U-shaped pattern for rank-order stability of Emotional Stability, Extraversion, Openness, and Agreeableness, with peak stability occurring in middle age and a decrease in stability occurring after age 60 in the German and Australian national representative samples (Lucas & Donnellan, 2011; Specht et al., 2011; Wortman, Lucas, & Donnellan, 2012). Yet discrepancies were observed concerning the direction of the relationship between certain personality traits and age in the US and Swiss nationally representative samples (Anusic, Lucas, & Donnellan, 2012).

The majority of the described studies on personality development in childhood and adulthood were based on cross-sectional data that examined cultural differences in personality trait levels. The sole reliance on cross-sectional study can be problematic in examining personality development as it confounds age and cohort effects. Yet it is important to point out that cross-sectional data provides us important information about the social and cultural changes between birth cohorts (Twenge, 2000, 2001). In the United States, for instance, mean levels of Extraversion and Neuroticism have increased in recent decades. The increases in narcissistic personality traits among American university students are theorized to be the result of larger culture-level changes in the United States involving parenting and education. The cultural shift toward encouraging very high self-esteem, individual achievement, money, and fame may have had far-reaching effects on psychological traits in recent generations. Thus exploring and measuring personality development using multimethod approaches may help us understand how genetic and environmental factors interact to influence average personality tendencies in different cultures, and how personality predicts different psychological outcomes across the life span.

# Future directions in personality development across cultures

For future research on culture and personality development, we have a number of recommendations. First, in terms of methods, it is important to consider language differences in intercultural comparisons. Thus measurement invariance needs to be established to ensure that the constructs measured are comparable across cultures. Two ways to accomplish this are (1) to establish measurement invariance before making cross-cultural comparisons and (2) to focus on bilingual immigrants and trace their personality development using two language versions of the same measure. Second, we would like to emphasize the importance of exploring intercultural similarities and differences at the facet level, which can provide a richer understanding of developing patterns of different cultures. The majority of previous cultural studies focused on personality changes at the trait level. However, some research provides important insights into cultural differences in personality at the facet level (e.g., positive emotion facet of Extraversion) and cultural differences in the relationship between personality and psychological outcomes at the facet level (Suh, Diener, Oishi, & Triandis, 1998). It is also crucial to consider systematic differences in response styles across cultures (Cheung & Rensvold, 2000). People may differ in the way they respond to items or provide inflated evaluations of themselves. Compared to individuals with Asian ethnic backgrounds, individuals with European ethnic backgrounds tended to show more overly positive self-evaluations whereas Asians were more likely to show ambivalent and moderate responses (Hamamura, Heine, & Paulhus, 2008), and/or less overly positive self-evaluations (H. Kim, Schimmack, Cheng, Webster, & Spectre, 2016; H. Kim, Schimmack, & Oishi, 2012). As these evaluation biases are systematic and highly reproducible, it is important to account for these cultural differences in evaluative biases in examining personality development.

# Conclusion

In this chapter, we reviewed cross-cultural research that used one (or more) of the three commonly used methods to understand personality development: (1) examining mean-level differences across different age cohorts, (2) examining mean-level changes in personality over time, and (3) examining rank-order changes in personality over time. These different methods help us understand the psychological reasons for the observed cultural similarities and differences in personality. For example, although age and cohort effects are confounded in a single cross-sectional study, it still provides valuable insights into the differences in personality development across various age groups.

Accumulated evidence has demonstrated the influence of genetic and environmental factors on personality development. People from countries that enter the labor force earlier than later showed an accelerated increase in maturity-related traits, such as Agreeableness, Conscientiousness, and Emotional Stability. Yet studies show a universal pattern of personality development across the life span: people becoming more conscientious, agreeable, and emotionally stable as they get older. Findings of cultural similarities in personality development should not be interpreted as a diminished role of culture. People in different cultures may show similar patterns of personality because they are engaging in "universal life tasks" at similar life stages (Bleidorn, 2012; Bleidorn et al., 2013; Lodi-Smith & Roberts, 2007), and even when studying personality within a single group, the role of culture is to be explained. Genes do not act in isolation from culture to build personality tendencies, but rather are in constant interaction with it. Indeed, cultural inputs are a necessary part of personality development everywhere.

One way to think about culture is as a form of social feedback about one's behaviors, including those based on personality traits. There seems to be consistent similarities in personality development across cultures, perhaps due to genetic variation within a population, but there are interesting differences between cultures as well (e.g., different timing of entry into labor force). Where cultural differences exist, these could be due to reinforcement or dampening of behaviors from cultural values. It is possible that certain personality types are approved or disapproved of depending on what is valued in a culture, and these values can work to maintain cultural patterns of personality over time.

# References

Ainsworth, M. D. S., Blehar, M. C., Waters, E., & Wall, S. (1978). *Patterns of attachment: A psychological study of the strange situation*. Hillsdale, NJ: Erlbaum.

Anusic, I., Lucas, R. E., & Donnellan, M. B. (2012). Cross-sectional age differences in personality: Evidence from nationally representative samples from Switzerland and the United States. *Journal of Research in Personality, 46*, 116–120.

Asendorpf, J. B., Denissen, J. J. A., & van Aken, M. A. G. (2008). Inhibited and aggressive preschool children at 23 years of age: Personality and social transitions into adulthood. *Developmental Psychology, 44*, 997–1011.

Bleidorn, W. (2012). Hitting the road to adulthood: Short-term personality development during a major life transition. *Personality and Social Psychology Bulletin, 38*, 1594–1608.

Bleidorn, W., Kandler, C., & Caspi, A. (2014). The behavioural genetics of personality development in adulthood—Classic, contemporary, and future trends. *European Journal of Personality, 28*, 244–255.

Bleidorn, W., Klimstra, T. A., Denissen, J. J., Rentfrow, P. J., Potter, J., & Gosling, S. D. (2013). Personality maturation around the world a cross-cultural examination of social-investment theory. *Psychological Science, 24*, 2530–2540.

Branje, S. J., Van Lieshout, C. F., & Gerris, J. R. (2007). Big Five personality development in adolescence and adulthood. *European Journal of Personality, 21*, 45–62.

Briley, D. A., & Tucker-Drob, E. M. (2014). Genetic and environmental continuity in personality development: A meta-analysis. *Psychological Bulletin, 140*, 1303–1331.

Bruner, J. S. (1990). *Acts of meaning*. Cambridge, MA: Harvard University Press.

Caspi, A., Roberts, B. W., & Shiner, R. L. (2005). Personality development: Stability and change. *Annual Review of Psychology, 56*, 453–484.

Caspi, A., Sugden, K., Moffitt, T. E., Taylor, A., Craig, I. W., Harrington, H., et al. (2003). Influence of life stress on depression: Moderation by a polymorphism in the 5-HTT gene. *Science, 301*, 386–389.

Cheung, G. W., & Rensvold, R. B. (2000). Assessing extreme and acquiescence response sets in cross-cultural research using structural equations modeling. *Journal of Cross-Cultural Psychology, 31*, 187–212.

Cohen, A. B. (2009). Many forms of culture. *American Psychologist, 64*, 194–204.

Cohen, A. B., & Rozin, P. (2001). Religion and the morality of mentality. *Journal of Personality and Social Psychology, 81*, 697–710.

Cohen, D., Nisbett, R. E., Bowdle, B. F., & Schwarz, N. (1996). Insult, aggression, and the Southern culture of honor: An "experimental ethnography." *Journal of Personality and Social Psychology, 70*, 945–960.

Denissen, J. J. A., Asendorpf, J. B., & van Aken, M. A. G. (2008). Childhood personality predicts long-term trajectories of shyness and aggressiveness in the context of demographic transitions in emerging adulthood. *Journal of Personality, 76*, 67−99.

De Raad, B., Barelds, D. P., Levert, E., Ostendorf, F., Mlačić, B., Blas, L. D., ... Church, A. T. (2010). Only three factors of personality description are fully replicable across languages: A comparison of 14 trait taxonomies. *Journal of Personality and Social Psychology, 98*, 160−173.

Donnellan, A. B., & Lucas, R. E. (2008). Age differences in the Big Five across the life span: Evidence from two national samples. *Psychology and Aging, 23*, 558−566.

Evertsson, M., England, P., Mooi-Reci, I., Hermsen, J., de Bruijn, J., & Cotter, D. (2009). Is gender inequality greater at lower or higher educational levels? Common patterns in the Netherlands, Sweden, and the United States. *Social Politics: International Studies in Gender, State & Society, 16*, 210−241.

Fraley, R. C., & Roberts, B. W. (2005). Patterns of continuity: A dynamic model for conceptualizing the stability of individual differences in psychological constructs across the life course. *Psychological Review, 112*, 60−74.

Gebauer, J. E., Bleidorn, W., Gosling, S. D., Rentfrow, P. J., Lamb, M. E., & Potter, J. (2014). Cross-cultural variations in Big Five relationships with religiosity: A sociocultural motives perspective. *Journal of Personality and Social Psychology, 107*, 1064−1091.

Grossmann, K., Grossmann, K. E., Spangler, G., Suess, G., & Unzner, L. (1985). Maternal sensitivity and newborns orientation responses as related to quality of attachment in Northern Germany. Growing points in attachment theory and research. *Child Development, 50*, 233−256.

Hamamura, T., Heine, S. J., & Paulhus, D. L. (2008). Cultural differences in response styles: The role of dialectical thinking. *Personality and Individual Differences, 44*, 932−942.

Henrich, J., Heine, S. J., & Norenzayan, A. (2010). The weirdest people in the world? *Behavioral and Brain Sciences, 33*, 61−135.

Ishii, K., Kim, H. S., Sasaki, J. Y., Shinada, M., & Kusumi, I. (2014). Culture modulates sensitivity to the disappearance of facial expressions associated with serotonin transporter polymorphism (5-HTTLPR). *Culture and Brain, 2*, 72−88.

John, O. P., Caspi, A., Robins, R. W., Moffitt, T. E., & Stouthamer-Loeber, M. (1994). The "Little Five": Exploring the nomological network of the five-factor model of personality in adolescent boys. *Child Development, 65*, 160−178.

Kandler, C., Bleidorn, W., Riemann, R., Spinath, F. M., Thiel, W., & Angleitner, A. (2010). Sources of cumulative continuity in personality: A longitudinal multiple-rater twin study. *Journal of Personality and Social Psychology, 98*, 995−1008.

Kim, H., Schimmack, U., Cheng, C., Webster, G. D., & Spectre, A. (2016). The role of positive self-evaluation on cross-cultural differences in well-being. *Cross-Cultural Research, 50*, 85−99.

Kim, H., Schimmack, U., & Oishi, S. (2012). Cultural differences in self- and other-evaluations and well-being: A study of European and Asian Canadians. *Journal of Personality and Social Psychology, 102*, 856−873.

Kim, H. S., Sherman, D. K., Mojaverian, T., Sasaki, J. Y., Park, J., Suh, E. M., & Taylor, S. E. (2011). Gene−culture interaction: Oxytocin receptor polymorphism (OXTR) and emotion regulation. *Social Psychological and Personality Science, 2*, 665−672.

Kim, H. S., Sherman, D. K., Sasaki, J. Y., Xu, J., Chu, T. Q., Ryu, C., ... Taylor, S. E. (2010). Culture, distress and oxytocin receptor polymorphism (OXTR) interact to influence emotional support seeking. *Proceedings of the National Academy of Sciences, 107*, 15717−15721.

Kim, H. S., Sherman, D. K., Taylor, S. E., Sasaki, J. Y., Chu, T. Q., Ryu, C., ... Xu, J. (2010). Culture, the serotonin receptor polymorphism (5-HTR1A), and locus of attention. *Social Cognitive and Affective Neuroscience, 5,* 212–218.

Kitayama, S., Ishii, K., Imada, T., Takemura, K., & Ramaswamy, J. (2006). Voluntary settlement and the spirit of independence: Evidence from Japan's "Northern Frontier." *Journal of Personality and Social Psychology, 91,* 369–384.

Leung, A. K.-Y., & Cohen, D. (2011). Within- and between-culture variation: Individual differences and the cultural logics of honor, face, and dignity cultures. *Journal of Personality and Social Psychology, 100,* 507–526.

Lodi-Smith, J., & Roberts, B. W. (2007). Social investment and personality: A meta-analysis of the relationship of personality traits to investment in work, family, religion, and volunteerism. *Personality and Social Psychology Review, 11,* 68–86.

Lucas, R. E., & Donnellan, M. B. (2011). Personality development across the life span: Longitudinal analyses with a national sample from Germany. *Journal of Personality and Social Psychology, 101,* 847–861.

McCartney, K., Harris, M. J., & Bernieri, F. (1990). Growing up and growing apart: A developmental meta-analysis of twin studies. *Psychological Bulletin, 107,* 226–237.

McCrae, R. R., Costa, P. T., de Lima, M. P., Simões, A., Ostendorf, F., Angleitner, A., ... Piedmont, R. L. (1999). Age differences in personality across the adult life span: Parallels in five cultures. *Developmental Psychology, 35,* 466–477.

McCrae, R. R., Costa, P. T., Jr., Ostendorf, F., Angleitner, A., Hrebickova, M., Avia, M. D., ... Smith, P. B. (2000). Nature over nurture: Temperament, personality, and life span development. *Journal of Personality and Social Psychology, 78,* 173–186.

McCrae, R. R., Costa, P. T., Jr, Terracciano, A., Parker, W. D., Mills, C. J., De Fruyt, F., & Mervielde, I. (2002). Personality trait development from age 12 to age 18: Longitudinal, cross-sectional and cross-cultural analyses. *Journal of Personality and Social Psychology, 83,* 1456–1468.

McCrae, R. R., & Terracciano, A. (2005). Universal features of personality traits from the observer's perspective: Data from 50 cultures. *Journal of Personality and Social Psychology, 88,* 547–561.

McCrae, R. R., Terracciano, A., & Members of the Personality Profiles of Cultures Project (2005). Universal features of personality traits from the observer's perspective: Data from 50 cultures. *Journal of Personality and Social Psychology, 88,* 547–561.

Miyake, K., Chen, S., & Campos, J. J. (1985). Infant temperament, mother's mode of interaction, and attachment in Japan: An interim report. In I. Bretherton, & E. Waters (Eds.), *Growing points of attachment theory and research* (pp. 276–297). Chicago, IL: Chicago University Press.

Morling, B., & Lamoreaux, M. (2008). Measuring culture outside the head: A meta-analysis of individualism–collectivism in cultural products. *Personality and Social Psychology Review, 12,* 199–221.

Na, J., Grossman, I., Varnum, M. E. W., Kitayama, S., Gonzalez, R., & Nisbett, R. E. (2010). Cultural differences are not always reducible to individual differences. *Proceedings of the National Academy of Sciences, 107,* 6192–6197.

Ozer, D. J., & Benet-Martínez, V. (2006). Personality and the prediction of consequential outcomes. *Annual Review of Psychology, 57,* 401–421.

Posada, G., Goa, Y., Wu, F., Posada, R., Tascon, M., Schoelmerich, A., ... Synnevaag, B. (1995). The secure-base phenomenon across cultures: Children's behavior, mothers' preferences, and experts' concepts. *Monographs of the Society for Research in Child Development, 60*(2–3), 27–47.

Roberts, B. W., & DelVecchio, W. F. (2000). The rank-order consistency of personality traits from childhood to old age: A quantitative review of longitudinal studies. *Psychological Bulletin, 126*, 3−25.

Roberts, B. W., Walton, K. E., & Viechtbauer, W. (2006). Patterns of mean-level change in personality traits across the life course: A meta-analysis of longitudinal studies. *Psychological Bulletin, 132*, 1−25.

Roberts, B. W., Wood, D., & Caspi, A. (2008). The development of personality traits in adulthood. In O. P. John (Ed.), *Handbook of personality: Theory and research* (3rd ed., pp. 375−398). New York, NY: Guilford Press.

Roberts, B. W., Wood, D., & Smith, J. L. (2005). Evaluating five factor theory and social investment perspectives on personality trait development. *Journal of Research in Personality, 39*, 166−184.

Robins, R. W., Fraley, R. C., Roberts, B. W., & Trzesniewski, K. H. (2001). A longitudinal study of personality change in young adulthood. *Journal of Personality, 69*, 617−640.

Rothbaum, F., Kakinuma, M., Nagaoka, R., & Azuma, H. (2007). Attachment and amae: Parent−child closeness in the United States and Japan. *Journal of Cross-Cultural Psychology, 38*, 465−486.

Rothbaum, F., Weisz, J., Pott, M., Miyake, K., & Morelli, G. (2000). Attachment and culture: Security in the United States and Japan. *American Psychologist, 55*, 1093−1104.

Sagi, A., Lamb, M. E., Lewkowicz, K. S., Shoham, R., Dvir, R., & Estes, D. (1985). Security of infant−mother, −father, and −metapelet attachments among kibbutz-reared Israeli children. *Monographs of the Society for Research in Child Development, 50*(1−2), 257−275, 209.

Sasaki, J. Y., Kim, H. S., & Xu, J. (2011). Religion and well-being: The moderating role of culture and the oxytocin receptor (OXTR) gene. *Journal of Cross-Cultural Psychology, 42*, 1394−1405.

Sasaki, J. Y., Kim, H. S., Mojaverian, T., Kelley, L. D., Park, I., & Janušonis, S. (2013). Religion priming differentially increases prosocial behavior among variants of dopamine D4 receptor (DRD4) gene. *Social Cognitive and Affective Neuroscience, 8*, 209−215.

Schmitt, D. P., Allik, J., McCrae, R. R., & Benet-Martínez, V. (2007). The geographic distribution of Big Five personality traits patterns and profiles of human self-description across 56 nations. *Journal of Cross-Cultural Psychology, 38*, 173−212.

Simpson, J. A. (1999). Attachment theory in modern evolutionary perspective. In J. Cassidy, & P. R. Shaver (Eds.), *Handbook of attachment* (pp. 115−140). New York, NY: Guilford.

Soto, C. J., John, O. P., Gosling, S. D., & Potter, J. (2011). Age differences in personality traits from 10 to 65: Big Five domains and facets in a large cross-sectional sample. *Journal of Personality and Social Psychology, 100*, 330−348.

Specht, J., Egloff, B., & Schmukle, S. C. (2011). Stability and change of personality across the life course: The impact of age and major life events on mean-level and rank-order stability of the Big Five. *Journal of Personality and Social Psychology, 101*, 862−882.

Srivastava, S., John, O. P., Gosling, S. D., & Potter, J. (2003). Development of personality in early and middle adulthood: Set like plaster or persistent change? *Journal of Personality and Social Psychology, 84*, 1041−1053.

Stephens, N. M., Markus, H. R., & Townsend, S. S. M. (2007). Choice as an act of meaning: The case of social class. *Journal of Personality and Social Psychology, 93*, 814−830.

Suh, E., Diener, E., Oishi, S., & Triandis, H. C. (1998). The shifting basis of life satisfaction judgments across cultures: Emotions versus norms. *Journal of Personality and Social Psychology, 74*, 482−493.

Tackett, J. L., Slobodskaya, H. R., Mar, R. A., Deal, J., Halverson, C. F., Baker, S. R., ... Besevegis, E. (2012). The hierarchical structure of childhood personality in five countries: Continuity from early childhood to early adolescence. *Journal of Personality, 80*, 847–879.

Takahashi, K. (1986). The role of the personal frame mark of social relationships in socialization studies. In H. Stevenson, H. Azuma, & K. Hakuta (Eds.), *Child development and education in Japan* (pp. 123–135). New York, NY: Freeman.

Terracciano, A., McCrae, R. R., & Costa, P. T. (2010). Intra-individual change in personality stability and age. *Journal of Research in Personality, 44*, 31–37.

Twenge, J. M. (2000). The age of anxiety? Birth cohort change in anxiety and neuroticism, 1952–1993. *Journal of Personality and Social Psychology, 79*, 1007–1021.

Twenge, J. M. (2001). Birth cohort changes in extraversion: A cross-temporal meta-analysis, 1966–1993. *Personality and Individual Differences, 30*, 735–748.

Viken, R. J., Rose, R. J., Kaprio, J., & Koskenvuo, M. (1994). A developmental genetic analysis of adult personality: Extraversion and neuroticism from 18 to 59 years of age. *Journal of Personality and Social Psychology, 66*, 722–730.

Vukasović, T., & Bratko, D. (2015). Heritability of personality: A meta-analysis of behavior genetic studies. *Psychological Bulletin, 141*, 769–785.

Wortman, J., Lucas, R. E., & Donnellan, M. B. (2012). Stability and change in the Big Five personality domains: Evidence from a longitudinal study of Australians. *Psychology and Aging, 27*, 867–874.

# Part Six

# Methods in Research on Personality Development

# Personality assessment in daily life: A roadmap for future personality development research

**27**

*Mathias Allemand[1] and Matthias R. Mehl[2]*
[1]University of Zurich, Zurich, Switzerland, [2]University of Arizona, Tucson, AZ, United States

## Introduction

Research in the field of personality development has shown that personality can change and continues to change in adulthood into old age (see McAdams & Olson, 2010; Roberts, Wood, & Caspi, 2008, for reviews). Changes in personality are typically accompanied by individual differences in change, implying that people differ in the direction and the amount or patterns of change as they move through adulthood (Allemand, Zimprich, & Martin, 2008; Roberts & Mroczek, 2008). These unique patterns of change may reflect the result of specific life experiences and events, exposure to diverse or varying environmental contexts, and a variety of adaptive processes and behaviors that people use in everyday life to maintain well-being and health. Regardless of individual differences in change, some general patterns of change have been consistently observed in previous research. For example, people tend to become more socially dominant (a facet of extraversion with attributes that are linked to self-confidence and independence), more agreeable and more conscientious, and less neurotic as they move through adulthood (Roberts, Walton, & Viechtbauer, 2006). These changes are often viewed as positive trends, given that higher levels of agreeableness and conscientiousness and lower levels of neuroticism are associated with desirable outcomes, such as greater success in work and family and better health and longevity (Roberts, Kuncel, Shiner, Caspi, & Goldberg, 2007). Research has also shown that both level and change of personality can predict greater success in work and family, and better health and longevity (Allemand, Steiger, & Fend, 2015; Mroczek & Spiro, 2007; Steiger, Allemand, Robins, & Fend, 2014).

Personality development is one of the most growing fields of research in personality science. But there is still a lot to be learned about the ways in which personality processes are assembled and unfold over time. One of the greatest challenges for future research refers to personality assessment, as the majority of previous research on personality development relied almost exclusively on self-report methods (e.g., questionnaires, interviews) to assess personality and to capture change (Baumeister, Vohs, & Funder, 2007). Although self-reports represent a popular and cheap way in terms of time and costs of obtaining data and are reliable and valid

Personality Development Across the Lifespan. DOI: http://dx.doi.org/10.1016/B978-0-12-804674-6.00027-2

assessment tools, the field of personality development would strongly profit from using multiple methods, such as combining self-report methods with observer ratings and partner reports, physiological assessment, behavioral and cognitive experiments, and daily life assessment paradigms. This is also important with respect to age-fair personality assessment, as young children and very old adults with functional impairments may not provide reliable self-reports.

A particular valuable approach is to assess personality processes outside the laboratory directly within people's natural environments (Reis & Gosling, 2010; Wrzus & Mehl, 2015; see Mehl & Conner, 2012, for a comprehensive review). Such a real-world assessment approach would help to capture the way in which lives are lived and experienced in their natural settings, in (close to) real time, and on repeated occasions, to better understand the processes underlying personality change and stability over time. What exactly does it mean in daily life to become more socially dominant, agreeable and conscientious, and less neurotic? How are personality changes manifested in daily life? What are the underlying processes that promote change or maintain stability? Do self-reported changes in personality reflect changes of perceptions and representations or do they also reflect actual and observable behavior changes? How can personality change processes be assessed or tracked in daily life as they occur? These questions call for research using daily life assessment paradigms. The goal of this chapter is thus to emphasize the relevance of assessing personality in daily life and to give a nontechnical overview of psychological and technological assessment advances that may provide novel and complementary assessment perspectives for the field of personality development.

## Conceptualizing personality

Personality can be conceptualized from multiple perspectives that may have differential implications for personality assessment in daily life. For example, McAdams (2013, 2015) offers a conceptual framework with three different albeit related standpoints or perspectives from which personality can be understood. Each standpoint focuses on unique units of analysis of personality. The first standpoint refers to personality characteristics that describe how people as social actors typically behave on the social stage of life, and encompasses personality characteristics such as traits, skills, and social roles. The second standpoint refers to characteristics that describe people as motivated agents and includes motivational characteristics such as personal goals, motives, values, and envisioned projects. The third standpoint conceptualizes people as autobiographical authors who narrate life stories as aspects of personality. Life narratives are the key units of analysis from this perspective. To assess constructs related to the three standpoints, researchers typically use a different set of methods such as self-reports and observer reports to assess traits and interview methods to assess life stories.

A real-world assessment approach would be particularly suited to capture the ways in which individuals behave as social actors on the social stage of life and how these behavioral patterns change over time. This chapter therefore focuses on the assessment of personality traits and especially their state manifestations in daily life as units of analysis. Personality traits are defined as relatively enduring tendencies for certain behaviors and experiences including thoughts and feelings (e.g., Roberts, 2009). Traits describe the most basic and general dimensions upon which individuals are typically perceived to differ. These individual differences are organized within the prominent conceptual framework of the Big Five dimensions (John, Naumann, & Soto, 2008).

In general, personality traits are thought to be relatively stable over time and thus reflect slow developmental processes. Assessing personality thus requires repeated assessments over longer periods of time to capture the long-term developmental processes. In contrast, the state manifestations of traits or how people behave in a given moment are more dynamic and fluctuating over shorter time periods. Unlike traits, states reflect dynamic processes of personality that show temporary changes in response to internal aspects such as motives and goals and external situations such as stress in a given situation or real-life context (Fleeson, 2001; Hooker & McAdams, 2003). States reflect the ways how individuals think, feel, or behave in a given situation, and thus reflect the manifestations of the traits. They are transient and involve change and variability over short periods of time. Assessing personality processes requires intensive, multiple repeated assessments over short periods of time to capture the short-term dynamics in daily life and the fluctuations over short time intervals. Such an approach provides information about the underlying processes of change or maintenance as they occur in addition to longer developmental change processes (Noftle & Fleeson, 2010, 2015).

## Contextualizing personality

Just as it is important to consider multiple perspectives on personality, it is important to consider personality in different life contexts and to assess personality at different levels of specificity. The appropriate level of specificity is important with respect to the assessment of contextualized personality constructs, as broader constructs such as the Big Five traits are typically less contextualized (Heller, Watson, Komar, Min, & Perunovic, 2007; Roberts, 2007; Roberts & Pomerantz, 2004). Only assessing constructs at a broad level may fail to capture the nuances present when evaluating specific life contexts or given situations. For example, when broad constructs are assessed, narrower facets that are correlated with criteria in the opposite directions may cancel each other out and mitigate the correlation with the criterion (Paunonen, 1998). In addition, the narrow personality characteristics associated with a broader personality trait have been shown to be negatively correlated, positively correlated, or not correlated at all with an outcome variable (Wood, Nye, & Saucier, 2010), a point that would be obscured by looking at the trait only at the broader level.

The appropriate breadth of personality assessment is important from a developmental perspective, as it may moderate age trends. For example, research has begun to investigate how age differences and age-related changes in the broad Big Five traits coincide with age differences and changes in narrower traits, or facet traits, that compose those domains (Jackson et al., 2009; Terracciano, McCrae, Brant, & Costa, 2005). Indeed, a study found that related but distinguishable facet traits within each broad trait domain show distinct age trends (Soto, John, Gosling, & Potter, 2011). These examples point to the need of using both broad and narrow measures of personality. If domain-specific personality aspects show identical or nearly identical chronological age and/or time trends, then a more generalized measure of personality would be sufficient to capture all of the important information about age differences in personality. If, however, domain-specific personality shows different age and/or time trends, then research is needed at the narrow level to achieve a full understanding of personality across adulthood.

Within the field of personality development some researchers assume a theoretical hierarchy of changeability, such that some attributes of personality such as the state manifestations of traits like discrete thoughts, feelings, and behaviors are assumed to be more contextualized, more changeable and variable, and more responsive to external and internal influences compared to broad and enduring personality traits. Several conceptualizations of personality make a distinction between different levels of specificity (e.g., Roberts & Pomerantz, 2004; Roberts & Jackson, 2008; Rosenberg, 1998; Wood & Roberts, 2006). For example, Roberts and Pomerantz' (2004) model includes three levels of person and contextual breadth ranging from narrow to broad levels. At the narrowest level, discrete trait-related thoughts, feelings, and behaviors (i.e., state manifestations of traits) may be more changeable than midlevel constructs such as habits or generalized emotional experiences, or broad constructs such as personality traits. Similarly, the proximal situation at the narrowest level is more changeable than the organizational climate at the medium level or the culture and geographic regions at the broad level. The level of discrete trait-related thoughts, feelings, and behaviors can be seen as the most dynamic as it reflects the ways how people think, feel, or behave in a given situation or daily life context. It is believed that person and situation constructs are at the broad level more general and enduring and at the narrow level more specific and passing or changeable due to specific circumstances and life contexts.

This chapter focuses primarily on the assessment of the state manifestations of personality traits in everyday life, because assessment at this level of specificity can provide more information about natural life contexts and social settings. The daily life contexts are the stages in which the development of each individual takes place. That is, individuals are embedded in dynamic social environments that create opportunities and constraints for individual developmental pathways. Thus the ultimate goal of personality (change) assessment must be to understand "what people actually do, think, and feel in the various contexts of their lives" (Funder, 2001, p. 213).

# Assessing personality in daily life contexts

With a few notable exceptions, existing longitudinal personality development studies covering years or decades relied most exclusively on single method assessment approaches based on self-reports or observer ratings. As such, improving and expanding personality assessment methods is one of the most important tasks necessary for creating a sustainable future for the field of personality development. Moreover, assessing personality processes in real-life contexts is an important avenue for the field of personality development for several reasons (cf. Wilhelm, Perrez, & Pawlik, 2012). First, assessing personality in daily life helps to better understand how people think, feel, and behave, and how changes in thoughts, feelings, and behaviors are manifested in everyday life and not only in the laboratory or with respect to retrospective or generalized responses in self-report questionnaires. Hence, collecting real-world evidence of people's unique everyday contexts, behaviors, resources, and ways of regulating the ongoing demands and challenges of daily life, well-being and health would help to better understand the ways in which personality processes are assembled and unfold in natural settings (close to) real time, and on repeated occasions. It would also help to better describe, explain, and predict the essential underlying processes and determinants of change and stability over time. Hence, a real-life assessment approach would increase ecological validity as the extent to which research findings on personality development such as increases in conscientiousness would generalize to settings typical of everyday life.

Second, assessing personality in daily life deals with the concern of the validity of retrospective or generalized responses obtained with questionnaires or interviews. Self-reports and interview methods are often biased by memory processes and cognitive heuristics, and they leave open the possibility that people respond on the basis of what they consider typical or socially desirable (Schwarz, 2012). Data captured in real-time tend to be less susceptible to such recall processes and memory distortions.

Third, assessing personality processes in real-life contexts requires repeated assessments for each person to better understand intraindividual variation of experience and behavior across unrestrained real-life conditions. Personality processes typically occur within people over time, but they also happen across people. Within-individual approaches may reveal different answers than between-individual approaches, because personality variables may vary across individuals for different reasons than why they may vary within individuals across repeated measurement occasions (Molenaar & Campbell, 2009). Both approaches are important. The between-individual variation reflects human individuality, whereas the within-individual variation may give important information about the experiences, behaviors, and processes of individuals' lives (Mroczek, Spiro, & Almeida, 2003). Importantly, age-fairness in personality assessment is most immediately concerned with the nature of between-individual variability; however, within-person processes can also be operating differentially at the measurement level across different age groups.

Finally, innovations and emerging technological developments in sensor-enable technologies, especially smartphones, create new opportunities for the assessment of personality in daily life and provide valuable data for the field of personality development (Intille, 2012; Mehl & Conner, 2012; Miller, 2012).

## *Assessing daily experiences and perceptions*

Ambulatory assessment is a powerful modern methodology that encompasses a wide range of methods to study people in their real-life contexts, including momentary self-reports by means of the experience-sampling method (ESM; Conner, Tennen, Flesson, & Barrett, 2009; Hektner, Schmidt, & Csikszentmihalyi, 2007), ecological momentary assessment (EMA; Shiffman, Stone, & Hufford, 2008), the diary method (Bolger, Davis, & Rafaeli, 2003; Nezlek, 2012), observational methods (e.g., audio or video recording, activity monitoring), and physiological methods (e.g., assessment of cardiac and respiratory activity using physiological sensors; Trull & Ebner-Priemer, 2013, 2014). Several specific research tools are available to assess thoughts and feelings on a moment-to-moment basis in daily life (see Wrzus & Mehl, 2015, for a review).

The key idea behind ambulatory self-report assessments is to collect in-the-moment or close-to-the-moment subjective data directly from people in their daily lives. Typically, people are asked repeatedly (e.g., five times per day) over a period of time (e.g., a week) to report on their current thoughts and feelings. These momentary questions typically refer to location (e.g., Where are you now?), social environment (e.g., With whom are you now?), activity (e.g., What are you currently doing?), and experiences (e.g., How are you feeling right now?). These momentary questions provide a snapshot of what is going on in people's lives at the time at which they are asked to report. A major technological and practical advance in this area has been the transition from paper-and-pencil assessments to time-stamped, digital data. Time-stamped digital data provide powerful means to handle otherwise common problems such as back-filling (i.e., completing a number of assessments retrospectively at a later, convenient time) and have given researchers important control over the assessment process. Finally, ambulatory self-report assessments allow for a relatively fine-grained assessment of within-person (personality) states and behaviors (Fleeson, 2004).

Despite the benefits of ambulatory self-report assessment, it is important to consider potential challenges such as acceptability, compliance, privacy concerns, and ethical issues (e.g., Trull & Ebner-Priemer, 2013). For example, older adults may have some reservations against the use of technology or may not feel fully comfortable with certain electronic devices; on the other hand, children, e.g., may have good general technology curiosity and acceptance but the use of specific electronic devices may pose challenges (e.g., carrying a smartphone with them throughout the day, attaching a wearable camera that stays in a good place). Other factors such as user-friendliness, burden of the assessment protocol, length of assessment period, and privacy concerns may also affect compliance. It is important thus to address potential challenges to provide age-fair personality assessments and to increase the compliance.

One way in which momentary self-reports have been creatively and successfully used in personality development research is to track the distribution of Big Five personality states in time, space, and people (e.g., Fleeson, 2001; Fleeson & Gallagher, 2009). In Fleeson's research on traits as density distributions of states, participants report on the extent to which, over the last half hour, they have acted in Big Five relevant ways (e.g., talkative, cooperative, irritable, hardworking). In an application of this model to personality development, Noftle and Fleeson (2010) found (in a cross-sectional study) clear age-related patterns in daily expressed agreeableness, neuroticism, extraversion, and conscientiousness. The trends derived from the moment-to-moment Big Five state levels mirrored in direction the trends obtained from participants' (global) Big Five self-reports, providing important behavioral confirmation of findings derived from personality scales (Noftle & Fleeson, 2015). Interestingly and importantly, the effect size for the moment-to-moment derived trajectories exceeded the effect size derived for the global trait questionnaire suggesting that cognitive mechanisms involved in personality survey responses (e.g., the stabilization of self-concept) may actually lead to an underestimation of actual personality change. Therefore, the field of personality development would strongly benefit from using multiple methods of assessment in general and incorporating momentary self-reports in particular. The systematic incorporation of momentary self-reports would also allow personality development researchers to better understand the environmental contexts in which personality development unfolds (Bleidorn, 2015).

## Assessing daily behavior

Several assessment methods exist to assess behaviors in naturalistic settings (see Wrzus & Mehl, 2015, for a review). On the one hand, ambulatory assessment methods described above can be easily used to sample everyday behavior including self-reported momentary social interactions and activities. As mentioned, this approach has proven successful for studying personality development from the perspective of traits as density distributions of states (Noftle & Fleeson, 2010). On the other hand, studying momentary personality-related behaviors through the lens of participants' self-perceptions still renders their responses subject to important self-report limitations such as impression management, self-deception, and, simply, the lack of conscious awareness (e.g., automatic behavioral expressions such as sighing or swearing; Robbins, Mehl, Holleran, & Kasle, 2011; Robbins et al., 2011). Observational methods can help circumvent these limitations. While behaviors can be relatively easily observed in the laboratory using video or sound recordings, the assessment of behaviors is much more difficult in daily life contexts (Wrzus & Mehl, 2015). Novel and innovative assessment methodologies based on mobile and sensor technologies are being developed to directly and unobtrusively track people's behaviors in their natural, spontaneous contexts of daily life using perceptual- and physical-sensor data (e.g., audio, video, location, and movement information; Mehl & Conner, 2012; Trull & Ebner-Priemer, 2013, 2014). Despite existing challenges including acceptability of technology, privacy concerns, and ethical issues (e.g., Trull & Ebner-Priemer, 2013), observational methods would be particularly well suited to track behaviors of people who cannot provide reliable self-reports such as young children and perhaps very old adults with severe impairments, given that the concrete handling of electronic devices is feasible in everyday life.

Ambulatory behavioral assessment reflects a particularly important supplementary methodology for personality development research beyond self-reports and observer reports. Personality changes as captured with self-reports may primarily reflect changes in a person's self-concept that do not necessarily reflect actual behavioral changes in everyday life. As such, observations of behaviors may reflect related albeit distinct sources of information about personality development and change processes and may provide personality information over and above the classical assessment methods.

**Sound**. One innovative assessment method is to collect auditory data (e.g., ambient sound) using portable audio recorders to assess personality and to track personality change processes over time. The electronically activated recorder (EAR; Mehl, Pennebaker, Crow, Dabbs, & Price, 2001) is a behavioral observation method that unobtrusively samples acoustic observations of people's momentary objective social interactions and environments within the natural flow of their lives (Mehl & Robbins, 2012). The EAR is a modified portable audio device (e.g., app on the smartphone) that registers thin slices of daily social interactions randomly or in a given order throughout the day. In tracking moment-to-moment ambient sounds, the EAR yields acoustic logs of the social behaviors and interactions as they naturally unfold. In sampling only a fraction of the time, it makes large naturalistic observation studies feasible and protects people's privacy, yielding enough sound bites to derive both reliable and valid data on people's habitual behavior patterns. The EAR is minimally bothersome for participants, and a large number of studies support its feasibility, reliability, validity, and utility (Mehl & Holleran, 2007; Mehl, Vazire, Ramírez-Esparza, Slatcher, & Pennebaker, 2007; Mehl, Robbins, & Deters, 2012). It has been used to investigate a number of interpersonally sensitive topics (e.g., Bollich et al., 2016) and has proven reliable in age groups from young adulthood to old age.

The brief snippets of recorded ambient sounds can be coded for a broad range of aspects of people's moment-to-moment social environments including their locations (e.g., at home, at a restaurant, outside), activities (e.g., listening to music, watching TV, eating), and interactions (e.g., alone, on the phone, with partner), and social interactions including content (e.g., health, food, politics), style (e.g., emotion words, past vs present tense, swearing), and emotional expression (e.g., laughing, crying, arguing) using a validated coding scheme, the Social Environment Coding of Sound Inventory (SECSI; Mehl & Robbins, 2012; Mehl & Pennebaker, 2003). Everyday sounds like speech and music can also be informative with respect to communication behaviors (Kraus & Slater, 2016). As such, the EAR method provides highly naturalistic, experientially vivid, and psychologically rich information about behaviors and contexts in daily life. Moreover, collecting auditory data may be a particularly useful assessment method with young children and very old adults, given that the audio recording does not provide a practical problem (Alisic, Barrett, Bowles, Conroy, & Mehl, 2016). An alternative approach to portable devices is to use room microphones.

Importantly, for the field of personality development, just like with Noftle and Fleeson's (2010) experience sampling study, it is possible for personality information derived from behavioral observation and personality information derived from traditional personality scales to yield discrepant information. In this regard, Ramirez-Esparza, Mehl, Alvarez-Bermudez, and Pennebaker (2009) used the EAR to study self-reported and behaviorally expressed personality in American and Mexican participants. Interestingly, they found that whereas American participants self-reported being more extraverted and sociable than Mexicans participants, Mexican participants spent significantly more time interacting with others and socializing (as recorded by the EAR). In fact, American participants scored significantly higher on the Big Five Inventory item "I consider myself to be a person who is talkative" but Mexican participants spent 9%, or almost a quarter, more time talking to others (43.2% vs 34.3%). This study suggests considerable potential gain when self-report measures, that primarily tap into aspects of a person's self-concept, are complemented with observational measures, that primarily tap into aspects of displayed behavior (an important source of a person's reputation) allowing together for a comprehensive assessment of the person from the inside and outside (Vazire, 2010).

**Sight**. A second assessment method is to collect visual data (e.g., video recordings, images/photos) using portable video recorders. For example, the Narrative Clip (getnarrative.com) is a recently developed behavioral observation method that collects visual data of people's momentary social interactions and environments. It is a small, wearable device that captures time-stamped and geo-located images or video recordings according to a predetermined interval (e.g., every 30 s). As such, it can provide unobtrusive insight into naturally occurring person−situation interactions. The video recordings or images/photos can be coded for aspects of participants' social environments and interactions (Mannay, 2016; Ray & Smith, 2012). The newly developed taxonomy of major dimensions of situational characteristics (the Situational Eight DIAMONDS, Rauthmann et al., 2014) can be used to code visual data. Photographs and visual methods hold great promise for tracking personality processes and change over time as well as accessing multiple levels of personality specificity. The assessment of visual data may represent a method that is particularly useful to track people who cannot or are unable to respond to self-report questions (Doherty et al., 2013). Naturally, capturing visual data also brings with it unique ethical challenges but researchers are working on ways to address them (Kelly et al., 2013).

**Smell**. A third assessment method is to collect olfactory data (e.g., body odors), because smell is an important sense in social interactions and may provide individual and contextual information. For example, the sense of smell can prime the experience of pleasure, can warn of danger, help identify suitable mates, locate food, or detect predators. Preliminary research findings demonstrated that some personality traits can be recognized using olfactory cues (i.e., body odor) and that olfaction supplements auditory and visual cues, contributing to the first impression accuracy of certain personality traits (Sorokowska, 2013; Sorokowska, Sorokowski, & Szmajke, 2012). Moreover, several technological tools are being developed to sample (body) odors. For example, the electrochemical nose (e-nose or micro nose) is an artificial olfaction device to sample, recognize, identify, and compare odors.

Whether this assessment method provides reliable and valid personality information over and above other classical and modern assessment approaches is a task for future empirical research.

**Smartphone sensing**. Recent technological advances (e.g., mobile technology, wearable sensor technology) in the field of computer science and the rapid growth in popularity of the use of various electronic devices in daily life have led to unlimited possibilities for personality science, especially for the assessment of state manifestations of personality traits in daily life (Intille, 2012; Mehl & Conner, 2012; Miller, 2012; Yarkoni, 2012). Mobile sensing systems and wearable devices are powerful and innovative methods for understanding people's life contexts, activities, behaviors, and social networks (Sazonov & Neuman, 2014; Schmid Mast, Gatica-Perez, Frauendorfer, Nguyen, & Choudhury, 2015). These systems can be used to sense social interaction behavior via ubiquitous computing devices followed by an automated extraction of verbal and nonverbal behavioral information with computational models and algorithms. For more information, including a critical discussion of the potentials and obstacles of current mobile sensing platforms, see Wrzus and Mehl (2015) and Harari et al. (2016).

## Assessing daily online behavior

An interesting domain of life that has only recently emerged is virtual daily behavior that refers to social behaviors and interactions on the Internet (Gosling & Mason, 2015). An Internet-based assessment method is to collect verbal behavioral data, including emailing, chatting, tweeting, blogging, and posting. For example, differences in the ways in which people use words (e.g., pronouns such as "I" and "we") have been found to carry a lot of psychological information (Pennebaker, Mehl, & Niederhoffer, 2003). Therefore, an interesting approach to assess online behavior is to sample virtual language behavior (e.g., verbal expressions and communications) and to conduct linguistic analyses using modern text analysis program such as the Linguistic Inquiry and Word Count (LIWC2015; Pennebaker, Boyd, Jordan, & Blackburn, 2015).

Another novel assessment method is to use social networking sites such as Facebook to observe behavior in naturalistic online settings, test hypotheses, and recruit a large number of study participants (Kosinski, Matz, Gosling, Popov, & Stillwell, 2015; Wilson, Gosling, & Graham, 2012). In a recent high-profile study, Youyou, Kosinski, and Stillwell (2015) demonstrated that computer-based personality judgments based entirely on patterns of Facebook Likes (in fact, only 90–100 were needed for the models) are more accurate in predicting life outcomes than informant reports and, in some cases, even more accurate than self-reports (e.g., participants' social network activity). Park et al. (2015) found a similar advantage of computer-based personality models over human personality judgments when the computer-based models were derived from participants' word use in their Facebook status-updates.

These studies have important implications for the field of personality development as they ultimately open up the possibility of estimating trajectories of personality change indirectly from archival online behavior without ever having directly collected explicit personality information (i.e., administered a personality question-naire). This, then, would open up the study of personality development beyond the limited number of existing and extensively mined longitudinal panel studies and thereby potentially dramatically broaden the data base for the field. Again, the fact that personality models based on online behavior have demonstrated unique predic-tive validity over self- and informant reports suggests that they may not only facilitate but also psychometrically complement the study of personality development.

## Assessing daily contexts

The environment plays an important role in personality development (Roberts & Pomerantz, 2004; Roberts et al., 2008). Despite its importance, however, the issue of conceptualizing and assessing the environment and real-life contexts is often ignored or poorly operationalized and is rather complex (Roberts, 2007). It seems appropriate to distinguish between objective characteristics of the environment (e.g., inside or outside a building) and subjective perceptions of the environment (e.g., perceiving the situation as dangerous). For example, Roberts et al. (2008) pro-posed a psychologically meaningful way to investigate contextual influences via the social role concept. They argued that rather than investigating the influence of objective contextual variables on personality development, it may be more mean-ingful to examine subjective environment in the form of social roles (e.g., worker role, parent role), and to investigate the relation between changes or stability in social roles and personality development. The idea is that roles contain cultural, societal, and individuals' expectations how to behave in social roles, and that an active, psychological commitment or investment to the roles might be associated with personality change (Lodi-Smith & Roberts, 2007). Self-report based ambula-tory assessment methods can be easily adapted to sample everyday experiences and behaviors with respect to the investment in specific social roles. Likewise, wearable sensor technologies discussed above can be used to assess objective environmental information through sound, sight, smell, taste, touch, and other senses (cf. Sazonov & Neuman, 2014). As mentioned earlier, the breadth of context information may range from the narrow proximal situation to broad geographical regions (cf. Roberts & Pomerantz, 2004).

**Situations**. Notable conceptual/theoretical and assessment efforts have been recently made to better psychologically understand proximal situations in daily life (Rauthmann, Sherman, & Funder, 2015) and to assess the major dimensions of situ-ation characteristics based on retrospective self-reports (Rauthmann et al., 2014) and in real-time using experience-sampling methods (Sherman, Rauthmann, Brown, Serfass, & Jones, 2015).

**Living contexts**. In addition, assessment strategies and tools have been devel-oped to examine physical contexts at the medium level such as home environments including people's personal (e.g., bedrooms) and professional (e.g., offices, class-rooms) living spaces (Graham, Gosling, & Travis, 2015) in order to understand how personality is expressed and detected in everyday real-life contexts (Gosling, Ko, Mannarelli, & Morris, 2002).

**Geographical contexts**. Finally, researchers also assess context data at the very broad geographical level of analysis (e.g., neighborhoods, cities; Rentfrow, 2014). The basic idea of this line of research is that the places where people live vary considerably in terms of their social, economic, political, climatic, physical, and personality characteristics (Rentfrow, Jokela, & Lamb, 2015). These conditions may affect how people from different geographical regions behave and interact with their environments and each other.

# Future directions

Future research needs to attach more importance to people's daily life contexts, as they are the stages in which personality processes are assembled and unfold over time. At the moment, it is clear that the field of personality development lags considerably behind other fields in assessing constructs and processes under real-life and real-time conditions and in their incorporation of ambulatory assessment methods. This is on some level little surprising, given that personality development researchers are traditionally concerned with relatively slow social and behavioral processes that unfold over periods of years and decades, whereas the field of ambulatory assessment tends to be concerned with relatively fast psychological processes that unfold over periods of days and weeks. Yet, one important future avenue for the field of personality development is to make better use of ambulatory assessment methods since they have the potential to enrich the field exactly in its Achilles heel, namely the characterization of the situational and environmental context in which personality development happens. One way to accomplish this would be to add ambulatory assessment components to existing longitudinal panel studies that are the prime target for personality development researchers. Of course, it would take some time and a few measurement time points until the momentary data could be fruitfully integrated into the analyses.

Following logically from this point, another important future avenue is to integrate personality processes across different time-scales. Historically, most personality studies employed cross-sectional designs and examine personality from the perspective of concurrent associations. The relatively few existing experience-sampling studies (e.g., Fleeson & Gallagher, 2009) have focused on personality dynamics as they unfold over the course of days and weeks or over months. Traditional developmental longitudinal studies, finally, are looking at long-term personality stability and change over years and decades. Clearly, personality dynamics unfold at the three levels and they unfold at the three levels nonindependently.

Measurement burst designs can help integrate slower acting and fast acting personality processes. A measurement burst research design involves longitudinal assessments that are planned around closely spaced successive "bursts" of assessments, rather than widely spaced successions of single time point assessments (see Stawski, MacDonald, & Sliwinski, 2015, for a review). It combines features of intensive short-term longitudinal methods such as ambulatory assessment with features of long-term longitudinal designs that are used to examine individuals over relatively long time intervals. Measurement burst designs provide researchers the unique opportunity to study long-term developmental changes in personality traits in combination with short-term dynamic personality processes that can only be measured on a daily or momentary basis, such as regulative and self-evaluative processes or emotional states in a given situation or real-life contexts (Stawski et al., 2015). Novel methodological approaches and statistical tools for studying personality processes across different time-scales are currently being developed (Gerstorf, Hoppman, & Ram, 2014; Nestler, Grimm, & Schönbrodt, 2015).

Finally, to have a full understanding of personality in different contexts over time, it is important to consider multiple perspectives of personality (McAdams, 2015; McAdams & Olson, 2010). Given space constraints, this chapter focused on the assessment of traits and states that are primarily descriptive for individuals as social actors (cf. McAdams, 2013). One important future avenue for the field of personality development is to use novel assessment methods to track motivational and narrative personality characteristics and processes over time (cf. McAdams, 2013). For example, a study used written narratives of personality change to understand how people conceptualize their changing personality over time (Lodi-Smith, Geise, Roberts, & Robins, 2009). Future research could use the EAR method to assess narratives and to study how and in which social situations in daily life people narrate personality change. More broadly, the use of novel psychological and technological assessment advances would significantly contribute to the existing personality assessment repertoire of the field of personality development. In particular, the collection of auditory, visual, olfactory, and social and smartphone sensing data may create new opportunities for the assessment of personality (change) processes in daily life. In addition, more efforts should be made for assessing daily life contexts at different levels of specificity including proximal situations, living spaces, and geographical regions.

## Conclusion

The goal of this chapter has been to discuss personality assessment in daily life as a complement to traditional assessment methods in the field of personality development. Assessing personality under real-life and real-time conditions would provide a better understanding about the ways in which personality processes are assembled and unfold over time. The use of ambulatory assessment to capture personality change processes in real-life contexts would offer interesting novel assessment perspectives for the field of personality development. Emerging developments in sensor-enabled mobile technologies to assess daily contexts and individual experiences, perceptions, and behaviors using auditory, visual, olfactory, and smartphone sensing data, will create new opportunities for researchers to study personality development and dynamics in daily life.

# References

Alisic, E., Barrett, A., Bowles, P., Conroy, R., & Mehl, M. (2016). Families coping with child trauma: A naturalistic observation methodology. *Journal of Pediatric Psychology*, *41*, 117−127.

Allemand, M., Steiger, A. E., & Fend, H. A. (2015). Empathy development in adolescence predicts social competencies in adulthood. *Journal of Personality*, *83*, 229−241.

Allemand, M., Zimprich, D., & Martin, M. (2008). Long-term correlated changes in personality traits in old age. *Psychology and Aging*, *23*, 545−557.

Baumeister, R. F., Vohs, K. D., & Funder, D. C. (2007). Psychology as the science of self-reports and finger movements: Whatever happened to actual behavior? *Perspectives on Psychological Science*, *2*, 396−403.

Bleidorn, W. (2015). What accounts for personality maturation in early adulthood? *Current Directions in Psychological Science*, *24*, 245−252.

Bolger, N., Davis, A., & Rafaeli, E. (2003). Diary methods: Capturing life as it is lived. *Annual Review of Psychology*, *54*, 579−616.

Bollich, K. L., Doris, J. M., Vazire, S., Raison, C. L., Jackson, J. J., & Mehl, M. R. (2016). Evesdropping on character: Assessing everyday moral behaviors. *Journal of Research in Personality*, *61*, 15−21.

Conner, T. S., Tennen, H., Fleeson, W., & Barrett, L. F. (2009). Experience sampling methods: A modern idiographic approach to personality research. *Social and Personality Psychology Compass*, *3*, 292−313.

Doherty, A. R., Hodges, S. E., King, A. C., Smeaton, A. F., Berry, E., Moulin, C. J., ... Foster, C. (2013). Wearable cameras in health. *American Journal of Preventive Medicine*, *44*, 320−323.

Fleeson, W. (2001). Towards a structure- and process-integrated view of personality: Traits as density distributions of states. *Journal of Personality and Social Psychology*, *80*, 1011−1027.

Fleeson, W. (2004). Moving personality beyond the person-situation debate: The challenge and the opportunity of within-person variability. *Current Directions in Psychological Science*, *13*, 83−87.

Fleeson, W., & Gallagher, P. (2009). The implications of the Big-Five standing for the distribution of trait manifestation in behavior: Fifteen experience-sampling studies and a meta-analysis. *Journal of Personality and Social Psychology*, *97*, 1097−1114.

Funder, D. C. (2001). Personality. *Annual Review of Psychology*, *52*, 197−221.

Gerstorf, D., Hoppman, C., & Ram, N. (2014). The promise and challenges of integrating multiple time-scales in adult developmental inquiry. *Research in Human Development*, *11*, 75−90.

Gosling, S. D., Ko, S. J., Mannarelli, T., & Morris, M. E. (2002). A room with a cue: Personality judgments based on offices and bedrooms. *Journal of Personality and Social Psychology*, *82*, 379−398.

Gosling, S. D., & Mason, W. (2015). Internet research in psychology. *Annual Review of Psychology*, *66*, 877−902.

Graham, L. T., Gosling, S. D., & Travis, C. K. (2015). The psychology of home environments: A call for research on residential space. *Perspectives on Psychological Science*, *10*, 346−356.

Harari, G.M., Lane, N.D., Wang, R., Crosier, B.S., Campbell, A.T., & Gosling, S.D. (2016). Using smartphone for collecting behavioral data in psychological science: Opportunities, practical considerations, and challenges. *Perspectives on Psychological Science*, *11*, 838−854.

Hektner, J. M., Schmidt, J. A., & Csikszentmihalyi, M. (2007). *Experience sampling method: Measuring the quality of everyday life*. Thousand Oaks, CA: Sage.

Heller, D., Watson, D., Komar, J., Min, J. A., & Perunovic, W. Q. E. (2007). Contextualized personality: Traditional and new assessment procedures. *Journal of Personality, 75,* 1229–1254.

Hooker, K., & McAdams, D. P. (2003). Personality reconsidered: A new agenda for aging research. *The Journals of Gerontology Series B: Psychological Sciences and Social Sciences, 58,* 296–304.

Intille, S. S. (2012). Emerging technology for studying daily life. In M. R. Mehl, & T. S. Conner (Eds.), *Handbook of research methods for studying daily life* (pp. 267–282). New York, NY: Guilford Press.

Jackson, J. J., Bogg, T., Walton, K. E., Wood, D., Harms, P. D., Lodi- Smith, J., ... Roberts, B. W. (2009). Not all conscientiousness scales change alike: A multi-method, multi-sample study of age differences in the facets of conscientiousness. *Journal of Personality and Social Psychology, 96,* 446–459.

John, O. P., Naumann, L. P., & Soto, C. J. (2008). Paradigm shift to the integrative Big Five trait taxonomy: History, measurement, and conceptual issues. In O. P. John, R. W. Robins, & L. A. Pervin (Eds.), *Handbook of personality: Theory and research* (3rd ed., pp. 114–158). New York, NY: Guilford.

Kelly, P., Marshall, S. J., Badland, H., Kerr, J., Oliver, M., Doherty, A. R., & Foster, C. (2013). An ethical framework for automated, wearable cameras in health behavior research. *American Journal of Preventive Medicine, 44,* 314–319.

Kosinski, M., Matz, S. C., Gosling, S. D., Popov, V., & Stillwell, D. (2015). Facebook as a research tool for the social sciences: Opportunities, challenges, ethical considerations, and practical guidelines. *American Psychologist, 70,* 543–556.

Kraus, N., & Slater, J. (2016). Beyond words: How humans communicate through sound. *Annual Review of Psychology, 67,* 83–103.

Lodi-Smith, J., Geise, A. C., Roberts, B. W., & Robins, R. W. (2009). Narrating personality change. *Journal of Personality and Social Psychology, 96,* 679–689.

Lodi-Smith, J., & Roberts, B. W. (2007). Social investment and personality: A meta-analysis of the relationship of personality traits to investment in work, family, religion, and volunteerism. *Personality and Social Psychology Review, 11,* 68–86.

Mannay, D. I. (2016). *Visual, narrative, and creative research methods: Application, reflection and ethics*. New York, NY: Routledge.

McAdams, D. P. (2013). The psychological self as actor, agent, and author. *Perspectives on Psychological Science, 8,* 272–295.

McAdams, D. P. (2015). *The art and science of personality development*. New York, NY: Guilford Press.

McAdams, D. P., & Olson, B. D. (2010). Personality development: Continuity and change over the life course. *Annual Review of Psychology, 61,* 517–542.

Mehl, M. R., & Conner, T. S. (2012). *Handbook of research methods for studying daily life*. New York, NY: Guilford Press.

Mehl, M. R., & Holleran, S. E. (2007). An empirical analysis of the obtrusiveness of and participants' compliance with the electronically activated recorder (EAR). *European Journal of Psychological Assessment, 23,* 248–257.

Mehl, M. R., & Pennebaker, J. W. (2003). The sounds of social life: A psychometric analysis of students' daily social environments and natural conversations. *Journal of Personality and Social Psychology, 84,* 857–870.

Mehl, M. R., Pennebaker, J. W., Crow, D. M., Dabbs, J., & Price, J. H. (2001). The Electronically Activated Recorder (EAR): A device for sampling naturalistic daily activities and conversations. *Behavior Research Methods, Instruments, & Computers*, *33*, 517−523.

Mehl, M. R., & Robbins, M. L. (2012). Naturalistic observation sampling: The Electronically Activated Recorder (EAR). In M. R. Mehl, & T. S. Conner (Eds.), *Handbook of research methods for studying daily life* (pp. 176−192). New York, NY: Guilford Press.

Mehl, M. R., Robbins, M. L., & Deters, F. G. (2012). Naturalistic observation of health-relevant social processes: The electronically activated recorder methodology in psychosomatics. *Psychosomatic Medicine*, *74*, 410−417.

Mehl, M. R., Vazire, S., Ramírez-Esparza, N., Slatcher, R. B., & Pennebaker, J. W. (2007). Are women really more talkative than men? *Science*, *317*, 82−82.

Miller, G. (2012). The smartphone psychology manifesto. *Perspectives on Psychological Science*, *7*, 221−237.

Molenaar, P. C. M., & Campbell, C. G. (2009). The new person-specific paradigm in psychology. *Current Directions in Psychological Science*, *18*, 112−117.

Mroczek, D. K., & Spiro, A. (2007). Personality change influences mortality in older men. *Psychological Science*, *18*, 371−376.

Mroczek, D. K., Spiro, A., & Almeida, D. M. (2003). Between- and within-person variation in affect and personality over days and years: How basic and applied approaches can inform one another. *Ageing International*, *28*, 260−278.

Nestler, S., Grimm, K. J., & Schönbrodt, F. D. (2015). The social consequences and mechanisms of personality: How to analyze longitudinal data from individual, dyadic, round-robin, and network designs. *European Journal of Personality*, *29*, 272−295.

Nezlek, J. B. (2012). Diary methods for social and personality psychology. In J. B. Nezlek (Ed.), *The SAGE library in social and personality psychology methods*. London: Sage Publications.

Noftle, E. E., & Fleeson, W. (2010). Age differences in big five behavior averages and variabilities across the adult life span: Moving beyond retrospective, global summary accounts of personality. *Psychology and Aging*, *25*, 95−107.

Noftle, E. E., & Fleeson, W. (2015). Intraindividual variability in adult personality development. In M. Diehl, K. Hooker, & M. J. Sliwinski (Eds.), *Handbook of intraindividual variability across the lifespan* (pp. 176−197). New York, NY: Routledge.

Park, G., Schwartz, H. A., Eichstaedt, J. C., Kern, M. L., Kosinski, M., Stillwell, D. J., ... Seligman, M. E. P. (2015). Automatic personality assessment through social media language. *Journal of Personality and Social Psychology*, *108*, 934−952.

Paunonen, S. V. (1998). Hierarchical organization of personality and prediction of behavior. *Journal of Personality and Social Psychology*, *74*, 538−556.

Pennebaker, J. W., Boyd, R. L., Jordan, K., & Blackburn, K. (2015). *The development and psychometric properties of LIWC2015*. Austin, TX: University of Texas at Austin.

Pennebaker, J. W., Mehl, M. R., & Niederhoffer, K. G. (2003). Psychological aspects of natural language use: Our words, our selves. *Annual Review of Psychology*, *54*, 547−577.

Ramirez-Esparza, N., Mehl, M. R., Alvarez-Bermudez, J., & Pennebaker, J. W. (2009). Are Mexicans more or less sociable than Americans? Insights from a naturalistic observation study. *Journal of Research in Personality*, *43*, 1−7.

Rauthmann, J. F., Gallardo-Pujol, D., Guillaume, E. M., Todd, E., Nave, C. S., Sherman, R. A., ... Funder, D. C. (2014). The Situational Eight DIAMONDS: A taxonomy of major dimensions of situation characteristics. *Journal of Personality and Social Psychology*, *107*, 677−718.

Rauthmann, J. F., Sherman, R. A., & Funder, D. C. (2015). Principles of situation research: Towards a better understanding of psychological situations. *European Journal of Personality, 29*, 363−381.

Ray, J. L., & Smith, A. D. (2012). Using photographs to research organizations: Evidence, considerations, and application in a field study. *Organizational Research Methods, 15*, 288−315.

Reis, H. T., & Gosling, S. D. (2010). Social psychological methods outside the laboratory. In S. T. Fiske, D. T. Gilbert, & G. Lindzey (Eds.), *Handbook of social psychology* (5th ed. Vol. 1). New York, NY: John Wiley.

Rentfrow, P. J. (2014). *Geographical psychology: Exploring the interaction of environment and behavior.* Washington, DC: American Psychological Association.

Rentfrow, P. J., Jokela, M., & Lamb, M. E. (2015). Regional personality differences in Great Britain. *PLoS ONE, 10*, e0122245.

Robbins, M. L., Focella, E. S., Kasle, S., Weihs, K. L., Lopez, A. M., & Mehl, M. R. (2011). Naturalistically observed swearing, emotional support and depressive symptoms in women coping with illness. *Health Psychology, 30*, 789−792.

Robbins, M. L., Mehl, M. R., Holleran, S. E., & Kasle, S. (2011). Naturalistically observed sighing and depression in rheumatoid arthritis patients: A preliminary study. *Health Psychology, 30*, 129−133.

Roberts, B. W. (2007). Contextualizing personality psychology. *Journal of Personality, 75*, 1071−1082.

Roberts, B. W. (2009). Back to the future: Personality and assessment and personality development. *Journal of Research in Personality, 43*, 137−145.

Roberts, B. W., & Jackson, J. J. (2008). Sociogenomic personality psychology. *Journal of Personality, 76*, 1523−1544.

Roberts, B. W., Kuncel, N. R., Shiner, R., Caspi, A., & Goldberg, L. R. (2007). The power of personality: The comparative validity of personality traits, socioeconomic status, and cognitive ability for predicting important life outcomes. *Perspectives on Psychological Science, 2*, 313−345.

Roberts, B. W., & Mroczek, D. (2008). Personality trait change in adulthood. *Current Directions in Psychological Science, 17*, 31−35.

Roberts, B. W., & Pomerantz, E. M. (2004). On traits, situations, and their integration: A developmental perspective. *Personality and Social Psychology Review, 8*, 402−416.

Roberts, B. W., Walton, K. E., & Viechtbauer, W. (2006). Patterns of mean-level change in personality traits across the life course: A meta-analysis of longitudinal studies. *Psychological Bulletin, 132*, 1−25.

Roberts, B. W., Wood, D., & Caspi, A. (2008). The development of personality traits in adulthood. *Handbook of personality: Theory and research, 3*, 375−398.

Rosenberg, E. L. (1998). Level of analysis and the organization of affect. *Review of General Psychology, 2*, 247−270.

Sazonov, E., & Neuman, M. (2014). *Wearable sensors: Fundamentals, implementation and application.* San Diego, CA: Elsevier Publishing.

Schmid Mast, M., Gatica-Perez, D., Frauendorfer, D., Nguyen, L., & Choudhury, T. (2015). Social sensing for psychology automated interpersonal behavior assessment. *Current Directions in Psychological Science, 24*, 154−160.

Schwarz, N. (2012). Why researchers should think "real-time." In M. R. Mehl, & T. A. Conner (Eds.), *Handbook of research methods for studying daily life* (pp. 22−42). New York, NY: Guilford Press.

Sherman, R. A., Rauthmann, J. F., Brown, N. A., Serfass, D. S., & Jones, A. B. (2015). The independent effects of personality and situations on real-time expressions of behavior and emotion. *Journal of Personality and Social Psychology, 109*, 872–888.

Shiffman, S., Stone, A. A., & Hufford, M. R. (2008). Ecological momentary assessment. *Annual Review of Clinical Psychology, 4*, 1–32.

Sorokowska, A. (2013). Seeing or smelling? Assessing personality on the basis of different stimuli. *Personality and Individual Differences, 55*, 175–179.

Sorokowska, A., Sorokowski, P., & Szmajke, A. (2012). Does personality smell? Accuracy of personality assessments based on body odour. *European Journal of Personality, 26*, 496–503.

Soto, C. J., John, O. P., Gosling, S. D., & Potter, J. (2011). Age differences in personality traits from 10 to 65: Big Five domains and facets in a large cross-sectional sample. *Journal of Personality and Social Psychology, 100*, 330–348.

Stawski, R. S., MacDonald, S. W. S., & Sliwinski, M. J. (2015). Measurement burst design. In S. K. Whitbourne (Ed.), *The Encyclopedia of adulthood and aging* (pp. 1–5). Hoboken, NJ: Wiley-Blckwell.

Steiger, A. E., Allemand, M., Robins, R. W., & Fend, H. A. (2014). Low and decreasing self-esteem during adolescence predict adult depression two decades later. *Journal of Personality and Social Psychology, 106*, 325–338.

Terracciano, A., McCrae, R. R., Brant, L. J., & Costa, P. T., Jr (2005). Hierarchical linear modeling analyses of the NEO-PI-R scales in the Baltimore Longitudinal Study of Aging. *Psychology and Aging, 20*, 493–506.

Trull, T. J., & Ebner-Priemer, U. (2013). Ambulatory assessment. *Annual Review of Clinical Psychology, 9*, 151–176.

Trull, T. J., & Ebner-Priemer, U. (2014). The role of ambulatory assessment in psychological science. *Current Directions in Psychological Science, 23*, 466–470.

Vazire, S. (2010). Informant reports. In S. D. Gosling, & J. A. Johnson (Eds.), *Advanced methods for conducting online behavioral research* (pp. 167–178). Washington, DC: American Psychological Association.

Wilhelm, P., Perrez, M., & Pawlik, K. (2012). Conducting research in daily life. In M. R. Mehl, & T. S. Conner (Eds.), *Handbook of research methods for studying daily life* (pp. 62–86). New York, NY: Guilford Press.

Wilson, R. E., Gosling, S. D., & Graham, L. T. (2012). A review of Facebook research in the social sciences. *Perspectives on Psychological Science, 7*, 203–220.

Wood, D., & Roberts, B. W. (2006). Cross-sectional and longitudinal tests of the Personality and Role Identity Structural Model (PRISM). *Journal of Personality, 74*, 779–810.

Wood, D., Nye, C. D., & Saucier, G. (2010). Identification and measurement of a more comprehensive set of person-descriptive trait markers from the English lexicon. *Journal of Research in Personality, 44*, 258–272.

Wrzus, C., & Mehl, M. R. (2015). Lab and/or field? Measuring personality processes and their social consequences. *European Journal of Personality, 29*, 250–271.

Yarkoni, T. (2012). Psychoinformatics new horizons at the interface of the psychological and computing sciences. *Current Directions in Psychological Science, 21*, 391–397.

Youyou, W., Kosinski, M., & Stillwell, D. (2015). Computer-based personality judgments are more accurate than those made by humans. *PNAS, 112*, 1036–1040.

# Analyzing processes in personality development

**28**

*Katharina Geukes, Maarten H.W. van Zalk, and Mitja D. Back*
University of Münster, Münster, Germany

How does personality stabilize and change and how can we capture personality development processes? There is compelling empirical evidence for personality changes across the entire lifespan (e.g., Roberts, Donnellan, & Hill, 2012). Moreover, according to the most prominent theoretical perspectives (see Specht et al., 2014, for a recent overview) and genetically informed longitudinal studies (see Bleidorn, Kandler, & Caspi, 2014, for a recent overview) both genetic and environmental factors contribute to personality development. Finally, on a macro-analytical level, specific factors related to personality change have been revealed, including life events (e.g., Lüdtke, Roberts, Trautwein, & Nagy, 2011; Specht, Egloff, & Schmukle, 2011) and social role investments (e.g., Denissen, Ulfers, Lüdtke, Muck, & Gerstorf, 2014; Lodi-Smith & Roberts, 2007).

In contrast, however, there is still limited insight into the mechanisms driving personality development. The goal of this chapter is twofold. First, we provide an integrative generic model describing three domains of specific micro-level state processes and how they are linked to a macro-level understanding of trait development. Second, we describe methodological challenges and solutions to the assessment of these state processes.

## Understanding processes in personality development: A generic model

A number of process-oriented models of personality define traits as individual differences in *state processes*, that is in the dynamic patterns of how people feel, think, strive for, and behave in circumscribed situations (e.g., Cervone, 2005; Cramer et al., 2012; Denissen & Penke, 2008; DeYoung, 2015; Fleeson & Jayawickreme, 2015; Mischel & Shoda, 1998; Read et al., 2010; Revelle & Condon, 2015; Robinson, 2007; Robinson & Wilkowski, 2015; Wood, Gardner, & Harms, 2015). These individual differences in state processes pertain to both differences in the *level of state expression*, that is, differences in how much a state variable is typically expressed (e.g., how much individuals feel joy; how much they differ in their expectations regarding valued outcomes) and differences in *state contingencies*, that is, differences in how much different state variables are contingent on each

Personality Development Across the Lifespan. DOI: http://dx.doi.org/10.1016/B978-0-12-804674-6.00028-4

other (e.g., how much positive feedback evokes joy; how much goal setting is aligned to one's outcome expectations). Following this rationale, personality development can be understood as changes and/or stabilization in both kinds of state processes (also see Roberts & Jackson, 2008).

A few conceptual approaches have been outlined that describe personality development as the result of the stabilization and change of state processes. Among them are the TESSERA framework (Wrzus & Roberts, in press), the PERSOC framework (Back, Baumert et al., 2011), and functional self-regulatory perspectives on personality development (Denissen, Wood, Penke, & van Aken, 2013; Hennecke, Bleidorn, Denissen, & Wood, 2014; Wood & Denissen, 2015). Below we provide a condensed generic overview building on and integrating these previous conceptual approaches. We describe three domains of state processes, outline how these state processes relate to personality trait stability and change, and link this process-based understanding to existing macro-perspectives on personality development.

## Three domains of state processes

We differentiate three broad domains of state processes: (1) Goals and strategies, (2) Actions and experiences, and (3) Evaluations and reflections. Existing personality differences can be understood as relatively enduring individual differences in the levels of state expressions and state contingencies within each of these domains (see Fig. 28.1). The three domains of state processes can be aligned to distinct phases of behavior regulation (i.e., (1) preaction, (2) action, and (3) postaction

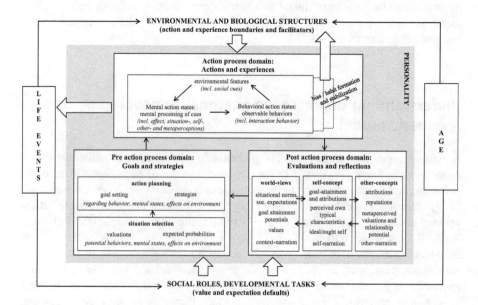

**Figure 28.1** A generic model of personality development processes.

phases; Carver & Scheier, 1981; Gollwitzer, 1990; Gross & Thompson, 2007; Heckhausen, 1991), and they reflect different research traditions on how personality is defined and assessed (via individual differences in (1) motives, (2) behaviors and cognitive-affective processing units, and (3) self-concepts/identity narratives).[1]

First, individual differences in *goals and strategies* regard processes underlying (1) the selection of situations and (2) the creation of action plans for a given situational choice (see Wood & Denissen, 2015). The selection of situations depends on valuations of desired outcomes (i.e., motives; desired end-states; reference values), as well as on expectations regarding one's abilities of performing certain actions, and regarding the effectiveness of these actions leading to desired outcomes (see Feather, 1959; Hastie, 2001; Rotter, 1954; Vroom, 1964). Individuals are assumed to aim at those actions that they think they are able to perform, and that they expect to have certain effects, which they evaluate positively. This idea is also contained in the TESSERA framework where Triggers (e.g., thoughts about existing motives or goals) and Expectations (e.g., about possible, useful, or appropriate states) are expected to precede further mental and behavioral states. When a situation has been selected, individuals create action plans involving the setting of goals and accompanying strategies on how these goals can be achieved. Individuals change in their personality the more they (1) change their situational valuations, (2) change their situational expectations (regarding the effectiveness of actions in given situations and their competence to perform these actions), and/or (3) create novel action plans to fit these adjusted valuations and expectations (e.g., Denissen et al., 2013; Hennecke, et al., 2014).

Imagine, e.g., Jack, a 16-year-old boy low in agreeableness (high in antagonism). He might be characterized by a high valuation of personal but a low valuation of group achievements, by expecting a low probability of personal achievements in collaborative group interactions and, therefore, a tendency to avoid or deselect collaborative group interactions. For Jack to become more agreeable, he might need to value group achievements more, to start to expect group achievements to increase by cooperative behavior, to feel more competent to perform cooperative actions, and create effective actions plans fitting these adjusted valuations and expectations, such as developing a strategy to listen to others and focus on other people's strengths and common goals.

Second, individual differences in *actions and experiences* pertain to differences in the dynamic interplay of (1) environmental features of the selected situation (including cues of social partners), (2) mental action states (e.g., affect, cognitions, evaluations, social perceptions), and (3) behavioral action states (i.e., observable behaviors that are influenced by the mental processing of and in turn shape environmental features). The central role of actually experienced and expressed states as well as their environmental precursors and consequences is also emphasized in the TESSERA framework (Wrzus & Roberts, in press), and, more specifically in the context of social interactions, in the PERSOC model (Back, Baumert et al., 2011;

---

[1] We should note that all of the described processes can be situated on a more or less impulsive versus reflective level (Back & Nestler, 2017; Wrzus & Roberts, in press).

also see Harris, 1995; Hutteman, Nestler, Wagner, Egloff, & Back, 2015; Leary & Baumeister, 2000; Reitz, Zimmerman, Hutteman, Specht, & Neyer, 2014; Swann & Bosson, 2008). Following these ideas, personality change is suggested to be initiated by (1) changes in the level of behavioral (e.g., smiling, behaving aggressively, working hard) and perceptional state expressions (e.g., perceiving yourself or others to be likeable, arrogant; experiencing positive affect) and/or by (2) changes in contingencies between environmental features and mental processing (e.g., how much negative feedback leads to anger; how much an intellectually stimulating task leads to joy) as well as between mental and behavioral states (e.g., how much anger leads to aggression; how much positive affect leads to hard working).

The more mental and behavioral states are repeated, the more they are thought to get automatized and independent of environmental cues and effects. Behavioral habits are formed and mental biases stabilize. Such learning processes are also key to self-regulatory approaches to personality development. Repetition and investment of self-regulatory resources are assumed to enhance self-regulatory competence, that is, the effectiveness with which self-regulatory mechanisms aimed at achieving certain reference values are performed (e.g., appraisal of situational features, behavioral expression control).

Within social interactions, Jack might, for instance, perceive more negative social feedback, experience more negative affect, behave in a more aggressive fashion, and evoke negative outcomes and negative feedback. Moreover, he might have stronger contingencies between perceived negative social feedback and negative affect and between negative affect and aggressive behavior. To change his personality, the self-enhancing negative spiral needs to be interrupted, whether by targeted interventions or by everyday incidences, in which he experienced a reduced level of aggressiveness, perceived negative social feedback with more ease, and was less reactive to perceived negative social feedback. Moreover, this might need to be repeated until alternative more lenient mental states and more prosocial behaviors have been automatized.

Third, individual differences in *evaluations and reflections* pertain to (1) individual's self-concepts, (2) their concepts of other individuals including the generalized other, and (3) their world views (i.e., their concepts about environmental contexts and circumscribed situations within these contexts). In the TESSERA framework, parts of this stage of evaluations and reflections are captured by reflective transformation processes (e.g., life reflection, self-narration) explaining manifestations of short-term state changes in permanent trait change. Such reflective processes do not only pertain to individuals' selves but also to reflections and the construction of coherent stories about their social counterparts and the environments and world they live in (also see Caspi & Roberts, 1999). The rich literature on self-narration (Bauer & McAdams, 2004; Dunlop, 2015; Lodi-Smith, Geise, Roberts, & Robins, 2009; Pasupathi, Mansour, & Brubaker, 2007) and the social structure of selves (e.g., actual vs ideal vs ought selves; Higgins, 1987) also relates to this domain of self-reflective processes.

Jack might, for example, attribute failures to others' stupidity, perceive others as incompetent and unfriendly, and see himself as entitled but not appropriately recognized. He might further perceive a social norm for collaboration but at the same time evaluate collaborative contexts as being uninteresting and useless for getting ahead. Jack might, therefore, proceed in telling his story of an unrecognized genius in a meaningless world of losers. To change this coherent story, Jack might need to be forced more explicitly to reflect on his own behaviors, on the specific ways it deviates from the behaviors of others, on his social reputations that are caused by this, and on how these reputations deviate from his intended effects on others.

State processes within each of the three domains set the stage for state processes in the next phase and the three phases themselves form a sequence of logically related processes. Goals and strategies guide individual's mental and behavioral states when entering an action unit. Individual's own experiences, own and others' behaviors, features of the environment, and how these were influenced by behaviors, all together build the basis of evaluations and reflections about oneself, others and inhabited environments. These evaluations and reflections then feed back into situational valuations and expectations.

# State processes and personality trait stability and change

We have defined personality characteristics as relatively enduring individual differences in a wide range of connected state processes. Consequently, personality development can be understood as stabilization and changes of these individual differences in state processes. Following our generic model, the existence of coherent personality differences and the comparatively strong stability of these differences can be well explained by the firm connection between processes within and across process domains. This is in line with the idea of personality stabilization due to individual differences in the reaction to and the selection, evocation, and manipulation of environmental information (Caspi & Roberts, 1999), and the self-reinforcing nature of social information processing mechanisms (e.g., Crick & Dodge, 1994; Nickerson, 1998). Similarly, individual state network perspectives conceptualize traits as individual differences in networks of connected state components. These state components are thought to be linked in a way that they mutually reinforce each other for causal, homeostatic, or logical reasons (see Cramer et al., 2012, for details). Thus, within individuals, states tend to develop into stable configurations (i.e., behavioral equilibriums) that underlie the strong temporal stability of globally assessed personality traits.

At the same time, the outlined personality processes point at potential ways of personality change. In principle, any of the outlined processes can be subject to change, thereby affecting other processes and potentially leading to a relatively enduring change in the levels of state expressions and in state contingencies (i.e., individual state networks reach a new equilibrium), that is, to personality trait change. The ease and effectiveness by which a given state change leads to personality change should depend on the strength and frequency of state change and on how strongly it is connected to other state aspects (i.e., the centrality of a state in an individual network). Changes in one state might push other states to similar levels (leading to permanent change) or, alternatively, these other states might pull the changed state back to its previous state level (leading to momentary fluctuations).[2]

# Linking macro- and micro-perspectives on personality development processes

Prior research on personality development processes has been mainly situated on a macro-level, focusing on the distal environmental and biological factors related to personality development (see Specht et al., 2014, for a recent overview) and less on the proximate mechanisms by which stabilization of and changes in personality are explained. We relate the micro-level approach to these macro-level analyses, thereby explaining how changes in biological structures (e.g., gene expression, hormonal levels; physical abilities) and environmental structures (e.g., probabilities of certain situational contexts, types of interaction partners), social roles (e.g., being a mother, friend, employee), age, and life events (e.g., marriage, birth of a child, accidents, death of significant others) lead to personality change (see Fig. 28.1).

Biological structures (e.g., individual differences in gene expression, hormonal levels) can restrict (or facilitate) the experience of mental states and the expression of state behaviors (e.g., Headey & Wearing, 1989; Ormel, Riese, & Rosmalen, 2012). According to a bottom-up approach to personality development, prolonged changes in personality states can lead to stable changes in general behavioral and mental tendencies that can in the long run affect neuroanatomical structures or gene expression, thereby permanently changing such biological set points for experiences and behaviors (see Roberts & Jackson, 2008; see arrow from "bias/habit formation and stabilization" to "environmental and biological structures" in Fig. 28.1). In addition, changes in biological structures can also be driven by ageing (e.g., genetically determined set-points are activated at a certain age, e.g., McCrae & Costa, 2008) and strong life events (e.g., effects of injuries, drug consumption, traumatic experiences).

Similarly, changes in environmental structures (e.g., culture and context differences in patterns of environmental cues) might change the range and intensity of expressed behavioral and experienced mental states, and thus, personality (i.e., socialization effects). Again, this can be triggered by ageing and life events. Importantly, the experience of life events can be actively driven by an individual's actions (i.e., selection effects; Caspi & Roberts, 1999). The proposed model can, thus, also be used to explain more complex genotype—environment effects (e.g., Scarr & McCartney, 1983), where genetic predispositions are suggested to affect

---

[2] In addition to identifying the specific kind of relevant state processes, future research should try to unravel in detail the time course and shape of personality change (see Luhmann, Orth, Specht, Kandler, & Lucas, 2014, for a recent detailed discussion) via state process changes.

people's typical actions which make certain life events more or less probable which changes the environmental structures in a way that further increases genetically determined actions. Another example concerns gene—environment interactions where repeated changes in action and experience states are caused by environmental changes but only in individuals with a specific biological make-up.

Social roles (Caspi, 1987; Roberts & Wood, 2006) and developmental tasks (Erikson, 1950; Havighurst, 1972; Hutteman, Hennecke, Orth, Reitz, & Specht, 2014) are among the most prominently discussed macro-analytical factors driving personality development. According to our model, this is due to the fact that they directly affect a number of specific state processes in the domain of evaluations and reflections (e.g., perceived social norms; comparison between actual, ideal, and ought selves) and goals and strategies (e.g., valuation of situational options; expected ability to perform certain actions). Social roles and developmental tasks change as individuals get older (i.e., they are age-graded) and are additionally related to life events (e.g., different social norms for individuals with or without kids).

In sum, the development of personality and the well-known effects of macro-analytical factors on personality development can be understood in terms of systematically related state processes. To gain fine-grained empirical insights on the stabilization of and changes in personality regarding different trait domains and developmental stages, these state processes, thus, need to be assessed.

## Assessing processes in personality development

The investigation of the described state processes involves considerable methodological challenges and the application of nonstandard assessment tools (see Harari et al., 2016; Lane, Miluzzo, Hong, Peebles, Choudury, & Campbell, 2010; Mehl & Conner, 2012; Reis & Gosling, 2010; Schmid Mast, Gatica-Perez, Frauendorfer, Nguyen, Choudhury, 2015; Trull & Ebner-Priemer, 2014; Wrzus & Mehl, 2015, for detailed overviews). Approaches to assess these states can be categorized according to two kinds of methodological options (see Table 28.1, e.g., Mehl, 2007). First, one can either try to assess the various processes in controlled laboratory sessions or within the field contexts they are experienced and acted out. Second, one can assess processes by subjective reports or more direct observations. Each of the resulting four assessment categories includes unique methodological strengths and limitations.[3]

---

[3] Here, we do not capture physiological recordings as another direct assessment method that can be applied to assess state processes in the lab (e.g., Dufner, Arslan, Hagemeyer, Schönbrodt, Denissen; 2015) or in the field (e.g., Bussmann, Ebner-Priemer, & Fahrenberg, 2009). Also, we do not consider statistical analyses needed to model personality development processes (see Nestler, Grimm, & Schönbrodt, 2015; and Voelkle & Wagner, Chapter 30, for overviews).

**Table 28.1  Categorization of methods for the assessment of state processes**

|                        | Laboratory-based | Field-based |
|------------------------|------------------|-------------|
| **Subjective reports** | Paper-pencil or computer-based self- and other-reports of one's own and other's mental states and behaviors; reports on situation characteristics | Time- and/or event-based experience-sampling of one's own and other's mental states and behaviors; reports on situation characteristics |
| **Direct observations** | Video-based behavior ratings and codings | Specific devices for behavior and situation capturing (e.g., Electronically Activated Recorder; Narrative Clip) |
|                        | Creation of objective situational features | Smartphone-based social sensing (e.g., of behavior, locations) |
|                        |                  | Online behavior (Twitter, Facebook, smartphone use) |

## Laboratory-based state assessments

Laboratory assessments provide researchers with control over the assessment context, thereby allowing to eliminate potentially confounding variables, to specify the environmental characteristics in a standardized way across individuals, and to directly access actually observable behaviors (Wrzus & Mehl, 2015). When being interested in Jack's and other's state processes, for example, one might design a laboratory-based study in which small groups of participants are videotaped while working on a number of relevant social interaction tasks (for an example see Geukes, Nestler, Küfner, & Back, 2016; osf.io/q5zwp).

## Subjective reports

Repeated state assessment of participants' mental states including their situational valuations, expectations, goals and strategies (preaction phase), their emotions, cognitions, and perceptions (action phase), and their attributions, evaluations of goal-attainment and reflections on their own, and the environments characteristics (postaction phase) can viably be realized via repeated paper-and-pencil or computer-/tablet-based questionnaires (e.g., before, during, and after each social interaction task). In the context of social interaction situations, one might also obtain relevant other-report information (e.g., liking, metaperceived affect and cognition, evaluations of relationship potential, reflections on others' personality characteristics) of multiple interaction partners, allowing to disentangle actor, partner, and relationship effects (Back & Kenny, 2010).

## Direct observations

Audiovisual recordings enable standardized quantifications of participants' behaviors by trained observers (see Bakeman, 2000; Furr & Funder, 2009, for overviews). Behavioral indicators might be realized in terms of behavioral ratings such as the friendliness of individuals' facial expression or the aggressiveness of their social reactions (i.e., molar level) and as specific behavioral codings such as the number/duration/intensity of smiles or of interruptions per event or time interval (i.e., molecular level).

## Methodological challenges

The main methodological challenges of capturing personality development processes in the lab pertain to resources, representativeness, and repetition. First, one needs a laboratory that allows for sufficiently detailed audiovisual recordings, potentially including multiple connected cameras and microphones that provide high-quality and time-stamped recordings of individuals verbal and nonverbal behaviors. Once behavior is recorded, one needs substantial time, organizing, and monetary and personal resources to obtain behavioral ratings and codings (Back & Egloff, 2009; Bakeman, 2000; Furr & Funder, 2009). Second, one needs to create laboratory situations that allow for the assessment of representative states that can be used as valid proxies for the participant's natural state responses. To this aim, one needs to carefully reflect on and pretest the psychologically active ingredients, trait-relevance and strength of situations, and on the natural variability of behavioral and mental states one is aiming at (see Back, Schmukle, & Egloff, 2009; Borkenau, Mauer, Riemann, Spinath, & Angleitner, 2004; Funder, Furr, & Colvin, 2000; Geukes, Breil et al., 2017; Ickes, 1983; Kirschbaum, Pirke, & Hellhammer, 1993, for existing examples). Third, as personality development processes unfold over longer periods of time, researchers need to use appropriately timed multisession designs in which participants repeatedly attend to laboratory assessments (Wrzus & Mehl, 2015).

## Field-based state assessments

Field assessments provide access to participants' momentary mental and behavioral states in their daily lives, i.e., in representative and relevant situations. They can capture the natural occurrences of states and how they unfold over time (i.e., their development; Bolger, Davis, & Rafaeli, 2003; Conner & Mehl, 2015; Mehl & Conner, 2012; Reis & Gable, 2000; Sbarra, 2006). One might, for example, try to assess Jack's state processes in his natural social environment, thereby longitudinally capturing the goals and strategies he pursues, the situations he encounters, the emotions, thoughts, and strivings he experiences and the behaviors he shows therein, and the evaluations and reflections that might be triggered by these interactive experiences (see Geukes, Hutteman, Nestler, Küfner, & Back, 2016, for an example; osf.io/2pmcr).

## Subjective reports

Repeated experience-sampling self-reports (Bolger & Laurenceau, 2013; Gosling & Johnson, 2010; Kubiak & Krog, 2012) of states can be realized in mobile ways (e.g., via smartphones) or in stationary ways (e.g., via online diaries) and they can be assessed contingent on specified events (i.e., event-based) or in regular time intervals (i.e., time-based). In case defined groups or complete networks of participants are investigated, one might additionally capture other perceptions of relevant states (e.g., how Jack's social partners perceive his behavior). For setting up an experience-sampling study, one might apply standard survey technologies (e.g., Qualtrics), or more powerful software solutions that allow for a highly flexible programming (e.g., Survey Signal, Hofmann & Patel, 2015; formr, Arslan & Tata, 2015; see Gunthert & Wenze, 2012; Moskowitz & Sadikaj, 2012; Wrzus & Mehl, 2015, for overviews).

## Direct observations

A few specific devices have been developed to more directly but unobtrusively assess behavioral and situational information within participants' daily lives. The Electronically Activated Recorder (EAR; Mehl, Pennebaker, Crow, Dabbs, & Price, 2001; Mehl, Robbins, & Deters, 2012), for example, intermittently registers snippets of ambient sounds, that can be used to infer information about the situational contexts people select (e.g., physical environment: at work or in a café; social environment: in a group, dyad or alone) and the state behaviors they engage in (e.g., arguing, laughing). Information on the situations people select in their daily lives and the detailed physical and social characteristics of these situations can also be inferred from visual observation devices attached to participants' clothes (e.g., the Narrative Clip, a wearable lifelogging camera; http://getnarrative.com) or worn as glasses (e.g., Google Glass; http://www.google.com/glass/).

An increasingly important way of assessing social behaviors targets individuals' online behavior, that is, on social and communication networks such as Twitter, Facebook, Instagram, or short message services. Using Jack's Facebook posts as an example, they allow to continuously record his online behavior (e.g., status updates or likes), and corresponding data produced by others (e.g., comments or likes by Jack's friends). To access Facebook data, for example, one could either use already assessed data such as from the myPersonality-project (mypersonality.org) or set up one's own Facebook study (http://developers.facebook.com; for details see Kosinski, Matz, Gosling, Popov, & Stillwell, 2015).

The rise of smartphone usage resulted in another powerful and potentially integrative approach to field-based assessments of personality processes: smartphone sensing methods (see Chittaranjan, Blom, & Gatica-Perez, 2013; Harari et al., 2016; Lane et al., 2010; Lathia et al., 2013; Miller, 2012; Schmid Mast et al., 2015, for overviews). Smartphones provide access to a variety of mobile sensor data (e.g., Wifi and GPS scans; accelerometer, light, microphone, and proximity sensors) and other phone data (e.g., call and sms logs) that can be used to infer rich information about individual's behaviors (e.g., social interactions, daily activities, mobility patterns) and the environment s/he selects (e.g., specific locations and context features). A particularly promising approach is to combine smartphone sensing methods with the automated extraction of behavioral information (for example, see Schmid Mast et al., 2015, for nonverbal, and Serfass & Sherman, 2015, for linguistic information) and the above-mentioned experience-sampling of subjective reports. One might, for example, automatically trigger event-based assessments of subjective mental states (e.g., momentary affect, cognitions, strivings) contingent on automatically collected and processed situational features (e.g., survey is triggered when iEAR is active, when Narrative Clip takes a picture, when SMS or voice contains negative affect, when present other people are identified).

# Methodological challenges

The main methodological challenges of capturing personality development processes in the field pertain to the technical implementation, the subjectivity of experience-sampling reports, the psychological meaning of objectively gathered information, and the timing of assessments.[4] The technical implementation of field-based assessments is a challenge in itself as the programming of assessment tools, data preparation and behavior extraction demand specialized programming and data processing expertise that neither is quickly developed nor is it inexpensive. In many cases, psychologist will have to collaborate with computer and information scientists.

Experience-sampling reports are a comparatively straightforward method that reduce common biases and maximize generalizability of individuals' self-reported mental states (e.g., retrospective biases; Bradburn, Sudman, & Wansink, 2004; Brose, Lindenberger, & Schmiedek, 2013; Schwarz & Oyserman, 2001). When it comes to the assessment of behaviors and situational features, however, one has to keep in mind that self-reported behaviors and situation perceptions might differ substantially from the behaviors actually shown and the situational characteristics actually present. The effect of shared self-report method variance is of particular importance, when being interested in the development of the dynamic relations between situation characteristics, behaviors, and mental states. Optimally, subjective reports of situations and behaviors are combined with more objective assessments.

A complementary challenge pertains to these more objective assessments. Most social sensing data for example is decontextualized and not directly associated with psychological meaning. Thus an additional task lies in the adequate combination and translation of objective environmental and behavioral data into psychologically meaningful units of analysis. There are two principle ways in which one can derive

---

[4] Online behavior and social sensing approaches to the assessment of personality processes also come along with a number of delicate privacy and ethical issues that need to be considered carefully (see Harari et al., 2016; Wrzus & Mehl, 2015).

such rules for data combination. One can apply machine learning to derive a predictive algorithm based on any existing objective features that best reproduces a more meaningful behavioral or situation state criteria (data-driven, bottom-up) and/or one can theoretically derive a combination of objective features that are conceptually related to a state of interest (theory-driven, top-down).

Finally, assessments of states in the field require nontrivial timing decisions. Self- and other reports as well as direct observations can be realized with time-based and/or event-based designs and with different time resolutions. Comparatively dynamic phenomena might require rather close monitoring and intensive designs to be adequately reflected in the data, whereas less dynamic phenomena can be appropriately captured in stationary online diaries (Conner, Barrett, Tugade, & Tenner, 2007). Social sensing and online platforms might even allow continuous assessments. Timing decisions should be made on the basis of theoretical assumptions regarding the hypothesized dynamics of the investigated phenomenon (see Luhmann et al., 2014) and might involve the combination of different schedules (e.g., measurement burst designs; see Sliwinski, 2008).

## Conclusion

Research on personality development has provided us with a wealth of insights on developmental patterns of traits across the life span, the joint influence of environmental and genetic factors, and more specific effects related to life events and social roles. It is now time to analyze in detail the processes underlying these patterns and effects. Unraveling the mechanisms of personality stabilization and change will lead to both more fine-grained theories and more effective interventions. The assessment of state process data, however, involves the investment of considerable resources and a number of nontrivial methodological challenges. We hold that it is worth the effort as this will help us to better understand what it means when a trait changes and what it takes to change a trait.

## References

Arslan, R.C., & Tata, C.S. (2015). formr.org survey software (Version v0.8.2). doi:10.5281/zenodo.32986.

Back, M. D., & Egloff, B. (2009). Yes we can! A plea for direct behavioral observation in personality research. *European Journal of Personality, 23*, 403−405.

Back, M. D., & Kenny, D. A. (2010). The social relations model: How to understand dyadic processes. *Social and Personality Psychology Compass, 4*, 855−870.

Back, M. D., & Nestler, S. (2017). Dual process approaches to personality. In R. Deutsch, B. Gawronski, & W. Hofmann (Eds.). *Reflective and impulsive determinants of human behavior* (pp. 137−154). New York, NY: Routledge.

Back, M. D., Baumert, A., Denissen, J. J. A., Hartung, F.-M., Penke, L., Schmukle, S. C., ... Wrzus, C. (2011). PERSOC: A unified framework for understanding the dynamic interplay of personality and social relationships. *European Journal of Personality*, *25*, 90−107.

Back, M. D., Schmukle, S. C., & Egloff, B. (2009). Predicting actual behavior from the explicit and implicit self-concept of personality. *Journal of Personality and Social Psychology*, *97*, 533−548.

Bakeman, R. (2000). Behavioral observation and coding. In H. T. Reis, & C. M. Judd (Eds.), *Handbook of research methods in social and personality psychology* (pp. 138−159). New York, NY: Cambridge University Press.

Bauer, J. J., & McAdams, D. P. (2004). Personal growth in adults' stories of life transitions. *Journal of Personality*, *72*, 573−602.

Bleidorn, W., Kandler, C., & Caspi, A. (2014). The behavioral genetics of personality development in adulthood—Classic, modern, and future trends. *European Journal of Personality*, *28*, 244−255.

Bolger, N., & Laurenceau, J.-P. (2013). *Intensive longitudinal methods: An introduction to diary and experience sampling research*. New York, NY: Guilford Press.

Bolger, N., Davis, A., & Rafaeli, E. (2003). Diary methods: Capturing life as it is lived. *Annual Review of Psychology*, *54*, 579−616.

Borkenau, P., Mauer, N., Riemann, R., Spinath, F. M., & Angleitner, A. (2004). Thin slices of behavior as cues of personality and intelligence. *Journal of Personality and Social Psychology*, *86*, 599−614.

Bradburn, N. N., Sudman, S., & Wansink, B. (2004). *Asking questions: The definitive guide to questionnaire design*. San Francisco, CA: Jossey-Bass.

Brose, A., Lindenberger, U., & Schmiedek, F. (2013). Affective states contribute to trait reports of affective well-being. *Emotion*, *13*, 940−948.

Bussmann, J. B. J., Ebner-Priemer, U. W., & Fahrenberg, J. (2009). Ambulatory activity monitoring: Progress in measurement of activity, posture, and specific motion patterns in daily life. *European Psychologist*, *14*, 142−152.

Carver, C. S., & Scheier, M. E. (1981). *Attention and self-regulation: A control theory approach to human behavior*. New York, NY: Springer.

Caspi, A. (1987). Personality in the life course. *Journal of Personality and Social Psychology*, *53*, 1203−1213.

Caspi, A., & Roberts, B. W. (1999). Personality continuity and change across the life course. In L. A. Pervin, & O. P. John (Eds.), *Handbook of personality: Theory and research* (2nd ed., pp. 300−346). New York, NY: Guilford Press.

Cervone, D. (2005). Personality architecture: Within-person structures and processes. *Annual Review of Psychology*, *56*, 423−452.

Chittaranjan, G., Blom, J., & Gatica-Perez, D. (2013). Mining largescale smartphone data for personality studies. *Personal and Ubiquitous Computing*, *17*, 433−450.

Conner, T., Barrett, L. F., Tugade, M. M., & Tenner, H. (2007). Idiographic personality: The theory and practice of experience sampling. In R. W. Robins, R. C. Fraley, & R. F. Krueger (Eds.), *Handbook of research methods in personality research* (pp. 79−96). New York, NY: Guildford Press.

Conner, T., & Mehl, M. R. (2015). Ambulatory assessment—Methods for studying everyday life. In R. A. Scott, S. M. Kosslyn, & M. Stephen (Eds.), *Emerging trends in the social and behavioral sciences* (pp. 1−15). Thousand Oaks, CA: SAGE Publications.

Cramer, A. O. J., van der Sluis, S., Noordhof, A., Wichers, M., Geschwind, N., Aggen, S. H., … Borsboom, D. (2012). Dimensions of normal personality as networks in search of equilibrium: You can't like parties if you don't like people. *European Journal of Personality*, *26*(4), 414−431.

Crick, N., & Dodge, K. (1994). A review and reformulation of social information-processing mechanisms in children's social adjustment. *Psychological Bulletin, 115*, 74−101.

Denissen, J. J., & Penke, L. (2008). Motivational individual reaction norms underlying the Five-Factor Model of personality: First steps towards a theory-based conceptual framework. *Journal of Research in Personality, 42*, 1285−1302.

Denissen, J. J. A., Ulfers, H., Lüdtke, O., Muck, P. M., & Gerstorf, D. (2014). Longitudinal transactions between personality and occupational roles: A large and heterogeneous study of job beginners, stayers, and changers. *Developmental Psychology, 50*, 1931−1942.

Denissen, J. J. A., Wood, D., Penke, L., & van Aken, M. A. G. (2013). Self-regulation underlies temperament and personality: An integrative developmental framework. *Child Development Perspectives, 7*, 255−260.

DeYoung, C. G. (2015). Cybernetic Big Five Theory. *Journal of Research in Personality, 56*, 33−58.

Dufner, M., Arslan, R. C., Hagemeyer, D., Schönbrodt, F. D., & Denissen, J. J. A. (2015). Affective contingencies in the affiliative domain: Physiological assessment, associations with the affiliation motive, and prediction of behavior. *Journal of Personality and Social Psycholog, 109*, 662−676.

Dunlop, W. L. (2015). Contextualized personality, beyond traits. *European Journal of Personality, 29*, 310−325.

Erikson, E. H. (1950). *Childhood and society*. New York, NY: Norton.

Feather, N. T. (1959). Subjective probability and decision under uncertainty. *Psychological Review, 66*, 150−164.

Fleeson, W., & Jayawickreme, E. (2015). Whole trait theory. *Journal of Research in Personality, 56*, 82−92.

Funder, D. C., Furr, R. M., & Colvin, C. R. (2000). The Riverside Behavioral Q-sort: A tool for the description of social behavior. *Journal of Personality, 68*, 451−489.

Furr, R. M., & Funder, D. C. (2009). Behavioral observation. In R. W. Robins, C. Fraley, & R. F. Krueger (Eds.), *Handbook of research methods in personality psychology* (pp. 273−291). New York, NY: Guilford Press.

Geukes, K., Breil, S. M., Hutteman, R., Küfner, A. C. P., Nestler, S., & Back, M. D. (2017). Explaining the longitudinal interplay of personality and social relationships in the laboratory and in the field: The PILS and CONNECT study. Manuscript in preparation.

Geukes, K., Hutteman, R., Nestler, S., Küfner, A. C. P., & Back, M. (2016, January 20). CONNECT. Retrieved from osf.io/2pmcr.

Geukes, K., Nestler, S., Küfner, A. C. P., & Back, M. (2016, January 26). PILS—Personality Interaction Laboratory Study. Retrieved from osf.io/q5zwp.

Gollwitzer, P. M. (1990). Action phases and mind-sets. In E. T. Higgins, & R. M. Sorrentino (Eds.), *Handbook of motivation and cognition: Foundations of social behavior* (Vol. 2, pp. 53−92). New York, NY: Guilford.

Gosling, S. D., & Johnson, J. A. (2010). *Advanced methods for conducting online behavioral research*. Washington, DC: American Psychological Association.

Gross, J. J., & Thompson, R. A. (2007). Emotion regulation: Conceptual foundations. In J. J. Gross (Ed.), *Handbook of emotion regulation* (pp. 3−24). New York, NY: Guilford.

Gunthert, K. C., & Wenze, S. J. (2012). Daily diary methods. In M. R. Mehl, & T. Connor (Eds.), *Handbook of research methods for studying daily life* (pp. 144−159). New York, NY: Guilford Press.

Harris, J. R. (1995). Where is the child's environment? A group socialization theory of development. *Psychological Review, 102*, 458−489.

Harari, G. M., Lane, N. D., Wang, R., Crosier, B. S., Campbell, A. T., Gosling, S. D. (2016). Using smartphones to collect behavioral data in psychological science: Opportunities, practical considerations, and challenges. *Perspectives on Psychological Science*, 11, 838−854.

Hastie, R. (2001). Problems for judgment and decision making. *Annual Review of Psychology*, *52*, 653−683.

Havighurst, R. J. (1972). *Developmental tasks and education*. New York, NY: McKay Company.

Headey, B., & Wearing, A. (1989). Personality, life events, and subjective well-being: Toward a dynamic equilibrium model. *Journal of Personality and Social Psychology*, *57*, 731−739.

Heckhausen, H. (1991). *Motivation and action*. New York, NY: Springer-Verlag.

Hennecke, M., Bleidorn, W., Denissen, J. J. A., & Wood, D. (2014). A three-part framework for self-regulated personality development across adulthood. *European Journal of Personality*, *28*, 289−299.

Higgins, E. T. (1987). Self-discrepancy: A theory relating self and affect. *Psychological Review*, *94*, 319−340.

Hofmann, W., & Patel, P. V. (2015). SurveySignal: A convenient solution for experience sampling research using participants' own smartphones. *Social Science Computer Review*, *33*, 235−253.

Hutteman, R., Hennecke, M., Orth, U., Reitz, A. K., & Specht, J. (2014). Developmental tasks as a framework to study personality development in adulthood and old age. *European Journal of Personality*, *28*, 267−278.

Hutteman, R., Nestler, S., Wagner, J., Egloff, B., & Back, M. D. (2015). Wherever I may roam: Processes of self-esteem development from adolescence to emerging adulthood in the context of international student exchange. *Journal of Personality and Social Psychology*, *108*, 767−783.

Ickes, W. (1983). A basic paradigm for the study of unstructured dyadic interaction. *New Directions for Methodology of Social & Behavioral Science*, *15*, 5−21.

Kirschbaum, C., Pirke, K. M., & Hellhammer, D. H. (1993). The "Trier Social Stress Test"—A tool for investigating psychobiological stress responses in a laboratory setting. *Neuropsychobiology*, *28*, 76−81.

Kosinski, M., Matz, S. C., Gosling, S. D., Popov, V., & Stillwell, D. (2015). Facebook as a research tool for social sciences: Opportunities, challenges, ethical considerations, and practical guidelines. *American Psychologist*, *70*, 543−556.

Kubiak, T., & Krog, K. (2012). Computerized sampling of experience and behavior. In M. R. Mehl, & T. Connor (Eds.), *Handbook of research methods for studying daily life* (pp. 124−143). New York, NY: Guilford Press.

Lane, N. D., Miluzzo, E., Hong, L., Peebles, D., Choudhury, T., & Campbell, A. T. (2010). A survey of mobile phone sensing. *Communications Magazine, IEEE*, *48*, 140−150.

Lathia, N., Pejovic, V., Rachuri, K. K., Mascolo, C., Musolesi, M., & Rentfrow, P. J. (2013). Smartphones for large-scale behavior change interventions. *Pervasive Computing, IEEE*, *12*, 66−73.

Leary, M. R., & Baumeister, R. F. (2000). The nature and function of self-esteem: Sociometer theory. *Advances in Experimental Social Psychology*, *32*, 1−62.

Lodi-Smith, J., Geise, A. C., Roberts, B. W., & Robins, R. W. (2009). Narrating personality change. *Journal of Personality and Social Psychology*, *96*, 679−689.

Lodi-Smith, J., & Roberts, B. W. (2007). Social investment and personality: A meta-analysis of the relationship of personality traits to investment in work, family, religion, and volunteerism. *Personality and Social Psychology Review, 11*, 68−86.

Lüdtke, O., Roberts, B. W., Trautwein, U., & Nagy, G. (2011). A random walk down university avenue: Life paths, life events, and personality trait change at the transition to university life. *Journal of Personality and Social Psychology, 101*, 620−637.

Luhmann, M., Orth, U., Specht, J., Kandler, C., & Lucas, R. E. (2014). Studying changes in life circumstances and personality: It's about time. *European Journal of Personality, 28*, 256−266.

McCrae, R. R., & Costa, P. T., Jr. (2008). The Five-Factor Theory of personality. In O. P. John, R. W. Robins, & L. A. Pervin (Eds.), *Handbook of personality: Theory and research* (3rd ed., pp. 159−181). New York, NY: The Guilford Press.

Mehl, M. R. (2007). Eavesdropping on health: A naturalistic observation approach for social-health research. *Social and Personality Psychology Compass, 1*, 359−380.

Mehl, M. R., & Conner, T. S. (2012). *Handbook of research methods for studying daily life*. New York, NY: Guilford Press.

Mehl, M. R., Pennebaker, J. W., Crow, D. M., Dabbs, J., & Price, J. H. (2001). The Electronically Activated Recorder (EAR): A device for sampling naturalistic daily activities and conversations. *Behavior Research Methods, Instruments, and Computers, 33*, 517−523.

Mehl, M. R., Robbins, M. L., & Deters, F. G. (2012). Naturalistic observation of health-relevant social processes: The electronically activated recorder methodology in psychosomatics. *Psychosomatic Medicine, 74*, 410−417.

Miller, G. (2012). The smartphone psychology manifesto. *Perspectives on Psychological Science, 7*, 221−237.

Mischel, W., & Shoda, Y. (1998). Reconciling processing dynamics and personality dispositions. *Annual Review of Psychology, 49*, 229−258.

Moskowitz, D. S., & Sadikaj, G. (2012). Event-contingent recording. In M. R. Mehl, & T. Connor (Eds.), *Handbook of research methods for studying daily life* (pp. 160−175). New York, NY: Guilford Press.

Nestler, S., Grimm, K. J., & Schönbrodt, F. D. (2015). The social consequences and mechanisms of personality: How to analyse longitudinal data from individual, dyadic, round-robin, and network designs. *European Journal of Personality, 29*, 272−295.

Nickerson, R. S. (1998). Confirmation bias: A ubiquitous phenomenon in many guises. *Review of General Psychology, 2*, 175−220.

Ormel, J., Riese, H., & Rosmalen, J. G. M. (2012). Interpreting neuroticism scores across the adult life course: Immutable or experience-dependent set points of negative affect? *Clinical Psychology Review, 32*, 71−79.

Pasupathi, M., Mansour, E., & Brubaker, J. R. (2007). Developing a life story: Constructing relations between self and experience in autobiographical narratives. *Human Development, 50*, 85−110.

Read, S. J., Monroe, B. M., Brownstein, A. L., Yang, Y., Chopra, G., & Miller, L. C. (2010). A neural network model of the structure and dynamics of human personality. *Psychological Review, 117*, 61−92.

Reis, H. T., & Gable, S. L. (2000). Event sampling and other methods for studying everyday experience. In H. T. Reis, & C. M. Judd (Eds.), *Handbook of research methods in social and personality psychology* (pp. 190−222). New York, NY: Cambridge University Press.

Reis, H. T., & Gosling, S. D. (2010). Social psychological methods outside the laboratory. In S. T. Fiske, D. T. Gilbert, & G. Lindzey (Eds.), *Handbook of social psychology* (5th ed., pp. 82–114). New York, NY: Wiley.

Reitz, A. K., Zimmermann, J., Hutteman, R., Specht, J., & Neyer, F. J. (2014). How peers make a difference: The role of peer groups and peer relationships in personality development. *European Journal of Personality, 28*, 279–288.

Revelle, W., & Condon, D. M. (2015). A model for personality at three levels. *Journal of Research in Personality, 56*, 70–81.

Roberts, B. W., & Jackson, J. J. (2008). Sociogenomic personality psychology. *Journal of Personality, 76*, 1523–1544.

Roberts, B. W., Donnellan, M. B., & Hill, P. L. (2012). Personality trait development in adulthood: Findings and implications. In H. Tennen, & J. Suls (Eds.), *Handbook of Psychology* (2nd ed., pp. 183–196). Wiley, Inc, Chapter 9.

Roberts, B. W., & Wood, D. (2006). Personality development in the context of the neo-socioanalytic model of personality. In D. K. Mroczek, T. D. Little, D. K. Mroczek, & T. D. Little (Eds.), *Handbook of personality development* (pp. 11–39). Mahwah, NJ: Lawrence Erlbaum Associates Publishers.

Robinson, M. D. (2007). Personality, affective processing, and self-regulation: Toward process-based views of extraversion, neuroticism, and agreeableness. *Social and Personality Psychology Compass, 1*, 223–235.

Robinson, M. D., & Wilkowski, B. M. (2015). Personality processes and processes as personality: A cognitive perspectiveIn M. Mikulincer, & P. R. Shaver (Eds.), *APA handbook of personality and social psychology* (Vol. 4, pp. 129–145). Washington, DC: American Psychological Association.

Rotter, J. B. (1954). *Social learning and clinical psychology*. New York, NY: Prentice-Hall.

Sbarra, D. A. (2006). Predicting the onset of emotional recovery following nonmarital relationship dissolution: Survival analyses of sadness and anger. *Personality and Social Psychology Bulletin, 32*, 298–312.

Scarr, S., & McCartney, K. (1983). How people make their own environments: A theory of genotype->environment effects. *Child Development, 54*, 424–435.

Schmid Mast, M., Gatica-Perez, D., Frauendorfer, D., Nguyen, L., & Choudhury, T. (2015). Social sensing for psychology: Automated interpersonal behavior assessment. *Current Directions in Psychological Science, 24*, 154–160.

Schwarz, N., & Oyserman, D. (2001). Asking questions about behavior: Cognition, communication, and questionnaire construction. *American Journal of Evaluation, 22*, 127–160.

Serfass, D. S., & Sherman, R. A. (2015). Situations in 140 characters: Assessing real-world situations on Twitter. *PLoS ONE, 10*(11), 1–19.

Sliwinski, M. J. (2008). Measurement-burst designs for social health research. *Social and Personality Psychology Compass, 2*, 245–261.

Specht, J., Bleidorn, W., Denissen, J. J., Hennecke, M., Hutteman, R., Kandler, C., ... Zimmermann, J. (2014). What drives adult personality development? A comparison of theories and empirical evidence. *European Journal of Personality, 28*, 216–230.

Specht, J., Egloff, B., & Schmukle, S. C. (2011). Stability and change of personality across the life course: The impact of age and major life events on mean-level and rank-order stability of the Big Five. *Journal of Personality and Social Psychology, 101*, 862–882.

Swann, W. B., Jr., & Bosson, J. K. (2008). Identity negotiation: A theory of self and social interaction. In O. P. John, R. W. Robins, & L. A. Pervin (Eds.), *Handbook of personality: Theory and research* (pp. 448–471). New York, NY: Guilford.

Trull, T. J., & Ebner-Priemer, U. (2014). The role of ambulatory assessment in psychological science. *Current Directions in Psychological Science*, *23*, 466–470.

Vroom, V. H. (1964). *Work and motivation*. Oxford: Wiley.

Wood, D., & Denissen, J. J. A. (2015). A functional perspective on personality trait development. In N. R. Branscombe, & K. Reynolds (Eds.), *Psychology of change: Life contexts, experiences, and identities*. New York, NY: Psychology Press.

Wood, D., Gardner, M. H., & Harms, P. D. (2015). How functionalist and process approaches to behavior can explain trait covariation. *Psychological Review*, *122*, 84–111.

Wrzus, C. & Roberts, B. W. (in press). Processes of personality development in adulthood: The TESSeRa framework. *Personality and Social Psychology Review*.

Wrzus, C., & Mehl, M. (2015). Lab and/or field? Measuring personality processes and their social consequences. *European Journal of Personality*, *29*, 250–271.

# Behavior genetics and personality development: A methodological and meta-analytic review

*Christian Kandler[1,2] and Michael Papendick[1]*
[1]Bielefeld University, Bielefeld, Germany, [2]Medical School Berlin, Berlin, Germany

## The nature of personality characteristics

Personality characteristics typically encompass conceptually broad dimensions to describe individual differences in adults' typical patterns of feeling, thinking, behaving, and regulating emotions and motivations. Behavior genetic studies have shown that about 40% to 50% of individual differences in personality characteristics are attributable to genetic differences (Johnson, Vernon, & Feiler, 2008; Vukasović & Bratko, 2015). That is, the heritability of personality characteristics ranges from about $h^2 = 0.40$ to 0.50. Estimates typically vary between $h^2 = 0.20$ and 0.70, depending on the accuracy of measurement (Kandler, 2012a; Kandler & Bleidorn, 2015), the validity of the personality constructs (Riemann & Kandler, 2010), and the personality characteristics investigated (Kandler, Zimmermann, & McAdams, 2014).

An average heritability of $h^2 = 0.50$ does not imply that 50% of personality differences are coded in genes, already observable after birth, or immutable. Genetic differences do not signify stable differences, just as environmental differences do not necessarily reflect changeability. From a developmental perspective, personality is a lifelong-developing configuration of psychological uniqueness, in which some (heritable) characteristics emerge during the development from infancy to adulthood, such as major life goals, interests, and value priorities, whereas other characteristics arise within the first years of life (McAdams, 2015). These early observable features are often referred to as temperament traits, which encompass the individual's characteristic style of expressing and regulating emotion (e.g., positive vs negative affect) and behavior (e.g., activation vs inhibition). Although adult personality traits may reflect broader and more elaborated features including typical thinking styles and the regulation of social acting, the fundamental concepts of child temperament and adult personality traits are more alike than different (Kandler et al., 2012; see Herzhoff, Kushner, & Tackett, Chapter 2). They are considered to be more stable and less environmentally malleable over years than characteristics emerging later in human development (cf. Kandler et al., 2014).

Several models of temperament and personality traits are useful in describing individual differences and development in both childhood and adulthood (Kandler,

Personality Development Across the Lifespan. DOI: http://dx.doi.org/10.1016/B978-0-12-804674-6.00029-6

Riemann, & Angleitner, 2013; Rothbart, Ahadi, & Evans, 2000; Shiner & Caspi, 2003). They can be organized in a common integrative framework (Bouchard & Loehlin, 2001; Markon, Krueger, & Watson, 2005). The most influential and most economic model (i.e., the best compromise between bandwidth and parsimony) integrates personality traits along five dimensions. Although these Big Five trait dimensions have been labeled in many ways, a common and integrative characterization may employ the following labels: (1) *neuroticism* (or negative affectivity/emotionality) versus emotional stability; (2) *extraversion* (or positive emotionality/surgency) versus introversion; (3) *openness to experiences* (or intellect/general interest) versus closed-mindedness/ traditionalism; (4) *agreeableness* (cooperativeness) versus aggressiveness; and (5) *conscientiousness* (or constraint/effortful control) versus neglect/irresponsibleness. Each of the five trait dimensions hierarchically subsumes a set of more specific traits (DeYoung, Guilty, & Petersen, 2007; John, Naumann, & Soto, 2008), such as activity and sociability as two early temperament aspects of extraversion.

Based on the integrative labeling of the Big Five personality trait dimensions, we provide a meta-analytic review on how genetic and environmental factors contribute to the variation, stability, and change in personality traits across the lifespan. We introduce developmental behavior genetic models to illustrate genetic and environmental contributions to the development of personality differences. We collected behavioral genetic studies (i.e., twin, adoption, and extended family designs), which should include either longitudinal data or cross-sectional data from one or more age cohorts with a minimal sample size of 100 family member dyads. These studies should be based on the Big Five personality trait model or empirically related temperament and personality models, such as Buss and Plomin's (Buss & Plomin, 1984) temperament model and Eysenck's (Eysenck & Eysenck, 1985) or Tellegen's (Tellegen & Waller, 2008) hierarchical personality models. Using Web of Science, PsycINFO, and Google Scholar, we identified 46 studies which were published before October 1, 2015. Sixteen studies have been excluded because of overlapping samples or incomplete information regarding the sample or measurement instruments. Table 29.1 gives a summary of included studies which are ordered according to the average age of the youngest cohort at first measurement occasion.

## Genetic and environmental variation in personality traits

Heritability estimates for personality characteristics are primarily based on the comparison of the similarity of monozygotic twins with the similarity of dizygotic twins. Therefore, we explain this design in more detail. Monozygotic (MZ) twins are genetically identical individuals and thus share all of the genetic factors (i.e., additive as well as nonadditive genetic factors $G_A$ and $G_{NA}$, see Fig. 29.1), which contribute to individual differences in personality. If MZ twins are or were reared together, they may also share or have experienced environmental factors ($E_S$), which can account for their resemblance. As a consequence, differences between MZ twin siblings must be attributable to nonshared environmental factors ($E_{NS}$).

**Table 29.1 Description of studies considered for meta-analysis**

| Authors | Design | | Age range | | Mean age | | Big Five personality traits | | | | |
|---|---|---|---|---|---|---|---|---|---|---|---|
| | $n_{Times}$ | $n_{Cohorts}$ | LO | HI | $M_{1,1}$ | $M_{i,j}$ | N | E | O | A | C |
| Plomin et al. (1993)[a] | 2 | 1 | 1.2 | 1.7 | 1.2 | 1.7 | EM | AC/SO | | | |
| Hudziak et al. (2003)[a,b] | 1 | 3 | 3 | 10 | 3.0 | | | | | Agg | |
| Hur (2009)[a] | 1 | 1 | 2 | 9 | 4.3 | | EM | AC/SO | | | |
| Goldsmith et al. (1997)[a] | 1 | 1 | 2.8 | 8.3 | 5.5 | | NA | SU | | | EC |
| Spinath & Angleitner (1998)[a] | 1 | 1 | 2 | 14 | 6.6 | | EM | AC/SO | | | |
| Matheny & Dolan (1980)[a] | 2 | 1 | 7 | 10 | 8.0 | 11.7 | EM | AC/SO | O | TM | CM |
| De Fruyt et al. (2006)[a] | 2 | 1 | 5 | 14 | 8.7 | 13.1 | N | E | O | A | C |
| Spengler et al. (2012)[c] | 2 | 1 | 7 | 14 | 9.1 | 16.0 | N | E | O | A | C |
| Gillespie et al. (2004)[c] | 1 | 1 | 12 | 16 | 12.0 | 15.5 | N | E | | | |
| Ganiban et al. (2008)[a] | 3 | 2 | 11 | 18 | 12.8 | | EM | AC/SO | | | |
| Rettew et al. (2006)[c] | 2 | 1 | 12 | 18 | 15.5 | | N | E | | | |
| Rettew et al. (2008)[c] | 1 | 1 | 12 | 18 | 15.5 | | N | E | | | |
| Hansell et al. (2012)[c] | 1 | 1 | 12 | 25.6 | 15.5 | | N | E | | | |
| Lewis et al. (2014)[c] | 1 | 1 | 16 | 16 | 16.0 | | NE | $PE_{A+C}$ | O | A | C |
| Hopwood et al. (2011)[c] | 1 | 1 | 16 | 30 | 17.0 | 29.0 | N | E | O | | CO |
| Bratko & Butkovic (2007)[c] | 3 | 1 | 15 | 23 | 17.3 | 21.3 | N | E | | | |
| Kupper et al. (2011)[c] | 2 | 1 | 14 | 75 | 17.3 | 29.6 | NA | SI | | | |
| Scarr et al. (1981)[c] | 3 | 1 | 16 | 22 | 18.5 | | N | E | | | |
| McGue et al. (1993)[c] | 1 | 1 | 17 | 37 | 19.8 | 29.6 | NE | PE | O | A | CO |
| Ono et al. (2000)[c] | 2 | 1 | 15 | 27 | 20.2 | | N | E | | | C |
| Viken et al. (1994)[c] | 1 | 6 | 18 | 29 | 20.5 | 56.5 | N | E | | A | |
| Kandler et al. (2010)[c,d] | 2 | 2 | 16 | 75 | 22.7 | 55.0 | N | E | O | A | C |
| Loehlin & Martin (2001)[c] | 3 | 2 | 17 | 92 | 23.2 | 61.4 | N | E | | | |
| Laceulle et al. (2013)[c] | 1 | 2 | 18 | 63 | 23.4 | 44.7 | N | E | | | |
| Bell & Kandler (in press)[c] | 4 | 1 | 52 | 61 | 56.5 | | N | E | O | A | C |
| Bergeman et al. (1993)[c] | 1 | 1 | 26 | 87 | 58.6 | | N | E | O | A | C |
| Johnson et al. (2005)[c] | 1 | 1 | 27 | 99 | 59.4 | 64.4 | NE | PE | | | |
| Pedersen & Reynolds (1998)[c] | 2 | 1 | 26 | 97 | 60.2 | 69.2 | N | E | O | | CO |
| Kandler et al. (2015)[c] | 4 | 1 | 64 | 85 | 71.3 | 75.6 | N | E | O | A | C |
| Read et al. (2006)[c] | 2 | 1 | >78 | | 82.3 | 86.3 | N | E | O | A | C |

Note: $n_{Times}$: Number of measurement occasions; $n_{Cohorts}$: number of cohorts; LO: lowest age; HI: highest age; $M_{1,1}$: average age of the youngest cohort at first measurement occasion; $M_{i,j}$: average age of the oldest cohort $i$ at the last measurement occasion $j$; N: neuroticism; E: extraversion; O: openness; A: agreeableness; C: conscientiousness; EM: emotionality; AC: activity; SO: sociability; EC: effortful control; SU: surgency; NA: negative affectivity; NE: negative emotionality; PE: positive emotionality; $PE_{A+C}$: positive emotionality averaged across agentic PE and communal PE; CO: constraint; SI: social inhibition; TM: tough-mindedness; CM: compliant morality.

[a]Mother/parents reports.
[b]Teacher reports.
[c]Self-reports.
[d]Peer reports.

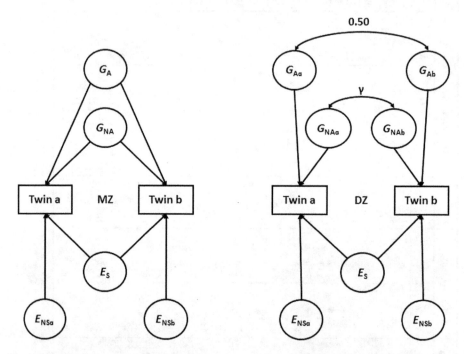

**Figure 29.1** Twin model for monozygotic (MZ) and dizygotic (DZ) twins: $G_A$ = additive genetic factors; $G_{NA}$ = nonadditive genetic factors; $E_S$ = environmental factors shared by twins; $E_{NS}$ = environmental factors not shared by twins (including measurement error); $\gamma$ = genetic correlation due to genetic dominance effects shared by DZ twins ($\gamma = 0.25$ in case of genetic dominance effects within gene loci; $\gamma = 0$ in case of genetic dominance effects between gene loci).

Dizygotic (DZ) twins are same-aged first-degree siblings, who share—like other (nontwin) first-degree siblings—on average 50% of their segregating genes, which can vary among humans. Thus DZ twins have a 50% probability of sharing additive genetic factors ($G_A$). In fact, additive genetic factors are correlated among biological family members as a function of their genetic relatedness. This is different with respect to nonadditive genetic factors ($G_{NA}$). DZ twins and other first-degree siblings but not other relatives can share genetic dominance effects, which can thus be correlated to some degree between DZ twins.[1] It can further be assumed that age-related influences and common environmental factors ($E_S$), which are not driven by the phenotypic (i.e., observable) similarity of twins, act to increase DZ twins' resemblance to the same degree as they contribute to the similarity of MZ twins.

[1] DZ twins have a 25% probability of sharing within-gene-loci dominance effects, because they get one of two gene variants within a gene locus from each parent resulting in four possible combinations of gene variants within this gene locus for first-degree siblings. However, the number of potential combinations between gene variants among gene loci is infinite. As a consequence, DZ twin pairs and other biological relatives (except genetically identical MZ twins) have a probability of sharing between-gene-loci dominance effects close to zero (i.e., epistatic gene interaction).

Thus the similarity and the dissimilarity of DZ twins are attributable to both genetic and environmental factors.

Assuming independence and additivity of genetic and environmental factors (cf. Kandler & Zapko-Willmes, Chapter 8), it follows from the logic of the twin design that the difference between the MZ and the DZ twin correlations informs about the heritability of a trait. The larger the difference, the larger the genetic contribution to the similarity of genetically identical individuals and to the differences among genetically unrelated individuals. As a rule of thumb, heritability can be broadly estimated as twice the MZ−DZ difference: $h^2 = 2 \times (r_{MZ} - r_{DZ})$. Personality correlations between MZ twins (uncorrected for error of measurement) typically range from $r = 0.30$ to $0.50$, whereas correlations between DZ twins or other first-degree relatives usually vary between $r = 0.10$ and $0.20$ (Johnson et al., 2008). The similarity between other biological relatives, such as half siblings, or biologically unrelated family members, such as adoptees or stepsiblings, is even smaller. This family correlation pattern with respect to personality traits is positively associated with the genetic relatedness and thus indicates a substantial heritability.

MZ twin correlations often tend to be larger than twice the DZ twin correlations indicating that both additive and nonadditive genetic factors contribute to twins' similarity in personality. The comparison between average broad-sense heritability estimates (additive + nonadditive genetic components) for personality traits based on studies including MZ twins ($h^2 = 0.47$) and narrow-sense heritability estimates (additive genetic component only) based on other genetically informative designs, such as adoption studies ($h^2 = 0.22$), suggests a significant contribution of epistatic gene interaction, because those influences are only shared by genetically identical twins (Vukasović & Bratko, 2015). Therefore, twin studies are essential to estimate the total genetic contribution to personality differences or, in other words, the broad-sense heritability including additive and nonadditive genetic contributions.

Heritability estimates are often underestimated to the degree to which personality traits are unreliably measured and twin correlations are not corrected for variance due to error of measurement. Random error of measurement is confounded with estimates of nonshared environmental factors ($E_{NS}$) that act to increase twin pairs' dissimilarity. After correcting for error variance ($\varepsilon^2$), the twin correlations, the differences between MZ and DZ twin correlations, and thus the heritability estimates are typically larger (as a rule of thumb: $h^2 = [2 \times (r_{MZ} - r_{DZ})]/[1 - \varepsilon^2]$). On the basis of results from 13 longitudinal studies, 14 cross-sectional studies on different age groups, and three cross-sequential studies (see Table 29.1), we estimated the average heritability of Big Five personality traits. Table 29.2 shows heritability estimates corrected and uncorrected for error variance. The estimates are comparable across the five trait dimensions.

MZ and DZ twin correlations within samples of twins reared apart, who do not share environmental influences after separation, are similar to twin correlations within samples of twins reared together indicating little contributions of shared environmental factors. The average estimates across the studies range between 0.01 (extraversion) and 0.06 (agreeableness) for uncorrected values and between 0.01

**Table 29.2  Average heritability estimates for Big Five personality traits**

|  | Uncorrected | | | Corrected | | |
|---|---|---|---|---|---|---|
|  | $h^2$ | | | $h^2/(1 - \varepsilon^2)$ | | |
|  | k | Ø | SE | k | Ø | SE |
| Neuroticism/negative affectivity | 61 | 0.39 | 0.11 | 67 | 0.49 | 0.13 |
| Extraversion/positive emotionality | 59 | 0.44 | 0.08 | 68 | 0.58 | 0.09 |
| Openness/intellect | 20 | 0.43 | 0.12 | 21 | 0.63 | 0.15 |
| Agreeableness/aggressiveness | 19 | 0.41 | 0.13 | 20 | 0.54 | 0.16 |
| Conscientiousness/constraint | 23 | 0.51 | 0.11 | 25 | 0.60 | 0.12 |

*Note*: Uncorrected estimates were attenuated due to error variance in personality measurement; corrected estimates were calculated as the proportion of the genetic variance to the reliability of personality measures; $k$ = number of estimates across studies; Ø = average estimate; SE = standard error of the average estimate.

and 0.09 for corrected values. Thus environments primarily act individually and affect the dissimilarity of twins. As a rule of thumb, the relative contribution of individual environmental influences to individual differences ($e^2$) can be estimated as follows: $e^2 = 1 - r_{MZ}$ (uncorrected for error of measurement) or $e^2 = (1 - \varepsilon^2) - r_{MZ}$ (corrected for error of measurement).

It is important to note that estimates of heritability and environmental contributions (i.e., environmentality $= 1 - h^2$) represent net effects of genetic and environmental factors on individual differences in a specific trait within a specific group or population at a specific point in time. Genetic and environmental variance components have few implications for developmental processes. Nevertheless, genetically informative (or environmentally sensitive) longitudinal studies and studies on different age groups can provide insights into the change of the relative contribution of genetic and environmental factors to individual differences in personality that can have implications for the etiology of personality development across the lifespan.

# Genetic and environmental contributions to personality differences across the lifespan

From a developmental view on the gene–environment interplay, genetic influences can drive experiences (Scarr & McCartney, 1983). People actively select niches and shape their environments, they evoke social reactions and construct experiences that are consistent with their genetic makeup (genotype). As a result, specific genotypes are associated with specific environments and thus with potential environmental factors. These genotype–environment correlations in terms of the genetic control of exposure to environmental influences act like genetic influences and, thus, would be confounded with estimates of the genetic contribution, if not explicitly modeled in quantitative genetic studies. With cumulative self-determination, genetically driven selection of environments (i.e., active genotype—environment correlation) may play an increasingly important role for the development of personality differences. As a consequence, the heritability estimates for personality traits should increase over time (see Fig. 29.2A).

In addition, individuals respond differently to the same environmental influences depending upon their genotypes. Some persons are more and others are less resilient against the same environmental stressors. If this type of genotype × environment interaction is not explicitly considered in behavior genetic models, it would be confounded with estimates of the genetic component, as genotype × shared environment interaction in terms of the genetic sensitivity to *same* environmental influences acts like genetic influences. Genotype × shared environment interaction may play a more important role for the siblings' resemblance during the first two decades of life, when siblings reared together share many environments (e.g., family, school, and neighborhood). As a consequence, correlations of MZ twins, whose genotypes are identical, should be larger in relation to the correlations of DZ twins and other siblings. In other words, if genotype × shared environment interaction plays an important role during childhood and adolescence, heritability of personality traits should be larger in these periods of life compared to other life stages. In adulthood, interactions between genotypes and environmental influences not shared by twins (e.g., own family, spouse, and working environment) are more common. These genotype × nonshared environment interactions in terms of the genetic sensitivity to *individual* environmental influences lead to a decline of the twins' similarity, because it would act like nonshared environmental influences, if not explicitly modeled in quantitative genetic studies. Consequently, the heritability of personality traits should be smaller in adulthood compared to younger life stages (see Fig. 29.2B).

The decreasing heritability from childhood to adulthood may also be attributable to cumulating unique environmental factors, since people gain different experiences. If these experiences accumulate across time, whether or not they interact with genetic influences, they would have the effect of making individuals, whether or not they are genetically related, less similar across the lifespan. In other words, with increasing environmental differences in personality and given stable genetic differences, the heritability of personality traits should decrease over time (see Fig. 29.2C).

Based on the heritability estimates reported in the 30 studies elected for the meta-analysis, we can visualize the age trends of heritability across the lifespan. For a better comparability across the studies and different measurement methods, all heritability estimates have been corrected for unreliability of personality measures ($h_{COR}^2 = h^2/[1-\varepsilon^2] = h^2/\text{Reliability}$) except for those studies which used factor scores. Fig. 29.3 illustrates a general (linear) decline of heritability across the lifespan. However, the age trend of heritability can best be described as a nonlinear (polynomial) function, which indicates an increasing heritability of personality traits during the development from infancy to adulthood, whereas heritability peaks in young adulthood and declines subsequently.

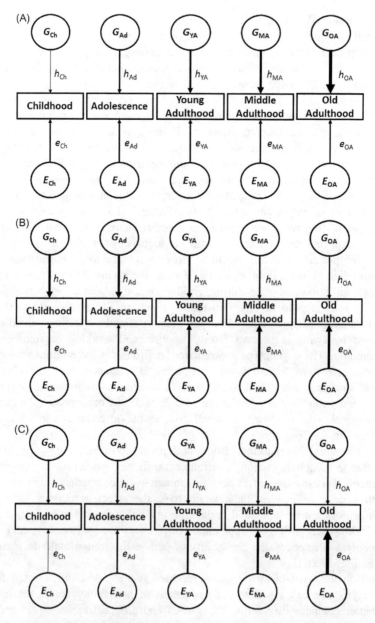

**Figure 29.2** Three different hypothetical age trends of genetic (*G*) and environmental (*E*) variation in personality: (A) the genetic variance and thus the heritability estimates increase due to active genotype—environment correlation across the lifespan; (B) the genetic variance and heritability estimates are larger in childhood and adolescence due to the important role of genotype × shared environment interaction during these life stages, but this switches in young adulthood, environmental variance is larger in middle and old adulthood and thus heritability estimates are smaller due to genotype × nonshared environment interaction in these adult ages; and (C) the environmental variance increases due to cumulative environmental influences and as a result the heritability estimates (given stable genetic differences) decline across the lifespan.

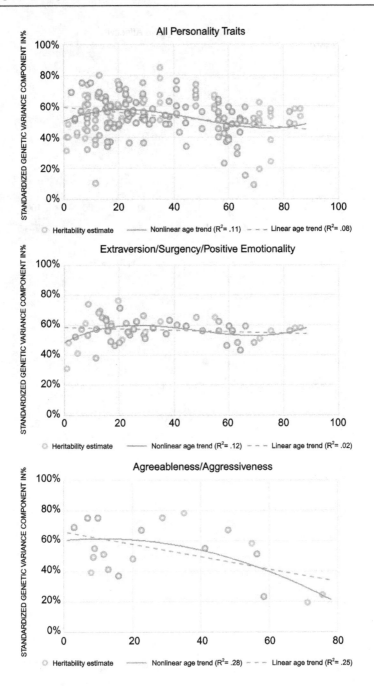

**Figure 29.3** Heritability (the proportion of individual differences due to genetic differences) for Big Five personality traits as a function of age. Estimates are based on the results of the 30 genetically informative longitudinal, cross-sequential, or age-cohort studies (see Table 29.1) and weighted by sample size (darker points carried more weight in the analysis).

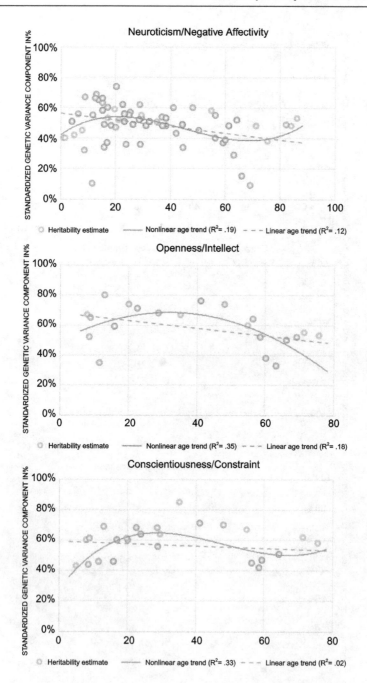

**Figure 29.3**  (Continued)

The increasing heritability during the first three decades of life may reflect active genotype—environment correlations in terms of niche picking and identity formation (cf. Fig. 29.2A). When children grow up to become independent young adults and to establish their role in society, the unfolding of the genotype in fitting environments appears to play an important role. However, the contributions of individual environmental influences and experiences, whether or not they interact with genetic factors, appear to become more important across the lifespan, leading to a decline of the heritability across adulthood (cf. Fig. 29.2B and C). For neuroticism, extraversion, and conscientiousness, heritability tends to increase again in old age. However, this trend is based on only two studies investigating samples with an average age beyond 70 (Kandler, Kornadt, Hagemeyer, & Neyer, 2015; Read, Vogler, Pedersen, & Johansson, 2006) and has to be replicated before drawing final conclusions.

# Stability of genetic and environmental differences in personality across the lifespan

Even though the change of genetic and environmental variation in personality traits across the lifespan reveals an important insight into the potential role of genotype—environment interplay as developmental mechanism, longitudinal twin studies can go beyond the variance decomposition and allow estimations of the stability and change of genetic and environmental differences (Bleidorn, Kandler, & Caspi, 2014). Longitudinal studies have provided robust evidence for a declining stability of individual differences in personality traits (i.e., the correlation within traits over time, in the following referred to as phenotypic stability) with an increasing interval between two measurement occasions (Conley, 1984; Fraley & Roberts, 2005). This indicates that the probability of individual differences in personality change increases with the timespan investigated. Given equal time intervals, longitudinal studies have also shown that the phenotypic stability of personality traits is low in childhood, rises across adolescence and young adulthood, reaches a relatively high plateau in middle adulthood, and appears to decline again in old age (Lucas & Donnellan, 2011; Specht, Egloff, & Schmukle, 2011; Wortman, Lucas, & Donnellan, 2012).

The patterns of relative personality stability are well known. However, the stability of genetic and environmental differences in personality traits (in the following referred to as genotypic and environmental stability) has just recently been investigated based on a restricted set of studies (Briley & Tucker-Drop, 2014; Kandler, 2012b). Our meta-analytic overview goes beyond these reviews by including new as well as older longitudinal twin studies on temperament and personality development, which were not yet considered in previous meta-analyses (e.g., Plomin et al., 1993; Kandler et al., 2015; Laceulle, Ormel, Aggen, Neale, & Kendler, 2013), and by excluding studies, which are not informative with respect to the Big Five personality traits (e.g., attention problems; cf. Briley & Tucker-Drop, 2014).

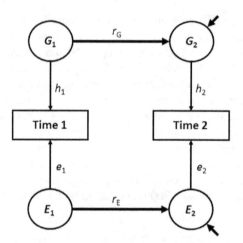

**Figure 29.4** Illustration of a genetically informative autoregressive model. For simplicity, the model is shown for only one twin and two measurement occasions; the correlation between the two measurement occasions $r_{1,2}$ can be estimated as $h_1 \times r_G \times h_2 + e_1 \times r_E \times e_2$ using the path coefficient approach (i.e., variances of latent factors are fixed to one); the coefficients $r_G$ and $r_E$ represent the stability of genetic and environmental differences; the terms $(h_1 \times r_G \times h_2)/r_{1,2}$ and $(e_1 \times r_E \times e_2)/r_{1,2}$ represent the genetic and environmental contributions to the stability of individual differences in personality.

Longitudinal twin studies of different age groups and cross-sequential studies with two or more measurement occasions allow estimates of the genotypic and environmental stability across time and reveal age trends of stability across the lifespan. The correlation between two measurement occasions ($r_{1,2}$) can be estimated as the sum of the genetic and environmental pathway's products: $r_{1,2} = h_1 \times r_G \times h_2 + e_1 \times r_E \times e_2$ (see Fig. 29.4), with the latent correlations $r_G$ and $r_E$ representing the genotypic and environmental stability.

Based on 16 longitudinal twin studies on personality traits, we estimated the phenotypic, genotypic, and environmental stability of Big Five personality traits for short-term (in years: $M = 4.08$; range $= 0.5$ to 7) and long-term (in years: $M = 10.06$; range $= 7$ to 13) intervals of time. The samples' average ages at first measurement occasions were neither significantly associated with the time intervals between measurement occasions ($r = -0.04$) nor with the availability of stability coefficients corrected for attenuation due to error of measurement ($r = 0.05$). Therefore, we took all estimates—whether or not they were corrected for measurement error—into account.

In line with previous research, short-term phenotypic stability is consistently larger compared to the stability of individual differences over longer periods of time (see Table 29.3). The average genotypic stability across age is almost perfect. Although the long-term genotypic stability tends to be smaller for neuroticism, agreeableness, and conscientiousness, the differences between short-term and long-term genotypic stability estimates are small. There are apparent and consistent differences between short-term and long-term environmental stabilities. The results

**Table 29.3 Phenotypic, genotypic, and environmental stability of individual differences in personality for short-term and long-term intervals between measurement occasions**

| Personality trait | k | Stability of individual differences | | | | | |
|---|---|---|---|---|---|---|---|
| | | Phenotypic $(r_P)$ | | Genotypic $(r_G)$ | | Environmental $(r_E)$ | |
| | | Ø | SE | Ø | SE | Ø | SE |
| *Short-term interval (about 4 years)* | | | | | | | |
| Neuroticism | 108 | 0.66 | 0.11 | 0.93 | 0.10 | 0.47 | 0.16 |
| Extraversion | 102 | 0.70 | 0.13 | 0.93 | 0.12 | 0.51 | 0.20 |
| Openness | 30 | 0.78 | 0.18 | 0.93 | 0.16 | 0.60 | 0.25 |
| Agreeableness | 21 | 0.82 | 0.12 | 0.96 | 0.05 | 0.65 | 0.23 |
| Conscientiousness | 30 | 0.77 | 0.14 | 0.90 | 0.14 | 0.59 | 0.13 |
| **ALL** | **291** | **0.71** | **0.14** | **0.93** | **0.11** | **0.52** | **0.19** |
| *Long-term interval (about 10 years)* | | | | | | | |
| Neuroticism | 24 | 0.57 | 0.11 | 0.85 | 0.13 | 0.37 | 0.11 |
| Extraversion | 21 | 0.64 | 0.14 | 0.92 | 0.13 | 0.35 | 0.17 |
| Openness | 9 | 0.77 | 0.11 | 1.00 | 0.00 | 0.42 | 0.13 |
| Agreeableness | 6 | 0.72 | 0.11 | 0.90 | 0.15 | 0.40 | 0.20 |
| Conscientiousness | 12 | 0.66 | 0.12 | 0.84 | 0.12 | 0.35 | 0.06 |
| **ALL** | **72** | **0.64** | **0.13** | **0.89** | **0.12** | **0.37** | **0.12** |

*Note:* Stability estimates are averaged across age; phenotypic and environmental stability estimates tend to be larger for Openness, Agreeableness, and Conscientiousness which is attributable to the fact that most studies, which provided stability estimates for these traits, corrected for measurement error; $k$ = number of stability estimates across studies; Ø = average estimate; SE = standard error of the average estimate.

indicate that genetic factors reflect the primary basis of long-term stability in personality differences, whereas environmental factors represent the primary source of variation in long-term personality change.

The following illustration of age trends of phenotypic, genotypic, and environmental stability is firstly based on all personality measures, given an equal interval of time (see Fig. 29.5A; time interval in years: $M = 4.08$; range $= 0.5$ to 7). Since the presence of measurement error attenuates phenotypic and environmental stability estimates, we also provide age trends of stability estimates corrected for error variance based on four longitudinal studies, which used Big Five personality trait measures (see Fig. 29.5B; time interval in years: $M = 5.27$; range $= 3$ to 6.5). Consistent with previous meta-analytic reviews, the phenotypic stability increases from childhood to middle adulthood reaching a plateau between the ages 40 and 70 (around $r_P = 0.70$ for uncorrected and around $r_P = 0.90$ for error-corrected personality trait measures), but tends to decline again in old age. This age trend of phenotypic stability is quite similar for all Big Five personality traits and can best be described as polynomial function of degree 2.

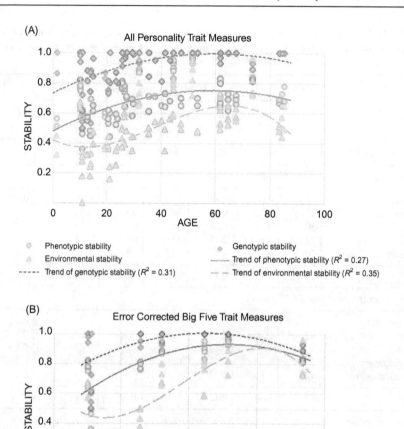

**Figure 29.5** Stability of phenotypic, genotypic, and environmental differences in personality traits as a function of age. Estimates are weighted by sample size (darker points, diamonds, and triangles carried more weight in the analysis) and based on (A) all 16 genetically informative longitudinal studies (see Table 29.1) or (B) the four selected studies which provided estimates for all Big Five traits corrected for error variance (De Fruyt et al., 2006; Kandler et al., 2010, 2015; Spengler et al., 2012).

The age trend of the genotypic stability appears to parallel the slope of the phenotypic stability across age but at a higher level. The genotypic stability increases from $r_G = 0.80$ in childhood across adolescence and young adulthood until it reaches almost perfect stability in middle adulthood. This trend is similar for all

**Table 29.4 Phenotypic, genotypic, and environmental stability of individual differences in personality for two age groups and error-corrected Big Five trait measures**

| Personality trait | k | Stability of individual differences | | | | | |
|---|---|---|---|---|---|---|---|
| | | Phenotypic $(r_P)$ | | Genotypic $(r_G)$ | | Environmental $(r_E)$ | |
| | | Ø | SE | Ø | SE | Ø | SE |
| *Age < 31* | | | | | | | |
| Neuroticism | 12 | 0.67 | 0.07 | 0.93 | 0.14 | 0.38 | 0.14 |
| Extraversion | 12 | 0.70 | 0.14 | 0.89 | 0.19 | 0.41 | 0.22 |
| Openness | 12 | 0.69 | 0.22 | 0.83 | 0.24 | 0.37 | 0.34 |
| Agreeableness | 12 | 0.69 | 0.08 | 0.93 | 0.10 | 0.40 | 0.17 |
| Conscientiousness | 12 | 0.68 | 0.16 | 0.82 | 0.20 | 0.44 | 0.18 |
| **ALL** | **60** | **0.69** | **0.13** | **0.88** | **0.17** | **0.40** | **0.20** |
| *Age > 30* | | | | | | | |
| Neuroticism | 15 | 0.86 | 0.07 | 0.99 | 0.03 | 0.69 | 0.18 |
| Extraversion | 15 | 0.91 | 0.05 | 0.96 | 0.08 | 0.83 | 0.11 |
| Openness | 15 | 0.91 | 0.04 | 0.99 | 0.03 | 0.69 | 0.15 |
| Agreeableness | 15 | 0.88 | 0.07 | 0.97 | 0.05 | 0.75 | 0.15 |
| Conscientiousness | 15 | 0.86 | 0.05 | 0.96 | 0.07 | 0.62 | 0.13 |
| **ALL** | **75** | **0.88** | **0.06** | **0.97** | **0.05** | **0.72** | **0.15** |

*Note:* Phenotypic and environmental stability estimates are corrected for variance due to measurement error assuming a 7-year time interval between assessments ($M_{AGE < 30} = 6.5$, range: 3.0–12.6; $M_{AGE < 31} = 7.2$, range: 4.5–12.6); $k$ = number of stability estimates across studies; Ø = average estimate; SE = standard error of the average estimate.

personality traits (see Table 29.4). Thus the steady increase in phenotypic stability from childhood to adulthood could be explained to some degree by stabilizing genetic differences. In other words, lower phenotypic stability in childhood and adolescence may be attributable to individual differences in genetically driven maturation, whereas larger phenotypic stability in adulthood can be attributed to largely stable genetic differences.

The stabilization of genetic differences from childhood to adulthood is in line with the concept of active genotype−environment correlation as propulsive developmental mechanism which becomes more important with increasing individual autonomy and environmental opportunities (see Kandler & Zapko-Willmes, Chapter 8). Individuals are attracted to, avoid, or manipulate their environments based upon their heritable personality traits that in turn reinforce personality differences. The almost perfect genotypic stability in middle adulthood may reflect the importance to maintain the selected and created environments based on genetic differences in this period of life. Some studies reported nonperfect genotypic stability in older age ($>70$; see Fig. 29.5B) indicating individual differences in genetically driven aging in later periods of life (see Kandler et al., 2015).

Environmental stability is comparatively low in childhood and adolescence (see Fig. 29.5). However, environmental factors stabilize across young and middle adulthood reaching a plateau around age 60 (between $r_E = 0.60$ and 0.70 for uncorrected and between $r_E = 0.80$ and 0.90 for error-corrected personality trait measures). Beyond retirement age, however, environmental stability appears to decline again. This pattern is comparable across all Big Five personality traits (see Table 29.4) and indicates that changing levels of phenotypic stability may also be attributable to changing environmental stability levels over the lifespan. Moreover, across all studies and age groups, the estimates of environmental stability were $r_E < 1$, indicating that environmental influences can affect individual personality change in every period of life.

The rather low environmental stability below age 30 may reflect individual differences in timing and experience of important life transitions and major life events in this period of life (e.g., transition to high school, first romantic partnership, leaving one's parental home, starting an apprenticeship or a job, and starting a family). In fact, adolescents and young adults experience more life transitions and major life events than mid-adults. Individual life events may be linked to major changes in life circumstances, daily routines, and social roles that require new individual adaptations. These individual changes may be associated with reversible or long-term individual personality changes. Similarly, older adults report and experience more changes in life circumstances (e.g., retirement, chronic diseases, care and death of partner and close peers) than middle-aged people. Even though most major life transitions and associated role changes are common to most people, they can occur sooner or later and act individually. Thus, life transitions, events, and role changes can affect both average slopes in personality traits and individual differences in personality maturation and change (Bleidorn, Kandler, Riemann, Angleitner, & Spinath, 2009; Specht et al., 2014).

# Genetic and environmental contributions to personality stability across the lifespan

The increasing environmental stability and the cumulative environmental contribution to personality differences from young to middle adulthood are consistent with the claim that life experiences can accumulate and solidify with age leading to an increasing environmental contribution to personality stabilization. This environmental component of the personality stability can be estimated using longitudinal quantitative genetic data (see Fig. 29.4). Age trends of the environmental influences to the phenotypic stability ($[e_1 \times r_E \times e_2]/r_P$) as well as the genetic stability component ($[h_1 \times r_G \times h_2]/r_P$) are illustrated in Fig. 29.6. As a previous meta-analysis (Briley & Tucker-Drop, 2014) reported, the absolute genetic contribution to the stability of personality differences appears to be largely constant across the lifespan ($[h_1 \times r_G \times h_2]/r_P \approx 0.40$), whereas the absolute environmental contribution constantly increases reaching the level of the genetic component in the second half

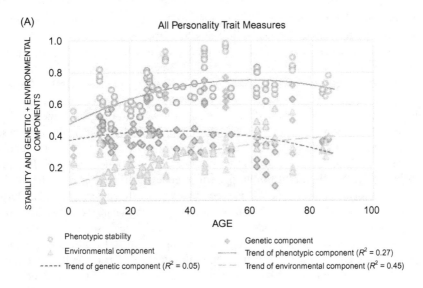

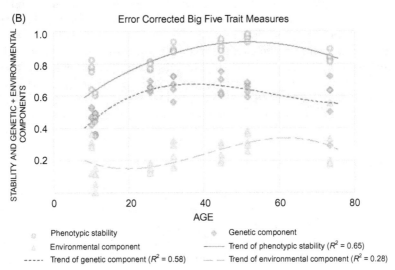

**Figure 29.6** Genetic and environmental contribution to the phenotypic stability of individual differences in personality traits as a function of age. Estimates are weighted by sample size (darker points, diamonds, and triangles carried more weight in the analysis) and based on (A) all 16 genetically informative longitudinal studies (see Table 29.1) or (B) the four selected studies which provided estimates for all Big Five traits corrected for error variance (De Fruyt et al., 2006; Kandler et al., 2010, 2015; Spengler et al., 2012).

of life (see Fig. 29.6A). That is, the relative genetic contribution to the phenotypic stability of personality traits declines, whereas the relative environmental component increases across the lifespan. On the one hand, this pattern indicates that personality stability in childhood is primarily due to genetic sources. On the other hand, however, personality differences stabilize across age due to environmental sources, which may reflect cumulative and solidifying life experiences.

Since the presence of measurement error variance would lead to an attenuation of heritability, an overestimation of the environmental variation within measurement occasions, as well as an underestimation of environmental stability between two points of time, the genetic and environmental contributions to the phenotypic stability can be biased to some degree. Therefore, we also examined age trends of genetic and environmental stability components corrected for error variance based on four longitudinal studies, which allow for error-corrected Big Five personality trait measures (see Fig. 29.6B). These trends are comparable across all Big Five traits but indicate a slightly different pattern of genetic and environmental contributions to phenotypic stability across age compared to the uncorrected trends. During the first three decades of life, the absolute genetic component increases from 0.40 to 0.60 and remains largely constant beyond age 30. The absolute environmental component primarily rises in the midlife from age 30 to 60 leading to a relative increase of the environmental contribution to the stability of personality differences. This pattern, again, is in line with the hypothesis that genetic differences drive the personality stabilization (in terms of active genotype—environment correlation) with increasing individual autonomy in the first third of life. When the child develops to an adult person, he or she selects suitable environments, avoids inappropriate contexts, tries to change given circumstances, and establishes his or her own identity based upon their genotypes. In midlife, adaptation mechanisms may change. People may increasingly try to stabilize and protect their established life circumstances and living environments, they rather change the self to adjust to limitations and constraints in the environment (McAdams, 2015).

## Conclusion

Developmental behavior genetic studies allow important insights into the etiology of personality differences, stability, and change over the life course. We introduced basic quantitative genetic modeling and examined the genetic and environmental variation in personality traits, the stability of the net effects of genetic and environmental factors, and the genetic and environmental contributions to the stability of personality differences. Both genetic and environmental factors contribute to the stability and change of individual differences in personality traits. Genetic factors primarily account for the long-term stability in personality differences, whereas environmental factors primarily affect individual differences in long-term personality change. Moreover, environmental influences can affect individual personality change in every period of life.

The illustration of age trends of genetic and environmental sources of variance and stability as separate components allows implications for how genetic and environmental factors can transact and interact in different phases of life accounting for personality development. The increasing heritability and the growing genotypic stability from childhood to young adulthood may reflect individual differences in genetically driven maturation. With increasing self-determination during the first third of life, genotypes drive the development of personality differences and increasing personality stabilization, they unfold within the various opportunities of the environment (genotype–environment correlation) in terms of niche picking and identity formation. Young people rather change the environment to fit their genotypes. In addition, individuals gain more and more individual life experiences—whether or not these experiences interact with genetic factors—across the lifespan. During the adult years, people may change their adaptation strategies. They try to maintain their social and living environments and rather change themselves to fit their environments, leading to an increase of the environmental contribution to personality differences and stability from young adulthood to old age.

## Funding

The authors received support from the Deutsche Forschungsgemeinschaft KA 4088/2-1.

## References[2]

Bell, E., & Kandler, C. (in press). The genetic and the sociological: Exploring the possibility of consilience. *Sociology*. http://dx.doi.org/10.1177/0038038516629908.

Bergeman, C. S., Chipuer, H. M., Plomin, R., Pedersen, N. L., McClearn, G. E., Nesselroade, J. R., & McCrae, R. R. (1993). Genetic and environmental effects on openness to experience, agreeableness, and conscientiousness: An adoption/twin study. *Journal of Personality*, *61*, 159–179.

Bleidorn, W., Kandler, C., & Caspi, A. (2014). The behavioural genetics of personality development in adulthood—Classic, contemporary, and future trends. *European Journal of Personality*, *28*, 244–255.

Bleidorn, W., Kandler, C., Riemann, R., Angleitner, A., & Spinath, F. (2009). Patterns and sources of adult personality development: Growth curve analyses of the NEO-PI-R scales in a longitudinal twin study. *Journal of Personality and Social Psychology*, *97*, 142–155.

Bouchard, T. J., Jr., & Loehlin, J. (2001). Genes, evolution, and personality. *Behavior Genetics*, *31*, 243–273.

[2] Studies included for meta-analysis: Bell & Kandler (in press); Bergeman et al. (1993); Bratko & Butkovic (2007); De Fruyt et al. (2006); Ganiban et al. (2008); Gillespie et al. (2004); Goldsmith et al. (1997); Hansell et al. (2012); Hopwood et al. (2011); Hudziak et al. (2003); Hur (2009); Johnson et al. (2005); Kandler et al. (2010); Kandler et al. (2015); Kupper et al. (2011); Laceulle et al. (2013); Lewis et al. (2014); Loehlin & Martin (2001); Matheny & Dolan (1980); McGue et al. (1993); Ono et al. (2000); Pedersen & Reynolds (1998); Plomin et al. (1993); Read et al. (2006); Rettew et al. (2006); Rettew et al. (2008); Scarr et al. (1981); Spengler et al. (2012); Spinath & Angleitner (1998); Viken et al. (1994).

Bratko, D., & Butkovic, A. (2007). Stability and genetic and environmental effects from adolescence to young adulthood: Results of Croatian longitudinal twin study of personality.
*Twin Research and Human Genetics, 10,* 151−157.

Briley, D., & Tucker-Drop, E. M. (2014). Genetic and environmental continuity in personality development: A meta-analysis. *Psychological Bulletin, 140,* 1303−1331.

Buss, A. H., & Plomin, R. (1984). *Temperament: Early developing personality traits.*
Hillsdale, NJ: Erlbaum.

Conley, J. J. (1984). The hierarchy of consistency: A review and model of longitudinal findings on adult individual differences in intelligence, personality, and self-opinion.
*Personality and Individual Differences, 5,* 11−25.

De Fruyt, F., Bartels, M., Van Leeuwen, K. G., De Clercq, B., Decuyper, M., & Mervielde, I.
(2006). Five types of personality continuity in childhood and adolescence. *Journal of
Personality and Social Psychology, 91,* 538−552.

DeYoung, C. G., Guilty, L. C., & Petersen, J. B. (2007). Between facets and domains: 10
aspects of the Big Five. *Journal of Personality and Social Psychology, 93,* 880−896.

Eysenck, H. J., & Eysenck, M. W. (1985). *Personality and individual differences: A natural
science approach.* New York, NY: Plenum Press.

Fraley, C., & Roberts, B. W. (2005). Patterns of continuity: A dynamic model for conceptualizing the stability of individual differences in psychological constructs across the life
course. *Psychological Review, 112,* 60−74.

Ganiban, J. M., Saudino, K. J., Ulbricht, J., Neiderhiser, J. M., & Reiss, D. (2008). Stability
and change in temperament during adolescence. *Journal of Personality and Social
Psychology, 95,* 222−236.

Gillespie, N. A., Evans, D. E., Wright, M. M., & Martin, N. G. (2004). Genetic simplex
modeling of Eysenck's dimensions of personality in a sample of young Australian twins.
*Twin Research, 7,* 637−648.

Goldsmith, H. H., Buss, K. A., & Lemery, K. S. (1997). Toddler and childhood temperament:
Expanded content, stronger genetic evidence, new evidence for the importance of environment. *Developmental Psychology, 33,* 891−905.

Hansell, N. K., Wright, M. J., Medland, S. E., Davenport, T. A., Wray, N. R., Martin, N. G.,
& Hickie, I. B. (2012). Genetic co-morbidity between neuroticism, anxiety/depression
and somatic distress in a population sample of adolescent and young adult twins.
*Psychological Medicine, 42,* 1249−1260.

Hopwood, C. J., Donnellan, M. B., Krueger, R. F., McGue, M., Iacono, W. G., Blonigen,
D. M., & Burt, S. A. (2011). Genetic and environmental influences on personality trait
stability and growth during the transition to adulthood: A three-wave longitudinal study.
*Journal of Personality and Social Psychology, 100,* 545−556.

Hudziak, J. J., van Beijsterveldt, C. E. M., Bartels, M., Rietveld, M. J. H., Rettew, D. C.,
Derks, E. M., & Boomsma, D. I. (2003). Individual differences in aggression: Genetic
analyses by age, gender, and informant in 3-, 7-, and 10-year-old Dutch twins. *Behavior
Genetics, 33,* 575−589.

Hur, Y.-M. (2009). Genetic and environmental contributions to childhood temperament in
South Korean twins. *Twin Research and Human Genetics, 12,* 549−554.

John, O. P., Naumann, L. P., & Soto, C. J. (2008). Paradigm shift to the integrative Big Five
trait taxonomy. In O. P. John, R. W. Robins, & L. A. Pervin (Eds.), *Handbook of personality: Theory and research* (3rd ed., pp. 114−158). New York, NY: Guilford.

Johnson, A. M., Vernon, P. A., & Feiler, A. R. (2008). Behavioral genetic studies of personality:
An introduction and review of the results of 50 +  years of research. In G. J. Boyle, G.
Matthews, & D. H. Saklofske (Eds.), *The Sage handbook of personality theory and assess-
ment. Vol. 1: Personality theories and models* (pp. 145−173). London, England: Sage.

Johnson, W., McGue, M., & Krueger, R. F. (2005). Personality stability in late adulthood: A behavioral genetic analysis. *Journal of Personality*, *73*, 523–551.

Kandler, C. (2012a). Knowing your personality is knowing its nature: The role of information accuracy of peer assessments for heritability estimates of temperamental and personality traits. *Personality and Individual Differences*, *53*, 387–392.

Kandler, C. (2012b). Nature and nurture in personality development: The case of neuroticism and extraversion. *Current Directions in Psychological Science*, *21*, 290–296.

Kandler, C., & Bleidorn, W. (2015). Personality differences and development: Genetic and environmental contributions. In J. D. Wright (Ed.), *International Encyclopedia of the Social & Behavioral Sciences* (2nd ed., Vol 17 pp.884–890). Oxford: Elsevier.

Kandler, C., Bleidorn, W., Riemann, R., Spinath, F. M., Thiel, W., & Angleitner, A. (2010). Sources of cumulative continuity in personality: A longitudinal multiple-rater twin study. *Journal of Personality and Social Psychology*, *98*, 995–1008.

Kandler, C., Held, L., Kroll, C., Bergeler, A., Riemann, R., & Angleitner, A. (2012). Temperamental traits of the Regulative Theory of Temperament and the Big Five: A multitrait–multimethod twin study. *Journal of Individual Differences*, *33*, 197–204.

Kandler, C., Kornadt, A. E., Hagemeyer, B., & Neyer, F. J. (2015). Patterns and sources of personality development in old age. *Journal of Personality and Social Psychology*, *109*, 175–191.

Kandler, C., Riemann, R., & Angleitner, A. (2013). Patterns and sources of continuity and change of energetic and temporal aspects of temperament in adulthood: A longitudinal twin study of self- and peer reports. *Developmental Psychology*, *49*, 1739–1753.

Kandler, C., Zimmermann, J., & McAdams, D. P. (2014). Core and surface characteristics for the description and theory of personality differences and development. *European Journal of Personality*, *28*, 231–243.

Kupper, N., Boomsma, D. I., de Geus, E. J. C., Denollet, J., & Willemsen, G. (2011). Nine-year stability of type D personality: Contributions of genes and environment. *Psychosomatic Medicine*, *73*, 75–82.

Laceulle, O. M., Ormel, J., Aggen, S. H., Neale, M. C., & Kendler, K. S. (2013). Genetic and environmental influences on the longitudinal structure of neuroticism: A trait-state approach. *Psychological Science*, *24*, 1780–1790.

Lewis, G. J., Haworth, C. M. A., & Plomin, R. (2014). Identical genetic influences underpin behavior problems in adolescence and basic traits of personality. *Journal of Child Psychology and Psychiatry*, *55*, 865–875.

Loehlin, J. C., & Martin, N. G. (2001). Age changes in personality traits and their heritabilities during the adult years: Evidence from Australian Twin Registry samples. *Personality and Individual Differences*, *30*, 1147–1160.

Lucas, R. E., & Donnellan, M. B. (2011). Personality development across the life span: Longitudinal analyses with a national sample from Germany. *Journal of Personality and Social Psychology*, *101*, 847–861.

Markon, K. E., Krueger, R., & Watson, D. (2005). Delineating the structure of normal and abnormal personality: An integrative hierarchical approach. *Journal of Personality and Social Psychology*, *88*, 139–157.

Matheny, A. P., Jr., & Dolan, A. B. (1980). A twin study of personality and temperament during middle childhood. *Journal of Research in Personality*, *14*, 224–234.

McAdams, D. P. (2015). *The art and science of personality development*. New York, NY: Guilford.

McGue, M., Bacon, S., & Lykken, D. T. (1993). Personality stability and change in early adulthood: A behavioral genetic analysis. *Developmental Psychology*, *29*, 96–109.

Ono, Y., Ando, J., Onoda, N., Yoshimura, K., Kanba, S., Hirano, M., & Asai, M. (2000). Genetic structure of the Five-Factor Model of personality in a Japanese twin population. *Keio Journal of Medicine, 49*, 152–158.

Pedersen, N. L., & Reynolds, C. A. (1998). Stability and change in adult personality: Genetic and environmental components. *European Journal of Personality, 12*, 365–386.

Plomin, R., Kagan, J., Emde, R. N., Reznick, J. S., Braungart, J. M., Robinson, J., & DeFries, J. C. (1993). Genetic change and continuity from fourteen to twenty months: The MacArthur longitudinal twin study. *Child Development, 64*, 1354–1376.

Read, S., Vogler, G. P., Pedersen, N. L., & Johansson, B. (2006). Stability and change in genetic and environmental components of personality in old age. *Personality and Individual Differences, 40*, 1637–1647.

Rettew, D. C., Rebollo-Mesa, I., Hudziak, J. J., Willemsen, G., & Boomsma, D. I. (2008). Non-additive and additive genetic effects on extraversion in 3314 Dutch adolescent twins and their parents. *Behavior Genetics, 38*, 223–233.

Rettew, D. C., Vink, J. M., Willemsen, G., Doyle, A., Hudziak, J. J., & Boomsma, D. I. (2006). The genetic architecture of neuroticism in 3301 Dutch adolescent twins as a function of age and sex: A study from the Dutch twin register. *Twin Research and Human Genetics, 9*, 24–29.

Riemann, R., & Kandler, C. (2010). Construct validation using multitrait–multimethod-twin data: The case of a general factor of personality. *European Journal of Personality, 24*, 258–277.

Rothbart, M. K., Ahadi, S. A., & Evans, D. E. (2000). Temperament and personality: Origins and outcomes. *Journal of Personality and Social Psychology, 78*, 122–135.

Scarr, S., & McCartney, K. (1983). How people make their own environments: A theory of genotype → environment effects. *Child Development, 54*, 424–435.

Scarr, S., Webber, P. L., Weinberg, R. A., & Wittig, M. A. (1981). Personality resemblance among adolescents and their parents in biologically related and adoptive families. *Journal of Personality and Social Psychology, 40*, 885–898.

Shiner, R. L., & Caspi, A. (2003). Personality differences in childhood and adolescence: Measurement, development, and consequences. *Journal of Child Psychology and Psychiatry, 44*, 2–32.

Specht, J., Bleidorn, W., Denissen, J., Hennecke, M., Huttman, R., Kandler, C., & Zimmermann, J. (2014). What drives adult personality development? A comparison of theoretical perspectives and empirical evidence. *European Journal of Personality, 28*, 216–230.

Specht, J., Egloff, B., & Schmukle, S. C. (2011). Stability and change of personality across the life course: The impact of age and major life events on mean-level and rank-order stability of the Big Five. *Journal of Personality and Social Psychology, 101*, 862–882.

Spengler, M., Gottschling, J., & Spinath, F. M. (2012). Personality in childhood: A longitudinal behavior genetic approach. *Personality and Individual Differences, 53*, 411–416.

Spinath, F. M., & Angleitner, A. (1998). Contrast effects in Buss and Plomin's EAS questionnaire: A behavioral-genetic study on early developing personality traits assessed through parental ratings. *Personality and Individual Differences, 25*, 947–963.

Tellegen, A., & Waller, N. G. (2008). Exploring personality through test construction: Development of the Multidimensional Personality Questionnaire. In G. J. Boyle, G. Matthews, & D. H. Saklofske (Eds.), *The Sage handbook of personality theory and assessment: Volume 2 personality measuring and testing* (pp. 262–292). London, England: Sage.

Viken, R. J., Rose, R. J., Kaprio, J., & Koskenvuo, M. (1994). A developmental genetic analysis of adult personality: Extraversion and neuroticism from 18 to 59 years of age. *Journal of Personality and Social Psychology, 66*, 722−730.

Vukasović, T., & Bratko, D. (2015). Heritability of personality: A meta-analysis of behavior genetic studies. *Psychological Bulletin, 141*, 769−785.

Wortman, J., Lucas, R. E., & Donnellan, M. B. (2012). Stability and change in the Big Five personality domains: Evidence from a longitudinal study of Australians. *Psychology and Aging, 27*, 867−874.

# Analyzing personality change: From average trajectories to within-person dynamics

Manuel C. Voelkle[1,2] and Jenny Wagner[1,3]
[1]Humboldt-Universität zu Berlin, Berlin, Germany, [2]Max Planck Institute for Human Development, Berlin, Germany, [3]Leibniz Institute for Science and Mathematics Education (IPN), Kiel, Germany

## Introduction

In 1937, one of the founders of modern personality psychology, Gordon Allport, introduced Wilhelm Windelbands famous distinction between *idiographic* and *nomothetic* sciences to the psychological literature (Allport, 1937). The idea of differentiating the nomothetic perspective, according to which the individual is just an exemplar of the population, from the focus on the uniqueness of an individual (idiographic perspective), became particularly prominent in personality research (Conner, Tennen, Fleeson, & Barrett, 2009; Mischel & Shoda, 1995). At around the same time, first voices were raised that called for a stronger emphasis on causal *explanation* in psychological research as opposed to the pure *description* by measures of central tendencies and covariation (e.g., Johnson, 1939). Although this argument concerned the entire field of psychology, in the sequel of Gordon Allport's, Raymond Cattell's, Hans Eysenck's, and other researcher's work on trait theory, the debate on the causal meaning of psychological traits became particularly controversial in personality psychology (e.g., Boag, 2011; Borsboom, Mellenbergh, & Van Heerden, 2003; John & Srivastava, 1999; McCrae & Costa, 1995).

At first glance, the two issues of *nomothetic versus idiographic* research and *description versus explanation* seem to be independent of each other. As illustrated in Fig. 30.1, it seems perfectly possible to describe an individual's personality profile, as well as to examine the causes that have led to a change in this person's personality. Likewise, we can assess the average personality structure across many individuals and determine the factors that affect this structure (e.g., in level, scatter, or shape; Cronbach & Gleser, 1953). This apparent orthogonality, however, begins to blur as soon as time is introduced as an additional dimension. As already noted by the famous philosopher John Stuart Mill (1848), temporal precedence is a necessary condition for establishing cause−effect relationships, so moving from description to explanation obviously requires some temporal information. Although extensively discussed in the methodological literature (e.g., Antonakis, Bendahan,

Personality Development Across the Lifespan. DOI: http://dx.doi.org/10.1016/B978-0-12-804674-6.00030-2

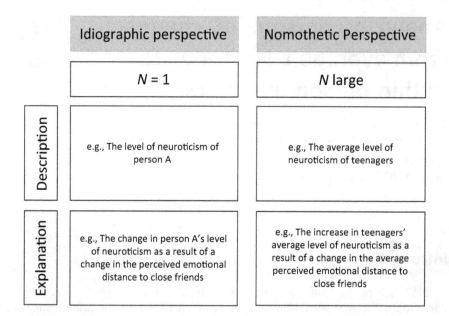

**Figure 30.1** The distinction of nomothetic versus idiographic research and description versus explanation. In contrast to description, (causal) explanation requires a temporal ordering. As discussed in the main text, in a longitudinal design with multiple time points and multiple individuals, heterogeneity due to different individuals may bias the identification of causal effects, unless adequately accounted for. Likewise parameter estimates may be biased if heterogeneity in sampling intervals is not adequately accounted for.

Jacquart, & Lalive, 2010; Halaby, 2004; Holland, 1986), what seems to be puzzling to many applied researchers, is the fact that the statistical models suitable to determine cause−effect relationships at the $N = 1$ level, may not be suitable for large $N$, and vice versa. For example, as will be discussed later in this chapter, an autoregressive parameter in an $N = 1$ time series model for a given Person A may be totally different in quantity and substantive meaning from an autoregressive parameter in a standard panel model. This holds true, even if every single individual in the panel would exhibit exactly the same autoregressive parameter as Person A. It will be shown that in order to arrive at meaningful conclusions when studying personality change, it is thus of utmost importance to carefully consider heterogeneity due to time and due to persons in our statistical analyses and substantive interpretations.

Taking the distinction between description versus explanation and the idiographic versus nomothetic perspective as a starting point, the goal of this chapter is to review common approaches to the analysis of personality change by means of longitudinal data. We will do so by focusing on the capabilities and limitations of some of the most prominent statistical models to address substantive research questions on personality change. This proceeding corresponds roughly to tracing the historical development that has led to the various statistical models (cf., Voelkle &

Adolf, 2015). Given the brevity of this chapter, we will focus on providing a bird's eye perspective, while giving key references for a more comprehensive introduction to the various methods and their mathematical—statistical foundations.

The structure of this chapter is as follows: we begin (1) with a short review of traditional models for the analysis of change and how their strict nomothetic perspective on change at the group level led to the development of latent trajectory models. These models opened up a new perspective on the individual by better accounting for individual differences. In the second part (2), we introduce dynamic models of change and show how their increasing popularity reflects the desire to move from a rather descriptive account of personality change toward an explanatory account of the underlying mechanisms. Interestingly, many of the dynamic models that are currently used for the analysis of sample data ($N$ large), such as the cross-lagged panel model, or the latent change score model, originate from single subject ($N = 1$) time series analysis. For this reason we begin this section with a short review of time series models. In the third part (3), we show how careless adoption of idiographic time series models to large sample panel models (nomothetic perspective), creates unique problems due to heterogeneity across individuals and time. If not adequately accounted for, such heterogeneity will lead to inappropriate results and incorrect conclusions. We will discuss recent developments to address these problems and illustrate selected models throughout this chapter by means of example data and R-code. The example dataset is generated using the R-script provided in Appendix A. It contains two variables $X_1$ and $X_2$ observed for $N = 500$ individuals across $T = 4$ measurement occasions, spanning a total of 7 years with measures taken after $\Delta t_1 = 1$, $\Delta t_2 = 3$, and $\Delta t_3 = 2$ years. For the sake of illustration, we may assume that $X_1$ represents neuroticism ($M_{t=1} = 2.42$, $SD_{t=1} = 1.41$) and $X_2$ the perceived emotional distance to friends ($M_{t=1} = 3.09$, $SD_{t=1} = 1.52$).

# Static models for the analysis of personality change

As compared to dynamic models, which will be discussed later on, the focus of static models lies not on detecting the inherent mechanisms that underlie a change process (e.g., a certain autoregressive process), but rather on describing change as a function of time, determining its significance and examining possible group differences therein (e.g., group differences in polynomial change).

## Traditional models for the analysis of change: Repeated measures (M)ANOVA

Deeply rooted in an experimental tradition, early approaches to study personality change focused primarily on changes in group means using (M)ANOVA-type approaches (e.g., Asendorpf & Wilpers, 1998; Helson & Soto, 2005; Roberts, Helson, & Klohnen, 2002). For an excellent introduction and overview from a broader perspective on model comparisons, see Maxwell and Delaney (2000). The basic idea of such approaches is to, first, decompose the overall variance into within-person

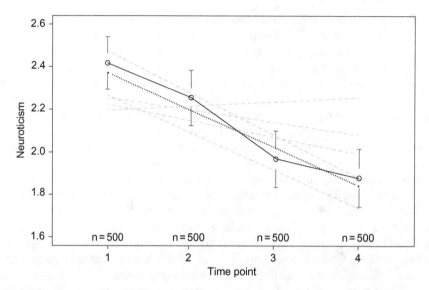

**Figure 30.2** Means, 95% confidence intervals, and estimated linear trajectory (dotted line) of variable $X_1$ (neuroticism), along with individual trajectories of five hypothetical cases (dashed lines).

(WP) and between-person (BP) variance. In a second step, the BP variance is controlled for, while the WP variance is further decomposed into variance that is due to differences in means over time and remaining residual variance. By comparing variance due to mean differences to remaining residual variance, various measures of effect sizes and inferential test statistics can be derived as described in most introductory statistics books (e.g., Hays, 1994). Although the basic approach can be extended in various ways—for example by introducing additional BP and/or WP factors and/or making different assumptions regarding the error structure—the focus is clearly on nomothetic change, that is, change in first-order moments that applies to the entire group. Any individual deviations are treated as nuisance. An example of a standard repeated measures ANOVA using the aov() function in R version 3.2.4 is provided in Appendix B. In this example, we look at mean changes in variable $X_1$ (neuroticism) over time and test whether the variability due to different means over time is significantly larger than what would be expected under chance conditions. If the reader runs the script, s/he will see that this is the case (Mean Sum of Squares due to time $= \text{MSS}_{\text{time}} = 31.37$ vs $\text{MSS}_{\text{error}} = 0.60$; $P < 0.001$). Means and 95% confidence intervals are shown in Fig. 30.2.

## Latent trajectory models for the analysis of change

(M)ANOVA-type approaches are still common in psychological research. With the advent of latent trajectory/linear mixed models in the 80s and 90s, however, the preference in personality psychology has slowly changed toward the latter. An excellent introduction to latent trajectory models is provided by Bollen and Curran (2006), Duncan, Duncan, and Strycker (2006), or Singer and Willett (2003). The reason for this change is a shift in focus from a purely nomothetic perspective on group means toward a more individualized conception of change in latent trajectory models (e.g., Mroczek & Spiro, 2005; Wagner, Lüdtke, Jonkmann, & Trautwein, 2013). Statistically, however, the two approaches are less different than often portrayed (cf. Meredith & Tisak, 1990; Voelkle, 2007). As illustrated in Fig. 30.3A, the decomposition of variance in a repeated measure ANOVA corresponds to a transformation of manifest variables to latent variables, which represent BP and WP differences ($\eta_1$, respectively $\eta_2$ to $\eta_T$ for the transformation matrix presented in Fig. 30.3A). In contrast, the latent trajectory model depicted in Fig. 30.3B uses a different transformation matrix $\Lambda$, with fewer latent variables. Similar to (M)ANOVA, $\Lambda$ is often chosen in a way that one factor represents a latent intercept and one or more factors represent the latent growth variables. Fig. 30.3B provides an example of a linear latent trajectory model. With fewer latent factors, the model becomes overidentified, which allows the separation of "true" variance and measurement error variance (depicted by the solid double-headed arrows on the manifest variables in Fig. 30.3B). The main difference between the two modeling approaches, however, is the change in emphasis. While in Fig. 30.3A, the variances of $\eta_{1t_1}$ to $\eta_{1T}$ are conceptualized as "noise" (i.e., systematic or unsystematic variance one is not interested in), this variance is of primary interest in Fig. 30.3B, because it is conceived of as representing systematic interindividual differences in level ($\eta_{int}$), and change over time ($\eta_{slp}$), respectively. An example of a linear latent trajectory model using the structural equation modeling (SEM) package lavaan

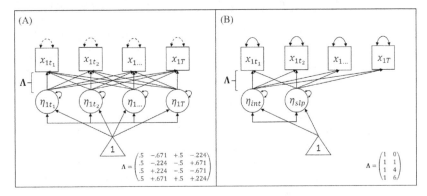

**Figure 30.3** Schematic illustration of a (M)ANOVA model (Panel A) and a latent growth curve model (Panel B). The primary difference between the two is the transformation matrix $\Lambda$, the number of factors, and the different conceptualization of the variance of the latent variables as "noise" in (M)ANOVA versus systematic interindividual differences in intercept and change in latent growth curve modeling. The triangle denotes the constant 1 (e.g., McArdle, 2009). The corresponding path coefficients represent means, intercepts, respectively. Double-headed arrows between different variables denote covariances among all connected variables. Double-headed arrows that begin and end at the same variable denote the variance of this variable.

version 0.5−20 (Rosseel, 2012) is provided in Appendix B. In this example, we looked at linear change in $X_1$ (neuroticism), which showed an average level of 2.38 ($P < 0.001$) at the first time point and an average decrease of about −0.09 ($P < 0.001$). The estimated average change trajectory is depicted as a dotted line in Fig. 30.2. In addition to the average trajectory, however, we now also obtain information about individual difference in initial status $SD(\eta_{int}) = 1.36$, and change over time $SD(\eta_{slp}) = 0.18$ (both $P < 0.001$). This additional information, which allows the description and possible prediction of individual differences, is illustrated by five exemplary cases in Fig. 30.2.

## Dynamic models for the analysis of personality change

The models discussed so far have in common that they describe change by using time as the predictor. In case of the repeated measures (M)ANOVA, a completely saturated model is employed, which limits the analysis to detecting differences in means over time. In this model, it remains unclear what "drives" the change. By limiting the range of possible trajectories to a prespecified function (e.g., a polynomial function), the shape of the trajectory becomes of key interest in latent growth curve modeling. In addition, individual difference in trajectories may be examined as described earlier. However, just like in (M)ANOVA, it remains unclear what "drives" the change, that is, the "causal" mechanisms behind any observed trajectory. Obviously time itself cannot be the true cause of change, but may only serve as a proxy of the actual causal mechanisms. In this sense, the models discussed so far are *static*, because they describe change, rather than modeling the (causal) dynamics that drive it. Dynamic models, in contrast, try to uncover the dynamics that underlie a change process, which develops in the time domain, without using time itself as the explanatory variable. This distinction is hardly ever made explicit in research on personality change, although researchers have used both approaches, in parts to address the same research questions.

One of the most popular dynamic models is certainly the autoregressive cross-lagged panel model. It has been used to address such diverse questions like what are the dynamic transactions between personality and social relationships (Lehnart & Neyer, 2006; Schaffhuser, Wagner, Lüdtke, & Allemand, 2014; Sturaro, Denissen, Aken, & Asendorpf, 2008), is low self-esteem an outcome or predictor of depression (Orth & Robins, 2013; Orth, Robins, Trzesniewski, Maes, & Schmitt, 2009), or what is the reciprocal association between self-concept and achievement (Trautwein, Lüdtke, Koller, & Baumert, 2006)? Interestingly, the key idea underlying the cross-lagged panel model originated from time series modeling with single subjects. For this reason, we quickly review the basic idea of time series models in the next paragraph, before discussing three selected classes of dynamic panel models for the analysis of personality change in the remainder of this chapter: autoregressive cross-lagged panel models, latent change score models, and continuous time models.

## Time series models

The probably simplest and most widely used example of an $N = 1$ time series model is the autoregressive model of order 1, the so-called AR(1) model. A schematic illustration of the AR(1) model is provided in Fig. 30.4A. Essentially the AR(1) model is

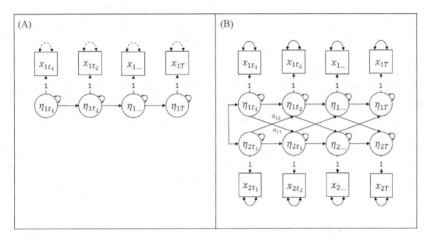

**Figure 30.4** Schematic illustration of a univariate AR(1) model (Panel A) and a bivariate cross-lagged-panel model (Panel B).

the mathematical representation of the well-known maxim in psychological research that past behavior is the best predictor of future behavior. The higher the autoregressive parameter $a$ (see Fig. 30.4A) and the lower the variance of the error term $\varepsilon_t$, the stronger depends the current behavior of an individual on his/her past behavior and the better can we predict his/her future behavior. Especially in recent psychological research, the autoregressive parameter, autocorrelation, respectively, has gained renewed attention in research on affect and affect regulation and has been interpreted as emotional inertia, with less inert people showing less unsystematic fluctuations in their affective experience (e.g., Brose, Schmiedek, Koval, & Kuppens, 2015; Kuppens, Allen, & Sheeber, 2010). From this perspective, a personality "trait" constitutes the upper limit of an AR(1) process, with the autoregressive parameter being one, or at least close to one. The AR(1) model described in this paragraph is just the most basic form of a time series model and a special case of the more general class of *autoregressive integrated moving average* ARIMA($p,d,q$) models, which are again a special case of the more general class of state−space models, both of which are beyond the scope of this chapter. For an excellent introduction to the former see Lütkepohl (2005), for the latter the book by Durbin and Koopman (2001).

## Cross-lagged panel models

Mathematically, the extension of time series models to panel models with multiple subjects is straightforward. In fact, in the simplest case of i.i.d.[1] observations and

---

[1] i.i.d. = independent and identically distributed

no random effects parameters, maximum likelihood parameter estimates are simply obtained by maximizing the sum of the log-likelihood across all individuals instead of the individual log-likelihood. This approach generalizes readily to the multivariate case as illustrated in Fig. 30.4B, which shows the autoregressive cross-lagged panel model that is widely used in the study of personality change as outlined above. Just like time series models, autoregressive cross-lagged panel models aim at capturing the dynamics of a change process rather than describing an average trajectory. Unfortunately, however, the mathematical similarity may be misleading, when it comes to the substantive interpretation of the parameter estimates. Typically, what researchers are interested in, are the "causal" effects of one variable on the other variable and vice versa. For example, if $\eta_1$ represents neuroticism and $\eta_2$ the perceived emotional distance to friends, we would like to conclude that the parameter $a_{12}$ in Fig. 30.4B represents the expected change in neuroticism if the perceived emotional distance to friends has changed by one unit over time. Unfortunately, such interpretation is often not justified. For example, using our example dataset and setting up a standard autoregressive cross-lagged panel model as illustrated in Fig. 30.4B yields cross-lagged parameter estimates of $a_{21} = -0.19$ and $a_{12} = -0.11$ (see Appendix B for the implementation in lavaan). The parameter estimate $a_{12} = -0.11$ suggests that an increase in the perceived emotional distance to friends slightly reduces neuroticism, while the parameter $a_{21} = -0.19$ suggests a stronger reciprocal effect from neuroticism on the perceived emotional distance to friends. As will be shown later on, despite a well-fitting model, nothing could be further from the truth.

There are (at least) two major problems in applying a panel model to the current data. First, the extension to multiple subjects has resulted in an additional source of BP variation. Unless explicitly accounted for, this will affect our parameter estimates. As a result, the substantive interpretation becomes ambiguous, because it remains unclear whether a parameter represents the effect due to a change in time or across individuals. This is what we refer to as the problem of *heterogeneity across individuals*. Second, $N = 1$ time series models have been developed for many time points, while panel models are typically used with only few measurement occasions. Furthermore, time series models are commonly used in situations in which the sampling is arbitrary and completely under the researchers' control, such as neurophysiological data (e.g., EEG) or econometric data (e.g., stock indices), typically resulting in equidistant time intervals. In contrast, in panel studies, time intervals between measurement occasions are often unequal.[2] This, however, may have severe implications for substantive interpretations unless explicitly accounted for. Given the unequal time intervals in our example dataset, does the effect $a_{21} = -0.19$ represent an effect over an interval of $\Delta t_1 = 1$, $\Delta t_2 = 3$, or $\Delta t_3 = 2$ years? What if another researcher would have chosen an interval of $\Delta t_1 = 0.5$ years? With a conventional cross-lagged panel model, it is not possible to address these questions and to compare results across studies. To this end, it is

---

[2] With increasing use of experience sampling studies, the problem of unequal time intervals also becomes more pressing in time series analysis of psychological data. This is an active field of research.

necessary to disentangle the effect of time intervals on parameter estimates from possible differences in the actual process. This is what we refer to as the problem of *heterogeneity in sampling intervals.*

To summarize, the popular class of cross-lagged parameter estimates has moved the field of research on personality away from the simple description of change toward a better understanding of the actual dynamics of change processes. Despite their intuitive appeal and apparent simplicity, however, common use of such models may be problematic due to *heterogeneity across individuals* and *heterogeneity in sampling intervals.*

# Accounting for heterogeneity: Toward a within-person perspective

In econometrics and sociology, there exists an extensive literature on how to best deal with—possibly unobserved—heterogeneity across individuals in panel data, dating back to the 70s and 80s (e.g., Hannan & Tuma, 1979; Hausman & Taylor, 1981; Hsiao, 2014). For an accessible introduction, see Halaby (2004). In contrast, in psychological research this topic has received far less attention and is only recently being rediscovered (e.g., Hamaker, Kuiper, & Grasman, 2015). Interestingly, however, in the 90s, so-called latent change score models were developed in psychology, which also gained increasing popularity in the analysis of personality change (e.g., McArdle & Hamagami, 2001; McArdle, 1988, 2009; Mund & Neyer, 2014; Ziegler, Cengia, Mussel, & Gerstorf, 2015). These models carefully distinguish between the actual within-person *change* (and potential relationships between WP changes across constructs) and heterogeneity across individuals, while at the same time allowing for the analysis of the dynamic nature of change processes.

## Accounting for heterogeneity across individuals: Latent change score models

An illustrative example of a latent change score model is provided in Fig. 30.5A. The exact specification is apparent from the lavaan code in Appendix B using $X_1 =$ neuroticism as an example. Although the graphical representation may look daunting, the model is actually quite simple. The additional row of latent variables denoted $\Delta\eta$ represents the changes in latent variables from one time point to the next. Although the analogy is not entirely correct, one can think of them as simple difference scores between time point $t$ and $t-1$. The parameter $a$ is the so-called proportional change score parameter, because it describes change as a proportional effect of the previous time point. The latent change variables may again be expressed as a function of another factor denoted $\eta_{slp}$. This factor captures stable interindividual differences in changes by simply adding a person specific value (possibly weighted by the parameter $b$) to each latent change variable. Although it may not be immediately apparent, because the constant is added to each *change* factor, this constant translates

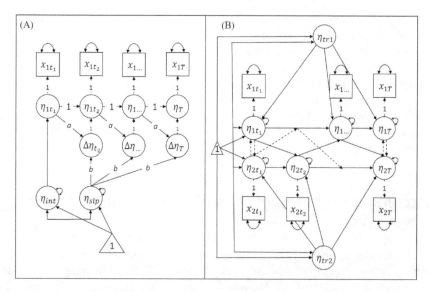

**Figure 30.5** Schematic illustration of a univariate latent change score model (i.e., dual change score model in Panel A) and a bivariate continuous time model including latent traits (Panel B).

into a *slope* when considering the actual process. Because of the dual representation of change via a slope factor and the change factors, the model is called a *dual* change sore model (McArdle, 2009, p. 597). Finally, $\eta_{int}$ represents interindividual differences at the first time point.

By explicitly representing WP changes as latent change variables, the model nicely separates BP and WP variance, while at the same time capturing the dynamic nature of the average WP changes by parameter $a$. It is insightful, however, to consider what happens if we set the parameter $a$ to 0 and fixing $b$ to 1. By doing so, we assume no temporal dynamics ($a = 0$) and linear change over time ($b = 1$). As a matter of fact, in this case, the model reduces exactly to the linear growth curve model introduced in Fig. 30.3B. The mathematical equivalence between the two models can be easily shown, although we refrain from doing so at this point. However, in order to gain a better understanding of the different ways to analyze change over time, we encourage the reader to test the equivalence of the two representations by imposing the constraints in the lavaan syntax provided in Appendix B.

## *Accounting for heterogeneity in sampling intervals: Continuous time models*

With the advent of latent change score models, researchers in personality psychology got increasingly aware of the importance of distinguishing WP change from BP differences, pushing the field one step further toward the study of within-person dynamics as opposed to the analysis of average trajectories. However, while latent change score models alleviate the problem of heterogeneity across individuals, they do not resolve the second problem, that is to adequately account for heterogeneity in sampling intervals. As pointed out above, unless we explicitly account for the length of time intervals, it is difficult to adequately interpret the resulting parameter estimates. As apparent from Fig. 30.5A, however, the actual time intervals are not part of the latent change score model. A common approach to deal with this problem is to artificially create equal intervals, by introducing so-called phantom variables. These are latent variables without underlying manifest variables that serve the only purpose of forcing the time intervals to be of the same length. Obviously, however, this cannot be a satisfying solution, because with increasing numbers of unequal time intervals the number of additional latent variables quickly becomes too large for the approach to be feasible (cf. Voelkle, Oud, Von Oertzen, & Lindenberger, 2012).[3]

By explicitly accounting for the actual time intervals between measurement occasions, continuous time models resolve the issue of heterogeneity in sampling intervals. For a more comprehensive introduction to continuous time modeling we refer the reader to Voelkle, Oud, Davidov, and Schmidt (2012). Fig. 30.5B provides a schematic illustration of a bivariate continuous time model with unequally spaced time intervals. The model looks similar to the autoregressive cross-lagged panel model in Fig. 30.4B, but contains two additional latent variables that capture stable interindividual differences—so-called trait variables—comparable to $\eta_{int}$ and $\eta_{slp}$ in Fig. 30.5A. By relating trait variables and state variables across different constructs, we may differentiate stable BP associations from actual WP dynamics. The similarity to the autoregressive cross-lagged panel model and the latent change score model is not coincidental. In fact, the former can be seen as a discrete time instantiation of the latter. Furthermore, Voelkle and Oud (2015) have shown how to translate a latent change score model into an autoregressive model and have demonstrated algebraically the equivalence of (common) latent change score models and continuous time models for the special case of equal time intervals of length $\Delta t = 1$. In other words, if all time intervals are equal and of the same length of exactly one unit, there exists a 1:1 relationship between the class of latent change score models, autoregressive and cross-lagged models and continuous time models. However, as soon as the time intervals are unequal and/or not equal to one, this relationship breaks down. In this case, continuous time models should be used. For details, see Voelkle and Oud (2015; e.g., Table 1).

As illustrated by the reciprocal dashed arrows at the first time point in Fig. 30.5B, another problem of discrete time models is the so-called instantaneous versus lagged effects dilemma. The dilemma states that in discrete time it is implausible that two constructs should be causally related over time but independent of each other at any given point in time (i.e., no reciprocal effects between $\eta_1$ and $\eta_2$

---

[3] For example, even in a moderate example with $T = 10$ time points and $N = 100$ individuals, one may end up with up to 900 different time intervals, if everyone was assessed at a different point in time. Depending on the actual time intervals between measurement occasions, this may easily require several thousand phantom variables.

at any given measurement occasion). This, however, is exactly, what models like the standard autoregressive cross-lagged panel model in Fig. 30.4B postulate. By using differential equations instead of difference scores, continuous time models resolve this dilemma. By conceptualizing cross-effects as the limiting case for infinitesimally small time intervals, there is no need for an arbitrary distinction between instantaneous and lagged effects in continuous time modeling, because the former simply constitute the limiting case of the latter for $\Delta t \rightarrow 0$.

Appendix B shows how to implement continuous time models via the R package ctsem version 1.1.5.2 (Driver, Oud, & Voelkle, in press), using our running example on neuroticism ($X_1$) and the perceived emotional distance to friends ($X_2$). As with all other code, the script can be easily adapted and may serve as a template for similar analyses. Although a comprehensive treatment is beyond the scope of this chapter, we want to pick out one result that is illustrated in Fig. 30.6. Based on the so-called drift matrix which represents the auto- and cross-effects in continuous time, we can compute discrete time autoregressive and cross-lagged effects as a function of the length of the time interval as shown in Fig. 30.6. Having accounted for heterogeneity across individuals via the inclusion of trait variables ($\eta_{tr1}$ and $\eta_{tr2}$), and having accounted for heterogeneity in sampling intervals via (stochastic) differential equations, the effects in Fig. 30.6 capture the actual within-person dynamics of the reciprocal interplay between neuroticism and perceived emotional distance to friends. Maybe most striking is the finding that the slightly negative effect of $X_2$ (perceived emotional distance to friends) on $X_1$ (neuroticism) has reversed in direction and strength. Rather than increases in neuroticism leading to decreases

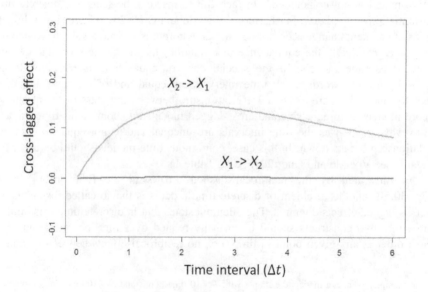

**Figure 30.6** Cross-lagged effects of $X_1$ on $X_2$ and vice versa as a function of the length of the time interval $\Delta t$.

in the perceived emotional distance to friends, just the opposite seems to be true. Neuroticism increases whenever the perceived emotional distance to friends is high (cross-lagged effect of 0.11 for $\Delta t = 1$). Likewise the strongly negative effect of $X_1$ on $X_2$ observed in the autoregressive cross-lagged panel model turns out to be close to zero (0.002 for $\Delta t = 1$) after accounting for heterogeneity across individuals and time intervals.[4]

Of course it is important to keep in mind that the data were simulated in order to illustrate a wide range of different longitudinal models with the same exemplary dataset. However, the simulation conditions were neither unrealistic nor extreme, but chosen in a way that closely mimics existing studies in personality psychology. Thus we hope that this little example was not only instrumental in illustrating a range of different "tools" for the analysis of personality change, but also helped to highlight the importance of asking the right questions, choosing the right tools to answer these questions, and carefully considering the conditions under which the tools function properly when interpreting ones results.

## Discussion

A comprehensive treatment of methods to study personality change is clearly beyond the scope of a book chapter. Rather, the purpose of this chapter was to provide a bird's eye perspective on popular approaches, identify some general trends, discuss common problems, and point the reader to ongoing developments. At the broadest level, we have argued that the study of personality change has progressed from the analysis of simple mean differences and average trajectories to the study of within-person (causal) dynamics. Likewise the methods used for longitudinal data analysis in personality psychology have changed over time and continue to develop. Accordingly, we have not only introduced different approaches, but have highlighted several shortcomings of existing methods and have pointed to recent developments that may help to overcome these problems. Rather than discussing technical details, however, we have limited ourselves to briefly sketch the general idea of each method, and to provide references for more detailed information. In addition, we used a simple example dataset to illustrate each approach and provide code for most of the models discussed. We encourage the reader to explore this code in order to gain a better understanding of each of the models. Furthermore, the code may be easily adapted to one's own research purposes. We thus hope, the chapter may not only provide an overview of existing approaches to study personality change, but may also serve as an inspiration to try out new—better—ways of data analysis.

---

[4] Although we do not discuss missing values in this chapter, it should be noted that from a continuous time perspective, missing values simply translate into unequal time intervals and may thus be easily handled, contingent on the usual assumptions of nonsystematic missings. For further information see Oud and Voelkle (2013).

# References

Allport, G. W. (1937). *Personality. A psychological interpretation*. New York, NY: Henry Holt.

Antonakis, J., Bendahan, S., Jacquart, P., & Lalive, R. (2010). On making causal claims: A review and recommendations. *The Leadership Quarterly*, *21*(6), 1086−1120. Available from http://dx.doi.org/10.1016/j.leaqua.2010.10.010.

Asendorpf, J. B., & Wilpers, S. (1998). Personality effects on social relationships. *Journal of Personality and Social Psychology*, *74*(6), 1531−1544. Available from http://dx.doi.org/10.1037/0022-3514.74.6.1531.

Boag, S. (2011). Explanation in personality psychology: "Verbal magic" and the Five-Factor Model. *Philosophical Psychology*, *24*(2), 223−243. Available from http://dx.doi.org/10.1080/09515089.2010.548319.

Bollen, K. A., & Curran, P. J. (2006). *Latent curve models: A structural equation perspective*. Hoboken, NJ: John Wiley.

Borsboom, D., Mellenbergh, G. J., & Van Heerden, J. (2003). The theoretical status of latent variables. *Psychological Review*, *110*(2), 203−219.

Brose, A., Schmiedek, F., Koval, P., & Kuppens, P. (2015). Emotional inertia contributes to depressive symptoms beyond perseverative thinking. *Cognition and Emotion*, *29*(3), 527−538. Available from http://dx.doi.org/10.1080/02699931.2014.916252.

Conner, T. S., Tennen, H., Fleeson, W., & Barrett, L. F. (2009). Experience sampling methods: A modern idiographic approach to personality research. *Social and Personality Psychology Compass*, *3*(3), 292−313. Available from http://dx.doi.org/10.1111/j.1751-9004.2009.00170.x.

Cronbach, L. J., & Gleser, G. C. (1953). Assessing similarity between profiles. *Psychological Bulletin*, *50*(6), 456−473. Available from http://dx.doi.org/10.1037/h0057173.

Driver, C.C., Oud, J.H.L., & Voelkle, M.C. (in press). Continuous time structural equation modeling with R Package ctsem. *Journal of Statistical Software*.

Duncan, T. E., Duncan, S. C., & Strycker, L. A. (2006). An introduction to latent variable growth curve modeling: Concepts, issues, and applications (2nd ed.). Mahwah, NJ: Lawrence Erlbaum Associates.

Durbin, J., & Koopman, S. J. (2001). *Time series analysis by state space methods*. Oxford: Oxford University Press.

Halaby, C. N. (2004). Panel models in sociological research: Theory into practice. *Annual Review of Sociology*, *30*(30), 507−544.

Hamaker, E. L., Kuiper, R. M., & Grasman, R. P. P. P. (2015). A critique of the cross-lagged panel model. *Psychological Methods*, *20*(1), 102−116. Available from http://dx.doi.org/10.1037/a0038889.

Hannan, M. T., & Tuma, N. B. (1979). Methods for temporal analysis. *Annual Review of Sociology*, *5*, 303−328. Retrieved from http://www.jstor.org/stable/2945957.

Hausman, J. A., & Taylor, W. E. (1981). Panel data and unobservable individual effects. *Econometrica*, *49*(6), 1377−1398. Available from http://dx.doi.org/10.2307/1911406.

Hays, W. L. (1994). *Statistics* (5th ed.). Orlando, FL: Harcourt Brace.

Helson, R., & Soto, C. J. (2005). Up and down in middle age: Monotonic and nonmonotonic changes in roles, status, and personality. *Journal of Personality and Social Psychology*, *89*(2), 194−204. Available from http://dx.doi.org/10.1037/0022-3514.89.2.194.

Holland, P. W. (1986). Statistics and causal inference. *Journal of the American Statistical Association*, *81*(396), 945−960. Available from http://dx.doi.org/10.1080/01621459.1986.10478354.

Hsiao, C. (2014). *Analysis of panel data* (3rd ed.). Cambridge: Cambridge University Press.

John, O. P., & Srivastava, S. (1999). The Big-Five trait taxonomy: History, measurement, and theoretical perspectives. In L. A. Pervin, & O. P. John (Eds.), *Handbook of personality: Theory and research* (pp. 102–139). New York, NY: Guilford Press.

Johnson, H. M. (1939). Rival principles of causal explanation in psychology. *Psychological Review*, *46*(6), 493–516. Available from http://dx.doi.org/10.1037/h0056121.

Kuppens, P., Allen, N. B., & Sheeber, L. (2010). Emotional inertia and psychological maladjustment. *Psychological Science*, *21*(7), 984–991. Available from http://dx.doi.org/10.1177/0956797610372634.

Lehnart, J., & Neyer, F. J. (2006). Should I stay or should I go? Attachment and personality in stable and instable romantic relationships. *European Journal of Personality*, *20*(6), 475–495. Available from http://dx.doi.org/10.1002/per.606.

Lütkepohl, H. (2005). *New introduction to multiple time series analysis*. Berlin: Springer.

Maxwell, S. E., & Delaney, H. D. (2000). *Designing experiments and analyzing data: A model comparison perspective*. Mahwah, NJ: Lawrence Erlbaum Associates.

McArdle, J. J. (1988). Dynamic but structural equation modeling of repeated measures data. In J. R. Nesselroade, & R. B. Cattell (Eds.), *Handbook of multivariate experimental psychology* (2nd ed., pp. 561–614). New York, NY: Plenum Press.

McArdle, J. J. (2009). Latent variable modeling of differences and changes with longitudinal data. *Annual Review of Psychology*, *60*, 577–605. Available from http://dx.doi.org/10.1146/annurev.psych.60.110707.163612.

McArdle, J. J., & Hamagami, F. (2001). Latent difference score structural models for linear dynamic analyses with incomplete longitudinal data. In L. Collins, & A. Sayer (Eds.), *New methods for the analysis of change* (pp. 139–175). Washington, DC: APA Press.

McCrae, R. R., & Costa, P. T. (1995). Trait explanations in personality psychology. *European Journal of Personality*, *9*(4), 231–252. Available from http://dx.doi.org/10.1002/per.2410090402.

Meredith, W., & Tisak, J. (1990). Latent curve analysis. *Psychometrika*, *55*(1), 107–122.

Mill, J. S. (1848). *A system of logic*. London: Parker.

Mischel, W., & Shoda, Y. (1995). A cognitive-affective system theory of personality: Reconceptualizing situations, dispositions, dynamics, and invariance in personality structure. *Psychological Review*, *102*(2), 246–268. Available from http://dx.doi.org/10.1037/0033-295X.102.2.246.

Mroczek, D. K., & Spiro, A., 3rd (2005). Change in life satisfaction during adulthood: Findings from the veterans affairs normative aging study. *Journal of Personality & Social Psychology*, *88*(1), 189–202. Available from http://dx.doi.org/10.1037/0022-3514.88.1.189.

Mund, M., & Neyer, F. J. (2014). Treating personality–relationship transactions with respect: Narrow facets, advanced models, and extended time frames. *Journal of Personality and Social Psychology*, *107*(2), 352–368. Available from http://dx.doi.org/10.1037/a0036719.

Orth, U., & Robins, R. W. (2013). Understanding the link between low self-esteem and depression. *Current Directions in Psychological Science*, *22*(6), 455–460. Available from http://dx.doi.org/10.1177/0963721413492763.

Orth, U., Robins, R. W., Trzesniewski, K. H., Maes, J., & Schmitt, M. (2009). Low self-esteem is a risk factor for depressive symptoms from young adulthood to old age. *Journal of Abnormal Psychology*, *118*(3), 472–478. Available from http://dx.doi.org/10.1037/a0015922.

Oud, J. H. L., & Voelkle, M. C. (2013). Do missing values exist? Incomplete data handling in cross-national longitudinal studies by means of continuous time modeling. *Quality & Quantity*, 1−18. Available from http://dx.doi.org/10.1007/s11135-013-9955-9.

Roberts, B. W., Helson, R., & Klohnen, E. C. (2002). Personality development and growth in women across 30 years: Three perspectives. *Journal of Personality*, *70*(1), 79−102. Available from http://dx.doi.org/10.1111/1467-6494.00179.

Rosseel, Y. (2012). Lavaan: An R package for structural equation modeling. *Journal of Statistical Software*, *48*(2), 1−36.

Schaffhuser, K., Wagner, J., Lüdtke, O., & Allemand, M. (2014). Dyadic longitudinal interplay between personality and relationship satisfaction: A focus on neuroticism and self-esteem. *Journal of Research in Personality*, *53*, 124−133. Available from http://dx.doi.org/10.1016/j.jrp.2014.08.007.

Singer, J. D., & Willet, J. B. (2003). *Applied longitudinal data analysis: Modeling change and event occurrence*. New York, NY: Oxford University Press.

Sturaro, C., Denissen, J. J. A., Aken, M. A. G. v, & Asendorpf, J. B. (2008). Person-environment transactions during emerging adulthood. *European Psychologist*, *13*(1), 1−11. Available from http://dx.doi.org/10.1027/1016-9040.13.1.1.

Trautwein, U., Lüdtke, O., Koller, O., & Baumert, J. (2006). Self-esteem, academic self-concept, and achievement: How the learning environment moderates the dynamics of self-concept. *Journal of Personality & Social Psychology*, *90*(2), 334−349. Available from http://dx.doi.org/10.1037/0022-3514.90.2.334.

Voelkle, M. C. (2007). Latent growth curve modeling as an integrative approach to the analysis of change. *Psychology Science Quarterly*, *49*(4), 375−414.

Voelkle, M. C., & Adolf, J. (2015). History of longitudinal statistical analyses. In N. A. Pachana (Ed.), *Encyclopedia of Geropsychology* (pp. 1−10). Singapore: Springer.

Voelkle, M. C., & Oud, J. H. L. (2015). Relating latent change score and continuous time models. *Structural Equation Modeling: A Multidisciplinary Journal*, *22*(3), 366−381. Available from http://dx.doi.org/10.1080/10705511.2014.935918.

Voelkle, M. C., Oud, J. H. L., Davidov, E., & Schmidt, P. (2012). An SEM approach to continuous time modeling of panel data: Relating authoritarianism and anomia. *Psychological Methods*, *17*, 176−192. Available from http://dx.doi.org/10.1037/a0027543.

Voelkle, M. C., Oud, J. H. L., Von Oertzen, T., & Lindenberger, U. (2012). Maximum likelihood dynamic factor modeling for arbitrary N and T using SEM. *Structural Equation Modeling*, *19*(3), 329−350. Available from http://dx.doi.org/10.1080/10705511.2012.687656.

Wagner, J., Lüdtke, O., Jonkmann, K., & Trautwein, U. (2013). Cherish yourself: Longitudinal patterns and conditions of self-esteem change in the transition to young adulthood. *Journal of Personality and Social Psychology*, *104*(1), 148−163. Available from http://dx.doi.org/10.1037/a0029680.

Ziegler, M., Cengia, A., Mussel, P., & Gerstorf, D. (2015). Openness as a buffer against cognitive decline: The Openness-Fluid-Crystallized-Intelligence (OFCI) model applied to late adulthood. *Psychology and Aging*, *30*(3), 573−588. Available from http://dx.doi.org/10.1037/a0039493.

# Appendix A

```
##############
# Preparation #
##############
#install.packages("ctsem")
#source('http://openmx.psyc.virginia.edu/getOpenMx.R')
library(gplots)
library(car)
library(ctsem)
library(lavaan)
set.seed(88)


##################
# Data generation #
##################
#Example: x1 = neuroticism; x2 = perceived presence of close friends
true_model    <- ctModel(Tpoints = 7, n.latent = 2, n.manifest = 2,
                         LAMBDA = matrix(c(1, 0, 0, 1), nrow = 2, ncol = 2),
                         DRIFT=matrix(c(-.3,0,.25,-.8),nrow=2),
                         MANIFESTVAR=diag(sqrt(0.15),2),
                         TRAITVAR=t(chol(matrix(c(1,-.5,-.5,1),nrow=2))),
                         DIFFUSION=t(chol(matrix(c(0.5,0.1,0.1,0.5),2))),
                         CINT=matrix(c(-0.1,2),nrow=2),
                         T0MEANS=matrix(c(2.5,3), ncol=1,nrow=2),
                         T0VAR=t(chol(matrix(c(1,0.5,0.5,1), ncol=2, nrow=2))))

expl_data_full <- ctGenerate(true_model, n.subjects = 500, burnin = 0, dT = 1, asymptotes = FALSE)
expl_data_full <- as.data.frame(expl_data_full)
#select five time points 1,2,5,7
expl_data          <- expl_data_full[c("Y1_T0", "Y2_T0", "Y1_T1", "Y2_T1", "Y1_T4", "Y2_T4", "Y1_T6", "Y2_T6")]
names(expl_data) <- c("Y1_T0", "Y2_T0", "Y1_T1", "Y2_T1", "Y1_T2", "Y2_T2", "Y1_T3", "Y2_T3")
expl_data$dT1     <- 1
expl_data$dT2     <- 3
expl_data$dT3     <- 2
head(expl_data)
mean(expl_data$Y1_T0)
sd(expl_data$Y1_T0)
mean(expl_data$Y2_T0)
sd(expl_data$Y2_T0)
```

# Appendix B

```
####################################
# Repeated measures (M)ANOVA for x1 #
####################################
temp            <- expl_data[,c(1,3,5,7)]
temp$id         <- 1:nrow(temp)
expl_data_long <- reshape(temp, idvar="id", varying=list(1:4), v.names="dv", direction="long")
# repeated measures anova
aov.out <- aov(dv ~ factor(time) + Error(factor(id)), data=expl_data_long)
summary(aov.out)
#manova
temp2           <- expl_data[,c(1,3,5,7)]
repeated.manova <- lm(cbind(Y1_T0, Y1_T1, Y1_T2, Y1_T3) ~ 1 , data=temp2)
summary(Anova(repeated.manova))
#plot
plotmeans(dv~time, xlab="Time point", ylab="dv", data=expl_data_long) #95% cI


#############################
# Latent growth curve model #
#############################
lgc <-    "i =~ 1*Y1_T0 + 1*Y1_T1 + 1*Y1_T2 + 1*Y1_T3
           s =~ 0*Y1_T0 + 1*Y1_T1 + 4*Y1_T2 + 6*Y1_T3
           Y1_T0 ~~ e*Y1_T0
           Y1_T1 ~~ e*Y1_T1
           Y1_T2 ~~ e*Y1_T2
           Y1_T3 ~~ e*Y1_T3"
fit_lgc <- growth(lgc, data=expl_data)
summary(fit_lgc, fit.measures=TRUE)


######################################################################
# Autoregressive cross-lagged panel model -- no trait no mean structure #
######################################################################
ARCL <-    "
#Measurment Model
x1T0 =~ 1*Y1_T0
x1T1 =~ 1*Y1_T1
x1T2 =~ 1*Y1_T2
x1T3 =~ 1*Y1_T3

x2T0 =~ 1*Y2_T0
x2T1 =~ 1*Y2_T1
x2T2 =~ 1*Y2_T2
x2T3 =~ 1*Y2_T3

Y1_T0 ~~ e1*Y1_T0
Y1_T1 ~~ e1*Y1_T1
Y1_T2 ~~ e1*Y1_T2
Y1_T3 ~~ e1*Y1_T3

Y2_T0 ~~ e2*Y2_T0
Y2_T1 ~~ e2*Y2_T1
Y2_T2 ~~ e2*Y2_T2
Y2_T3 ~~ e2*Y2_T3

#Structural Model
x1T3 ~ a11*x1T2 + a12*x2T2
x2T3 ~ a22*x2T2 + a21*x1T2

x1T2 ~ a11*x1T1 + a12*x2T1
x2T2 ~ a22*x2T1 + a21*x1T1

x1T1 ~ a11*x1T0 + a12*x2T0
x2T1 ~ a22*x2T0 + a21*x1T0
```

```
#Dynamic Error
x1T3 ~~ q11*x1T3
x1T2 ~~ q11*x1T2
x1T1 ~~ q11*x1T1

x2T3 ~~ q22*x2T3
x2T2 ~~ q22*x2T2
x2T1 ~~ q22*x2T1

x1T3 ~~ q12*x2T3
x1T2 ~~ q12*x2T2
x1T1 ~~ q12*x2T1

#T0 covariance matrix
x1T0  ~~ start(2)*x1T0
x2T0  ~~ start(2)*x2T0
x1T0  ~~ x2T0"

fit_ar <- sem(ARCL, meanstructure=F, data=expl_data[,1:8])
summary(fit_ar, fit.measures=TRUE)

#######################################
# Univariate dual change score model x1 #
#######################################
LCS <-    "
#Measurment Model
x1T0 =~ 1*Y1_T0
x1T1 =~ 1*Y1_T1
x1T2 =~ 1*Y1_T2
x1T3 =~ 1*Y1_T3

Y1_T0 ~~ e*Y1_T0
Y1_T1 ~~ e*Y1_T1
Y1_T2 ~~ e*Y1_T2
Y1_T3 ~~ e*Y1_T3

#Dynamic Model
x1T1 ~ 1*x1T0
x1T2 ~ 1*x1T1
x1T3 ~ 1*x1T2

d_T1 =~ 1*x1T1
d_T2 =~ 1*x1T2
d_T3 =~ 1*x1T3

d_T1 ~ a*x1T0
d_T2 ~ a*x1T1
d_T3 ~ a*x1T2

slp =~ 1*d_T1 + 1*d_T2 + 1*d_T3
int =~ 1*x1T0
int ~~ slp

#Mean structure
Y1_T0 ~ 0*1
Y1_T1 ~ 0*1
Y1_T2 ~ 0*1
Y1_T3 ~ 0*1
```

```
x1T0 ~ 0*1
x1T1 ~ 0*1
x1T2 ~ 0*1
x1T3 ~ 0*1

d_T1 ~ 0*1
d_T2 ~ 0*1
d_T3 ~ 0*1

slp ~ mslp*1

int ~ mint*1

#Dynamic Error
d_T1 ~~ 0*d_T1
d_T2 ~~ 0*d_T2
d_T3 ~~ 0*d_T3

x1T0 ~~  0*slp
x1T0 ~~  0*x1T0"

fit_lcs <- sem(LCS, meanstructure=T, data=expl_data[,c(1,3,5,7)])
summary(fit_lcs, fit.measures=TRUE)


#########################
# Continuous time model #
#########################
ctmodel_est    <- ctModel(Tpoints = 4, n.latent = 2, n.manifest = 2,
                     LAMBDA = matrix(c(1, 0, 0, 1), nrow = 2, ncol = 2),
                     DRIFT=matrix(c("a11","a21","a12","a22"),nrow=2),
                     MANIFESTVAR=matrix(c("manvar1",0,0,"manvar2"),nrow=2),
                     TRAITVAR=matrix(c("trvar1","trvar21",0,"trvar2"),nrow=2),
                     DIFFUSION=matrix(c("q1","q21",0,"q2"),2),
                     CINT=matrix(c("cint1","cint2"),nrow=2, ncol=1),
                     T0MEANS=matrix(c("m1","m2"), nrow=2, ncol=1),
                     T0VAR=matrix(c("T0var1","T0var12",0,"T0var2"), ncol=2, nrow=2))

ctmodel_fit    <- ctFit(expl_data, ctmodel_est, optimizer = "SLSQP")
summary(ctmodel_fit, verbose=T)
plot(ctmodel_fit, AR=T, CR=T, standardiseCR=F, withinVariance=F, mean=F, wait=F, CRylim=c(-0.1,0.3))
```

# Part Seven

# New Areas of Research on Personality Development

# Cohort differences in personality

## 31

*Gizem Hülür*
University of Zurich, Zurich, Switzerland

The sociocultural environment surrounding us, including living circumstances, attitudes, values, and material standards, is different today than it was years, decades, and centuries ago and will probably be different in the future. According to lifespan psychological and life course sociological perspectives (Baltes, Cornelius, & Nesselroade, 1979; Bronfenbrenner, 1986; Caspi, 1987; Elder, 1974; Riley, 1973; Ryder, 1965; Schaie, 1965), individual lives are embedded in and shaped by broader societal and historical contexts. It is well documented that average levels of cognitive performance considerably increased across the last century (Flynn, 2007; Pietschnig & Voracek, 2015). Accumulating evidence suggests that other psychological traits, such as Big Five personality (e.g., Mroczek & Spiro, 2003; Smits, Dolan, Vorst, Wicherts, & Timmerman, 2011; Terracciano, McCrae, Brant, & Costa, 2005; Twenge, 2000, 2001a), do also differ across generations. My objective in this chapter is to highlight key issues in research on cohort differences in personality. Following the broad definition of personality in this book, I will focus on a number of psychological individual difference characteristics, including Big Five traits, cognitive function, perceived control, self-esteem, and well-being; while acknowledging that it is under debate whether some of these characteristics can be classified as personality traits (for overviews, see DeYoung, 2011; Diener, 1996; Hooker & McAdams, 2003; Kandler, Zimmermann & McAdams; 2014; Trzesniewski, Donnellan, & Roberts, 2003). This chapter is organized into four sections. First, I will give a definition of cohort differences and highlight some methodological considerations. Second, I will address why we expect personality to differ across cohorts. Third, I will give a selective overview of research on cohort differences in a number of psychological traits. Fourth, I will outline open questions and avenues for future research.

## What are cohort differences and how can we study them?

Conceptually, a cohort is a group of individuals who experience the same event at the same time (Ryder, 1965). Studies of cohort differences in personality typically examine differences between birth cohorts, that is, people born in the same historical time who share common life experiences. Developmental scientists have long been concerned with conceptual and methodological issues in the study of cohort differences (Baltes & Nesselroade, 1979; Schaie, 1965; Schaie & Baltes, 1975). According to the age-cohort-period model (Schaie, 1965, 2011), each observation

Personality Development Across the Lifespan. DOI: http://dx.doi.org/10.1016/B978-0-12-804674-6.00031-4

made at a specific time point is a function of age, cohort, and time period, or a combination of these factors. *Age effects* refer to ontogenetic changes associated with the chronological age of individuals. For example, conscientiousness typically shows longitudinal increases in young adulthood (Roberts, Walton, & Viechtbauer, 2006), which can be considered an age effect that signifies maturation (Bleidorn, 2015). *Cohort effects* indicate how accumulated life experiences associated with being born in a certain cohort shape personalities of individuals across the lifespan. For example, if accumulated common life experiences of 20-year-olds born in the 1990s would make them less (or more) conscientious than 20-year-olds born in the 1980s, this would be considered a cohort effect. A *period effect* refers to effects associated with living through a certain time period. Period effects may be of more transient nature than cohort effects and may affect multiple cohorts. If unemployment (which is associated with declines in conscientiousness: Boyce, Wood, Daly, & Sedikides, 2015), would increase during an economic crisis, lower levels of conscientiousness observed during this specific time period at population level would be considered a period effect. Effects of age, cohort, and period are not independent of one another; they can interact in multiple ways. For example, cohorts may differ in how their conscientiousness changes with age: an *age × cohort interaction*.

The majority of studies in this selective review utilized *time lag analyses* (Schaie, 1965) to examine cohort differences. To examine cohort differences in conscientiousness in a time-lag analysis, one would compare two sets of cross-sectional data obtained from, for example, 20-year-olds in 2000 (born in 1980) and 20-year-olds in 2010 (born in 1990). In this type of design, age is being held constant, while cohort and time period are confounded. Each birth cohort is examined at a different time period. Although we sometimes interpret differences between cross-sectional samples as differences between birth-cohorts (related to being born in 1980 vs 1990), it is important to note that period effects (related to being in year 2000 vs 2010) may also be relevant. *Cross-temporal meta-analysis* (e.g., Twenge, 2000, 2001a) is a meta-analytic method based on the same principle as time lag analyses, i.e., age is being held constant, while time of measurement varies. In cross-temporal meta-analyses, researchers collect information on studies using the same measure in similar age groups (e.g., college students) in different time periods. If scores differ over time, this would indicate existence of cohort (or period) differences.

The *longitudinal sequence* method (also called cohort sequences; Schaie, 1965) follows two (or more) cohorts over same age ranges, enabling to examine age−cohort interactions, e.g., whether changes in conscientiousness from age 20 to 30 are similar in those born in 1980 versus 1990. Again we sometimes interpret these differences as age × cohort interactions, but period effects could also be relevant, as we observe each birth cohort growing older during a different time period (e.g., 2000 to 2010 for the 1980 birth cohort, and 2010 to 2020 for the 1990 birth cohort).

Studies utilizing time lag and longitudinal sequence designs offer insights into generational shifts in personality, while specific events taking place at time of measurement may also be relevant.

# Why can we expect cohort differences in personality?

Industrialized countries have undergone many sociocultural changes over the last century, some of which may be relevant for personality development across the lifespan. First, living circumstances changed considerably. Different cohorts went through different experiences from early childhood to old age which may have shaped their personalities in different ways. For example, after the post World-War II Baby Boom, birth rates declined and families became smaller (e.g., Martin, Hamilton, Osterman, Curtin, & Mathews, 2015). Furthermore, parenting styles may have changed, with children being granted more autonomy for self-expression (Rutherford, 2009). Both the quality of education and its quantity (i.e., years spent in education) increased (Blair, Gamson, Thorne, & Baker, 2005; Schaie, Willis, & Pennak, 2005). Work experiences also differed between cohorts. For example, women's labor force participation increased (Juhn & Potter, 2006). Also, relationship experiences changed, with divorce becoming more common (see Amato, 2010) and marriage and childbirth being postponed into later ages (Martin et al., 2015; US Census Bureau, 2015). Cohorts probably also differed in experiences in old age: People today live longer (Vaupel, 2010), and physical functioning has improved (Crimmins, 2015). At the same time, diseases became more prevalent because treatments increased length of life for those with disease (Crimmins, 2015). This is of course only a selective list of changing life circumstances. All of these factors mentioned above, including family structure (e.g., Zajonc, 1976), parenting styles (e.g., Baumrind, 1971), education (e.g., Schaie et al., 2005), work experiences (e.g., Schooler, Mulatu, Oates, 1999), intimate relationships (e.g., Hoppmann, Gerstorf, Luszcz, 2011), length of life (e.g., Baltes & Smith, 2003), and health (e.g., Wagner, Ram, Smith, & Gerstorf, 2015) were proposed to profoundly shape individual development across the lifespan.

Second, people in different cohorts did not only make different experiences in various life domains, they were also confronted with different social norms and expectations. Thus the same personality traits may be associated with different consequences in different cohorts. For example, George, Helson, and John (2011) found that, among women born in the 1930s, being conscientious was unrelated to work involvement, satisfaction with work, or status level in young and middle adulthood. Instead, higher conscientiousness predicted commitment to wife and mother roles. The authors argued that due to shifts in social norms, they would expect conscientious women today to pursue both career and family goals. This would mean that being conscientious would relate to different outcomes based on societal expectations. Also, perceptions of what is considered a desirable personality trait may change across cohorts: For example, Liu, Chen, Li, and French (2012) argued that while shyness may have been considered a positive personality trait in traditional Chinese society valuing group harmony, it may become a less desirable trait in a market economy. In line with this reasoning, they found that shyness was associated with positive developmental outcomes such as leadership and academic achievement in 1994. However, in 2008, shyness predicted only negative outcomes, such as lower peer preference or higher loneliness. Taken together, these findings suggest that the same personality traits may impact individuals' lives differently depending on the historical time they live in.

In conclusion, several factors proposed to shape personality development changed over recent decades and personality traits probably also changed in how adaptive they are for certain outcomes. As a result, a growing body of research examines cohort differences in personality.

# What is known about cohort differences in personality?

In this section, I will give a selective overview of research on cohort differences in personality. As noted in the introduction, following the broad definition of personality in this book (see Part IV), I refer to personality as a wide range of psychological traits that show meaningful between-person differences.

**Big Five personality**. The Five-Factor Theory of personality (McCrae & Costa, 2003) is currently one of the most influential theories in personality psychology (see Mõttus, Chapter 7). Although research on Big Five personality pays considerable attention to the broader sociocultural context in terms of cross-cultural differences (e.g., Costa, Terracciano, & McCrae, 2001), relatively few studies examined how personality differs across historical contexts.

Twenge (2000, 2001a) was among the first to examine cohort differences in Big Five traits and demonstrated increases in extraversion and neuroticism in US college students based on cross-temporal meta-analyses. Twenge's (2001a) finding of increased extraversion was replicated in other studies. Extraversion (or some of its facets) increased across cohorts in predominantly middle-aged and older US (Mroczek & Spiro, 2003; Terracciano et al., 2005) and Swedish (Billstedt et al., 2013) samples and in Dutch freshman psychology students (Smits et al., 2011). Twenge (2001a) provided several explanations for increasing extraversion, including emphasis on social skills in schools and the shift to a service economy. These experiences may also explain higher extraversion among later-born cohorts of middle-aged and older individuals, who may be able to maintain previous levels of extraversion because of historical improvements in health (Crimmins, 2015; Wagner et al., 2015).

Research is less conclusive with regard to cohort differences in neuroticism in young adults. Twenge (2000) reports increases in neuroticism among US college students, whereas Smits et al. (2011) found declines among Dutch students. In middle-aged and older adults, available findings point to a historical decline in neuroticism (Mroczek & Spiro, 2003; Terracciano et al., 2005; but see Billstedt et al., 2013; no significant difference). These findings are consistent with studies observing higher levels of psychosocial function among later-born cohorts of older adults (e.g., Gerstorf et al., 2015; Hülür et al., 2016; Sutin et al., 2013).

Few studies examined cohort differences in other Big Five traits (for exceptions, see Smits et al., 2011; Terracciano et al., 2005). Furthermore, relatively less is known about cohort differences in age-related change. Terracciano et al. (2005) found no cohort differences in change, whereas Mroczek and Spiro (2003) found that later-born participants showed relatively less decline in extraversion and more decline in neuroticism. It is important to note that the different birth cohorts in both studies showed little overlap in the age range examined. For example, in Mroczek and Spiro's study (2003), because of the study design, differences between an earlier-born (1897–1919) and a later-born (1920–29) cohort in age-related trajectories could only be observed between 70 and 75 years of age. It is an open question whether similar cohort differences in longitudinal change can be found at other ages.

**Cognitive performance**. It is well documented that cognitive test scores, especially in tests of fluid cognitive performance, increased dramatically in many industrialized countries across the last century (Flynn, 2007: Pietschnig & Voracek, 2015). Several factors have been proposed to underlie this development, including improvements in nutrition and healthcare (Lynn, 1998), education (Schaie et al., 2005), or resources available per child (Sundet, Borren, & Tambs, 2008), all of which are related to economic prosperity. In line with this reasoning, increases in test scores were associated with gross domestic product growth per capita (Pietschnig & Voracek, 2015). Furthermore, test scores increased more steeply in countries that started industrializing more recently (Nisbett et al., 2012; Wongupparaj, Kumari, & Morris, 2015), suggesting that cohort differences in cognitive performance could be based on broader societal changes resulting from industrialization.

The research outlined above mainly focused on historical gains in children, adolescents, and young adults. Because of demographic changes toward an older population, it is important to know whether these gains are maintained in older ages. Accumulating evidence suggests that historical gains are also observed among older adults (e.g., Bowles, Grimm, & McArdle, 2005; Christensen et al., 2013; Gerstorf et al., 2015; Gerstorf, Ram, Hoppmann, Willis, & Schaie, 2011; Skirbekk, Stonawski, Bonsang, & Staudinger, 2013). However, it is less clear whether cohort differences also exist in rates of change, that is, whether later cohorts show less steep decline of cognitive performance. So far, available findings are inconclusive and show that older adults in later-born cohorts show less (Dodge, Zhu, Lee, Chang, & Ganguli, 2014; Gerstorf et al., 2011; Schaie et al., 2005), equal (Finkel, Reynolds, McArdle, & Pedersen, 2007; Zelinski & Kennison, 2007), or more decline (Karlsson, Thorvaldsson, Skoog, Gudmundsson, & Johansson, 2015). Furthermore, initial evidence suggests that advantages of later cohorts may disappear at the end of life (Gerstorf et al., 2011; Hülür, Infurna, Ram, & Gerstorf, 2013).

**Perceived control**. Perceived control, i.e., the general sense of having control over one's life (Rotter, 1966; Skinner, 1995) can apply to multiple situations and may be considered a personality characteristic (see Specht, Egloff, & Schmuckle, 2013). Control beliefs can be differentiated into two independent dimensions (Lachman, Neupert, & Agrigoroaei, 2011). People with higher *internal control* beliefs think that their life outcomes depend on their own efforts, while those with higher *external control* beliefs think that external circumstances are crucial. An individual may hold the belief that working hard will lead to success, while also thinking that external factors beyond their control may hamper reaching important goals. Thus a person may be high both in external and internal control beliefs.

Research on cohort differences in high school and college students is inconclusive. In a cross-temporal meta-analysis, Twenge, Zhang, and Im (2004) found that control beliefs became more external between 1960 and 2002 in college students. However, Trzesniewski and Donnellan (2010) showed that perceived control remained stable between 1976 and 2006 among high school seniors. Methodological differences may have contributed to the discrepancy: While Trzesniewski and Donnellan's (2010) measure assessed perceived *personal* control ("When I make plans, I am almost certain I can make them work"), Twenge et al. (2004) measure included items assessing perceived control both over personal and *societal* outcomes ("In the long run the people are responsible for bad government on a national as well as on a local level"). It is possible that perceived control over societal outcomes is more susceptible to historical change. It is also important to note that both studies used one-dimensional scales of perceived control. Individuals could be high in either external or internal control beliefs, but not in both.

In a recent study, we found that older adults today reported substantially lower levels of external control compared to older adults 20 years ago, while no cohort difference was found in internal control beliefs (Hülür et al., 2016). One potential explanation is that lives of earlier-born participants were impacted more by major historical events on which most of them probably had no or little direct personal control, such as World War II. Thus it is an open question whether our finding is specific to a geographical location (Berlin or Germany) or whether similar trends exist elsewhere. Furthermore, declines in religiosity across cohorts may be relevant because more religious individuals may believe that events are predetermined (Fiori, Brown, Cortina, & Antonucci, 2006; Wolf, 2008). Although we controlled for religious affiliation, cohort differences in subjective importance of religion may still have existed.

**Subjective well-being**. Subjective well-being can be considered as a summary measure of how well an individual is doing in multiple life domains (Diener, 1984). Well-being involves trait-like components and shows some degree of stability across the lifespan (Diener & Lucas, 1999). Studies examining population trends in large-scale annual cross-sectional surveys such as the General Social Survey found that cohort and period effects were relatively minor (e.g., Blanchflower & Oswald, 2004; Twenge, Sherman, & Lyubomirsky, 2016; Yang, 2008). Furthermore, historical trends differed by age group with adolescents showing slight increases and people older than 30 years showing slight declines between 1972 and 2014 (Twenge et al., 2016). In population-based samples of high school seniors between 1976 and 2006, happiness and life satisfaction were relatively stable (Trzesniewski & Donnellan, 2010). Also, differences in well-being based on gender and ethnicity declined across time (Yang, 2008).

Studies of mental health trends in high school and college students suggest that more subtle depressive symptoms increased, whereas more severe symptoms such as suicidal ideation (or suicide rates) declined (Twenge, 2015; Twenge et al., 2010). Also, access to mental healthcare increased, which may explain declines in more severe mental health issues (Twenge, 2015). At the population level, little evidence for cohort differences in mental health was found in the annual cross-sectional National Psychiatric Morbidity Surveys in England between 1993 and 2007 (Spiers et al., 2011, 2012). Taken together, available evidence points to relative stability of well-being across cohorts.

Studies focusing on older adults generally find that later-born cohorts report higher levels of well-being, conceptualized as higher life satisfaction or fewer depressive symptoms (Gerstorf et al., 2015; Hülür, Ram, & Gerstorf, 2015; Sutin et al., 2013; Zivin, Pirraglia, McCammon, Langa, & Vijan, 2013; but see Schilling, 2005). However, initial evidence suggests that cohort-related increases in well-being may disappear at the end of life (Hülür et al., 2015).

It is important to note that these findings were obtained in participants from the United States, the United Kingdom, and Germany. Different trends may exist in other sociocultural contexts. For example, studies from China show that depressive symptoms increased both in adolescents and older adults over the last two decades (Shao et al., 2013; Xin, Niu, & Chi, 2012). Authors of both studies argue that challenges to traditional family structures due to industrialization and urbanization may be relevant. Thus different historical trends may be at play based on geographical and sociocultural context.

**Self-esteem**. Self-esteem refers to an individual's global evaluations and feelings of his or her own worth (Orth & Robins, 2014). Cross-temporal meta-analyses showed increases in elementary, middle school, and college students' self-esteem as measured by the Rosenberg Self-Esteem Scale (Rosenberg, 1965) over the recent decades (Gentile, Twenge, & Campbell, 2010; Twenge & Campbell, 2001). Findings were inconclusive with regard to high school students' self-esteem: While Gentile et al. (2010) found increases, Twenge and Campbell (2001) observed an increase only in boys. Furthermore, in a time-lag analysis with population-based samples of high school seniors between 1976 and 2006, Trzesniewski and Donnellan (2010) found no cohort differences in self-esteem.

Available evidence on age-related trajectories of self-esteem suggests that cohorts did not differ in trajectories of change (Erol & Orth, 2011; Orth, Trzesniewski, & Robins, 2010; Orth, Robins & Widaman, 2012). Because of longitudinal design features, cohorts did not completely overlap in age ranges examined. For example, Orth et al. (2012) examined differences in self-esteem trajectories between four generations (children, parents, grandparents, and great-grandparents). With each participant contributing data over up to 12 years, some generations showed overlap in longitudinal age ranges examined, whereas others did not. Children showed some overlap with parents (children: 16 to 47 years, parents: 19 to 68 years), whereas they showed little overlap with grandparents (41 to 90 years) and no overlap with great grandparents (61 to 97 years). Thus the study provides insights on cohort differences within overlapping ages; however, it is possible that differences may have existed outside these age ranges.

In conclusion, available evidence indicates that self-esteem was either stable or increased over the last two to three decades, while age-related trajectories were similar across cohorts. Again, these studies were based on US samples and different trends were observed elsewhere (e.g., China: Liu & Xin, 2015). Also, given that some aspects of psychosocial function improved across cohorts in old age (e.g., Gerstorf et al., 2015; Hülür et al., 2016; Sutin et al., 2013), it is an open question whether similar trends will be observed for self-esteem.

# Open questions

Taken together, available evidence clearly supports the idea that psychological traits are shaped by the time periods people live in. As psychologists were usually interested in identifying processes that generalize across historical periods, cohort differences were often considered nuisances (Caspi, 1987). Thus with the exception of cohort differences in cognition and well-being, empirical evidence is beginning to accumulate and a number of questions are still open. According to lifespan psychological and life course sociological developmental perspectives, individual development is shaped by both historic and ontogenetic processes and their interactions. As Caspi (1987) noted, "the changing environmental context of development must be thoroughly understood and analyzed before an adequate account of individual behavior is possible" (p. 1211) (see also Caspi & Roberts, 2001). Below, I will address some open questions and outline avenues for future research.

**Linking cohort differences to developmental theory**. Since various societal and cultural changes took place over recent decades, it is not too difficult to find post hoc explanations for any finding. For example, because more employees engage in teamwork (Inanc, Felstead, Gallie, & Green, 2013), one may predict increases in agreeableness, as it may be beneficial for working in groups (Barrick, Stewart, Neubert, & Mount, 1998). On the other hand, declines in collectivistic values (Park, Twenge, & Greenfield, 2014) may predict declines in agreeableness, as agreeableness is related to collectivism (Benet-Martinez & Karakitapoglu-Aygün, 2003). Thus it is becoming important to tie research on cohort differences more closely to theory. For example, the theory of emerging adulthood proposes that younger adults are beginning to enter adult roles at later ages (Arnett, 2000). Based on this theory, one could develop the hypothesis that cohorts of late adolescents and young adults differ in developmental trajectories of personality traits that are considered to signify maturation (Bleidorn, 2015), such as emotional stability, conscientiousness, and agreeableness. Fig. 31.1 illustrates two hypotheses based on the theory of emerging adulthood (Arnett, 2000). In Panel A, it is hypothesized that personality maturation (illustrated here as increase in conscientiousness) is postponed to a later age for individuals in the later-born cohort, because they enter adult roles at a later age. Once processes of personality maturation set in, both cohorts follow the same trajectory with a similar rate of increase. In contrast, in Panel B, both cohorts start personality maturation at the same age. However, the later-born cohort shows slower increases in conscientiousness than the earlier-born cohort, because of, for example, a prolonged period of identity exploration.

Also, hypotheses of compression of morbidity versus manufactured survival make different predictions regarding cohort differences in old age (Fries, 1980, 2005; Olshansky, Hayflick, & Carnes, 2002; for an overview and illustration, see Hülür,

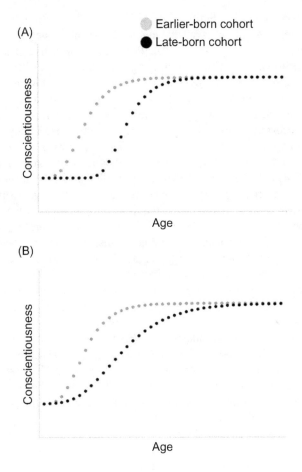

**Figure 31.1** A graphical illustration of two hypotheses based on the theory of emerging adulthood (Arnett, 2000). Panel A: According to the hypothesis illustrated in Panel A, personality maturation (here: increase in conscientiousness) shifted to later ages in the later-born cohort (in black) as compared to the earlier-born cohort (in gray). However, once processes of personality maturation set in, both cohorts undergo this process at the same rate. Panel B: According to the hypothesis illustrated in Panel B, personality maturation starts at the same age for both cohorts. However, personality maturation occurs at a faster rate for the earlier-born cohort (in gray) as compared to the later-born cohort (in black) that experiences a prolonged period of identity formation. Please note that for the sake of simplicity, this illustration assumes that levels of conscientiousness at baseline (e.g., childhood or adolescence conscientiousness) and levels of conscientiousness after maturation are equal in both cohorts. Both of these assumptions are testable in empirical data.

Ram, & Gerstorf, 2016). For example, according to the compression of morbidity hypothesis, older adults today would live longer lives and experience declines in function at relatively later ages compared to previous cohorts. On the other hand, according to the manufactured survival hypothesis, increased length of life would go along with expansion of morbidity, that is, older adults today would spend more years in poor health. As of yet, available evidence does not conclusively support one or the other scenario (see Vaupel, 2010). Potentially, these historical trends carry important implications for personality development, since health has been proposed to affect personality late in life (Wagner et al., 2015). Taken together, a number of specific hypotheses on cohort differences can be derived based on developmental theory to further our understanding of personality development across the lifespan.

**Subgroup differences**. Some historical developments differentially impacted specific subgroups of the population. For example, Twenge (2001b) found that women's assertiveness varied across historical time synchronously with women's social status in society (see also André et al., 2010), while similar trends were not observed in men. With regard to cognitive performance, researchers extensively studied whether historical improvements were stronger at the lower or upper end of the test score distribution (Nisbett et al., 2012). Subgroup differences in test score gains can provide insights into potential mechanisms responsible for historical developments. For example, Nisbett et al. (2012) argued that if cohort differences were based on improvements in nutrition, this should translate into stronger gains at the lower end of the distribution, because upper classes probably had access to a nutritious diet as well in the past. In summary, the study of subgroup differences can provide important insights into mechanisms involved in individual development.

**Issues of measurement**. Another open question is whether observed historical differences reflect changes in the underlying psychological traits or if they are related to response behaviors. This issue has been thoroughly discussed in the study of cohort differences in cognitive performance: Do the observed increases in tests scores reflect cohort differences at the level of cognitive *performance* in single tests, or at the level of the underlying *ability* that the tests were designed to measure (Pietschnig & Voracek, 2015; Wicherts et al., 2004)? Available evidence suggests that test-taking skills may partially explain historical trends; however, substantial improvements nevertheless remain after controlling for cohort differences in test-taking behavior (see Pietschnig & Voracek, 2015).

Also, cohorts may differ in how they perceive and evaluate their personalities. For example, Costa et al. (2001) surprisingly found larger gender differences in personality in societies with higher gender equality. Research suggests that people more often engage in between-gender comparisons in more gender-equal societies, whereas in societies with more rigid gender roles same-gender comparisons are more common (Guimond et al., 2007). With gender roles becoming more egalitarian over time, between-gender comparisons may be more frequent among later-born cohorts. That women's self-reports of assertiveness nevertheless increased from the late 1960s to 1990s (Twenge, 2001b) may imply that increases in the underlying personality trait of assertiveness may be even more substantial.

Tests of measurement invariance, i.e., whether instruments are suited to measure the same underlying construct in different cohorts, may help with some of these issues (see Smits et al., 2011). For example, Smits et al. (2011) found that the item "I think it is important to dress to fit the occasion" was biased with respect to cohort.

This finding is probably based on changing social norms regarding dress codes (see Smits et al., 2011). The decision to exclude such biased items had impact on the size of observed cohort differences (Smits et al., 2011). In summary, it is a largely open question whether observed historical changes took place at the level of underlying traits. Studies of measurement invariance across cohorts can provide some information in this regard.

## Conclusion

The sociocultural environment surrounding us has undergone many important historical changes in recent decades. As outlined in this chapter, cohort differences were documented in a number of between-person difference characteristics. From a theoretical perspective, these findings clearly demonstrate that personality is shaped by the broader historical and sociocultural context individuals are embedded in. Thus to better understand personality development across the lifespan, future research needs to consider both historical and ontogenetic processes and their interplay.

## References

Amato, P. R. (2010). Research on divorce: Continuing trends and new developments. *Journal of Marriage and Family*, *72*, 650–666. Available from http://dx.doi.org/10.1111/j.1741-3737.2010.00723.x.

André, M., Lissner, L., Bengtsson, C., Hällström, T., Sundh, V., & Björkelund, C. (2010). Cohort differences in personality in middle-aged women during a 36-year period. Results from the Population Study of Women in Gothenburg. *Scandinavian Journal of Public Health*, *38*, 457–464.

Arnett, J. J. (2000). Emerging adulthood: A theory of development from the late teens through the twenties. *American Psychologist*, *55*, 469–480. Available from http://dx.doi.org/10.1037/0003-066X.55.5.469.

Baltes, P. B., Cornelius, S. W., & Nesselroade, J. R. (1979). Cohort effects in developmental psychology. In J. R. Nesselroade, & P. B. Baltes (Eds.), *Longitudinal research in the study of behavior and development* (pp. 61–87). New York, NY: Academic Press.

Baltes, P. B., & Nesselroade, J. R. (1979). History and rationale of longitudinal research. In J. R. Nesselroade, & P. B. Baltes (Eds.), *Longitudinal research in the study of behavior and development* (pp. 1–39). New York, NY: Academic Press.

Baltes, P. B., & Smith, J. (2003). New frontiers in the future of aging: From successful aging of the young old to the dilemmas of the fourth age. *Gerontology*, *49*, 123–135. Available from http://dx.doi.org/10.1159/000067946.

Barrick, M. R., Stewart, G. L., Neubert, M. J., & Mount, M. K. (1998). Relating member ability and personality to work-team processes and team effectiveness. *Journal of Applied Psychology*, *83*, 377–391. Available from http://dx.doi.org/10.1037/0021-9010.83.3.377.

Baumrind, D. (1971). Current patterns of parental authority. *Developmental Psychology*, *4*, 1–103. Available from http://dx.doi.org/10.1037/h0030372.

Benet-Martínez, V., & Karakitapoglu-Aygun, Z. (2003). The interplay of cultural values and personality in predicting life-satisfaction: Comparing Asian- and European-Americans. *Journal of Cross-Cultural Psychology, 34*, 38−61. Available from http://dx.doi.org/10.1177/0022022102239154.

Billstedt, E., Waern, M., Duberstein, P., Marlow, T., Hellström, T., Ostling, S., & Skoog, I. (2013). Secular changes in personality: Study on 75-year-olds examined in 1976−1977 and 2005−2006. *International Journal of Geriatric Psychiatry, 3*, 298−304. Available from http://dx.doi.org/10.1002/gps.3825.

Blair, C., Gamson, D. A., Thorne, S., & Baker, D. P. (2005). Rising mean IQ: Cognitive demand of mathematics education for young children, population exposure to formal schooling, and the neurobiology of the prefrontal cortex. *Intelligence, 33*, 93−106. Available from http://dx.doi.org/10.1016/j.intell.2004.07.008.

Blanchflower, D. G., & Oswald, A. J. (2004). Well-being over time in Britain and the USA. *Journal of Public Economics, 88*, 1359−1386. http://dx.doi.org/10.1016/S0047-2727(02)00168-8.

Bleidorn, W. (2015). What accounts for personality maturation in early adulthood? *Current Directions in Psychological Science, 24*, 245−252 Available from http://dx.doi.org/10.1177/0963721414568662.

Bowles, R. P., Grimm, K. J., & McArdle, J. J. (2005). A structural factor analysis of vocabulary knowledge and relations to age. *Journals of Gerontology: Series B: Psychological Sciences and Social Sciences, 60*, P234−P241. Available from http://dx.doi.org/10.1093/geronb/60.5.P234.

Boyce, C. J., Wood, A. M., Daly, M., & Sedikides, C. (2015). Personality change following unemployment. *Journal of Applied Psychology, 100*, 991−1011. Available from http://dx.doi.org/10.1037/a0038647.

Bronfenbrenner, U. (1986). Ecology of the family as a context for human development research perspectives. *Developmental Psychology, 22*, 723−742. Available from http://dx.doi.org/10.1037/0012-1649.22.6.723.

Caspi, A. (1987). Personality in the life course. *Journal of Personality and Social Psychology, 53*, 1203−1213. Available from http://dx.doi.org/10.1037/0022-3514.53.6.1203.

Caspi, A., & Roberts, B. W. (2001). Personality development across the life course: The argument for change and continuity. *Psychological Inquiry, 12*, 49−66. Available from http://dx.doi.org/10.1207/S15327965PLI1202_01.

Christensen, K., Thinggaard, M., Oksuzyan, A., Steenstrup, T., Andersen-Ranberg, K., Jeune, B., ... Vaupel, J. W. (2013). Physical and cognitive functioning of people older than 90 years: A comparison of two Danish cohorts born 10 years apart. *The Lancet, 382*, 1507−1513. Available from http://dx.doi.org/10.1016/S0140-6736(13)60777-1.

Costa, P. T., Jr., Terracciano, A., & McCrae, R. R. (2001). Gender differences in personality traits across cultures: Robust and surprising findings. *Journal of Personality and Social Psychology, 81*, 322−331. Available from http://dx.doi.org/10.1037/0022-3514.81.2.322.

Crimmins, E. M. (2015). Lifespan and healthspan: Past, present, and promise. *Gerontologist, 55*, 901−911. Available from http://dx.doi.org/10.1093/geront/gnv130.

DeYoung, C. (2011). Intelligence and personality. In R. J. Sternberg, & S. B. Kaufman (Eds.), *The Cambridge handbook of intelligence* (pp. 711−737). New York, NY: Cambridge University Press.

Diener, E. (1984). Subjective well-being. *Psychological Bulletin, 95*, 542−575. Available from http://dx.doi.org/10.1037/0033-2909.95.3.542.

Diener, E. (1996). Traits can be powerful, but are not enough: Lessons from subjective well-being. *Journal of Research in Personality*, *30*, 389−399. Available from http://dx.doi.org/10.1006/jrpe.1996.0027.

Diener, E., & Lucas, R. (1999). Personality, and subjective well-being. In D. Kahneman, E. Diener, & N. Schwarz (Eds.), *Well-being: The foundations of hedonic psychology* (pp. 213−229). New York, NY: Sage.

Dodge, H. H., Zhu, J., Lee, C.-W., Chang, C.-C. H., & Ganguli, M. (2014). Cohort effects in age-associated cognitive trajectories. *Journals of Gerontology: Series A: Biological Sciences and Medical Sciences*, *69*, M687−M694. Available from http://dx.doi.org/10.1093/gerona/glt181.

Elder, G. H., Jr. (1974). *Children of the Great Depression: Social change in life experience.* Chicago, IL: University of Chicago Press.

Erol, R. Y., & Orth, U. (2011). Self-esteem development from age 14 to 30 years: A longitudinal study. *Journal of Personality and Social Psychology*, *101*, 607−619. Available from http://dx.doi.org/10.1037/a0024299.

Finkel, D., Reynolds, C. A., McArdle, J. J., & Pedersen, N. L. (2007). Cohort differences in trajectories of cognitive aging. *The Journals of Gerontology: Series B. Psychological Sciences and Social Sciences*, *62*, P286−P294. Available from http://dx.doi.org/10.1093/geronb/62.5.P286.

Fiori, K. L., Brown, E. E., Cortina, K. S., & Antonucci, T. (2006). Locus of control as a mediator of the relationship between religiosity and life satisfaction: Age, race, and gender differences. *Mental Health, Religion and Culture*, *9*, 239−263. Available from http://dx.doi.org/10.1080/13694670600615482.

Flynn, J. R. (2007). Solving the IQ Puzzle. *Scientific American Mind*, *18*, 24−31. Available from http://dx.doi.org/10.1038/scientificamericanmind1007-24.

Fries, J. F. (1980). Aging, natural death, and the compression of morbidity. *New England Journal of Medicine*, *303*, 130−135.

Fries, J. F. (2005). The compression of morbidity. *Milbank Quarterly*, *83*, 801−823. Available from http://dx.doi.org/10.1111/j.1468-0009.2005.00401.x.

Gentile, B., Twenge, J. M., & Campbell, W. K. (2010). Birth cohort differences in self-esteem, 1988−2008: A crosstemporal meta-analysis. *Review of General Psychology*, *14*, 261−268. Available from http://dx.doi.org/10.1037/a0019919261.

George, L. G., Helson, R., & John, O. P. (2011). The "CEO" of women's work lives: How Big Five Conscientiousness, Extraversion, and Openness predict 50 years of work experiences in a changing sociocultural context. *Journal of Personality and Social Psychology*, *101*, 812−830. Available from http://dx.doi.org/10.1037/a0024290.

Gerstorf, D., Hülür, G., Drewelies, J., Eibich, P., Duezel, S., Demuth, I., . . . Lindenberger, U. (2015). Secular changes in late-life cognition and well-being: Towards a long bright future with a short brisk ending? *Psychology and Aging*, *30*, 301−310. Available from http://dx.doi.org/10.1037/pag0000016.

Gerstorf, D., Ram, N., Hoppmann, C. A., Willis, S. L., & Schaie, K. W. (2011). Cohort differences in cognitive aging and terminal decline in the Seattle Longitudinal Study. *Developmental Psychology*, *47*, 1026−1041. Available from http://dx.doi.org/10.1037/a0023426.

Guimond, S., Branscombe, N., Brunot, S., Buunk, A. P., Chatard, A., Désert, M., . . . Yzerbyt, V. (2007). Culture, gender, and the self: variations and impact of social comparison processes. *Journal of Personality and Social Psychology*, *92*, 1118−1134. Available from http://dx.doi.org/10.1037/0022-3514.92.6.1118.

Hooker, K., & McAdams, D. P. (2003). Personality reconsidered: A new agenda for aging research. *Journal of Gerontology: Psychological Sciences*, *58B*, P296–P304. Available from http://dx.doi.org/10.1093/geronb/58.6.P296.

Hoppmann, C. A., Gerstorf, D., & Luszcz, M. (2011). Dyadic interrelations in lifespan development and aging: How does 1 + 1 make a couple? *Gerontology*, *57*, 144–147. Available from http://dx.doi.org/10.1159/000320324.

Hülür, G., Drewelies, J., Eibich, P., Düzel, S., Demuth, I., Ghisletta, P., ... Gerstorf, D. (2016). Cohort differences in psychosocial function over 20 years: Current older adults feel less lonely and less dependent on external circumstances. *Gerontology*. Available from http://dx.doi.org/10.1159/000438991.

Hülür, G., Infurna, F. J., Ram, N., & Gerstorf, D. (2013). Cohorts based on decade of death: No evidence for secular trends favoring later cohorts in cognitive aging and terminal decline in the AHEAD study. *Psychology and Aging*, *28*, 115–127. Available from http://dx.doi.org/10.1037/a0029965.

Hülür, G., Ram, N., & Gerstorf, D. (2015). Historical improvements in well-being do not hold in late life: studies of birth-year and death-year cohorts in national samples from the US and Germany. *Developmental Psychology*, *51*, 998–1012. Available from http://dx.doi.org/10.1037/a0039349.

Hülür, G., Ram, N., & Gerstorf, D. (2016). Terminal decline of function. In V. L. Bengtson & R. A. Settersten, Jr. (Eds.), *Handbook of theories of aging* (3rd ed., pp. 277–300). New York, NY: Springer.

Inanc, H., Felstead, A., Gallie, D., & Green, F. (2013). *Job control in Britain: First findings from the Skills and Employment Survey 2012*. London, UK: Centre for Learning and Life Chances in Knowledge Economies and Societies, Institute of Education.

Juhn, C., & Potter, S. (2006). Changes in labor force participation in the United States. *Journal of Economic Perspectives*, *20*, 27–46. Available from http://dx.doi.org/10.1257/jep.20.3.27.

Kandler, C., Zimmermann, J., & McAdams, D. (2014). Core and surface characteristics for the description and theory of personality differences and development. *European Journal of Personality*, *28*, 231–243. Available from http://dx.doi.org/10.1002/per.1952.

Karlsson, P., Thorvaldsson, V., Skoog, I., Gudmundsson, P., & Johansson, B. (2015). Birth cohort differences in fluid cognition in old age: Comparisons of trends in levels and change trajectories over 30 years in three population-based samples. *Psychology and Aging*, *30*, 83–94. Available from http://dx.doi.org/10.1037/a0038643.

Lachman, M., Neupert, S., & Agrigoroaei, S. (2011). The relevance of control beliefs for health and aging. In K. W. Schaie, & S. L. Willis (Eds.), *Handbook of the Psychology of Aging* (7th ed., pp. 175–190). New York, NY: Elsevier.

Liu, D., & Xin, Z. (2015). Birth cohort and age changes in the self-esteem of Chinese adolescents: A cross-temporal meta-analysis, 1996–2009. *Journal of Research on Adolescence*, *25*, 366–376. Available from http://dx.doi.org/10.1111/jora.12134.

Liu, J., Chen, X., Li, D., & French, D. (2012). Shyness-sensitivity, aggression, and adjustment in urban Chinese adolescents at different historical times. *Journal of Research on Adolescence*, *22*, 393–399. Available from http://dx.doi.org/10.1111/j.1532-7795.2012.00790.x.

Lynn, R. (1998). In support of the nutrition theory. In U. Neisser (Ed.), *The rising curve: Long-term gains in IQ and related measures* (pp. 207–218). Washington, DC: American Psychological Association.

Martin, J. A., Hamilton, B. E., Osterman, M. J. K., Curtin, S. C., & Mathews, T. J. (2015). Births: Final Data for 2013. *National Vital Statistics Reports* (64, p. 1). Hyattsville, MD: National Center for Health Statistics.

McCrae, R. R., & Costa, P. T., Jr. (2003). *Personality in adulthood: A Five-Factor Theory perspective* (2nd ed.,). New York, NY: Guilford Press.

Mroczek, D. K., & Spiro, A. (2003). Modeling intraindividual change in personality traits: Findings from the Normative Aging Study. *Journals of Gerontology: Series B. Psychological Sciences and Social Sciences, 58,* P153−P165. Available from http://dx. doi.org/10.1093/geronb/58.3.P153.

Nisbett, R. E., Aronson, J., Blair, C., Dickens, W., Flynn, J., Halpern, D. F., & Turkheimer, E. (2012). Intelligence: New findings and theoretical developments. *American Psychologist, 67,* 130−159. Available from http://dx.doi.org/10.1037/a0026699.

Olshansky, S. J., Hayflick, L., & Carnes, B. A. (2002). Position statement on human aging. *Journals of Gerontology: Series A: Biological Sciences and Medical Sciences, 57,* M292−M297. Available from http://dx.doi.org/10.1093/gerona/57.8.B292.

Orth, U., & Robins, R. W. (2014). The development of self-esteem. *Current Directions in Psychological Science, 23,* 381−387. Available from http://dx.doi.org/10.1177/ 0963721414547414.

Orth, U., Robins, R. W., & Widaman, K. F. (2012). Life-span development of self-esteem and its effects on important life outcomes. *Journal of Personality and Social Psychology, 102,* 1271−1288. Available from http://dx.doi.org/10.1037/a0025558.

Orth, U., Trzesniewski, K. H., & Robins, R. W. (2010). Self-esteem development from young adulthood to old age: A cohort-sequential longitudinal study. *Journal of Personality and Social Psychology, 98,* 645−658. Available from http://dx.doi.org/10.1037/a0018769.

Park, H., Twenge, J. M., & Greenfield, P. M. (2014). The great recession: Implications for adolescent values and behavior. *Social Psychology and Personality Science, 5,* 310−318. Available from http://dx.doi.org/10.1177/1948550613495419.

Pietschnig, J., & Voracek, M. (2015). One century of global IQ gains: A formal meta-analysis of the Flynn effect (1909−2013). *Perspectives on Psychological Science, 10,* 282−306. Available from http://dx.doi.org/10.1177/1745691615577701.

Riley, M. W. (1973). Aging and cohort succession: Interpretations and misinterpretations. *Public Opinion Quarterly, 37,* 35−49. Available from http://dx.doi.org/10.1086/268058.

Roberts, B. W., Walton, K., & Viechtbauer, W. (2006). Patterns of mean-level change in personality traits across the life course: A meta-analysis of longitudinal studies. *Psychological Bulletin, 132,* 1−25. Available from http://dx.doi.org/10.1037/0033-2909.132.1.1.

Rosenberg, M. (1965). *Society and the adolescent self-image.* Princeton, NJ: Princeton University Press.

Rotter, J. B. (1966). Generalized expectancies for internal versus external control of reinforcement. *Psychological Monographs: General and Applied, 80,* 1−28. Available from http://dx.doi.org/10.1037/h0092976.

Ryder, N. B. (1965). The cohort as a concept in the study of social changes. *American Sociological Review, 30,* 843−861. Available from http://dx.doi.org/10.1007/978-1-4613-8536-3_2.

Rutherford, M. B. (2009). Children's autonomy and responsibility: An analysis of childrearing advice. *Qualitative Sociology, 32,* 337−353. Available from http://dx.doi.org/ 10.1007/s11133-009-9136-2.

Schaie, K. W. (1965). A general model for the study of developmental problems. *Psychological Bulletin, 64,* 92−107. Available from http://dx.doi.org/10.1037/h0022371.

Schaie, K. W. (2011). Historical influences on aging and behavior. In K. W. Schaie, & S. L. Willis (Eds.), *Handbook of the psychology of aging* (pp. 41−55). San Diego, CA: Elsevier.

Schaie, K. W., & Baltes, P. B. (1975). On sequential strategies in developmental research. *Human Development*, *18*, 384−390. Available from http://dx.doi.org/10.1159/000271498.

Schaie, K. W., Willis, S. L., & Pennak, S. (2005). An historical framework for cohort differences in intelligence. *Research in Human Development*, *2*, 43−67. Available from http://dx.doi.org/10.1207/s15427617rhd0201&2_3.

Schilling, O. K. (2005). Cohort- and age-related decline in elder's life satisfaction: Is there really a paradox? *European Journal of Ageing*, *2*, 254−263. Available from http://dx.doi.org/10.1007/s10433-005-0016-7.

Schooler, C., Mulatu, M. S., & Oates, G. (1999). The continuing effects of substantively complex work on the intellectual functioning of older workers. *Psychology and Aging*, *14*, 483−506. Available from http://dx.doi.org/10.1037/0882-7974.14.3.483.

Shao, J., Li, D., Zhang, D., Zhang, L., Zhang, Q., & Qi, X. (2013). Birth cohort changes in the depressive symptoms of Chinese older adults: A cross-temporal meta-analysis. *International Journal of Geriatric Psychiatry*, *28*, 1101−1108. Available from http://dx.doi.org/10.1002/gps.3942.

Skinner, E. A. (1995). *Perceived control, motivation, and coping*. Thousand Oaks, CA: Sage.

Skirbekk, V., Stonawski, M., Bonsang, E., & Staudinger, U. M. (2013). The Flynn effect and population aging. *Intelligence*, *41*, 169−177. Available from http://dx.doi.org/10.1016/j.intell.2013.02.001.

Smits, I. A. M., Dolan, C. V., Vorst, H. C. M., Wicherts, J. M., & Timmerman, M. E. (2011). Cohort differences in Big Five personality factors over a period of 25 years. *Journal of Personality and Social Psychology*, *100*, 1124−1138. Available from http://dx.doi.org/10.1037/a0022874.

Specht, J., Egloff, B., & Schmukle, S. C. (2013). The effects of age, gender, and education on trajectories of perceived control in a nationally representative German sample. *Developmental Psychology*, *49*, 353−364. Available from http://dx.doi.org/10.1037/a0028243.

Spiers, N., Bebbington, P., McManus, S., Brugha, T. S., Jenkins, R., & Meltzer, H. (2011). Age and birth cohort differences in the prevalence of common mental disorder in England: National Psychiatric Morbidity Surveys 1993−2007. *British Journal of Psychiatry*, *198*, 479−484. Available from http://dx.doi.org/10.1192/bjp.bp.110.084269.

Spiers, N., Brugha, T. S., Bebbington, P., McManus, S., Jenkins, R., & Meltzer, H. (2012). Age and birth cohort differences in depression in repeated cross-sectional surveys in England: The National Psychiatric Morbidity Surveys, 1993 to 2007. *Psychological Medicine*, *42*, 2047−2055. Available from http://dx.doi.org/10.1017/S003329171200013X.

Sundet, J. M., Borren, I., & Tambs, K. (2008). The Flynn effect is partly caused by changing fertility patterns. *Intelligence*, *36*, 183−191. Available from http://dx.doi.org/10.1016/j.intell.2007.04.002.

Sutin, A. R., Terracciano, A., Milaneschi, Y., An, Y., Ferrucci, L., & Zonderman, A. B. (2013). Cohort effect on well-being: The legacy of economic hard times. *Psychological Science*, *24*, 379−385. Available from http://dx.doi.org/10.1177/0956797612459658.

Terracciano, A., McCrae, R. R., Brant, L. J., & Costa, P. T., Jr. (2005). Hierarchical linear modeling analyses of the NEO-PI−R scales in the Baltimore Longitudinal Study of Aging. *Psychology and Aging*, *20*, 493−506. Available from http://dx.doi.org/10.1037/0882-7974.20.3.493.

Trzesniewski, K. H., & Donnellan, M. B. (2010). Rethinking "Generation Me": A Study of cohort effects from 1976−2006. *Perspectives in Psychological Science*, *5*, 58−75. Available from http://dx.doi.org/10.1177/1745691609356789.

Trzesniewski, K. H., Donnellan, M. B., & Robins, R. W. (2003). Stability of self-esteem across the lifespan. *Journal of Personality and Social Psychology*, *84*, 205−220. Available from http://dx.doi.org/10.1037/0022-3514.84.1.205.

Twenge, J. M. (2000). The age of anxiety? Birth cohort change in anxiety and neuroticism, 1952−1993. *Journal of Personality and Social Psychology*, *79*, 1007−1021. Available from http://dx.doi.org/10.1037/0022-3514.79.6.1007.

Twenge, J. M. (2001a). Birth cohort changes in extraversion: A cross-temporal meta-analysis, 1966−1993. *Personality and Individual Differences*, *30*, 735−748. http://dx.doi.org/10.1016/S0191-8869(00)00066-0.

Twenge, J. M. (2001b). Changes in women's assertiveness in response to status and roles: A cross-temporal meta-analysis, 1931−1993. *Journal of Personality and Social Psychology*, *81*, 133−145. Available from http://dx.doi.org/10.1037/0022-3514.81.1.133.

Twenge, J. M. (2015). Time period and birth cohort differences in depressive symptoms in the U.S., 1982−2013. *Social Indicators Research*, *121*, 437−454. Available from http://dx.doi.org/10.1007/s11205-014-0647-1.

Twenge, J. M., & Campbell, W. K. (2001). Age and birth cohort differences in self-esteem: A cross-temporal meta-analysis. *Personality and Social Psychology Review*, *5*, 321−344. Available from http://dx.doi.org/10.1207/S15327957PSPR0504_3.

Twenge, J. M., Gentile, B., DeWall, C. N., Ma, D. S., Lacefield, K., & Schurtz, D. R. (2010). Birth cohort increases in psychopathology among young Americans, 1938−2007: A cross-temporal meta-analysis of the MMPI. *Clinical Psychology Review*, *30*, 145−154. Available from http://dx.doi.org/10.1016/j.cpr.2009.10.005.

Twenge, J. M., Sherman, R. A., & Lyubomirsky, S. (2016). More happiness for young people, and less for mature adults: Time period differences in subjective well-being in the U.S., 1972−2014. *Social Psychological and Personality Science*, *7*, 131−141. Available from http://dx.doi.org/10.1177/1948550615602933.

Twenge, J. M., Zhang, L., & Im, C. (2004). It's beyond my control: A cross-temporal meta-analysis of increasing externality in Locus of Control, 1960−2002. *Personality and Social Psychology Review*, *8*, 308−319.

US Census Bureau (2015), Median age at first marriage: 1890 to present. Retrieved from https://www.census.gov/hhes/families/files/graphics/MS-2.pdf.

Vaupel, J. W. (2010). Biodemography of human ageing. *Nature*, *464*, 536−542. Available from http://dx.doi.org/10.1038/nature08984.

Wagner, J., Ram, N., Smith, J., & Gerstorf, D. (2015). Personality trait development at the end of life: Antecedents and correlates of mean-level trajectories. *Journal of Personality and Social Psychology*. Available from http://dx.doi.org/10.1037/pspp0000071.

Wicherts, J. M., Dolan, C. V., Hessen, D. J., Oosterveld, P., Baal, G. C. M., van, Boomsma, D. I., & Span, M. M. (2004). Are intelligence tests measurement invariant over time? Investigating the nature of the Flynn effect. *Intelligence*, *32*, 509−537. Available from http://dx.doi.org/10.1016/j.intell.2004.07.002.

Wolf, C. (2008). How secularized is Germany? Cohort and comparative perspectives. *Social Compass*, *55*, 111−126. Available from http://dx.doi.org/10.1177/0037768608089733.

Wongupparaj, P., Kumari, V., & Morris, R. A. (2015). Cross-temporal meta-analysis of Raven's Progressive Matrices: Age groups and developing versus developed countries. *Intelligence*, *49*, 1−9. Available from http://dx.doi.org/10.1016/j.intell.2014.11.008.

Xin, Z., Niu, J., & Chi, L. (2012). Birth cohort changes in Chinese adolescents' mental health. *International Journal of Psychology*, *47*, 287−295. Available from http://dx.doi.org/10.1080/00207594.2011.626048.

Yang, Y. (2008). Social inequalities in happiness in the United States, 1972 to 2004: An age-period-cohort analysis. *American Sociological Review*, *73*, 204−226. Available from http://dx.doi.org/10.1177/000312240807300202.

Zajonc, R. B. (1976). Family configuration and intelligence. *Science*, *192*, 227−236. Available from http://dx.doi.org/10.1126/science.192.4236.227.

Zelinski, E. M., & Kennison, R. F. (2007). Not your parents' test scores: Cohort reduces psychometric aging effects. *Psychology and Aging*, *22*, 546−557. Available from http://dx.doi.org/10.1037/0882-7974.22.3.546.

Zivin, K., Pirraglia, P. A., McCammon, R. J., Langa, K. M., & Vijan, S. (2013). Trends in depressive symptom burden among older adults in the United States from 1998 to 2008. *Journal of General Internal Medicine*, *28*, 1611−1619. Available from http://dx.doi.org/10.1007/s11606-013-2533-y.

# Development of implicit personality

**32**

*John F. Rauthmann*
Wake Forest University, Winston-Salem, NC, United States

This chapter deals with a new frontier in personality development research virtually unexplored so far: the stability and change of implicit or automatic aspects of personality. First, the literature is reviewed that conceives personality traits as automatized habits of acting, thinking, feeling, and desiring. Second, the measurement of implicit personality traits is briefly reviewed, especially regarding two central questions: Do measures of implicit traits and self-reports capture the same construct? How stable and malleable are implicit traits? Lastly, some directions for future research on the development of implicit personality traits are sketched.

## The automaticity of personality

### The definition and measurement of traits

What is a personality trait? The most parsimonious (and grossly oversimplifying) answer would be that traits are temporally stable average levels or patterns of affect, behavior, cognition, and desire (ABCDs) (Funder, 2001; Ortony, Norman, & Revelle, 2005). For example, extraverted people experience more positive affect (A), act sociable when meeting strangers (B), think optimistically about the future (C), and need excitement (D) (Wilt & Revelle, 2008). Traits cannot be directly observed, but need to be inferred from manifest variables that are measurable via different data sources (Fig. 32.1): Behavior (i.e., objectively measured behavioral output), Indirect measures (i.e., projective tests, implicit association tasks),[1] Observation (i.e., observational codings by experts), Physiology (i.e., biological, physiological, and chemical assessments), Stranger-impressions (i.e., strangers' ratings of a person), Informant-ratings (i.e., friends' and family's ratings of a person), Experience-sampling (i.e., people report mental states and behavior several times a day for weeks), and Self-reports/ Narratives (i.e., people's explicit self-concepts and identities). These BIOPSIES data sources provide a biopsy of a personality trait, and each source may grant different

---

[1] There is some debate about how to name this category. For example, De Houwer (2005) would use "implicit tests" or "indirect measures," Schultheiss (2007) "nondeclarative personality tests," and Bornstein (2007) probably "performance-based tests." This work uses "indirect measures" as the umbrella term. Implicit measures such as the Implicit Association Task are a subset of indirect measures (which also span projective tests).

*Personality Development Across the Lifespan.* DOI: http://dx.doi.org/10.1016/B978-0-12-804674-6.00032-6

**Figure 32.1** The BIOPSIES data sources of personality assessment. *Note*: This depiction is not intended to be a measurement model. The eight BIOPSIES data sources can be thought of overlapping with each other to the extent that they measure the same underlying personality trait. For clarity sake, the BIOPSIES are not depicted as overlapping, but besides each other tapping the same trait. Apart from such shared variance, there may also be method-specific variance.

and unique information about a trait. Most personality research, however, still relies only on self-reports, but since they can be distorted in various ways (e.g., by social desirability, impression management, self-deception), other data sources should be used also. This is especially true for personality development research.

The literature on personality stability and change has yielded important findings on how stable *self-reports* are and how they change across the lifespan (for an overview, see Specht et al., 2014). Thus we have a relatively good understanding of how people's explicitly formulated understanding about themselves develop across time (see McAdams, 2015, for a developmental framework around people's narratives). However, relatively little is known about the development of personality *as measured by different data sources* than people's reports. This is particularly true for indirect measures which supposedly capture automatic and implicit aspects of traits. Automatic processes operate in the absence of consciously formulated goals, a full capacity of cognitive resources, substantial amount of time, or awareness of the triggering situational stimuli, the automatic process itself, or the outcome of the process (Bargh, 1994; De Houwer, Teige-Mocigemba, Spruyt, & Moors, 2009; Moors & De Houwer, 2006). Accordingly, measures have often been termed "indirect" if participants are not aware of and cannot consciously or willfully take influence on what is being measured, hence not requiring any introspection or eliciting self-presentational tendencies.

Roberts, Walton, and Viechtbauer (2006, p. 7) noted in their meta-analysis on mean-level change that there were too few longitudinal studies that employed peer-reports or projective tests (which is a subset of indirect measures) so that they could not examine whether methods different than self-reports would impact mean levels of traits across the lifespan. Further, Roberts and DelVecchio (2000) conducted a meta-analysis on studies that reported rank-order stabilities with time intervals 1 year or longer. Self-reports comprised 50%, peer-reports 41%, and projective tests only 9% of studies (which were mostly restricted to high school students and college age samples). Using only eight studies ($N = 489$) that used projective tests, they found an estimated population rank-order stability correlation of $\rho = 0.43$ (95% CI $= 0.34-0.52$), which rose to 0.45 when controlling for age of participants and time interval of the longitudinal study. It is also telling that virtually no longitudinal data on personality stability or change exist that would have used indirect measures other than projective tests such as implicit association tasks.

This state of affairs may have something to do with how traits have been traditionally conceptualized. Most trait conceptualizations focus more on deliberate and conscious ABCDs (Funder, 1991) as well as on people's broad descriptions of themselves (John, Naumann, & Soto, 2008). However, the sociogenomic model of personality (Roberts & Jackson, 2008) presented an intriguing contrarian view (Roberts, 2009, p. 9):

> [T]raits are relatively non-conscious, non-motivational entities. By definition, the repetitive nature of traits and their constituent elements means that the entire system of thoughts, feelings, and behaviors has been habituated. That is to say, the repetitions arise because of the non-conscious stimulus-response patterns—a "readiness to respond" (. . .)

This definition thus conceives traits as *automatic* patterns of ABCDs in relation to triggering environmental or situational stimuli. For example, the association between certain stimuli (e.g., many people in a room) and reactions (e.g., behaving assertive) will become habitual if there are positive consequences (personal rewards or reinforcement: e.g., standing in the center of attention and being complimented), if stimuli—reactions—consequences concatenations occur with a certain regularity. Indeed, such concatenations constitute a basic form of learning and development (Ericsson & Lehmann, 1996; Wood & Neal, 2007) where behaviors will become automatized habits and consolidated into traits (Paulhus, 1993). For example,

Thornike (1913) referred to the tendency of selecting increasingly efficient (i.e., less time, energy, attention, etc.) and automatic behaviors into an organism's behavioral repertoire as the *law of habit* or *law of exercise*. The automatization of behavior into habits and traits is also incorporated into newer functionalistic formulations of traits (Wood, Gardner, & Harms, 2015) and personality development (Wood & Denissen, 2015). Further, it is also reflected in Magidson, Roberts, Collado-Rodriguez, and Lejuez (2014) theory-driven intervention approach for changing personality where the authors propose to target state-level behaviors (and their contingencies with rewards) so that they can be, via repeated enactment, become habitualized and automatized—and thus ingrained into a person's trait. Moreover, it has been argued that much of our daily lives *in general* are dependent on automatic, "unconscious" mechanisms and processes (e.g., Bargh & Chartrand, 1999). In spite of all of this, there is still a lack of empirical research that addresses the stability and change of implicitly measured traits.

## Dual-process conceptions

Personality psychology in general has had a varied history with unconscious aspects of traits. For example, psychodynamic theories (e.g., from Freud, Jung, Adler, Horney) were explicitly concerned with latent desires, wishes, and anxieties that would produce unconscious dynamics within persons and govern their behavior. Ironically, in early behaviorism's neglect of any such subjective, internal person variables (e.g., Watson, Skinner), learning theorists also stressed automatized behavior that, more often than not, may have occurred due to implicit learning. Humanism, however, has emphasized more controlled aspects of persons who have a free will and decide deliberately what to do in or with their lives (e.g., May, Maslow, Frankl), thus deemphasizing uncontrollable, unconscious processes. In contrast to these "three forces," cognitive approaches to personality have reconciled conscious and automatic aspects. Particularly *dual-process models of information processing*, developed in cognitive psychology and social cognition research, are relevant here (for details, see Strack & Deutsch, 2004). These essentially posit that there are two systems of information processing: impulsive (hot, affective, emotional, intuitive, spontaneous, automatic, effortless, uncontrollable) processing in an associative system versus reflective (cold, cognitive, rational, analytical, deliberate, effortful, controlled) processing in a propositional system. The impulsive system could be thought of as an autopilot that constantly and efficiently processes information. Upon the perception and recognition of stimuli, associative networks are activated and behavioral schemata triggered (i.e., spread of activation processes). The output is spontaneous and automatic reactions to situational stimuli (e.g., being yelled at and infuriatingly yelling back). In contrast, the reflective system employs deliberate and consciously available thinking, reasoning, and decision processes to formulate more long-term and complex behavioral intentions. Thus its output is controlled behavior (e.g., deciding what to say in an apology because one has yelled at somebody). These cognitive psychological models have been most notably implemented into attitude research that distinguishes between explicit and implicit attitudes (e.g., Bassili & Brown, 2005; Nosek, 2007). Explicit attitudes (e.g., I endorse a vegan lifestyle) stem from the reflective system and are stored in declarative/propositional memory systems, are consciously available to the attitude holder, can be measured in questionnaires or interviews, and predict conscious and controlled behavior. In contrast, implicit attitudes stem from the impulsive system and are stored in associative networks, are usually not consciously available, need to be measured by indirect measures, and predict spontaneous and automatic (as well as socially undesirable) behavior.

Because people's self-concepts about themselves and their traits may be conceptualized as attitudes toward the self, it is possible to distinguish between explicit and implicit self-concepts (Schnabel & Asendorpf, 2010; Schnabel, Asendorpf, & Greenwald, 2008a). Thus, when specifically referring to personality, propositional representations may be termed explicit personality self-concepts (e.g., "I am a sociable person"), and associative representations implicit personality self-concepts (e.g., strong association between "I, me" and "sociable"). Back, Schmukle, and Egloff (2009) extended these ideas in their *Behavioral Process Model of Personality (BPMP)*, as visualized in Fig. 32.2. Personality is conceptualized as the typical

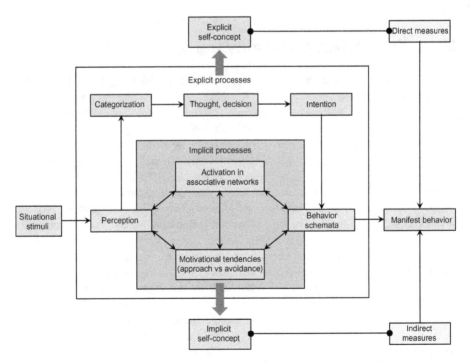

**Figure 32.2** The behavioral process model of personality.
*Source*: Adapted from Back M.D., Schmukle S.C. and Egloff B., Predicting actual behavior from the explicit and implicit self-concept of personality, *Journal of Personality and Social Psychology* **97**, 2009, 533−548 (Fig. 32.1, p. 535).

functioning of reflective and impulsive processes. Typical reflective information processing (e.g., world-views, standards, and knowledge) leads to explicit self-concepts which can be captured by direct measures (e.g., questionnaire items) that ask the person about his/her views about him-/herself. However, there can be various kinds of biases in people's self-descriptions (e.g., limits in self-knowledge or introspection, memory distortions, impression management, and willful faking). Typical impulsive information processing in the form of associative networks leads to implicit self-concepts which can be captured by indirect measures (e.g., projective tests, implicit association tasks) that circumvent people's self-reports in favor of subtler measurement. Directly measured traits are better for predicting controlled and deliberate behavior, while indirectly measured traits seem better for predicting uncontrolled and automatic behavior (Back et al., 2009; Steffens & Schulze König, 2006). Because of limited overlaps between directly and indirectly measured traits (see "Convergent Validity" section later), each offer a unique window into understanding personality and its effects on behavioral, social, and life outcomes. Nonetheless, research on personality development has so far almost exclusively relied on self-reports. The development (or stability and change) of automatic aspects of personality has thus not received sufficient theoretical or empirical attention.

## Measuring implicit personality traits

There are several different forms of indirect measures (De Houwer, 2006), but projective tests (e.g., revised versions of the Rorschach test), affective priming tasks, and implicit association tasks (IATs; Fazio, Jackson, Dunton, & Williams, 1995; Greenwald, McGhee, & Schwartz., 1998) are probably among the most prominent ones. The remainder of this chapter will focus on IATs because of their favorable psychometric properties (e.g., internal consistencies of 0.70−0.90; Hofmann, Gawronski, Gschwendner, Le, & Schmitt, 2005; Nosek, Greenwald, & Banaji, 2007; Schmukle & Egloff, 2004; Schnabel, Asendorpf, & Greenwald, 2008b; Schnabel, Asendorpf, & Greenwald, 2008c) and good applications to personality constructs, such as anxiety, shyness, self-esteem, and the Big Five (Asendorpf, Banse, & Mücke, 2002; Back et al., 2009; Schmukle, Back, & Egloff, 2008). Nonetheless, it is not always easy to discern what exactly IATs tell us (for common misconceptions, see Gawronski, LeBel, & Peters, 2007), and there have also been critiques of persistent conceptual and methodological issues with IATs (e.g., Fiedler, Mess, & Bluemke, 2006). Regardless, IATs offer a good way of measuring more automatic aspects of personality (Back et al., 2009), and it has been argued that "implicit" is best understood in terms of "automatic" (De Houwer, 2006; De Houwer & Moors, 2007). De Houwer et al. (2009, p. 347) summarize the key idea behind IATs (for details on procedures and scoring methods, especially if self-concepts are concerned, see Schnabel et al. 2008a, 2008b, 2008c):

*During a typical IAT, participants see stimuli that belong to one of four categories and are asked to categorize each stimulus by pressing one of two keys. Two of the*

*four categories are assigned to the first key, and the two other categories are
assigned to the second key. The core idea underlying the IAT is that categorization
performance should be a function of the degree to which categories that are
assigned to the same key are associated in memory. Hence, by examining which
combinations of categories result in the best categorization performance, one
should be able to infer which categories are more closely associated in memory.*

To apply IATs to personality development, two questions become immediately
important. First, to what extent do IAT measures and self-reports of supposedly the
same construct tap the same latent space (convergent construct validity)? If implicit
and explicit assessments of traits measure essentially "the same thing," then examinations of the stability and change of implicit personality traits might yield similar
findings to what we already know from self-reports. Second, how stable are IAT
scores across time (retest reliability and stability)? If implicit assessments of traits
do not show substantial retest correlations, then erroneous measurement error and/
or a lack of stability of implicit traits may be the culprits. The next paragraphs
review extant findings on convergent validity and retest associations of IAT scores.

## Convergent validity

Several studies have examined to what extent IATs and self-reports of the same construct correlate. First, two meta-analyses found average convergent correlations of
0.19 (corrected for measurement error: 0.24; SD = 0.14; Hofmann, Gschwendner,
Nosek, & Schmitt, 2005) and 0.37 (for attitude domains; Nosek, 2005). Specifically,
Hofmann et al. (2005) found that 44% of variance in implicit—explicit correlations
were due to measurement error. This meant that potentially 56% of true variation
could be accounted for by moderator variables (see Hofmann et al. 2005). Second
studies utilizing Big Five traits in explicit and implicit assessment may be most
informative because much of the personality development literature used the Big
Five (Specht et al., 2014). Findings of this literature seem to be mixed, however.
For example, Steffens and Schulze König (2006) found statistically significant correlations (<0.29) only for neuroticism and conscientiousness. In contrast, Schmukle
et al. (2008) found in two studies convergent correlations around 0.30 only for extraversion and conscientiousness. Further, Back et al. (2009) found significant correlations only for neuroticism (0.25) and extraversion (0.31).

Taken together, all of these findings on small to moderate convergent validity
indicate that related but distinct aspects of traits are measured by implicit and
explicit assessment (see also Nosek & Smyth, 2007, who found the same for attitudes). Thus we cannot a priori expect that extant findings on mean-level and rank-
order stability of self-reported personality traits can be applied to the development
of implicit personality. Rather, new and separate research is needed that examines
personality-related IAT scores across the lifespan (for developmental perspectives
on implicit cognition, see Cvencek & Meltzoff, 2015 and Olson & Dunham, 2010).

# Retest reliability and stability

Given the low convergent explicit–implicit correlations, it is also worth noting at this point that IATs typically correlate only very weakly or not at all with other indirect measures which themselves are also not or only weakly correlated (Schnabel et al., 2008a, 2008b). This speaks for highly method-specific constructs being sampled, rather than a common class of "implicit constructs." However, even if method variance can be reduced or controlled for (for details, see Mierke & Klauer, 2003), IATs seem to be influenced by contextual variations. For example, Mitchell, Nosek, and Banaji's (2003) findings suggested "automatic attitudes being continuous, online constructions that are inherently flexible and contextually appropriate, despite being outside conscious control" (p. 455). Similar findings and conclusions have also been reported elsewhere (e.g., Blair, 2002; Ferguson & Bargh, 2007). Indeed, automatic processes and implicit cognition (e.g., attitudes, beliefs, identity) have been described as malleable and conditional upon present contexts and situations (e.g., Dasgupta & Asgari, 2004; Dasgupta & Greenwald, 2001; Foroni & Mayr, 2005; Kahneman & Treisman, 1984; Lowery, Hardin, & Sinclair, 2001; Mitchell et al. 2003; Nosek et al., 2007; Richeson & Ambady, 2003; Rudman, Ashmore, & Gary, 2001; Teachman & Woody, 2003; Wittenbrink, Judd, & Park, 2001).

If implicit self-concepts are treated as automatic attitudes toward the self or certain trait domains (e.g., extraversion and neuroticism) associated with the self, then they may also be relatively "flexible." Such flexibility would be demonstrated in two findings. First, cross-temporal stability (most notably in the form of retest correlations) would be diminished because contextual factors may contribute at each measurement point to fluctuations in implicit self-concepts. Second, implicit self-concepts should be more malleable and prone to change. Both of these implications are explored below.

## *Retest correlations*

Nosek et al. (2007) found a median retest correlation of 0.56 across different studies, and Hofmann et al. (2005) reported a meta-analytic estimate of 0.51. Fig. 32.3 plots retest correlations as a function of retest interval in days from several studies (Banse, Seise, & Zerbes, 2001; Bosson, Swann, & Pennebaker, 2000; Cunningham, Preacher, & Banaji, 2001a; Dasgupta & Greenwald, 2001; Egloff & Schmukle, 2002; Egloff, Schwerdtfeger, & Schmukle, 2005; Gamer, Schmukle, Luka-Krausgrill, Egloff, 2008; only control group: Gschwendner, Hofmann, & Schmitt, 2008; Greenwald & Farnham, 2000; Hofmann et al., 2005; Schmukle & Egloff, 2004, 2005; Steffens & Buchner, 2003). The 27 retest correlations plotted averaged to $M_r = 0.51$ ($SD_r = 0.21$, range: 0.16–0.72). Interestingly, though there is a slight downward decline as the time interval in days increases, retest correlations seem to produce similar retest correlations in short time and longer ones. For example, Egloff et al. (2005) found retest correlations for an Anxiety IAT of 0.58 (after 1 week), 0.62 (after 1 month), and 0.47 (after 1 year; not included in

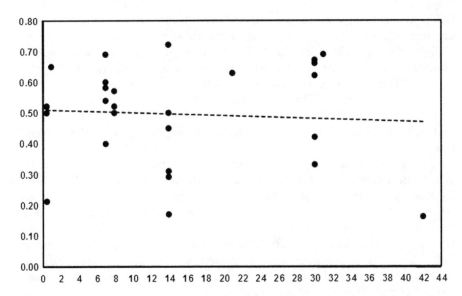

**Figure 32.3** Retest correlations of IATs. *Note*: *x*-axis: Retest interval in days, *y*-axis = retest correlation (*r*). The dotted line represents the linear trend of retest correlations as a function of retest interval in days.

Fig. 32.1 because an outlier). Taken together, retest correlations were moderate in degree, but fall behind those computed from explicit self-report measures (e.g., Roberts & DelVecchio, 2000). This suggests that whatever trait-related IAT measure, they seem to not only pick up reliable and stable interindividual differences, but also other factors that may be the source of variation in people's rank-orders.

It is important to understand that "simple" retest correlations, usually indexed by zero-order Pearson product−moment correlations, confound two actually distinct phenomena: reliability and stability. Reliability is commonly defined as the (degree of) absence of measurement error. A perfectly stable construct (i.e., one where rank-orders of persons do not change across time) would not yield a retest *r* of 1.0 if there was substantial measurement error (causing perturbations in the rank-ordering of persons in the sample and thus attenuating the *r* estimate). Stability can be defined in different ways (Ozer, 1986; Fleeson & Noftle, 2008), but one of the more prominent ways is in which the rank-ordering of persons in a given sample remains the same across two measurement points. This is commonly indexed by a correlation, such as *r*. A perfectly reliable measure with no measurement error and maximum precision would not yield an *r* of 1.0 if the measured construct is not stable (i.e., there are systematic differential changes between persons that cause rank-orders to change independently from capricious error and random fluctuations of the measurement method). One way to separate reliability from stability would be to disattenuate retest correlations according to internal consistencies. This yields upper-boundary *r*s that would be obtained if the measure was perfectly reliable. In contrast, a more sophisticated data-analytical technique would be to model associations latently with structural equation modeling (using a measurement model for each time point and associating latent implicit variables with each other). The latent retest correlation yields a better estimate of stability that is independent of measurement errors (see Cunningham et al., 2001a). This is important to note because, using multiple IATs, Cunningham, Nezlek, and Banaji (2001b) demonstrated that a substantial proportion of variance in each IAT stemmed from measurement error which will restrict finding high stability coefficients. Furthermore, latent state trait (LST) models (Steyer, Ferring, & Schmitt, 1992) take these ideas even further because they cannot only be used to separate error from true variance, but true variance is also separated into reliable state and trait variance. Extant LST analyses (Schmukle & Egloff, 2004, 2005; Steffens & Buchner, 2003) found that IATs not only capture reliable trait variance (interindividual differences) but also systematic measurement occasion as well as person × occasion interaction effects. The question then is which occasion-specific factors instill variations. For example, Schmukle and Egloff (2004) concluded for an anxiety IAT that it was not (induced) state anxiety. Thus more research will be needed to understand method- and context-specific effects that reside within IATs.

## Malleability

IAT scores seem to be flexible and plastic as participants are able to fake (Kim, 2003; Steffens, 2004). Faking per se does not provide strong evidence for plasticity, but it may be an indicator that the measure or the construct is malleable. Stronger evidence comes from studies that demonstrate changes in IATs after some "treatment," including short-term changes after experimental manipulations and particularly middle- to longer term changes after (psychotherapeutic) interventions. First, it has been demonstrated that IAT scores can vary depending on experimental conditions (e.g., Foroni & Mayr, 2005; Lowery et al., 2001) as well as extraneous influences (e.g., order of measures, previous experiences with IATs; for an overview, see Nosek et al., 2007). Second, it has been demonstrated that changes in IAT scores (of moderate to high effect size) can be achieved via psychotherapeutic interventions (e.g., social anxiety: Gamer et al., 2008; spider phobia: Teachman & Woody, 2003) and cognitive trainings (e.g., social rejection: Schnabel & Asendorpf, 2015). Accordingly, rank-order stabilities may be reduced which index change (e.g., Gamer et al., 2008; control group = 0.66 vs social anxiety group = 0.31). Thus IAT scores appear to be malleable with appropriate interventions. However, they do not seem to track conditioned Pavlovian learning (anxiety: Boschen, Parker, Neuman, 2007) and have also been shown to remain constant across different age groups (racial attitudes in 6- and 10-year olds as well as adults: Baron & Banaji, 2006). Regarding age, it also seems that IAT effects are larger in older adults than younger persons (Greenwald & Nosek, 2001; Hummert, Garstka, O'Brien, Greenwald, & Mellott, 2002), though such age effects may be explainable by IAT scoring algorithms (Greenwald, Nosek, & Banaji, 2003) and perhaps increased cognitive fluency with more age (Nosek et al., 2007).

## Summary

Taken together, IAT scores appear to be little to somewhat stable in terms of pre-served rank-orders among studied participants, though there is considerable method- and occasion-specific variance contained in them. Additionally, not much is known about the developmental trajectories of IAT scores so far, except that they can be stable but are also changeable via experimental manipulations and interventions. However, much more research is needed, particularly in the domain of IATs pertaining to basic personality traits such as the Big Five where virtually no studies exist so far.

# Future directions

## Summary

Several conclusions can be gleaned. First, personality traits can and should be measured with different data sources (Fig. 32.1). Single-trait multimethod approaches can be used to examine the common latent variance that is tapped for a construct as measured by different data sources. Particularly for the personality development literature, it will be generally important to employ other data sources than self-reports. A good starting point is indirect measures, most notably in the form of IATs. Second, personality traits may be understood in terms of automatic ABCDs and thus be studied under the lens of dual-process models (Fig. 32.2). Focusing on the implicit side of traits should complement our fairly advanced understanding of their explicit sides (as measured by traditional self-reports). Third, IATs and self-reports pertaining to major dimensions of personality traits, such as the Big Five, show small to moderate convergent construct validity. In general, it seems prudent to conclude that at least two different aspects of the same trait construct are measured—if the same construct is measured at all. Thus we cannot conclude that developmental patterns and trajectories of trait-related IAT scores will be the same as uncovered in self-reports. This makes it necessary to examine the development of implicit personality to contrast mean-level and rank-order stability of IAT scores with what we know from self-reports (Roberts & DelVecchio, 2000; Roberts et al., 2006). Fourth, retest correlations of IAT scores are, on average, moderate in size with only little variations as a function of time interval between testings (Fig. 32.3). This fits to the literature demonstrating state-, occasion-, and method-specific variances in IAT scores besides reliable interindividual differences. Thus latent state trait models may be a good solution because they untangle reliable state and trait from unreliable variance in IAT scores across measurement occasions. Additionally, IAT scores seem to be flexible and malleable according to given contexts, experimental manipulations, and psychotherapeutic interventions. Attending to a stable yet longitudinally changing construct that is measured by multiple methods at multiple occasions, recent developments in distinguishing state variability from trait change in longitudinal multitrait multimethod data within latent state trait analytical frameworks should be utilized (e.g., Geiser, Eid, Nussbeck, Courvoisier, & Cole, 2010a, 2010b; Geiser et al. 2015). Despite such advances and their potential for understanding the development of implicit personality, the development of IAT scores in general and for trait constructs in particular remains an understudied topic so far.

## Questions to be addressed

Several questions surrounding the development of implicit personality seem ripe to be addressed. For example, Does the development of implicit personality show parallels to the developmental course of self-reports regarding mean-level and rank-order stability and change? How are implicit and explicit measures of traits correlated with each other as well as other data sources measuring the same construct across the lifespan (age-dependent convergent construct validity)? Do they influence each other in cross-lagged ways, such that when one changes the other also changes (temporo-sequential and causal contiguities)? How are they (differentially) related to different life outcomes across the lifespan (age-dependent criterion validity and nomological networks)? Which biological mechanisms and environmental conditions as well as their interactions operate for stability and change in implicit traits?

In addition to these basic research questions revolving around "normative" personality change that takes place automatically and naturally across life, more applied questions targeting the voluntary and purposefully induced change of traits may be addressed also. For example, do interventions targeted at personality (Magidson et al. 2014; Hudson & Fraley, 2015) and people's explicit goals to change their traits (Hudson & Roberts, 2014) result in changes of implicit traits also? If yes, why is this the case, how sustainable and long lasting is implicit trait change, and which consequences and trajectories does it entail? According to Magidson et al. (2014, p. 1443), automatic aspects of traits may be the key to lasting personality change as the challenge for any intervention to changing personality traits is not only to overcome the nonconscious nature of personality traits but also to inculcate a level of change that is so complete it is automatic and instantiated over time in an enduring way.

All of the preceding questions can be addressed in a *general sense*, targeting population estimates for groups of people, as well as in a *differential sense*, targeting individual deviations from normative group estimates. For example, are there interindividual differences in intraindividual change of implicit traits? If so, which underlying biological, psychological, and environmental mechanisms and processes drive such differential change within persons? And which short-, middle-, and long-term consequences do such differences have?

# Conclusion

To date, personality development studies have focused mainly on self-reports as data sources on people's personality traits. However, there are multiple sources, and one particularly informative source may be indirect measures that capture implicit, automatic aspects of traits. Though the importance of automaticities in traits has already been understood (Back et al., 2009; Roberts, 2009; Wood & Denissen, 2015), tracking implicit traits across the lifespan with their stability and change has not been undertaken sufficiently so far. Thus there is yet a lot to be theorized about and data to be gathered on in a hopefully emerging field of the development of implicit personality.

# References

Asendorpf, J. B., Banse, R., & Mücke, D. (2002). Double dissociation between implicit and explicit personality self-concept: The case of shy behavior. *Journal of Personality and Social Psychology*, *83*, 380–393.

Back, M. D., Schmukle, S. C., & Egloff, B. (2009). Predicting actual behavior from the explicit and implicit self-concept of personality. *Journal of Personality and Social Psychology*, *97*, 533–548.

Banse, R., Seise, J., & Zerbes, N. (2001). Implicit attitudes toward homosexuality: Reliability, validity, and controllability of the IAT. *Zeitschrift für Experimentelle Psychologie*, *48*, 145–160.

Bargh, J. A. (1994). The four horsemen of automaticity: Awareness, intention, efficiency, and control in social cognition. In R. S. Wyer, Jr., & T. K. Srull (Eds.), *Handbook of social cognition* (2nd ed., pp. 1–40). Hillsdale, NJ: Lawrence Erlbaum Associates, Inc.

Bargh, J. A., & Chartrand, T. L. (1999). The unbearable automaticity of being. *American Psychologist*, *54*, 462–479.

Baron, A. S., & Banaji, M. R. (2006). The development of implicit attitudes: Evidence of race evaluations from ages 6 and 10 and adulthood. *Psychological Science*, *17*, 53–58.

Bassili, J. N., & Brown, R. D. (2005). Implicit and explicit attitudes: research, challenges, and theory. In D. Albarracin, B. Johnson, & M. Zanna (Eds.), *The handbook of attitudes* (pp. 543–574). Hillsdale, NJ: Erlbaum.

Blair, I. V. (2002). The malleability of automatic stereotypes and prejudice. *Personality and Social Psychology Review*, *6*, 242–261.

Bornstein, R. F. (2007). Toward a process-based framework for classifying personality tests: Comment on Meyer and Kurtz (2006). *Journal of Personality Assessment*, *89*, 202–207.

Boschen, M. J., Parker, I., & Neumann, D. L. (2007). Changes in implicit associations do not occur simultaneously to Pavlovian conditioning of physiological anxiety responses. *Journal of Anxiety Disorders*, *21*, 788–803.

Bosson, J. K., Swann, W. B., & Pennebaker, J. W. (2000). Stalking the perfect measure of implicit self-esteem: The blind men and the elephant revisited? *Journal of Personality and Social Psychology*, *79*, 631–643.

Cunningham, W. A., Nezlek, J. B., & Banaji, M. R. (2001b). Conscious and unconscious ethnocentrism: Revisiting the ideologies of prejudice. *Unpublished manuscript*, Yale University, New Haven, CT.

Cunningham, W. A., Preacher, K. J., & Banaji, M. R. (2001a). Implicit attitude measures: Consistency, stability, and convergent validity. *Psychological Science, 12*, 163−170.

Cvencek, D., & Meltzoff, A. N. (2015). Developing implicit social cognition in early childhood: Methods, phenomena, prospects. In S. Flannery Quinn, & S. Robson (Eds.), *The Routledge international handbook of young children's thinking and understanding* (pp. 43−53). Abingdon, England: Routledge.

Dasgupta, N., & Asgari, S. (2004). Seeing is believing: Exposure to counterstereotypic women leaders and its effect on the malleability of automatic gender stereotyping. *Journal of Experimental Social Psychology, 40*, 642−658.

Dasgupta, N., & Greenwald, A. G. (2001). On the malleability of automatic attitudes: Combating automatic prejudice with images of admired and disliked individuals. *Journal of Personality and Social Psychology, 81*, 800−814.

De Houwer, J. (2005). What are implicit measures and indirect measures of attitude? *Social Psychology Review, 7*, 18−20.

De Houwer, J. (2006). What are implicit measures and why are we using them. In R. W. Wiers, & A. W. Stacy (Eds.), *The handbook of implicit cognition and addiction* (pp. 11−28). Thousand Oaks, CA: Sage Publishers.

De Houwer, J., & Moors, A. (2007). How to define and examine the implicitness of implicit measures. In B. Wittenbrink, & N. Schwarz (Eds.), *Implicit measures of attitudes: Procedures and controversies* (pp. 179−194). New York, NY: Guilford Press.

De Houwer, J., Teige-Mocigemba, S., Spruyt, A., & Moors, A. (2009). Implicit measures: A normative analysis and review. *Psychological Bulletin, 135*, 347−368.

Egloff, B., & Schmukle, S. C. (2002). Predictive validity of an Implicit Association Test for measuring anxiety. *Journal of Personality and Social Psychology, 83*, 1441−1455.

Egloff, B., Schwerdtfeger, A., & Schmukle, S. C. (2005). Temporal stability of the Implicit Association Test—Anxiety. *Journal of Personality Assessment, 84*, 82−88.

Ericsson, K. A., & Lehmann, A. C. (1996). Expert and exceptional performance: Evidence of maximal adaptation to task constraints. *Annual Review of Psychology, 47*, 273−305.

Fazio, R. H., Jackson, J. R., Dunton, B. C., & Williams, C. J. (1995). Variability in automatic activation as an unobtrusive measure of racial attitudes: A bona fide pipeline? *Journal of Personality and Social Psychology, 69*, 1013−1027.

Ferguson, M. J., & Bargh, J. A. (2007). Beyond the attitude object. In B. Wittenbrink, & N. Schwarz (Eds.), *Implicit measures of attitudes: Procedures and controversies* (pp. 216−246). New York, NY: Guilford.

Fiedler, K., Messner, C., & Bluemke, M. (2006). Unresolved problems with the "I," the "A," and the "T": A logical and psychometric critique of the Implicit Association Test (IAT). *European Review of Social Psychology, 17*, 74−147.

Fleeson, W., & Noftle, E. E. (2008). Where does personality have its influence? A supermatrix of consistency concepts. *Journal of Personality, 76*, 1355−1385.

Foroni, F., & Mayr, U. (2005). The power of a story: New, automatic associations from a single reading of a short scenario. *Psychonomic Bulletin and Review, 12*, 139−144.

Funder, D. C. (1991). Global traits: A Neo-Allportian approach to personality. *Psychological Science, 2*, 31−39.

Funder, D. C. (2001). Personality. *Annual Review of Psychology, 52*, 197−221.

Gamer, J., Schmukle, S. C., Luka-Krausgrill, U., & Egloff, B. (2008). Examining the dynamics of the implicit and the explicit self-concept in social anxiety: Changes in the Implicit Association Test-Anxiety and the Social Phobia Anxiety Inventory following treatment. *Journal of Personality Assessment, 90*, 476−480.

Gawronski, B., LeBel, E. P., & Peters, K. R. (2007). What do implicit measures tell us? Scrutinizing the validity of three common assumptions. *Perspectives on Psychological Science, 2,* 181−193.

Geiser, C., Eid, M., Nussbeck, F. W., Courvoisier, D. S., & Cole, D. A. (2010a). Multitrait-multimethod change modeling. *AStA—Advances in Statistical Analysis, 94,* 185−201.

Geiser, C., Eid, M., Nussbeck, F. W., Courvoisier, D. S., & Cole, D. A. (2010b). Analyzing true change in longitudinal multitrait−multimethod studies: Application of a multi-method change model to depression and anxiety in children. *Developmental Psychology, 46,* 29−45.

Geiser, C., Keller, B. T., Lockhart, G., Eid, M., Cole, D. A., & Koch, T. (2015). Distinguishing state variability from trait change in longitudinal data: The role of measurement (non)invariance in latent state-trait analyses. *Behavior Research Methods, 47,* 172−203.

Greenwald, A. G., & Farnham, S. D. (2000). Using the Implicit Association Test to measure self-esteem and self-concept. *Journal of Personality and Social Psychology, 79,* 1022−1038.

Greenwald, A. G., McGhee, D. E., & Schwartz, J. L. K. (1998). Measuring individual differences in implicit cognition: The Implicit Association Test. *Journal of Personality and Social Psychology, 74,* 1464−1480.

Greenwald, A. G., & Nosek, B. A. (2001). Health of the Implicit Association Test at age 3. *Zeitschrift für Experimentelle Psychologie, 48,* 85−93.

Greenwald, A. G., Nosek, B. A., & Banaji, M. R. (2003). Understanding and using the Implicit Association Test: I. An improved scoring algorithm. *Journal of Personality and Social Psychology, 85,* 197−216.

Gschwendner, T., Hofmann, W., & Schmitt, M. (2008). Differential stability: The effects of acute and chronic construct accessibility on the temporal stability of the Implicit Association Test. *Journal of Individual Differences, 29,* 70−79.

Hofmann, W., Gawronski, B., Gschwendner, T., Le, H., & Schmitt, M. (2005). A meta-analysis on the correlation between the Implicit Association Test and explicit self-report measures. *Personality and Social Psychology Bulletin, 31,* 1369−1385.

Hofmann, W., Gschwendner, T., Nosek, B. A., & Schmitt, M. (2005). What moderates implicit−explicit consistency? *European Review of Social Psychology, 16,* 335−390.

Hudson, N. W., & Fraley, R. C. (2015). Volitional personality trait change: Can people choose to change their personality traits? *Journal of Personality and Social Psychology, 109,* 490−507.

Hudson, N. W., & Roberts, B. W. (2014). Goals to change personality traits: Concurrent links between personality traits, daily behavior, and goals to change oneself. *Journal of Research in Personality, 53,* 68−83.

Hummert, M. L., Garstka, T. A., O'Brien, L. T., Greenwald, A. G., & Mellott, D. S. (2002). Using the implicit association test to measure age differences in implicit social cognitions. *Psychology and Aging, 17,* 482−495.

John, O. P., Naumann, L. P., & Soto, C. J. (2008). Paradigm shift to the Integrative Big-Five Trait Taxonomy: History, measurement, and conceptual issues. In O. P. John, R. W. Robins, & L. A. Pervin (Eds.), *Handbook of personality: Theory and research* (pp. 114−158). New York, NY: Guilford Press.

Kahneman, D., & Treisman, A. (1984). Changing views of attention and automaticity. In R. Parasuraman, & D. R. Davies (Eds.), *Varieties of attention* (pp. 29−61). San Diego, CA: Academic Press.

Kim, D. Y. (2003). Voluntary controllability of the Implicit Association Test (IAT). *Social Psychology Quarterly, 66*, 83–96.

Lowery, B. S., Hardin, C. D., & Sinclair, S. (2001). Social influence effects on automatic racial prejudice. *Journal of Personality and Social Psychology, 81*, 842–855.

Magidson, J. F., Roberts, B. W., Collado-Rodriguez, A., & Lejuez, C. W. (2014). Theory-driven intervention for changing personality: Expectancy value theory, behavioral activation, and conscientiousness. *Developmental Psychology, 50*, 1442–1450.

McAdams, D. P. (2015). *The art and science of personality development.* New York, NY: Guilford Press.

Mierke, J., & Klauer, K. C. (2003). Method-specific variance in the Implicit Association Test. *Journal of Personality and Social Psychology, 85*, 1180–1192.

Mitchell, J. P., Nosek, B. A., & Banaji, M. R. (2003). Contextual variations in implicit evaluation. *Journal of Experimental Psychology: General, 132*, 455–469.

Moors, A., & De Houwer, J. (2006). Automaticity: A theoretical and conceptual analysis. *Psychological Bulletin, 132*, 297–326.

Nosek, B. A. (2005). Moderators of the relationship between implicit and explicit evaluation. *Journal of Experimental Psychology: General, 134*, 565–584.

Nosek, B. A. (2007). Implicit–explicit relations. *Current Directions in Psychological Science, 16*, 65–69.

Nosek, B. A., Greenwald, A. G., & Banaji, M. R. (2007). The Implicit Association Test at age 7: A methodological and conceptual review. In J. A. Bargh (Ed.), *Automatic processes in social thinking and behavior* (pp. 265–292). Hove, England: Psychology Press.

Nosek, B. A., & Smyth, F. L. (2007). A multitrait–multimethod validation of the Implicit Association Test: Implicit and explicit attitudes are related but distinct constructs. *Experimental Psychology, 54*, 14–29.

Olson, K. R., & Dunham, Y. D. (2010). The development of implicit social cognition. In B. Gawronski, & B. Keith Payne (Eds.), *Handbook of implicit social cognition: Measurement, theory, and applications.* New York, NY: Guilford.

Ortony, A., Norman, D. A., & Revelle, W. (2005). Effective functioning: A three level model of affect, motivation, cognition, and behavior. In J. Fellous, & M. Arbib (Eds.), *Who needs emotions? The brain meets the machine* (pp. 173–202). New York, NY: Oxford Univeristy Press.

Ozer, D. J. (1986). *Consistency in personality: A methodological framework.* New York, NY: Springer.

Paulhus, D. L. (1993). Bypassing the will: The automatization of affirmations. In D. M. Wegner, & J. W. Pennebaker (Eds.), *Handbook of mental control* (pp. 573–587). Hillsdale, NJ: Psychology.

Richeson, J. A., & Ambady, N. (2003). Effects of situational power on automatic racial prejudice. *Journal of Experimental Social Psychology, 39*, 177–183.

Roberts, B. W. (2009). Back to the future: Personality and assessment and personality development. *Journal of Research in Personality, 43*, 137–145.

Roberts, B. W., & DelVecchio, W. F. (2000). The rank-order consistency of personality from childhood to old age: A quantitative review of longitudinal studies. *Psychological Bulletin, 126*, 3–25.

Roberts, B. W., & Jackson, J. J. (2008). Sociogenomic personality psychology. *Journal of Personality, 76*, 1523–1544.

Roberts, B. W., Walton, K., & Viechtbauer, W. (2006). Patterns of mean-level change in personality traits across the life course: A meta-analysis of longitudinal studies. *Psychological Bulletin, 132*, 1–25.

Rudman, L. A., Ashmore, R. D., & Gary, M. L. (2001). "Unlearning" automatic biases: The malleability of implicit prejudice and stereotypes. *Journal of Personality and Social Psychology, 81,* 856–868.

Schmukle, S. C., Back, M. D., & Egloff, B. (2008). Validity of the Five-Factor Model for the implicit self-concept of personality. *European Journal of Psychological Assessment, 24,* 263–272.

Schmukle, S. C., & Egloff, B. (2004). Does the Implicit Association Test for assessing anxiety measure trait and state variance? *European Journal of Personality, 18,* 483–494.

Schmukle, S. C., & Egloff, B. (2005). A latent state-trait analysis of implicit and explicit personality measures. *European Journal of Psychological Assessment, 21,* 100–107.

Schnabel, K., & Asendorpf, J. B. (2010). The self-concept: New insights from implicit measurement procedures. In B. Gawronski, & B. K. Payne (Eds.), *Handbook of implicit social cognition* (pp. 408–425). New York, NY: Guilford Press.

Schnabel, K., & Asendorpf, J. B. (2015). Cognitive trainings reduce implicit social rejection associations. *Journal of Social and Clinical Psychology, 34,* 365–391.

Schnabel, K., Asendorpf, J. B., & Greenwald, A. G. (2008a). Using Implicit Association Tests for the assessment of implicit personality self-concept. In G. J. Boyle, G. Matthews, & D. H. Saklofske (Eds.), *Personality theory and assessment: Vol 2 Personality measurement and testing* (pp. 508–528). Thousand Oaks, CA: Sage.

Schnabel, K., Asendorpf, J. B., & Greenwald, A. G. (2008b). Assessment of individual differences in implicit cognition: A review of IAT measures. *European Journal of Psychological Assessment, 24,* 210–217.

Schnabel, K., Asendorpf, J. B., & Greenwald, A. G. (2008c). Understanding and using the Implicit Association Test: V. Measuring semantic aspects of trait self-concepts. *European Journal of Personality, 22,* 695–706.

Schultheiss, O. (2007). A memory-systems approach to the classification of personality tests: Comment on Meyer and Kurtz (2006). *Journal of Personality Assessment, 89,* 197–201.

Specht, J., Bleidorn, W., Denissen, J. J. A., Hennecke, M., Hutteman, R., Kandler, C., ... Zimmermann, J. (2014). What drives adult personality development? A comparison of theoretical perspectives and empirical evidence. *European Journal of Personality, 28,* 216–230.

Steffens, M. C. (2004). Is the Implicit Association Test immune to faking? *Experimental Psychology, 51,* 165–179.

Steffens, M. C., & Buchner, A. (2003). Implicit Association Test: Separating transsituationally stables and variable components of attitudes toward gay men. *Experimental Psychology, 50,* 33–48.

Steffens, M. C., & Schulze König, S. (2006). Predicting spontaneous Big Five behavior with implicit association tests. *European Journal of Psychological Assessment, 22,* 13–20.

Steyer, R., Ferring, D., & Schmitt, M. J. (1992). States and traits in psychological assessment. *European Journal of Psychological Assessment, 8,* 79–98.

Strack, F., & Deutsch, R. (2004). Reflective and impulsive determinants of social behavior. *Personality and Social Psychology Review, 8,* 220–247.

Teachman, B. A., & Woody, S. R. (2003). Automatic processing in spider phobia: Implicit fear associations over the course of treatment. *Journal of Abnormal Psychology, 112,* 100–109.

Thornike, E. L. (1913). *The psychology of learning (Vol. 2).* New York, NY: Mason-Henry Press.

Wilt, J., & Revelle, W. (2008). Extraversion and emotional reactivity. In M. Leary, & R. H. Hoyle (Eds.), *Handbook of individual differences in social behavior*. New York, NY: Guilford Press.

Wittenbrink, B., Judd, C. M., & Park, B. (2001). Spontaneous prejudice in context: Variability in automatically activated attitudes. *Journal of Personality and Social Psychology, 81*, 815−827.

Wood, D, & Denissen, J. J. (2015). A functional perspective on personality trait development. In K. J. Reynolds & N. R. Branscombe (Eds.), *Psychology of change. Life contexts, experiences, and identities* (pp. 97−115).

Wood, D., Gardner, M. H., & Harms, P. D. (2015). How functionalist and process approaches to behavior can explain trait covariation. *Psychological Review, 122*, 84−111.

Wood, W., & Neal, D. T. (2007). A new look at habits and the habit−goal interface. *Psychological Review, 114*, 843−863.

# Volitional personality change

## 33

Nathan W. Hudson[1] and R. Chris Fraley[2]
[1]Michigan State University, East Lansing, MI, United States,
[2]University of Illinois at Urbana-Champaign, Champaign, IL, United States

Charles Dickens's classic novel, *A Christmas Carol*, chronicles the tale of an embittered, compassionless miser named Ebenezer Scrooge. One cold, bleak Christmas Eve, Ebenezer is haunted by three apparitions. These spirits reveal that—should he fail to fundamentally alter his harsh, penurious ways—Scrooge's life will end in a lonely and unmourned death. Desperate to avoid this wretched fate, Scrooge pledges to change his personality. And true to his word, in the novel's final pages, Ebenezer transforms from a tightfisted and coldhearted antagonist into an extraordinarily generous, fatherly, and compassionate benefactor.

But can *real* people actually transform core personality traits simply because they believe that doing so would be valuable? In recent years, psychological scientists have begun to tackle this question (Hudson & Fraley, 2015; Robinson, Noftle, Guo, Asadi, & Zhang, 2015). Research has attempted to understand whether people, like Scrooge, want to change their personality traits—and if so, which traits they desire to change and why. Research has also begun to examine whether people are able to successfully change their personality traits—and if so, what kinds of factors facilitate this process. The purpose of this chapter is to overview theory and research on *volitional personality change*—people's desires and attempts to change their own personality traits. After reviewing existing theory and research, we conclude by highlighting what we believe to be the most important questions for future research to address.

## Do people want to change their personality traits?

Ebenezer Scrooge's story is admittedly extreme; most people are not motivated to change their personality traits courtesy of spectral threats of imminent doom. Do real people actually want to change their personality traits? How common are *trait change goals*? Several recent studies have examined this question. Hudson and Roberts (2014) created the 44-item Change Goals Big Five Inventory (C-BFI; see Appendix) by asking college students to rate the extent to which they wanted to increase, decrease, or stay the same with respect to each of the items contained within the standard Big Five Inventory (BFI; John & Srivastava, 1999). They found that participants' trait change goals were organized by the Big Five personality dimensions (for an overview of the Big Five, see Goldberg, 1993). That is, participants tended to express desires to change with respect to the five broad dimensions,

Personality Development Across the Lifespan. DOI: http://dx.doi.org/10.1016/B978-0-12-804674-6.00033-8

rather than specific, unique attributes. For example, if a participant indicated a desire to become more assertive—an attribute related to extraversion—that person was also likely to express goals to increase with respect to other attributes subsumed by extraversion, such as sociability, enthusiasm, and energy. Thus the Big Five personality dimensions can be used to summarize not only personality traits themselves, but also the ways in which most people wish to change.

Within the Big Five framework, Hudson and Roberts (2014) found that the *vast majority* of college students wanted to increase with respect to each positively keyed Big Five personality dimension—extraversion, agreeableness, conscientiousness, emotional stability (the opposite of neuroticism), and openness to experience. Specifically, as can be seen in Fig. 33.1, a minimum of 87% of people wanted to increase with respect to each dimension; and no more than 3% of participants expressed a desire to decrease with respect to any dimension. In a similar study using a shorter, 5-item measure of people's trait change goals (one item per dimension), Robinson et al. (2015) found that a minimum of 56% of college students desired to increase with respect to each Big Five personality dimension—and no more than 7% of their participants wanted to decrease in any dimension.

Taken together, research suggests that the majority of college students want to change aspects of their personality traits. These findings, however, are not limited in their generalizability to American college students. Students in the United Kingdom, Iran, and China also express goals to increase with respect to each Big Five personality dimension (Robinson et al., 2015). Finally—although older adults do tend to express less of a desire to change their personality traits, as compared with younger adults—individuals as old as 70 years of age still indicate goals to increase with respect to each Big Five personality dimension (Hudson & Fraley, 2016b). Taken together, these findings clearly suggest that it does not require anything as extreme as spectral coercion to motivate people to want to change their personality traits. Irrespective of how trait change goals are measured, the majority of adults wish to increase with respect to each Big Five personality dimension (Hudson & Fraley, 2016b; Hudson & Roberts, 2014; Robinson et al., 2015).

## Why do people want to change their personality traits?

Generally, theorists have argued that trait change goals are primarily *extrinsically motivated* (for an overview of intrinsic vs extrinsic motivation, see Deci & Ryan, 1985, 2000). Stated differently, people desire to change their personality traits as an instrumental means to promote valued external outcomes or prevent feared ones (Baumeister, 1994; Hennecke, Bleidorn, Denissen, & Wood, 2014; Hudson & Roberts, 2014; Kiecolt, 1994). For example, individuals may want to become more thorough, hardworking, and responsible as a means to improve their grades or earn promotions at work. Supporting this notion, research has found that students who are dissatisfied with their academic experience are more likely to express desires to

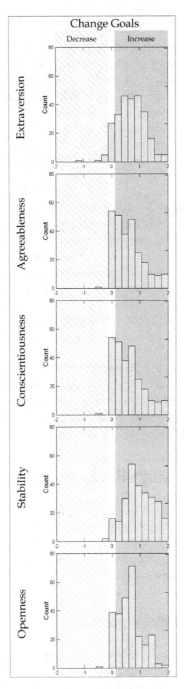

**Figure 33.1** Histograms of Hudson and Roberts' (2014) participants' trait change goals, as measured using the C-BFI. Positive values (solid background shading) represent goals to increase. Negative values (striped background shading) represent goals to decrease. Zero values (no background shading) represent goals to remain the same.

increase in conscientiousness (Hudson & Roberts, 2014). Similarly, people who are unhappy with their social lives tend to articulate goals to increase in extraversion—presumably because they believe that being more outgoing, sociable, and enthusiastic would assuage their interpersonal dissatisfaction (Hudson & Roberts, 2014). In fact, individuals who fear even *potentially* being ostracized in the future may formulate goals to alter their personality traits in ways that will minimize the probability of their fears becoming realized (Quinlan, Jaccard, & Blanton, 2006). Across all of these examples, individuals—like Scrooge—may desire to change their personality traits as a means to attain a variety of external goals.

It is also possible, however, that some individuals are *intrinsically motivated* (Deci & Ryan, 1985, 2000) to change their personality traits (Hennecke et al., 2014; Hudson & Roberts, 2014). Specifically, some personality traits, such as extraversion and conscientiousness, are socially desirable in and of themselves (Dunlop, Telford, & Morrison, 2012). Thus some people may want to increase with respect to those traits—not to attain a specific external outcome—but rather for the purpose of possessing the trait *per se* (Hennecke et al., 2014; Hudson & Roberts, 2014). Supporting this notion, research has found that people who are low with respect to socially desirable traits (e.g., extraversion, conscientiousness; Dunlop et al., 2012) are the most likely to report goals to increase with respect to those traits (Hudson & Roberts, 2014).

To summarize, most people—especially young adults—desire to change their personality traits. Theoretically, these goals are primarily extrinsically motivated—individuals want to change their personality traits as a means to attain other, external, valued goals. However, some people may also be intrinsically motivated to grow in socially desirable traits that they lack.

## Can people volitionally change their personality traits?

The fact that most people *want* to change aspects of their personality (Hudson & Fraley, 2016b; Hudson & Roberts, 2014) raises an important question: Can people *actually* change their traits simply in virtue of wanting to do so? Before explicitly addressing this question, it is important to review how personality traits are thought to develop more generally in adulthood.

## Adult personality development

Research demonstrates that personality traits change during adulthood (for an overview, see Roberts, Wood, & Caspi, 2008). On average, adults tend to become more agreeable, conscientious, and emotionally stable with age (Roberts, Walton, & Viechtbauer, 2006). These normative maturational trends are believed to result from a combination of genetically predetermined maturation (analogous to biologically predetermined physical maturation; Bleidorn, Kandler, Riemann, Angleitner, & Spinath, 2009) in addition to the effects of commonly shared life experiences (e.g., the fact that most people invest in careers in young adulthood may cause most people to increase in conscientiousness over time; see Roberts & Wood, 2006; Roberts et al., 2008).

In addition to these normative maturational trends, individuals' personality traits also change in idiosyncratic ways, as a function of their experiences. For example, the individuals who most deeply invest in their careers are the ones who increase the most in conscientiousness over time (Hudson & Roberts, 2016; Hudson, Roberts, & Lodi-Smith, 2012). People who invest in romantic relationships tend become emotionally stable at a faster rate than their peers who remain single (Lehnart, Neyer, & Eccles, 2010). Even factors as seemingly trivial as completing daily crossword and Sudoku puzzles have been linked to changes in personality traits over time (Jackson, Hill, Payne, Roberts, & Stine-Morrow, 2012).

Theoretically, people's personality traits change as a function of their experiences because those experiences serve as strong, consistent presses that evoke certain state-level patterns of thoughts, feelings, and behaviors (Hennecke et al., 2014; Hutteman, Nestler, Wagner, Egloff, & Back, 2015; Magidson, Roberts, Collado-Rodriguez, & Lejuez, 2012; Roberts & Jackson, 2008). For example, workplaces presumably reinforce conscientious behaviors (e.g., responsibility, punctuality, thoroughness) and punish nonconscientious ones (e.g., shoddy workmanship, absenteeism). As a consequence, workplaces cause people to engage in more conscientious state-level thoughts, feelings, and behaviors. Theoretically, any changes to state-level thoughts, feelings, and behaviors that are sustained for a long enough period of time can coalesce into enduring trait-level changes (Hennecke et al., 2014; Magidson et al., 2012; Roberts & Jackson, 2008). Supporting this notion, several longitudinal studies have found that state-level changes to thoughts, feelings, and behavior predict corresponding subsequent trait development (Hudson & Fraley, 2015; Hutteman et al., 2015). Thus, for example, the experience of deeply investing in one's career can lead to lasting gains in conscientiousness—through the process of shaping one's state-level conscientious thoughts, feelings, and behaviors over an extended period of time (Hudson & Roberts, 2016; Hudson et al., 2012; Lodi-Smith & Roberts, 2007).

That said, the precise mechanisms through which state-level thoughts, feelings, and behaviors educe trait development are not well understood. However, scholars have argued that state-level changes may simply become learned, habitual, and automatized over time (Hennecke et al., 2014). As a nonmutually exclusive possibility, it may also be the case that state-level changes to thoughts, feelings, and behavior alter individuals' physiology (perhaps including the epigenome), leading to corresponding trait changes (Roberts & Jackson, 2008).

# Volitional trait change

On the simplest level, life experiences (including social roles) are thought to shape people's personality traits by consistently evoking state-level patterns of thoughts, feelings, and behaviors over an extended period of time—and those state-level changes eventually coalesce into enduring trait change (Hennecke et al., 2014; Hutteman et al., 2015; Magidson et al., 2012; Roberts & Jackson, 2008). This raises the question: Can individuals *volitionally* regulate their own thoughts, feelings, and behaviors over extended periods of time in ways that enable them to change their own traits (Hennecke et al., 2014; Hudson & Fraley, 2015)? Although it seems obvious that people can make changes to their behavior at least over short periods of time, actually changing one's personality traits may be considerably more difficult. For instance, it may be the case that genetic or situational forces exert stronger influences on trait levels than do volitional forces, leading to an outcome in which volitional trait changes are meager, short-lived, or even impossible to attain.

To date, a total of four studies have explicitly examined whether people can volitionally change their own personality traits. In three separate samples, Hudson and Fraley (2015, 2016a) assessed college students' trait change goals via the C-BFI at the beginning of a semester. Over the following 4 months, they collected self-report measures of participants' personality traits. Across all three samples, students' trait change goals, as reported at the beginning of the semester, generally predicted corresponding subsequent trait growth over the course of 4 months. As can be seen in Fig. 33.2, participants who expressed desires to become more extraverted at Time 1, for example, experienced faster growth in trait extraversion over the course of the semester, as compared with their peers who did not wish to change with respect to extraversion.[1] In one study, this phenomenon was corroborated using daily behavior checklists (Hudson & Fraley, 2015). For example, students who—at the beginning of the semester—indicated goals to become more extraverted tended to increase in extraverted daily behaviors at a faster rate over the course of the semester, as compared with their peers who did not wish to become more extraverted. Importantly, however, participants' personality traits and daily behaviors changed at only a slow-to-moderate pace. Across all of Hudson and Fraley's studies, participants were predicted to increase a maximum of approximately 0.25−0.50 standard deviations in desired traits over the course of 4 months (albeit this amount is still substantially higher than meta-analytic estimates of the normative changes that occur during a 4-month period in young adulthood; Roberts et al., 2006).

It is important to note that, in one of Hudson and Fraley's (2015) studies, as students' personality traits changed in ways that aligned with their goals, their trait change goals tended to dissipate. For example, if an individual wanted to become more extraverted—and then actually increased in extraversion over the course of the semester—s/he tended to express *less intense* goals to continue increasing in extraversion at the end of the semester. This is consistent with the idea that people were actually fulfilling their goals—and thus the goal to continue increasing was sated and dissipated.

---

[1] Notably, in later studies, Hudson and Fraley demonstrated that this is not merely an artifact of experimental demand. Hudson and Fraley (2017) assessed participants' personality traits repeatedly *before* and after administering a change goals measure. Exposure to the change goals measure did not moderate growth in participants' traits. Stated differently, people were changing in ways that aligned with their desires *before* Hudson and Fraley asked them about how they would like to change their personality traits—a scenario that is impossible to explain as having occurred due to acquiescence to experimental demand.

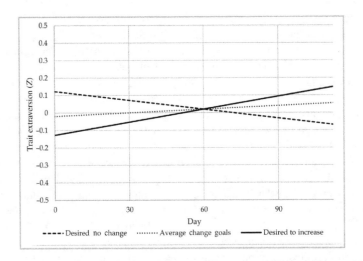

**Figure 33.2** Model-predicted growth in trait extraversion for Hudson and Fraley's (2015) participants who, at the beginning of the study, expressed goals to increase or stay the same with respect to extraversion.
*Source:* Reproduced from Hudson, N. W., & Fraley, R. C. (2015). Volitional personality trait change: Can people choose to change their personality traits? Journal of Personality and Social Psychology, 109, 490−507.

In contrast to the studies discussed earlier, there is at least one study of which we are aware that suggests that people may *not* be able to volitionally change their personality traits. Robinson et al. (2015) assessed students in the United Kingdom who were graduating from college. They measured students' trait change goals using a five-item measure (one item per dimension). They subsequently measured participants' self-reported personality traits twice—once when the students graduated, and once 1 year later. They found that participants' trait change goals predicted either no trait change or trait changes *opposite* the desired direction.

To summarize, the limited empirical evidence available suggests that people do, at the very least, *tend to change* in ways that align with their desires (Hudson & Fraley, 2015, 2016a; cf. Robinson et al., 2015). This may support the notion that people are, in fact, able to *volitionally change* their own personality traits.

# How can people change their own personality traits?

Theoretically, trait change occurs when state-level thoughts, feelings, and behaviors are changed over a sufficiently long period of time to educe corresponding trait development (Hennecke et al., 2014; Hudson & Fraley, 2015; Magidson et al., 2012; Roberts & Jackson, 2008). Supporting this notion, in one of Hudson and Fraley's (2015) studies, the association between trait change goals and corresponding trait development was partially mediated by trait-relevant daily behavior. For example, goals to increase in extraversion predicted subsequent increases in extraverted daily behaviors—which, in turn, predicted increases in trait extraversion. This is consistent with the idea that modifying one's state-level thoughts, feelings, and behaviors over an extended period of time can evoke enduring trait changes.

Moreover, in one of their studies, Hudson and Fraley (2015) experimentally tested the notion that state-level changes to thoughts, feelings, and behaviors might coalesce into trait-level changes. They randomly assigned their participants to intervention and control groups. The intervention group was guided on a weekly basis in modifying their state-level thoughts, feelings, and behaviors to match their ideal traits. Specifically, these participants generated "small steps" and implementation intentions (Gollwitzer & Brandstätter, 1997) that would help them pull their thoughts, feelings, and behaviors in line with their desired traits. For example, someone who wanted to become more extraverted might be coached to create a small step similar to, "I will invite Aaron and Megan to lunch on Tuesday"; that same person might be guided to author an implementation intention similar to, "If I have an opinion on what's being discussed in my philosophy class, then I will voice my thoughts." In contrast, participants in the control group simply wrote about their existing personality traits each week.

Although participants in both groups tended to change in ways that aligned with their trait change goals (e.g., people who wanted to become more conscientious tended to experience faster increases in conscientiousness over time), participants who received coaching in shaping their state-level thoughts, feelings, and behaviors experienced up to *double* the growth in desired traits, as compared with participants in the control group (see Fig. 33.3). Thus it appears that successfully regulating

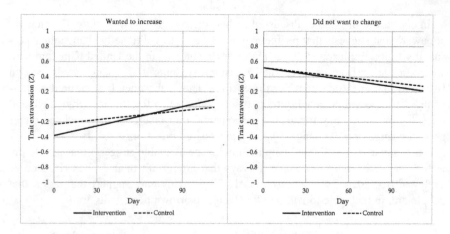

**Figure 33.3** Model-predicted growth in trait extraversion for Hudson and Fraley's (2015) participants in the intervention and control groups who, at the beginning of the semester, expressed goals to increase or stay the same with respect to extraversion. Participants who wanted to increase in extraversion and partook in a weekly goal-setting intervention to pull their thoughts, feelings, and behaviors in line with their desired levels of extraversion experienced up to double the amount of growth in trait extraversion over the course of the semester. In contrast, the intervention had no statistically significant effect on individuals who did *not* wish to change. *Source:* Reproduced from Hudson, N. W., & Fraley, R. C. (2015). Volitional personality trait change: Can people choose to change their personality traits? Journal of Personality and Social Psychology, 109, 490–507.

one's own thoughts, feelings, and behaviors—*faking it until you make it*, as it were—may be viable strategy for volitionally changing one's own traits.

That being said, there may be other viable strategies that people can employ to obtain desired changes to their personality traits. Moreover, individual differences in ability to regulate thoughts, feelings, and behaviors may influence whether people are able to successfully change their own personality traits *a fiat*. Thus other strategies, such as committing to social roles that will instill desired traits within oneself, may prove fruitful (Lodi-Smith & Roberts, 2007; Roberts & Wood, 2006; Stevenson & Clegg, 2011). Finally, there may be other strategies that people use to successfully change their personality traits that researchers have not yet anticipated. Clearly, *much* future research is needed to understand the types of strategies people use in attempt to change their traits, and which strategies are the most efficacious.

## What are the implications of volitional personality change?

Ebenezer Scrooge was motivated to change his personality traits in order to avoid a feared future—a bitter, lonely, and unmourned death. But in volitionally changing his personality, Scrooge also accrued a variety of additional psychological benefits. Despite once being characterized by greed, isolation, regret, and negative affect, in the novel's final pages, Ebenezer transforms into a character that is better described as abundantly overflowing with generosity, meaningful relationships, and positive affect and joy. Research suggests that, like Scrooge, people want to change their personality traits (Hudson & Fraley, 2016b; Hudson & Roberts, 2014; Robinson et al., 2015) and may be able to find some degree of success in doing so (Hudson & Fraley, 2015, 2016a; cf. Robinson et al., 2015). But *should* individuals attempt to change their personality traits? What are the psychological *implications* of desiring and pursuing trait change? Can individuals, like Scrooge, improve their lives and psychological well-being through volitional personality change? Or does desiring and pursuing self-change actually entail greater psychological costs than benefits?

There are competing theoretical perspectives regarding the psychological implications of desiring and attempting self-change. On one hand, theorists have argued that change goals are frequently motivated by *dissatisfaction* with aspects of one's life (Baumeister, 1994; Kiecolt, 1994). For example, college students who are dissatisfied with their academic experience tend to report desires to become more conscientious (Hudson & Roberts, 2014). Because conscientiousness is associated with academic performance (e.g., Richardson & Abraham, 2009), to the extent that people are able to successfully increase in conscientiousness, they may experience corresponding boosts to academic outcomes. Thus successful volitional personality change may have the potential to assuage the sources of people's woes, improve their life outcomes, and consequently boost their psychological well-being (Hudson & Fraley, 2016a).

In contrast, other theorists have argued that desires and attempts to change oneself may have the potential to *harm* psychological well-being (Herman & Polivy, 2003; Polivy & Herman, 2002; Trottier, Polivy, & Herman, 2009). For one, focusing on how one falls short of one's ideals may promote negative affect (Higgins, 1987). People who expect unrealistic amounts of self-change—or that self-change will be a panacea—may only set themselves up for psychologically damaging disappointment (Polivy & Herman, 2002). Moreover—especially if volitional personality change is difficult to realize—people may accrue opportunity costs by failing to disengage from their trait change goals in lieu of pursing other, more fruitful ambitions (King & Hicks, 2007). Finally, even if individuals are able to successfully change their personality traits, those changes may be accompanied by unanticipated "side effects" that have the potential to worsen well-being. For example, to the extent that one's time is held constant, efforts to become extremely extraverted may bring boons to one's social well-being at the cost of time and energy focused into one's career. Consequently, it may simply be better to learn to want the traits that one has, rather than to try to attain the traits that one wants (Polivy & Herman, 2002).

Although there is currently extremely limited empirical data on these issues, in one intensive longitudinal study, Hudson and Fraley (2016a) found preliminary evidence for both perspectives. Holding constant their personality traits—including growth therein—participants who expressed desires to become more conscientious or open to experience at the beginning of the semester tended to experience relative declines in psychological well-being, as compared with their peers who did not wish to change with respect to these traits. This may suggest that focusing on the negative aspects of oneself—how one falls short of one's ideals—is counterproductive to psychological well-being (e.g., Higgins, 1987). Perhaps students expected that increases in conscientiousness or openness to experience would hold panacean implications for their collegiate experience—expectations that seemingly inevitably must lead to disappointment (Polivy & Herman, 2002). Or possibly students who were focused on changing their levels of conscientiousness and openness simply missed opportunities to pursue other goals that might have otherwise improved their lives and psychological well-being (e.g., King & Hicks, 2007).

In contrast, Hudson and Fraley (2016a) found that participants who actually increased in any of the Big Five personality dimensions over the course of the study—irrespective of whether the trait changes were desired—tended to experience simultaneous gains in well-being. Thus participants who became more extraverted, for example, were likely to also increase in life satisfaction. Moreover, participants' change goals moderated the link between trait growth and increases in well-being, such that *desired* trait changes were especially predictive of boosts to well-being.

Collectively, these findings might suggest that, like Scrooge, people may be able to improve their life circumstances and psychological well-being through volitional changes to their personality traits. That said, simply desiring change may lead to decrements in well-being over time. Thus especially unfruitful desires and attempts to change oneself may backfire, leading to worsened well-being. The question, therefore, of whether individuals *should* pursue self-change may depend on a variety of factors—including what types of change people desire, the feasibility of actually attaining those changes, and the beliefs and expectations individuals hold regarding the impact self-change will have on their lives.

# Future directions

The empirical literature on volitional personality development is in its infancy. Thus many critical questions remain unexplored. For the remainder of this chapter, we highlight what we believe to be the most crucial questions for future research.

# Methodological issues

**Multimethod triangulation**. One of the biggest limitations of existing research on volitional personality change is that all studies to date have relied exclusively on self-reports of personality trait change. Several studies have attempted to address some of the limitations of self-report measures by collecting self-report daily behavior checklists—which are ostensibly more objective than self-reported trait ratings— or by ruling out experimental demand as an explanation for the observed correlations between participants' trait change goals and subsequent corresponding trait development (Hudson & Fraley, 2015, 2017). Nevertheless, the fact remains that self-report measures suffer numerous limitations (Paulhus & Vazire, 2007). For example, experimental demand aside, the self may be biased to see illusory/placeboic personality growth in the desired direction over time.

We believe it is therefore critical for future studies to employ a variety of personality measures, including self-reports, observer reports, and perhaps even objective behavioral measures. Although observer reports, for example, are not necessarily superior to self-reports (e.g., the self has the greatest amount of insight and information in evaluating its own personality; Paulhus & Vazire, 2007), they can partially address and overcome the limitations of self-reports (e.g., self-favoring bias). That said, the use of observer reports may require studying volitional personality change over a longer period of time. As compared with the self, observers may be less motivated or able to detect changes in the self's personality (Paulhus & Vazire, 2007). Moreover, observers might discount "true" changes in the self's personality as "merely" being due to situational forces (Hennecke et al., 2014). For example, observers might attribute increases in the self's gregariousness, activity, energy, and enthusiasm as being due to the self associating with a more partying crowd of friends, rather than "true" changes to the self's level of extraversion. Thus it may require greater changes—and changes that are sustained for a longer period of time—for volitional change to be detectable to observers.

**More thorough longitudinal studies**. To date, all of the longitudinal studies examining volitional change processes have been relatively short in duration: 16 measurement occasions over 4 months (Hudson & Fraley, 2015, 2016a, 2017) or two measurement occasions over 12 months (Robinson et al., 2015). Although most studies have found that people tend to change in ways that align with their trait change goals (Hudson & Fraley, 2015, 2016a, 2017), it is unclear (1) how much trait change people can attain and (2) whether those trait gains can be sustained over an extended period of time. Specifically, it is unlikely that individuals can increase with respect to any trait *ad infinitum*. Thus it seems reasonable that individuals would eventually reach a point of diminishing returns in their attempts to change their own personalities. Moreover, it remains an open question whether individuals can *maintain* volitional trait changes over time. It may be the case that once individuals stop actively pursuing volitional change, they revert to their baseline levels of each trait.

Pertaining to this issue—as we have already discussed—Robinson et al. (2015) measured people's personality traits twice, 1 year apart, and found that people did *not* change according to their desires. This raises the possibility that, although people can volitionally change their personalities over the short-term and in a relatively invariant context (a semester of college), such changes might get disrupted—or may even fail to persist—over important life transitions (e.g., graduation), or over extended periods of time. We believe it is therefore absolutely critical for future research to examine volitional change processes over longer time periods and across important social and developmental transitions.

**Generalizability**. To date, most research on volitional change has focused on young, American, college samples. Although there is evidence that non-Americans and older adults express *trait change goals* (Hudson & Fraley, 2016b; Robinson et al., 2015), future research should explore whether noncollege aged adults can also *volitionally change* their personality traits in desired ways. On one hand, personality traits appear to become less plastic with age (Roberts et al., 2006)—which might lead one to expect that older adults may attain less success in their volitional change efforts. On the other hand, empirical evidence suggests that personality remains an open, malleable system well into adulthood (e.g., Hudson & Roberts, 2016; Jackson et al., 2012), and that its plasticity may actually *increase* in the latter years of life (Specht et al., 2014)—which might lead one to expect that older adults (perhaps especially the elderly) would experience similar success in changing their traits, as compared with college students.

## Theoretical issues

**What are the obstacles to volitional change?** Future research should explore the obstacles that may interfere with people's ability to change their personality traits as desired. For example, people may underestimate the value that trait change could bring (Hennecke et al., 2014), or they may believe that it would be impossible to change personality traits (Chiu, Hong, & Dweck, 1997; Dweck, 2008). With respect to the latter, research on mindsets suggests that people vary in the extent to which they believe that personality is immutable versus changeable—and these beliefs have implications for personality functioning (Chiu et al., 1997; Dweck, 2008). Hudson and Fraley (2017) examined whether generalized lay theories about personality change moderate people's abilities to attain desired trait changes. In their studies, participants' beliefs about the malleability of personality did *not* moderate trait growth; people who desired to change in specific traits tended to do so regardless of whether they believed personality can change.

Nonetheless, the basic idea still rings true. There should be specific attitudes or mindsets that people hold that will facilitate or impair their ability to change in desired directions. One potential way to explore these ideas in the future is to examine the extent to which more granular *expectancy* (e.g., beliefs that *extraversion* can change) and *value* (e.g., beliefs regarding how one's life would be improved by becoming more extraverted) are related to change goals and actual change. Furthermore, the factors that *motivate* people's trait change goals may predict their ability to successfully change. For example, intrinsically motivated trait change goals may garner greater success in attaining trait change, as compared with extrinsically motivated goals (Deci & Ryan, 1985, 2000).

Beyond beliefs, expectations, and motives, other individual differences may also moderate people's abilities to engender desired changes to their personality traits. For instance, individuals with greater variability in their within-person personality states (e.g., Fleeson, 2001) may be more easily able to shift their thoughts, feelings, and behaviors toward ideal levels, as compared with individuals whose personality states are more constant.

**What change strategies work best?** Existing studies suggest that changing state-level thoughts, feelings, and behaviors over a long enough period of time may be one way to successfully attain volitional change goals (Hudson & Fraley, 2015; Hutteman et al., 2015; Magidson et al., 2012; Roberts & Jackson, 2008). That said, individual differences in people's ability to regulate their own behavior may determine the success of attempting to "brute force" cognitive, affective, and behavioral changes (Hennecke et al., 2014). Moreover, there may be a variety of other strategies that people might use to attempt to change their traits. For example, committing to social roles that instill desired traits within oneself may be a viable means to attain volitional change (Lodi-Smith & Roberts, 2007; Roberts & Wood, 2006; Stevenson & Clegg, 2011). Future research should first identify the strategies that appear to be most promising in helping people volitionally change their traits. The efficacy of these strategies should then be formally tested using intensive longitudinal experiments (e.g., Hudson & Fraley, 2015).

# Conclusion

Recent research suggests that Ebenezer Scrooge's journey of self-change reflects some trappings of truth. Like Ebenezer, many people are motivated to change their personality traits in order to attain external goals—including improving their psychological well-being. And moreover, an emerging body of studies suggests that people can, in fact, follow in Scrooge's footsteps and *actually* change their personality traits in moderate, albeit psychologically meaningful ways. It is our hope that future research will begin to elucidate more fully which strategies and circumstances best enable individuals to realize their trait change goals—and to more completely understand the long-term implications of people's active attempts to volitionally change their own personality traits.

# References

Baumeister, R. F. (1994). The crystallization of discontent in the process of major life change. In T. F. Heatherton, & J. L. Weinberger (Eds.), *Can personality change?* (pp. 281−297). Washington, DC: American Psychological Association.

Bleidorn, W., Kandler, C., Riemann, R., Angleitner, A., & Spinath, F. M. (2009). Patterns and sources of adult personality development: Growth analyses of the NEO PI-R scales in a longitudinal twin study. *Journal of Personality and Social Psychology, 97,* 142−155.

Chiu, C. Y., Hong, Y., & Dweck, C. S. (1997). Lay dispositionism and implicit theories of personality. *Journal of Personality and Social Psychology, 73,* 19−30.

Deci, E. L., & Ryan, R. M. (1985). *Intrinsic motivation and self-determination in human behavior.* New York, NY: Plenum.

Deci, E. L., & Ryan, R. M. (2000). The "what" and "why" of goal pursuits: Human needs and the self-determination of behavior. *Psychological Inquiry, 11,* 227−268.

Dunlop, P. D., Telford, A. D., & Morrison, D. L. (2012). Not too little, but not too much: The perceived desirability of responses to personality items. *Journal of Research in Personality, 46,* 8−18.

Dweck, C. S. (2008). Can personality be changed? *Current Directions in Psychological Science, 17,* 391−394.

Fleeson, W. (2001). Toward a structure- and process-integrated view of personality: Traits as density distributions of states. *Journal of Personality and Social Psychology, 80,* 1011−1027.

Goldberg, L. R. (1993). The structure of phenotypic personality traits. *American Psychologist, 48,* 26−34.

Gollwitzer, P. M., & Brandstätter, V. (1997). Implementation intentions and effective goal pursuit. *Journal of Personality and Social Psychology, 73,* 186−199.

Hennecke, M., Bleidorn, W., Denissen, J. J. A., & Wood, D. (2014). A three-part framework for self-regulated personality development across adulthood. *European Journal of Personality, 28,* 289−299.

Herman, C. P., & Polivy, J. (2003). Realistic and unrealistic self-change efforts. *American Psychologist, 58,* 823−824.

Higgins, E. T. (1987). Self-discrepancy: A theory relating self and affect. *Psychological Review, 94,* 319−340.

Hudson, N. W., & Fraley, R. C. (2016a). Changing for the better? Longitudinal associations between volitional personality change and psychological well-being. *Personality and Social Psychology Bulletin, 42,* 603−615.

Hudson, N. W., & Fraley, R. C. (2016b). Do people's desires to change their personality traits vary with age? An examination of trait change goals across adulthood. *Social Psychological and Personality Science, 7,* 847−856.

Hudson, N. W., & Fraley, R. C. (2017). To what extent do beliefs and expectations moderate volitional change processes? Under Review.

Hudson, N. W., & Fraley, R. C. (2015). Volitional personality trait change: Can people choose to change their personality traits? *Journal of Personality and Social Psychology, 109,* 490−507.

Hudson, N. W., & Roberts, B. W. (2014). Goals to change personality traits: Concurrent links between personality traits, daily behavior, and goals to change oneself. *Journal of Research in Personality, 53,* 68−83.

Hudson, N. W., & Roberts, B. W. (2016). Social investment in work reliably predicts change in conscientiousness and agreeableness: A direct replication and extension of Hudson, Roberts, and Lodi-Smith (2012). *Journal of Research in Personality, 60,* 12−23.

Hudson, N. W., Roberts, B. W., & Lodi-Smith, J. (2012). Personality trait development and social investment in work. *Journal of Research in Personality, 46,* 334−344.

Hutteman, R., Nestler, S., Wagner, J., Egloff, B., & Back, M. D. (2015). Wherever I may roam: Processes of self-esteem development from adolescence to emerging adulthood in the context of international student exchange. *Journal of Personality and Social Psychology, 108,* 767−783.

Jackson, J. J., Hill, P. L., Payne, B. R., Roberts, B. W., & Stine-Morrow, E. A. L. (2012). Can an old dog learn (and want to experience) new tricks? Cognitive training increases openness to experience in older adults. *Psychology and Aging, 27,* 286−292.

John, O. P., & Srivastava, S. (1999). The Big-Five trait taxonomy: History, measurement, and theoretical perspectives. In L. A. Pervin, & O. P. John (Eds.), *Handbook of personality: Theory and research* (2nd ed., pp. 102−138). New York, NY: Guilford Press.

Kiecolt, K. J. (1994). Stress and the decision to change oneself: A theoretical model. *Social Psychology Quarterly, 57,* 49−63.

King, L. A., & Hicks, J. A. (2007). Whatever happened to "What might have been?" Regrets, happiness, and maturity. *American Psychologist, 62,* 625−636.

Lehnart, J., Neyer, F. J., & Eccles, J. (2010). Long-term effects of social investment: The case of partnering in young adulthood. *Journal of Personality, 78,* 639−670.

Lodi-Smith, J., & Roberts, B. W. (2007). Social investment and personality: A meta-analysis of the relationship of personality traits to investment in work, family, religion, and volunteerism. *Personality and Social Psychology Review, 11,* 68−86.

Magidson, J. F., Roberts, B. W., Collado-Rodriguez, A., & Lejuez, C. W. (2012). Theory-driven intervention for changing personality: Expectancy value theory, behavioral activation, and conscientiousness. *Developmental Psychology, Advance online publication.*

Paulhus, D. L., & Vazire, S. (2007). The self-report method. In R. W. Robins, R. C. Fraley, & R. F. Krueger (Eds.), *Handbook of research methods in personality psychology* (pp. 224−239). New York, NY: The Guilford Press.

Polivy, J., & Herman, C. P. (2002). If at first you don't succeed: False hopes of self-change. *American Psychologist, 57,* 677−689.

Quinlan, S. L., Jaccard, J., & Blanton, H. (2006). A decision theoretic and prototype conceptualization of possible selves: Implications for the prediction of risk behavior. *Journal of Personality, 74,* 599−630.

Richardson, M., & Abraham, C. (2009). Conscientiousness and achievement motivation predict performance. *European Journal of Personality, 23,* 589−605.

Roberts, B. W., & Jackson, J. J. (2008). Sociogenomic personality psychology. *Journal of Personality, 76,* 1523−1544.

Roberts, B. W., Walton, K. E., & Viechtbauer, W. (2006). Patterns of mean-level change in personality traits across the life course: A meta-analysis of longitudinal studies. *Psychological Bulletin, 132,* 1−25.

Roberts, B. W., & Wood, D. (2006). Personality development in the context of the neo-socioanalytic model of personality. In D. K. Mroczek, & T. D. Little (Eds.), *Handbook of personality development* (pp. 11−39). Mahwah, NJ: Lawrence Erlbaum Associates.

Roberts, B. W., Wood, D., & Caspi, A. (2008). The development of personality traits in adulthood. In O. P. John, R. W. Robins, & L. A. Pervin (Eds.), *Handbook of personality: Theory and research* (3rd ed., pp. 375−398). New York, NY: The Guilford Press.

Robinson, O. C., Noftle, E. E., Guo, J., Asadi, S., & Zhang, X. (2015). Goals and plans for Big Five personality trait change in young adults. *Journal of Research in Personality*, *59*, 31−43.

Specht, J., Bleidorn, W., Denissen, J. J. A., Hennecke, M., Hutteman, R., Kandler, C., & Zimmermann, J. (2014). What drives adult personality development? A comparison of theoretical perspectives and empirical evidence. *European Journal of Personality*, *28*, 216−230.

Stevenson, J., & Clegg, S. (2011). Possible selves: Students orientating themselves towards the future through extracurricular activity. *British Educational Research Journal*, *37*, 231−246.

Trottier, K., Polivy, J., & Herman, C. P. (2009). Effects of resolving to change one's own behavior: Expectations vs. experience. *Behavior Therapy*, *40*, 164−170.

# Appendix. Change Goals Big Five Inventory (C-BFI; Hudson & Roberts, 2014)

## Instructions

How much do you want to change yourself? Here are a number of personality traits that you may or may not want to change within yourself. Please rate the extent to which you want to change each trait.

## Response scale

All items are rated using the following response scale:

Much more than I currently am (+2)
More than I currently am (+1)
I do not want to change in this trait (0)
Less than I currently am (−1)
Much less than I currently am (−2)

## Items

1. I want to be someone who is talkative
2. I want to be someone who is reserved (r)
3. I want to be someone who is full of energy
4. I want to be someone who generates a lot of enthusiasm
5. I want to be someone who tends to be quiet (r)
6. I want to be someone who has an assertive personality

7. I want to be someone who is sometimes shy, inhibited (r)
8. I want to be someone who is outgoing, sociable
9. I want to be someone who tends to find fault with others (r)
10. I want to be someone who is helpful and unselfish with others
11. I want to be someone who starts quarrels with others (r)
12. I want to be someone who has a forgiving nature
13. I want to be someone who is generally trusting
14. I want to be someone who can be cold and aloof (r)
15. I want to be someone who is considerate and kind to almost everyone
16. I want to be someone who is sometimes rude to others (r)
17. I want to be someone who likes to cooperate with others
18. I want to be someone who does a thorough job
19. I want to be someone who can be somewhat careless (r)
20. I want to be someone who is a reliable worker
21. I want to be someone who tends to be disorganized (r)
22. I want to be someone who tends to be lazy (r)
23. I want to be someone who perseveres until the task is finished
24. I want to be someone who does things efficiently
25. I want to be someone who makes plans and follows through with them
26. I want to be someone who is easily distracted (r)
27. I want to be someone who is depressed, blue (r)
28. I want to be someone who is relaxed, handles stress well
29. I want to be someone who can be tense (r)
30. I want to be someone who worries a lot (r)
31. I want to be someone who is emotionally stable, not easily upset
32. I want to be someone who can be moody (r)
33. I want to be someone who remains calm in tense situations
34. I want to be someone who gets nervous easily (r)
35. I want to be someone who is original, comes up with new ideas
36. I want to be someone who is curious about many different things
37. I want to be someone who is ingenious, a deep thinker
38. I want to be someone who has an active imagination
39. I want to be someone who is inventive
40. I want to be someone who values artistic, esthetic experiences
41. I want to be someone who prefers work that is routine (r)
42. I want to be someone who likes to reflect, play with ideas
43. I want to be someone who has artistic interests
44. I want to be someone who is sophisticated in art, music, or literature

## Administration and scoring

Items should be presented in randomized order. Reverse items are indicated above with (r). Average items to form composites as follows:

Items 1—8: goals to change extraversion
Items 9—17: goals to change agreeableness
Items 18—26: goals to change conscientiousness
Items 27—34: goals to change emotional stability
Items 35—44: goals to change openness to experience.

# Index

CPSIA information can be obtained
at www.ICGtesting.com
Printed in the USA
LVHW03*2058110818
586684LV00010B/209/P

9  780128  046746